THE OFFICIAL
TOUR DE FRANCE
1903-2004

THE OFFICIAL
TOUR DE FRANCE
1903-2004

WEIDENFELD & NICOLSON

CONTENTS

RENÉ POTTIER

JACQUES ANQUETIL

EDDY MERCKX

BERNARD HINAULT

GREG LEMOND

MIGUEL INDURÁIN

LANCE ARMSTRONG

THE HIGH
MOUNTAINS
1947, in the first
post-War Tour de
France, Ronconi and
Rossello cross the
Col de Galibier
together during
the Grenoble to
Briançon stage.

1903–2004

100 years of the Tour de France

JEAN-MARIE LEBLANC
DIRECTOR OF THE TOUR DE FRANCE

How could it not be a pleasure, as well as a duty, to commemorate a century of the Tour de France? To take an introspective pause in a hectic, and therefore sometimes uncaring, present? To rest my eyes on the rear-view mirror of the sporting epopoeia? For Henri Desgrange and his successors Jacques Goddet and Félix Lévitan fathered an uncommon human adventure, a peerless cycle race, and a great national celebration each July; these three aspects have gradually merged into a single unity.

The infant, fragile and restless from birth, had a stormy childhood. 'The Tour de France is over and its second edition will, I greatly fear, have been its last. It will have been killed by its own success, by the blind passions it has unleashed and by abuse and suspicion worthy only of the ignorant and the mischievous.'

So wrote Desgrange in the 25 July 1904 edition of *L'Auto*. Happily, he was wrong. But what anguish must have tormented the first director of the Tour, a demanding, fastidious man smitten as much by the sporting ideal as by great athletic exploits, an ideal already under threat from sordid conspiracies.

Desgrange's resolve and charisma, and his tireless quest for the best possible – or the least bad – formula for the Tour allowed him to overcome the risks. With the introduction of national teams in 1930, he achieved all, or nearly all, of his goals, boosting the sales of *L'Auto*, attracting advertising partners (he was, after all, a press baron), and offering the French public the best imaginable array of winners with Leducq, Magne, Speicher, and Lapébie (we should not forget Vietto, either).

Taking up the baton from Desgrange wasn't easy for Jacques Goddet and Félix Lévitan in 1947. Goddet, Desgrange's heir, had almost seen the Tour slip out of his control; the penury that characterized the troubled period after the War greatly complicated its revival. Once again, it was a question of finding the best formula and balancing the books. This meant the inevitable return of commercial teams, the creation of the

Prologue, the green and the polka-dot jerseys, foreign *Grands Départs*, and so on. Goddet couldn't bear to be idle and invented new stimuli – bonuses, mountain finishes – and with Anquetil, then Merckx, then Hinault, the Tour achieved equilibrium, at least in sporting terms.

Goddet and Lévitan, like Desgrange before them, consolidated the Tour without abandoning greater ambitions. For example, in 1982, Goddet, echoing France's success in the FIFA World Cup, had the idea of holding an 'internationalized' Tour every four years, contested by national teams. Goddet, a lyrical and elegiac visionary like Desgrange, could carry his readers with him, but this intellectually attractive idea was, in practice, quite infeasible.

As we celebrate the centenary of the Tour, we can legitimately speculate what the future holds in store. Yet, 'Recollection is our strength. Let us never efface memorable anniversaries. When the night attempts to close in, we should rekindle these memories as we would light torches.' The pages that follow, the images and exploits they bring back to life, are the torches evoked by Victor Hugo, the author of those lines. Does the night presage some sombre destiny threatening the Tour de France to the point that we may need the support of these grand moments?

Now is not the time for pessimism, with record numbers of roadside spectators (in France and neighbouring countries), record media coverage, record viewing figures. Yet no French rider has won the Tour since 1985 and our dear Bernard Hinault. How, then, to explain this success?

First with the depth and strength of its roots. A hundred years of epic and glorious history, of exploits and drama, of tradition and passion, of the second most popular sport in the countries of Western Europe, where the most famous road races in the world were created.

Then, there are the Tour's inherent assets: its place in the calendar (thank you, Henri Desgrange, for choosing July; thank you, Léon Blum, France's first Socialist premier, for introducing paid holidays in 1936) and its geography which, with the Alps and Pyrenees, offers marvellous terrain for world-class cyclists.

I should also stress the care paid to the itinerary and the amenities: the first is a complex alchemy of tasks designed to allow victory to go to a climber or a time-triallist or a *rouleur*, without favouring any specific rider or type; the second means guaranteeing the riders physical and psychological comfort, recovery time, and regulations that preserve, as far as possible, the sporting ethic, and equality of opportunity for all.

Following Desgrange and Goddet, this supreme concern with honest competition has broadly speaking been achieved (despite the 1998 Festina scandal) and is an indispensable pre-condition for the credibility of the Tour.

Another factor underlying the success of the Tour de France today is television. Television magnifies the race. The backdrops are incomparable, the actors are excellent, always courageous, sometimes heroic. But the workers who provide the images and the perfection of their technology bring to the small screen every tiny, enticing morsel of boldness and suspense from this daily soap opera. Television and the Tour seem made for each other, just as in the past printed narratives (text and photos), then radio broadcasts, fired the public imagination. We imagine that internet surfers in Australia and North America will soon enjoy the Tour live.

Last, but by no means least in importance, the social function of the Tour de France scarcely needs emphasizing. It is a bringer of festivities, dreams and gladness; it is free of violence, and unites people of all generations and backgrounds. It allows TV viewers to discover, or rediscover, France's rivers and bridges, châteaux and churches, mountains and valleys. It is the best ambassador France could have.

These extra-sporting concerns imply, in turn, putting a great deal of energy into engaging the young, whether by encouraging them to take up cycling, or by inspiring them to support the Tour at the roadside. Yes, the Tour de France is flourishing; yes, it is popular and prosperous; yes,

increasing numbers of towns want to welcome the Tour – its economic partners are plentiful, and so too are its television outlets – for the excellent value for money the Tour de France offers. But above all, the *people* love the Tour. In return, the Tour brings competitors and spectators together in such intimate proximity, allowing the public to be heard more clearly, and promotes greater respect for the riders and a better understanding of sport.

But every coin has two sides, and although they are happily few and far between, dramas do occur: the deaths of Simpson in 1967 and Casartelli in 1995. And the Tour has other demons, and today they are at least three: drugs, overexpansion and money.

Recent experience has shown that event organizers have little control over the use of drugs, beyond showing vigilance and using whatever means they have at their disposal to support the work of the public and sporting authorities.

However, we must control our growth and be prepared to say no to more media coverage, to an even greater caravan, to more sponsors, vehicles and guests. All of these would impose such rigid logistical constraints that it would end up grotesquely obese, being made to run from town to town for twenty-three days in succession! That would signal the end of small host towns, even the end of the event's spirit of conviviality. Obsessed by profit and security, the Tour would soon risk losing its soul.

As I write this, it seems an absurd paradox: the Tour de France being forced to restrain its own prosperity when, in other times, Desgrange, Goddet and Lévitan could scarcely keep the wolf from the door. However, it is important to prevent the short-term frenzy of the immediate moment from jeopardizing their conscientious, long-term project. However, by paying the price of maintaining a constant and sustained lucidity, the Tour de France, this precious jewel, will be able to go as far as possible into the second century of its existence. Need I say that I hope it does so with all my heart and all my strength...?

From 1967 to 1971, Jean-Marie Leblanc was a professional rider (seen here leading Eddy Merckx).

... from 1971 to 1988, he was a reporter, first for *La Voix du Nord* and then on *L'Équipe*...

... and since 1988, he has been director of the Tour de France: a unique career!

1903–2004

Foreword
BY LANCE ARMSTRONG

I can remember beginning to watch or pay attention to the Tour back in the mid-80s when Greg Lemond was starting to really excel there. This was the time when the American media first began to cover the race and give it some attention. It was viewed more as a 'freak event' or an 'extreme sport'. The real breakthrough was Greg's ride in the 1989 Tour that was capped off by what could be argued as one of the greatest days in sport. I remember watching the final time trial on the Champs-Élysées and being blown away by what I had just seen. At that point in time, I was still basically a full-time professional triathlete but it's no wonder that I decided shortly thereafter to devote almost all of my time to cycling. The Tour had become an event the Americans could follow and truly care about.

For me, the Tour is the greatest annual sporting event in the world. It has everything... difficulty, colour, pain, suffering, victory, emotion, and even death at times. It's a product of many, many years of hard work by the French. The race belongs to them and I realize that more than ever now. The French love it and protect it like it's their baby.

The Tour has also become the most famous race in America. If you ask someone on the streets of New York City, San Francisco, or Austin, Texas, to name one bike race they know of, then I'm sure the near 100 percent answer is 'the Tour de France'. They love it, they follow it now, and they're even beginning to understand the tactics! *Mon Dieu..!*

And finally, I live for this race. I love it. I want to win in more ways than most will ever know. I cherish so much my days in yellow that it keeps me busy almost 365 days a year. To lose a Tour and have to face my team, who have worked so hard, would be heart wrenching. I don't want to see that day and I'll do whatever I can to prevent it.

Long live the Tour!

How the Tour was born

BY SERGE LAGET

The Paris-Rouen, first run in 1869, the Bordeaux-Paris and the Paris-Brest-Paris, both 1891, were the creations of three visionaries, enthusiasts and newspapermen: Richard Lesclide, Maurice Martin and Pierre Giffard. These pioneers were motivated as much by necessity as by idealism: Lesclide, Martin and Giffard certainly believed in the potential first of the velocipede and then of the bicycle, but they also needed to sell newspapers – *Vélocipède Illustrated*, *Véloce Sport* and *Le Petit Journal*.

A humanist committed to developing new technologies (e.g. the telephone and automobile) to improve humanity's lot, Giffard had also been deeply affected by the French defeat in the Franco-Prussian War (1870). He believed the bicycle could help reclaim Alsace-Lorraine.

He organized cycle races as much to boost the cycling industry as to develop French muscle in a field hitherto dominated by Britons: the rider George Pilkington Mills and the manufacturers Humber and Dunlop. The future, he hoped, would see the heirs of cyclist Charles Terront and industrialists Adolphe Clément and Edouard Michelin surge into Strasbourg. The bicycle was transport, sport, freedom, revolution. It fascinated figures like journalist and premier Georges Clemenceau, novelist and political activist Émile Zola and painter Maurice de Vlaminck. It also fired the imagination of a young legal clerk from Paris named Henri Desgrange. Intrigued by extremes, exertion and the outdoors, Desgrange mounted his bicycle and joined the new religion.

The bicycle acquired its bible at the end of 1892 when Giffard created *Le Vélo*, a daily sports journal printed on green paper. Giffard launched new ideas which Desgrange, twelve years his junior, put into practice. He set the first world hour record – 35.325 km (21.937 miles) unpaced. Then, he took up his pen.

At that moment, the Dreyfus affair broke. Alfred Dreyfus, a French Army officer and a Jew from Alsace, was falsely accused of spying for Germany. Between his imprisonment in 1894 and re-trial in 1899, France was divided: conservatives opposed Dreyfus; progressives like Giffard supported him. Outraged by the injustice, Giffard championed Dreyfus in *Le Vélo*, denouncing anti-Dreyfusard industrialists like De Dion, Michelin and Clément, whose advertising kept *Le Vélo* afloat. De Dion and his friends decided to found their own paper, one worthy of their copious advertising budget.

On 16 October 1900, *L'Auto-Vélo*, printed on yellow paper, was established at 10, rue du Faubourg, Montmartre. Its direction had been entrusted to Desgrange and a meticulous accountant named Victor Goddet. Desgrange, a winner, not just a player, was capable of matching and beating Giffard at his own game; green versus yellow, one was bound to lose.

Desgrange had once predicted the demise of road racing. Now, he championed it, and scored a decisive point in 1901 when *Le Petit Journal* asked him to organize the second Paris-Brest race (created by Giffard), won by Maurice Garin for bicycle manufacturer La Française. Desgrange pressed home his advantage in 1902 by organizing a race from Marseille to Paris, then a breakaway Bordeaux-Paris, weeks after the version backed by *Le Vélo*. The winner was Garin, in a faster time than the *Le Vélo* race. Giffard retaliated through the courts, obtaining an order obliging Desgrange to remove the term 'Vélo' from his title. But both journals were in trouble, with tiny 25,000 circulations.

The difference between them was one of enthusiasm: Desgrange's determination, work ethic and his status as a former champion had attracted a small team of devotees, including several defectors from Giffard's *Le Vélo*. One of them, Géo Lefèvre, had the idea that would spell the end for his former employer. It came to him over lunch with Desgrange and Goddet at the Zimmer Madrid in Boulevard Montmartre, near *L'Auto-Vélo*'s offices, on 20 November 1902. 'What about a Tour de France in several stages with rest days?'

The zany idea, perhaps the product of pre-lunch drinks, appealed more to Goddet than to

Desgrange, but on 17 January 1903, the day after *L'Auto-Vélo* became *L'Auto*, among fourteen different sporting events promoted by the journal, the counterattack was launched with a reference to a mysterious 'major road race'. The 19 January front-page headline declared: 'The Tour de France, the greatest cycle race in the world.' It was to be a geographical and athletic extension of the Eiffel Tower, that symbol of French majesty and aspiration. Yet the *L'Auto* team didn't quite know how to go about it.

The idea of a Tour de France was not new. Catherine de Medici had completed one in 1564; the Compagnons du Tour de France were apprentice craftsmen who took three years to complete theirs. In sporting terms, however, it was unheard of, in spite of 'tours' by Louis Gillet's *draisienne* (hobby horse) in 1830, and Adolphe Clément's velocipede in 1870. In 1893, *Le Journal* had planned a tour through Nantes, Bordeaux, Toulouse, Marseille, Lyon and Troyes, but there was no sponsorship; at the time, sponsors funded only long-distance solo riders like Charles Terront, who cycled from Saint-Petersburg to Paris in 1894.

In 1895, Théophile Joyeux covered 4,429 km (2,750 miles) around France in nineteen days and Jean Corre, 5,102 km (3,168 miles) in twenty-five days. A major race was a different proposition. The only model was the Tour de France car race organized by the French daily *Le Matin* between 16 and 25 July 1899. René de Knyff, driving a Panhard-Levassor, roared through the seven stages of the 2,291-km (1,423-mile) route at an average speed of over 51 kph (32 mph).

The only bicycle races that covered more than 2,000 km (1,242 miles) were the Six Days, track races first held in 1899. It was therefore a matter, in Géo Lefèvre's words, of 'transforming France into a velodrome' by taking six of the one-day classics which had already, or almost, been created, and placing them end to end. Lefèvre became a sort of one-man band: starter, timekeeper, finish judge, controller and special envoy,

travelling by bicycle or train to perform his multiple roles.

Desgrange faced different teething troubles from the Baron de Coubertin or Jules Rimet. The first Olympic Games, held in Greece in 1896, and the first World Cup, held in Uruguay in 1930, were organized by public bodies, charged admission, and changed venue every four years. The Tour was private, annual, free and drew 15 million spectators to the most beautiful stadium on earth. This was the challenge the *L'Auto* team had to meet.

While Giffard, whose departure from the world of sport was welcomed by an exasperated Desgrange, was discovering China, the director and chief editor of *L'Auto* was tearing his hair out trying to find fifty cyclists prepared to spend 31 May to 5 July competing for 20,000 francs of prize money from Paris to Lyon, Marseille, Toulouse, Bordeaux, Nantes and back to Paris. It was like asking them to cycle off into the unknown, although Desgrange's colleague Georges Abran had reconnoitred all 2,200 km (1,366 miles). On 21 April, the project nearly fell apart: only fifteen riders had signed on. No. 1 was Desgrange's friend Maurice Garin.

Desgrange quickly rescheduled the race to 1 to 18 July, halved its length and the entry fee (from 20 to 10 francs), increased the prize money and allocated 5 francs expenses per day. His changes were announced on 6 May; by 30 June 1903, there were seventy-eight entries. As Georges Méliès amazed cinema audiences with his *Voyage dans la Lune* (Trip to the Moon), Desgrange, Lefèvre and Co. were moving heaven and earth to get the Tour, more crusade or adventure than road race, off the ground.

Late in 1904, *Le Vélo* became *Le Journal de l'Automobile*. Having fought Giffard, Desgrange invited him to work as a reporter for *L'Auto*. When Giffard died in 1923, Desgrange paid him a moving tribute and financed a monument to him. The Tour de France was a reality; the passion and enthusiasm of its creators never faltered.

Henri Desgrange and Victor Goddet, in O'Galop's caricatures, were as different and as complementary as fire and water. Their partnership made it possible to put Géo Lefèvre's idea into practice.

Although Desgrange believed firmly in the interest of the Tour, he was so overcautious that, without Lefèvre's enthusiasm, the first race would have been a disaster.

In this poster by Noël Dorville (1902), the fantasy girl of La Française cycles presents the various components of the future Tour. Lefèvre's idea was to lay the six classics end to end.

THE PATRONS OF THE TOUR

1903-1939 :	Henri Desgrange.
1947-1961 :	Jacques Goddet.
1962-1986 :	Jacques Goddet and Félix Lévitan.
1987 :	Jean-François Naquet-Radiguet and Xavier Louy.
1988 :	Jean-Pierre Courcol and Xavier Louy.
1989-1993 :	Jean-Pierre Carenso and Jean-Marie Leblanc.
1994-2000 :	Jean-Claude Killy and Jean-Marie Leblanc.
2001 :	Patrice Clerc and Jean-Marie Leblanc.

Garin opens the epic

The La Française team and its leader Maurice Garin couldn't afford to lose the first Tour de France. In 1901 Garin had won the Paris-Brest-Paris, all 1,200 non-stop kilometres of it; in July 1902, he had taken the second Bordeaux-Paris of the year, organized by the sports paper *L'Auto-Vélo* to spike the version convened a month earlier by rival publication *Le Vélo*. To step up to the next level, Garin's team needed a successful Tour de France. For *L'Auto*, the Tour de France was a means of boosting sales and scoring points against *Le Vélo*. For bicycle manufacturer La Française, success in the six-stage Tour also meant sales; their red, white and blue finish captured the pervading national sentiment perfectly.

The Tour de France was the ultimate test of courage. Its stages effectively added six gruelling one-day Classics to the cycling calendar, although only the hard men of the Six-Day races, held on the track, not the open road, had ever covered distances like these, approaching 2,500 kilometres. To attract the 59 swashbuckling fortune-hunters who started alongside Garin, the organizers had to offer wealthy prizes and bonuses. All of the entrants were professional or semi-professional cyclists, although many had other trades; race winnings alone would have provided a meagre living.

The first Tour de France left Paris on 1 July 1903. With some riders taking 35 hours or more to finish the longer stages, it did not return until 19 July. There were seven much-needed rest days; the rest was an odyssey of suffocating dust, blinding sun, buffeting mistral, bone-breaking vibrations, not to mention punctures, falls and losing the way. Not surprisingly, only a third of the riders made it to the race finish at the Parc des Princes velodrome on 19 July. The first riders to sign the register at the race start beneath the Réveil-Matin bar, Henri Ellinamour and Léon Pernette, had simply disappeared during the race. Others had been disqualified for all manner of cheating. Special edition after special edition of *L'Auto* rolled off the presses. As well as Garin's exploits on the way to Lyon and Nantes, they told the tale of Aucouturier's abandon on stage one, his subsequent withdrawal from the overall classification, and his 'unclassified' wins on stages two and three to Marseille and Toulouse. *L'Auto* went from strength to strength, slowly securing its place as the greatest sports paper of the century. France, meanwhile, watched from the thresholds of its home-steads as these extraordinary men conferred a new dignity on those who performed such feats of endurance, prompting Desgrange to baptize them the *noblesse du muscle*.

GENERAL CLASSIFICATION

1. **Maurice Garin** (FRA)
   2,428 km in 94h.33m.14s; Average Speed: 25.679 kph
2. **Lucien Pothier** (FRA) at 2h.59m.2s
3. **Fernand Augereau** (FRA) at 4h.29m.24s
4. Rodolphe Muller (ITA) at 4h.39m.30s
5. Jean Fischer (FRA) at 4h.58m.44s
6. Marcel Kerff (BEL) at 5h.52m.24s
7. Julien 'Samson' Lootens (BEL) at 8h.31m.8s
8. Georges Pasquier (FRA) at 10h.24m.4s
9. François Beaugendre (FRA) at 10h.52m.14s
10. Aloïs Catteau (BEL) at 12h.44m.57s
11. Jean Dargassies (FRA) at 13h.49m.10s
12. Ferdinand Payan (FRA) at 19h.9m.2s
13. Julien Girbe (FRA) at 23h.16m.52s
14. Isidore Lechartier (FRA) at 24h.5m.13s
15. Josef Fischer (GER) at 25h.14m.26s
16. Alexandre Foureaux (FRA) at 31h.50m.52s
17. René Salais (FRA) at 32h.34m.43s
18. Émile Moulin (FRA) at 49h.43m.15s
19. Georges Borot (FRA) at 51h.37m.38s
20. Pierre Desvages (FRA) at 62h.53m.54s

1ˢᵗ TOUR DE FRANCE, 6 STAGES – 2,428 KILOMETRES

Stage	Date	Distance	STAGE	STAGE WINNER	YELLOW JERSEY
Stage 1	Wednesday 1 July	467 km	Paris – Lyon	M. Garin (FRA)	M. Garin
Stage 2	Sunday 5 July	374 km	Lyon – Marseille	H. Aucouturier (FRA)	M. Garin
Stage 3	Wednesday 8 July	423 km	Marseille – Toulouse	H. Aucouturier (FRA)	M. Garin
Stage 4	Sunday 12 July	268 km	Toulouse – Bordeaux	C. Laeser (SUI)	M. Garin
Stage 5	Monday 13 July	425 km	Bordeaux – Nantes	M. Garin (FRA)	M. Garin
Stage 6	Saturday 18 July	471 km	Nantes – Paris	M. Garin (FRA)	M. Garin

Marcel Kerff

Julien Lootens

Lucien Pothier

The riders were signed in at the Réveil-Matin by Alphonse Steinès, but due to roadworks the Tour was actually started further down the road, by Georges Abran, at precisely sixteen minutes past three.

Garin takes charge

The first Tour was already an international event, with Swiss, Belgian and German riders. Here Germany's Josef Fischer, 38, samples Boumboum Liquorice and a cigar.

LYON (2 July): The finish? Well, since you ask... I missed it! Garin and Pagie were on rude bicycles; I'd taken the express train and still they beat me to Lyons! I'd seen them replenish themselves at Moulins and plunge into the night, and, discerning the astonishing vigour in these two demons of the road, I'd calculated their advance on my already-optimistic timetable and intuited that I'd miss them. My train pulled in at 8.50, I leapt into a car, and from a distance made out a crowd of thousands on the Quai de Vaise, shouting, applauding and thronging around two figures white with dust. It was them! They'd just finished, had boarded a car and were making off in the direction from which I'd just arrived. In the nick of time, our two august colleagues, correspon-dent Lassagne and chief inspector Abran, provided me with their first-hand accounts of the finish. 'It was quite simple: at 7.20am a telephone call from Tarare announced the passing of Garin and Pagie. We hastened to prepare the checkpoint and soon, at 9 o'clock, we heard the 'tara-ta-ta' of distant horns. A flag was waved and Garin arrived, bounding like a cat over the fat cobblestones of the quay, a worthy victory of the first stage of the Tour de France.'

Garin makes a habit of mistiming his finishes. After Paris-Brest, he breached the Parc des Princes velodrome in the morning while the huge crowd didn't expect him until the afternoon. In Bordeaux-Paris 1902, he was within minutes of entering the velodrome before it had even opened to the public. This time too, the conqueror of the first stage of our race, an opening test that on its own is worth a Bordeaux-Paris, arrived in Lyon before the checkpoint was manned and while the streets were still clear, but for a hundred or so devotees who had come out early to inform themselves of the competitors' progress.

Pagie, the rider from Tourcoing, finished a valiant second, less than a minute behind his famous rival, happily presenting us with the prospect of a closely faught battle in the days to come. Half-an-hour later, Léon Georget arrived to a fanfare of horns. This son of Châtellerault wore a mask of fury; without a word, he spoke in gestures and allowed himself to be conducted to the nearby baths where Garin and Pagie were already installed.

The crowd was gathering by the minute in the outlying Faubourg of Vaise, swollen by sportsmen, children, young women in light, summery outfits and loud-voiced housewives without even the decorum to sport a bonnet. Just how much further could we be from Paris?

Now, although well spaced, the arrivals became regular. First Augereau, then Jean Fischer, who narrated his tribulations with some composure for once, passing up his customary breast-beating, and as the classification table below shows, after a rather dense series of arrivals, a lull occurred, which allowed the officials to luncheon, at the *Brasserie Comte*, of course,

since it was there that the stylish checkpoint for the finish line had been installed.

During the morning, as one cyclist succeeded another, I went to see Garin and Pagie and the other leaders, whose first thought had been to visit the baths. I found the champion stretched out over a camp bed, completely naked beneath a thick woollen blanket, as calm, relaxed and proud now as he had been full of energy the previous night at Moulins.

The man is a marvel! He showed me his posterior, on which the saddle marks had already disappeared. He had no scars beyond a slight graze to the knee and elbow after a fall while leaving Moulins. With great precision, in astonishing detail that betrayed a prodigious memory and surprising lucidity after such efforts, he recalled: 'a chaotic, turbulent start. I moved ahead of the confusion and heard crashes behind me.

'Someone shouted out that Josef Fischer had gone down. Poor lad! We all looked after ourselves – *c'est la guerre* – as far as Fontainebleau! Chapperon, Trippier, Georget and Aucouturier attacked relentlessly. They were after my scalp, that much was obvious – but they weren't having it! Two kilometres from the checkpoint at Fontainebleau, Georget and Aucouturier attacked again. Chapperon and Trippier were left behind, but Pagie and I were quickly back with the leaders. Further on, Aucouturier said to me "The two of you should save yourselves," but I told him, "Wait, this isn't the time to be dropping anyone." The heat was unbearable.

'After Briare, the leading group agreed to stop at the next village to wash in fresh water, but no one dismounted. I didn't care! I could see that devil Aucouturier was labouring more and more. Muller was wilting and Pasquier was groaning and gasping for breath. Now, to complete my joy, it was getting tough! We reached Cosne. They were all struggling except Georget and Pagie. I heard them agreeing to take a rest, and I said to Pagie, who is a protégé of mine: "Listen, I'm telling you not to dismount outside an inn."

'They all dismounted in a flurry, but we continued, Pagie and I. Only Georget left the inviting cold water to pursue us. He reached us after 100 metres. Aucouturier was dropped and has lost already the Tour de France. Beyond Pouilly, Georget said: "Look.

After 17 hours in the saddle, two mobile controls and three signing-in points, Garin won the stage to Lyon, beside 33, Quai de Vaise, where the crowd was as great as the previous afternoon at the Réveil-Matin.

Léon Georget, after a series of punctures and having ridden alone from Nevers, finished third with a 35-minute deficit. He was fuelled by Bordeaux and biscuits.

Pacers were forbidden, but a crowd of enthusiastic fans on bicycles joined Garin, 'the White Bulldog', when he dropped Pagie in the closing stages.

I think I've got a rear-wheel puncture." He had to stop to repair it. From that point on, it didn't feel like a race. I saved my energy, and helped Pagie so that I wouldn't be alone. Then Lyon, and those cobblestones. That was stage one. Roll on stage two.'

And Maurice Garin smiled merrily. As for his indefatigable manager, our friend Delattre, with whom I spent the whole night at Moulins and then on the train, he was elated. His man had won, and nine out of the twelve members of his team, La Française, are still in the race: It's a marvellous result! Bravo, Delattre! Bravo, 'La Française'!

Victory goes to the favourite

Above: Garin savours victory, and a cigarette, accompanied by his son (right).

A storm-surge overwhelming a handful of madmen trying to build a dam: this was the image brought to mind yesterday by the crowds that invaded the road at Ville d'Avray at 2 o'clock, as the controllers tried in vain to direct them to the sides of the road. It was an impossible fight from the start, and we recognised this no more starkly than just before 2pm, when stewards spread the word that the competitors were just a few pedal-strokes from the finishing post.

The crowd surged forward for a better view and no human force could have held them back, although a shoulder-width gap remained to allow the cyclists to pass.

Thanks to dispatches from the previous checkpoints, we knew that the leading peloton consisted of ten cyclists and that all ten would no doubt fight head-on to win the last stage of this colossal *randonnée*.

What was going to happen? We hardly dared think. With every passing second, the crowd bulged, the mass of spectators became more compact. There were people everywhere, at windows, on rooftops, in trees, on bicycles, in cars, on horseback, on foot; never before had such enthusiasm been seen.

The final episode in the Tour's great drama was unfolding. An overexcited spectator brought Jean Fischer down, who could have

won the stage with a well-timed attack. But then Garin unleashed his sprint, thrust through the crowd and passed under the finishing banner at exactly nine minutes past two. Behind him, Augereau and Samson fought for second place. Passions were at their zenith. The crowd noise intensified and a prodigious uproar greeted the race finish. Ladies brandished parasols, men wielded hats; I even saw spectators in tears. There, the emotions that sport can arouse! In the heat of battle, Augereau couldn't avoid a photographer and careered head-first into his lens.

Once they had finished, the valiant *routiers* were swept into the gardens flanking the offices of *L'Auto* for champagne and a swift wash before leaving for the Parc des Princes. This procession, which I can only describe as triumphal, did not please all these devourers of kilometres. Garin asked if he could make the journey to the velodrome by car, declaring that he did not want to perish at the hands of an over-enthusiastic crowd. We informed him that bicycles were compulsory. Deafening applause from the thousands who were watching greeted his departure. Having transformed France into a gigantic velodrome, it was time for Garin to savour his apotheosis in the Parc des Princes.

DESGRANGE'S CONCLUSION

And that was the first Tour de France! All my colleagues are exhausted. I'm delighted and I only wish that the hours of work and great satisfaction that the race has meant for us could go on indefinitely, so delicious is the work, so sweet are its satisfactions. I have dreamed many sporting dreams in my life but never have I conceived of anything as worthy as this reality.

In the outskirts of Bordeaux, the Swiss rider Charles Laeser was proclaimed winner of the fourth stage. It was the first foreign stage win in the Tour de France.

His labours over, Maurice Garin takes a lap of honour around the cinder track at the Parc de Princes.

Pothier (2nd) dismounts to receive a bouquet from his father; while Augereau (3rd) seems to have recovered from his finish-line collision with a photographer.

Cornet's lucky break

The 1904 Tour was one of the most scandalous and sinister in history, tainted by plots, scams, booby-traps made of nails, surreptitious train journeys and crowds so partisan that, especially in Saint-Etienne and Alès, they hurled abuse and more at riders from other regions. Henri Desgrange had turned a blind eye to some of the abuses, and bitten his tongue when perhaps he would have preferred to speak. But the day after the race finish, disgusted at the incessant cheating, the regional prejudice and the monotonous dominance of Maurice Garin and the La Française team, he made up his mind. The event had become a victim of its own success; the passions it aroused were too fervent to be controlled. This second Tour de France, he decided, would be the last.

Then came the ratification of the race results. This normally took a fortnight or less for major events. This time, however, the Union Vélocipédique de France was in no hurry. Desgrange and *L'Auto* observed perplexed silence until 2 December when the Union announced its decision: the first four finishers in the provisional classification were to be disqualified and suspended for repeated contraventions of the race regulations. Maurice Garin was stripped of his stage win and the overall title; the hapless Hippolyte Aucouturier saw four stage wins struck from the records. Lucien Pothier, the provisional runner-up, was banned for life. The new winner was the fifth-placed rider, Henri Cornet, aged only 20.

The Union Vélocipédique had already flexed its muscles after participants in the 1904 Bordeaux-Paris race had hitched lifts on their coaches' motorbikes. Now, by making an example of riders at the Tour, the Union Vélocipédique did what the incensed Desgrange couldn't have done even if he had wanted to, and for a man known for his derisive turn of phrase, his response was somewhat muted. The penalties, he proffered, failed to take into account 'the profound and conflicting interests' that underlay the two events. The Union's verdict, he fudged, was rather heavy-handed for his tastes and those of his newspaper: granted, there may have been some small excesses, stretching the rules regarding food consumption, but were such harsh penalties really warranted? Desgrange, however, was probably more relieved than angry. He picked himself up, dusted himself off and was soon planning the next year's Tour.

GENERAL CLASSIFICATION

1. **Maurice Garin** (FRA) La Française, 2,429 km in 93h.6m.24s; Average Speed: 26.081 kph
2. **Lucien Pothier** (FRA) at 3h.28m
3. **César Garin** (FRA) at 1h.51m.13s
4. Hippolyte Aucouturier (FRA) at 2h.52m.26s
5. Henri Cornet (FRA), at 2h.59m.31s
6. Jean-Baptiste Dortignacq (FRA) at 5h.15m.45s
7. Philippe Jousellin (FRA) at 8h.34m.24s
8. Aloïs Catteau (BEL), at 12h.0m.56s
9. Camille Fily (FRA) at 15h.38m.42s
10. Jean Dargassies (FRA) at 16h.4m.1s

FINAL GENERAL CLASSIFICATION 2 nd DECEMBER

1. **Henri Cornet** (FRA) 2,429 km in 96h.5m.55s; Average Speed: 25.265 kph
2. **Jean-Baptiste Dortignacq** (FRA) at 2h.16m.14s
3. **Aloïs Catteau** (BEL) at 9h.1m.25s
4. Jean Dargassies (FRA) at 13h.4m.30s
5. Julien Maitron (FRA) at 19h.6m.15s
6. Auguste Daumain (FRA) at 22h.44m.36s
7. Louis Coolsaet (BEL) at 23h.44m.20s
8. Achille Colas (FRA) at 25h.9m.50s
9. René Saget (FRA) at 25h.55m.16s
10. Gustave Drioul (BEL) at 30h.54m.49s

2nd TOUR DE FRANCE, 6 STAGES – 2,429 KILOMETRES

			STAGE	STAGE WINNER	YELLOW JERSEY
Stage 1	Saturday 2 July	467 km	Paris – Lyon	M. Garin (FRA)	M. Garin
Stage 2	Saturday 9 July	374 km	Lyon – Marseille	H. Aucouturier (FRA)	M. Garin
Stage 3	Wednesday 13 July	424 km	Marseille – Toulouse	H. Aucouturier (FRA)	M. Garin
Stage 4	Sunday 17 July	268 km	Toulouse – Bordeaux	L. Pothier (FRA)	M. Garin
Stage 5	Wednesday 20 July	425 km	Bordeaux – Nantes	H. Aucouturier (FRA)	M. Garin
Stage 6	Saturday 23 July	471 km	Nantes – Paris (Ville-d'Avray)	H. Aucouturier (FRA)	M. Garin

			STAGE	STAGE WINNER	YELLOW JERSEY
Stage 1	Saturday 2 July	467 km	Paris – Lyon	M. Frederick (SUI)	M. Frederick
Stage 2	Saturday 9 July	374 km	Lyon – Marseille	A. Faure (FRA)	E. Lombard
Stage 3	Wednesday 13 July	424 km	Marseille – Toulouse	H. Cornet (FRA)	H. Cornet
Stage 4	Sunday 17 July	268 km	Toulouse – Bordeaux	F. Beaugendre (FRA)	F. Beaugendre
Stage 5	Wednesday 20 July	425 km	Bordeaux – Nantes	J.-B. Dortignacq (FRA)	H. Cornet
Stage 6	Saturday 23 July	471 km	Nantes – Paris	J.-B. Dortignacq (FRA)	H. Cornet

Above right: At Paris, in the courtyard of *L'Auto*, wheels, frames and components were stamped before a testing 2,428 kilometres (1,508 miles) of racing.
Right: At Lyon, the riders arrived at the *Délices à la Demi-Lune* restaurant to a twenty-five trumpet fanfare.

Garin from the word go! Just like in 1903...

I'm here again, in the depths of the countryside and the night, waiting with feverish impatience for the sudden, phantasmagorical rush of riders to appear, each rendered identical by a thick layer of white dust.

I'm standing in the fields before the town of Briare where we have set up the famous secret checkpoint; every competitor will have to dismount and sign in here. This isolated corner presents a peculiar aspect; the road is barred by lanterns that speckle the night sky. Stencils spell out the words 'Stop, Checkpoint!' in huge letters. With me, beneath the acetylene flares, are race officials and a crowd of villagers, cyclists and drivers who populate our picturesque encampment.

A trail of light approaches; it is Ouzou and Miral, the dusty drivers with whom I'll be dashing to Lyon. They have news: a dozen cyclists are leading at a furious pace. Pothier has been dropped after a puncture. Aucouturier appears to be out of the race already; he has fallen three times and has lost 45 minutes. Then, on the horizon, the agreed signal: a green Bengal light. As it emits its pale glow, a thick cloud comes towards us; inside, there are bodies, steel and legs pumping frantically. A cry goes up: 'Checkpoint!' The rivals hesitate for a second, then throw themselves on the pencils and papers prepared in advance in an inextricable tangle of machines. After a feverish rush, the leaders are soon free; the rest give chase.

We are following them now; the peloton sheds the occasional rider, but Garin's little white jacket is always at the front. The night begins to brighten, the stars are extinguished, the sky is tinged with blue, a pink glow rises and the sun appears.

Pougues is soon behind us and we reach Nevers and another battle for pens. Garin shouts for food. Pothier, dropped after several crashes, has made up the lost terrain magnificently, he throws down a bicycle he had borrowed to be able to carry on: 'A bicycle! Give me a bicycle that's the right size!' By the time they reach Moulins only six riders remain. Soon it is only five: Garin, Pothier, Gerbi (the Italian), Frédérick and Chevalier. Chevalier is dropped first, then, faced with a climb that rises like a wall before them, Gerbi asks if everyone will agree to climb it on foot. Frédérick agrees. Garin puts his head down and attacks; Pothier, always so light in the saddle, follows easily; Gerbi grits his teeth and dons his crampons; Frédérick loses contact and gives up the struggle.

Garin senses that the game will be won here and persists with his effort, an admirable effort, an effort equal to the finest he has sown the great roads of France with. Gerbi admits defeat. Only Pothier remains in the slipstream of the king of the road. The two men climb the hill beyond Roanne as the panorama opens beneath us, then hurtle down, cornering at top speed on the improbable bends that only end at Tarare.

The crowds are thickening, distant flags flap in the wind, a banner stretches across the road and the stands are full. Garin chooses that moment to attack, dodging spectators on bikes. As Pothier hesitates, his adversary gains a decisive lead. Garin has won his first stage, and, as in 1903, he may even have won the Tour, for the great Aucouturier didn't reach Lyon unscathed.

Aged 33, Maurice Garin's second Tour victory was faster than his first.

THE WILD BOAR
BY HENRI DESGRANGE

What a superb fighting beast Maurice Garin is, armed with all the qualities to neutralize his adversaries and guarantee victory. He is the racing cyclist, the great *routier*, in every sense of the word: with a turn of speed fast enough to capture resounding victories on the track, and with a shrewd mind. Men fade away behind him. When there is a big fall, Garin avoids it almost every time. He has an admirable stomach too, and can, when he has to, cover 200 kilometres (124 miles) without eating. And when his parched opponents stop at roadside fountains, he arches his back, leans into the pedals and presses on towards the finish. He can resist any speed, no one can drop him and when he takes the lead, the average speed always rises.

His victory in stage one seems to have been much less easy than last year. Whereas in 1903 he had taken command of the race as early as Briare, 150 kilometres (93 miles) from Paris, and had kept Pagie with him in order not to ride alone, this year a veritable pack of riders attacked him throughout the night, laying traps and probing him for signs of weakness. At Montargis, more than fifty riders passed the checkpoint like a whirlwind; at Cosne, there were still fifteen left; but by Nevers the strain was beginning to tell. Man and muscle had already done part of their task. There were no more than six riders at his heels, chasing frantically, stretched to breaking point. By the time they reached Moulins, he'd left another body by the wayside.

At Roanne, the drama had almost run its course; just one desperate rider clung on: Pothier, second in the 1903 Tour.

The others, nearer or further, suffered bottomless fatigue and the lassitude of their muscles, as the 'wild boar' pulled away, increasing the distance that separated them from him. Chevalier was three minutes behind at Roanne; at Tarare, 40 km (25 miles) on, the gap was 23 minutes.

Only Pothier kept up the pace and it seems that at the end of this first stage the general classification should be the same as last year.

Halfway there, and enough's enough

If we were the sort titillated by scandal, we might have taken pleasure in both the attempted murder committed at St-Étienne and the brawl that happened near Alès last night.

But that is not our intention, and if the success of the 1903 Tour de France led us to count on even greater success this year, we didn't dream it would be of this nature. We didn't imagine that communities would turn out to support their local champion with such passion that they would ease his path to victory by demolishing his rivals, or take revenge for a just disqualification on his fellow riders.

There was, nevertheless, a considerable difference between the incidents that took place at St-Étienne and Nîmes. At St-Étienne it was planned in secret; the would-be assassins waited at the Col de la République

with the simple intention of helping Faure to win by knifing his opponents. There are times when the most courageous thing to do is to simply turn around and leave, and for this reason we have decided that next year the Tour will no longer pass through the Loire.

The Nîmes incident was of a different type altogether. In the first place, the townsfolk from Nîmes are strangers to fighting; better still, they fought valiantly to prevent supporters from Alès from carrying out a dirty trick. At St-Étienne it was a knife in the back; at Nîmes it was a brutal and stupid attack that requires a response. We shall deliver it in 1905; the Tour will pass through Nîmes but Payan will no more be allowed to take part next year than this, unless he is able to produce categorical proof of his innocence.

SURVEILLANCE BY AUTOMOBILE

The two *L'Auto* motor cars have ensured rigorous surveillance. No peccadillo, however small, can be attributed to the competitors, who all rode an absolutely fair race. Ouzou's marvellous 3-cylinder will certainly finish the Tour de France without the slightest mechanical hitch, and for those who understand what it takes for a motor car to follow the riders at speeds between 15 and 25 kph (9 and 15 mph), then to maintain high speed jumping from one group to the other and moving to the front to take on fuel or announce the impending arrival of the peloton to the checkpoint marshals, the achievement of Ouzou's Cottereau vehicle will be highly appreciated.

Here we should also mention the motorcycle with a gear change and front-axle assembly ridden by Gaston Rivierre, who didn't lose the front pack throughout, which no doubt reminded him of the days when he won the Bordeaux-Paris race.

Recognizable by their white jackets, Maurice Garin, his brother César and Lucien Pothier pull out to avoid a cart, under the gaze of the Tour officials.

The last Tour?

The Tour de France is over and its second celebration will also, I deeply fear, be its last. It will have been killed by its own success, by the blind passions that it unleashed, and the slurs and filthy suspicions worthy only of the ignorant and malicious. Yet it seemed, and it still seems, that with this great contest we had built the most enduring and impressive monument in the sport of cycling. We had hoped that we would be able to use it to bring a little sporting virtue to most of France. The results last year seemed to confirm that we were right. Yet after only the second Tour de France we are disheartened and discouraged after three weeks of lies and infamy.

Maurice Garin won the Tour de France for the second time, followed only seconds later by Pothier, who took second place as he did last year. In third place was another Garin, one of Maurice's younger brothers. We have long known the ardour with which the La Française company, whose machines are used by these three riders, contest bicycle races – especially the great road races. While complimenting La Française on its great success, which its three champions could certainly have achieved by valour alone, I have a cordial reproach to submit; to whit, that they entrusted their organization at the Tour de France to individuals too involved in previous, regrettable incidents at road races, lacking the calm, impartiality and clarity of vision to understand the rising public distaste caused by deception during road races.

I should not forget those modest, little known, diminutive men who have accomplished the work of giants: anyone who has beheld the delicate silhouettes of Dortignacq, Cornet, Fily and Maitron is left baffled, wondering how far energy and willpower can take humanity. These are the men who could have ensured the greatest success for our contest, if only the passions unleashed there had allowed it to be seen by calmer eyes.

The December verdict

The ratification of the Tour de France. We will look in a moment at the decisions taken by the Union Vélocipédique de France, the sanctions the Union has imposed on a number of riders, the disqualification of the leading riders, and the considerations that accompanied their sentences.

With full knowledge of the facts, it is extremely difficult to grasp whether the heavy penalties meted out to the leading riders were motivated by sound reasoning, since their decision was announced without indicating which documents formed its basis. It is not unreasonable to believe that public opinion will demand an explanation and that the Union should provide it.

We approached the Union as the supreme power in cycling, entirely independent and uniquely competent in the last resort to intervene in a case as sensitive as this – a sporting event that for a month aroused unprecedented feeling among the public. In front of me, the chiefs of the two leading manufacturers affected by the Union's decision gave the strictest instructions to every member of their staff involved with racing to follow the race regulations to the letter.

I followed two complete stages in person and confirm that no breach was committed that would justify any such measure against any rider from these two marques. I should add that the file given to the Union by the commissaires contained no material to justify such severe penalties.

Since the judgement has now been made public, there is no reason not to say that my own verdict would have been different. I would have upheld the disqualification of Chevalier and Payan, both caught *in flagrante delicto*, I would have associated Pothier with their fate. To the others, I would have issued fines, nothing more.

The Union must now prove to the public, those I will term both the victims and the instigators of events, that it can distinguish between the spirit and the letter of the law.

Despite the large number of fixed and mobile checkpoints like this one at Versailles, the second Tour de France was marked by cheating and shortcuts, leading to the disqualification of the four highest-placed cyclists.

Trousselier puts the Tour back *en route*

Considerably longer than the first two Tours, with eleven stages instead of six, and a new rulebook that converted time differentials into points, the 1905 Tour de France represented a new departure. More importantly, it was peaceful, relatively law-abiding – despite the estimated 125 kg (276 lb) of tintacks strewn across the roads – and fell to a worthy champion, Louis Trousselier, aged barely 24. The good-natured Trousselier won five stages for the team sponsored by Peugeot bikes. Runner-up Hippolyte Aucouturier, with three stage wins, rode on the same team, a clear indication of the strength in depth at the disposal of the canny Peugeot manager Léopold Alibert.

Peugeot could have completed a clean sweep of podium places if René Pottier had not been forced to drop out on stage three. Pottier had made light work of the first ascent in Tour de France history of the Ballon d'Alsace, speeding up it at 20 kph (12 mph) to take the race lead on the end of day two. The next day, injuries sustained during a fall in the finale of the first stage to Nancy, exacerbated by the pace of his ascent, forced his withdrawal. Trousselier returned to the head of the general classification by winning stage three at Grenoble, on the very day he had been due to start his military service.

The 1905 Tour attracted massive crowds despite sometimes blistering temperatures, their attention caught by the inclusion of the Ballon d'Alsace and the Tour's first excursion into the Alps, which Aucouturier sprinted up at 25 kph (15 mph). With riders like Jean-Baptiste Dortignacq, Émile Georget and Lucien Petit-Breton, the opposition was extremely strong. Dortignacq took three stages on his way to third place overall, while Petit-Breton, described as an Argentine from Buenos Aires but actually born in France, harried the Peugeot team, and complained to the organizers over their bike changes in the mountains. He also rode into fifth place despite rotten luck. The nails thrown over the road had cost him dearly and caused scores of other racers to puncture, although, fortunately, they did not put a stop to the race.

GENERAL CLASSIFICATION

1. **Louis Trousselier** (FRA) 35 points
   2,994 km in 109h.55m.39s; Average Speed: 27.107 kph
2. **Hippolyte Aucouturier** (FRA) 61
3. **Jean-Baptiste Dortignacq** (FRA) 64
4. Émile Georget (FRA) 123
5. Lucien Petit-Breton (FRA) 155
6. Augustin Ringeval (FRA) 202

7. Paul Chauvet (FRA) 231
8. Philippe Pautrat (FRA) 248
9. Julien Gabory (FRA) 255
10. Julien Maitron (FRA) 304
11. Alois Catteau (BEL) 355
12. Martin Soulie (FRA) 358
13. Léon Leygoute (FRA) 394

14. Camille Fily (FRA) 415
15. Antony Wattelier (FRA) 441
16. Henri Lignon (FRA) 488
17. Maurice Decaup (FRA) 490
18. Maurice Carriere (FRA), 497
19. Gustave Guillarme (FRA) 509
20. Julien 'Samson' Lootens (BEL) 515

3rd TOUR DE FRANCE,
11 STAGES – 2,994 KILOMETRES

			STAGE	STAGE WINNER	YELLOW JERSEY
Stage 1	Sunday 9 July	340 km	Paris – Nancy	L. Trousselier (FRA)	L. Trousselier
Stage 2	Tuesday 11 July	299 km	Nancy – Besançon	H. Aucouturier (FRA)	R. Pottier
Stage 3	Saturday 15 July	327 km	Besançon – Grenoble	L. Trousselier (FRA)	L. Trousselier
Stage 4	Sunday 16 July	348 km	Grenoble – Toulon	H. Aucouturier (FRA)	L. Trousselier
Stage 5	Tuesday 18 July	192 km	Toulon – Nîmes	L. Trousselier (FRA)	L. Trousselier
Stage 6	Thursday 20 July	307 km	Nîmes – Toulouse	J.-B. Dortignacq (FRA)	L. Trousselier
Stage 7	Sunday 23 July	268 km	Toulouse – Bordeaux	L. Trousselier (FRA)	L. Trousselier
Stage 8	Tuesday 25 July	257 km	Bordeaux – La Rochelle	H. Aucouturier (FRA)	L. Trousselier
Stage 9	Thursday 27 July	263 km	La Rochelle – Rennes	L. Trousselier (FRA)	L. Trousselier
Stage 10	Saturday 29 July	167 km	Rennes – Caen	J.-B. Dortignacq (FRA)	L. Trousselier
Stage 11	Sunday 30 July	253 km	Caen – Paris	J.-B. Dortignacq (FRA)	L. Trousselier

The winner of the Tour is normally happier than this, but Louis Trousselier. aged 24, was conscripted by the army the moment he dismounted. He didn't even have time to enjoy his winnings of 6,950 francs.

Trou-trou's triumph and return

Trousselier, a member of the Vélo-Club de Levallois, was unstoppable. He treated the perils of his first Tour as a game, from the scorching heat at Nîmes to the cobbles between Paris and Roubaix.

Born into a family of cycling enthusiasts, 'Trou-trou' mastered the finer points of the bicycle at an early age and became a real acrobat. His tricks would make him a star.

PARIS (30 July): A marvellous finale! The Tour de France ended yesterday as an indisputable success. Absorbing from start to finish, it gave us three weeks of the liveliest sporting emotions, offering successive, captivating struggles often unresolved until the finish-line. Just as no rose is without its thorns, so no success is without its shadows, yet these serve ultimately to accentuate the splendour. The third Tour de France survived its demise on its first stage by the very narrowest of margins, and I imagine that this was the exact purpose of the sinister brute who sowed the road with fistfuls of nails.

Yet we have reaped great satisfactions this year. Where last year we saw competitors ready at any moment to box each other's ears, excitable crowds threatening to set upon them, scandals erupting beneath their feet and the race enveloped in ill repute, this year, in equal measure, everything passed off admirably.

Everyone has embraced their responsibility to compete honestly and not to act destructively with regard to his fellows. Those who contributed to the success of this Tour de France have provided the clearest proof that a race of this scale need not awaken humanity's worst instincts.

Indeed, comparing our spirits at the end of this third Tour de France with those of a year ago, we discover such a difference that, whereas last year we announced our decision never again to recommence an event that resembled all too often a form of torture, now, even before we have recovered from our labours, we are looking forward to another Tour de France in 1906. For every action contains its end result within itself; each human creation will know happy tomorrows, provided it has not suffered the

harmful effects of people or circumstances. What lessons emerge from such a contest disputed with such spirit? This, above all else: that henceforth anything can be asked of the riders; and second, that nothing is any longer impossible when the interested parties work towards the success of the whole.

Will the 1906 Tour de France be identical to this year's? The results this year will most likely lead us to adopt regulations that will closely resemble those of 1904. We have also suggested that the route could very well be extended to introduce new obstacles and provide the riders with the opportunity to conquer new challenges. Yet let us never overlook the prodigious exertions of these men who have, on each stage over the past three weeks, provided ceaseless acts of daring and heroism. Their mission is now complete, and it is right to express our admiration for their spirit and valour. To remember the keenness with which we have followed their smallest efforts and our

The way is finally clear for Trousselier, who went on to win with ease at Bordeaux, as he had at Nancy, Grenoble and Nîmes.

happiness at the success of each of them. *Oui!* Everyone triumphed yesterday. Wherever they finished on the stage or over-all, they were all winners, and the crowds that lined the roads and in the velodrome told them so with their unquenchable zest.

Trousselier's victory overflows the bounds of eulogy. Never has one man collected so many victories in a season. Winner of Paris-Roubaix, forced to abandon Bordeaux-Paris when he was still among the first three, he came back to the Tour de France in finer fettle than at the start of the season and somehow summoned the strength to win five stages without a moment's weakness. He accepted the implacable sun and the rudest climbs with the unfailing Parisian humour. So easy and relaxed was his victory, achieved by a rider of such class and quality, that it has no precedents in the annals of cycling.

INTERVIEW WITH THE CHAMPION

With Trousselier, who marches out of the shower looking fresh, spruce, with the sparkling eyes of a champion and a moustache at battle stations, all we have to do is listen: 'I'm not sorry it's over – at least I'll be able to sleep till noon. That bore Albert won't be knocking at my door at 2 o'clock in the morning with his, "Let's go, Louis, it's time." I've never felt needlessly emotional; I was always sure that, barring accidents, I'd win by a decent margin. My legs are strong; the engine works pretty well; my appetite's ferocious and I'm hale and hearty. I owe a vote of thanks to those who've contributed to my victory: Monsieur Sicot, the director at Peugeot; Albert, who gave me first-class advice throughout; Lesna, who has looked after me like a father; and my rivals, who haven't taken it too badly; my coaches and *L'Auto*, who have popped a modest fortune into the palm of my hand.'

Having avoided unpleasant surprises in the general classification, Trousselier, in complete control of the race, savours his coffee at Rouen in the company of the ubiquitous Abran (left).

Pottier, the first of the eagles

The fourth Tour de France was revolutionary in both the quality of the field and the conception of the route. By increasing the number of stages from 11 to 13, and the length from 3,000 to 4,500 km (less than 2,000 to nearly 2,800 miles), with detours through Germany, Spain and Italy, Desgrange finally transformed his race into *La Grande Boucle*: a majestic 'great loop' that policed the nation's perimeter. Leaving the buzzing Buffalo velodrome in north Paris one 4 July evening, this colossal event mobilized 76 first-class athletes. There was Trousselier, the reigning champion; René Pottier, forced to abandon with injury as race leader the previous year; Émile Georget, fourth in 1905, and his brother Léon; the old-hand Aucouturier and the youngster Petit-Breton. And for the first time in Tour history, the mountain stages proved decisive. René Pottier, the king of the Ballon d'Alsace in 1905, used the climb to launch a heroic solo 220-km (137-mile) breakaway to Dijon, where he gained a 48-minute margin. He increased his lead by tearing through the Alps and winning at Grenoble by a quarter of an hour and at Nice by 26 minutes. He then defended his lead all the way to Paris. By winning the final stage at the Parc des Princes, Pottier earned an ecstatic welcome, thanks to the manner in which he had contained the threat of Trousselier, who had won the stages finishing at Toulouse, Bordeaux, Nantes and Brest, and his own team-mate, the promising Georges Passerieu. Passerieu, who finished first at Marseille and again at Caen, reached Paris with Pottier and encouraged his leader to abandon his customary reserve and sprint for the finishing line to take his fifth stage win in style. Despite finishing among the top five in ten out of the thirteen stages, Petit-Breton had to be content with fourth place overall. Only fourteen riders ended a race diminished once again by punctures caused by roads deliberately strewn with nails, but brightened by Dortignacq's win close to his home in Bayonne. It was a surprisingly eventful race that recorded the poorest average speed since 1903: little more than 24.460 kph (15.199 mph).

GENERAL CLASSIFICATION

1. **René Pottier** (FRA) 31 pts
   4,543 km; Average Speed 24.463 kph
2. **Georges Passerieu** (FRA) 39
3. **Louis Trousselier** (FRA) 59
4. **Lucien Petit-Breton** (FRA) 65
5. Émile Georget (FRA) 80
6. Aloïs Catteau (BEL) 129
7. Édouard Wattelier (FRA) 137
8. Léon Georget (FRA) 152
9. Eugène Christophe (FRA) 156
10. Antony Wattelier (FRA) 168
11. Georges Fleury (FRA) 201
12. Ferdinand Payan (FRA) 222
13. Léon Winant (FRA) 241
14. Georges Bronchard (FRA) 256

4ᵗʰ TOUR DE FRANCE, 13 STAGES – 4,543 KM

			STAGE	STAGE WINNER	YELLOW JERSEY
Stage 1	Wednesday 4 July	275 km	Paris – Lille	É. Georget (FRA)	É. Georget
Stage 2	Friday 6 July	400 km	Douai – Nancy	R. Pottier (FRA)	R. Pottier
Stage 3	Sunday 8 July	416 km	Nancy – Dijon	R. Pottier (FRA)	R. Pottier
Stage 4	Tuesday 10 July	311 km	Dijon – Grenoble	R. Pottier (FRA)	R. Pottier
Stage 5	Thursday 12 July	345 km	Grenoble – Nice	R. Pottier (FRA)	R. Pottier
Stage 6	Saturday 14 July	292 km	Nice – Marseille	G. Passerieu (FRA)	R. Pottier
Stage 7	Monday 16 July	480 km	Marseille – Toulouse	L. Trousselier (FRA)	R. Pottier
Stage 8	Wednesday 18 July	300 km	Toulouse – Bayonne	J.-B. Dortignacq (FRA)	R. Pottier
Stage 9	Friday 20 July	338 km	Bayonne – Bordeaux	L. Trousselier (FRA)	R. Pottier
Stage 10	Sunday 22 July	391 km	Bordeaux – Nantes	L. Trousselier (FRA)	R. Pottier
Stage 11	Tuesday 24 July	321 km	Nantes – Brest	L. Trousselier (FRA)	R. Pottier
Stage 12	Thursday 26 July	415 km	Brest – Caen	G. Passerieu (FRA)	R. Pottier
Stage 13	Sunday 29 July	259 km	Caen – Paris	R. Pottier (FRA)	R. Pottier

Dressed in the black and white colours of the Vélo-Club de Levallois and his own choice of unusual headgear, Pottier, 27, rode 650 kilometres (404 miles) in solo breakaways on his way to victory. Unprecedented!

King René, crowned on the Ballon d'Alsace

At the hint of a hill, Pottier attacked, whether at Pont-l'Éveque (above) or on the Ballon d'Alsace.

DIJON (8 July): A cloud of dust announces the riders' approach, until, *voilà!*, they zip around a bend and unleash their assault on the mountain. With a turn of the starting crank, our motor growls and we are on their heels. What happens next is easy to tell. At the foot of the slope, Pottier powers ahead at unheard of speed, as if he'd heard the final lap bell at a track race. He hasn't reached the first hairpin before the peloton is torn apart and we witness a superb spectacle. One by one or in bunches, Pottier shakes off the pack, as a wild boar does a pack of hounds. The first to cry mercy are Catteau and Fleury. Trousselier, Decaup and Privat follow, sickened by the startling pace of the leader, who persists in his endeavour without a backward glance. After a kilometre (0.6 miles) of this infernal obstacle, Winant is dropped, followed almost immediately by the quartet of Léon Georget, Tuvache, Aucouturier and the elder of the Watteliers. Twenty seconds later, Cadolle, Émile Georget, Gabory, Beaugendre and the younger of the Watteliers suffer the same fate. Go on, Pottier! You'll have them all! Just beyond the three-kilometre post, Petit-Breton and Dortignacq watch in wide-eyed fatigue as the leader darts away. Two men still resist the onslaught: Ringeval and Passerieu. For a while we nurture the illusion that they may cling on to the top. It is not to be. Pottier's trunk, wrapped in black and white hoops, remains curled over his powerful cadence, and suddenly it is Passerieu's turn to fall away. Pottier and Ringeval are alone now. A brief but terrifying duel breaks out, until, making a final demand from his boundless reserves, the leader pulls away in to the teeth of the gradient. Ringeval loses ground, makes it up again with a magnificent effort, then drops back again, done for!

Pottier broached the climb with eighteen other riders. He concludes it alone with an enormous lead, in front of a hundred impassioned spectators, driven, like us, into raptures by his exploit. Despite riding alone for the second half of the climb, Pottier has never let up. At the summit, he is exactly four-and-a-half minutes ahead of Passerieu and Ringeval. Determined not to relinquish his advantage, he plunges vertiginously down the Ballon's gigantic buttress to begin the 220 kilometres (136 miles) that still separate him from Dijon.

Those of us who witnessed his interminable, solitary, high-speed ride were left wondering whether it had not all been a dream, and asking ourselves what mysterious force it is that possesses the human organism and allows it to push back the boundaries of the possible.

Pottier: the bike is mightier than the pen

'Let me assure you, never has a race been so rigorously marshalled. It wouldn't have been easy to cheat, even if I'd wanted to. Look, here's one example out of ten I could give you: on the stage from Nancy to Dijon I'd dropped the peloton early, climbing the Ballon d'Alsace, and then I did more than 200 kilometres (124 miles) alone at the front, relying on my own resources and without any assistance whatsoever, except at the checkpoints. After following me for a long time, the official car had stopped and I was left to cross a plain that seemed to go on for ever followed by a squadron of riding spectators, for we were approaching the finish.

'Suddenly, 'tuff, tuff, tuff': I hear the car drawing alongside me. I threw a quick look over the occupants and my eyes met those of Monsieur Breyer, who gave me a very inquisitorial look which obviously meant: "My old chum, what are all these cyclists up to? There wouldn't perchance be any surreptitious drafting going on here?" In faith, I didn't say a word, but I was cut to the quick, so much so that I took off and rode like a

man possessed. Two kilometres (1.2 miles) later not a single cyclist remained on my wheel. On the other hand, I'm wrong to mock the commissaires' vehicle, which performs an inestimable service by updating me regularly on the interval separating me from my rivals.

'This may seem peculiar, but before the race, the man I feared the most was my old rival Marcel Cadolle. He'd beaten me too often on the road when we were amateurs for me not to be wary of him. You'll understand why, after opening up a lead over the first five stages, I eased back from full effort. Well advised by my devoted manager Alibert, I had two objectives: to build up reserves in case my strength failed me, as it could have after my exertions between Paris and Nice; and to keep watch over those like Cadolle, from whom I feared an aggressive counterattack. For example, once Cadolle had been left behind, I thought that the whole thing was in the bag, excepting an unlikely surprise from Passerieu. I kept an eye on him to the finish, especially as we

were riding for the same manufacturer.

'Look, there was nothing as hard as the stage from Brest to Caen. It started on a freezing night and continued into a day of suffocating heat, during which we had more than 400 km (248 miles) of undulating roads: hills, more hills, and still more hills! I thought we'd never get to the end. The final stage, on the other hand, I found easy and even pleasant. All the way from Caen to Paris there was spectacular applause and cheering before the final lap at the Parc des Princes.

'Apart from all that, all my opponents are tough nuts, starting with Passerieu, who hasn't said his last, and poor old Louis Trousselier, who inherited some of my bad luck from last year at the start. It's true that on the uphill stretches I would always have the advantage over him in any case. Climbing, you see, is my forte; speeding over the Ballon d'Alsace is much easier for me than writing a newspaper article.'

14 July, 6th stage, Nice-Marseille: Despite a strong wind, crowds of enthusiasts rode with Passerieu and Pottier, leading alone after the punctures of Cadolle and Christophe. With a huge lead in the general classification, Pottier gave the stage win to his team-mate.

Petit-Breton seizes the day

The climber René Pottier, hero of the 1906 Tour, would have been perfectly suited to the 1907 Tour, which crossed the Chartreuse massif via the Col de Porte and Le Sappey, on the way to Grenoble. Fate decided otherwise; in January that year, aged just 28, Pottier took his own life. The tragedy opened the race to an army of ambitious pretenders. The 1905 champion Louis Trousselier won the first stage to Roubaix, then shared a rare dead-heat with Émile Georget in German-occupied Metz. Then Georget took over the race lead by winning at Belfort, taking second behind Marcel Cadolle at Lyon, and taking the stage win at Grenoble after a magnificent duel on the Col de Porte with François Faber. Cadolle represented the main threat; a former French amateur champion and winner of two Bordeaux-Paris titles, Cadolle had abandoned in 1906 on stage 11, lying third overall. This year, he was in second place until stage seven approached Nîmes. A serious accident there robbed him not just of his hopes of victory, but of his cycling career.

Georget, meanwhile, added stage win after stage win. Victory looked his, until he accepted a borrowed bike on the stage to Bayonne. The organizers imposed a massive points penalty, leaving him in third place. The Alcyon team, including the well-placed Trousselier, withdrew in protest, leaving the field clear for another Peugeot cyclist, Lucien Mazan, a.k.a. Petit-Breton, a.k.a. the Argentine, to take the race in hand. In fairness, Petit-Breton had begun to clear the field himself, with a winning 250-km (155-mile) breakaway to Bayonne. He consolidated his advantage two days later with a second stage win in his hometown of Nantes. Petit-Breton was certainly an opportunist and, with his spectacular accelerations, something of a showman, but his overall victory at a record average speed of over 28 kph (17 mph) owed little to luck.

His rise to fame had begun in 1904, when he caught the eldest Georget brother, Léon, in the Bol d'Or; in 1905 he had finished fifth in his first Tour and set a world hour record of 41.110 km (25.546 miles). A year later, after coming fourth behind Pottier in the Tour de France, he had won the Paris-Tours, followed by the Milan-San Remo in Spring 1907. On equipment supplied by Peugeot, like Trousselier and Pottier before him, the 24-year-old was at the pinnacle of his profession. The well-informed Claude Lenoir confessed to being thrilled by 'the rapid, alert and calm fashion in which he tends to his machine and to himself'. For Lenoir, Petit-Breton was simply 'the greatest road racer we have'.

GENERAL CLASSIFICATION

1. **Lucien Petit-Breton** (FRA) Peugeot, 47 pts
   4,488 km; Average Speed: 28.470 kph
2. **Gustave Garrigou** (FRA) 66
3. **Émile Georget** (FRA) 74
4. Georges Passerieu (FRA) Peugeot, 85
5. François Beaugendre (FRA) 123
6. Eberardo Pavesi (ITA) 150

7. François Faber (LUX) 156
8. Augustin Ringeval (FRA) 184
9. Alois Catteau (BEL) 196
10. Ferdinand Payan (FRA) 227
11. Pierre-Gonzague Privat (FRA) 251
12. Georges Fleury (FRA) 274
13. François Lafourcade (FRA) 299

14. Marius Vilette (FRA) 333
15. Alzir Vivier (FRA) 340
16. Gaston Tuvache (FRA) 348
17. Eugène Delhaye (BEL) 378
18. Baptiste Roux (FRA) 389
19. Philippe Pautrat (FRA) 393
20. Henri Timmermann (FRA) 411

5th TOUR DE FRANCE, 14 STAGES – 4,488 KM

			STAGE	STAGE WINNER	YELLOW JERSEY
Stage 1	Monday 8 July	272 km	Paris – Roubaix	L. Trousselier (FRA)	L. Trousselier
Stage 2	Wednesday 10 July	398 km	Roubaix – Metz (GER)	É. Georget (FRA) & L. Trousselier (FRA)	L. Trousselier
Stage 3	Friday 12 July	259 km	Metz (GER) – Belfort	É. Georget (FRA)	É. Georget
Stage 4	Sunday 14 July	309 km	Belfort – Lyon	M. Cadolle (FRA)	É. Georget
Stage 5	Tuesday 16 July	311 km	Lyon – Grenoble	É. Georget (FRA)	É. Georget
Stage 6	Thursday 18 July	345 km	Grenoble – Nice	G. Passerieu (FRA)	É. Georget
Stage 7	Saturday 20 July	345 km	Nice – Nîmes	É. Georget (FRA)	É. Georget
Stage 8	Monday 22 July	303 km	Nîmes – Toulouse	É. Georget (FRA)	É. Georget
Stage 9	Wednesday 24 July	299 km	Toulouse – Bayonne	L. Petit-Breton (FRA)	É. Georget
Stage 10	Friday 26 July	269 km	Bayonne – Bordeaux	G. Garrigou (FRA)	L. Petit-Breton
Stage 11	Sunday 28 July	391 km	Bordeaux – Nantes	L. Petit-Breton (FRA)	L. Petit-Breton
Stage 12	Tuesday 30 July	321 km	Nantes – Brest	G. Garrigou (FRA)	L. Petit-Breton
Stage 13	Thursday 1 August	415 km	Brest – Caen	É. Georget (FRA)	L. Petit-Breton
Stage 14	Sunday 4 August	251 km	Caen – Paris	G. Passerieu (FRA)	L. Petit-Breton

A massive penalty following an illegal bicycle change saw Émile Georget lose his lead to Petit-Breton, the eventual winner.

Petit-Breton hosts a Peugeot exhibition

No fewer than 110 cyclists started the sixth Tour, a 4,488-kilometre (2,789-mile) epic over 14 stages. In *L'Auto*, Desgrange wrote: 'With their legs and courage, they express more eloquently than others can with words the beauty of effort and the august splendour of the will.'

They included the close-knit Peugeot team, their sights set on repeating Lucien Petit-Breton's 1907 triumph. Under the direction of the redoubtable Léopold Alibert, Peugeot had assembled most of the greatest talents in the sport, including, alongside the reigning champion, Émile Georget, François Faber, Georges Passerieu, Hippolyte Aucouturier, Henri Cornet, Jean-Baptiste Dortignacq and Georges Paulmier. Between them, they had already won 21 stages and two Tours de France. The only competition came from the poorly organized Alcyon and Labor teams, which included the former Peugeot rider and 1905 winner Louis Trousselier, the Belgian Van Hauwaert, the Italian Luigi Ganna, and Frenchman Gonzague Privat, under an apprentice manager, Alphonse Baugé. All the signs were that it would be a Peugeot walkover. Nonetheless, the Tour drew masses of spectators curious to see whether Faber, Passerieu or Garrigou would have the opportunity to capitalize on any mishap or moment of weakness that

might befall Petit-Breton. In the event, Faber accumulated four stage wins, Passerieu took three, and Garrigou led the field over the Ballon d'Alsace. But there was no touching Petit-Breton, who rode with his head as well as his legs, was an expert mechanic, and was, above all, consistent. He won five stages, including the finish in his hometown of Nantes, where he won in spite of a crash caused by a fan on a bike. In just one stage did he finish outside the first four. He could break away at will, and when he punctured, he invariably had enough reserves to catch the leading group and fight out the final sprint, as was the case in Bordeaux, where he finished tenth out of eleven, his worst placing of the event. In the thirteen other stages, he came first five times, second three times and third five times. Petit-Breton only lost 2 kg (4 lb) in an event utterly dominated by Peugeot, which made a clean sweep of the 14 stages and took the first four places in the overall classification. When it rained, Peugeot led with Faber; when it was hot, with Dortignacq; when the road was steep, with Garrigou; and always with Petit-Breton in attendance. The Peugeot leader was awarded the first Mountain Prize, improved his average speed from the 1907 Tour, and became the first winner of two Tours, and two consecutive Tours at that.

GENERAL CLASSIFICATION

1. **Lucien Petit-Breton** (FRA) Peugeot, 36 pts
   4,488 km; Average Speed: 28.740 kph
2. **François Faber** (LUX) 68
3. **Georges Passerieu** (FRA) 75
4. **Gustave Garrigou** (FRA) 91
5. Luigi Ganna (ITA) 120
6. Georges Paulmier (FRA) 125
7. Georges Fleury (FRA) 134
8. Henri Cornet (FRA) 142
9. Marcel Godivier (FRA) 153
10. Giovanni Rossignoli (ITA) 160
11. Paul Duboc (FRA) 163
12. Clemente Canepari (ITA) 183
13. François Beaugendre (FRA) 195
14. Paul Chauvet (FRA) 209
15. Eugène Forestier (FRA) 231
16. Achille Germain (FRA) 236
17. André Pottier (FRA) 237
18. Ernest Paul (FRA) 243
19. Aldo Bettini (ITA) 243
20. Giovanni Gerbi (ITA) 246

6th TOUR DE FRANCE, 14 STAGES - 4,488 KM

			STAGE	STAGE WINNER	YELLOW JERSEY
Stage 1	Monday 13 July	272 km	Paris – Roubaix	G. Passerieu (FRA)	G. Passerieu
Stage 2	Wednesday 15 July	398 km	Roubaix – Metz (GER)	L. Petit-Breton (FRA)	G. Passerieu
Stage 3	Friday 17 July	259 km	Metz (GER) – Belfort	F. Faber (LUX)	L. Petit-Breton
Stage 4	Sunday 19 July	309 km	Belfort – Lyon	F. Faber (LUX)	L. Petit-Breton
Stage 5	Tuesday 21 July	311 km	Lyon – Grenoble	G. Passerieu (FRA)	L. Petit-Breton
Stage 6	Thursday 23 July	345 km	Grenoble – Nice	J.-B. Dortignacq (FRA)	L. Petit-Breton
Stage 7	Saturday 25 July	345 km	Nice – Nîmes	L. Petit-Breton (FRA)	L. Petit-Breton
Stage 8	Monday 27 July	303 km	Nîmes – Toulouse	F. Faber (LUX)	L. Petit-Breton
Stage 9	Wednesday 29 July	299 km	Toulouse – Bayonne	L. Petit-Breton (FRA)	L. Petit-Breton
Stage 10	Friday 31 July	269 km	Bayonne – Bordeaux	G. Paulmier (FRA)	L. Petit-Breton
Stage 11	Sunday 2 August	391 km	Bordeaux – Nantes	L. Petit-Breton (FRA)	L. Petit-Breton
Stage 12	Tuesday 4 August	321 km	Nantes – Brest	F. Faber (LUX)	L. Petit-Breton
Stage 13	Thursday 6 August	415 km	Brest – Caen	G. Passerieu (FRA)	L. Petit-Breton
Stage 14	Sunday 9 August	251 km	Caen – Paris	L. Petit-Breton (FRA)	L. Petit-Breton

The two men who dominated the race broke away on the final stage.
They passed this checkpoint at Rouen in the same order they finished in the
general classification: first Petit-Breton; second Faber.

François Faber, the hungry giant

In 1908, Petit-Breton had predicted the advent of Luxembourg's François Faber, who proved him right with a brilliant ride in 1909. The man they called the 'Giant from Colombes' won the Tour with such panache that he entered the public imagination alongside René Pottier, the climber who had won the 1906 Tour. Faber rode for Alcyon, the new super-team, managed by the master tactician Alphonse Baugé, although he could have won the race alone. Even the weather favoured him; this was a cold, wet Tour – there was even snow in the Ballon d'Alsace – but Faber, who worked as a labourer on the Seine, was inured to the elements. In any case, at nearly six foot and carrying 91 kg (14 stone 3 lb), he was better equipped than most to withstand the conditions.

The first stage to Roubaix unfolded into the teeth of a storm. Faber emerged unscathed, and celebrated by winning the next five stages, an unprecedented achievement in the Tour's short history, and one he achieved thanks to long solo breakaways and heroic exploits over the Ballon d'Alsace and the three greats cols of the early Tours: Porte, Laffrey and Bayard. Seventy-seven riders abandoned during the first six stages through mud, snow and driving rain. Faber simply ploughed on.

Only the pounding of the Southern sun and a nasty fall took the edge off his performance; he was relegated to fifth place on the stage into Toulouse and tenth on the Bayonne stage. By Bordeaux, he was back at his best, winning his sixth stage at an incredible 33 kph (20.5 mph). Faber had started the Tour 5 kg (11 lb) over his race weight, and finished it at the top of his form, without ever being put into serious difficulty. His Alcyon team-mates mopped up the final stages, giving the team 13 stage wins out of a possible 14, and put their seal on their domination by filling the top five places in the final stage to the Parc des Princes. They did the same in the final classification, with the 22-year-old Faber followed by Garrigou, Alavoine, Duboc and Van Houwaert. In sixth place overall was Faber's half-brother Ernest Paul, who won the 'independents' category. For the record, Faber was said to have ridden alone for 255 km (158 miles) on stage three to Belfort, arriving 33 minutes ahead of Garrigou in second place; he had already achieved a similar time advantage over Lapize the previous day. As the classification was still based on points, as in the Peugeot years from 1905 to 1908, these extraordinary feats never made it into the record books.

GENERAL CLASSIFICATION

1. **François Faber** (LUX) Alcyon, 37 pts
   4,488 km; Average Speed: 28.658 kph
2. **Gustave Garrigou** (FRA) Alcyon, 57
3. **Jean Alavoine** (FRA) Alcyon, 66
4. Paul Duboc (FRA) Alcyon, 70
5. Cyrille Van Houwaert (BEL) Alcyon, 92
6. Ernest Paul (FRA) Independent, 95

7. Constant Menager (FRA) Le Globe, 102
8. Louis Trousselier (FRA) Alcyon, 114
9. Eugène Christophe (FRA) Independent, 139
10. Aldo Bettini (ITA) Independent, 142
11. Julien Maitron (FRA) Le Globe, 148
12. Georges Fleury (FRA) Le Globe, 152
13. Alfred Faure (FRA) Independent, 205

14. Mario Gajoni (ITA) Legnano, 210
15. Attilio Zavatti (ITA), Legnano, 241
16. Jules Deloffre (FRA), Nil Supra, 252
17. Joseph Habierre (FRA,) Independent, 296
18. Ildebrando Gamberini (ITA) Felisina, 305
19. Alfred Le Bars (FRA) Independent, 317
20. Émile Lachaise (FRA) Independent, 327

7th TOUR DE FRANCE, 14 STAGES – 4,488 KM

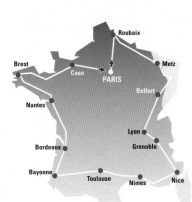

		STAGE		STAGE WINNER	YELLOW JERSEY
Stage 1	Monday 5 July	272 km	Paris – Roubaix	C. Van Houwaert (BEL)	C. Van Houwaert
Stage 2	Wednesday 7 July	398 km	Roubaix – Metz (GER)	F. Faber (LUX)	F. Faber
Stage 3	Friday 9 July	259 km	Metz (GER) – Belfort	F. Faber (LUX)	F. Faber
Stage 4	Sunday 11 July	309 km	Belfort – Lyon	F. Faber (LUX)	F. Faber
Stage 5	Tuesday 13 July	311 km	Lyon – Grenoble	F. Faber (LUX)	F. Faber
Stage 6	Thursday 15 July	345 km	Grenoble – Nice	F. Faber (LUX)	F. Faber
Stage 7	Saturday 17 July	345 km	Nice – Nîmes	E. Paul (FRA)	F. Faber
Stage 8	Monday 19 July	303 km	Nîmes – Toulouse	J. Alavoine (FRA)	F. Faber
Stage 9	Wednesday 21 July	299 km	Toulouse – Bayonne	C. Ménager (FRA)	F. Faber
Stage 10	Friday 23 July	269 km	Bayonne – Bordeaux	F. Faber (LUX)	F. Faber
Stage 11	Sunday 25 July	391 km	Bordeaux – Nantes	L. Trousselier (FRA)	F. Faber
Stage 12	Tuesday 27 July	321 km	Nantes – Brest	G. Garrigou (FRA)	F. Faber
Stage 13	Thursday 29 July	415 km	Brest – Caen	P. Duboc (FRA)	F. Faber
Stage 14	Sunday 1 August	251 km	Caen – Paris	J. Alavoine (FRA)	F. Faber

The 1909 Tour, reputed to be the hardest in history, was a mere jaunt for the phenomenal François Faber. A six-litre lung capacity kept his massive physique well-oxygenated from Paris to Paris.

Victory for the Giant from Colombes

PARIS (1 August): Faber has outdone even Petit-Breton. In atrocious conditions, he equalled him by playing the protagonist's role in thirteen of the Tour's fourteen stages, and surpassed him by winning in five consecutive stages, and, let it be added, in the five rightly considered the most demanding of the event. Indeed, Faber proved himself superior to Petit-Breton, and at least equal to the much lamented Pottier. His merit is all the greater in that Faber, as a *routier*, represents a remarkable exception to the norm. It is scarcely comprehensible how a man standing 1.78 m (5 ft 10 in) and carrying 91 kg (14 st 3 lb) at the start of a race like the Tour de France could accomplish what he has. This constitution would suit him perfectly to sprinting at the highest levels, but meets none of the demands made by road racing. Yet the astonishing facts say otherwise and demonstrate quite clearly that we're in the presence of a true phenomenon.

François Faber's Tour de France will long remain in the memory. His feats will find no imitators in the near future. He has become the King of the Road just as Arthur Zimmerman was the uncontested King of the Sprint, John Michael the Middle-Distance King and Constant Huret the Long-Distance King.

Let us praise the Giant from Colombes because he was from start to finish the master of every situation. Let us praise him because, throughout the entire 4,488 kilometres (2,789 miles) of the Tour, he remained invincible and unflinching. Let us praise this 22-year-old as a great man who deserves the triumphant greeting that met him everywhere.

The seventh Tour de France was Faber's definitive apotheosis. If *L'Auto's* classic race has, since its creation, always found the man it needed to remain the most absorbing of all bicycle races, let us recognize, without prejudice, that it has never known a winner more deserving than Faber.

Even more than Petit-Breton, Faber has become the man of the Tour de France. Bravo, Faber! And bravo, Baugé! For we should not forget, on this triumphant day, that it is the capable *directeur sportif* of the great Alcyon marque to whom we owe our opportunity to applaud the success of this superb athlete, the most admirable we have seen in the Tour to date.

But enough about the man; let us turn to the end of the race. The stage from Caen to Paris gave nothing away in excitement to the preceding stages, and was marred by no regrettable incidents. From the first kilometre to the last, it retained the peculiar flavour of the triumphal final stage, and it was truly, for the valiant survivors of the Tour de France, a race to glory, a contest of consolation after 28 days of heroic toil. Along the length of the route from Caen to Paris, via Pont-Audemer, Rouen, Vernon, Mantes and Versailles, thousands and thousands of spectators hastened to the roadside to witness the heroes of this great trek.

Everywhere, a storm of enthusiasm lifted the riders on wings of public acclamation. At the magnificent Parc des Princes, both within and without, at Boulogne, Saint Cloud and Ville d'Avray, the cohorts we have come to expect turned out, allowing us, the people of Paris, to break the most astonishing public records, thanks in part to our devoted correspondents Damez, Danglard, Chaussin, Lassagne, Guérin, Ardoin, Crès, Pons and Saint-Vanne, not to mention Bardet, Capelle, Huby and Machurey, all artisans of the formidable success of the Tour de France, year after year.

The 1909 Tour de France closed against a glorious backdrop. The weather was radiant; the final stage superb, and if the supporters of the Giant from Colombes were denied the pleasure of seeing him take first place on the final stage, they could at least take consolation in seeing the well-deserved ovation that met him at the Parc des Princes.

The Tour has lost none of its huge appeal. Let us record that fact with pride. With men like those brought forth by the Tour de France, what would be the point of hiding behind false modesty?

Behind the giant of the road, Garrigou took second place in the general classification. This former champion of France has gained in endurance without losing any of his brilliance and speed. A sympathetic and loyal rider, we believe we see in him a future winner of the Tour de France.

Aged just 22, François Faber stands by a handsome head and broad shoulders
above a hellish Tour, attracting the admiration of the French public.

Lapize takes the Tour to the Pyrenees

The great innovation of the 1910 Tour de France was the entry into the Pyrenees, proposed to Henri Desgrange by his assistant, Alphonse Steinès. Early in the New Year, Steinès had ventured up the Col de Tourmalet by car only to find the way blocked by impenetrable snowdrifts. That evening he addressed a telegram to Desgrange, claiming that the road up the Tourmalet was very good and perfectly accessible.

In July that year, 106 independent riders and just three ten-man teams representing bicycle manufacturers started the Tour. Yet despite the challenge posed by Legnano, with Petit-Breton, Dortignacq and Georget, and Le Globe, with Cornet, Paulmier and Crupelandt, Alcyon again proved invincible, achieving a sensational clean-sweep of the first four places in the final classification and taking nine stage wins from a possible fifteen. Once again, the main source of interest was the internecine warfare between the Alcyon riders, who occupied the top three places in the general classification at the end of every day's racing.

Faber headed the race for eleven stages from Metz to Nantes, but at Nîmes a collision with a dog brought him down and left him to ride the remaining 2,498 kilometres (1,551 miles) carrying a severe injury. On the road to Perpignan the following day, the curly-haired Octave Lapize, third overall, began to eat into his lead. Their duel kept *L'Auto* readers all over France on tenterhooks. Over the following days, Lapize clawed back more of the deficit thanks to magnificent wins on stage nine, from Perpignan to Luchon over the Col de Porte, the Portet d'Aspet and the Portet des Ares, and on the epic stage ten to Bayonne over the four classic cols of the Peyresourde, Aspin, Tourmalet and Aubisque. As Lapize led the riders up the gruelling Aubisque, he spat bitter words at the organizers in nearby vehicles which immediately entered the lore of the Tour de France: '*Vous êtes des assassins!*' – 'Murderers!'

Faber finally lost his race lead on stage thirteen to Brest. Lapize maintained his advantage to Paris, where he finished the Tour for the first and only time in his career. Victory was the just reward for the 22-year-old, who had given a stunning performance in the Alps and surprised his critics with his great stamina over long distances as well as his superb climbing skills.

Yet Faber had been cursed by bad luck, and so too had Émile Georget, the stage winner in Belfort, and the two-time champion Petit-Breton, whose challenges were brought to an abrupt halt by crashes. At least one independent deserves a mention: the Pyrenean native Lafourcade, who led the way for much of the terrible Luchon-Bayonne stage.

GENERAL CLASSIFICATION

1. **Octave Lapize** (FRA) Alcyon, 63 pts
   4,737 km; Average speed: 28.680 kph
2. **François Faber** (LUX) Alcyon, 67
3. **Gustave Garrigou** (FRA) Alcyon, 86
4. Cyrille Van Houwaert (BEL) Alcyon, 97
5. Charles Cruchon (FRA) Independent, 119
6. Charles Crupelandt (FRA) Le Globe, 148
7. Ernest Paul (FRA) Independent, 154
8. André Blaise (BEL) Alcyon, 166
9. Julien Maitron (FRA) Le Globe, 171
10. Aldo Bettini (ITA) Alcyon, 175
11. Pierino Albini (ITA) Legnano, 176
12. Georges Paulmier (FRA) Le Globe, 182
13. Ernesto Azzini (ITA) Legnano, 194
14. François Lafourcade (FRA) Independent, 205
15. Jules Deloffre (FRA) Le Globe, 213
16. Henri Cornet (FRA) Le Globe, 214
17. Luigi Azzini (ITA) Legnano, 220
18. Constant Menager (FRA) Legnano, 222
19. Augustin Ringeval (FRA) Independent, 241
20. Frédéric Saillot (FRA) Le Globe, 258

8TH TOUR DE FRANCE, 15 STAGES – 4,737 KM

			STAGE	STAGE WINNER	YELLOW JERSEY
Stage 1	Sunday 3 July	272 km	Paris – Roubaix	C. Crupelandt (FRA)	C. Crupelandt
Stage 2	Tuesday 5 July	398 km	Roubaix – Metz (GER)	F. Faber (LUX)	F. Faber
Stage 3	Thursday 7 July	259 km	Metz (GER) – Belfort	É. Georget (FRA)	F. Faber
Stage 4	Saturday 9 July	309 km	Belfort – Lyon	F. Faber (LUX)	F. Faber
Stage 5	Monday 11 July	311 km	Lyon – Grenoble	O. Lapize (FRA)	F. Faber
Stage 6	Wednesday 13 July	345 km	Grenoble – Nice	J. Maitron (FRA)	F. Faber
Stage 7	Friday 15 July	345 km	Nice – Nîmes	F. Faber (LUX)	F. Faber
Stage 8	Sunday 17 July	216 km	Nîmes – Perpignan	G. Paulmier (FRA)	F. Faber
Stage 9	Tuesday 19 July	289 km	Perpignan – Luchon	O. Lapize (FRA)	F. Faber
Stage 10	Thursday 21 July	326 km	Luchon – Bayonne	O. Lapize (FRA)	F. Faber
Stage 11	Saturday 23 July	269 km	Bayonne – Bordeaux	E. Paul (FRA)	F. Faber
Stage 12	Monday 25 July	391 km	Bordeaux – Nantes	L. Trousselier (FRA)	F. Faber
Stage 13	Wednesday 27 July	321 km	Nantes – Brest	G. Garrigou (FRA)	O. Lapize
Stage 14	Friday 29 July	424 km	Brest – Caen	O. Lapize (FRA)	O. Lapize
Stage 15	Sunday 31 July	262 km	Caen – Paris	E. Azzini (ITA)	O. Lapize

Sensational in the Alps, unbeatable in the Pyrenees, where he pushed and pedalled in turn to scale the summits, Octave Lapize dominated the Tour and his team-mate François Faber.

1910 TOUR DE FRANCE

What a battle! *Magnifique!*

Not without some surprise, we inform our readers that the much anticipated duel between François Faber and Émile Georget, two former heroes of the Col de Porte, failed to materialize. Faber, with a heavy cold, was dropped before Nantua; only superhuman courage allowed him to finish the stage sixth. Georget, still suffering stomach pains, couldn't defend his position and finished just nineteenth. They can't be blamed for abstaining from the final battle between Lapize, Crupelandt and Van Houwaert through the mountains of the Chartreuse. It was an admirable encounter and confirmed Crupelandt's fine reputation as a climber. Initially dropped by Lapize and Van Houwaert, Crupelandt fought like a demon on the formidable slope, caught them and dropped them. It would be remiss of me to report the stage without offering him our congratulations, first over the top of the Col de Porte and first among those deserving special mention. On the descent Lapize regained the lead and snatched the stage win from the valiant Roubaisien. Lapize, winner of Paris-Roubaix and Paris-Brussels, put on a staggeringly courageous and energetic performance.

Despite atrocious pain in his feet, Lapize was determined to show what he was made of and demonstrated remarkable courage by giving very little ground on the climb of the Chartreuse, before finally gaining the upper hand on the descent and the final few kilometres on the flat. We have too often remarked that Lapize sometimes has less spirit than many of his colleagues. Today, we congratulate him on yesterday's achievement. His great exploit will go down in memory, and we'll remind him of it each time he fails to ride like the true champion he is.

1

2 3

4

1. At the checkpoint in Rouen on the road to Paris, it looked like Lapize's Tour was slipping away from him. Due to punctures he was 11min 40sec down on Faber.

2. A day off. Lapize, Trousselier and Blaise take the air in Biarritz. Later, on a rest day in Nice, the riders were shocked by the death of their colleague Helière, stung by a jellyfish while swimming.

3. Italy's Ernesto Azzini won at the Parc des Princes. The real winner, of course, was Lapize.

4. At the Hôtel du Pot d'Étain checkpoint 183 kilometres (114 miles) from Paris, it seemed as if Lapize (here with Blaise) had lost the Tour to Faber. But Faber's puncture enabled Lapize to fight back.

5. At Bordeaux, the stage winner, Crupelandt, was disqualified for obstructing Azzini. The win went to Ernest Paul. Inexperienced and swayed by Lapize, Paul later contributed to the defeat of his half-brother Faber.

6. Forty-one survivors line up at the start of the final stage at Caen, with the Alcyon team (left to right: Faber, Van Houwaert, Blaise and Lapize) on the front row.

7. The 345 kilometres (214 miles) from Nice to Nîmes, in scorching heat, ended in victory for Faber. At the checkpoint in Cannes, Faber was already ahead with Petit-Breton.

5

6 7

Lapize's crowning moment

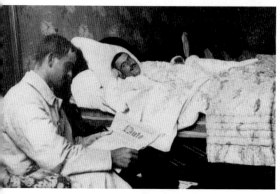

Lapize laughs as Garrigou reads out *L'Auto* to him. Either that, or he can hear Baugé in the next bedroom, playing his violin to Faber.

If Faber had had the advice of wise old Charles Terront, the cunning winner of Paris-Brest-Paris in 1891, earlier in the race, the smiling giant might yet have won the 1910 Tour.

Garrigou (wearing No. 2) was the first Tour rider to cross the Col de Tourmalet without dismounting, but as he reached the brow of the col, Lapize was still 500 metres ahead of him.

PARIS (31 July): The 1910 Tour de France came to a close yesterday after one last battle, magnificent and deeply moving. Two valiant opponents, Faber and Lapize, did the lion's share of the work, and with the unquestionable victory of Lapize, the hero of the Pyrenees, the wonderful champion of Alcyon and Dunlop, the general classification took its definitive form.

The glory goes to Lapize, who's been the rider of the year – remember that he's already won Paris-Roubaix and Paris-Brussels. He has surprised even those who considered him exceptional, unbeatable even, in races of up to 400 km (250 miles), but incapable of administering his effort over a construction as great as the Tour. He has

proved that the best over those distances is also the best over any distance.

Lapize is due further congratulations since the race was extremely trying for him in the early stages. He was not himself as far as Belfort, and even in stage four, he succumbed to a moment of despair and finished twenty-fifth. However, from that point on, we rediscovered the great rider he is, and received immediate proof between Lyon and Grenoble that he was the best climber.

Lapize's exploit on the Tourmalet will enter Tour de France legend. The Ballon d'Alsace was the making of Pottier, sorely missed; the Pyrenees have raised Lapize to the top level of today's cyclists. It would have been a shame if the victor in the Pyrenees had not also won the Tour.

So, once more, bravo, Lapize! Bravo for your brilliant victory, your excellent race finish, your Pyrenean stages, your Brest-Caen, which will long remain in our memory. Bravo for everything that you have achieved, and especially for the thrill of excitement we felt on the final stage when even two punctures couldn't keep you from triumph.

Fate did not want a second Faber victory, yet we can hardly say he has been defeated. The name of Lapize, champion of the Union des Cyclistes de Paris, will forever bring to mind the Giant from Colombes, winner of the 1909 Tour, and second by four points in this year's enthralling contest.

Faber should take consolation from the knowledge that his defeat has lost him no public esteem. He is as worthy of praise as Lapize, and we shall remain eternally grateful to him for being a worthy opponent of the Alcyon-Dunlop leader in a duel that has no equal in the history of cycling.

Despite, or perhaps because of, the stretches where he walked his bike, Octave Lapize crossed the great cols of the Pyrenees at the head of the race.

INTERVIEW WITH THE WINNER

To record his impressions of the Tour as a whole, I approached the overwhelming victor of the Tour de France. He's radiant, of course; radiant and loquacious, which may come as something of a surprise to those who know the champion from the Union des Cyclistes de Paris, a club dear to our friend Steinès.

'*Eh bien, Monsieur L'Auto*! What do you think I'm thinking?' Lapize called out when he saw me.

'That's exactly what I'd like to know.'

'That's simple. I was thinking, at the start of the Tour de France, that I didn't think it was my kind of race! Then, after a while, I realised I wasn't out of touch with the leaders. Finally, after I'd won quite a few stages, I told myself I might be in with a chance after all. Yesterday, as I was going to bed, I told myself that I could win, all the same. And today, I won!

'Only one impression of the race sticks in my mind, quite a big one, at that. It is that the Pyrenees are incredible, and I'd much rather be on the banking of the Parc des Princes velodrome than on the descent from the Col d'Aubisque.

'Anyway, you can see that I haven't lost too much weight: look, my detachable collars are still a perfect fit. That was my only real worry, to have to go out and buy some smaller ones. That's in the past now.'

'You didn't have any problems with your eyes?'

'Pah! Just the same as my comrades, but all in all I've nothing to complain about in that regard.'

'What about punctures?'

'Punctures, *mon Dieu*! I wasn't blessed with good luck on the final stage. Three kilometres (nearly 2 miles) from the start, I punctured on some broken glass and lost ten minutes or more that I couldn't make up. At Aubergenville, I managed to find a nail right in my trajectory, and some nail it was, too. But nothing could stop me: I was playing my final card and I couldn't afford to lose too many places. Is there anything else you have to ask me? No? *Bonsoir, Monsieur!*'

Lapize is about to take his leave when one of his supporters calls out: 'You're just taking "la pize" out of that chap, aren't you, Octave?'

Questions like this must be an occupational hazzard for Lapize, but he took it in his stride – just as he did the Pyrenees.

Garrigou and the Galibier

The ninth Tour de France followed the previous year's fifteen-stage model, but substantially lengthened the route to a new record of 5,344 kilometres (3,321 miles). There were fourteen rest days and the riders would need them: this was the first Tour to take in the high Alps, and specifically, the towering Galibier. Alcyon's winning streak, which had begun two years earlier with victory for François Faber, owed much to the expert direction of Alphonse Baugé. This year, Baugé placed his faith in Gustave Garrigou, one of the great protagonists of the Tour de France for years (second in 1907 and 1909, third in 1910, and fourth in 1908). Baugé's protégé seized the lead by a hair's breadth from his team-mate Jules Masselis at the end of the first stage in Dunkerque. A day later, he lost it, also to Masselis, by a similar margin before another team-mate, the voracious François Faber, escaped on stage three and took over the race lead with a spectacular solo break of 206 km (128 miles) launched on the Ballon d'Alsace.

Faber's efforts were in vain, however, for in Chamonix, Garrigou snatched the race lead back and kept it. The following day Émile Georget became the first Tour de France hero to cross the Galibier. Georget, however, was already out of contention after a fall on the Ballon d'Alsace. Garrigou would have had an easy ride, had Paul Duboc not begun to whittle away his lead. On the morning of stage seven, Garrigou's advantage was sixteen points; Duboc reduced it to fifteen between Nice and Marseille, thirteen between Marseille and Perpignan, and ten by winning the stage from Perpignan to Luchon. Then, near the town of Argelès the following day, Duboc collapsed, ill. Garrigou put him to the sword, gaining three hours on the stage and stretching his lead to 26 points. He added to his lead when the stage winner, Maurice Brocco, was disqualified. Brocco's crime? Riding within himself for days to save energy for the stage win, raged Henri Desgrange. Garrigou was awarded the win. Still Duboc didn't give up. At La Rochelle, he won the stage by twelve minutes. Garrigou retaliated with a stage win at Cherbourg, two days later. Duboc escaped with Georget the following day and took the stage win at Le Havre. In Normandy, Duboc's supporters intended to teach Garrigou a lesson, but the race leader simply changed his shirt and disappeared into the peloton. Duboc's brave defiance continued with second place in the final stage behind his team-mate Godivier. And in second place he stayed, 18 points behind the untouchable Garrigou and 23 ahead of the unfortunate Émile Georget, who had already finished third in 1907.

GENERAL CLASSIFICATION

1. **Gustave Garrigou** (FRA) Alcyon, 43 pts
   5,344 km; Average speed: 27,322 kph
2. **Paul Duboc** (FRA) La Française, 61
3. **Émile Georget** (FRA) La Française, 84
4. Charles Crupelandt (FRA) La Française, 119
5. Louis Heusghem (BEL) Alcyon, 135
6. Marcel Godivier (FRA) La Française, 141
7. Charles Cruchon (FRA) La Française, 145
8. Ernest Paul (FRA) Alcyon, 153
9. Albert Dupont (FRA) Le Globe, 157
10. Henri Devroye (BEL) Le Globe, 171
11. Firmin Lambot (BEL) Le Globe, 178
12. Henri Cornet (FRA) Le Globe, 178
13. Paul Deman (BEL) Independent, 198
14. Julien Maitron (FRA) La Française, 216
15. Jules Deloffre (FRA) Independent, 217
16. Georges Paulmier (FRA) Automoto, 226
17. Ottavio Pratesi (ITA) Independent, 251
18. Alfred Faure (FRA) Automoto, 255
19. Vincent Dhulst (FRA) Independent, 265
20. Lucien Pothier (FRA) Le Globe, 284

9TH TOUR DE FRANCE, 15 STAGES – 5,344 KM

			STAGE	STAGE WINNER	YELLOW JERSEY
Stage 1	Sunday 2 July	351 km	Paris – Dunkerque	G. Garrigou (FRA)	G. Garrigou
Stage 2	Tuesday 4 July	388 km	Dunkerque – Longwy	J. Masselis (BEL)	J. Masselis
Stage 3	Thursday 6 July	331 km	Longwy – Belfort	F. Faber (LUX)	F. Faber
Stage 4	Saturday 8 July	344 km	Belfort – Chamonix	C. Crupelandt (FRA)	G. Garrigou
Stage 5	Monday 10 July	366 km	Chamonix – Grenoble	É. Georget (FRA)	G. Garrigou
Stage 6	Wednesday 12 July	348 km	Grenoble – Nice	F. Faber (LUX)	G. Garrigou
Stage 7	Friday 14 July	334 km	Nice – Marseille	C. Crupelandt (FRA)	G. Garrigou
Stage 8	Sunday 16 July	335 km	Marseille – Perpignan	P. Duboc (FRA)	G. Garrigou
Stage 9	Tuesday 18 July	289 km	Perpignan – Luchon	P. Duboc (FRA)	G. Garrigou
Stage 10	Thursday 20 July	326 km	Luchon – Bayonne	M. Brocco (FRA)	G. Garrigou
Stage 11	Saturday 22 July	379 km	Bayonne – La Rochelle	P. Duboc (FRA)	G. Garrigou
Stage 12	Sunday 23 July	470 km	La Rochelle – Brest	M. Godivier (FRA)	G. Garrigou
Stage 13	Wednesday 26 July	405 km	Brest – Cherbourg	G. Garrigou (FRA)	G. Garrigou
Stage 14	Friday 28 July	361 km	Cherbourg – Le Havre	P. Duboc (FRA)	G. Garrigou
Stage 15	Sunday 30 July	317 km	Le Havre – Paris	M. Godivier (FRA)	G. Garrigou

On the snow-swept Galibier, where Georget had attacked, Garrigou limited his losses, alternately walking and riding on a bike equipped with a freewheel and one gear, developing 4.2 metres (13 ft 8 in) per turn of the pedal.

Garrigou: victory with a sense of humour

After 11,737 minutes of suffering, Garrigou finds deliverance at the Parc des Princes. The decision to leave Peugeot for Alcyon proved to be the right one.

PARIS (30 July): 'My impressions? That's like asking me to embark on another stage. However, since it will entertain your readers, who've been so charming towards me, I'll gladly remount my machine and do it, not perhaps with a smile, but showing willing!

'I should start by saying I was very confident on stage one after I saw Lapize puncture and Petit-Breton fall. After various accidents, I reached the finish line at Dunkerque alone, except for Masselis. I won by good fortune, but I was nonetheless pleased for that. What do you expect? Other people's misfortunes are your own happiness, especially when, like me, you haven't been spared your share of bad luck.

'I was still more confident at the start of stage two, and in spite of a number of difficulties, I was riding with surprising ease until the sprint, when it suddenly felt like I was pushing a wheelbarrow. Masselis sprang away from under my nose with improbable strength. Faber caught me up and with his usual elegance he beat me by a nose, although he couldn't reach Masselis.

'I started stage four from Belfort to Chamonix downhearted. How wrong I was. God is just: the stage went well for me, despite what Alavoine calls an attack of the rowboats a few kilometres from the finish. I was with my friend François at the time. We were fighting like men possessed, almost as if we were being paid to, when Heusghem flashed past, followed by Crupelandt, who leapt forward like a jack in a box. We

realized there and then that we'd simply run out of gas. Luckily for me, Faber, with his six-litre engine, was in even direr straits than your humble servant. He dropped to a snail's pace, so slow that without even noticing I dropped him on the climb at Le Fayet.

'At that moment, I rediscovered an insane kind of courage. Massetts was no longer well placed in the general classification. I had only to make up time on Faber to regain the race lead. I didn't waste any time; I pushed on like a lunatic and finished on all fours. At the foot of Mont Blanc I had the joyful realization (and this doesn't happen every day) that the hunger knock isn't all bad. On the next day but one, I rode my best race. We had to cross the Galibier. The stage start was amusing; downhill all the way! But soon the fun began, and by fun I refer to the tasteless prank of slipping mountains under the roads of our beautiful country. They might suit riders like Georget or Duboc, but for a boy like me who likes his Tours de France nice and easy, getting by without exceptional graft, *eh bien*, it hardly bears thinking about.

'I'd scarcely had a chance to say "Ouch!" before Georget and Duboc slipped by without the slightest effort to politely bid me *adieu*. It didn't go down well, and I set off in pursuit. At Annecy, I was four minutes behind. At Aix-les-Bains, I had made up a little more time, and I was alone. The other shipmates, including Faber, were behind me. At Chambéry I was no more than two minutes behind. Finally, at Saint-Michel-de-Maurienne, contemplating the beauty of nature as I went, I had the further delight of seeing the two rascals at the checkpoint.

'I pounced on them in one fell swoop, but did they greet me like old friends? *Au contraire!* On the pretext that we were on the Col du Télégraphe, Georget made off, claiming that he had a message to dispatch to a lady friend in Châtellerault. Then Duboc followed him, on the grounds that Georget wouldn't know the way. In short, I was on my own again, standing on my pedals and saying to myself that Desgrange had to be a real assassin to force us to spend our holidays like this. After more than two-and-a-half hours of continuous toil, plus several kilometres on foot, I

reached the tunnel at the summit of the Galibier. What a bizarre idea to build a tunnel at an altitude of 2,600 metres (8,530 feet).

'On the stage from Grenoble to Nice, Faber saw fit to pull ahead. I let him go in the company of Nempon and Dupont. Then Nempon and Dupont came back into view. As for the big François, he was waiting for me at the hotel in Nice. Does friendship mean nothing any more? I finished second, defeated, dejected, and with an unhappy memory of the Col de Valgelaye.

'At Marseille, Crupelandt, Georget and Nempon were playing cards when I arrived. At Perpignan, Duboc and Heusghem, who I had tried to interest in a boxing match with a yokel who had knocked me down, arrived ahead of me to announce my arrival. At Luchon, this same Duboc, plus Georget, plus Godivier, had ordered a nice, hot bath for the leader of the big race. I was beginning to get worried about all this consideration, because, after all, Duboc was hot on my heels. Between Luchon and Bayonne, I resolved to deliver a major attack, which didn't prevent me from being dropped while showing too much caution on the descent from the Col de Peyresourde. I regularly lost sight of Duboc, Georget or Brocco as they put distance between us.

'Fate decided otherwise. I started by catching Duboc, who was lying in a ditch sick as a dog. You know the rest. I arrived second at Bayonne, ahead of Georget, who didn't expect to see me again. From then on, barring accidents, I couldn't be beaten. I had some bad luck on the Bayonne-La Rochelle stage, but I'd rather not remember the fact that I eventually finished fourth after lying in last place. On the leg from La Rochelle to Brest, I rode cautiously, keeping a close watch on Duboc, and finished seventh. Between Brest and Cherbourg it was Duboc's turn to be plagued with punctures, and I won my second stage. Between Cherbourg and Le Havre, I had to dig deep after flints on the roads had given me a handicap. Finally, I was pretty mediocre on the final stage; the one thing on my mind was to avoid an accident like the one in 1908 that nearly killed Petit-Breton.

'And that was my Tour!'

Slow at changing his freewheel and prone to damaging his brakes while descending, Garrigou relied heavily on the organizational skills of Baugé, who oversaw everything for Alcyon. After winning the race, Gustave paid vibrant homage to his ten *soigneurs*, especially Manchon, Thémar and Panosetti. Also key to the collective effort was Pierre Labat, enveloped in Dunlop tyres (right).

Defraye coasts to victory

The tenth Tour de France followed the established formula (15 stages, 5,319 km [3,305 miles], 14 rest days, with the overall classification decided on points). The only major change was that it departed for the first time from the Luna Park, Porte Maillot in Paris.

On 30 June 1912, 131 team riders and independents sped past the Arc de Triomphe. The leading bicycle marques – Alcyon, Peugeot, La Française, Griffon, J.-B. Louvet, Automoto, Armor and Thomann – had assembled their finest riders: there were former winners like Petit-Breton, Lapize, Garrigou and Faber, and worthy contenders like Duboc, Crupelandt and Émile Georget. The race looked more open than ever. Charles Crupelandt immediately marked out his territory by winning in Dunkerque, close to his Roubaix home, where he had triumphed in 1910. This set the tone for the Tour, which proved yet another unlucky one for Petit-Breton, who fell foul of a cow in Armentières on stage two and abandoned. Odile Defraye, the Belgian, announced his intentions by winning the stage, with Garrigou, the reigning champion, on his wheel. Armor rider Eugène Christophe, the winner of the 1910 Milan-San Remo, won the next three stages, including

two in the Alps, despite having shorn himself of his characteristic handlebar moustache. As the race left Grenoble, Christophe and Defraye shared the race lead. By the end of the next stage, Defraye was sharing the lead with Octave Lapize. Desgrange was tipping the Belgian: on the Ballon d'Alsace, he had been amazed at the dexterity with which Defraye had removed and flipped his rear wheel to change gear for the climb. Having paced himself through the Alps, Defraye opened a significant gap on the first stage of the Pyrenees. Christophe fought heroically, bursting up the Col d'Oschquis at such speed that the mountain specialist Lapize, recognizing his inferiority, abandoned the race. In the second Pyrenean stage, Louis Mottiat sped to victory through the pouring rain with Christophe on his wheel. Defraye, however, was in complete control, and from then on kept the leading group under close surveillance all the way to Paris. Jean Alavoine won three of the closing stages by putting a pioneering derailleur to excellent use. Christophe, with no such technology, had reason to regret that Desgrange had lifted the ban on freewheels. He could finish no better than second behind Alphonse Baugé's most recent protégé, and the first Belgian ever to win the Tour de France.

GENERAL CLASSIFICATION

1. **Odile Defraye** (BEL) Alcyon, 49 pts
   5,319 km in 190h.34m; Average Speed: 27.894 kph
2. **Eugène Christophe** (FRA) Armor, 108
3. **Gustave Garrigou** (FRA) Alcyon, 140
4. Marcel Buysse (BEL) Peugeot, 147
5. Jean Alavoine (FRA) Armor, 148
6. Philippe Thys (BEL) Peugeot, 148
7. Hector Tiberghien (BEL) Griffon, 149
8. Henri Devroye (BEL) Le Globe, 163
9. Félicien Salmon (BEL) Peugeot, 166
10. Alfons Spiessens (BEL) J.B. Louvet, 167
11. Louis Heusghem (BEL) Alcyon, 167
12. René Vanderberghe (BEL) Thomann, 194
13. Vincenzo Borgarello (ITA) J.-B. Louvet, 212
14. François Faber (LUX) Automoto, 229
15. Louis Engel (FRA) Aiglon, 241
16. Charles Deruyter (BEL) Peugeot, 255
17. Jacques Coomans (BEL) Thomann, 260
18. Firmin Lambot (BEL) Le Globe, 265
19. Ottavio Pratesi (ITA) Independent, 304
20. Charles Guyot (SUI) Aiglon, 309

10TH TOUR DE FRANCE, 15 STAGES – 5,319 KM

			STAGE	STAGE WINNER	YELLOW JERSEY
Stage 1	Sunday 30 June	351 km	Paris – Dunkerque	C. Crupelandt (FRA)	C. Crupelandt
Stage 2	Tuesday 2 July	388 km	Dunkerque – Longwy	O. Defraye (BEL)	V. Borgarello
Stage 3	Thursday 4 July	331 km	Longwy – Belfort	E. Christophe (FRA)	O. Defraye
Stage 4	Saturday 6 July	344 km	Belfort – Chamonix	E. Christophe (FRA)	O. Defraye
Stage 5	Monday 8 July	366 km	Chamonix – Grenoble	E. Christophe (FRA)	O. Defraye, E. Christophe
Stage 6	Wednesday 10 July	323 km	Grenoble – Nice	O. Lapize (FRA)	O. Defraye, O. Lapize
Stage 7	Friday 12 July	334 km	Nice – Marseille	O. Defraye (BEL)	O. Defraye
Stage 8	Sunday 14 July	335 km	Marseille – Perpignan	V. Borgarello (ITA)	O. Defraye
Stage 9	Tuesday 16 July	289 km	Perpignan – Luchon	O. Defraye (BEL)	O. Defraye
Stage 10	Thursday 18 July	326 km	Luchon – Bayonne	L. Mottiat (BEL)	O. Defraye
Stage 11	Saturday 20 July	379 km	Bayonne – La Rochelle	J. Alavoine (FRA)	O. Defraye
Stage 12	Monday 22 July	470 km	La Rochelle – Brest	L. Heusghem (BEL)	O. Defraye
Stage 13	Wednesday 24 July	405 km	Brest – Cherbourg	J. Alavoine (FRA)	O. Defraye
Stage 14	Friday 26 July	361 km	Cherbourg – Le Havre	V. Borgarello (ITA)	O. Defraye
Stage 15	Sunday 28 July	317 km	Le Havre – Paris	J. Alavoine (FRA)	O. Defraye

Stewards monitored the tenth Tour from six official cars. Only a third of the starters completed the Tour, after weathering icy temperatures, driving rain, the Alps, the Pyrenees and rivals assisted by the revolutionary freewheel.

Thys, Peugeot's lion

Marked by sudden changes of fortune, the eleventh Tour de France, classified according to time for the first time since 1904, was one of the most eventful in history, although victory still favoured the rider with the most complete palette of skills and the least susceptibility to bad luck.

1913 had seen some frantic changes of dancing partners. Trousselier, Petit-Breton and Alibert, the director, had all left Peugeot, Trousselier for the J.-B. Louvet team, Petit-Breton and Alibert for Automoto. Peugeot had poached Alcyon strategist Alphonse Baugé and two former winners, Faber and Garrigou. It was a blow for Alcyon, who had lost Lapize to La Française a year earlier and were left with Defraye. The teams appeared evenly matched, and those representing Griffon (with Micheletto), Alcyon (with Masselis, Henri Pélissier and Defraye) and Libérator (with the independent Vanlerberghe) shared the early stage wins and the race lead. Stage four (Brest to La Rochelle, 470 km [292 miles]), with freewheels permitted, proved the exception, allowing Peugeot, through the Belgian stage winner Marcel Buysse, to state its intent. The anti-Peugeot coalition had lost Lapize on stage three; he felt his La Française team was too disorganized to be of any

use. The illusion of a close contest lasted to stage six from Bayonne to Luchon, when Peugeot blew the race apart. Its riders finished first, second and third on the stage and in the general classification, despite losing Christophe, leader on the road at the top of the Aubisque until he had fallen and been forced to repair his forks at the forge in Sainte-Marie-de-Campan. The Belgian Philippe Thys seized the race lead; Defraye had abandoned because of the ban on freewheels. On the second Pyrenean stage, Buysse took his second and Peugeot's third stage win. He lost the race lead to Thys at Nice after lengthy bike repairs and a time penalty. Thys had already taken category wins as an Independent at three major stage races, including the Tour de France. Not yet 24, he calmly took control, despite a late challenge from Petit-Breton assisted by a derailleur and Alibert's wise advice, until he crashed out of the race on stage fourteen.

By the time the race reached Paris, Peugeot riders filled all the podium places and had won ten stages out of a possible fifteen, thanks to the efforts of François Faber (two stage wins) and Marcel Buysse (six), who were clearly better team-players than Garrigou. The Lions of Peugeot had, once again, lived up to their own high standards.

GENERAL CLASSIFICATION

1. **Philippe Thys** (BEL) Peugeot, 5,388 km in 197h.54m; Average Speed: 26.715 kph
2. **Gustave Garrigou** (FRA) Peugeot, at 8h.37m.
3. **Marcel Buysse** (BEL) Peugeot, at 3h.30m.55s.
4. Firmin Lambot (BEL) Griffon, at 4h.12m.45s.
5. François Faber (LUX) Peugeot, at 6h.26m.4s.
6. Alfons Spiessens (BEL) J.-B. Louvet, at 7h.57m.52s.

7. Eugène Christophe (FRA) Peugeot, at 14h.6m.35s.
8. Camillo Bertarelli (ITA) independent, at 16h.21m.38s.
9. Joseph Van Daele (BEL) J.-B. Louvet, at 16h.39m.53s.
10. Émile Engel (FRA) Peugeot, at 16 h.52m.34s.
11. Louis Trousselier (FRA) J.-B. Louvet, at 18h.11m.30s.
12. Jules Deloffre (FRA) independent, at 18h.31m.31s.
13. Clemente Canepari (ITA) J.-B. Louvet, at 19h.11m.13s.

14. Paul Deman (BEL) Automoto, at 19h.27m.2s.
15. Vincent Dhulst (FRA) independent, at 20h.10m.12s.
16. Louis Petitjean (BEL) independent, at 22h.0m.27s.
17. Paul Hostein (FRA) Peugeot, at 25h.41m.6s.
18. Maurice Leliaert (BEL) independent, at 26h.18m.25s.
19. Jean Alavoine (FRA) Peugeot, at 27h.43m.47s.
20. Giuseppe Contesini (ITA) independent, at 30h.37m.34s.

11TH TOUR DE FRANCE, 15 STAGES – 5,388 KM

			STAGE	STAGE WINNER	YELLOW JERSEY
Stage 1	Sunday 29 June	388 km	Paris – Le Havre	G. Micheletto (ITA)	G. Micheletto
Stage 2	Tuesday 1 July	364 km	Le Havre – Cherbourg	J. Masselis (BEL)	J. Masselis
Stage 3	Thursday 3 July	405 km	Cherbourg – Brest	H. Pélissier (FRA)	O. Defraye
Stage 4	Saturday 5 July	470 km	Brest – La Rochelle	M. Buysse (BEL)	O. Defraye
Stage 5	Monday 7 July	379 km	La Rochelle – Bayonne	H. Vanlerberghe (BEL)	O. Defraye
Stage 6	Wednesday 9 July	326 km	Bayonne – Luchon	P. Thys (BEL)	P. Thys
Stage 7	Friday 11 July	324 km	Luchon – Perpignan	M. Buysse (BEL)	M. Buysse
Stage 8	Sunday 13 July	325 km	Perpignan – Aix-en-Provence	G. Garrigou (FRA)	M. Buysse
Stage 9	Tuesday 15 July	356 km	Aix-en-Provence – Nice	F. Lambot (BEL)	P. Thys
Stage 10	Thursday17 July	333 km	Nice – Grenoble	F. Faber (LUX)	P. Thys
Stage 11	Saturday 19 July	325 km	Grenoble – Genève (SUI)	M. Buysse (BEL)	P. Thys
Stage 12	Monday 21 July	335 km	Genève (SUI) – Belfort	M. Buysse (BEL)	P. Thys
Stage 13	Wednesday 23 July	325 km	Belfort – Longwy	F. Faber (LUX)	P. Thys
Stage 14	Friday 25 July	393 km	Longwy – Dunkerque	M. Buysse (BEL)	P. Thys
Stage 15	Sunday 27 July	340 km	Dunkerque – Paris	M. Buysse (BEL)	P. Thys

The 1913 Tour was different. A new classification system, a new direction –
anticlockwise – and a new technology: the three-speed Sturmey-Archer, which
helped Petit-Breton negotiate every obstacle, including sheep.

Christophe's curse

LUCHON (9 July, by telegraph): I will be very brief today, first, because I lost two hours trying to find out from Defraye the circumstances of his abandon; second, because I arrived here at an impossible hour; and third, because the Luchon telegraph, which normally works very slowly, is not working at all today, it seems, and the only hope I have of getting this dispatch to you is to keep it very short.

WITH A DEFICIT OF 2HRS 5MINS DEFRAYE ABANDONS

On the Col d'Oschquis, after Saint-Jean-Pied-de-Port, four men literally flew past the pack: Christophe, Buysse, Alavoine and Rossius. Alavoine punctured at the top of the pass and was replaced by Thys. Garrigou then joined this group along with Spiessens and Engel. At Oloron, our seven men led Defraye by 11mins: at Eaux-Bonnes, they still led by 11mins. At Argelès, Defraye passed 1hr 7mins behind; the Alcyon leader abandoned at Barèges, 2hrs 5mins behind the leaders.

ON THE COL D'AUBISQUE

We shall follow, in brief, the leading group through the Pyrenean passes, and finish with some considerations on Defraye's abandon. At the Eaux-Bonnes checkpoint, Engel has lost contact and no longer figures in the lead pack. Within minutes, Garrigou and Spiessens, in that order, also lose contact; Garrigou finishes a little higher and steals a march on Spiessens. We therefore have in the lead: Christophe, leading the dance all the way to the summit; Buysse, climbing all over his bike but not ceding an inch; Rossius, slighter than the first two, following without a hint of fatigue; and finally Thys, who loses ground, makes it up, leads for a while, but is finally dropped about halfway up. A little higher, it was Rossius's turn; he is quickly caught and dropped by Thys, full of energy again. Let's go back to Christophe and Buysse: Christophe pedals calmly but as powerfully as on the Galibier last year.

On the steepest part, he even takes a hand off the handlebars to signal to Baugé, following at a distance. Thys, who has dismounted to push his bike, doesn't want to lose contact. He sprints up frantically, remounts, pedals to within five lengths of the leaders, then dismounts again. The road surface, already poor, has become dreadful, and both Buysse and Christophe are thrown to the ground and have to complete the ascent on foot. They are both very fresh, however, and Christophe tells me, 'It's a shame the road was so bad; I could easily have done it all on my bike!' At Argelès, Thys, who had rejoined the two leaders, Christophe and Buysse, passes at 11.21am; Rossius passes ten minutes later, followed by Garrigou, three minutes after Christophe's accident.

At Barèges, that is, at the foot of the Tourmalet, Christophe and Thys signed in at 12.46pm, Buysse at 12.50, Garrigou at 12.59 and Rossius at 1.01. I am informed that the two leaders, Christophe and Thys, climbed the Tourmalet beautifully and that Thys, whose cadence on the Aubisque, in my opinion, seemed more erratic than Christophe's, managed to gain nearly five minutes over his rival. It was then that Christophe broke the fork on his bicycle and had to walk the 14-kilometre (8.7-mile) descent to Sainte-Marie-de-Campan. As I send this telegraph, he is already more than two hours behind and I have no news of him. Since Defraye's abandon, Christophe has been leading the general classification. After Christophe's accident, however, Buysse briefly inherited the race lead, before Thys finished the stage with such an advantage that he took over at the head of the Tour de France. Note, however, that Garrigou came in third at Luchon, Faber is not badly placed at all and Alavoine, had he not punctured high on the Col d'Oschquis, would have regained several places.

WHAT WILL ALCYON DO?

At the time of this dispatch, I still don't know Alcyon's decision, but, in their place, and this was also Ludovie's opinion at the Barèges control point, I would continue to fight. Suppose Lapize hadn't dropped out the other day, do you doubt he would now have a first-class chance? The accident that befell Christophe today is proof that anything can

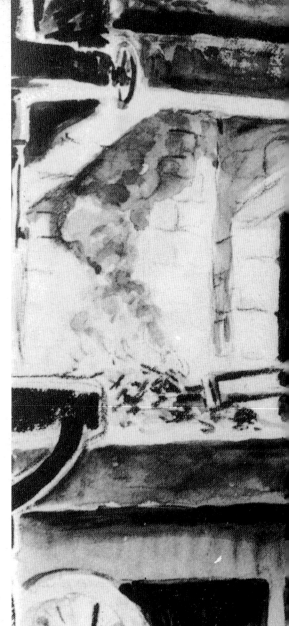

happen. At the stage start in Bayonne this morning, Thys was fifth in the general classification, and now he's first. Who was the man immediately behind him? It was Mottiat, just two minutes behind him. True, Mottiat hasn't improved his situation here, but he is extraordinarily fresh; he won the Bordeaux-Paris last year, and the stage from Luchon to Bayonne. The Pyrenees are not over yet; the Alps are still to come. Rossius rode a splendid race today, which bodes well, and Coomans, despite his stomach trouble, cannot have lost too many places.

There are still nine stages of the Tour de France to ride, and even Napoleon was defeated the morning before he won the Battle of Marengo.

Photographers were still rare, and none were at the forge at Sainte-Marie-de-Campan. However, the scene was re-created some years later by Paul Ordner. In addition to the hours he lost, Christophe was given a three-minute penalty for asking assistance from Automoto!

THE FORGE

Luchon (from one of our special correspondents): In a lost corner of the Pyrenees, after descending 14 kilometres (8.7 miles) from the Tourmalet's summit on foot with his bicycle on his back, a man arrives, masked in tragedy. Like a madman, he asks after a blacksmith. This man knows that he should have won the Tour, that the die has rolled for him. He has one desire left: to take his machine back to Paris, with the other seven riders of the Peugeot team. The man is Eugène Christophe, and no one knows the Tour de France better. On the Col d'Aubisque, he was joyous, with victory almost guaranteed. Now, he is here, in the forge at Sainte-Marie-de-Campan. His fork is broken. Being an expert mechanic, he asks, 'Do you have a 22mm tube?' Christophe sets to work, so weary that he struggles to lift his machine, and his cries fill the smoky, dirty space of the forge. He has finished the piece, and, refusing all help, tries to insert it into the tube; it won't fit. He has to start again. Now, he has filed the piece down: it fits! It just needs pinning, and he passes it under the stamp. 'Let me give you a hand,' insists the blacksmith, but Christophe replies, 'No, I can't.' Then, he asks for bread, and stuffs it into the pockets of his jersey. He has had to lose time for his machine, but he has not even a minute to spare on his exhausted physique. A last gesture: he asks the time. 'I still have four hours to finish,' he says, knowing to the minute the hours of the checkpoints. Christophe mounts his bicycle, climbs the Col d'Aspin, scrambles up the Col de Peyresourde like a man possessed, and sweeps into Luchon at top speed. On the summit of the Col d'Aubisque, this man was first in the general classification. He did what you have just read to ensure that the Peugeot team will return to Paris complete.

Belgium's second triumph

PARIS (27 July): The 11th Tour de France ended yesterday to the constant cheering of a delirious crowd, in the presence of more than 200,000 Parisians, scattered along the road from Poissy and gathered in the immense Parc des Princes, the only sporting arena worthy of hosting the finish of this great and famous race. This triumphant reception was to be expected, for this year's Tour de France has been extraordinarily compelling. From the start, the major contenders played a waiting game, before, one by one, we saw them leading the overall placing. Then came the first abandons: Lapize, Émile Georget, Crupelandt. From the first Pyrenean stage onwards, the battle assumed fantastic proportions and at Perpignan we witnessed the abandons of the 1912 champion Defraye, Rossius, Mottiat and Coomans, leaving Thys, Buysse, Garrigou and Faber with an enormous advantage. The unlucky Christophe had already dropped out of contention after a ridiculous accident on the Tourmalet.

A decimated field reached the Alps, but despite the large numbers of abandons, the valiant athletes who remained assumed the responsibility of charging the battle with vigour, passion and the unexpected. It was here that Petit-Breton began a magnificent defence, one against all.

Buysse, at the head of the general classification, abandoned, leaving his place to his compatriot Philippe Thys. Thys led the dance

Trained by Peugeot, directed by Baugé, Thys, from Brussels, owed his victory as much to his athletic gifts as to the misadventures of Christophe, M. Buysse and Petit-Breton. He is not yet 23.

ahead of Garrigou and Petit-Breton. It was between these two men that the ensuing battles were fought and followers still remember the extraordinary courage and energy that finally allowed Petit-Breton to claim second place in the general classification.

But that was before the dramatic penultimate stage from Longwy to Dunkerque, which was to prove fatal for Petit-Breton, fallen in the field of honour, and during which Thys nearly lost his overall lead.

Then, yesterday, in Dunkerque, two men separated by just eight minutes after more than 5,000 kilometres (3,105 miles) lined up at the start. At the finish, it was the Belgian, Thys, who had victoriously defended his lead.

I will come back to Philippe Thys, a man who owes his fortune, and the proud reputation he enjoys today, to our great national marque, Peugeot. But for now, don't let us abandon the race itself.

Two great modifications had been made to the regulations of the Tour de France and, on 29 June, we waited expectantly to see what surprises they would bring. Today, we must acknowledge that, for the most part, they have been extraordinarily successful.

The time-based classification has proven itself the only system capable of maintaining interest from start to finish, and as the most consistent system, it is also the most logical.

It has delivered a consistently brutal campaign and moments of great anxiety – it was evidently the cause of the dramatic events that punctuated the end of the race. And thanks to the new anti-clockwise itinerary, we have been far from the monotonous final stages of previous years.

Thys's victory deserves to be welcomed with great enthusiasm. It is the triumph of a champion who is as modest as he is courageous; it is the definitive blossoming of a young man. Peugeot, our national marque, can be proud to have led this rider to brilliant victory in the most important bicycle race.

For, *nota bene*, Thys is a Peugeot product. He made his debut in 1911 in the Paris-Toulouse, which he won. Then he won Paris-Turin and finally Peugeot's Circuit Français. In 1912, in his first appearances alongside the great road racers, Thys was superb, taking sixth place in the Tour de France.

After such a result, Thys could only target the very greatest success. Integrated into the Peugeot team, directed flawlessly by the excellent Baugé, Philippe Thys is today champion of the 1913 Tour de France; there is nothing astonishing about this young Peugeot rider's upward march to glory: it merely obeyed the rules of logic.

WINNERS' SASHES

We are delighted to announce to the valiant competitors of the Tour de France that tomorrow at the Parc des Princes, thanks to the kindness of four enthusiasts belonging to the firm Coeur, of 50, rue de Turenne, we will be awarding the winner in the team category and the winner in the Independent category with a superb sash with a silver cartouche. All our thanks go to these generous supporters. Thanks to them, the winners of our great race will have a precious souvenir of their 1913 Tour de France.

Left: 'On the descent from the Tourmalet, as soon as I realized I was alone, I pushed as hard as I could,' confided Philippe Thys, on whom fortune was smiling. Thys was merely the first of Peugeot's yellow bicycles to finish, followed 18 minutes later by Buysse and then a revived Garrigou.

HOW MANY DAYS IN THE SADDLE?

For the amusement of our readers, here is a record, to be continued tomorrow, of the number of days each competitor would have taken to complete all 5,388 kilometres (3,346 miles) of the race if they had been cycling non-stop:

**Thys: 8 days and 5 hours
Garrigou: 8 days and 6 hours
Buysse: 8 days and 9 hours
Lambot: 8 days and 10 hours
Faber: 8 days and 12 hours
Spiessens: 8 days and 14 hours
Christophe: 8 days and 20 hours
Bertarelli: 8 days and 22 hours
Van Daele: 8 days, 22 hours and 30 minutes
Engel: 8 days, 22 hours and 30 minutes
Trousselier: 9 days
Deloffre: 9 days**

Tomorrow we shall amuse ourselves further with the final riders who, over the 29 days of the Tour de France, have been in the saddle nearly half this length of time.

Philippe the Wise

Good sense prevailed and the classification system based on time was retained for the 1914 Tour. Another constant was the dominance of the Peugeot team, still managed by the shrewd Alphonse Baugé. He had guided Belgium's Philippe Thys to victory in 1913 and, in 1914, the two men set out to repeat the feat. During the night of 28 June, lit by the headlamps of the ever-increasing number of race vehicles, 147 riders left the west Paris suburb of Saint-Cloud. Virtually all the cyclists now used the two-speed Eadie hub gear and freewheel. Twenty-eight days later, on 26 July, only 54 of them made it back to the Parc des Princes. Several of those who did left for military service less than eight days later; 'le grand match', as Desgrange called the Great War, had already started. Desgrange himself signed up at over 50 years of age; among the millions who lost their lives in the terrible carnage that followed were Lucien Petit-Breton, Octave Lapize, who had won in Marseille, and the headstrong François Faber. In typical fashion, Faber had won in Longwy and Dunkerque by virtue of the long-distance solo breakaways that were his speciality. But by then, he was way out of contention.

Thys had lost no time getting started; he struck his first blow at Le Havre where he won stage one. He shared the race lead with Alcyon's Jean Rossius for four stages, as wins by his Peugeot team-mates Émile Engel and Oscar Egg strengthened his position. Then, by following the swashbuckling Lambot into the Pyrenees, Thys gained an apparently unassailable advantage. The young Italian Costante Girardengo dropped out of the race and Rossius, an all-round Belgian racer, seized his opportunity in Nice for a second stage win. From then on, the only threat to Thys's plans came from his team-mates Garrigou (who rode brilliantly over the Galibier and the Aravis) and Henri Pélissier (who dominated the Col d'Allos and the roads into Belfort). But these were just scraps left over by Thys, 'the Basset hound', who continued to keep a wary eye out for trouble. It came on the penultimate stage when he made an unauthorized wheel change as he chased Faber's irresistible attack. The infringement cost him a 30-minute penalty, leaving Henri Pélissier less than two minutes off his winning pace. The sanction added spice to the final stage, which Pélissier won. Thys, however, avoided any unpleasant surprises by finishing on his rival's wheel. It would be five years before the next Tour de France, and many of the athletes spent the intervening period making other exertions in a less metaphorical form of conflict; many – too many – made the ultimate sacrifice.

GENERAL CLASSIFICATION

1. **Philippe Thys** (BEL) Peugeot, 5,405 km in 200h.28m.48s; Average Speed: 27.028 kph
2. **Henri Pélissier** (FRA) Peugeot, at 1m.50s.
3. **Jean Alavoine** (FRA) Peugeot, at 36m.53s.
4. Jean Rossius (BEL) Alcyon, at 1h.57m.5s.
5. Gustave Garrigou (FRA) Peugeot, at 3h.0m.21s.
6. Émile Georget (FRA) Peugeot, at 3h.20m.59s.
7. Alfons Spiessens (BEL) J.-B. Louvet, at 3h.53m.55s.
8. Firmin Lambot (BEL) Peugeot, at 5h.8m.54s.
9. François Faber (LUX) Peugeot, at 6h.15m.53s.
10. Louis Heusghem (BEL) Peugeot, at 7h.49m.2s.
11. Eugène Christophe (FRA) Peugeot, at 8h.31m.58s.
12. Ernest Paul (FRA) Delage, at 9h.42m.51s.
13. Oscar Egg (SUI) Peugeot, at 10h.0m.40s.
14. Léon Scieur (BEL) Thomann, at 10h.2m.30s.
15. Camille Botte (BEL) Independent, at 10h.14m.33s.
16. Angelo Erba (ITA) Alleluia, at 11h.21m.22s.
17. Donald Kirkham (AUS) Phebus, at 11h.53m.39s.
18. Hector Tiberghien (BEL) Delage, at 12h.23m.21s.
19. Jacques Coomans (BEL) Thomann, at 12h.24m.15s.
20. Ivor Munro (AUS) Phebus, at 12h.34m.57s.

12TH TOUR DE FRANCE, 15 STAGES – 5,405 KM

			STAGE	STAGE WINNER	YELLOW JERSEY
Stage 1	Sunday 28 June	388 km	Paris – Le Havre	P. Thys (BEL)	P. Thys
Stage 2	Tuesday 30 June	364 km	Le Havre – Cherbourg	J. Rossius (BEL)	J. Rossius, P. Thys
Stage 3	Thursday 2 July	405 km	Cherbourg – Brest	É. Engel (FRA)	J. Rossius, P. Thys
Stage 4	Saturday 4 July	470 km	Brest – La Rochelle	O. Egg (SUI)	J. Rossius, P. Thys
Stage 5	Monday 6 July	379 km	La Rochelle – Bayonne	O. Egg (SUI)	J. Rossius, P. Thys
Stage 6	Wednesday 8 July	326 km	Bayonne – Luchon	F. Lambot (BEL)	P. Thys
Stage 7	Friday 10 July	323 km	Luchon – Perpignan	J. Alavoine (FRA)	P. Thys
Stage 8	Sunday 12 July	370 km	Perpignan – Marseille	O. Lapize (FRA)	P. Thys
Stage 9	Tuesday 14 July	338 km	Marseille – Nice	J. Rossius (BEL)	P. Thys
Stage 10	Thursday 16 July	333 km	Nice – Grenoble	H. Pélissier (FRA)	P. Thys
Stage 11	Saturday 18 July	325 km	Grenoble – Genève (SUI)	G. Garrigou (FRA)	P. Thys
Stage 12	Monday 20 July	335 km	Genève (SUI) – Belfort	H. Pélissier (FRA)	P. Thys
Stage 13	Wednesday 22 July	325 km	Belfort – Longwy	F. Faber (LUX)	P. Thys
Stage 14	Friday 24 July	390 km	Longwy – Dunkerque	F. Faber (LUX)	P. Thys
Stage 15	Sunday 26 July	340 km	Dunkerque – Paris	H. Pélissier (FRA)	P. Thys

Saint-Cloud, 3 am. Abran is just about to give the starting signal to the 147 racers. Freewheel and tin *bidons* in place, Petit-Breton, Defraye and Faber prepare to devour the 388 km (241 miles) that separate them from Le Havre.

Lambot, by default

The thirteenth Tour was especially demanding, and not only because it took the riders through the war-torn regions of northern and eastern France. Scarcity was widespread, and the shortage of tyres and material forced the cycle manufacturers to form La Sportive, a consortium which equipped almost half of the participants.

Rain and cold compounded the difficulties of the 5,560-km (3,452-mile) route. The riders lacked race condition, and only eleven of the 67 starters made it back to Paris. The suffering began on stage one; the stony roads from Paris to Le Havre finished off 26 riders, including 1913 and 1914 champion Thys, hampered by stomach problems. It was an eventful stage: Rossius, who won it, earned a thirty-minute penalty by handing Thys a water bottle; Jean Alavoine, meanwhile, suffered a long succession of punctures, and lay in a ditch for half an hour before pulling himself together. The fact that Alavoine finished second in Paris, an hour and three-quarters behind the winner, is indicative of the strange unfolding of the 1919 Tour. The arrogance of the Pélissier brothers after winning stages two and three made them so many enemies in the peloton that they had to withdraw before the start of stage five, though not before they had compared the riders to convict labourers in the

celebrated expression, 'les forçats de la route'. Eugène Christophe became the first rider ever to wear the *maillot jaune*, the coveted yellow jersey, introduced this year, before breaking his fork, just as he had in 1913. A fall in Nice had weakened the fork; and 468 km (290 miles) of bone-shaking cobbles on the penultimate stage between Metz and Dunkerque had finished it off, costing Christophe the Tour. He had been leading Belgium's Firmin Lambot by 28mins 5secs; the repair cost him seventy minutes. A further fall added to his deficit, and 'Cricri' eventually limped into Paris the moral winner, but third in the official standings. To console him, *L'Auto* launched a collection for him that reached monumental proportions.

As the embittered but eloquent Pélissier brothers put it, the 1919 Tour had been a race for cart horses; rude beasts with little sense of restraint, who even attacked while Christophe was relieving himself. Despite the loss of Thys and Masson, the favourites, Belgium still had the last word with the ironman Lambot. The French had achieved eleven stage wins out of fifteen, and although it had been an uninspiring Tour with the lowest average speed yet, it also signalled a rebirth, symbolized by the appearance of the new leader's jersey, the colour of the sun. The perfect symbol for an age in need of regeneration.

GENERAL CLASSIFICATION

1. **Firmin Lambot** (BEL) La Sportive
   5,560 km in 231h.7m.15s; Average Speed: 24.054 kph
2. **Jean Alavoine** (FRA) La Sportive, at 1h.42m.54s.
3. **Eugène Christophe** (FRA) La Sportive, at 2h.26m.31s.
4. Léon Scieur (BEL) La Sportive, at 2h.52m.15s.
5. Honoré Barthélemy (FRA) La Sportive, at 4h.14m.22s.

6. Jacques Coomans (BEL) La Sportive, at 15h.21m.34.
7. Luigi Lucotti (ITA) Bianchi, at 16h.1m.12s.
8. Joseph Van Daele (BEL) La Sportive, at 18h.23m.2s.
9. Alfred Steux (BEL) La Sportive, at 20h.29m.1s.
10. Jules Nempon (FRA) Louvet, at 21h.44m.12s.

Note: On 12 August, after a commissaires' appeal, Paul Duboc (n° 44), eighth overall, was disqualified for borrowing a car to go and repair his pedal axle. Otherwise there would have been 11 finishers at the Parc des Princes.

13TH TOUR DE FRANCE, 15 STAGES – 5,560 KM

			STAGE	STAGE WINNER	YELLOW JERSEY
Stage 1	Sunday 29 June	388 km	Paris – Le Havre	J. Rossius (BEL)	J. Rossius
Stage 2	Tuesday 1 July	364 km	Le Havre – Cherbourg	H. Pélissier (FRA)	H. Pélissier
Stage 3	Thursday 3 July	405 km	Cherbourg – Brest	F. Pélissier (FRA)	H. Pélissier
Stage 4	Saturday 5 July	412 km	Brest – Les Sables-d'Olonne	J. Alavoine (FRA)	E. Christophe
Stage 5	Monday 7 July	482 km	Les Sables-d'Olonne – Bayonne	J. Alavoine (FRA)	E. Christophe
Stage 6	Wednesday 9 July	326 km	Bayonne – Luchon	H. Barthélemy (FRA)	E. Christophe
Stage 7	Friday 11 July	323 km	Luchon – Perpignan	J. Alavoine (FRA)	E. Christophe
Stage 8	Sunday 13 July	370 km	Perpignan – Marseille	J. Alavoine (FRA)	E. Christophe
Stage 9	Tuesday 15 July	338 km	Marseille – Nice	H. Barthélemy (FRA)	E. Christophe
Stage 10	Thursday 17 July	333 km	Nice – Grenoble	H. Barthélemy (FRA)	E. Christophe
Stage 11	Saturday 19 July	325 km	Grenoble – Genève (SUI)	H. Barthélemy (FRA)	E. Christophe
Stage 12	Monday 21 July	371 km	Genève (SUI) – Strasbourg	L. Lucotti (ITA)	E. Christophe
Stage 13	Wednesday 23 July	315 km	Strasbourg – Metz	L. Lucotti (ITA)	E. Christophe
Stage 14	Friday 25 July	468 km	Metz – Dunkerque	F. Lambot (BEL)	F. Lambot
Stage 15	Sunday 27 July	340 km	Dunkerque – Paris	J. Alavoine (FRA)	F. Lambot

It took the Tour to convince France that the war was truly over. The handful of riders who made it through the deluge embodied hope. And who could fail to be moved by the sight of Mrs Lambot kissing her husband in the yellow jersey?

The road and the sun

It's the most beautiful peloton of *routiers* that you could dream of. See them start their exertions tomorrow morning, see the energy that will drive them to assault the most redoubtable obstacles, and tell me what spirit drives them on. Is it not our bright youth that you will see pass, with the charming smiles of young gods, the white teeth of wolves eager to bite, legs like magnificent pistons that will power over the Tourmalet and the Galibier, with harmonious backs and indomitable wills? This is the France of tomorrow, spirited, energized, determined and healthy, which will begin the most beautiful of crusades, sowing along the route, with potent, graceful gestures, the good news of sport. I will spend a whole month watching them, studying them, admiring them. They will free me from my austere daily toil, cleanse my mind, elevate me over life's inanities, separate me from the indifferent and the loutish. I will give myself to them for the delights they will bring me and the crusade that they will wage across our war-torn nation.

I would like the crowds that gather from afar along the way to give them the warm acclaim they deserve; to come more as pilgrims than spectators; to meet these valiant men with respect; to see in them someone to replace our loved ones, cruelly abducted from our tenderness by the Boche.

Strasbourg! Metz! It isn't a dream! We'll go there, *chez nous*! From Belfort to Haguenau, we'll see the blue Vosges that before we could only contemplate from afar. We'll travel along the Rhine. I cannot resist recalling our first Tour de France in 1903 with its ridiculously small itinerary: Lyon, Marseille, Toulouse, Bordeaux, Nantes, Paris. From the peaks of the Pyrenees, the peaks of the Alps, the peaks of the Jura, towns like Lyon, Toulouse, Rennes and Nancy appear to us today like indistinct points in the deepest part of a basin. With Strasbourg and Metz, our ambitions are fulfilled; the Tour de France is complete. This is what we were lacking, after the Normandy patois, the Breton dialect, the southern tongues that sing like cicadas, the harshness of Flemish – the joy of Alsatian speech, the triumphal entry into Strasbourg, welcomed by the graceful flights of storks and the wingèd headdresses of the girls of Alsace!

Let us welcome challenges that only yesterday we feared. There can be no joy without a struggle: this must be the sportsman's motto.

Saturday 19 July. Stage 11. Grenoble-Genève. Eugène Christophe (right), the race leader, has swapped the grey jersey of La Sportive for the yellow jersey to distinguish the race leader. Scieur, Alavoine and Lambot (from left to right) witness this historic moment.

Lambot, a worthy winner

PARIS (27 July): Every sports enthusiast in Paris must have squeezed into the immense arena of the Parc des Princes to celebrate, as was only fitting, the achievement of the eleven brave survivors of the Tour de France 1919. *L'Auto's* great race, a veritable World Championship of road racing, has counted another magnificent year, and Firmin Lambot, the glorious Belgian champion, has triumphed and now adds his name to its immortal *palmarès*. How perfect! Naturally, we must deplore the mechanical incident during stage 14 that cost our brave Christophe first place in the general classification. However, we must also recognize with impartiality that the name of Firmin Lambot, after all that this brave young man has achieved in the 13th Tour de France, is in no way a lesser champion than the previous winners of this formidable trial. Our first gesture, the day after his phenomenal victory and the unforgettable finale at a Parc des Princes crammed with enthusiasts, must be to stand before him and congratulate, from the bottom of our hearts, this small but athletic Belgian who has known nothing but resounding success in our Tour de France since 1912.

His success this year was certainly not as clear-cut as in previous years and doubtless all followers, whatever their nationality, would have preferred a smoother, more decisive victory. Although richly deserved, Lambot himself is certainly not overwhelmed

Beleaguered by bad luck, Christophe received a delirious reception at the Parc, consolation from his wife, and a job offer as foreman from the boss of the factory where he repaired his fork.

by his triumph. He is worthy of it! During this 13th Tour de France, he had shown truly extraordinary qualities. He was quick when he needed to be, had incredible stamina, was an excellent climber and would have won the 14th stage even if Christophe's forks hadn't collapsed. We offer you respect, then, Firmin Lambot, winner of the 1919 Tour de France, unconditionally! The winner of the Bayonne-Luchon stage in 1914 and the 1913 Tour de Sospel was one of the best athletes in this difficult, agonizing Tour that demanded so much bravery and energy. Let's also be proud of our unfortunate Christophe; let's show him compassion and console him in his misfortune, as is only right. But don't let us diminish Lambot's victory, which nothing can legitimately challenge.

Bravo, Lambot! Along with Christophe and Jean Alavoine, you have been the best in a Tour de France that dispatched five-sixths of its competitors. You are one of the heroes of a Tour that many quickly found to be

beyond human endurance, with its bad roads, infrequent provisions, all the usual problems aggravated by a far too obvious lack of equipment and tyres. French sports followers welcome you as the successor to Garin, Cornet, Trousselier, Pottier, Petit-Breton, Faber, Lapize, Garrigou, Defraye and Philippe Thys.

We celebrate this, as we celebrate the fact that, contrary to the opinion of some, the crowds today remain as interested as they were when the Tour de France was in its infancy and had not yet attained its status as the true World Championship of road racing that it now enjoys.

Applause resounded all around the immense arena of the Parc. Incessant cries went up as soon as a 'Tour de France' (his arrival announced by the roar of the crowd who had been unable to get into the arena) appeared at the start of the final straight. Following the majestic arrival of Jean Alavoine, winner of five stages, of little Lucotti, of that bulldog Barthélemy, the swarthy Scieur and the slight Coomans, who raised a storm of bravos, a touching reception was given to brave little Nempon, sole survivor from Category B. Then, after Lambot, Van Daele, Steux and Duboc came the unforgettable arrival of Christophe, the unluckiest rider the world has ever seen. The crowd's passion overflowed into delirium! It was fantastic! Christophe was fêted like a god, and our 'Vieux Gaulois', normally so calm and composed, felt tears of recognition wash over his eyes.

Yes, this finale of the 13th Tour de France has been a success without precedent, a triumph to demonstrate that sports enthusiasts truly appreciate the outstanding performance of each of our courageous competitors. *L'Auto* sincerely wishes to thank all aficionados of sport everywhere. Today we are as proud of those who cheered on the 11 survivors of our race as we will always be of the brave men who made it possible for the 1919 Tour de France to bridge the gap so majestically between the uncertain present and the glorious past. *L'Auto* has no more doubts: the Tour de France is still the Tour de France – the most tremendous and passionate contest there is!

RIDERS' WEIGHTS

	At the start	At the finish
Lambot	64 kg	63 kg
Alavoine	74 kg	69.5 kg
Christophe	67 kg	67 kg
Scieur	81 kg	78 kg
Barthélemy	69 kg	68 kg
Coomans	63 kg	61 kg
Lucotti	67.5 kg	67 kg
Duboc	69 kg	63.6 kg
Van Daele	73 kg	69 kg
Steux	70.5 kg	64.5 kg
Nempon	61 kg	58 kg

Steux lost the most weight: 6 kg (13 lb) – there must be hardly anything left of him! Christophe lost the least, weighing the same at the finish as when he started. This shows how carefully our 'Vieux Gaulois' prepared himself for the race.

Number three for Thys

When Philippe Thys, the Belgian from Anderlecht, gave the journalists a conspiratorial wink, they knew he was on song. In 1913 and 1914, he had won the Tour. In 1919 he hadn't had time to blink before abandoning on stage one. In 1920, Thys, at the heart of the manufacturers' group La Sportive, was in fine fettle, and had the confidence of Alphonse Baugé, La Sportive's manager. Baugé had directed Thys at Peugeot and knew that when his man was in condition, he was unbeatable. He also knew Thys was capable of winning in the mountains, or at the very least containing the best climbers. So this year, as in 1914, the Belgian saved energy in the hills, restricted the winners of the mountain stages to narrow time gains, and worked on extending his lead only when the time was right. Baugé's theory translated perfectly into practice: the first of four stage wins, from Le Havre to Cherbourg, gave Thys the joint race lead alongside Goethals, Mottiat, Rossius and Masson. Mottiat lost his place among them on stage three. Stage four, from Brest to Les Sables-d'Olonne, whittled the leaders down to the two Belgians, Thys and Masson. Henri Pélissier, after consecutive stage wins, weighed up his chances, found them wanting and abandoned on the marathon stage five from Les

Sables to Bayonne (482 kilometres [301.25 miles]). By sticking on Lambot's wheel through stages five and six, Thys notched up two second places and in Luchon became the sole race leader. He had crossed the formidable Pyrenees, which once again undid the unfortunate Christophe. After five successive second places, Thys put his foot down into Nice, gained almost an hour on his closest rival, Hector Heusghem, and at last earned the yellow jersey that the organizer, overwhelmed by events, had been forgetting to award. In the Alps he maintained his lead comfortably, especially after the best French rider, Honoré Barthélemy, who had given a master class in climbing on the slopes of the Galibier, broke his collarbone. The injured Frenchman ultimately finished eighth overall, the highest placed non-Belgian. Thys, meanwhile, deservedly took a victory demanded by logic. Baugé had chosen him, and that meant he couldn't lose, despite puncture after puncture after puncture. Aged almost 30, the Belgian had achieved the first hat-trick in Tour de France history. But it had been no cakewalk; proof of just how hard the 1920 Tour had been lay in Thys's average speed, the second lowest in its history after 1919. The 1920 Tour had taken a terrible toll on the riders; out of 113 starters, just 22 made it back to Paris.

GENERAL CLASSIFICATION

1. **Philippe Thys** (BEL) La Sportive, 5,519 km in 228h.36m.13s; Average speed: 24.132 kph
2. **Hector Heusghem** (BEL) La Sportive, at 57m.21s.
3. Firmin Lambot (BEL) La Sportive, at 1h.39m.35s.
4. L. Scieur (BEL) La Sportive, at 1h.44m.58s.
5. É. Masson 'Senior' (BEL) La Sportive, at 2h.56m.52s.
6. L. Heusghem (BEL) La Sportive, at 3h.40m.47s.
7. J. Rossius (BEL) La Sportive, at 3h.49m.55s.
8. H. Barthélemy (FRA) La Sportive, at 5h.35m.19s.
9. F. Goethals (FRA) La Sportive, at 9h.23.7s.
10. J. Van Daele (BEL) La Sportive, at 10h.45m.41s.
11. E. Dhers (FRA), La Sportive, at 11h.15m.9s.
12. J. Pelletier (FRA) Delage, at 20h.4m.32s.
13. T. Wynsdau (BEL) J.-B. Louvet, at 25h.14m.2s.
14. N. Amenc (FRA) Devaux, at 33h.25m.47s.
15. J. Muller (FRA) J.-B. Louvet, at 33h.48m.53s.
16. H. Ferrara (FRA) Devaux, at 34h.32m.27s.
17. G. Ceccherelli (ITA) Radior, at 48h.40m.35s.
18. M. Matheron (FRA) Martin, at 51h.11m.4s.
19. É. Dorfeuille (FRA) Delage, at 53h.10m.
20. P. Hudsyn (BEL) Automoto, at 55h.36m.42s.

14TH TOUR DE FRANCE, 15 STAGES – 5,519 KM

			STAGE	STAGE WINNER	YELLOW JERSEY
Stage 1	Sunday 27 June	388 km	Paris – Le Havre	L. Mottiat (BEL)	L. Mottiat (BEL)
Stage 2	Tuesday 29 June	364 km	Le Havre – Cherbourg	P. Thys (BEL)	P. Thys (BEL)
Stage 3	Thursday 1 July	405 km	Cherbourg – Brest	H. Pélissier (FRA)	P. Thys (BEL)
Stage 4	Saturday 3 July	412 km	Brest – Les Sables-d'Olonne	H. Pélissier (FRA)	P. Thys (BEL)
Stage 5	Monday 5 July	482 km	Les Sables-d'Olonne – Bayonne	P. Lambot (BEL)	P. Thys (BEL)
Stage 6	Wednesday 7 July	326 km	Bayonne – Luchon	P. Lambot (BEL)	P. Thys (BEL)
Stage 7	Friday 9 July	323 km	Luchon – Perpignan	J. Rossius (BEL)	P. Thys (BEL)
Stage 8	Sunday 11 July	325 km	Perpignan – Aix-en-Provence	L. Heusghem (BEL)	P. Thys (BEL)
Stage 9	Tuesday 13 July	356 km	Aix-en-Provence – Nice	P. Thys (BEL)	P. Thys (BEL)
Stage 10	Thursday 15 July	333 km	Nice – Grenoble	H. Heusghem (BEL)	P. Thys (BEL)
Stage 11	Saturday 17 July	362 km	Grenoble – Gex	L. Scieur (BEL)	P. Thys (BEL)
Stage 12	Monday 19 July	354 km	Gex – Strasbourg	P. Thys (BEL)	P. Thys (BEL)
Stage 13	Wednesday 21 July	300 km	Strasbourg – Metz	P. Thys (BEL)	P. Thys (BEL)
Stage 14	Friday 23 July	433 km	Metz – Dunkerque	F. Goethals (FRA)	P. Thys (BEL)
Stage 15	Sunday 25 July	340 km	Dunkerque – Paris	J. Rossius (BEL)	P. Thys (BEL)

As the Belgian national anthem rang out in honour of Philippe Thys,
the public invaded the Parc des Princes to congratulate the survivors,
who were forced to finish the 1920 Tour de France on foot.

Above: First crossed in 1910, the high mountains brought an epic dimension to the Tour. Below: Faber had stamped his signature on the Col d'Allos in 1911. Lapize, Petit-Breton and Barthélemy followed. In 1920, Lambot conquered the peak as he had six years earlier.

Above: The gaps between riders become massive in the mountains. Halfway up the Tourmalet, Noel Amenc and Romain Bellenger were more than an hour behind the leader. Below: In the Nice-Grenoble stage, the race turned into a demonstration by the Belgians, particularly on the Col d'Allos (2,230 m [7,316 ft]).

Thys, a truly great champion

PARIS (25 July): Another glorious chapter entered the annals of the Tour de France yesterday afternoon, when the 14th edition ended in a blaze of glory, before a vast and vociferous crowd overflowing the Parc des Princes, which, however capacious, was inadequate to contain the numbers come to welcome the cyclists home.

For the third time, Philippe Thys inscribed his name on the prestigious *palmarès*, surpassing the record set by Petit-Breton. His achievement hardly comes as a shock. Those who know him, who've seen him at work, who recall with what mastery and brio he won in 1913 and 1914, can only regard his triumph as unsurprising. But for the war, this citizen of Anderlecht might have been celebrating not his third Tour de France victory, but his fifth or sixth. Indeed, it is clear that, since Garrigou, cycling has known none so courageous and complete as Thys. He has it all: an orderly mind, great stage-racing experience, superior athleticism, plus, in a small frame, sufficient power to meet any and every challenge.

We have known for a long, long time that Thys is gifted with every skill. He is as quick as the quickest, he's a fine climber, he has an outstanding kick and he knows when and how to expend his energy. The proof of his superiority shone through clearly during this most recent Tour de France. He was present in every move, at every finish, and continually playing a protagonist's role. In short, he proved himself the best by far. Thanks to his friend Baugé whose advice he continues to value and follow, Thys has become the champion he was before the war. In the general classification, six other Belgians follow Thys, making a clean and victorious sweep for the black, red and yellow colours of our friends across the border in this 14th Tour de France.

Hector Heusghem, who we didn't imagine so strong, came second, having ridden with remarkable consistency, and won the extremely tough stage from Nice to Grenoble, which involves, as we all know, climbing Saint-Michel and the Col d'Allos. Lambot, last year's hero, the King of the Mountains and the best climber we've ever seen, took third place, adding wins in stage five, Les Sables to Bayonne, the longest in this year's Tour, and stage six, Bayonne to Luchon, the first Pyrenean stage, to his *palmarès*.

Lambot ends this Tour de France with a magnificent collection of honours. He was unquestionably the finest climber of the race, first over the Aubisque, first over the Tourmalet, first over the Aspin, first over the Portet-d'Aspet, first over the Col de Braus, first over the Col d'Allos, first to the summit of gigantic Galibier – first everywhere, he has clearly shown absolute authority as a climber. Without his poor start, without the proximity of Thys, a redoubtable specialist himself on the long climbs, he could easily have repeated his feat of last year.

The colours of France have not seen such celebrations this year. After winning two stages, Henri Pélissier withdrew voluntarily, in circumstances we all know. Then it was Christophe's turn, exhausted by a season that had been perhaps too full of success, and the victim of illness. Barthélemy, Goethals and Dhers saved French national pride. All rode with great courage and we would be ungrateful if, the day after their triumphal reception at the Parc des Princes, we did not say a few words in their praise.

1

2   3

4

1. The finish line at Aix. The Belgian contest continues before soldiers of the 55th Infantry Regiment. Behind Louis Heusghem, seven men fight for second place. Thys wins as Mottiat impedes Van Daele.

2. Aix-en-Provence: Joseph Van Daele is helped across the finish line following his clash with Louis Mottiat. Van Daele finished 8th on the stage.

3. On the Col de Braus (between Aix and Nice), José Pelletier, Louis Heusghem and Henri Ferrara, a regional rider, dropped their following car.

4. Fabio Orlandini of the *Gazzetta dello Sport* didn't have a good Tour. After losing Belloni, Gremo and Jean Alavoine of Bianchi, invincible at the Tour of Italy, he broke down between Gex and Strasbourg.

5. Guillaume Ceccherelli struggles over the summit of the Galibier; he would reach Gex 2hrs 40mins behind stage winner Scieur.

6. Rest day in Nice. Alphonse Baugé, director of La Sportive, and his protégés Thys and Lambot, recover. Thys has finally been officially awarded a yellow jersey, and his lead is over an hour.

7. On the road to Strasbourg, Joseph Van Daele, still in his raincoat and finishing his lunch, takes on a local enthusiast.

8. At Gap, after refuelling on bananas and sandwiches, (and an omelette for Lambot) the five leaders devoured the 103 kilometres (64 miles) separating them from Grenoble in four hours.

5

6   7

8

Scieur, the locomotive

Eighth overall and the first French finisher in 1920, despite a fractured shoulder and dislocated wrist, Honoré Barthélemy was the favourite for the 1921 Tour, ahead of Romain Bellenger and Eugène Christophe. Desgrange, the Tour organizer, was counting on him to recapture the glory that had shone on the Belgians since 1912. It didn't look a complicated task; Thys, the winner of three Tours, was recovering from illness contracted after the Six-Days in Brussels (which, incidentally, he had won) and Lambot had also been sick.

These ambitions disintegrated on stage one when Barthélemy punctured on the way to Le Havre and lost his chance of the first yellow jersey. Thys and Rossius finished far behind and abandoned, but another Belgian leapt into the breach. Virtually unknown at the start of the Tour, Léon Scieur was a protégé of Firmin Lambot, the 1919 champion; both men came from the same Walloon village, and Lambot had brought Scieur to professional cycling. Scieur donned the yellow jersey at Cherbourg and consolidated his lead at Brest, where he triumphed in the velodrome. Bellenger abandoned on stage seven, suffering from dysentery. The 36-year-old Christophe, whose creaking back could cope no better with the Pyrenees in 1921 than the previous year, followed him on stage eight.

Hector Heusghem seemed determined to miss every chance to overtake his compatriot, while Scieur consolidated his lead by finishing fourth at Toulon, reinforced it by finishing third in Nice, and copper-bottomed it with a stage win at Grenoble. Barthélemy didn't let Desgrange down completely; in spite of bad luck he was to finish third overall, winning the Strasbourg stage after a long breakaway with Scieur and Heusghem, which he settled with a sprint. Desgrange then relegated Lambot and Mottiat to last place in the stage for not trying hard enough to chase down the leading trio. With his characteristically idiosyncratic viewpoint, Desgrange's articles in *L'Auto* bristled with poetry, passion and protest. He coined picturesque new phrases to describe the race, railed against the invasive queues of following vehicles, applauded the rider Jules Deloffre who entertained the crowds at the stage starts with his acrobatics, and made proposal after proposal to bring the Tour to the whole of the French national territory, and allow it to heal the scars left by the conflict. He also bade farewell to Ernest Paul and Lucien Pothier who had ridden their final Tour. For Paul, it was a false farewell: he would be back for one more Tour. Not so for Pothier: thirty-second overall in 1921, he had finished second in the first Tour de France in 1903. It was the end of an era.

GENERAL CLASSIFICATION

1. **Léon Scieur** (BEL) La Sportive, 5,484 km in 221h.50m.26s; Average speed: 24.720 kph
2. **Hector Heusghem** (BEL) La Sportive, at 18m.36s.
3. **Honoré Barthélemy** (FRA) La Sportive, at 2h.1m.
4. Luigi Lucotti (ITA) Ancora, at 2h.39m.18s.
5. Hector Tiberghien (BEL) La Sportive, at 4h.33m.19s.
6. Victor Lenaers (BEL) Delage, at 4h.53m.23s.
7. Léon Despontin (BEL) La Sportive, at 5h.1m.54s.
8. Camille Leroy (BEL) Delage, at 7h.56m.27s.
9. Firmin Lambot (BEL) La Sportive, at 8h.26m.25s.
10. Félix Goethals (FRA) La Sportive, at 8h.42m.26s.
11. Louis Mottiat (BEL) La Sportive, at 8h.51m.24s.
12. Eugène Dhers (FRA) La Sportive, at 9h.44m.36s.
13. Henri Ferrara (FRA) La Sportive, at 11h.58m.34s.
14. Noël Amenc (FRA) La Sportive, at 12h.37m.23s.
15. Joseph Muller (FRA) Delage, at 12h.59m.8s.
16. Félix Sellier (BEL) Delage, at 13h.56m.45s.
17. Henri Colle (SUI) J.-B. Louvet, at 15h.2m.22s.
18. Enrico Sala (ITA) Ancora, at 19h.9m.18s.
19. Guillaume Ceccherelli (ITA) Chimene, at 22h.49m.12s.
20. Auguste Meyer (FRA) J.-B. Louvet, at 22h.53m.44s.

15TH TOUR DE FRANCE, 15 STAGES – 5,484 KM

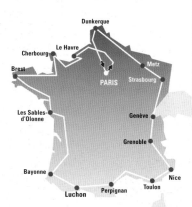

			STAGE	STAGE WINNER	YELLOW JERSEY
Stage 1	Sunday 26 June	388 km	Paris – Le Havre	L. Mottiat (BEL)	L. Mottiat (BEL)
Stage 2	Tuesday 28 June	364 km	Le Havre – Cherbourg	R. Bellenger (FRA)	L. Scieur (BEL)
Stage 3	Thursday 30 June	405 km	Cherbourg – Brest	L. Scieur (BEL)	L. Scieur (BEL)
Stage 4	Saturday 2 July	412 km	Brest – Les Sables-d'Olonne	L. Mottiat (BEL)	L. Scieur (BEL)
Stage 5	Monday 4 July	482 km	Les Sables-d'Olonne – Bayonne	L. Mottiat (BEL)	L. Scieur (BEL)
Stage 6	Wednesday 6 July	326 km	Bayonne – Luchon	H. Heusghem (BEL)	L. Scieur (BEL)
Stage 7	Friday 8 July	323 km	Luchon – Perpignan	L. Mottiat (BEL)	L. Scieur (BEL)
Stage 8	Sunday 10 July	411 km	Perpignan – Toulon	L. Lucotti (ITA)	L. Scieur (BEL)
Stage 9	Tuesday 12 July	272 km	Toulon – Nice	F. Lambot (BEL)	L. Scieur (BEL)
Stage 10	Thursday 14 July	333 km	Nice – Grenoble	L. Scieur (BEL)	L. Scieur (BEL)
Stage 11	Saturday 16 July	325 km	Grenoble – Genève (SUI)	F. Goethals (FRA)	L. Scieur (BEL)
Stage 12	Monday 18 July	371 km	Genève (SUI) – Strasbourg	H. Barthélemy (FRA)	L. Scieur (BEL)
Stage 13	Wednesday 20 July	300 km	Strasbourg – Metz	F. Sellier (BEL)	L. Scieur (BEL)
Stage 14	Friday 22 July	433 km	Metz – Dunkerque	F. Goethals (FRA)	L. Scieur (BEL)
Stage 15	Sunday 24 July	340 km	Dunkerque – Paris	F. Goethals (FRA)	L. Scieur (BEL)

1. 1921's Tour matched Hector Heusghem (left) against Léon Scieur. Despite Heusghem's efforts, it was Scieur who gained the upper hand.
2. 'Winning the Tour was easy with my "La Sportive" bicycle, my masseur, Varnier, and Baugé, my *directeur sportif*,' confided Scieur.
3. At Strasbourg, after 400 kilometres (250 miles) and over 16 hours in the saddle, Antony Wattelier is still an acrobat.
The legs may be tired but the arms...

1

2   3

Lambot's luck

This year's race saw so many twists and turns that it exhausted four potential winners before finally finding its master at the last gasp. As usual, Desgrange's predictions were wildly inaccurate. He had envisaged 1922 Paris-Roubaix winner Berten Dejonghe or, at a pinch, Christophe or Barthélemy victorious at the Parc des Princes, but certainly not one of the men he referred to caustically as 'those old Belgian chargers'. But it was the old Belgian chargers who took the race by the horns after a broken fork ended the ambitions of that old campaigner, Eugène Christophe, for the *third* time in his Tour de France career. Jean Alavoine took over the yellow jersey in the Pyrenees and wore it for five stages until a series of punctures lost him his lead and left him out of contention. Three successive stage wins would have put another of Peugeot's Belgians, Philippe Thys, on track for a historic fourth Tour de France win, had a broken wheel in the Pyrenees not already ruled him out. Unlike Léon Scieur, Thys refused to quit, picking up five stage wins and becoming the first conqueror of the Col de Izoard in Tour history.

By the end of stage 12 the Belgian Hector Heusghem was in the yellow jersey, with his compatriot Firmin Lambot just three minutes behind. Lambot had profited from Eugène Christophe's misfortune in 1919, during stage 14, when a broken fork at Raismes had cost the Frenchman the Tour and handed the yellow jersey to Lambot, a man of more reliable fortunes. Now aged 36 years, Lambot was the chosen leader of the discerning Alphonse Baugé, whose Peugeot team ran rings around the opposition, winning 12 stages out of 15. To his great surprise, his combination of consistency and good fortune was rewarded. Lambot's luck appeared to be focussed on the unlucky number *par excellence*; he wore the number 13, and it was on stage 13 that Heusghem received a one-hour penalty for swapping his machine after an accident, and Lambot inherited the race lead, despite the fact that he hadn't won a stage!

Some claimed that if Heusghem had belonged to a better team than Thomann, it might have been a different story. Yet Firmin was so fortunate and his team-mates and adversaries so ill-fated that if Heusghem had not lost his jersey after being sanctioned for his offence, who says he would not have found another way to lose it?

GENERAL CLASSIFICATION

1. **Firmin Lambot** (BEL) Peugeot
   5,372 km in 222h.8m.6s; Average speed: 24.202 kph
2. **Jean Alavoine** (FRA) Peugeot at 41m.15s.
3. **Félix Sellier** (BEL) Alcyon, at 42m.2s.
4. Hector Heusghem (BEL) Thomann, at 43m.56s.
5. Victor Lenaers (BEL) Automoto, at 45m.32s.
6. Hector Tiberghien (BEL) Peugeot, at 1h.21m.35s.
7. Léon Despontin (BEL) Peugeot, at 2h.24m.29s.
8. Eugène Christophe (FRA) Automoto, at 3h.25m.39s.
9. Jean Rossius (BEL) La Française, at 3h.26m.6s.
10. Federico Gay (ITA) Automoto, at 3h.51m.59s.
11. Émile Masson (BEL) Alcyon, at 4h.0m.21s.
12. Gaston Degy (BEL) Peugeot, at 4h.49m.13s.
13. Arsène Alancourt (FRA) Armor, at 5h.20m.56s.
14. Philippe Thys (BEL) Peugeot, at 5h.48m.58s.
15. José Pelletier (FRA) Austral, at 5h.53m.29s.
16. Joseph Muller (FRA) Peugeot, at 7h.51m.23s.
17. Giuseppe Santhia (ITA) Devaux, at 8 h.57m.35s.
18. Théophille Beeckman (BEL) Delage, at 9 h.40m.32s.
19. Louis Heusghem (BEL) Peugeot, at 9h.50m.34s.
20. Jules Nempon (FRA) Nempon, at 12h.11m.56s.

16TH TOUR DE FRANCE,
15 STAGES – 5,372 KM

			STAGE	STAGE WINNER	YELLOW JERSEY
Stage 1	Sunday 25 June	**388 km**	Paris – Le Havre	R. Jacquinot (FRA)	R. Jacquinot
Stage 2	Tuesday 27 June	**364 km**	Le Havre – Cherbourg	R. Bellenger (FRA)	R. Jacquinot
Stage 3	Thursday 29 June	**405 km**	Cherbourg – Brest	R. Jacquinot (FRA)	R. Jacquinot
Stage 4	Saturday 1 July	**412 km**	Brest – Les Sables-d'Olonne	P. Thys (BEL)	E. Christophe
Stage 5	Monday 3 July	**482 km**	Les Sables-d'Olonne – Bayonne	J. Alavoine (FRA)	E. Christophe
Stage 6	Wednesday 5 July	**326 km**	Bayonne – Luchon	J. Alavoine (FRA)	E. Christophe
Stage 7	Friday 7 July	**323 km**	Luchon – Perpignan	J. Alavoine (FRA)	J. Alavoine
Stage 8	Sunday 9 July	**411 km**	Perpignan – Toulon	P. Thys (BEL)	J. Alavoine
Stage 9	Tuesday 11 July	**284 km**	Toulon – Nice	P. Thys (BEL)	J. Alavoine
Stage 10	Thursday 13 July	**274 km**	Nice – Briançon	P. Thys (BEL)	J. Alavoine
Stage 11	Saturday 15 July	**260 km**	Briançon – Genève (SUI)	É. Masson 'Senior' (BEL)	J. Alavoine
Stage 12	Monday 17 July	**371 km**	Genève (SUI) – Strasbourg	É. Masson 'Senior' (BEL)	H. Heusghem
Stage 13	Wednesday 19 July	**300 km**	Strasbourg – Metz	F. Gay (ITA)	F. Lambot
Stage 14	Friday 21 July	**432 km**	Metz – Dunkerque	F. Sellier (BEL)	F. Lambot
Stage 15	Sunday 23 July	**325 km**	Dunkerque – Paris	P. Thys (BEL)	F. Lambot

Above: To take on the unknown Izoard, Alavoine, Beekmann, Thys, Sellier and Heusghem stayed together.
Below: Stage 5, Les Sables-d'Olonne – Bayonne, 482 kilometres (299 miles), was the longest stage since 1919, and it was also one of the hottest.

The Pélissier brothers: France at last!

No Tour de France since 1912 had been won by a Frenchman. Of course, there had been the war, and Christophe had twice come close, but the hard men of Flanders always seemed to have the last laugh. The consensus was that riders who thought too much – men like the Pélissier brothers – would never be able to win. 'Exit the thoroughbreds, enter the cart horses,' was the thought in many people's minds. Although Barthélemy and Alavoine had given grounds for optimism, France's greatest hope remained the Pélissiers, its most popular riders, if only they could finish the race.

The Belgians were hit by sometimes self-imposed setbacks. The unfortunate Thys abandoned on stage nine to go home to his new wife. Lambot and Scieur were jaded and suffering from too much stardom. The valiant Robert Jacquinot, Romain Bellenger, and especially the Pélissiers, put the Belgian disarray to their advantage. The brothers were finally riding together in the slipstream of Lucien Buysse and Ottavio Bottecchia, a lively Italian *domestique* trawled up by Baugé for the Automoto team. But Henri and Francis were determined to prove their critics wrong. They started the job at Brest, breaking away together and finishing Henri, first, Francis, second. It was a good omen that Francis, carrying a knee injury, continued for the sake of

his brother. Their team worked to keep Henri in touch with the leaders until the race reached the Alps, chasing Bellenger down the west coast, then Alavoine and Bottecchia over the Pyrenees. At Nice, Bottecchia was in the yellow jersey, almost 30 minutes ahead of Henri. Then, the brothers turned the tables between Nice and Geneva, using the Izoard, Galibier and Aravis to paint a new French masterpiece. Desgrange was overjoyed; Henri emerged from the Alps with a half-hour lead. A miracle had happened, as it often does in the Tour.

The race was won, France was blazoned in glory and the carnival was completed by symbolic victories in Strasbourg and Dunkerque for local riders Muller and Goethals. Sales of *L'Auto* soared, well-wishers flooded into the publication's Montmartre offices for the results and lined the roadside to express their gratitude to the champions who had brought such honour to France. Francis and Henri became symbols of brotherhood, courage and intelligence. The writer André Reuze pronounced: 'The thoroughbreds have got the better of the workhorses,' despite the fact that the victory owed much to the discreet Henri Manchon, who dosed his two champions with pick-up pills to prevent them from drinking insatiably at every fountain like their team-mate Bottecchia, second overall.

GENERAL CLASSIFICATION

1. **Henri Pélissier** (FRA) Automoto
   5,386 km in 222h.15m.30s; Average speed: 24.428 kph
2. **Ottavio Bottecchia** (ITA) Automoto, at 30m.41s.
3. **Romain Bellenger** (FRA) Peugeot, at 1h.4m.43s.
4. Hector Tiberghien (BEL) Peugeot, at 1h.29m.16s.
5. Arsène Alancourt (FRA) Armor, at 2h.6m.40s.
6. Henri Colleé (SUI) Griffon, at 2h.28m.43s.

7. Léon Despontin (BEL) Peugeot, at 2h.39m.49s.
8. Lucien Buysse (BEL) Automoto, at 2h.40m.11s.
9. Eugène Dhers (FRA) Armor, at 2h.59m.9s.
10. Marcel Huot (FRA) Griffon, at 3h.16m.56s.
11. Joseph Muller (FRA) Peugeot, at 3h.26m.46s.
12. Ottavio Pratesi (ITA) Liggi, at 3h.35m.6s.
13. Félix Goethals (FRA) Thomann, at 4h.21m.38s.

14. Théophille Beeckman (BEL) Griffon, at 5h.0m.4s.
15. Joseph Normand (FRA) Davy, at 5h.9m.59s.
16. Gaston Degy (FRA) Peugeot, at 5h.35m.57s.
17. Lucien Rich (FRA) Christophe, at 6h.35m.6s.
18. Paul Duboc (FRA), Allelulia, at 6h.56m.41s.
19. Camille Botte (BEL) Delage, at 7h.13m.56s.
20. Georges Cuvelier (FRA) Lapize, at 7h.30m.47s.

17TH TOUR DE FRANCE, 15 STAGES – 5,386 KM

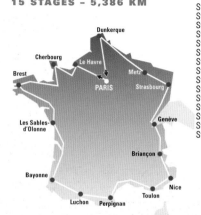

Stage	Date	Distance	STAGE	STAGE WINNER	YELLOW JERSEY
Stage 1	Sunday 24 June	381 km	Paris – Le Havre	R. Jacquinot (FRA)	R. Jacquinot (FRA)
Stage 2	Tuesday 26 June	371 km	Le Havre – Cherbourg	O. Bottecchia (ITA)	O. Bottecchia (ITA)
Stage 3	Thursday 28 June	405 km	Cherbourg – Brest	H. Pélissier (FRA)	O. Bottecchia (ITA)
Stage 4	Saturday 30 June	412 km	Brest – Les Sables-d'Olonne	A. Dejonghe (BEL)	R. Bellenger (FRA)
Stage 5	Monday 2 July	482 km	Les Sables-d'Olonne – Bayonne	R. Jacquinot (FRA)	R. Bellenger (FRA)
Stage 6	Wednesday 4 July	326 km	Bayonne – Luchon	J. Alavoine (FRA)	O. Bottecchia (ITA)
Stage 7	Friday 6 July	323 km	Luchon – Perpignan	J. Alavoine (FRA)	O. Bottecchia (ITA)
Stage 8	Sunday 8 July	427 km	Perpignan – Toulon	L. Buysse (BEL)	O. Bottecchia (ITA)
Stage 9	Tuesday 10 July	281 km	Toulon – Nice	J. Alavoine (FRA)	O. Bottecchia (ITA)
Stage 10	Thursday 12 July	275 km	Nice – Briançon	H. Pélissier (FRA)	H. Pélissier (FRA)
Stage 11	Saturday 14 July	260 km	Briançon – Genève (SUI)	H. Pélissier (FRA)	H. Pélissier (FRA)
Stage 12	Monday 16 July	377 km	Genève (SUI) – Strasbourg	J. Muller (FRA)	H. Pélissier (FRA)
Stage 13	Wednesday 18 July	300 km	Strasbourg – Metz	R. Bellenger (FRA)	H. Pélissier (FRA)
Stage 14	Friday 20 July	433 km	Metz – Dunkerque	F. Goethals (FRA)	H. Pélissier (FRA)
Stage 15	Sunday 22 July	343 km	Dunkerque – Paris	F. Goethals (FRA)	H. Pélissier (FRA)

From Montretout to the Parc des Princes, hundreds of thousands of spectators cheered on the riders who squeezed through with the official cars at a snail's pace.

Henri Pélissier is crowned King Henry of France

Henri and Francis Pélissier had one mission: to complete the Tour together. They began to take flight at Brest, where they won their fourth Tour stage.

Thanks to Baugé's careful handling (right) and Manchon's support behind the scenes, the Pélissiers reached the end of the Tour this time.

Next to Henri, Francis is huge – he fits the plans of the Automoto team better than he fits the hotel beds.

The 17th Tour de France is over. It ended yesterday afternoon at the Parc des Princes in the magnificent surroundings that befit such a splendid race, and which must count among the most compelling ever seen. I believe that only the 1910 Tour de France, with its fabulous duel between François Faber and Octave Lapize, can be ranked beside the event which has just unfolded its enthralling designs. My preference swings resolutely towards this year's race, which

saw, in turn, Jacquinot, Bottecchia, Bellenger, Bottecchia and Henri Pélissier lead the general classification. Just one black mark marred the event: the stupid accident between Nice and Briançon that put the likeable Jean Alavoine, one of the most remarkable specialists in the sport, out of the race, depriving us of a clash between this young man from Versailles and Henri Pélissier, a battle that would certainly have fired the public's imagination. Looking at the

17th Tour de France in detail, we have to acknowledge that not one of the 15 stages was superfluous. We've seen a truly pre-War Tour, a Tour that provided the swift, noble whippets victory over the hardy, resistant grafters. It also allowed a man of the very first order to show himself: I'm referring, of course, to the Italian Ottavio Bottecchia.

However, fortunately for France, we have Henri Pélissier, and we are delighted to see his name in the final *palmarès*, which has

Henri did not win his first yellow jersey until his sixth attempt, and Francis is well aware what it cost him. For the benefit of the cameras, he threatens to defend it tooth, nail and big stick against the exuberant or the careless who, he claimed, had broken two of his wheels and lost him hours.

not featured a single French name since 1912. Do I really need to deliver a panegyric in praise of Henri Pélissier? Abroad, too, great happiness has greeted his victory. Everywhere, those who follow the Tour de France are of one mind in recognizing that, when he truly wants to be so, Henri Pélissier is indisputably the king of the *routiers*. This year we saw him as we had not since the War. At the start of the race, Henri Pélissier no longer enjoyed the confidence of any follower of the Tour de France, or even of his own supporters. No one believed he would ever finish the Tour, nor even get past the Pyrenees. Yet that was where Henri surprised us all, dominating completely at Bayonne, then at Luchon and Perpignan. We saw him reach Nice with a half-hour deficit after suffering all sorts of mishaps. However, he was never prey to the kind of mental weakness that he showed in 1919 and 1920. At Briançon, after an unforgettable ride over the Izoard, we witnessed a victory worthy of a true ace as he resolutely claimed his place as leader.

IN THE SADDLE
BY HENRI PÉLISSIER

I remember the torture that my friends put me through, shouting and clapping me on the back, their enthusiasm overflowing but their faces tense with anxiety. How many times I prayed to God to protect me from my friends! But when you have the chance to win an event like the Tour de France, it's wrong to complain, there can only be joy. I am happy: that's my story in three words. But I must also say how I marvelled at the brio of my comrade Bottecchia and wondered at his astonishing performance. Don't forget either that I did not win the Tour de France alone; I was supported by my brother Francis who, severely hampered from the second stage by a blow to his knee, continued the Tour in spite of his suffering, giving me an example of what can be achieved through determination and energy.

11th stage. The Pélissiers broke away on the Aravis, finishing 16 minutes ahead of Bottecchia, who lost 41 minutes in total. At Geneva, with the Tour won, Henri embraces his brother.

Forza Bottecchia!

After his fine victory in 1923, the logical favourite for the 1924 Tour de France was Henri Pélissier. But in Cherbourg at the end of the second stage, he let slip the truth: 'In this form, Bottecchia is head and shoulders above the rest of us.' It was true: the Italian was dazzling, even more than during the previous year's trial run, when he finished second. Bottecchia was their Automoto team-mate, but the Pélissier brothers preferred a strategic withdrawal than a Tour as Bottecchia's lackeys. In any case, at 35, Henri was closer to his dotage than his athletic prime and, after 32 abandons in the first two stages, he opted to stage a protest against the exploitation of riders by the dictatorial Tour organization, rather than risk his reputation. The truth was that the Pélissier brothers were facing decline, but they put up a cunning smoke screen for the real reason for their withdrawal. They stepped down at Coutances on stage three, after receiving a sanction for abandoning a jersey (riders were supposed to finish the race with all the equipment they started with). They had the good fortune to have a witness to their mischief: Albert Londres, the brilliant but outspoken special correspondent for the *Petit Parisien*, recently returned from a trip to the French penal colonies in Cayenne. In his hands, the Pélissiers' story was transformed from a damp squib into a bombshell, all the more dangerous as popular expectations were running high. Londres' article depicted a race run in dictatorial, almost prison-like circumstances. After all the fuss in Coutances the *forçats* made way for Bottecchia. Ottavio, a stonemason from Friuli in North-East Italy, hogged the limelight, wearing the yellow jersey from start to finish, sharing it for two days with the Belgian Théophile Beeckman between Brest and Les Sables. The Pyrenees allowed Bottecchia to showcase his prodigious capacities, levelling the Aubisque, Aspin and Tourmalet from the front. Such was his power that Desgrange compared him to Faber, the giant himself. Bottecchia avoided injury at the hands of the following vehicles – Desgrange's despised 'automobilistical saraband' – but lost three minutes when he was attacked by a dog. However, when he wasn't tearing off burst tyres with his teeth, he sang as he pedalled. Bottecchia and runner-up Nicolas Frantz may have devoured the Tour, in Desgrange's words, 'like a glass of water', but it wasn't the same for everyone. Jean Alavoine summed up the general lot even better than the Pélissiers when he said: 'If I'm going well, my tyres burst. If my tyres don't burst, I feel like I'm the one who's breathing my last.'

GENERAL CLASSIFICATION

1. **Ottavio Bottecchia** (ITA) Automoto, 5,425 km in 226h.18m.21s; Average speed: 24.250 kph
2. **Nicolas Frantz** (LUX) Alcyon, at 35m.36s.
3. **Lucien Buysse** (BEL) Automoto, at 1h.32m.13s.
4. Bartolomeo Aimo (ITA) Legnano, at 1h.32m.47s.
5. Théophile Beeckman (BEL) Griffon, at 2h.11m.12s.
6. Joseph Muller (FRA) Peugeot, at 2h.35m.33s.
7. Arsène Alancourt (FRA) Armor, at 2h.41m.31s.
8. Romain Bellenger (FRA) Peugeot, at 2h.51m.9s.
9. Omer Huyse (BEL) Lapize, at 2h.58m.13s.
10. Hector Tiberghien (BEL) Peugeot, at 3h.5m.4s.
11. Philippe Thys (BEL) Peugeot, at 3h.15m.24s.
12. Georges Cuvelier (FRA) Peugeot, at 3h.21m.45s.
13. Ermano Vallazza (ITA) Legnano, at 3h.48m.24s.
14. Jean Alavoine (FRA) Peugeot, at 3h.55m.45s.
15. Gaston Degy (BEL) Aiglon, at 5h.11m.48s.
16. Raymond Engelbert (BEL) Alcyon, at 5h.20m.11s.
17. Alfons Standaert (BEL) Armor, at 5h.41m.48s.
18. Louis Mottiat ((BEL) Alcyon, at 5h.54m.19s.
19. Ottavio Pratesi (ITA) Ostende, at 6h.0m.4s.
20. Lucien Rich (FRA) Automoto, at 6h.26m.21s.

18TH TOUR DE FRANCE, 15 STAGES – 5,425 KM

	STAGE		STAGE WINNER	YELLOW JERSEY
Stage 1 Sunday 22 June	381 km	Paris – Le Havre	O. Bottecchia (ITA)	O. Bottecchia
Stage 2 Tuesday 24 June	371 km	Le Havre – Cherbourg	R. Bellenger (FRA)	O. Bottecchia
Stage 3 Thursday 26 June	405 km	Cherbourg – Brest	P. Thys (BEL) & T. Beeckman (BEL)	O. Bottecchia
Stage 4 Saturday 28 June	412 km	Brest – Les Sables-d'Olonne	F. Goethals (FRA)	O. Bottecchia
Stage 5 Monday 30 June	482 km	Les Sables-d'Olonne – Bayonne	O. Huyse (BEL)	O. Bottecchia
Stage 6 Wednesday 2 July	326 km	Bayonne – Luchon	O. Bottecchia (ITA)	O. Bottecchia
Stage 7 Friday 4 July	323 km	Luchon – Perpignan	O. Bottecchia (ITA)	O. Bottecchia
Stage 8 Sunday 6 July	427 km	Perpignan – Toulon	L. Mottiat (BEL)	O. Bottecchia
Stage 9 Tuesday 8 July	280 km	Toulon – Nice	P. Thys (BEL)	O. Bottecchia
Stage 10 Thursday 10 July	275 km	Nice – Briançon	G. Brunero (ITA)	O. Bottecchia
Stage 11 Saturday 12 July	307 km	Briançon – Gex	N. Frantz (LUX)	O. Bottecchia
Stage 12 Monday 14 July	360 km	Gex – Strasbourg	N. Frantz (LUX)	O. Bottecchia
Stage 13 Wednesday 16 July	300 km	Strasbourg – Metz	A. Alancourt (FRA)	O. Bottecchia
Stage 14 Friday 18 July	433 km	Metz – Dunkerque	R. Bellenger (FRA)	O. Bottecchia
Stage 15 Sunday 20 July	343 km	Dunkerque – Paris	O. Bottecchia (ITA)	O. Bottecchia

In the Pyrenees, conquered Cyrano-style with a wave of his imperial nose, Bottecchia won the admiration of Albert Londres: 'regular as a clock's pendulum, he was the only one who didn't seem to be pushing himself beyond his powers'.

Bottecchia shows a safe pair of hands

The 1925 Tour, contested by 209 riders divided into trade teams and independents known as *touristes-routiers*, swept over the contours of France in no less than 18 stages, and became a classic in Tour history. It was a Tour worthy of a craftsman, and fell to one in the stonemason Ottavio Bottecchia, who mastered it with skilled, sober hands, avoiding unnecessary haste or superfluous gestures. Now pushing 31 and riding his third Tour, the Automoto champion knew the workings of the great Tour de France machine perfectly. The youthful mistakes of 1923 belonged to the past. He no longer drank insatiably, he knew how to ride strategically unimportant stages with the minimum of effort, and didn't hesitate to make his team-mates work for him, within the rules. Thanks to this complete apprenticeship, and the fact that sharing a room with his compatriot Alfonso Piccin left him much more relaxed than in the past, the shy Ottavio claimed his second Tour with four vigorous blows of the hammer at the start and finish of the race.

At Le Havre, the eagle-nosed Italian won stage one by three minutes from Francis Pélissier, securing the yellow jersey for two stages. At Bordeaux, his sprint speed brought him the stage win, and at Bayonne, he regained the yellow jersey temporarily from Belgium's Adelin Benoît. After taking definitive possession of the jersey at Perpignan, Ottavio delegated his brilliant team-mate Lucien Buysse to take the lead, and hugged his wheel all the way back to Paris. As the *Miroir des Sports* graciously put it, more than mere assistance, Buysse offered the champion an alter ego. Buysse rode alongside him on the road to Toulon, opened the way for him through the hairpins of the Col de Braus, and turned the Aravis and Galibier into a Via Bottecchia. Despite the dominance of the Automoto team, there were still opportunities for Alcyon, directed by Ludovic Feuillet, to gain some lesser glory. Italy's Bartolomeo Aimo was king in the Alps, while the Luxembourger Nicolas Frantz became the prince of the stage finishes with four wins. But for Bottecchia, the Tour ran smoothly, without crises or slip-ups. His shepherd Buysse even had enough juice left in the closing stages to grab second place overall and give Automoto a one-two victory in the final classification. It faithfully reflected the team's solidity and superiority. According to custom, the Pélissier brothers abandoned, Alavoine and Christophe were treated as heroes, and the leader had more than an hour's advantage by Toulon. Now over 40, Christophe joined Alavoine, Heusghem, Jacquinot, Mottiat, Thys and Henri Pélissier in bidding adieu to a race that had changed their lives.

GENERAL CLASSIFICATION

1. **Ottavio Bottecchia** (ITA) Automoto, 5,430 km in 219h.10m.18s; Average speed: 24.820 kph
2. **Lucien Buysse** (BEL) Automoto, at 54m.20s.
3. **Bartolomeo Aimo** (ITA) Alcyon, at 56m.37s.
4. Nicolas Frantz (LUX) Alcyon, at 1h.11m.24s.
5. Albert Dejonghe (BEL) J.-B. Louvet, at 1h.27m.42s.
6. Théophile Beeckman (BEL) Thomann, at 2h.24m.43s.
7. Omer Huyse (BEL) Armor, at 2h.33m.38s.
8. Auguste Verdijck (BEL) Christophe, at 2h.44m.36s.
9. Felix Sellier (BEL) Alcyon, at 2h.45m.59s.
10. Federico Gay (ITA) Meteore, at 4h.6m.3s.
11. Romain Bellenger (FRA) Alcyon, at 4h.26m.10s.
12. Adelin Benoît (BEL) Thomann, at 4h.37m.14s.
13. Jean Alavoine (FRA) J. Alavoine, at 4h.39m.48s.
14. Hector Martin (BEL) J.-B. Louvet, at 4h.48m.44s.
15. Jules Buysse (BEL) Automoto, at 5h.7m.33s.
16. Léon Despontin (BEL) *touriste-routier*, at 5h.28m.7s.
17. Émile Hardy (BEL) Christophe, at 6h.39m.1s.
18. Eugène Christophe (FRA) J.-B. Louvet, at 6h.55m.31s.
19. Giovanni Rossignoli (ITA) *touriste-routier*, at 7h.18m.13s.
20. Raymond Engelbert (BEL) Labor, at 7h.30m.6s.

19TH TOUR DE FRANCE, 18 STAGES - 5,430 KM

			STAGE	STAGE WINNER	YELLOW JERSEY
Stage 1	Sunday 21 June	340 km	Paris – Le Havre	O. Bottecchia (ITA)	O. Bottecchia
Stage 2	Tuesday 23 June	371 km	Le Havre – Cherbourg	R. Bellenger (FRA)	O. Bottecchia
Stage 3	Thursday 25 June	405 km	Cherbourg – Brest	L. Mottiat (BEL)	A. Benoît
Stage 4	Friday 26 June	208 km	Brest – Vannes	N. Frantz (LUX)	A. Benoît
Stage 5	Saturday 27 June	204 km	Vannes – Les Sables d'Olonne	N. Frantz (LUX)	A. Benoît
Stage 6	Sunday 28 June	293 km	Les Sables-d'Olonne – Bordeaux	O. Bottecchia (ITA)	A. Benoît
Stage 7	Monday 29 June	189 km	Bordeaux – Bayonne	O. Bottecchia (ITA)	O. Bottecchia
Stage 8	Wednesday 1 July	326 km	Bayonne – Luchon	A. Benoît (BEL)	A. Benoît
Stage 9	Friday 3 July	323 km	Luchon – Perpignan	N. Frantz (LUX)	O. Bottecchia
Stage 10	Saturday 4 July	215 km	Perpignan – Nîmes	T. Beeckman (BEL)	O. Bottecchia
Stage 11	Sunday 5 July	215 km	Nîmes – Toulon	L. Buysse (BEL)	O. Bottecchia
Stage 12	Tuesday 7 July	280 km	Toulon – Nice	L. Buysse (BEL)	O. Bottecchia
Stage 13	Thursday 9 July	275 km	Nice – Briançon	B. Aimo (ITA)	O. Bottecchia
Stage 14	Saturday 11 July	303 km	Briançon – Évian	H. Martin (BEL)	O. Bottecchia
Stage 15	Monday 13 July	373 km	Évian – Mulhouse	N. Frantz (LUX)	O. Bottecchia
Stage 16	Wednesday 15 July	334 km	Mulhouse – Metz	H. Martin (BEL)	O. Bottecchia
Stage 17	Friday 17 July	433 km	Metz – Dunkerque	H. Martin (BEL)	O. Bottecchia
Stage 18	Sunday 19 July	343 km	Dunkerque – Paris	O. Bottecchia (ITA)	O. Bottecchia

As handy with a syphon as he is with his gears, Bottecchia takes advantage of a three-minute break at Abbeville for some refreshment. It was obviously just the tonic; he went on to triumph in Paris.

Unfinished business for the Buysse brothers

On 20 June 1926, the Tour de France started outside Paris for the first time. Évian was the departure point for a record 5,745-kilometre (3,567-mile) route. The 126 who set off faced 17 gruelling stages and 13 rest days. Just 41 would reach Paris. Not knowing quite where Évian was, the riders were shepherded across France in a special train. Then, unsure how the race would unfold, they set off at a gentle pace, to Desgrange's great annoyance. No less than ten stages ended in a bunch sprint. If Jules Buysse hadn't stirred things up by winning stage one at Mulhouse, the race would have consisted of little more than monotonous grinds with a sprint finish. Jules was just one of a family of brilliant brothers. Lucien Buysse had progressed through the ranks of the Automoto team and helped Ottavio Bottecchia to victory in the 1924 and 1925 Tours, finishing, respectively, third and second overall. Nonetheless, at 33, he wasn't among Henri Desgrange's favourites. The Tour director considered him a slow starter, and fancied another Belgian, Adelin Benoît, for the yellow jersey.

Thirteen years before, another Buysse brother, Marcel, had been leading the Tour de France when a broken handlebar had robbed him of his chances. Despite winning four of the six remaining stages, he could only claw his way back to third

place. Lucien and Jules aimed to right that distant wrong, and from the moment Jules won stage one, the brothers constructed victory like expert architects.

By winning stage three at Dunkerque after 17 hours and 433 kilometres (269 miles) of torment, their fellow Belgian Gustave Van Slembrouck borrowed the yellow jersey from the Buysses and wore it down to the Pyrenees. There, the experienced Lucien Buysse took advantage of hellish conditions on stage ten from Bayonne to Luchon to gain nearly two hours on Van Slembrouck and take over the race lead. It was a gruelling ordeal, but two days later, he had recovered sufficient strength to win stage eleven from Luchon to Perpignan and lengthen his lead; his brother Jules finished second in the stage. At Perpignan, after a victorious solo breakaway over 150 kilometres (93 miles), Lucien had the Tour in his pocket, and savoured a glass of Cinzano as the other riders battled through the elements. Ludovic Feuillet's Alcyon team did its best, but Frantz was ill and Aimo had his limits. Besides, Lucien Buysse was in complete control; he kept his nerve and refused to get involved in the dangerous sprints. Van Slembrouck, an inveterate smoker, abandoned in the Alps, allowing Buysse an easy ride to the capital.

GENERAL CLASSIFICATION

1. **Lucien Buysse** (BEL) Automoto, 5,745 km in 238h.44m.25s; Average speed: 24.063 kph
2. **Nicolas Frantz** (LUX) Alcyon, at 1h.22m.25s.
3. Bartolomeo Aimo (ITA) Alcyon, at 1h.22m.51s.
4. Théophile Beeckman (BEL) Armor, at 1h.43m.54s.
5. Félix Sellier (BEL) Alcyon, at 1h.49m.13s.
6. Albert Dejonghe (BEL) J.-B. Louvet, at 1h.56m.15s.
7. Léon Parmentier (BEL) J.-B. Louvet, at 2h.9m.20s.
8. Georges Cuvelier (FRA) Météore, at 2h.28m.32s.
9. Jules Buysse (BEL) Automoto, at 2h.37m.3s.
10. Marcel Bidot (FRA) Thomann, at 2h.53m.54s.
11. Odile Taillieu (BEL) J.-B. Louvet, at 3h.9m.8s.
12. Joseph Van Dam (BEL) Automoto, at 4h.0m.35s.
13. Omer Huyse (BEL) Automoto, at 4h.7m.24s.
14. Camille Van de Casteele (BEL) J.-B. Louvet, at 4h.28m.19s.
15. Aimé Dossche (BEL) Christophe, at 5h.23m.19s.
16. Émile Hardy (BEL) Christophe, at 6h.2m.20s.
17. Raimond Engelbert (BEL) Alcyon, at 6h.3m.10s.
18. Henri Colle (SUI) J.-B. Louvet, at 7h.10m.35s.
19. Georges Detreille (FRA) Météore, at 7h.48m.17s.
20. Omer Vermeulen (BEL) Météore, at 7h.49m.44s.

20TH TOUR DE FRANCE, 17 STAGES – 5,745 KM (THE LONGEST TOUR)

Dunkerque
Cherbourg
Brest
Le Havre
Metz
PARIS
Mulhouse
Dijon
Les Sables-d'Olonne
Évian
Bordeaux
Briançon
Bayonne
Nice
Luchon
Perpignan
Toulon

			STAGE	STAGE WINNER	YELLOW JERSEY
Stage 1	Sunday 20 June	373 km	Évian – Mulhouse	J. Buysse (BEL)	J. Buysse
Stage 2	Tuesday 22 June	334 km	Mulhouse – Metz	A. Dossche (BEL)	J. Buysse
Stage 3	Thursday 24 June	433 km	Metz – Dunkerque	G. Van Slembrouck (BEL)	G. Van Slembrouck
Stage 4	Friday 26 June	361 km	Dunkerque – Le Havre	F. Sellier (BEL)	G. Van Slembrouck
Stage 5	Sunday 28 June	357 km	Le Havre – Cherbourg	A. Benoît (BEL)	G. Van Slembrouck
Stage 6	Tuesday 30 June	405 km	Cherbourg – Brest	J. Van Dam (BEL)	G. Van Slembrouck
Stage 7	Thursday 2 July	412 km	Brest – Les Sables-d'Olonne	N. Frantz (LUX)	G. Van Slembrouck
Stage 8	Friday 3 July	285 km	Les Sables-d'Olonne – Bordeaux	J. Van Dam (BEL)	G. Van Slembrouck
Stage 9	Sunday 4 July	189 km	Bordeaux – Bayonne	N. Frantz (LUX)	G. Van Slembrouck
Stage 10	Tuesday 6 July	326 km	Bayonne – Luchon	L. Buysse (BEL)	L. Buysse
Stage 11	Thursday 8 July	323 km	Luchon – Perpignan	L. Buysse (BEL)	L. Buysse
Stage 12	Saturday 10 July	427 km	Perpignan – Toulon	N. Frantz (LUX)	L. Buysse
Stage 13	Monday 12 July	280 km	Toulon – Nice	N. Frantz (LUX)	L. Buysse
Stage 14	Wednesday 14 July	275 km	Nice – Briançon	B. Aimo (ITA)	L. Buysse
Stage 15	Friday 16 July	303 km	Briançon – Évian	J. Van Dam (BEL)	L. Buysse
Stage 16	Saturday 17 July	321 km	Évian – Dijon	C. Van de Casteele (BEL)	L. Buysse
Stage 17	Sunday 18 July	341 km	Dijon – Paris	A. Dossche (BEL)	L. Buysse

Third in 1924, second – and, some said, the moral victor – in 1925, Lucien Buysse
owed his categorical victory, in the words of team director Karel Steyaert, to his
'profound comprehension of the Tour'.

What a way to win the yellow jersey!

LUCHON (Tuesday 6 July): The stage from Bayonne to Luchon, the toughest of all the stages in this year's Tour de France, is over. The Automoto team unleashed its formidable assault at the foot of Aubisque and pursued it all the way to the finishing post, in catastrophic weather and on roads swamped with mud and scarred with furrows. As everyone had foreseen, today's general classification bears no relation to that of two days ago. Van Slembrouck has lost the yellow jersey. Too heavy for the climb, he was one of the first to succumb when Lucien Buysse gave the signal to commence hostilities, and it is almost certain that he will never wear it again. But it will always have been a great and glorious honour for Van Slembrouck and his team, J.-B. Louvet-Wolber, to have worn the jersey from Dunkerque to Luchon. On the Aubisque, three men took flight and dominated the race: Lucien Buysse, Dejonghe and Huyse. Bottecchia, however, suffering from backache, lost contact, announced his abandon, then resumed the stage. Adelin Benoît, meanwhile, of whom much was expected, fell and was obliged to withdraw from the race that he had hoped to win.

At the Tourmalet, it was Huyse's turn to drop off the pace, leaving Lucien Buysse and Dejonghe alone at the head of the race. Behind them, Taillieu, Devos and Aimo chased frantically; the rest were no longer in the fight. Finally, the remarkable Lucien Buysse managed to shake off Dejonghe, and raced off bulldog-like towards the finish-line, and it was with a lead of over 25 minutes that he triumphally cut the tape at Luchon. Aimo came in second, Devos third. In one decisive blow, Lucien Buysse made up his deficit in the general classification and triumphantly seized the yellow jersey

Sellier, one of the Alycon leaders, has a puncture. Debusschere, his team-mate, helps him repair it, as the regulations now allow.

of the race leader. It's in good hands; his victory will clearly not have surprised anyone. But how he must have wanted this victory! How spiritedly he attained it! It was quite simply magnificent; he has produced the finest performance of his career.

We offer him our sincerest congratulations. We especially applaud him for being prepared to risk everything with such fortitude and passion. It will now require someone truly exceptional to prise the trophy from Buysse's grasp. I would like to close by underlining that yesterday was also a day of celebration for two marques dear to the Tour de France, Automoto and Hutchinson. Three times winners of this colossal odyssey, this pairing had never yet allowed an athlete to achieve such an inspired tour de force as that achieved yesterday by Lucien Buysse. For a champion of Lucien's class, the support of two marques like Automoto and Hutchinson was just what was needed to defeat all his rivals by such a distance and make good a deficit of more than 22 minutes at a single stroke. Automoto and Hutchinson, who made this feat possible, deserve to be honoured as much as Lucien Buysse himself. One more word: think for a moment of what those wretched independents must have suffered during the storm... And how could we end this report without applauding once more the magnificent performance of Rossignoli and Touzard, first and second *touristes routiers* in the stage.

Our final wish is that fate should not be too cruel, and should spare a few more of our brave men.

At Dunkerque, Buysse swore he would be race leader at Luchon. He was, crossing the storm, the Aubisque and Peyresourde to triumph over Aimo and Parmentier.

The fog and the cold made fingers too numb to change tyres, so Van Dam, Huyse and Jules Buysse shelter Lucien as he makes the repairs at Goodfordom (opposite).

It should have been Tesi's day of glory with the Tour passing through his native city of Toulouse, but he fell at the Les Guignes crossroads.

Jules Buysse (in front), Lucien's younger brother, launches a victorious attack in which the Italian Ottavio Bottecchia (behind) is destined to lose ground.

Having conquered the elements at Luchon, Lucien Buysse holds Aimo and Frantz in check. Above, they pursue him over the Puymorens.

The Tour de Frantz

The 1927 Tour de France began without the two outstanding favourites. Buysse, the 1926 winner, did not start for personal reasons; Bottecchia, the 1925 winner, had died a tragic and mysterious death. In these circumstances, it couldn't have been a normal Tour, and in any case, Desgrange wanted to see a more dynamic race, one that would not be decided on the traditional marathon through the Pyrenees between Bayonne and Luchon. His fine-tuning meant 24 shorter stages, with teams starting the 16 flat stages separately, like team time-trials in which individual riders could break away to obtain a better time. The result was a Tour to follow with pen, paper and stopwatch in hand. It confused the spectators, and didn't achieve its aims: not even Desgrange could have anticipated Alcyon's brilliant renaissance, or Dilecta's pathetic collapse. After an excellent start, winning stages one and five and taking the yellow jersey for six days, first with Francis Pélissier and then Ferdinand Le Drogo, the Dilecta team simply fell apart. On stage six, Pélissier abandoned, sick; on stage nine, the rest of the team withdrew.

Fortunately, the Belgian riders who spearheaded J.-B. Louvet stepped into the breach with stage wins for Van Slembrouck, Decorte, Verhaegen, Geldhof and Martin, who wore the yellow jersey down the west coast until the all-important Pyrenean stages. Then, in the time-honoured fashion, and contrary to Desgrange's plans, Luxembourg's Nicolas Frantz, hardened by the experience of three Tours de France, took control of the race on the customary decisive stage to Luchon. At the stage start in Bayonne, Frantz lay seventeen minutes behind race leader Martin; at the stage finish in Luchon, Martin lay twenty-second overall, an hour and forty minutes adrift. It was the first yellow jersey of Frantz's Tour career and he had no intention of giving it up. Van Slembrouck took his second stage win at Perpignan, although with Frantz and team-mate Adelin Benoît on his wheel, it was a victory for Alcyon's new strategist Ludovic Feuillet. In the stage from Toulon to Nice, Frantz tightened his grip even more, allowing him to control the race until Metz, where a stage win put the finishing touch on his dominance.

There was plenty of incident, including surprising, sustained attacks by two *touristes-routiers*, the Italian Gordini in the Pyrenees and the Swiss Martinet in the Alps, and two bright young French riders, André Leducq and Antonin Magne, finished in the top six. But with eleven stage wins, Alcyon rode away with the race, and in the buccaneering Nicolas Frantz, Luxembourger François Faber found a worthy successor.

GENERAL CLASSIFICATION

1. **Nicolas Frantz** (LUX) Alcyon, 5,321 km in 198h.16m.42s; Average speed: 27.224 kph
2. **Maurice De Waele** (BEL) Labor, at 1h.48m.21s.
3. **Julien Vervaecke** (BEL) Armor, at 2h.25m.6s.
4. André Leducq (FRA) Thomann, at 3h.2m.5s.
5. Adelin Benoit (BEL) Alcyon, at 4h.45m.1s.
6. Antonin Magne (FRA) Alleluia, at 4h.48m.23s.

7. Pé Verhaegen (BEL) J.-B. Louvet, at 6h.18m.36s.
8. Julien Moineau (FRA) Alleluia, at 6h.36m.17s.
9. Hector Martin (BEL) J.-B. Louvet, at 7h.7m.34s.
10. Maurice Geldhof (BEL) J.-B. Louvet, at 7h.16m.2s.
11. Raymond Decorte (BEL) J.-B. Louvet, at 8h.17m.12s.
12. Louis Muller (BEL) Armor, at 8h.27m.49s.
13. Jan Debusschere (BEL) Alcyon, at 10h.51m.56s.

14. Gustaaf Van Slembrouck (BEL) J.B. Louvet, at 11h.1m.54s.
15. Pierre Magne (FRA) Alleluia, at 12h.12m.37s.
16. Louis Delannoy (BEL) Labor, at 13h.28m.2s.
17. Jos Hemelsoet (BEL) J.-B. Louvet, at 14h.8m.18s.
18. Secundo Martinetto (ITA) touriste-routier, at 14h.37m.12s.
19. Henri Touzard (FRA) touriste-routier, at 15h.8m.3s.
20. José Pelletier (FRA) touriste-routier, at 15h.52m.28s.

21ST TOUR DE FRANCE, 24 STAGES – 5,321 KM

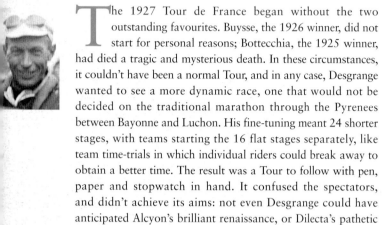

STAGE				STAGE WINNER	YELLOW JERSEY
Stage 1	Sunday 19 June	180 km	Paris – Dieppe	F. Pélissier (FRA)	F. Pélissier
Stage 2	Monday 20 June	103 km	Dieppe – Le Havre	M. De Waele (BEL)	F. Pélissier
Stage 3	Tuesday 21 June	225 km	Le Havre – Caen	H. Martin (BEL)	F. Pélissier
Stage 4	Wednesday 22 June	140 km	Caen – Cherbourg	C. Van de Casteele (BEL)	F. Pélissier
Stage 5	Thursday 23 June	199 km	Cherbourg – Dinan	F. Le Drogo (FRA)	F. Pélissier
Stage 6	Friday 24 June	206 km	Dinan – Brest	A. Leducq (FRA)	F. Le Drogo
Stage 7	Saturday 25 June	207 km	Brest – Vannes	G. Van Slembrouck (BEL)	H. Martin
Stage 8	Sunday 26 June	204 km	Vannes – Les Sables-d'Olonne	R. Decorte (BEL)	H. Martin
Stage 9	Monday 27 June	285 km	Les Sables-d'Olonne – Bordeaux	A. Benoît (BEL)	H. Martin
Stage 10	Tuesday 28 June	189 km	Bordeaux – Bayonne	P. Verhaegen (BEL)	H. Martin
Stage 11	Thursday 30 June	326 km	Bayonne – Luchon	N. Frantz (LUX)	N. Frantz
Stage 12	Sunday 2 July	323 km	Luchon – Perpignan	G. Van Slembrouck (BEL)	N. Frantz
Stage 13	Monday 4 July	360 km	Perpignan – Marseille	M. De Waele (BEL)	N. Frantz
Stage 14	Tuesday 5 July	120 km	Marseille – Toulon	A. Magne (FRA)	N. Frantz
Stage 15	Wednesday 6 July	280 km	Toulon – Nice	N. Frantz (LUX)	N. Frantz
Stage 16	Friday 8 July	275 km	Nice – Briançon	J. Vervaecke (BEL)	N. Frantz
Stage 17	Sunday 9 July	283 km	Briançon – Évian	P. Verhaegen (BEL)	N. Frantz
Stage 18	Monday 11 July	213 km	Évian – Pontarlier	A. Benoît (BEL)	N. Frantz
Stage 19	Tuesday 12 July	119 km	Pontarlier – Belfort	M. Geldhof (BEL)	N. Frantz
Stage 20	Wednesday 13 July	145 km	Belfort – Strasbourg	R. Decorte (BEL)	N. Frantz
Stage 21	Thursday 14 July	165 km	Strasbourg – Metz	N. Frantz (LUX)	N. Frantz
Stage 22	Friday 15 July	159 km	Metz – Charleville	H. Martin (BEL)	N. Frantz
Stage 23	Saturday 16 July	270 km	Charleville – Dunkerque	A. Leducq (FRA)	N. Frantz
Stage 24	Sunday 17 July	344 km	Dunkerque – Paris	A. Leducq (FRA)	N. Frantz

On the Aravis, Vervaecke, Benoît, Leducq and Frantz in the yellow jersey, limit the lead of the winning breakaway of Magne, De Waele, Verhaegen and Martinet.

Frantz lacked the style and agility to be a truly great climber but with his handlebars raised high he had enough power to give a climbing masterclass between Bayonne and Luchon and take the yellow jersey.

On a stage that started at night, Italy's Michele Gordini, a *touriste-routier*, led by 58 minutes at Eaux-Bonnes. But mechanical problems on the Aubisque meant he finished only fifth at Luchon.

Frantz, from beginning to end

Certain *directeurs sportifs* have made immense contributions to the history of the Tour de France. If Alphonse Baugé was the magician during the heroic early Tours, the Twenties belong to Ludovic Feuillet. The brilliant weather that accompanied the 1928 Tour suited the sky-blue colours of his Alcyon team perfectly, and Feuillet, clad in his characteristic white coat, directed his team and his leader, Luxembourg's Nicolas Frantz, to an overwhelming victory. Nine French regional formations rode beside the *touristes-routiers* and eight trade teams, one of which, the four-man Ravat-Wonder, comprised three Australians and a New Zealander, the first antipodeans to ride the Tour de France.

The start was brought forward to 17 June due to the Olympic Games in Amsterdam, and Desgrange unleashed a record peloton of 162 riders divided into no less than three categories: manufacturers' teams, regional teams and *touristes-routiers*. As in 1927, teams started separately on the fifteen flat stages, which destroyed the chances of the *touristes-routiers*, but allowed the tough Australians to show their mettle. The trade teams representing Alleluia, Elvish, Thomann and J.-B. Louvet sent out Antonin Magne, Marcel and Jean Bidot, Julien Moineau, Marcel Huot and Victor Fontan to complicate Feuillet's task; they made an impression on individual stages, but none on the general classification. Alcyon's dominance was absolute, with brilliant riders like Maurice De Waele and André Leducq supporting an inspirational and meticulous leader. Nicolas Frantz, who wore fresh shorts and socks on every stage and the yellow jersey from start to finish, rode so impeccably that Henri Desgrange had to maintain the interest of his readers with tales of an artificial contest between the French and foreign riders. It was a foretaste of what the Tour would be like when national teams replaced trade teams in 1930, but it was also a distortion of the truth. French riders won thirteen stages out of twenty-two, but none looked likely to repeat Henri Pélissier's success. Desgrange momentarily turned on Antonin Magne in the Pyrenees when the 24-year-old couldn't turn the tables on Frantz, but it was pique, no more.

Only a last gasp accident three stages from Paris threatened to deprive Frantz of overall victory. The style with which he recovered and chased to the stage finish at Metz half an hour behind his closest rival, Leducq, finally earned him Desgrange's admiration; that, and victory in the five key stages of the Tour. The final podium of Alcyon team-mates Frantz, Leducq and De Waele accurately reflected Alcyon's supremacy.

GENERAL CLASSIFICATION

1. **Nicolas Frantz** (LUX) Alcyon, 5,375 km in 192h.48m.58s; Average speed: 27.876 kph
2. **André Leducq** (FRA) Alcyon, at 50m.7s.
3. **Maurice De Waele** (BEL) Alcyon, at 56m.16s.
4. Jan Mertens (BEL) Thomann, at 1h.19m.18s.
5. Julien Vervaecke (BEL) Armor, at 1h.53m.32s.
6. Antonin Magne (FRA) Alleluia, at 2h.14m.2s.
7. Victor Fontan (FRA) Elvish, at 5h.7m.47s.
8. Marcel Bidot (FRA) Alleluia, at 5h.18m.28's.
9. Marcel Huot (FRA) Alleluia, at 5h.37m.33s.
10. Pierre Magne (FRA) Alleluia, at 5h.41m.20s.
11. Joseph Mauclair (FRA) Armor, at 5h.44m.1s.
12. Gaston Rebry (BEL) Alcyon, at 5h.53m.44s.
13. Louis Delannoy (BEL) Armor, at 6h.11m.35s.
14. Camille Van de Casteele (BEL) J.-B. Louvet, at 7h.3m.2s.
15. Salvador Cardona (SPA) Elvish, at 7h.33m.47s.
16. Pé Verhaegen (BEL) J.-B. Louvet, at 7h.39m.56s.
17. Julien Moineau (FRA) Alleluia, at 8h.3m.23s.
18. Hubert Opperman (AUS) Ravat-Wonder, at 8h.34m.25s.
19. Désiré Louesse (BEL) Alcyon, at 9 h.27m.21s.
20. Odile Taillieu (BEL) J.-B. Louvet, at 10 h.23m.18s.

22ND TOUR DE FRANCE, 22 STAGES – 5,375 KM

Malo-les-Bains · Charleville · Dieppe · Cherbourg · Metz · Brest · Caen · PARIS · Strasbourg · Dinan · Belfort · Vannes · Pontarlier · Les Sables-d'Olonne · Évian · Bordeaux · Grenoble · Bayonne · Nice · Marseille · Luchon · Perpignan

			STAGE	STAGE WINNER	YELLOW JERSEY
Stage 1	Sunday 17 June	207 km	Paris – Caen	N. Frantz (LUX)	N. Frantz
Stage 2	Monday 18 June	140 km	Caen – Cherbourg	A. Leducq (FRA)	N. Frantz
Stage 3	Tuesday 19 June	199 km	Cherbourg – Dinan	G. Rebry (BEL)	N. Frantz
Stage 4	Wednesday 20 June	206 km	Dinan – Brest	P. Verhaegen (BEL)	N. Frantz
Stage 5	Thursday 21 June	208 km	Brest – Vannes	M. Bidot (FRA)	N. Frantz
Stage 6	Friday 22 June	204 km	Vannes – Les Sables-d'Olonne	N. Frantz (LUX)	N. Frantz
Stage 7	Saturday 23 June	285 km	Les Sables-d'Olonne – Bordeaux	V. Fontan (FRA)	N. Frantz
Stage 8	Sunday 24 June	225 km	Bordeaux – Hendaye	M. De Waele (BEL)	N. Frantz
Stage 9	Tuesday 26 June	387 km	Hendaye – Luchon	V. Fontan (FRA)	N. Frantz
Stage 10	Thursday 28 June	323 km	Luchon – Perpignan	A. Leducq (FRA)	N. Frantz
Stage 11	Saturday 30 June	363 km	Perpignan – Marseille	A. Leducq (FRA)	N. Frantz
Stage 12	Monday 2 July	330 km	Marseille – Nice	N. Frantz (LUX)	N. Frantz
Stage 13	Wednesday 4 July	333 km	Nice – Grenoble	A. Magne (FRA)	N. Frantz
Stage 14	Friday 6 July	329 km	Grenoble – Évian	J. Moineau (FRA)	N. Frantz
Stage 15	Sunday 8 July	213 km	Évian – Pontarlier	P. Magne (FRA)	N. Frantz
Stage 16	Monday 9 July	119 km	Pontarlier – Belfort	A. Leducq (FRA)	N. Frantz
Stage 17	Tuesday 10 July	145 km	Belfort – Strasbourg	J. Mauclair (FRA)	N. Frantz
Stage 18	Wednesday 11 July	165 km	Strasbourg – Metz	N. Frantz (LUX)	N. Frantz
Stage 19	Thursday 12 July	139 km	Metz – Charleville	M. Huot (FRA)	N. Frantz
Stage 20	Friday 13 July	271 km	Charleville – Malo-les-Bains	M. De Waele (BEL)	N. Frantz
Stage 21	Saturday 14 July	234 km	Malo-les-Bains – Dieppe	A. Magne (FRA)	N. Frantz
Stage 22	Sunday 15 July	330 km	Dieppe – Paris	N. Frantz (LUX)	N. Frantz

Above: The Alcyon team was merciless, over all terrain. Here, De Waele leads Vervaecke, Frantz, Rebry and Mertens.
Below: At Dinan, Alcyon riders take a break after dominating the first stages. From left to right: Rebry, Mertens, Vervaecke, De Waele, Frantz and Delannoy.

De Waele and the end of an era

In 1929, further changes were introduced: the separate starts were discontinued in stages with a forecast average speed of 30 kph (18.6 mph), and there was a return to riders repairing their own punctures, whether or not they were on trade teams. For two years the public had awaited a duel between the two favourites, Nicolas Frantz (Alcyon) and Lucien Buysse (Lucifer). At last, they were riding against each other, and expectations of an epic contest were high. The hiccup was that another Alcyon rider, a solid 28-year-old from Flanders named Maurice De Waele, had resolved to conquer the Tour after finishing second in 1927 and third in 1928. The quiet, self-effacing De Waele had been the eternal runner-up, his talent and courage overlooked. Yet if he benefited from his adversaries' problems (Frantz suffered no less than five punctures between Luchon and Perpignan; Buysse was getting on, and Fontan was bitterly unlucky when he was wearing the yellow jersey), it was only by riding impeccably, heroically, even during illness, and with Feuillet's clear-sighted direction.

Nor was De Waele spared misfortune. He won the yellow jersey at Brest following an escape with his compatriot Delannoy, but lost it three days later thanks to two punctures on the way to Bordeaux. Through the Pyrenees from Bayonne

to Luchon he was in the breakaway with Fontan and the stage winner Cardona, but lost contact after another burst tyre. Finally, between Luchon and Perpignan, Fontan abandoned in the yellow jersey after an encounter with a dog, which gave the stage to Demuysère by ten seconds and the *maillot jaune* to De Waele who then kept it all the way to Paris.

Demuysère, his compatriot and team-mate, and indeed the entire Alcyon team, protected his lead on the roads back to Paris. The lack of appetite of the Alleluia riders also contributed to his easy ride home. Above all, the valiant De Waele had a comfortable fifteen-minute lead as the race left the Pyrenees, enough to stave off even the most bellicose rival, and he did nothing but build on it. He may have been considered a workhorse, but he was a hardy one. In Grenoble he was so ill that he could only take a few spoonfuls of sugar dissolved in water, yet he held on. For Desgrange, the sight of a sick man winning the Tour de France was almost too much. De Waele's triumph prompted the *Miroir des Sports* to write: 'The most logical rider has won.' But the logic was largely dictated by the all-powerful cycle manufacturers. Feeling that he was losing control of the Tour, Desgrange had had enough. De Waele, an exemplary winner in spite of everything, had unwittingly sparked a revolution.

GENERAL CLASSIFICATION

1. **Maurice De Waele** (BEL) Alcyon, 5,276 km in 186h.39m.15s; Average speed 28.32 kph,
2. **Giuseppe Pancera** (ITA) La Rafale, at 44m.23s.
3. **Joseph Demuysère** (BEL) Lucifer, at 57m.10s.
4. Salvador Cardona (SPA) Fontan, at 57m.46s.
5. Nicolas Frantz (LUX) Alcyon, at 58m.
6. Louis Delannoy (BEL) La Française, at 1h.6m.9s.
7. Antonin Magne (FRA) Alleluia, at 1h.8m.
8. Julien Vervaecke (BEL) Alcyon, at 2h.1m.37s.
9. Pierre Magne (FRA) Alleluia, at 2h.3m.
10. Gaston Rebry (BEL) Alcyon, at 2h.17m.49s.
11. André Leducq (FRA) Alcyon, at 2h.24m.51s.
12. Frans Bonduel (BEL) Dilecta, at 2h.52m.35s.
13. Désiré Louesse (BEL) Fontan, at 3h.3m.
14. Bernard Van Rysselberghe (BEL) Dilecta, at 3h.6m.23s.
15. Benoît Faure (FRA) Sud-Est, at 3h.33m.29s.
16. Marcel Bidot (FRA) La Française, at 3h.40m.49s.
17. Armand Van Bruaene (BEL) De Dion, at 4h.11m.54s.
18. Charles Govaerts (BEL) Elvish, at 4h.14m.24s.
19. Francis Bouillet (FRA) Lucifer, at 5h.7m.51s.
20. Ernest Neuhard (FRA) De Dion, at 5h.45m.12s.

23RD TOUR DE FRANCE, 22 STAGES – 5,276 KM

			STAGE	STAGE WINNER	YELLOW JERSEY
Stage 1	Sunday 30 June	203 km	Paris – Caen	A. Dossche (BEL)	A. Dossche
Stage 2	Monday 1 July	140 km	Caen – Cherbourg	A. Leducq (FRA)	A. Dossche
Stage 3	Tuesday 2 July	199 km	Cherbourg – Dinan	O. Taverne (BEL, touriste-routier)	A. Dossche
Stage 4	Wednesday 3 July	206 km	Dinan – Brest	L. Delannoy (BEL)	M. De Waele
Stage 5	Thursday 4 July	208 km	Brest – Vannes	G. Van Slembrouck (BEL)	M. De Waele
Stage 6	Friday 5 July	204 km	Vannes – Les Sables-d'Olonne	P. Le Drogo (FRA)	M. De Waele
Stage 7	Saturday 6 July	285 km	Les Sables-d'Olonne – Bordeaux	N. Frantz (LUX)	N. Frantz
Stage 8	Sunday 7 July	182 km	Bordeaux – Bayonne	J. Moineau (FRA)	G. Rebry
Stage 9	Tuesday 9 July	363 km	Bayonne – Luchon	S. Cardona (SPA)	V. Fontan
Stage 10	Thursday 11 July	323 km	Luchon – Perpignan	J. Demuysère (BEL)	M. De Waele
Stage 11	Saturday13 July	366 km	Perpignan – Marseille	A. Leducq (FRA)	M. De Waele
Stage 12	Monday 15 July	207 km	Marseille – Cannes	M. Bidot (FRA)	M. De Waele
Stage 13	Tuesday 16 July	133 km	Cannes – Nice	B. Faure (FRA, touriste-routier)	M. De Waele
Stage 14	Thursday 18 July	333 km	Nice – Grenoble	G. Rebry (BEL)	M. De Waele
Stage 15	Saturday 20 July	329 km	Grenoble – Évian	J. Vervaecke (BEL)	M. De Waele
Stage 16	Monday 22 July	283 km	Évian – Belfort	C. Pélissier (FRA)	M. De Waele
Stage 17	Tuesday 23 July	152 km	Belfort – Strasbourg	A. Leducq (FRA)	M. De Waele
Stage 18	Wednesday 24 July	165 km	Strasbourg – Metz	A. Leducq (FRA)	M. De Waele
Stage 19	Thursday 25 July	159 km	Metz – Charleville	B. Van Rysselberghe (BEL)	M. De Waele
Stage 20	Friday 26 July	270 km	Charleville – Malo-les-Bains	M. De Waele (BEL))	M. De Waele
Stage 21	Saturday 27 July	234 km	Malo-les-Bains – Dieppe	A. Leducq (FRA)	M. De Waele
Stage 22	Sunday 28 July	332 km	Dieppe – Paris	N. Frantz (LUX)	M. De Waele

As in 1928, Ludovic Feuillet (white coat) directed Alcyon to victory. The difference was that Frantz and Leducq (centre) stepped down a notch, and De Waele, the metronome, triumphed.

Leducq becomes a national hero

In Henri Desgrange's view, the excessive interference of the cycle manufacturers had often distorted the Tour. Desgrange repeatedly observed that the Tour was meant to be 'for the riders'. The constant feuding between the teams, poisoned by transfers and poaching, irritated Desgrange, and in his journalism he shifted the emphasis to Franco-Belgian or Franco-Italian rivalries. It worked in the short term, but it was really confounding chalk with cheese. With his organization running smoothly, *L'Auto* firmly established and the Tour in a settled pattern, the patriotic former champion can hardly have been unaware of the excitement aroused by the achievements of the national tennis team. In 1927 France had defeated the United States to win the Davis Cup and then defended it in true musketeer fashion on the clay courts of the Roland Garros stadium. The idea of establishing national teams, sending them round the countryside of France, and funding the whole enterprise through an attractive publicity caravan sounded highly ambitious, but Desgrange believed it could be done. And it was: forty top riders were divided into five eight-man teams and dressed in the national colours of Belgium, France, Germany, Italy and Spain. Sixty *touristes-routiers* were organized into regional teams. The Tour would keep its audience transfixed by following the rules of classical theatre – the action would occur in one place (France), at one time (July), and have one aim (everyone against the French). Everyone rode the same yellow bikes, but if a team leader broke something or fell, his teammates could assist him. In the blue of their national team, much-loved French riders like Dédé (André Leducq), Charlot (Charles Pélissier), and the brothers Antonin and Pierre Magne, who had been stagnating in their trade teams, suddenly sprouted wings. The three favourites, Belgium's Demuysère, Italy's Binda and the veteran Frenchman Fontan, all gave way before André Leducq. The Frenchman was pushed all the way to Paris by the Italian Learco Guerra and by *touristes-routiers* like Benoît Faure, who took flight over the mountains, and Louis Péglion, who won a stage at Nice. Yet, transformed by *directeur sportif* Henri Manchon, France emerged victorious. In *L'Auto*, Jacques Goddet wrote, 'a Pélissier can always forge a champion,' and he was right: Charlot Pélissier shepherded Leducq to victory, while delighting his own supporters with eight stage wins. Thanks to the use of telephone lines to transmit photographs, a development as French as the Tour, Goddet's pronouncements were illustrated with photographs and on the streets in hours. A new atmosphere pervaded the race that would last until 1934.

GENERAL CLASSIFICATION

1. **André Leducq** (FRA) France, 4,818 km in 172h.12m.16s; Average speed: 27.978 kph
2. **Learco Guerra** (ITA) Italy, at 14m.13s.
3. **Antonin Magne** (FRA) France, at 16m.3s.
4. Joseph Demuysère (BEL) Belgium, at 21m.34s.
5. Marcel Bidot (FRA) France, at 41m.18s.
6. Pierre Magne (FRA) France, at 45m.42s.
7. Frans Bonduel (BEL) Belgium, at 56m.19s.
8. Benoît Faure (FRA) touriste-routier, at 58m.34s.
9. Charles Pélissier (FRA) France, at 1h.4m.37s.
10. Adolf Schon (GER) Germany, at 1h.21m.39s.
11. Louis Delannoy (BEL) Belgium, at 1h.27m.23s.
12. Aimé Dossche (BEL) Belgium, at 1h.28m.14s.
13. Oskar Thierbach (GER) Germany, at 1h.35m.34s.
14. Louis Péglion (FRA) touriste-routier, at 1h.44m.14s.
15. Jan Mertens (BEL) Belgium, at 1h.49m.24s.
16. Salvador Cardona (SPA) Spain, at 1h.59m.43s.
17. Valeriano Riera (SPA) Spain, at 2h.23m.9s.
18. Marcel Mazeyrat (FRA) touriste-routier, at 2h.25m.23s.
19. Georges Laloup (BEL) Belgium, at 2h.31m.37s.
20. Giuseppe Pancera (ITA) Italy, at 2h.33m.51s.

24TH TOUR DE FRANCE, 21 STAGES – 4,818 KM

			STAGE	STAGE WINNER	YELLOW JERSEY
Stage 1	Wednesday 2 July	206 km	Paris – Caen	C. Pélissier (FRA)	C. Pélissier
Stage 2	Thursday 3 July	203 km	Caen – Dinan	L. Guerra (ITA)	L. Guerra
Stage 3	Friday 4 July	206 km	Dinan – Brest	C. Pélissier (FRA)	L. Guerra
Stage 4	Saturday 5 July	210 km	Brest – Vannes	O. Taverne (BEL)	L. Guerra
Stage 5	Sunday 6 July	202 km	Vannes – Les Sables-d'Olonne	A. Leducq (FRA)	L. Guerra
Stage 6	Monday 7 July	285 km	Les Sables-d'Olonne – Bordeaux	J. Aerts (BEL)	L. Guerra
Stage 7	Tuesday 8 July	222 km	Bordeaux – Hendaye	J. Merviel (FRA)	L. Guerra
Stage 8	Wednesday 9 July	146 km	Hendaye – Pau	A. Binda (ITA)	L. Guerra
Stage 9	Thursday 10 July	231 km	Pau – Luchon	A. Binda (ITA)	A. Leducq
Stage 10	Saturday 12 July	322 km	Luchon – Perpignan	C. Pélissier (FRA)	A. Leducq
Stage 11	Monday 14 July	164 km	Perpignan – Montpellier	C. Pélissier (FRA)	A. Leducq
Stage 12	Tuesday 15 July	209 km	Montpellier – Marseille	A. Magne (FRA)	A. Leducq
Stage 13	Wednesday 16 July	181 km	Marseille – Cannes	L. Guerra (ITA)	A. Leducq
Stage 14	Thursday 17 July	132 km	Cannes – Nice	L. Péglion (FRA) touriste-routier	A. Leducq
Stage 15	Saturday 19 July	333 km	Nice – Grenoble	L. Guerra (ITA)	A. Leducq
Stage 16	Monday 21 July	331 km	Grenoble – Évian	A. Leducq (FRA)	A. Leducq
Stage 17	Wednesday 23 July	282 km	Évian – Belfort	F. Bonduel (BEL)	A. Leducq
Stage 18	Thursday 24 July	223 km	Belfort – Metz	C. Pélissier (FRA)	A. Leducq
Stage 19	Friday 25 July	159 km	Metz – Charleville	C. Pélissier (FRA)	A. Leducq
Stage 20	Saturday 26 July	271 km	Charleville – Malo-les-Bains	C. Pélissier (FRA)	A. Leducq
Stage 21	Sunday 27 July	300 km	Malo-les-Bains – Paris	C. Pélissier (FRA)	A. Leducq

The turning point: on the Col du Télégraphe, André Leducq in the yellow jersey sets off again after a second fall, pushed by Pierrot Magne. Downcast, he came close to abandoning, but with encouragement and a new pedal, he regained his resolve and his dominance.

André Leducq, darling of France

His sense of humour, his good looks and his talent had already made Leducq France's most popular rider. After overcoming terrible bad luck and making friends throughout the race, 'Dédé' became irresistible. Isn't that so, Mme Leducq?

PARIS (27 July): André Leducq, the brilliant victor of the 24th Tour de France, is unquestionably the man of the moment. Everyone is talking about him and our offices have been inundated with telephone calls asking for information of every sort about the champion. We therefore thought we would oblige all our readers by providing some biographical notes about the ever-smiling 'Dédé'. Leducq was born 27 February 1904 in Saint-Ouen, Paris, and as his parents were sports enthusiasts – his

father even raced bicycles in 1899 – the young André was not yet five when his parents presented him with a bicycle, on which he immediately showed remarkable ability. Every Sunday, Mr Leducq would take his little lad riding on the roads of Saint-Ouen. Some Sundays, he also took him to the Vélodrome, so, as you can imagine, the desire to take part in races didn't take long to seize young André who, aged 15, didn't hesitate to sign up for an event organized by the local racing club where, on a bike fitted

with fat pneumatic tyres – 32 mm, if you please – he finished in the brilliant position of 86th. But the result didn't discourage him and in 1919 he joined the Montmartre Sportif where, with good advice, he began to excel in category and club races. In fact, he made such a good impression, even without winning anything major, that a Monsieur Souchard, a rider with the Levallois Cycling Club, spotted him and decided to enrol him in Paul Ruinart's school. It was not long, therefore, before André Leducq began to realize his brilliant potential and, in a race from Nanterre to Mantes and back, achieved his first victory, to the great joy of Leducq senior who, following the example of Michard's father, became and continues to be the most devoted of managers.

The victories continued. That same year, 1922, André Leducq took the *Petit Journal* trophy and the French Junior National Championship. In 1923, he continued to distinguish himself, winning, among other

OUR NATIONAL FESTIVAL OF CYCLING

For the last month, millions of intrigued onlookers, some new to the Tour, others already great enthusiasts, have gathered at the roadside throughout France to cheer on men mounted on bicycles. Far beyond the city limits of Paris, these men had to navigate between two human waves lining the way. At the velodrome, 40,000 spectators bombarded them with 'Bravos!' and other passionate invocations. This is now indisputably our national cycling festival. Henceforth, each year we will celebrate this festival in the same way, rejoicing in the greater glory of this divine instrument. Our entire cycling industry is the beneficiary of this tremendous publicity, not just one or two manufacturers.

In order not to incur the ire of those who reproach us for changing the regulations every year, next year's will remain largely the same, trusting the riders greater freedom on the basis that they made wise use of this year's conditions. In this way the Tour de France will now become a great international and peaceful competition to which the cycling nations will come each year to measure the merits of their finest athletes.

Passing through Mainville, the French team had the race under control: Leducq and Charles Pélissier lead at great speed. Pélissier went on to win the stage.

titles, the Étoiles de Paris in five stages, beating his friend Souchard. However, like Michard, 1924 was Leducq's most important year. Once again winner of the *Petit Journal* trophy, that year he was also awarded two championship titles: champion of France and world amateur champion. In 1925, he left for his military service and naturally became the French military road-racing champion. At the end of 1926, back in civvies, he rested all winter, turned professional at the beginning of 1927 and you know the rest.

In 1927, Leducq won three stages in the Tour de France. In 1928, in addition to his wins in Paris-Le Havre and Paris-Roubaix, he finished second overall. Last year he won five Tour stages. Now he has finally won the Tour de France. Finishing in front of a crowd of 30,000 in a Parc des Princes that is soon to be expanded, you can rest assured that 'Dédé' will not stop there.

Having already fallen while descending the Galibier, Leducq fell again at the foot of the Télégraphe. Overwhelmed, he wept, called for his mother and was about to abandon when friends arrived...

The first Tour for national teams started well for France. Here, one national hero congratulates another: boxer Georges Carpentier with Charles Pélissier, holder of the first yellow jersey.

Magne, a volcano from the Auvergne

The perfectionist Desgrange had fine-tuned the Tour's great engine again to increase the tension. There were twenty-four stages, later start times and, most importantly, three-minute time bonuses for stage winners, with larger bonuses for winning margins greater than three minutes.

The Tour started with a surprise from the most unexpected quarter when an Austrian *touriste-routier* named Max Bulla won stage two and spent the following day in the yellow jersey. Then Antonin Magne, a man who had ridden four good Tours, and was thought of as a Tour rider but not a potential winner, emerged as the principal player. Having overcome illness and the bankruptcy of his manufacturer, Magne, from the volcanic landscapes of the Auvergne, proved himself a determined, methodical, talented and courageous champion. He prepared well, building up his fitness by riding the ninteenth Giro d'Italia in May, and spending twelve days training in the Pyrenees with his friend Fontan to familiarize himself with the terrain.

On the descent from the Tourmalet, Magne caught the riders in the leading group, then dropped them to pursue the leader, Demuysère. In fact, Demuysère had punctured and was far behind him, but by the time Fontan could alert him, Magne was on fire, alone at the head of the race. The Auvergne volcano was awakening, and the French national team had a new leader. As Magne rode into Luchon, to collect the stage win, the yellow jersey and his time bonus, there was delirium among the crowds. His lead over Antonio Pesenti, the Italian who finished second on the stage and moved into second in the general classification, was 9mins 32secs. It was an important margin, given the threat posed by the Italians. On stage fourteen from Cannes to Nice, their best of the race, Italian riders finished first, second and third, although Magne, with Louis Péglion's support, kept their advantage in check, then launched a solo counterattack, keeping his overall lead at 5mins 31secs. Two days later, on the road to Gap, Pesenti and Di Paco seemed to have Magne on the ropes when providence considerably put a powerful Charlot Pélissier at his side. By taking the wheel of this luxury locomotive, Magne again managed to limit the damage.

The Tour was finally won by the team spirit that united the French. On the Galibier, Benoît Faure was Magne's guide. On the freezing stage from Évian to Belfort, Leducq brought him a flask of piping hot coffee. From then on, Magne resisted the final onslaught of the Belgians Rebry and Demuysère single-handedly. The Parc des Princes offered the champion a warm welcome, who, two weeks later, collapsed from his exertions.

GENERAL CLASSIFICATION

1. **Antonin Magne** (FRA) France, 5,095 km in 177h.10m.3s; Average speed: 28.758 kph
2. **Joseph Demuysère** (BEL) Belgium, at 12m.56s.
3. **Antonio Pesenti** (ITA) Italy, at 22m.51s.
4. Gaston Rebry (BEL) Belgium, at 46m.40s.
5. Maurice De Waele (BEL) Belgium, at 49m.46s.
6. Julien Vervaecke (BEL) Belgium, at 1h.10m.11s.
7. Louis Péglion (FRA) France, at 1h.18m.33s.
8. Erich Metze (GER) Germany, at 1h.20m.59s.
9. Albert Buchi (SUI) Australia-Switzerland, at 1h.29m.29s.
10. André Leducq (FRA) France, at 1h.30m.8s.
11. Oskar Thierbach (GER) Germany, at 1h.34m.3s.
12. Hubert Opperman (AUS) Australia-Switzerland, at 1h.36m.43s.
13. Benoît Faure (FRA) France, at 1h.40m.38s.
14. Charles Pélissier (FRA) France, at 1h.45m.11s.
15. Max Bulla (AUT), touriste-routier, at 1h.51m.32s.
16. Kurt Stoepel (GER) Germany, at 2h.5m.58s.
17. Raffaele Di Paco (ITA) Italy, at 2h.11m.11s.
18. Alfons Schepers (BEL) Belgium, at 2h.15m.27s.
19. Ludwig Geyer (GER) Germany, at 2h.16m.22s.
20. Herbert Sieronski (GER) Germany, at 2h.33m.40s.

25TH TOUR DE FRANCE, 24 STAGES – 5,095 KM

Stage	Date	Dist	STAGE	STAGE WINNER	YELLOW JERSEY
Stage 1	Tuesday 30 June	208 km	Paris – Caen	A. Hamerlinck (BEL)	A. Hamerlinck
Stage 2	Wednesday 1 July	212 km	Caen – Dinan	M. Bulla (AUT) touriste-routier	M. Bulla
Stage 3	Thursday 2 July	206 km	Dinan – Brest	F. Battesini (ITA)	L. Le Calvez
Stage 4	Friday 3 July	211 km	Brest – Vannes	A. Godinat (FRA) touriste-routier	R. Di Paco
Stage 5	Saturday 4 July	202 km	Vannes – Les Sables-d'Olonne	C. Pélissier (FRA)	R. Di Paco & C. Pélissier
Stage 6	Sunday 5 July	338 km	Les Sables-d'Olonne – Bordeaux	A. Hamerlinck (BEL)	R. Di Paco
Stage 7	Monday 6 July	180 km	Bordeaux – Bayonne	G. Loncke (BEL) touriste-routier	R. Di Paco
Stage 8	Tuesday 7 July	106 km	Bayonne – Pau	C. Pélissier (FRA)	C. Pélissier
Stage 9	Wednesday 8 July	231 km	Pau – Luchon	A. Magne (FRA)	A. Magne
Stage 10	Friday 10 July	322 km	Luchon – Perpignan	R. Di Paco (ITA)	A. Magne
Stage 11	Sunday 12 July	164 km	Perpignan – Montpellier	R. Di Paco (ITA)	A. Magne
Stage 12	Monday 13 July	207 km	Montpellier – Marseille	M. Bulla (AUT) touriste-routier	A. Magne
Stage 13	Tuesday 14 July	181 km	Marseille – Cannes	C. Pélissier (FRA)	A. Magne
Stage 14	Wednesday 15 July	132 km	Cannes – Nice	E. Gestri (ITA)	A. Magne
Stage 15	Friday 17 July	233 km	Nice – Gap	J. Demuysère (BEL)	A. Magne
Stage 16	Saturday 18 July	102 km	Gap – Grenoble	C. Pélissier (FRA)	A. Magne
Stage 17	Sunday 19 July	230 km	Grenoble – Aix-les-Bains	M. Bulla (AUT) touriste-routier	A. Magne
Stage 18	Monday 20 July	204 km	Aix-les-Bains – Évian	J. Demuysère (BEL)	A. Magne
Stage 19	Tuesday 21 July	282 km	Évian – Belfort	R. Di Paco (ITA)	A. Magne
Stage 20	Wednesday 22 July	209 km	Belfort – Colmar	A. Leducq (FRA)	A. Magne
Stage 21	Thursday 23 July	192 km	Colmar – Metz	R. Di Paco (ITA)	A. Magne
Stage 22	Friday 24 July	159 km	Metz – Charleville	R. Di Paco (ITA)	A. Magne
Stage 23	Saturday 25 July	271 km	Charleville – Malo-les-Bains	G. Rebry (BEL)	A. Magne
Stage 24	Sunday 26 July	313 km	Malo-les-Bains – Paris	C. Pélissier (FRA)	A. Magne

Encouraged by the soldiers, Magne powers up the Col de Braus alone, chasing the Italians Gestri, Pesenti and Gremo.

Luckily, the stage from Luchon to Perpignan was comparatively relaxed. Antonin Magne, the yellow jersey, could calmly replace a punctured tyre at the foot of the Col d'Aspet.

At Gap, exhausted, Pélissier and Magne recover. After a frantic chase led by Charlot, Magne kept the yellow jersey.

Turmoil at the summit of the Tourmalet as Desgrange and Goddet protect Magne (no. 33) and Pesenti (drinking). The Frenchman caught the Italian on the climb.

Magne and France

Antonin Magne: 'You won't settle for a "I'm happy I won" will you? Even if I'm dashed sincere when I say it. Tell your readers that if I had to suffer the mental anguish of this last month again, I wouldn't start it again for all the money in the world. The fatigue is nothing, the pain isn't much more, but the fear of not winning was truly horrible for me. I don't know how you're going to explain it, phrase it how you want, but if I were a journalist, it would take me a long time to find the right words. I've been suffering dreadfully for a number of stages, but I haven't breathed a word, not even to my team-mates, because all the strength and determination that they used to help me to win depended on the confidence they had in me. That might begin to explain why I found it so difficult to defend my yellow jersey. It was terrible, I can assure you. Yes, that's what I'd like to say to the the public who have cheered me on so well.'

Charles Pélissier: 'I rode the Tour de France because everyone told me it was necessary for the French team. I've done my best. I've done what I was asked conscientiously, but I don't think I will be taking part in another Tour de France.'

André Leducq: 'This year, there were better climbers, although towards the end I was as strong as Demuysère. However, it's not right to think about anything other than Tonin's victory.'

On the cobbles of Northern France, Magne blocks Demuysère's final attack. In the Pyrenees and in the Alps, where he was the yellow jersey on the road, the Belgian was Magne's main rival.

Dédé Leducq, heart-throb of France

Time bonuses of four minutes for stage winners, two minutes for runners-up and one minute for third place were decisive in the 1932 Tour. Once again, the pre-race favourites – three Belgians in Alfons Schepers, Jef Demuysère and Jean Aerts, and the Frenchman Marcel Bidot – flopped. The Italians rode brilliantly in the mountains and reaped seven stage wins, four of which fell to the valiant Raffaele Di Paco, who had taken five the previous year. Nonetheless, they never challenged for overall victory. The opening salvo came from Jean Aerts, who won in Caen. However, deep divisions at the heart of the Belgian team kept the Flemish and the Walloons from working together, and Aerts soon found himself isolated. Kurt Stoepel, the unexpected leader of a surprising German team, took over the yellow jersey the following day and sustained his challenge for the rest of the race. But the surprise of the Tour was French heart-throb André 'Dédé' Leducq who seized the reins two days later by winning the stage into Bordeaux and assuming the race lead. In the Pyrenees, the Italian Antonio Pesenti, third in the 1931 Tour and fresh from victory in the Giro d'Italia, stormed across the landscape with his team-mate Camusso. But Leducq defended his lead, then struck back with consecutive second places at Perpignan and

Montpellier. On the punishing ride from Cannes to Nice, taking in the Col de Braus and Col de Castillon, he rode out an off-day with the help of his team-mates. Georges Speicher, a future Tour champion, made the ultimate cycling sacrifice by handing his leader a wheel from his own bike. Days later, a revitalized Leducq disappeared into the snow and fog and emerged victorious at Aix-les-Bains. It was a decisive stage; his closest rivals, Stoepel and Camusso, lost more than thirteen minutes that day.

Leducq's perfect knowledge of the route and excellent humour contributed to his composure. He hummed the melodies of Fredo Gardoni and Jean Cyrano, lent his name to toe-straps, watches, tyre patches and hair grease, even swigged from a bottle of white wine before attacking the Col de Bayard.

The Tour's finish coincided with the opening of the Los Angeles Olympics, and on 31 July, Leducq became the first winner to celebrate at the rebuilt Parc des Princes. To the delight of Henri Desgrange, Leducq, with six stage wins, two second places and three thirds, had reaped the benefit from the new time bonuses. Stoepel, second overall with a twenty-four-minute deficit, had won seven bonus minutes, compared with Leducq's thirty-one. Leducq had enjoyed twenty-three days in the yellow jersey, accessorized this year with a matching yellow cap.

GENERAL CLASSIFICATION

1. **André Leducq** (FRA) France, 4,520 km in 154h.11m.49s; Average speed: 29.313 kph
2. **Kurt Stoepel** (GER) Germany, at 24m.3s.
3. **Francesco Camusso** (ITA) Italy, at 26m.21s.
4. Antonio Pesenti (ITA) Italy, at 37m.8s.
5. Georges Ronsse (BEL) Belgium, at 41m.4s.
6. Frans Bonduel (BEL) Belgium, at 45m.13s.

7. Oskar Thierbach (GER) Germany, at 58m.44s.
8. Joseph Demuysère (BEL) Belgium, at 1h.3m.24s.
9. Luigi Barral (ITA) touriste-routier, at 1h.6m.57s.
10. Georges Speicher (FRA) France, at 1h.8m.37's.
11. Albert Buchi (SUI) Switzerland, at 1h.13m.33s.
12. Benoît Faure (FRA) touriste-routier, at 1h.14m.12s.
13. Jean Aerts (BEL) Belgium, at 1h.16m.24s.

14. Michele Orecchia (ITA) Italy, at 1h.18m.45s.
15. Georges Lemaire (BEL) Belgium, at 1h.19m.18s.
16. Maurice Archambaud (FRA) France, at 1h.25m.27s.
17. Jan Wauters (BEL) Belgium, at 1h.29m.21s.
18. René Bernard (FRA) touriste-routier, at 1h.35m.28s.
19. Max Bulla (AUT) Germany-Austria, at 1h.38m.23s.
20. Gaston Rebry (BEL) Belgium, at 1h.39m.1s.

26TH TOUR DE FRANCE, 21 STAGES – 4,520 KM

			STAGE	STAGE WINNER	YELLOW JERSEY
Stage 1	Wednesday 6 July	208 km	Paris – Caen	J. Aerts (BEL)	J. Aerts
Stage 2	Thursday 7 July	300 km	Caen – Nantes	K. Stoepel (GER)	K. Stoepel
Stage 3	Saturday 9 July	387 km	Nantes – Bordeaux	A. Leducq (FRA)	A. Leducq
Stage 4	Monday 11 July	206 km	Bordeaux – Pau	G. Ronsse (BEL)	A. Leducq
Stage 5	Tuesday 12 July	229 km	Pau – Luchon	A. Pesenti (ITA)	A. Leducq
Stage 6	Thursday 14 July	322 km	Luchon – Perpignan	F. Bonduel (BEL)	A. Leducq
Stage 7	Saturday 16 July	168 km	Perpignan – Montpellier	F. Bonduel (BEL)	A. Leducq
Stage 8	Sunday 17 July	206 km	Montpellier – Marseille	M. Orecchia (ITA)	A. Leducq
Stage 9	Monday 18 July	191 km	Marseille – Cannes	R. Di Paco (ITA)	A. Leducq
Stage 10	Tuesday 19 July	132 km	Cannes – Nice	F. Camusso (ITA)	A. Leducq
Stage 11	Thursday 21 July	233 km	Nice – Gap	A. Leducq (FRA)	A. Leducq
Stage 12	Friday 22 July	102 km	Gap – Grenoble	R. Lapebie (FRA)	A. Leducq
Stage 13	Saturday 23 July	230 km	Grenoble – Aix-les-Bains	A. Leducq (FRA)	A. Leducq
Stage 14	Sunday 24 July	204 km	Aix-les-Bains – Évian	R. Di Paco (ITA)	A. Leducq
Stage 15	Monday 25 July	291 km	Évian – Belfort	A. Leducq (FRA)	A. Leducq
Stage 16	Tuesday 26 July	145 km	Belfort – Strasbourg	G. Loncke (BEL)	A. Leducq
Stage 17	Wednesday 27 July	165 km	Strasbourg – Metz	R. Di Paco (ITA)	A. Leducq
Stage 18	Thursday 28 July	159 km	Metz – Charleville	R. Di Paco (ITA)	A. Leducq
Stage 19	Friday 29 July	271 km	Charleville – Malo-les-Bains	G. Rebry (BEL)	A. Leducq
Stage 20	Saturday 30 July	212 km	Malo-les-Bains – Amiens	A. Leducq (FRA)	A. Leducq
Stage 21	Sunday 31 July	159 km	Amiens – Paris	A. Leducq (FRA)	A. Leducq

With the arrival of the charming Dédé Leducq, the Tour found a new audience. Thousands of young women, fascinated by the champion's adventures, applauded him at the roadside and the stage finishes.

André Leducq wraps it up

Desgrange had seen some riders in his time, yet was enchanted by this new Leducq, 'relentless on the flat, a sprinter, a climber when necessary, but also, with such an organized head, a team leader who thinks of everything'.

GAP (21 July): At the Barcelonnette checkpoint Camusso, third in the general classification and in reality Leducq's most threatening opponent, signed in 2mins 15secs ahead of 'Dédé'. In fact, Leducq was accompanied by Pesenti, fourth in the general classification, and Stoepel came in another 30 seconds after Leducq, the yellow jersey. Leducq had to catch Camusso at all costs to neutralize the danger.

So how are they dispersed along the road from Barcelonnette to Gap? In first place is Benoît Faure, alone over the brow of the Col d'Allos and the first to pass the Barcelonnette control point, 35 seconds ahead of Camusso. What hope does he have of finishing alone more than 60 kilometres (37 miles) further on, in the teeth of a fierce headwind? In reality, we should expect

Camusso, if he knows Leducq has lost time behind him, to make every effort to catch up with Faure.

We can do better than that, however – we're going to go back through the entire peloton, starting with these fine fellows, and you will understand what is going to happen.

Right at the back is Moineau, riding solo. Much further on, perhaps a kilometre ahead we find Kutzbach and Haas; 500 metres further on are Muller, Erne and Altenburger; another 300 metres further up is an entire peloton including Aerts, Loncke, Schepers, Demuysère and Rebry – that is, practically all the Belgian team, with Goulême; Vanzenried, Alfred Buchi, Simoni, Venot, Albert Bula, Barthélemy, Buttafocchi and Bernard. At least a good kilometre ahead we find another pack, this time consisting of Speicher, Neuhard, Lapébie, Péglion, Frantz and Guiramand. This is where we find our first French contingent, whose sole task is to try to repeat Charles Pélissier's feat of 1931.

All we have to do now is catch up with the leaders; you can imagine our feelings as we wonder what we will find. We have to find out nothing less than whether the young demon Camusso has stripped Leducq of his yellow jersey, and whether fortune will finally smile on our Italian friends. Perhaps Stoepel, behind at Barcelonnette, has caught up with Leducq; but is Leducq still with Pesenti? As we draw nearer, we can discern from afar Leducq's yellow jersey. Things look better already, but we still don't know whether Camusso and Benoît Faure, riding

together now, have pushed on to Gap alone. We are quickly reassured, however, as on closer inspection, we can make out the graceful silhouette of Camusso; and that tiny rider must be none other than Benoît Faure. They've been caught and slow down wisely, especially Camusso, wary of an effort that could disadvantage them in stages to come. Stoepel is there too, which means that the first four men in the overall placing are neck and neck. This peloton, the leading group, contains 17 riders.

THE FINAL STRETCH

At the risk of finishing in a large pack – which I still believe puts the leaders in danger of a serious fall – the pace drops, as the wind seems to redouble in strength. Then the inevitable occurs: first Thierbach and Orecchia catch up, then it was the turn of the Archambaud group, which, thanks to its perseverance, finally catches sight of the yellow jersey and regains contact. Getting ahead of ourselves, I can tell you that the other group containing Speicher, Péglion and Lapébie, will not be as fortunate and will not catch up. The leading group therefore consists of the following: Ronsse, Lemaire, Bonduel, Pesenti, Morelli, Camusso, Orecchia, Marchisio, Albert Bula – the star of the Swiss team – Umbenhauer, Max Bulla, Thierbach, Geyer, Stoepel, Leducq, Marcel Bidot in person, Archambaud; and, among the Individuals, Benoît Faure, Fayolle, Mazeyrat, Buysse, Wauters, Decroix, Zanzi, Barral, Vierengo and Trueba.

You already know that Leducq wins the stage and improves his placing by four bonus minutes, as the regulations stipulate. And what an achievement, to succeed against a peloton of 27 men – first to break away, then not to allow himself to be caught, and above all to arrive first.

From our Hotchkiss, some distance away, it seemed that Leducq attacked intelligently, leaving the group at just the right moment. On the other hand we noticed, again from a distance, a sturdy hand push a jersey in German colours, to assist him in his task, no doubt. Thankfully, the commissaires were paying attention at the time.

'Dédé', who hated the cold, gritted his teeth through this storm on the Galibier. A frozen finger or two was a small price to pay for limiting Camusso's advantage and defending his chances of becoming champion again.

Leducq recovers after beating Di Paco in Bordeaux. With this victory and his time bonus, he'll soon be dressed in the yellow jersey.

Leducq has unequivocally consolidated his position. Having left Nice this morning with a lead of only 3mins 13secs, he will set off tomorrow morning for Grenoble with a lead of 7mins 13secs. However, the memory of his misfortunes in the previous stage should serve as a reminder of the fragility of such a lead. *Memento quia pulvis es*: remember that you are dust.

KURT STOEPEL, A HARD MAN

It's very simple: Stoepel is a brave man. Rugged face, slender legs: good type for a cyclist. When I see him catch up with the leading group again and again, sticking with Leducq, I dream of those nights during the war spent in ramshackle trenches as the enemy troops launched disciplined attacks. To think we were once at war! If we had played a little more sport together, we would no doubt have understood, admired, loved each other better. The highly disciplined Stoepel accepted his declassification without a murmur. In fact, according to Charles Pélissier, he was aware of his unfair advantage and so freewheeled over the finishing line. From here to Paris, there will be plenty of opportunities for revenge.

What a fine creature, this Leducq!

PARIS (31 July): There: the final few turns of the pedal of this great, 5,000-kilometre (3,000-mile) race are over. The final cheers are still ringing in our ears and our 'Dédé', with Madame Dédé on his arm, can at last go home to enjoy some home cooking and sleep without dreaming of level crossings, rain, snow, punctures and photographers.

However, I haven't quite said my last, as I feel duty bound to express exhaustively how much André Leducq deserves his victory and how vastly superior he was to his rivals. We'll leave aside for the moment, if you don't mind, the fact that the time bonuses forced him to race in a different, more thinking manner than two years ago. Nor do I wish, in his case, to emphasize the traditional resourcefulness that has always allowed the French, when desperation calls, to find the emergent champion they need to ensure victory.

It is merely to pay homage to Truth to say that, at the beginning of the race, the French team showed not the slightest sign of any hope of success. There were three youngsters who looked too young, three others there, let's put it like this, for want of better riders; Bidot, on whom we were betting for the last time, and finally Leducq, the champion in 1930, but bad in 1931, and this year looking more 'not good enough'

than 'promising'. The situation was only aggravated by a Belgian team that looked as formidable as you could hope for and began as the great favourites, a team assembled with great care and attention to detail by the Italian Federation and a German team in which we recognized all the qualities for which this nation is famous. I should add that the organizer would not have been displeased to see the home team fall short of monopolizing victory over the teams from rival nations. And yet, from the very first stages, André Leducq gave the lie to the predictions. The mischievous, cheeky Leducq, with a poor service record over the last year, launched a crushing stampede that flattened this tangled undergrowth of frustrated ambition underfoot.

Two weeks before the race, no one even imagined a Leducq victory. However, his form suddenly peaked, the butterfly emerged from the cocoon, and for three weeks our stunned and delighted eyes witnessed without a doubt the finest, most graceful athletic beast we have ever seen. Even before Pau, even before the cols of the Pyrenees, the yellow jersey was adorning his back. In the first four stages, he consistently finished at the head of affairs. We then saw him employ a tactic that he repeated with great clarity of thought in the mountain stages. Instead of

risking his all on the Aubisque and the Tourmalet, as he did in 1930, we saw him on these two ascents, as on the Braus, the Allos, the Col Bayard and the Galibier, ride with great wisdom, stealth and reason, as his position dictated. The Tour was already his. He had won the yellow jersey; he no longer had to fight to win it – only to keep it.

Was this the Leducq of 1930? Not at all. In 1930 he was a pedantic clerk on pedals, stingily counting his few minutes' lead, protecting his yellow jersey and judiciously avoiding the ruckus of 40 or so other madmen battling it out for each stage win.

This year, nothing of the sort! You saw him at every party: every sprint, every victory, every time bonus. Without Barthélemy's push before the stage finish at Charleville – still a mystery to us – Leducq easily gained more than 50 percent of the bonus points available over the 21 stages. He finished on the podium 12 times (including Charleville). The crowds cheered him on madly all along the road. As our cars went by, we could hear a constant rumble as they chanted 'Leducq...Leducq...Ducq... Ducq! Ducq! Ducq! Ducq! Ducq!'.

I shall conclude by saying that a champion, a great champion, has been born just when we thought all was lost.

Above. On the new track at the Parc des Princes, Leducq beat Speicher and finished in style. This was Dédé's 21st stage victory since his Tour debut in 1927.
Opposite: At the Parc des Princes, the biggest smile belonged to Leducq, the champion; the shy Stoepel finished runner-up. Coincidentally, both were relegated in the rankings after benefiting from pushes during sprints.

Speicher: all for one, and won for France

According to *L'Auto*'s tips for the 1933 Tour de France, the inheritor of Léon Scieur's soubriquet 'Locomotive', Italy's Learco Guerra, would top the podium beside Leducq and Magne. In keeping with the Tour's commercial ethos, Guerra endorsed Martini-Rossi, the sponsors of the first official King of the Mountains competition, while Pélissier and Archambaud lent their names to Gomina brilliantine.

1933 saw the twenty-seventh Tour, which started on 27 June and lasted twenty-seven incredible days. Eighty policemen on bikes accompanied the eighty competitors, equally split between teams and Independents, to the *Grand Départ*, where the exotic Josephine Baker started the race. But the race didn't need facile mnemonics to find a permanent place in the collective memory. The war between the Belgians, the Italians and the French was relentless and absorbing. Charles Pélissier abandoned early, but Maurice Archambaud wore the yellow jersey all the way from Lille in the North-East to Gap in the Alps, and again from Cannes to Marseille. When his personal hopes of victory dissolved, Archambaud became a willing and valuable *domestique*, as did 1931 victor Antonin Magne, whose hopes of victory never really materialized. With their help, and more from men like Dédé Leducq and future winner

Roger Lapébie, a former swimmer named Georges Speicher was able to consolidate the race lead he had taken with a stage win in Marseille, and defend it with great authority.

The team spirit among the French riders contrasted starkly with the open hostility dividing the Belgians; Georges Lemaire seized the yellow jersey for two stages in the Alps, and entered the Pyrenees fifteen seconds behind Speicher. With assistance, Lemaire might have put Speicher in difficulty, but his team-mate Jean Aerts, betrayed the previous year, abandoned him without a second thought. Aerts had no hope of overall victory; by targeting stage wins, he sabotaged Lemaire's efforts.

The most dangerous Italian turned out not to be Guerra but Giuseppe Martano, who threatened Speicher in the Pyrenees and earned an unexpected podium place in Paris. Guerra, the favourite, consoled himself with five stage wins; the final two-minute time bonus he earned on the final stage propelled him into second place. And so the Tour ended, with a Frenchman and two Italians on the podium, and the Spaniard Vicente Trueba as the first King of the Mountains. For *L'Auto*, it had been an unqualified success; its tips had been as wayward as ever, but they didn't prevent it from achieving a record circulation of 854,000 during the Tour.

GENERAL CLASSIFICATION

1. **Georges Speicher** (FRA) France, 4,396 km in 147h.51m.37s; Average speed: 29.730 kph
2. **Learco Guerra** (ITA) Italy, at 4m.1s.
3. **Giuseppe Martano** (ITA) touriste-routier, at 5m.8s.
4. Georges Lemaire (BEL) Belgium, at 21m.22s.
5. Maurice Archambaud (FRA) France, at 21m.22s.
6. Vicente Trueba (SPA) touriste-routier, at 27m.27s.
7. Léon Level (FRA) touriste-routier, at 35m.23s.
8. Antonin Magne (FRA) France, at 36m.37s.
9. Jean Aerts (BEL) Belgium, at 42m.53s.
10. Kurt Stoepel (GER) Germany-Austria, at 45m.28s.
11. Fernand Fayolle (FRA) touriste-routier, at 56m.11s.
12. Ludwig Geyer (GER) Germany-Austria, at 57m.4s.
13. Albert Buchi (SUI) Switzerland, at 1h.7m.59s.
14. Gaston Rebry (BEL) Belgium, at 1h.20m.16s.
15. Gaspard Rinaldi (FRA) touriste-routier, at 1h.28m.12s.
16. Eugène Le Goff (FRA) touriste-routier, at 1h.24m.59s.
17. Léon Le Calvez (FRA) France, at 1h.38m.44s.
18. Alfons Schepers (BEL) Belgium, at 1h.39m.49s.
19. René Le Grevès (FRA) France, at 1h.48m.31s.
20. Alfred Buchi (SUI) Switzerland, at 1h.49m.59s.

27TH TOUR DE FRANCE, 23 STAGES – 4,396 KM

Stage	Date	Distance	STAGE	STAGE WINNER	YELLOW JERSEY
Stage 1	Tuesday 27 June	262 km	Paris – Lille	M. Archambaud (FRA)	M. Archambaud
Stage 2	Wednesday 28 June	192 km	Lille – Charleville	L. Guerra (ITA)	M. Archambaud
Stage 3	Thursday 29 June	166 km	Charleville – Metz	A. Schepers (BEL)	M. Archambaud
Stage 4	Friday 30 June	220 km	Metz – Belfort	J. Aerts (BEL)	M. Archambaud
Stage 5	Saturday 1 July	293 km	Belfort – Évian	L. Louyet (BEL)	M. Archambaud
Stage 6	Monday 3 July	207 km	Évian – Aix-les-Bains	L. Guerra (ITA)	M. Archambaud
Stage 7	Tuesday 4 July	229 km	Aix-les-Bains – Grenoble	L. Guerra (ITA)	M. Archambaud
Stage 8	Wednesday 5 July	102 km	Grenoble – Gap	G. Speicher (FRA)	M. Archambaud
Stage 9	Thursday 6 July	227 km	Gap – Digne	G. Speicher (FRA)	G. Lemaire
Stage 10	Friday 7 July	156 km	Digne – Nice	F. Cornez (FRA)	G. Lemaire
Stage 11	Sunday 9 July	128 km	Nice – Cannes	M. Archambaud (FRA)	M. Archambaud
Stage 12	Monday 10 July	208 km	Cannes – Marseille	G. Speicher (FRA)	G. Speicher
Stage 13	Tuesday 11 July	168 km	Marseille – Montpellier	A. Leducq (FRA)	G. Speicher
Stage 14	Wednesday 12 July	166 km	Montpellier – Perpignan	A. Leducq (FRA)	G. Speicher
Stage 15	Friday 14 July	158 km	Perpignan – Ax-les-Thermes	J. Aerts (BEL)	G. Speicher
Stage 16	Saturday 15 July	165 km	Ax-les-Thermes – Luchon	L. Louyet (BEL)	G. Speicher
Stage 17	Sunday 16 July	91 km	Luchon – Tarbes	J. Aerts (BEL)	G. Speicher
Stage 18	Monday 17 July	185 km	Tarbes – Pau	L. Guerra (ITA)	G. Speicher
Stage 19	Wednesday 19 July	233 km	Pau – Bordeaux	J. Aerts (BEL)	G. Speicher
Stage 20	Thursday 20 July	183 km	Bordeaux – La Rochelle	J. Aerts (BEL)	G. Speicher
Stage 21	Friday 21 July	266 km	La Rochelle – Rennes	J. Aerts (BEL)	G. Speicher
Stage 22	Saturday 22 July	169 km	Rennes – Caen	R. Le Grevès (FRA)	G. Speicher
Stage 23	Sunday 23 July	222 km	Caen – Paris	L. Guerra (ITA)	G. Speicher

To change gear, the cyclists had to reverse their rear wheel,
as Speicher has just done here.

That's the Tour!

'So what is this Tour de France I hear so much about?' asked the grandson of Monsieur Homais, pharmacist to Madame Bovary and her creator Gustave Flaubert. I replied, 'The Tour de France is an event that specifically gives pharmacists an annual opportunity to leave their dispensaries behind and see a little fine, healthy youth fly past as gracefully as swallows.

'The Tour de France is a slice of life, of magnificent life, offered to the sedentary; something with the power to cleanse their minds, distract them from their daily tasks, give them a taste for movement, the need to travel, the desire for new skies, the will, before they pass away, to do something else on this earth other than sell sulphate of soda or potassium permanganate.

'The Tour de France is the need, each day more pressing, to achieve better public health through exercise. It is the dream, in perspective, of a better society where each person will forge his own place following the barometer of his determination and strength.

'The Tour de France is, for the crowds, a rustling that runs like a frisson over the entire world, and is picked up by the antennas of the wireless service.

'The Tour de France is each of our beautiful regions charged with emotion, eagerly awaiting the hiss on asphalt of dozens of pneumatic tyres, powered by so many vigorous pistons; it's the sound of a march to the Arc de Triomphe, of immense populations creating "the roar of the sea made by a great people as it marches".

'The Tour de France is a crusade, a pilgrimage, an example, a lesson and an education. It's an opportunity for the country to come together in the great religion of sport, the chance to speak a common language that is understood the world over, and to sing the world hymn of courage and will.

'The Tour de France is the French nation opening its borders to our foreign friends.

'The Tour de France is, for a 20-year-old kid if he completes it, a small fortune waiting for him.

'The Tour de France is noise, movement, crowds making unimaginable journeys, the expression of the need we all have to express ourselves and raise up ephemeral idols.

'The Tour de France is a race lasting one month, but with 11 months of anticipation for this inconceivable contest, each episode of which holds millions of sports enthusiasts in rapt suspense.

'That is the Tour de France,' I explained to Monsieur Homais's grandson.

I didn't tell him, of course, that for the organizer, the Tour de France is also a terrible headache!

1

HOW I WON THE TOUR...

BY GEORGES SPEICHER

Over the last few stages, I sensed my form coming back, slowly but surely. As soon as we left Grenoble, I knew I was going to fly. And I reasoned as follows: 'Georges,' I said, 'if you ride well, you'll have to do something to help Maurice [Archambaud] break away and make up some minutes on Guerra.' I did fly, too, and how! At no time did I feel tired, either climbing or on the flat. And then, knowing that Guerra was behind us and that we were eating second by second into his lead, well, that really gave us heart. When I broke away, it was because I knew Maurice would easily be able to finish. In fact, he actually encouraged me to go on, because he didn't want to risk falling on the descent to Gap. I never had the feeling I was going to end up face down in the hay, so I tore down the hill at an insane speed. That cooled me down a bit.

Two or three times, I thought I would faint because of the heat. But that never lasted more than a few seconds and each time I managed to pull myself together.

1. Josephine Baker, famous for dancing naked but for a girdle of bananas, came to the starting point at Vésinet to present flowers to the popular champion Charles Pélissier. The race was aptly sponsored by Fyffes bananas, much appreciated by the competitors. A little comfort for 'Charlot', who was often over-criticized by the press.

2. Speicher, the 'greyhound', on the Galibier with Archambaud in the yellow jersey, in his wake. He broke away on the Col Bayard, but only to deprive the Belgian Lemaire of a two-minute time bonus.

3. During the rest day in Perpignan, Jacques Goddet has lunch with the French team. Leducq is recognizable (from the back), with Speicher on the left and Lapébie on the right.

4. Archambaud, affectionately nicknamed 'Le Poupard', or 'Chubby Cheeks', by Desgrange, wore the yellow jersey for several days. Here, he makes an ardent fan very happy.

5. Vicente Trueba, the 'Flea from Torrelavega', made lighter work of the Tourmalet than of this level crossing at Bielle.

6. Speicher had a big female following that flocked to the Parc des Princes to see him become the champion at his second attempt, aged 25. There, he received a sash from the Levallois Cycling Club, of which he was a member, with Trousselier, Pottier, Thys and Leducq.

Magne, with a little help from his friends

Team spirit and national pride gave Leducq, Magne and Speicher victory from 1930 to 1933. That, and the self-lessness of men like Charles Pélissier, Pierre Magne and Antonin Magne. In 1934, the suppression of one individual's ambitions for the greater good reached controversial extremes involving a former bellboy riding his first Tour: René Vietto.

Vietto's team leader was Antonin Magne, who had taken the yellow jersey from Georges Speicher, the race favourite, on stage two. Magne's performance in the Alps and on the Col de Braus confirmed his strength, although Italy's Giuseppe Martano was on his wheel. On the stage to Cannes, Vietto made a timely contribution by beating the Italian in the sprint and depriving him of the two-minute time bonus. Magne took full advantage of the time bonuses awarded on each of the fourteen peaks in the King of the Mountains competition, gathering enough between Marseille and Perpignan to push Martano back to 3mins 42secs. Two broken frames set Martano back even further.

Then the Tour reached the Pyrenees, and Vietto's tribulations began. He had waltzed over the Alps; through the Pyrenees, he had been staging a virtuoso performance when team duties cut his recital short. Between Perpignan and Ax-les-Thermes, he gave up a wheel to his leader. Between Ax and Luchon, he actually had to turn round, ride back along the route and hand Magne his bike. The frustration was suffocating, both for Vietto and for the public watching from the roadside or following the race through the pages of *L'Auto*.

Without Vietto's twin acts of renunciation, Magne would certainly have lost the jersey. The question that no one could answer was whether Vietto would have been able to recover it. He had already reduced his disadvantage from fifty-four to twenty-nine minutes.

The time bonuses would prove decisive. Vietto served his leader by cleaning up the bonuses in the mountains, Lapébie did the same on the flat. Magne, meanwhile, was free to concentrate on his two great master strokes: the gruelling stage from Luchon to Tarbes and the time trial at Nantes. His ruthless domination of both knocked the stuffing out of Martano, who lost seventeen minutes on stage eighteen and eleven during the Nantes time trial. Vietto did no better, and lost his place on the final podium to Lapébie.

André Leducq, following the Tour as a journalist, predicted that Vietto would one day win the Tour. He was wrong, and Vietto had already lost his best chance.

GENERAL CLASSIFICATION

1. **Antonin Magne** (FRA) France, 4,363 km in 147h.13m.58s; Average speed: 31.233 kph
2. **Giuseppe Martano** (ITA) Italy, at 27m.31s.
3. **Roger Lapébie** (FRA) France, at 52m.15s.
4. Félicien Vervaecke (BEL) touriste-routier, at 57m.40s.
5. René Vietto (FRA) France, at 59m.2s.
6. Ambrogio Morelli (ITA) touriste-routier, at 1h.12m.2s.
7. Ludwig Geyer (GER) Germany, at 1h.12m.51s.
8. Sylvère Maes (BEL) touriste-routier, at 1h.20m.56s.
9. Mariano Canardo (SPA) Switzerland-Spain, at 1h.29m.2s.
10. Vicente Trueba (SPA) Switzerland-Spain, at 1h.40m.39s.
11. Georges Speicher (FRA) France, at 1h.52m.21s.
12. Raymond Louviot (FRA) France, at 2h.3m.21s.
13. Edoardo Molinar (ITA) touriste-routier, at 2h.16m.52s.
14. Eugenio Gestri (ITA) Italy, at 2h.21m.9s.
15. Adriano Vignoli (ITA) Italy, at 2h.21m.58s.
16. Giovanni Cazzulani (ITA) Italy, at h.32h.38s.
17. Albert Buchi (SUI) Switzerland, at 2h.35m.17s.
18. Frans Bonduel (BEL) Belgium, at 2h.44m.47s.
19. Federico Ezquerra (SPA) Switzerland-Spain, at 2h.53m.3s.
20. August Erne (SUI) Switzerland-Spain, at 2h.55m.26s.

28TH TOUR DE FRANCE, 23 STAGES - 4,363 KM

			STAGE	STAGE WINNER	YELLOW JERSEY
Stage 1	Tuesday 3 July	262 km	Paris – Lille	G. Speicher (FRA)	G. Speicher
Stage 2	Wednesday 4 July	192 km	Lille – Charleville	R. Le Grevès (FRA)	A. Magne
Stage 3	Thursday 5 July	161 km	Charleville – Metz	R. Lapébie (FRA)	A. Magne
Stage 4	Friday 6 July	220 km	Metz – Belfort	R. Lapébie (FRA)	A. Magne
Stage 5	Saturday 7 July	293 km	Belfort – Évian	G. Speicher & R. Le Grevès (FRA)	A. Magne
Stage 6	Monday 9 July	207 km	Évian – Aix-les-Bains	G. Speicher (FRA)	A. Magne
Stage 7	Tuesday 10 July	229 km	Aix-les-Bains – Grenoble	R. Vietto (FRA)	A. Magne
Stage 8	Wednesday 11 July	102 km	Grenoble – Gap	G. Martano (ITA)	A. Magne
Stage 9	Thursday 12 July	227 km	Gap – Digne	R. Vietto (FRA)	A. Magne
Stage 10	Friday 13 July	156 km	Digne – Nice	R. Le Grevès (FRA)	A. Magne
Stage 11	Sunday 15 July	126 km	Nice – Cannes	R. Vietto (FRA)	A. Magne
Stage 12	Monday 16 July	195 km	Cannes – Marseille	R. Lapébie (FRA)	A. Magne
Stage 13	Tuesday 17 July	172 km	Marseille – Montpellier	G. Speicher (FRA)	A. Magne
Stage 14	Wednesday 18 July	177 km	Montpellier – Perpignan	R. Lapébie (FRA)	A. Magne
Stage 15	Friday 20 July	158 km	Perpignan – Ax-les-Thermes	R. Lapébie (FRA)	A. Magne
Stage 16	Saturday 21 July	165 km	Ax-les-Thermes – Luchon	A. Vignoli (ITA)	A. Magne
Stage 17	Sunday 22 July	91 km	Luchon – Tarbes	A. Magne (FRA)	A. Magne
Stage 18	Monday 23 July	172 km	Tarbes – Pau	R. Vietto (FRA)	A. Magne
Stage 19	Wednesday 25 July	215 km	Pau – Bordeaux	E. Meini (ITA)	A. Magne
Stage 20	Thursday 26 July	183 km	Bordeaux – La Rochelle	G. Speicher (FRA)	A. Magne
Stage 21 (1)	Friday 27 July	81 km	La Rochelle – La Roche-sur-Yon	R. Le Grevès (FRA)	A. Magne
Stage 21 (2)	Friday 27 July	83 km	La Roche-sur-Yon – Nantes (TT)	A. Magne (FRA)	A. Magne
Stage 22	Saturday 28 July	275 km	Nantes – Caen	R. Louviot (FRA)	A. Magne
Stage 23	Sunday 29 July	221 km	Caen – Paris	S. Maes (BEL)	A. Magne

In the 1930s, the Tour not only meant sport but also Fredo Gardoni, the
famous accordionist, seated here with Antonin Magne. Magne loved
the 'poor-man's piano'; it reminded him of his origins in the Auvergne.

Magne's second Tour

PARIS (July 29): 'After riding the Six Days, I'd taken part in all the one-day classics, which meant I'd made many, hard efforts. I therefore feared when the Tour de France began that all those sprints and breakaways since February would take their toll. However, I had an almost violent longing to place well in this race. I was under no illusions that my task would be easy, and I knew that the man I was going to have to beat was Martano. He had prepared specifically for the Tour, and I was well aware of his abilities. I won't pretend that I was emotional leaving Paris. I have never had a good ride on stage one, from Paris to Lille; I still don't understand why. The memory of the terrible crisis I suffered on stage one last year came insistently to mind. When I found myself riding through Lille in the leading peloton, I said to myself, "Tonin, you've started well; you're going to have to finish well too." And at the end of the second stage, they threw the yellow jersey at me. I'd have preferred Speicher to have kept it!

'So I wasn't thrilled to be first in the general classification after the second stage. I'd promised myself to keep my efforts to a minimum, and even to allow the yellow jersey to be taken from me if it proved too difficult to keep, but a race is a race, and once you get started, despite yourself you give everything you have to remain in the lead.

'Climbing the Aravis, I realized my strength was equal to Martano's. That gave me hope, although I also knew that the most difficult task would be to hold out against him in the Alps. Being close to his home and with the encouragement of his fans, who had turned out in force, I didn't doubt for a second that he'd do everything possible to take the lead. But I also knew that if I tried to respond to Martano's accelerations and to stay with him at any cost, both of us would eventually suffer a crisis. So I decided to ride it my way without worrying about him. Despite what people are saying, it was the first time I'd decided to ride according to my own strategy, I risked everything to gain everything. I came within a hair's breadth of losing the yellow jersey but I felt my form getting better and better, and I waited for Martano to weaken.

'Unfortunately, the Pyrenees started badly for me. I fell at the foot of the Puymorens, just before arriving in Ax-les-Thermes, and the following day I broke my bike within sight of Luchon. But just as I began to despair, it happened: we were climbing the Col de Peyresourde, and I realized Martano was labouring hard. I didn't hesitate for a second: it was time to strike and, for the first time since leaving Paris, I really gave it everything I had, trying to put as much distance as possible between myself and Martano. The end result was more than I could have hoped for, and from that

Vietto may have been indispensible, but Magne laid the foundation for his win by breaking away alone on Aspin (above) and gaining seventeen minutes on Martano.

Stage fifteen, Perpignan to Ax-les-Thermes (20 July): Leading at Puymorens, Vietto was descending with Magne when Magne fell and broke his wheel...

... after giving him his own wheel, Vietto had to wait several minutes for the repair vehicle. In any case, Magne's frame had been bent; he had to borrow Speicher's bike.

Brilliant on the Soulor (above), Vietto could only aspire to be King of the Mountains, after losing 54 minutes at Evian after getting tar in his eye.

moment, I really began to entertain the possibility of victory.

'Day by day, I tried to lose as little time as possible and waited impatiently for the time trial. I was truly dreading each stage because any one could have cost me the yellow jersey. Oh yes, I could have lost it: all it would have taken was to blow a tyre a couple of times, break a wheel, or damage the bike itself and, left behind and riding alone, I would have lost precious minutes. However, I also knew that, barring incidents and accidents, I'd ride a good time because I'd never been in such good shape as this year at the Tour de France. Obviously, it was hard work, but I recovered much more quickly than I had ever done before in my career. Finally, during the time trial, I gave it everything I had for the second time. Then, the finish line in Paris loomed and I breathed a sigh of relief as soon as I crossed it. Over the closing stages, I'd been terrified of an accident, of falling and being unable to get up again. But, here I am, I've won my second Tour, and I must thank all my team-mates, from Louviot to Vietto. Tonight, I can assure you, there is one more happy man on Earth.'

VIETTO SAVES MAGNE AGAIN!

On stage sixteen, Ax-les-Thermes to Luchon (21 July), the yellow jersey, once again victim of a mechanical problem, was saved by Vietto, just as he had been the previous day. Two perspectives of the event: Antonin Magne: 'It happened on a little descent after the Portet d'Aspet. I was trying to accelerate and catch up with Gissels and Martano who were ahead of me when my back wheel locked and my chain wrapped around my derailleur; I couldn't repair it.

'All my team-mates were ahead, the truck was far behind and, for a few seconds, I really thought that it was all over. I was desperate. Then suddenly René Vietto came flying round a bend, climbing at full speed; he'd turned round and was coming back to give me his bike. I mounted immediately, and a little further along, Roger Lapébie was waiting for us. He led right to the top of the Col des Ares. On the descent, he continued to lead me out, and I don't know to whom I owe the most today, Vietto or Lapébie.'

Jacques Goddet gave us the rest of the story: 'Vietto was fuming like a mortally wounded bull. But he was still very much alive, and his tongue was sharp. "That Antonin, he doesn't know how to ride a bike. Lapébie is riding his own race, and I'm stuck here. You can see that this bike is in pieces. And that truck is taking for ever, I'm going to lose ten minutes. I'm not going to play the slave for ever, you know." Lapébie had left in search of bonus points, after Vietto had secured the ranking on the top of the passes. That's logical, isn't it? Vietto can say that he was the principal element in the victory if Magne wins the Tour.'

The unknown Romain

The 1935 Tour began with high hopes of the Spanish climbers, and even greater expectations of the race favourites Magne, Speicher and Vietto for France, and the Italians Bergamaschi, Camusso and Martano. The Spaniards, however, had mostly abandoned before the race reached the Alps; the favourites too were destined to disappoint. France's recent string of victories had depended on an indomitable team spirit; this year, it had evaporated. Without Charles Pélissier, who had chosen to enter in the Individual category, and Antonin Magne, who was injured, the French lacked the morale to succeed. The team, and its leader, Georges Speicher, could do no more than call their opponents' bluff.

As it was, the early leader emerged not from a magician's hat but from a first stage from Paris to Lille which was so demanding that the Tour expert Raymond Huttier could call it 'tough, decisive – a killer'. A lucky level crossing gave Romain Maes, described by Desgrange as a 'compact ball of muscle', a fifty-three second lead. It disheartened his rivals, and, more importantly, transformed Maes. No one considered the 22-year-old Belgian, the thirteenth of fifteen children, a likely candidate for even fleeting acquaintance with the yellow jersey. No one, that is, except Ludovic Feuillet, the legendary coach who had discovered him. The sceptics, forgetting Feuillet's expert eye for talent, awaited Maes' collapse. It didn't come in the Alps, where he overcame his fear of descending and took an unexpected stage win at Cannes. It didn't come in the time trial from Narbonne to Perpignan where he almost beat Archambaud. That left the Pyrenees, where the Italians Morelli and Teani had him on the ropes between Luchon and Pau. Slipping into the wake of his team-mates Lowie and the master climber Vervaecke, Maes escaped with a lead of a few minutes at Pau. The Tour as good as won, Belgium broke into euphoria. On the Sunday of the final stage, the parish priest of Lourdes cited the riders of the Tour de France as an example of perseverance. Romain Maes' perseverance was certainly exemplary.

The 1935 Tour de France was also marked by tragedy. On the descent from the Galibier on 11 July, the Spanish climber Francesco Cepeda fell and fractured his skull. Three days later, he became the first Tour rider to die during the race.

GENERAL CLASSIFICATION

1. **Romain Maes** (BEL) Belgium, 4,338 km in 141h.32m; Average speed: 30.650 kph
2. **Ambrogio Morelli** (ITA) Independent, at 17m.52s.
3. **Félicien Vervaecke** (BEL) Belgium, at 24m.6s.
4. Sylvère Maes (BEL) Independent, at 35m.24s.
5. Jules Lowie (BEL) Independent, at 51m.26s.
6. Georges Speicher (FRA) France, at 54m.29s.
7. Maurice Archambaud (FRA) France, at 1h.9m.28s.
8. René Vietto (FRA) France, at 1 h 21m.3s.
9. Gabriel Ruozzi (FRA) touriste-routier, at 1h.34m.2s.
10. Oskar Thierbach (GER) Germany, at 2h.0m.4s.
11. Pierre Cogan (FRA) touriste-routier, at 2h.11m.56s.
12. Benoît Faure (FRA) touriste-routier, at 2h.21m.1s.
13. Charles Pélissier (FRA) Independent, at 2h.29m.21s.
14. René Bernard (FRA) touriste-routier, at 2h.30m.47s.
15. René Le Grevès (FRA) France, at 2h.40m.5s.
16. Fernand Fayolle (FRA) touriste-routier, at 2h.48m.7s.
17. André Leducq (FRA) France, at 2h.56m.14s.
18. Pierre Cloaerc (FRA) touriste-routier, at 3h.19m.55s.
19. Joseph Mauclair (FRA) touriste-routier, at 3h.20m.36s.
20. Antoine Dignef (BEL) Independent, at 3h.24m.52s.

29TH TOUR DE FRANCE, 21 STAGES – 4,338 KM

Stage	Date	Distance	Stage	Stage Winner	Yellow Jersey
Stage 1	Thursday 4 July	262 km	Paris – Lille	R. Maes (BEL)	R. Maes
Stage 2	Friday 5 July	192 km	Lille – Charleville	C. Pélissier (FRA) individual	R. Maes
Stage 3	Saturday 6 July	161 km	Charleville – Metz	R. Di Paco (ITA)	R. Maes
Stage 4	Sunday 7 July	220 km	Metz – Belfort	J. Aerts (BEL)	R. Maes
Stage 5 (1)	Monday 8 July	262 km	Belfort – Genève (SUI)	M. Archambaud (FRA)	R. Maes
Stage 5 (2)	Monday 8 July	58 km	Genève (SUI) – Évian (TT)	R. Di Paco (ITA)	R. Maes
Stage 6	Wednesday 10 July	207 km	Évian – Aix-les-Bains	R. Vietto (FRA)	R. Maes
Stage 7	Thursday 11 July	229 km	Aix-les-Bains – Grenoble	R. Camusso (ITA)	R. Maes
Stage 8	Friday 12 July	102 km	Grenoble – Gap	J. Aerts (BEL)	R. Maes
Stage 9	Saturday 13 July	227 km	Gap – Digne	R. Vietto (FRA)	R. Maes
Stage 10	Sunday 14 July	156 km	Digne – Nice	J. Aerts (BEL)	R. Maes
Stage 11	Tuesday 16 July	126 km	Nice – Cannes	R. Maes (BEL)	R. Maes
Stage 12	Wednesday 17 July	195 km	Cannes – Marseille	C. Pélissier (FRA) individual	R. Maes
Stage 13 (1)	Thursday 18 July	112 km	Marseille – Nîmes	V. Bergamaschi (ITA)	R. Maes
Stage 13 (2)	Thursday 18 July	56 km	Nîmes – Montpellier (TTT)	G. Speicher (FRA)	R. Maes
Stage 14 (1)	Friday 19 July	103 km	Montpellier – Narbonne	R. Le Grevès (FRA)	R. Maes
Stage 14 (2)	Friday 19 July	63 km	Narbonne – Perpignan (TT)	M. Archambaud (FRA)	R. Maes
Stage 15	Saturday 20 July	325 km	Perpignan – Luchon	S. Maes (BEL)	R. Maes
Stage 16	Monday 22 July	194 km	Luchon – Pau	A. Morelli (ITA)	R. Maes
Stage 17	Wednesday 24 July	224 km	Pau – Bordeaux	J. Moineau (FRA)	R. Maes
Stage 18 (1)	Thursday 25 July	159 km	Bordeaux – Rochefort	R. Le Grevès (FRA)	R. Maes
Stage 18 (2)	Thursday 25 July	33 km	Rochefort – La Rochelle (TT)	A. Leducq (FRA)	R. Maes
Stage 19 (1)	Friday 26 July	81 km	La Rochelle – La Roche-sur-Yon	R. Le Grevès (FRA)	R. Maes
Stage 19 (2)	Friday 26 July	95 km	La Roche-sur-Yon – Nantes (TTT)	J. Aerts (BEL)	R. Maes
Stage 20 (1)	Saturday 27 July	220 km	Nantes – Vire	R. Le Grevès (FRA)	R. Maes
Stage 20 (2)	Saturday 27 July	55 km	Vire – Caen (TTT)	A. Morelli (ITA)	R. Maes
Stage 21	Sunday 28 July	221 km	Caen – Paris	R. Maes (BEL)	R. Maes

As fresh and energetic at the close of the Tour as at the start, Maes won the final stage from Caen to Paris. Like Bottecchia and Frantz before him, he had worn the yellow jersey from start to finish.

A cycling holiday for Sylvère Maes

Desgrange made minor modifications to ensure the 1936 Tour de France ran smoothly. There were fewer cars authorized to follow the race; six rest days rather than four, five time trials instead of six, two motorbike gendarmes, and only ninety riders. The team selection was also tweaked, with three ten-man national teams representing Germany, Belgium and France (Italy did not take part for political reasons), a combined Spain-Luxembourg team, and five four-man national teams representing Switzerland, Holland, Yugoslavia, Romania and Austria. There were also thirty *touristes-routiers*, including René Vietto.

Record numbers of spectators saw the Tour, thanks to the paid workers' holidays created by the Popular Front, in power since June. Desgrange fell ill on stage two, and was forced to abandon, while relentless rain prevented the racing from beginning in earnest before the Alps. Until then, the crowds were entertained by long-range sorties by riders from Switzerland and Luxembourg; the abandon of Romain Maes followed by outraged recriminations; the vanishing act by the novice Yugoslavs and Romanians; Vietto's abandon after two broken

chains, and Speicher's after a fall while descending the Galibier.

Archambaud struggled to unite the French, but the previous year's ill-feeling was exacerbated by Magne, who played a waiting game while Belgium's Sylvère Maes – no relation to 1935's winner – slowly awoke to his own strength. After dispossessing Archambaud of the yellow jersey at Briançon, Maes consolidated his lead by repelling Magne's attack on the Izoard, included on the route for the first time since 1927, then snuffing him out two days later on the way to Nice.

Belgium's dominance was challenged only by Luxembourg, Spain's climbers and the flamboyant French *touristes-routiers*. On the mountain passes of the Pyrenees between Luchon and Pau, where Magne believed he could recover his losses, he cracked. On 27 July, Sylvère Maes' twenty-seventh birthday, he won the Pau stage and built a twenty-seven minute lead. With a tranquillity that matched that of predecessors like Frantz and Magne, Maes controlled the race for the remaining week. His gallant adversary, Antonin Magne, applauded the untouchable Belgian, and his country was once more in rapture, not least in the café Maes owned at Ghistelles, aptly named 'Tourmalet'.

GENERAL CLASSIFICATION

1. **Sylvère Maes** (BEL) Belgium, 4,414 km in 142h.47m.32s; Average speed: 30.912 kph
2. **Antonin Magne** (FRA) France, at 26m.55s.
3. **Félicien Vervaecke** (BEL) Belgium, at 27m.53s.
4. Pierre Clemens (LUX) Spain-Lux, at 42m.42s.
5. Arsène Mersch (LUX) Spain-Lux, at 53m.24s.
6. Mariano Canardo (SPA) Spain-Lux, at 1h.3m.4s.

7. Mathias Clemens (LUX) Spain-Lux, at 1h.10m.44s.
8. Léo Amberg (SUI) Switzerland, at 1h.19m.13s.
9. Marcel Kint (BEL) Belgium, at 1h.22m.25s.
10. Léon Level (FRA) touriste-routier, at 1h.27m.57s.
11. Julian Berrendero (SPA) Spain-Lux, at 1h.34m.37s.
12. Sylvain Marcaillou (FRA) touriste-routier, at 1h.38m.6s.
13. Louis Thietard (FRA) touriste-routier, at 1h.47m.47s.

14. Raoul Lesueur (FRA) France, at 1h.50m.15s.
15. Albert Van Schendel (HOL) Holland, at 1h.52m.23s.
16. Pierre Cogan (FRA) France, at 1h.52m.48s.
17. Federico Ezquerra (SPA) Spain-Lux, at 1h.54m.39s.
18. Robert Tanneveau (FRA) France, at 1h.57m.9s.
19. François Neuville (BEL) Belgium, at 2h.1m.16s.
20. René Le Grevès (FRA) France, at 2h.7m.45s.

30TH TOUR DE FRANCE, 21 STAGES - 4,414 KM

Stage	Date	Distance	STAGE	STAGE WINNER	YELLOW JERSEY
Stage 1	Tuesday 7 July	258 km	Paris – Lille	P. Egli (SUI)	P. Egli
Stage 2	Wednesday 8 July	192 km	Lille – Charleville	R. Wierinckx (BEL)	M. Archambaud
Stage 3	Thursday 9 July	161 km	Charleville – Metz	M. Clemens (LUX)	A. Mersch
Stage 4	Friday 10 July	220 km	Metz – Belfort	M. Archambaud (FRA)	M. Archambaud
Stage 5	Saturday 11 July	298 km	Belfort – Évian	R. Le Grevès (FRA)	M. Archambaud
Stage 6	Monday 13 July	212 km	Évian – Aix-les-Bains	E. Meulenberg (BEL)	M. Archambaud
Stage 7	Tuesday 14 July	224 km	Aix-les-Bains – Grenoble	T. Middelkamp (HOL)	M. Archambaud
Stage 8	Wednesday 15 July	194 km	Grenoble – Briançon	J.-M. Goasmat (FRA)	S. Maes
Stage 9	Thursday 16 July	202 km	Briançon – Digne	L. Level (FRA)	S. Maes
Stage 10	Saturday 18 July	156 km	Digne – Nice	P. Maye (FRA)	S. Maes
Stage 11	Sunday 19 July	126 km	Nice – Cannes	F. Ezquerra (SPA)	S. Maes
Stage 12	Tuesday 21 July	195 km	Cannes – Marseille	R. Le Grevès (FRA)	S. Maes
Stage 13 (1)	Wednesday 22 July	112 km	Marseille – Nîmes	R. Le Grevès (FRA)	S. Maes
Stage 13 (2)	Wednesday 22 July	52 km	Nîmes – Montpellier (TTT)	S. Maes (BEL)	S. Maes
Stage 14 (1)	Thursday 23 July	103 km	Montpellier – Narbonne	R. Le Grevès (FRA)	S. Maes
Stage 14 (2)	Thursday 23 July	63 km	Narbonne – Perpignan (TTT)	S. Maes (BEL)	S. Maes
Stage 15	Saturday 25 July	325 km	Perpignan – Luchon	S. Ducazeaux (FRA)	S. Maes
Stage 16	Monday 27 July	194 km	Luchon – Pau	S. Maes (BEL)	S. Maes
Stage 17	Wednesday 29 July	229 km	Pau – Bordeaux	R. Le Grevès (FRA)	S. Maes
Stage 18 (1)	Thursday 30 July	117 km	Bordeaux – Saintes	E. Meulenberg (BEL)	S. Maes
Stage 18 (2)	Thursday 30 July	75 km	Saintes – La Rochelle (TTT)	S. Maes (BEL)	S. Maes
Stage 19 (1)	Friday 31 July	81 km	La Rochelle – La Roche-sur-Yon	M. Kint (BEL)	S. Maes
Stage 19 (2)	Friday 31 July	65 km	La Roche-sur-Yon – Cholet (TTT)	F. Vervaecke (BEL)	S. Maes
Stage 19 (3)	Friday 31 July	67 km	Cholet – Angers	P. Maye (FRA)	S. Maes
Stage 20 (1)	Saturday 1 August	204 km	Angers – Vire	R. Le Grevès (FRA)	S. Maes
Stage 20 (2)	Saturday 1 August	55 km	Vire – Caen (TTT)	A. Magne (FRA)	S. Maes
Stage 21	Sunday 2 August	234 km	Caen – Paris	A. Mersch (LUX)	S. Maes

Above: Thanks to the Popular Front, many French workers were able to enjoy their first paid holidays. Thousands took this opportunity to encourage their Tour de France heroes.
Below: Between Briançon and Digne, Maes reinforced his lead on the slopes of the Izoard.

Lapébie derails the Belgians

The universal use of the derailleur revolutionized the 1937 Tour; nationalistic zeal came close to derailing it. Two days after his sublime ascent of the Galibier, the yellow jersey Gino Bartali slid off the road into a torrent of Alpine melt-water. Chilled to the bone, he had to abandon. His misfortune changed the complexion of the race, clearing the way for an acrimonious fight between the Frenchman Roger Lapébie, and Belgium's reigning champion Sylvère Maes.

During week one, riders from Luxembourg, Switzerland, Italy, Germany and Belgium had shared the stages. Bartali's climbing brilliance had set a new star in cycling's firmament, and shaken up the general classification. His withdrawal had left Maes in the yellow jersey; by defending it through the Alps and the decisive Pyrenean stages, the Belgians felt the race had been won. However, Maes' lead after the stage between Luchon and Pau depended on a 1min 30sec time penalty against Lapébie, after he had profited from too much assistance from his team-mates, despite the fact that even Belgian *directeur*

sportif Karel Steyaert admitted that Lapébie had gained the upper hand on the Aubisque. With his 2min 45sec time gain cancelled out, Lapébie considered abandoning. Two days later, however, the tables were turned when Maes was penalized fifteen seconds after the Belgians riding as Individuals had assisted him following a puncture. Maes' penalty, further time lost due to a closed level crossing, and Lapébie's bonus for finishing second on the stage left only twenty-five seconds between them. With feelings running high, Maes abandoned the Tour at Bordeaux, taking the Belgian team with him. Lapébie took over the jersey, while expressing deep regret at Maes' absence.

During the Vire-Caen time trial, Lapébie's form failed catastrophically. Only judicious use of the newly approved derailleur allowed him to come through with his lead intact. Then, at the gate of the Parc des Princes, he lost his chain. Heart in mouth, he rectified the fault and pedalled off to become the first Tour de France victor to have ridden every stage using a derailleur.

GENERAL CLASSIFICATION

1. **Roger Lapébie** (FRA) France, 4,415 km in 138h 58m.31s; Average speed: 31.768 kph
2. **Mario Vicini** (ITA) Independent, at 7m.17s.
3. **Léo Amberg** (SUI) Switzerland at 26m.13s.
4. Francesco Camusso (ITA) Italy, at 26m.53s.
5. Sylvain Marcaillou (FRA) France, at 35m.36s.
6. Édouard Vissiers (BEL) Independent, at 38m.13s.
7. Paul Chocque (FRA) France, at 1h.5m.19s.
8. Pierre Gallien (FRA) Independent, at 1h.6m.33s.
9. Erich Bautz (GER) Germany, at 1h.6m.41s.
10. Fabien Frechaut (FRA) Independent, at 1h.24m.34s.
11. Herbert Muller (BEL) Independent, at 1h.26m.51s.
12. Raymond Passat (FRA) Independent, at 1h.27m.58s.
13. Marcel Laurent (FRA) Independent, at 1h.31m.57s.
14. Oskar Thierbach (GER) Germany, at 1h.34m.27s.
15. Julian Berrendero (SPA) Spain, at 1h.34m.48s.
16. Gustaaf Deloor (BEL) Independent, at 1h.36m.3s.
17. Victor Cosson (FRA) Independent, at 1h.38m.55s.
18. Jean-Marie Goasmat (FRA) Independent, at 1h.39m.36s.
19. Sauveur Ducazeaux (FRA) Independent, at 1h.41m.21s.
20. Robert Oubron (FRA) Independent, at 1h.46m.9s.

31ST TOUR DE FRANCE, 20 STAGES – 4,415 KM

	STAGE		STAGE WINNER	YELLOW JERSEY
Stage 1	Wednesday 30 June	263 km	Paris – Lille	J. Majerus (LUX)	J. Majerus
Stage 2	Thursday 1 July	192 km	Lille – Charleville	M. Archambaud (FRA)	J. Majerus
Stage 3	Friday 2 July	161 km	Charleville – Metz	W. Generati (ITA)	M. Kint
Stage 4	Saturday 3 July	220 km	Metz – Belfort	E. Bautz (GER)	E. Bautz
Stage 5 (1)	Sunday 4 July	175 km	Belfort – Lons-le-Saunier	H. Puppo (FRA)	E. Bautz
Stage 5 (2)	Sunday 4 July	34 km	Lons-le-Saunier – Champagnole (TTT)	S. Maes (BEL)	E. Bautz
Stage 5 (3)	Sunday 4 July	93 km	Champagnole – Genève (SUI)	L. Amberg (SUI)	E. Bautz
Stage 6	Tuesday 6 July	180 km	Genève (SUI) – Aix-les-Bains	G. Deloor (BEL)	E. Bautz
Stage 7	Wednesday 7 July	228 km	Aix-les-Bains – Grenoble	G. Bartali (ITA)	G. Bartali
Stage 8	Thursday 8 July	194 km	Grenoble – Briançon	O. Weckerling (GER)	G. Bartali
Stage 9	Friday 9 July	220 km	Briançon – Digne	R. Lapébie (FRA)	S. Maes
Stage 10	Sunday 11 July	251 km	Digne – Nice	F. Vervaecke (BEL)	S. Maes
Stage 11 (1)	Tuesday 13 July	169 km	Nice – Toulon	E. Meulenberg (BEL)	S. Maes
Stage 11 (2)	Tuesday 13 July	65 km	Toulon – Marseille (TTT)	G. Danneels (BEL)	S. Maes
Stage 12 (1)	Wednesday 14 July	112 km	Marseille – Nîmes	A. Antoine (FRA)	S. Maes
Stage 12 (2)	Wednesday 14 July	51 km	Nîmes – Montpellier	R. Pedroli (SUI)	S. Maes
Stage 13 (1)	Thursday 15 July	103 km	Montpellier – Narbonne	F. Camusso (ITA)	S. Maes
Stage 13 (2)	Thursday 15 July	63 km	Narbonne – Perpignan	E. Meulenberg (BEL)	S. Maes
Stage 14 (1)	Saturday 17 July	99 km	Perpignan – Bourg-Madame	E. Meulenberg (BEL)	S. Maes
Stage 14 (2)	Saturday 17 July	59 km	Bourg-Madame – Ax-les-Thermes	M. Canardo (SPA)	S. Maes
Stage 14 (3)	Saturday 17 July	167 km	Ax-les-Thermes – Luchon	E. Meulenberg (BEL)	S. Maes
Stage 15	Monday 19 July	194 km	Luchon – Pau	J. Berrendero (SPA)	S. Maes
Stage 16	Wednesday 21 July	235 km	Pau – Bordeaux	P. Chocque (FRA)	S. Maes
Stage 17 (1)	Thursday 22 July	123 km	Bordeaux – Royan	E. Bautz (GER)	R. Lapébie
Stage 17 (2)	Thursday 22 July	37 km	Royan – Saintes	A. Braeckeveldt (BEL) & H. Wengler (GER)	R. Lapébie
Stage 17 (3)	Thursday 22 July	67 km	Saintes – La Rochelle	R. Lapébie (FRA)	R. Lapébie
Stage 18 (1)	Friday 23 July	81 km	La Rochelle – La Roche-sur-Yon (TT)	R. Lapébie (FRA)	R. Lapébie
Stage 18 (2)	Friday 23 July	172 km	La Roche-sur-Yon – Rennes	P. Chocque (FRA)	R. Lapébie
Stage 19 (1)	Saturday 24 July	114 km	Rennes – Vire	R. Passat (FRA)	R. Lapébie
Stage 19 (2)	Saturday 24 July	59 km	Vire – Caen (TT)	L. Amberg (SUI)	R. Lapébie
Stage 20	Sunday 25 July	234 km	Caen – Paris	E. Vissers (BEL)	R. Lapébie

The Tour was a family affair for Roger Lapébie who was encouraged by his daughter in Nice, supported by his brother in the Pyrenees and congratulated by his wife in the Parc des Princes.

Derailleur: Lapébie uses one and wins

The derailleur played a major role in this year's Tour de France, and made a huge contribution to Roger Lapébie's victory; he was always in the right gear at the right time. Being more athletic than Sylvère Maes, Lapébie was also able to push big gears when necessary. When he broke away before Digne, he had the strength to push a seven-metre gear (7.66 yards). On the first twists and turns of the Soulor road, he didn't hesitate to select a 5.76-metre (6.3-yard) gear. It was this ratio, enormous given the gradient and the distance already covered, that allowed Lapébie back into the race.

Unlike Marcaillou, Lapébie always listened to me when it came to selecting his gears.

On the Izoard, I indicated the right places to change gear, and where several of the Belgians had difficulty changing cogs, and made violent, nervous manoeuvres, Lapébie, who had changed gear in the right place, sped past.

On the stage from Vire to Caen, I'm convinced that Vicini would have beaten him if he hadn't changed gear more than forty times. Roger therefore allowed himself to be led blindly, and leaning out the door, I shouted to him, '15, 17, 16, 18.'

His rhythm always remained the same, while Vicini, having to back-pedal to force the chain to jump, could not change gears as often...

Above: Crossing the Landes in searing heat, Lapébie gave Maes a cooling shower. Further on, when the yellow jersey blew a tyre and the French attacked, it was an altogether colder shower.

Below: Feeling unjustly penalized, Sylvère Maes, the yellow jersey, and his team came close to not setting off again from Bordeaux. The peloton awaited their decision.

Opposite: The Belgians didn't attack Lapébie when he broke his bike. Either he was too strong, or they weren't in good form, or perhaps it was for reasons of fair play.

Bartali, on wings of prayer

The principal innovation at the 1938 Tour de France was the suppression of the Individual category. Three twelve-man teams represented France, Belgium, Germany and Italy, while Spain, Austria, Switzerland, the Netherlands and Luxembourg fielded six riders each.

Roger Lapébie didn't defend his title. Attending the Tour as an apprentice journalist, he saw a mirror image of the 1937 Tour, in which Gino Bartali didn't fall and the Belgians battled hard to the end. Italy's *directeur sportif*, the great Costante Girardengo, was assisted by Mussolini's General Antonelli; the riders were under orders to demonstrate the beneficial effects of Fascism. The Belgians merely wanted to resume their string of victories, broken at Bordeaux the previous year.

A tense contest developed between the mountain specialists Vervaecke and Bartali. On the classic stage from Pau to Luchon, Félicien Vervaecke won the stage and the jersey; Bartali finished nearly a minute later, and jumped from nineteenth to second in the general classification. Far behind, 1933 champion Georges Speicher was seen being towed by a car and

thrown off the race. The following day on the Portet d'Aspet climb, Bartali gained a 1min 25sec bonus to move within 53 seconds of Vervaecke; by winning the time trial from Narbonne to Béziers, the Belgian stretched his lead again to 3mins 45secs. On 18 July, the day of his twenty-fourth birthday, victory and a one-minute time bonus at Marseille brought Bartali closer. Three days later, a hair's breadth separated them after Vervaecke obstructed Bartali in the sprint for the time bonus on the Col de Braus and incurred a 30-second sanction.

The following day's Alpine marathon from Digne to Briançon was one of the great stages in Tour history. Climbing like an angel but descending like a devil, the devout Catholic Bartali won the stage seventeen minutes ahead of Vervaecke. By crossing three cols at the head of the field and taking the stage win, he added 5mins 43secs of time bonuses to his lead.

On the final stage the veterans Magne and Leducq escaped alone. They entered the Parc des Princes together and crossed the line arm in arm. It was a fitting end to the Tour de France careers of two fine champions.

GENERAL CLASSIFICATION

1. **Gino Bartali** (ITA) Italy, 4,680.5 km in 148h.29m.12s; Average speed: 31.565 kph
2. **Félicien Vervaecke** (BEL) Belgium, at 18m.27s.
3. **Victor Cosson** (FRA) France, at 29m.26s.
4. Edward Vissers (BEL) Belgium, at 35m.8s.
5. Mathias Clemens (LUX) Luxembourg, at 42m.8s.
6. Mario Vicini (ITA) Italy, at 44m.59s.
7. Jules Lowie (BEL) Belgium, at 48m.56s.
8. Antonin Magne (FRA) France, at 49m.
9. Marcel Kint (BEL) Belgium, at 59m.49s.
10. Dante Gianello (FRA) Bleuets, at 1h.6m.47s.
11. Jean-Marie Goasmat (FRA) France, at 1h.7m.34s.
12. Albertin Disseaux (BEL) Belgium, at 1h.12m.16s.
13. Robert Tanneveau (FRA) Cadets, at 1h.13m.54s.
14. Sylvère Maes (BEL) Belgium, at 1h.21m.11s.
15. Pierre Gallien (FRA) France, at 1h.24m.34s.
16. Mariano Canardo (SPA) Spain, at 1h.26m.48s.
17. François Neuville (BEL) Belgium, at 1h.35m.43s.
18. Jean Fréchaut (FRA) France, at 1h.37m.24s.
19. Rafael Ramos (SPA) Spain, at 1h.37m.40s.
20. Glauco Servadei (ITA) Italy, at 1h.41m.38s.

32ND TOUR DE FRANCE
21 STAGES – 4,680.5 KM

	STAGE				STAGE WINNER	YELLOW JERSEY
Stage 1	Tuesday 5 July	215 km	Paris – Caen		W. Oberbeck (GER)	W. Oberbeck
Stage 2	Wednesday 6 July	237 km	Caen – Saint-Brieuc		J. Majerus (LUX)	J. Majerus
Stage 3	Thursday 7 July	238 km	Saint-Brieuc – Nantes		G. Schulte (HOL)	J. Majerus
Stage 4 (1)	Friday 8 July	62 km	Nantes – La Roche-sur-Yon		E. Meulenberg (BEL)	J. Majerus
Stage 4 (2)	Friday 8 July	83 km	La Roche-sur-Yon – La Rochelle		E. Meulenberg (BEL)	J. Majerus
Stage 4 (3)	Friday 8 July	83 km	La Rochelle – Royan		F. Vervaecke (BEL)	J. Majerus
Stage 5	Sunday 10 July	198 km	Royan – Bordeaux		E. Meulenberg (BEL)	J. Majerus
Stage 6 (1)	Monday 11 July	52 km	Bordeaux – Arcachon		G.J. Rossi (ITA)	J. Majerus
Stage 6 (2)	Monday 11 July	171 km	Arcachon – Bayonne		G. Servadei (ITA)	A. Leducq
Stage 7	Tuesday 12 July	115 km	Bayonne – Pau		T. Middelkamp (HOL)	A. Leducq
Stage 8	Thursday 14 July	193 km	Pau – Luchon		F. Vervaecke (BEL)	F. Vervaecke
Stage 9	Saturday 16 July	260 km	Luchon – Perpignan		J. Fréchaut (FRA)	F. Vervaecke
Stage 10 (1)	Sunday 17 July	63 km	Perpignan – Narbonne		A. Van Schendel (HOL)	F. Vervaecke
Stage 10 (2)	Sunday 17 July	27 km	Narbonne – Béziers (TT)		F. Vervaecke (BEL)	F. Vervaecke
Stage 10 (3)	Sunday 17 July	73 km	Béziers – Montpellier		A. Magne (FRA)	F. Vervaecke
Stage 11	Monday 18 July	223 km	Montpellier – Marseille		G. Bartali (ITA)	F. Vervaecke
Stage 12	Tuesday 19 July	199 km	Marseille – Cannes		J. Fréchaut (FRA)	F. Vervaecke
Stage 13	Thursday 21 July	284 km	Cannes – Digne		D. Gianello (FRA)	F. Vervaecke
Stage 14	Friday 22 July	219 km	Digne – Briançon		G. Bartali (ITA)	G. Bartali
Stage 15	Saturday 23 July	311 km	Briançon – Aix-les-Bains		M. Kint (BEL)	G. Bartali
Stage 16	Monday 25 July	284 km	Aix-les-Bains – Besançon		M. Kint (BEL)	G. Bartali
Stage 17 (1)	Tuesday 26 July	89.5 km	Besançon – Belfort		E. Masson 'Junior' (BEL)	G. Bartali
Stage 17 (2)	Tuesday 26 July	143 km	Belfort – Strasbourg		J. Fréchaut (FRA)	G. Bartali
Stage 18	Wednesday 27 July	186 km	Strasbourg – Metz		M. Kint (BEL)	G. Bartali
Stage 19	Thursday 28 July	196 km	Metz – Reims		F. Galateau (FRA)	G. Bartali
Stage 20 (1)	Saturday 30 July	48 km	Reims – Laon		G. Servadei (ITA)	G. Bartali
Stage 20 (2)	Saturday 30 July	42 km	Laon – Saint-Quentin (TT)		F. Vervaecke (BEL)	G. Bartali
Stage 20 (3)	Saturday 30 July	107 km	Saint-Quentin – Lille		F. Neuville (BEL)	G. Bartali
Stage 21	Sunday 31 July	279 km	Lille – Paris		A. Leducq (FRA) & A. Magne (FRA)	G. Bartali

'We've both won,' Gino told his *directeur*, the old *Campionissimo* Girardengo (kissing him). 'I brought my muscles and my capacity for suffering and you, your wisdom and experience.'

Gino,
a *campionissimo*

'Before leaving for France, Costante Girardengo, our technical director, called a meeting to tell us his strategy. Depending on the result, the team would back Vicini, Cottur or Bartali. I don't think I commit the sin of pride when I say that I was sure he would play my card. And Girardengo himself repeatedly stated his belief that Italy would win the Tour with Bartali.

'The time bonuses awarded to the first rider over the summit of the mountain passes would dictate our race.

'I did my utmost to stay close to Sylvère Maes as far as Pau. There, I was eighteenth in the general classification, seven minutes behind Leducq, who I didn't consider a potential winner, four minutes behind Lowie, and three behind Vervaecke and Cosson. I had the same time as Vissers and was five minutes up on Sylvère Maes. On 14th July, we celebrated the French national holiday in our own way – it was the day of the Pau-Luchon stage with four mountain passes. This, in my opinion, is the most gruelling stage, because it's your first confrontation with the mountains. They are suddenly there in front of you; there's no gradual transition.

'Sticking to the strategy of the Italian national team, I didn't attack. But a kilometre (0.6 miles) from the Aubisque summit, I reflected that Gianello might jump me in the sprint. So I increased the pace slightly, and my rivals dropped off my wheel. I looked back. Vissers was 100 metres (328 feet) behind me. The others were nowhere to be seen. At the top, I was 40 seconds ahead according to Girardengo, who joined me in the tunnel before Argelès. I had just earned a 1min 40sec bonus and had carried out my plan to the letter.

'I made the descent gently and, one by one, Vissers, Berrendero, Vervaecke, Carini, Gallien and Gianello joined me. With no team-mates, it was in my interests to wait. Mollo reached us, but I was waiting for Vicini, of whom I had no news.

Yellow jersey on the road since the Col du Vars, Gino Bartali forced open the doors of legend on the Izoard, breaking away alone and completing an amazing feat.

Between Digne and Briançon, Bartali, seen leading Clemens and Vicini, showcased his talents as a climber, particularly on the Izoard, where he dispersed the last survivors.

On the Allos, the first col of the day, Bartali attacked and gained 1min 9secs over the Belgian rider Vissers, whose fellow countryman Vervaecke, the yellow jersey holder, was beginning to weaken.

Then, on the Vars, Gino, on the offensive, gained 1min 19secs on Cosson, who then suffered four punctures. Each one cost three minutes.

'Then, it was the Tourmalet. Halfway up the pass, there were only four of us left: Gianello, Vervaecke, Vissers and me. Gianello made several accelerations, but each time I caught him easily. Finally, just a kilometre (0.6 miles) from the top, I attacked, shaking off Gianello and then Vissers. Vervaecke stayed on my wheel, and I can still feel at my back his powerful, rhythmic breathing. I pushed hard, but he stuck close. Nine hundred metres from the top, he was still there. I sprinted and finally dropped him. I arrived at the top alone and plunged into the descent, still determined not to expend any energy in vain.

'In Sainte-Marie-de-Campan, Vervaecke,

Vissers and Gianello, my three shadows, were back. I got on their wheels and waited for the Aspin. Finally, I saw the *flame rouge*, the red flag that marks the last kilometre before the top of the passes, shifted into a high gear and sprinted, taking the lead alone. Head down, I hurtled down the descent. I was going to take 16 seconds from Vervaecke, for a 1min-16sec bonus. To recapitulate, I'd taken 1min 40secs on the Aubisque, 1min 15secs on the Tourmalet and 1min 16secs on the Aspin. That's a total of 4mins 11secs. I was already in the yellow jersey. On the descent, I did some thinking: one minute at the Peyresourde summit, one minute at the finish line, at least, and

I'd be leaving Luchon with a big lead.

'Some say I'm not prudent enough on the descents. Whatever the truth, I took a bend too sharply, skidded, broke my wheel and fell flat on my face. I got up, saw that I wasn't hurt, and thanked Heaven. I needed to change my wheel, which would cost me time, but I didn't get impatient, particularly since Jacques Goddet's car arrived and pulled to a halt. Jean Leulliot quickly handed me a wheel: I lost only 1min 40secs replacing it. Of course, while all this was happening Vervaecke and Vissers passed me by. My plan went out the window. All it would take now would be for one of them to take the time bonuses on the Peyresourde and at the finish and my lead would be reduced to nothing. I finished the Aspin descent less quickly. It's always the same. When you've just fallen, it's hard to fight off your fear. But I climbed Peyresourde quite easily, magnificently encouraged by the crowd. The French public really are wonderful.

'At Luchon, I had lost 55 seconds to Vervaecke and Vissers. This meant I'd regained 45 seconds on my two fellow competitors on the descent from Aspin and on the climb up the Peyresourde. But I had lost the jersey, which went to Félicien [Vervaecke] instead. At the stage start in Pau, I had been 3mins 57secs behind Vervaecke. By Luchon, even though I had accumulated an individual bonus of 4mins 11secs, I was still 2mins 18secs behind the leader and in second place. In a way, we had cancelled each other out. The next day consisted of three semi-stages: Perpignan to Narbonne, the Narbonne to Béziers time trial, and then Béziers to Montpellier.

Vervaecke and Cosson (left and right) smile at the 50,000 spectators in the Parc des Princes, while Gino (centre) gives thanks to Heaven, his scapular hanging from his pocket.

At the summit of the Iseran (2,769m [9,085ft], 10 percent gradient), Bartali, seen leading Kint, Magne and Cosson, limited Vervaecke's lead before the descent where, plummeting away after being hemmed in by the Belgian team, he caught him.

Vaervaecke beat me in the time trial fair and square. I hope no one thinks for an instant that it was this defeat that incites me to declare that the regulations governing the time trials need to be revised.

'We arrived in Cannes for the joy of a rest day. I met up with my father who had come over from Florence bringing news of home.

THE NEVER-ENDING ALPS

'If I had to name the toughest stage of the Tour, I would say it's the one between Cannes and Digne. I'm sure that will come as a surprise to many. The Sospel loop has already required a reputation as "a wicked piece of pedalling", in Leducq's words. But add to that 200 kilometres (124 miles) of false flat and you'll see that the effort is draining. In all honesty, I have to recognize that I found this stage from Cannes to Digne desperately boring. On the morning of 22 July, a date that will stay in my memory for a long time, I set out to win the yellow jersey that I'd missed in the Pyrenees. Or rather, that Saint Teresa had not wanted me to take over just yet.

'The Aubisque and the Tourmalet had convinced me that I was the best climber in the peloton and I also knew that only a crash could keep me from winning the Tour. I didn't need hypnosis to work that out; the facts alone had led me to the obvious conclusion.

'The Allos, the Vars and the Izoard represented three great opportunities for me; I had to exploit them. I was sure of my strength: nobody could get to the top ahead of me, except in the case of an accident. Was I sure that I wouldn't puncture? No; but my custom is not to fight the decisions of destiny. I had nothing to lose and everything to

gain. Girardengo and General Antonelli had already orchestrated the piece. I played my part to their tempo, without missing a note.

'From the lowest slopes of the Allos, I was part of the small group in the lead. After the red flag, I sprinted to shake off Vissers, the only rider still on my wheel, then took my first time bonus, with nine seconds on top. On the Vars, I increased the pace, not to open a big gap, but to have a clear advantage over the group at the top of the descent, where I played my trump card. For it was on the descent from the Vars that I won the Tour de France. Reading back through the reports of my win, I noted that at the top of the Vars I was 19secs up on Cosson, 31 up on Vicini, 46 up on Mollo and 118 up on Vervaecke. At Guillestre, at the bottom of the Vars descent, I was 7 minutes up on Vervaecke and 9 minutes up on Cosson. Work it out. You'll say: punctures. True, but it's forgotten that I punctured too and nobody gave me a wheel. I repaired it alone, then went after Vicini, who had passed me. So I believe I'm in the right to say I won the jersey on the descent from the Vars.

'Someone will object that I had to be in the lead at the top to descend without the handicap of the dust stirred up by the back-up vehicles. There's truth in that, too. On the Izoard, I dropped Mathias Clemens – a fine athlete I'm glad to recognize here – and my compatriots Mollo and Vicini. Girardengo had told me the jersey was mine. It's curious, but it gave me no joy. I had already exhausted that sweet surprise in the Pyrenees, and I knew that it was better to get to Briançon before celebrating.

'I could have been a complete bundle of nerves on the Izoard descent, at the mercy of

the slightest accident. Saying to myself that I was on the way to victory in the Tour and that I was at the mercy of the slightest accident, I could have thought of the melt-water at Digne, or my broken wheel the other day on the Aspin. But I didn't think at all. I plunged into the valley thinking only of the cool glass of milk that I'd asked Villa to have ready for me in my hotel room when I arrived. That is what was going through my mind when I achieved the dream of my life. But I won't dwell on that. I am sure you will have understood that, once my initial joy was past, a number of emotions were running high in our camp with five Italians among the first six... and the yellow jersey.

'Followers from Turin had flocked to Briançon in their thousands, and there was an explosion of excitement. General Antonelli hugged me and cried for joy, Girardengo was ecstatic and Villa sent telegraphs the length and breadth of Italy.

THE ISERAN COUP

'After all these friendly celebrations, I slept badly. I was anxious. I tossed and turned in bed without finding sleep until just three hours before the race was to start again. I was in a poor physical state. I told Girardengo, who advised me to try not to show it and not to chase if I was dropped. There were enough descents and flat sections from the summit of the Iseran to Aix-les-Bains to allow me to come back. But the truth is that I felt I was in inferior condition compared to the stage start at Digne. And you must now understand why I implore Mr. Desgrange to schedule a rest day in the Alps.

'On top of this, making a gentle ascent of the Galibier, I must have caught a slight cold. When I reached the Iseran, I grimaced: there was nothing I could do. I was beaten. I remembered Girardengo's advice and I didn't force the pace. However, on the descent from the Iseran I rode for all I was worth. Even before we reached the valley, I rejoined my opponents. They had ridden well, but you can't shake off a man who is out to win the yellow jersey and who knows that in eight days it will all be over. There's only one conclusion: I won my jersey descending from the Vars and defended it descending from the Iseran... in spite of which I won the prize as the best climber!

Sylvère, a final celebration before war

The absence of Italy, and therefore the reigning champion Bartali, and of Lapébie, the 1937 champion, due to an accident, left the Belgians Edward Vissers and Félicien Vervaecke as favourites for the 1939 Tour. With no German delegation, the organizers invited ten eight-man teams: two teams represented Belgium; France sent a national team plus four French regional formations; Luxembourg, the Netherlands and Switzerland completed the roster.

Following recent trends, six racing days were divided into two short semi-stages; on two days, three semi-stages were held. The Col d'Iseran hosted the Tour's first mountain time trial. Another innovation, the disqualification of the last-placed rider in the general classification, was applied only between stages two and seven; after a fall put the first yellow jersey of the 1939 Tour, Amédée Fournier, in last place, the rule was suspended, then forgotten for the rest of the Tour.

On day two, Fournier had handed his yellow jersey to 1935 champion Romain Maes for a matter of hours when Maes won the first time trial on day two. By the time the race reached the Pyrenees, however, Romain Maes had had enough; he abandoned exhausted on the time-trial stage to Pau, never to start another Tour. By then, the yellow jersey had been gracing René Vietto's shoulders for five days. Vietto had ridden for France in 1934 and 1935, as a *touriste-routier* in 1936 and for the France B team in 1938. Now on the regional South-East team, Vietto was hit by bronchitis in Royan, and was still suffering in the Pyrenees. On the stage from Pau to Toulouse, Vervaecke, Bartali's vanquisher in the Pyrenees a year earlier, was forced to abandon with back pain. His team-mate Edward Vissers rode alone for 200 kilometres (125 miles) to win the stage; four minutes later, Vietto and Sylvère Maes finished together.

It was a brilliant win, but over the gruelling Izoard, Vissers' team-mate Sylvère Maes took the yellow jersey, dropping Vissers by twelve minutes and finishing seventeen minutes ahead of Vietto. The following day Maes won the mountain time trial up the Iseran by a massive four minutes. Maes' twenty-seven-minute lead in the general classification was deserved and unassailable. At the finish in Paris, Maes had won the general classification, the mountains competition, and improved the average speed to 31.994 kph (19.89 mph).

GENERAL CLASSIFICATION

1. **Sylvère Maes** (BEL) Belgium, 4,225 km in 132h.3m.17s; Average speed: 31.994 kph
2. René Vietto (FRA) South-East, at 30m.38s.
3. Lucien Vlaemynck (BEL) Belgium B, at 32m.8s.
4. Mathias Clemens (LUX) Luxembourg, at 36m.9s.
5. Edward Vissers (BEL) Belgium, at 38m.5s.
6. Sylvain Marcaillou (FRA) France, at 45m.16s.
7. Albertin Disseaux (BEL) Belgium B, at 46m.54s.
8. Jan Lambrichs (HOL) Holland, at 48m.1s.
9. Albert Ritserveldt (BEL) Belgium B, at 48m.27s.
10. Cyriel Vanoverberghe (BEL) Belgium B at 49m.44s.
11. Dante Gianello (FRA) France, at 55m.55s.
12. Raymond Passat (FRA) South-West at 57m.23s.
13. Auguste Mallet (FRA) France, at 1h.2m.5s.
14. M. Archambaud (FRA) North-East-Île-de-France, at 1h.6m.24s.
15. Albert Van Schendel (HOL) Holland, at 1h.10m.1s.
16. P. Gallien (FRA) North-East-Île-de-France, at 1h.10m.22s.
17. L. Thietard (FRA) North-East-Île-de-France, at 1h.13m.33s.
18. Christophe Didier (LUX) Luxembourg, at 1h.19m.7s.
19. Georges Naisse (FRA) France, at 1h.23m.53s.
20. Pierre Clemens (LUX) Luxembourg, at 1h.24m.48s.

33RD TOUR DE FRANCE
18 STAGES - 4,225 KM

			STAGE	STAGE WINNER	YELLOW JERSEY
Stage 1	Monday 10 July	215 km	Paris – Caen	A. Fournier (FRA)	A. Fournier
Stage 2 (1)	Tuesday 11 July	63.5 km	Caen – Vire (TT)	R. Maes (BEL)	R. Maes
Stage 2 (2)	Tuesday 11 July	119.5 km	Vire – Rennes	E. Tassin (FRA)	J. Fontenay
Stage 3	Wednesday 12 July	244 km	Rennes – Brest	P. Cloarec (FRA)	J. Fontenay
Stage 4	Thursday 13 July	174 km	Brest – Lorient	R. Louviot (FRA)	R. Vietto
Stage 5	Friday 14 July	207 km	Lorient – Nantes	A. Fournier (FRA)	R. Vietto
Stage 6 (1)	Saturday 15 July	144 km	Nantes – La Rochelle	L. Storme (BEL)	R. Vietto
Stage 6 (2)	Saturday 15 July	107 km	La Rochelle – Royan	E. Pages (FRA)	R. Vietto
Stage 7	Monday 17 July	198 km	Royan – Bordeaux	R. Passat (FRA)	R. Vietto
Stage 8 (1)	Tuesday 18 July	210.5 km	Bordeaux – Salies-de-Béarn	M. Kint (BEL)	R. Vietto
Stage 8 (2)	Tuesday 18 July	68.5 km	Salies-de-Béarn – Pau (TT)	K. Litschi (SUI)	R. Vietto
Stage 9	Wednesday 19 July	311 km	Pau – Toulouse	E. Vissers (BEL)	R. Vietto
Stage 10 (1)	Friday 21 July	148.5 km	Toulouse – Narbonne	P. Jaminet (FRA)	R. Vietto
Stage 10 (2)	Friday 21 July	27 km	Narbonne – Béziers (TT)	M. Archambaud (FRA)	R. Vietto
Stage 10 (3)	Friday 21 July	70.5 km	Béziers – Montpellier	M. Archambaud (FRA)	R. Vietto
Stage 11	Saturday 22 July	212 km	Montpellier – Marseille	F. Galateau (FRA)	R. Vietto
Stage 12 (1)	Sunday 23 July	157 km	Marseille – Saint-Raphaël	F. Neuens (LUX)	R. Vietto
Stage 12 (2)	Sunday 23 July	121.5 km	Saint-Raphaël – Monaco	M. Archambaud (FRA)	R. Vietto
Stage 13	Monday 24 July	101.5 km	Monaco – Monaco	P. Gallien (FRA)	R. Vietto
Stage 14	Tuesday 25 July	175 km	Monaco – Digne	P. Cloarec (FRA)	R. Vietto
Stage 15	Wednesday 26 July	219 km	Digne – Briançon	S. Maes (BEL)	S. Maes
Stage 16 (1)	Thursday 27 July	126 km	Briançon – Bonneval-sur-Arc	P. Jaminet (FRA)	S. Maes
Stage 16 (2)	Thursday 27 July	64.5 km	Bonneval-sur-Arc – Bourg-St-Maurice (TT)	S. Maes (BEL)	S. Maes
Stage 16 (3)	Thursday 27 July	103.5 km	Bourg-St-Maurice – Annecy	A. Van Schendel (HOL)	S. Maes
Stage 17 (1)	Saturday 29 July	226 km	Annecy – Dole	F. Neuens (LUX)	S. Maes
Stage 17 (2)	Saturday 29 July	59 km	Dole – Dijon (TT)	M. Archambaud (FRA)	S. Maes
Stage 18 (1)	Sunday 30 July	151 km	Dijon – Troyes	R. Le Grevès (FRA)	S. Maes
Stage 18 (2)	Sunday 30 July	201 km	Troyes – Paris	M. Kint (BEL)	S. Maes

Followed by the car carrying Leducq, now a journalist, Sylvère Maes
reaches the summit of the Izoard. He'd forewarned his opponents
of this devastating ride which placed him among the greats.

A victory for Maes and the Tour

Sylvère has won. For five days, we've known it. Since the first twisted hairpin that, as you turn, marks the sudden, brutal gradient of the Izoard. There, in an instant, Vietto, gaunt and intoxicated with his impotence, paid for his vain defiance of nature's laws. And, despite our sorrow, it seems more just this way, for today, as yesterday, it is Sylvère Maes whom we celebrate. Not just the vivid, vigorous man himself (despite calves as flat as a Breton crêpe and shoulders that scarcely stretch beyond the limits of his jaw), but the qualities he represents, qualities without which the Tour will spurn you and

slip out of your grasp. He doses his energies well, by all accounts. But one must prepare for the Tour, reject life's pleasures, its ease and comfort. Maes rejected the marvellous heritage of those Flemish farmers, hardy by upbringing; that is even better. One must observe the discipline of those three weeks of racing for months, that's the truth of the Tour. And, still more, one must obey. For this enormous battle opposes not just athletes, but also methods and systems. When a greater authority emerges, official with Monsieur Fernand Adant, spiritual with Karel Steyaert, to distribute roles, you have

to be able to accept a year of servitude in order, the following year, to be served. In 1938, Sylvère wore the livery of a lackey and polished the boots of his black-clad Belgian team-mates. This year, as in 1936, Sylvère Maes wore the tunic of the master. Yet the most striking thing about this fine Tour de France is that the protégé of Mr. Gentil and Ludovic Feuillet managed to win without the help of his team. Not that his team did not do its duty, but Vissers, the only man who could really have helped his leader, had earned, with his fabulous performance in the Pyrenees, a degree of freedom.

A man of few words, Sylvère Maes takes advantage of a Belgian radio reporter to greet his wife in Flemish, and to tell her to serve the beers at their bar, the 'Tourmalet' in Ghistelles.

INNOVATION: THE MOUNTAIN TIME TRIAL
BY JEAN LEULLIOT

BONNEVAL (27 July): It was the first time that a time trial had been staged in the high mountains. What was the verdict? That it was, in principle, a success, but, like all innovations, it requires some improvements. To realize its full significance and role, it might be better if the finish-line were fixed at 15 or 20 kilometres (9 to 12 miles), at most, and on a climb. This would avoid the bunching that inevitably occurs on a slight descent or when there is too much flat road. But who could put into words the suffering inherent in a race against the clock in the mountains? Who could make it comprehensible to people who have never climbed a mountain pass? The physical effort required simply to climb a pass is considerable. The heart beats so fast you feel it's going to burst. Breathing is hard, and breathing becomes increasingly noisy and rapid. Your temples are squeezed in a vice and your legs tremble. But you have to keep on and on, without a moment's respite. Add to that the freezing currents of mountain air that alternate with layers of warm air and make you shiver as if you had a fever. It's a terrifying effort, without compare. Witness Maes, Vissers, Marcaillou, Mallet, Vanoverberghe, and many others, who climbed the 13 kilometres (8 miles) of the Iseran out of the saddle the entire time. They were so tired after this part of the stage that none of them had the strength, or the will, to attack on the Col de Tamié where, previously, someone has almost always broken away.

On the prearranged day and at the appointed hour, in the great alpine stage, Sylvère Maes (bare-headed) arrives right on time. The French are split, but Maes was supported by two compatriots: Vissers, the favourite, is leading, Ritserveldt is moving onto his wheel.

The other three survivors on the team contributed their help only on rare occasions, although these proved very useful. Kint's punch, Neuville's robust health and Hendrickx's loyalty constituted an adequate barricade. Lyautey said that a demonstration of strength is sufficient in order not to have to use it. Even this strategy was not needed by the Belgians this month. Sylvère's Tour was made still more individual by the large number of time trials, and finally and above all by the fact that the mountains this year completely isolated the leading riders from their team-mates. We even witnessed a fratricidal struggle between Maes and Vissers from the Tourmalet to Toulouse!

Maes, a citizen of Ghistelles, commandingly won the Tour de France. He'll share his direct takings with the other men in black.

Finally, the most important question in the aftermath of a Tour de France won in the same conditions and at the same place as the previous Tour is: 'Isn't there just one way of winning the Tour, and just one system?'

As long as the Belgian team has climbers, and strong climbers, it will adopt, broadly speaking, the method that brought it victory yesterday. But our marvellous friend Karel Steyaert acknowledged how difficult it is to read a race when he said to me: 'This year, we made no mistake regarding Vietto's potential. But last year, right up to the last pass, right up to that terrible Izoard, we thought that Bartali would crack...'

The truth varies with the identity of the riders. What can be appreciated, thanks to the Tour, is that the riders need to love the ordeal they have undertaken to be able to accept everything that it throws at them: the changes, the setbacks and the snubs as well as the joy, the good fortune and the bouquets that success brings.

THE TOUR DE FRANCE IN TWENTY WRITERS
BY HENRI TROYAT (PRIX GONCOURT 1938)

Every day, a different writer recounts his experience of the Tour. They include Mac Orlan, Fayard, Scize, Dereme, Coolus, Tristan Bernard and Henri Jeanson:

There are sports events that resemble pretty women. First you love them with passion, and later with affection, and it's then that they become most indispensable to us. Today, it's with affection that I love the Tour de France. An affection that is lasting, warm and tender. I like the idea that, as the holidays approach, a pure subject of enthusiasm is offered to spirits wearied by the doleful drumbeat of political events. On the front pages of the newspapers headlines promising invasions, mobilizations and massacres, are replaced by the welcome announcement of the Tour de France.

Images of government ministers, their brows furrowed with anxiety, dictators with disturbing moustaches and monumental jaws, and criminals, retail and wholesale, part before the image of a rider, his eyes wide like a fish from the depths of the ocean balanced on the weightless glint of his bicycle. Behind him lies a peaceful landscape of plains, or a backdrop of sugar-loaf mountains, or some corner of a village. He is roasted by the sun, or beaten by the rain. His name matters little. He is a cyclist, and that is enough. Tomorrow, we will see him prostrate at the side of the road, beside his broken bike. The day after, we recognize him in a portrait, his head thrown back, his Adam's apple bulging, drinking from his bidon while steering with one hand. Later, we will see him again, pushing his way through a forest of raised arms and yelling faces as he races towards the triumphal banner across the finishing line.

Days pass, and this group of men, powering along the roads of France, carry in their wake the enthusiastic camaraderie of the regions through which they pass. The Tour de France is an armistice called before the gathering storm.

The ersatz tours

Due to war, restrictions, patriotism, and then post-War restructuring, no Tour de France was organized between 1939 and 1947. Despite the consent of the occupying forces, Jacques Goddet regarded the Tour, a symbol of 'peace in July', as too powerful and too susceptible of appropriation by the enemies of France, to allow it to be held. Henri Desgrange would not have done it: why should his spiritual son? Elsewhere, other Tours went ahead: the Tours of Switzerland, Spain and Italy. French riders took part there. But in France there were only 'Circuits de France', 'Rondes de France', miniature or rationed Tours. Just as swedes and artichoke replaced the potato, and cars ran on natural gas rather than petrol, there were ersatz Tours de France, which had the merit of keeping the embers glowing beneath the ashes.

The crisis began on 24 August 1939 when the Circuit de L'Ouest in Lorient, Brittany was called to a halt. The race had completed just five of its eight scheduled stages. The Belgian Albéric Schotte was declared the winner, thanks to the growing crisis which culminated with Hitler's invasion of Poland on 1 September. French troops were mobilized the following day and France declared war on Germany on 3 September at 5 pm.

It was through *L'Auto-Soldat* (first edition dated 16 September) that we learn that the Union de Cyclisme Internationale (UCI) had ratified the results of the Tour, that half of the 900,000 francs in prize money had been dispatched to Belgium, and that René Vietto had visited the journal's offices in the Faubourg, the first to collect his winnings. We also

The first and only edition of the Circuit de France was only 1,515 km (941 miles) instead of the planned 1,650 km (1,025 miles). It was just as well, or the gas-powered back-up vehicle would have broken down even more.

learned about the appearance of the term 'Kraut' instead of 'Boche', and the enlistment of Maye, Leducq, Magne, Archambaud, Degy and Cloarec as cook, cyclist, chauffeur, artilleryman, explosives expert, etc. The last giants of the Thirties would be fighting on all fronts in this war. Robert Oubron (20th in 1937, 41st in 1938) became a light infantryman, allowing him to capture, at the beginning of December, Kurt Stoepel, the runner-up behind Leducq in 1932! At the same moment, in Brussels, the UCI issued the dates for the 1940 Tour. It was to run from 26 June to 21 July, with four major summits and the route taking an easterly direction, although it would coincide with the Tour of Germany! Expressing absolute disgust at this devious ruse by Hitler, to whom he referred to as 'the house painter', Desgrange retired and refused to countenance a 34th Tour. Meanwhile, the parents of 1939's riders reported to the offices of *L'Auto* to collect their sons' prize money and, like Mme Archambaud, return the organization's suitcase and rain cape so that the cost of these wouldn't be deducted from the cheque. Deprived of his beloved competition, Desgrange fell ill and died in 1940.

Competition slowly recommenced. In 1941, Dante Gianello won the Critérium du Midi, and in mid-July 1942, the 25th edition of the race, held over four stages, was won by Louis Gauthier, a former miner. Around the same time, Kubler rode brilliantly in the Swiss Tour, where Egli, seen hitching a lift in a car, was disqualified. Jacques Goddet kept the flame alive by inviting the 100,000 readers of *L'Auto* to vote for a fantasy French team to ride a fantasy 1942 Tour de France. As there was no Tour, he maintained contact with the Aspin and the Tourmalet with a one-stage Grand Prix des Pyrénées, which was won by Eugène Galliussi, who also won the Circuit du Mont Ventoux. But the big race, involving the major French manufacturers (Génial, Dilecta, Helyett, Alcyon, Mercier and France-Sport), was organized by La France Socialiste and Jean Leulliot. It was held between 28 September and 4 October, covering over 1,650 kilometres (1,025 miles) divided into six stages, from Paris to Paris, via Le Mans, Poitiers, Limoges, Clermont, Saint-Étienne, Lyon and Dijon. Sixty-nine riders were taken aback by rain, cold, poor food and accommodation (in seminaries), punctures, makeshift night-time arrivals, and the neutralization of the border between occupied and free France. President Laval endorsed its organization, despite the victory of the Belgian François Neuville, but in Goddet's words, 'We barely avoided disaster'. Goddet patiently continued with his popular fantasy Tour de France in 1943, while planning a

Neither the Circuit de France, in 1942, nor the Ronde de France, in 1946, could replace the Tour, despite the beautiful poster designs of Cello and Paul Ordner.

Grand Prix du Tour de France with stages chosen in relation to the classic Tours. The first edition was won by Jo Goutorbe; the second, in 1944, went to Belgium's Maurice De Simpelaere.

But with the end of the conflict on 8 May 1945, the big year of the rebirth would really be 1946. A truncated Tour of Italy saw Bartali dominate Coppi and then win the Tour of Switzerland. The president of the new French Cycling Federation, Achille Joinard, had no Tour de France, for *L'Auto* had published during the occupation and was now suppressed, and its successor, *L'Equipe*, was not yet *persona grata*.

Francis Pélissier joined the management of team La Perle, Georges Géminiani rode superbly in the Circuit des Six Provinces won by Georges Martin, Pierre Molinéris won the Grand Prix du Vercors, and René Vietto, always enamoured of uncompromising racing, made sparks fly on the Ventoux-Méditerranée, even if he had lost a little of his sparkle. In any case, he had trained a pupil named Apo Lazaridès, an aspiring youngster of 20, who, in a Ronde de France between Bordeaux and Grenoble, saved French honour in the Alps (as Raymond Louviot had in Montpellier) after a 300-kilometre (186-mile) breakaway that saw him reach Grenoble with a nine-minute lead. It wasn't enough to catch the Italians Giulio Breschi and Ezio Bertocchi who, broken in by the Giro, had taken a decisive lead over the first two stages, for, in accordance with the restriction regulations, there were only five stages (10–14 July). The Ronde was organized by *Ce Soir*, which, with its eye on the Tour de France, was keen to show the public authorities its organizational capacities.

This ruling also affected the Course du Tour de France, organized by the Parc des Princes and the *Parisien Libéré*, again with an eye to the Tour. Run from 23 to 28 July from Monaco to Paris via the Alps, it was a partial return to the past, with regional and national teams. The old rivalry between Jean-Marie Goasmat and Vietto was continued through their pupils, the former counting on Jean Robic, the latter, handicapped by a saddle sore after a fabulous win between Digne and Briançon, backing Apo Lazaridès. In the Parc des Princes, revisited at last, Apo wore the first yellow jersey of the renaissance, despite terrible stomach pains.

The last stage of the race saw the return of Steyaert, Fernand Paul, Ronsse, Gyssels and Romain Maes as apprentice journalists. Vietto came in second as in the 1939 Tour, but with Frenchmen like Apo, Teisseire, Cogan, Piot and Fachleitner, he proclaimed: 'We will be unbeatable next year. And if the Tour escapes us, I'll start pedalling a sewing machine.' France was once again ready for the real Tour to begin.

Liberation at last

Ever since he fractured his skull at the Paris-Roubaix classic, Jean Robic wore a leather helmet from which his two cabbage ears protruded. He was no Adonis and his rivals used to call him 'Biquet', a sarcastic term of endearment meaning 'Lovey', or 'Ducky', or 'Sweetie-Pie'! This ridiculous soubriquet fitted Robic, in a strange, inverted way: he was bellicose, obstinate, and taunted the big names of the peloton in his Breton brogue: 'Bobet? Bartali? I've got one in each leg!' He was only joking, of course. But he was never more serious than when he was joking. On 2 July 1947, his team-mates on the regional team from West France tipped René Vietto, already in the yellow jersey since stage two, for overall victory. Biquet flew into a rage, launched a blistering attack in the Chartreuse and won the stage at Grenoble by nearly five minutes.

When Vietto responded by storming over the Izoard and winning at Digne, Robic, held up by a puncture on the descent from the Col de Vars, wasn't downhearted. 'I feel unstoppable,' he trumpeted, and immediately lost the support of his team, just as the race reached the Pyrenees. 'If he's so strong, he can manage by himself,' complained his team-mate Eloi Tassin. More alone than ever, Robic dropped Vietto and Brambilla on

the Peyresourde and covered the remaining 190 kilometres (119 miles) on his own. The tea towel flapping round his neck to avoid sunstroke made him look like a Tuareg tribesman.

By the time he reached Pau, eleven minutes before Vietto and with an armful of time bonuses, he had gained fifteen minutes on the yellow jersey. Vietto was holding on by the skin of his teeth; he finally lost the yellow jersey to Italy's Pierre Brambilla on the time trial, two days before the Paris finale. Robic lay fifty-three seconds behind. Stage twenty passed without incident. There was one more stage to go, and it was pure theatre. Robic opened the hostilities just outside Rouen, on the Bonsecours climb. France's Édouard Fachleitner chased across to him and piled on the pressure. Brambilla failed to react and the gap grew. Robic, entirely at ease, made his compatriot an offer. 'You can't win the Tour, Fach, because I won't let you go. So let's ride together and I'll give you 100,000 francs...'

At Paris, Robic's victory came as a huge surprise to the massive crowds gathered to greet the race. Under the direction of Jacques Goddet, who had taken over from Henri Desgrange, Jean Robic, 'Biquet', had won the Tour of the Liberation, the biggest Tour of all. All without ever having worn the yellow jersey.

GENERAL CLASSIFICATION

1. **Jean Robic** (FRA) West
   4,642 km in 148h.11m.25s; Average speed 31.412 kph
2. **Édouard Fachleitner** (FRA) France, at 3m.58s.
3. **Pierre Brambilla** (ITA) Italy, at 10m.7s.
4. Aldo Ronconi (ITA) Italy, at 11m.
5. René Vietto (FRA) France, at 15m.23s
6. Raymond Impanis (BEL) Belgium, at 18m.14s.
7. Fermo Camellini (ITA) Holland-Mixed, at 24m.8s.
8. Giordano Cottur (ITA) Italy, at 1h.6m.3s.
9. Jean-Marie Goasmat (FRA) West, at 1h.16m.3s.
10. Jean-Apôtre 'Apo' Lazaridès (FRA) South-East, at 1h.18m.44s.
11. Lucien Teisseire (FRA) France, at 1h.32m.16s.
12. Pierre Cogan (FRA) West, at 1h.44m.55s.
13. Albéric 'Brik' Schotte (BEL) Belgium, at 1h.56m.45s.
14. Giuseppe Tacca (ITA) Italy, at 2h.05m.7s.
15. Jean 'Bim' Diederich (LUX) Switz-Lux, at 2h.10m.43s.
16. Daniel Thuayre (FRA) Ile-de-France, at 2h.13m.4s.
17. Gottfried Weilenmann (SUI) Switz-Lux, at 2h.18m.23s.
18. Jean Kirchen (LUX) Switz-Lux, at 2h.20m.26s.
19. Paul Giguet (FRA) South-East, at 2h.26m.25s.
20. Jean Goldschmit (LUX) Switz-Lux, at 2h.32m.24s.

34TH TOUR DE FRANCE, 21 STAGES – 4,642 KM

			STAGE	STAGE WINNER	YELLOW JERSEY
Stage 1	Wednesday 25 June	236 km	Paris – Lille	F. Kübler (SUI)	F. Kübler
Stage 2	Thursday 26 June	182 km	Lille – Bruxelles (BEL)	R. Vietto (FRA)	R. Vietto
Stage 3	Friday 27 June	314 km	Bruxelles (BEL) – Luxembourg (LUX)	A. Ronconi (ITA)	R. Vietto
Stage 4	Saturday 28 June	223 km	Luxembourg (LUX) – Strasbourg	J. Robic (FRA)	R. Vietto
Stage 5	Sunday 29 June	248 km	Strasbourg – Besançon	F. Kubler (SUI)	R. Vietto
Stage 6	Tuesday 1 July	249 km	Besançon – Lyon	L. Teisseire (FRA)	R. Vietto
Stage 7	Wednesday 2 July	172 km	Lyon – Grenoble	J. Robic (FRA)	A. Ronconi
Stage 8	Thursday 3 July	185 km	Grenoble – Briançon	F. Camellini (ITA)	A. Ronconi
Stage 9	Saturday 5 July	217 km	Briançon – Digne	R. Vietto (FRA)	R. Vietto
Stage 10	Sunday 6 July	255 km	Digne – Nice	F. Camellini (ITA)	R. Vietto
Stage 11	Tuesday 8 July	230 km	Nice – Marseille	É. Fachleitner (FRA)	R. Vietto
Stage 12	Wednesday 9 July	165 km	Marseille – Montpellier	H. Massal (FRA)	R. Vietto
Stage 13	Thursday 10 July	172 km	Montpellier – Carcassonne	L.Teisseire (FRA)	R. Vietto
Stage 14	Friday 11 July	253 km	Carcassonne – Luchon	A. Bourlon (FRA)	R. Vietto
Stage 15	Sunday 13 July	195 km.	Luchon – Pau	J. Robic (FRA)	R. Vietto
Stage 16	Monday 14 July	195 km	Pau – Bordeaux	G. Tacca (FRA)	R. Vietto
Stage 17	Tuesday 15 July	272 km	Bordeaux – Les Sables-d'Olonne	E. Tassin (FRA)	R. Vietto
Stage 18	Wednesday 16 July	236 km	Les Sables-d'Olonne – Vannes	P. Tarchini (FRA)	R. Vietto
Stage 19	Friday 18 July	139 km	Vannes – Saint-Brieuc (TT)	R. Impanis (BEL)	P. Brambilla
Stage 20	Saturday 19 July	235 km	Saint-Brieuc– Caen	M. Diot (FRA)	P. Brambilla
Stage 21	Sunday 20 July	257 km	Caen – Paris	A. Schotte (BEL)	J. Robic

In the intense heat of 1947's summer the peloton takes a pit-stop to drink, wash and cool down.

Jean Robic, King of the Pyrenees

PAU: In a cool old house, passing through interminable corridors, we reach the room in which masseur Julien is working on Fermo Camellini. All the leaders in the general classification arrived together at Pau, although they had fought each other mercilessly in the high mountains. All, that is, except Fermo Camellini, who, from his 2min-11sec deficit on Vietto, dropped tonight to 14mins 46secs. The man with the drawn features and sunken eyes on the massage table has a pained, distant look. We imagine him again on the ochre road to the Soulor, his legs heavy, greedily gorging on the water he was offered, his powerful breathing like a blacksmith's bellows. 'I couldn't see clearly any more and I was knocked over twice by the follow-up cars that passed too close,' he said. He showed us his stomach. 'It hurts, it's burning,' he added, to complete his inventory of tribulations. And yet, grimacing in pain as the alcohol stung his skin, he was disappointed: 'It's a shame we've passed the Pyrenees.' The mountains had delivered their verdict. Gradients will play no further role in the result. And Camellini, today's big loser, has plenty of reasons for regret.

Vietto, Brambilla, Ronconi, Fachleitner and Robic, dispersed over eight minutes, have reason not to consider the race over. The verdict of the Pyrenees is open to appeal. 'I need an old-style Tour de France,' René Vietto told us, 'with long stages. I don't start easily. I dread the short stages.' Nonetheless, he preserved his yellow jersey, although even he doubted he'd hold on to it on the Tourmalet, when he informed Léo Véron that he wanted Fachleitner to launch a big attack, 'to the death!' in his own words. From now on, he can count on the devoted support of the entire French team. Although we shouldn't dismiss the danger coming from the Italian or Breton quarter, we have to say that the French are likely to bring their leader into Paris victorious.

After 78 kilometres (48 miles) of the stage, Robic led over the Tourmalet, 4mins 28secs ahead of Brambilla, and 12 minutes ahead of Vietto. This magnificent feat laid the foundations of his overall success.

In 30 kilometres, Jean Robic seizes the jersey from Brambilla

It was too much! This astonishing Tour had already drained us of our stocks of emotions and our stocks of superlatives, only, on this final day, to push against the very limits of fantasy. We announced that there was bound to be a battle, that the jersey really could change hands and that the last kilometres would count for as much as an entire mountain stage. We believed it, of course, but we thought that tradition would be stronger, that the riders' energy would diminish in the face of the cheering crowds, or that Brambilla would rather die on the spot than allow himself to be overthrown by anyone...

But a tiny Breton, fierce, stubborn, doubting nothing, least of all his own capabilities, wanted to win the Tour, and never gave up hope of doing so. A plan had been drawn up, but he took no notice of it and took off at the first opportunity, obeying only his violent impetus, tearing the jersey from Brambilla's back in scarcely 30 kilometres (18.6 miles). From then on, he ruled the Tour. A unique feat, unforgettable, crowning a Tour like no other. It all started on the road out of Rouen. Barely had the riders started climbing the Côte de Bonsecours when Robic attacked. Then, performing his duty, Brambilla extracted his yellow jersey from the peloton, chest heaving, already defeated, and made an extraordinary effort to catch his opponent. But then a third man appeared. Just where the gradient was steepest, he rocketed past his two rivals like a racing car. It was Fachleitner, a stupefying Fachleitner, exceptional, like a spirit of the air, marvellous and powerful. He covered the steep slope at a sprint. How did Robic have enough punch left to chase him, you wonder! Grimacing, 'Biquet' accelerated in desperation and jumped on this providential wheel. He had just won the Tour!

Fachleitner and Breton were riding at speeds the like of which we've never seen before on the road, knocking back the kilometres at nearly 50 kph (31 mph), Brambilla had to pay for his earlier efforts. His collapse was tragic and pitiful.

Brambilla was being brutally punished for his brave attempts over the last three weeks to steal victory. But his defeat, which in his honest simplicity he didn't attempt to excuse in any way, was touched by the sublime: it was Brambilla who, for the most part, made this the greatest and best of the Tours de France.

The Tour also says thank you to René Vietto, although he had condemned his team-mates to mere servitude since Brussels. Fachleitner's lamentable attitude in the blazingly hot stage from Brussels to Luxembourg later justified trading the chances of a rider without great character for those of a brilliant champion, passionate about the Tour. Aside from these riders who triumphed over the pitfalls and the difficulties of the route; aside from Robic, a winner who seized his victory head-on and held it tight, there is another magnificent winner: the Tour itself. Yet again, words are meaningless when confronted with the welcome that the people of France extended to the Tour. Desgrange's dream for the Tour has been magnified: to entertain and to demonstrate through the example of a sincere sporting battle, that man can endure anything, and overcome any obstacle, to attain his goal.

2 3

1. The attack by Robic (left) on the Côte de Bonsecours was fatal for Brambilla and Ronconi. Teisseire and Fachleitner (leading) fared rather better.

2. The Italian Pierre Brambilla chats and smiles with Italian journalists before the start of the fateful final stage.

3. In intense heat, the riders rush for refreshment as race officials attempt to organize them.

4. Luchon to Pau: The Tour narrowly avoided a catastrophe when three kilometres (1.8 miles) from the summit of the Tourmalet, a plane belonging to L'Équipe crashed into the road just before the peloton arrived (led by Vietto, weakening). Only the pilot, Georges de Seversky, was hurt and had to be hospitalized.

5. Lille to Brussels: After a 180-kilometre (112-mile) breakaway, Vietto rode the closing half an hour at 47 kph (29 mph), an incredible speed that sent this motorcycle and sidecar spinning out of control.

6. Robic fulfilled his dream by taking the Tour. At the Parc des Princes, he shared his joy with his wife.

4

5 6

Bartali, ten years later

By 1948, Bartali was 34. Ten years had passed since he had won the Tour de France. His hair was receding, he was less talkative and the war had robbed him of some of his best years. Bartali had used the Giro d'Italia as preparation for the Tour, and had finished eighth.

By the end of stage twelve, Bartali lay 21mins 20secs behind the race leader, a brilliant young Frenchman named Bobet, universally known as Louison. True, the Italian had won Lourdes, and had prayed before the Virgin's shrine there. He was convinced that divine assistance would come, unlike the Italian press corps, which packed its bags and left.

The following day was a rest day for the riders. In Italy, Domenico Pallante, a slightly-built Sicilian packing a Smith and Wesson, decided that it would be a rest day of a more definitive kind for Palmiro Togliatti, the chairman of Italy's powerful Communist Party. At 11.30 that morning, before he could be overpowered, Pallante fired four bullets into Togliatti's neck, spleen and close to his heart. He was rushed to hospital in critical condition. By late afternoon, Italy was paralysed by a General Strike. At night, there were disturbances; some feared civil war was only hours away.

At 6am the following morning, with Italy in crisis, the Tour resumed. By 3.30pm Bartali was soaring over the Col d'Izoard, the highest and steepest climb of the day, more than 18 minutes ahead of Bobet. At 4.29, Bobet crossed the line. Bartali now lay second overall, 51secs behind the yellow jersey. Italy, instead of fighting in the streets, had gathered around its wirelesses. The following day, newsflashes kept the nation informed of Bartali's progress. At 8.30am, crossing the Col du Lauteret, he trailed Bobet by 20secs. On the Galibier, both riders attacked. Not an inch separated them as they wrestled over the next 80 kilometres, perfectly matched. At the summit of the Croix-de-Fer, Bartali had clawed back just two seconds. Then, leaving Grenoble, Bobet cracked. On the Col de Porte, Bartali had a lead of 6mins 37secs. By the time he reached Aix-les-Bains, his lead over Bobet in the general classification was 8mins 3secs.

Italy was ecstatic. On Saturday 17 July, the Communist newspaper *L'Unità* called off the general strike. Over the page, it carried a dry account of the ultra-Catholic Bartali's victories. At hospital in Rome, Togliatti was stable, and awake, and asked his son for news of the Tour de France. Bartali won a third consecutive stage from Aix to Lausanne; at Liège six days later, he won his seventh stage of the Tour and extended his overall lead to 26mins 16 secs. Cycling had worked its healing power.

GENERAL CLASSIFICATION

1. **Gino Bartali** (ITA) Italy, 4,922 km in 147h.10m.36s; Average speed 33.404 kph
2. **Albéric 'Brik' Schotte** (BEL) Belgium, at 26m.16s.
3. **Guy Lapébie** (FRA) South-West-Central, at 28m.48s.
4. Louison Bobet (FRA) France, at 32m.59s.
5. Jean Kirchen (LUX) Holland-Luxembourg, at 37m.53s.
6. Lucien Teisseire (FRA) France, at 39m.57s.
7. Roger Lambrecht (BEL) International, at 49m.56s.
8. Fermo Camellini (ITA) International, at 51m.36s.
9. Louis Thiétard (FRA) Paris, at 55m.23s.
10. Raymond Impansi (BEL) Belgium, at 1h.0m.3s.
11. Constant 'Stan' Ockers (BEL) Belgium, at 1h.0m.13s.
12. André Brulé (FRA) Paris, at 1h.2m.30s.
13. Kléber Piot (FRA) Paris, at 1h.24m.28s.
14. Edward Van Dyck (BEL) Belgium, at 1h.32m.13s.
15. Raphaël Geminiani (FRA) South-West-Central, at 1h.39m.49s.
16. Jean Robic (FRA) France, at 1h.41m.26s.
17. René Vietto (FRA) France, at 1h.42m.48s.
18. Édouard Klabinsky (FRA) International, at 1h.45m.30s.
19. Bruno Pasquni (ITA) Italy, at 1h.48m.50s.
20. Marcel Dupont (BEL) Belgium B, at 1h.59m.47s.

35TH TOUR DE FRANCE, 21 STAGES – 4,922 KM

			STAGE	STAGE WINNER	YELLOW JERSEY
Stage 1	Wednesday 30 June	237 km	Paris – Trouville	G. Bartali (ITA)	G. Bartali
Stage 2	Thursday 1 July	259 km	Trouville – Dinard	V. Rossello (ITA)	J. Engels
Stage 3	Friday 2 July	251 km	Dinard – Nantes	G. Lapébie (FRA)	L. Bobet
Stage 4	Saturday 3 July	166 km	Nantes – La Rochelle	J. Pras (FRA)	R. Lambrecht
Stage 5	Sunday 4 July	262 km	La Rochelle – Bordeaux	R. Rémy (FRA)	R. Lambrecht
Stage 6	Monday 5 July	244 km	Bordeaux – Biarritz	L. Bobet (FRA)	L. Bobet
Stage 7	Wednesday 7 July	219 km	Biarritz – Lourdes	G. Bartali (ITA)	L. Bobet
Stage 8	Thursday 8 July	261 km	Lourdes – Toulouse	G. Bartali (ITA)	L. Bobet
Stage 9	Saturday 10 July	246 km	Toulouse – Montpellier	R. Impanis (BEL)	L. Bobet
Stage 10	Sunday 11 July	248 km	Montpellier – Marseille	R. Impanis (BEL)	L. Bobet
Stage 11	Monday 12 July	245 km	Marseille – San Remo (ITA)	G. Sciardis (ITA)	L. Bobet
Stage 12	Tuesday 13 July	170 km	San Remo (ITA) – Cannes	L. Bobet (FRA)	L. Bobet
Stage 13	Thursday 15 July	274 km	Cannes – Briançon	G. Bartali (ITA)	L. Bobet
Stage 14	Friday 16 July	263 km	Briançon – Aix-les-Bains	G. Bartali (ITA)	G. Bartali
Stage 15	Sunday 18 July	256 km	Aix-les-Bains – Lausanne (SUI)	G. Bartali (ITA)	G. Bartali
Stage 16	Monday 19 July	243 km	Lausanne (SUI) – Mulhouse	E. Van Dyck (BEL)	G. Bartali
Stage 17	Wednesday 21 July	120 km	Mulhouse – Strasbourg (TT)	R. Lambrecht (BEL)	G. Bartali
Stage 18	Thursday 22 July	195 km	Strasbourg – Metz	G. Corrieri (ITA)	G. Bartali
Stage 19	Friday 23 July	249 km	Metz – Liège (BEL)	G. Bartali (ITA)	G. Bartali
Stage 20	Saturday 24 July	228 km	Liège (BEL) – Roubaix	B. Gauthier (FRA)	G. Bartali
Stage 21	Sunday 25 July	286 km	Roubaix – Paris	G. Corrieri (ITA)	G. Bartali

Briançon to Aix-les-Bains. On the ascent of the Croix-de-Fer, Louison Bobet and André Brule try in vain to hang on to Gino Bartali's wheel. Despite a puncture on the descent, the Tuscan took the stage by an immense margin.

Bartali, magnificent from Paris to Paris

'I hope that Desgrange can see me from Paradise and still esteems me.' Even in victory, 'Gino the Pious' didn't forget the first Tour de France director, who had offered him his friendship.

Ten years after his first win, Bartali took his second Tour de France. It was a total victory for the Italian team, managed masterfully by Binda.

It's over. Gino Bartali has won his second Tour de France ten years after the first. He won it with such distinction and superiority that can admit no criticism or reservations. At a given moment, it might have been possible to suppose that without his technical problem in the Guil Valley, before the Izoard climb, Bobet might have kept his yellow jersey. The way Gino rode the rest of the race brought proof to the contrary.

We, on the other hand, had insisted on Ockers' chances on several occasions and, when he collapsed with a food-related crisis at the stage start at Toulouse, we succumbed to the temptation to write that 'Stan' had just lost a Tour de France that, in reality, should have been his.

Gino once again brought a decisive refutation: although the Belgian Schotte distinguished himself, he never put the Italian in difficulty. He could clearly only aspire to a podium placing. He was lucky that Guy Lapébie had tendon problems. As for Guy, he started off to finish, and to finish, if possible, with a high placing, but not to win: under these circumstances, he could never have become a serious rival for Gino. Finally, Lambrecht, although delighting us with his fluid style, never for an instant gave the impression of being able to triumph over a Bartali in great condition. Consequently, Bartali's victory admits no discussion.

What is admirable about the Italian champion is that he won the race as a complete rider, where before the war he won it as a climber, a specialist. Of course, the mountains were still his strong point, but his sprint victories at the end of some very tough breakaways helped him towards this final result, which everyone applauds.

Consult the *palmarès* of the Tour: never before has any man achieved a second victory ten years after his first. Until now Philippe Thys was the record holder, with seven years. It has been accomplished by a rider who is extraordinarily dedicated, particularly intelligent and remarkably talented. Gino is only 34 years old. If he wants to, he may perhaps win another Tour, although his task will be that much more difficult in that we have in Bobet a future champion, and next year, the Maestro Fausto Coppi will, in all probability, be the man to be celebrated.

Having achieved his position as leader and comfortably settled into a lead that oscillated between 25 and 50 minutes, Bartali could have locked himself into a defensive corner. On the contrary, he was determined to show everyone that it was quite useless to attack him. He took advan-

Bobet hangs on: in the stage from Cannes to Briançon, he has to dig deep in order not to collapse and ends up eighteen minutes behind the winner... Gino Bartali.

Briançon to Aix-les-Bains: Climbing the Col de la Croix-de-Fer, on a road worthy of a cyclo-cross circuit, Louison Bobet showed extraordinary energy and determination as he attempted, in vain, to shake off Gino Bartali.

tage of a long but unchallenging slope, before Lausanne to ride into the city on Lake Geneva alone. A little later he encountered the 'mountains' of the Ardennes and there again, darted away to first place in Liège.

To our eyes, these two great feats are as valuable as the Izoard, the Croix-de-Fer, and the solitary epic of the Chartreuse. They are as valuable because they belong to that set of gestures that are considered more beautiful, the more unnecessary they are: the Briançon and Aix-les-Bains stages were good for earning minutes, whereas the Lausanne and Liège stages (and Gino is the only man to have won on these three different territories, monopolizing all the foreign stages but San Remo) were solely to increase Gino's prestige and authority in the peloton.

Truly, no one has ever accomplished what Bartali has achieved.

HOW GINO BARTALI WON UNDER THE GUIDANCE OF A MASTER
THE ITALIAN POINT OF VIEW FROM GUIDO GIARDINI OF *LA GAZZETTA DELLO SPORT*

So Bartali has won his second Tour de France, ten years later. Look at the two dates: 1938, 1948. How can a man defy all the laws of nature and, after ten years, appear far and away the best of all the Tour de France contenders? To understand this, we need to investigate this exceptional feat. Athletes have the right to ask if Bartali is a phenomenon. No, Bartali is not a phenomenon. He won because he is still the strongest in the mountains; he won because he was clearly the best. How to explain this superiority? With the observation that, in my view, this Tour contained very few top class riders. The 1947 Tour gave rise to illusions: the 1948 Tour put order back into things and showed that cycling worldwide is on the lookout for new blood. The proof of this is Lapébie, a talented rider but more a track cyclist than a road racer. His abilities have allowed him to finish third overall. From the Italian point of view, the Tour has been a success, though above all for Bartali, since his team-mates had a mission to accomplish and we know that the Italians are capable of sacrificing their personal ambition when the good of the team requires it. In his role as technical director, Alfredo Binda, a man accustomed to triumph, added this Italian victory to his personal *palmarès*. He has proved himself a master, as much of a master as when he won the World Championship.

Peace between the bold

The impossible fragility of Fausto Coppi's physique belied his extraordinary abilities. His huge hands waved like albatross wings, and his timid, dark eyes always seemed to gaze downwards, resting on something no one else could see. He'd won the Giro d'Italia in 1940 and 1947; in 1942, he'd set a new world hour record on the track. Five years younger than reigning yellow jersey Gino Bartali, Coppi was also the most complete cyclist who had ever lived.

Arbitrating between the two champions was a third legend. Italian *directeur sportif* Alfredo Binda, the winner of five pre-War Tours of Italy and three World Championships, was perhaps the greatest rider in history never to have won the Tour de France. In 1930, the organizers of the Giro d'Italia paid him the equivalent of the winner's prize money, six stage wins and his employer's bonus not to ride, because his presence would have made the result a foregone conclusion. Binda had spent most of his career riding in Italy for the manufacturer Legnano, which had no French interests, and rode only one Tour. In 1930, he'd been third overall when a fall on stage seven lost him forty-five minutes. He won the following two stages for pride, then devoted himself to his leader, Learco Guerra.

It was a significant victory on Binda's part to secure both Bartali and Coppi for Italy's 1949 Tour de France team. After days of negotiation, Bartali and Coppi agreed a pact. Then Coppi made a disastrous start, falling and destroying his bike on stage five. When a substandard replacement was wheeled out, Coppi, dejected, came close to abandoning. Only Binda could persuade him to continue. He reached Saint-Malo more than half an hour behind the race leader.

Coppi won the 92-kilometre (58-mile) time trial two days later, then marked time through the Pyrenees and across southern France. Then, on Bartali's thirty-fifth birthday, the two greatest climbers in the sport attacked on the Izoard; at Briançon, Bartali took the stage victory and the yellow jersey. The following day, they attacked again. Plummeting down the slopes of the Petit-Saint-Bernard, Bartali punctured. Binda convinced Coppi to leave Bartali behind. Gaining five minutes on his rival, Coppi took the yellow jersey. On the penultimate stage, a 137-kilometre (86-mile) time trial, Coppi increased his lead to nearly eleven minutes, and maintained it to Paris. He had won the Tour at his first attempt, and become the first to win the Tours of Italy and France in the same year.

GENERAL CLASSIFICATION

1. **Fausto Coppi** (ITA) Italy, 4,808 km in 149h.40m.49s; Average speed: 32.119 kph
2. **Gino Bartali** (ITA) Italy, at 10m.55s.
3. **Jacques Marinelli** (FRA) Île-de-France, at 25m.13s.
4. Jean Robic (FRA) North-West, at 34m.28s.
5. Marcel Dupont (BEL) Belgium B, at 38m.59s.
6. Fiorenzo Magni (ITA) Italy B, at 42m.10s.
7. Constant 'Stan' Ockers (BEL) Belgium, at 44m.35s.
8. Jean Goldschmitt (LUX) Luxembourg, at 47m.24s.
9. Jean-Apôtre 'Apo' Lazaridès (FRA) France, at 52m.28s.
10. Pierre Cogan (FRA) North-West, at 1h.8m.55s.
11. Roger Lambrecht (BEL) Belgium, at 1h.17m.21s.
12. Gino Sciardis (ITA) Italy, at 1h.22m.1s.
13. Jean Kirchen (LUX) Luxembourg, at 1h.28m.14s.
14. Lucien Teisseire (FRA) France, at 1h.34m.56s.
15. Jean 'Bim' Diederich (LUX) Luxembourg, at 1h.35m.54s.
16. Robert Chapatte (FRA) France, at 1h.38m.40s.
17. Serafino Biagioni (ITA) Italy, at 1h.38m.47s.
18. Nello Lauredi (FRA) South-East, at 1h.43m.22s.
19. Georges Aeschlimann (SUI) Switzerland, at 1h.47m.52s.
20. Pierre Tacca (FRA) Île-de-France, at 1h.48m.1s.

36TH TOUR DE FRANCE, 21 STAGES – 4,808 KM

		STAGE	STAGE WINNER	YELLOW JERSEY
Stage 1	Thursday 30 June	Paris – Reims	M. Dussault (FRA)	M. Dussault
Stage 2	Friday 1 July	Reims – Bruxelles (BEL)	R. Lambrecht (BEL)	R. Lambrecht
Stage 3	Saturday 2 July	Bruxelles (BEL) – Boulogne-sur-Mer	N. Callens (BEL)	N. Callens
Stage 4	Sunday 3 July	Boulogne-sur-Mer – Rouen	L. Teisseire (FRA)	J. Marinelli
Stage 5	Monday 4 July	Rouen – Saint-Malo	F. Kübler (SUI)	J. Marinelli
Stage 6	Tuesday 5 July	Saint-Malo – Les Sables-d'Olonne	A. Deledda (FRA)	J. Marinelli
Stage 7	Thursday 7 July	Les Sables-d'Olonne – La Rochelle (TT)	F. Coppi (ITA)	J. Marinelli
Stage 8	Friday 8 July	La Rochelle – Bordeaux	G. Lapébie (FRA)	J. Marinelli
Stage 9	Saturday 9 July	Bordeaux – Saint-Sébastien (SPA)	L. Caput (FRA)	J. Marinelli
Stage 10	Sunday 10 July	Saint-Sébastien (SPA) – Pau	F. Magni (ITA)	F. Magni
Stage 11	Tuesday 12 July	Pau – Luchon	J. Robic (FRA)	F. Magni
Stage 12	Wednesday 13 July	Luchon – Toulouse	R. Van Steenbergen (BEL)	F. Magni
Stage 13	Thursday 14 July	Toulouse – Nîmes	E. Idée (FRA)	F. Magni
Stage 14	Friday 15 July	Nîmes – Marseille	J. Goldschmitt (LUX)	F. Magni
Stage 15	Saturday 16 July	Marseille – Cannes	D. Keteleer (BEL)	F. Magni
Stage 16	Monday 18 July	Cannes – Briançon	G. Bartali (ITA)	G. Bartali
Stage 17	Tuesday 19 July	Briançon – St-Vincent-d'Aosta (ITA)	F. Coppi (ITA)	F. Coppi
Stage 18	Thursday 21 July	St-Vincent-d'Aosta (ITA) – Lausanne (SUI)	V. Rossello (ITA)	F. Coppi
Stage 19	Friday 22 July	Lausanne – Colmar	R. Géminiani (FRA)	F. Coppi
Stage 20	Saturday 23 July	Colmar – Nancy	F. Coppi (ITA)	F. Coppi
Stage 21	Sunday 24 July	Nancy – Paris	R. Van Steenbergen (BEL)	F. Coppi

The cohabitation between the two Italian champions, Coppi (right) and Bartali (left), was masterfully managed by their *directeur sportif*, Alfredo Binda. Quite an achievement!

An unnecessary truce

CANNES: Yesterday, we envisioned that today would bring a powerful attack from Fausto Coppi. Naturally, we had excellent reasons to support this prediction. But we hadn't reckoned on the diplomatic talents of Binda and the Italian managers. For them, it was essential to start with a glowing demonstration of friendship, to satisfy national opinion. There was certainly no need to pounce on victory like a cat on a mouse; that would not be good manners! The result was the spectacle of Fausto and Gino making absolutely no attempt to break away from each other. Coppi calmly waited for Bartali after the latter had punctured on the descent from the Izoard, not 10 kilometres (6.2 miles) from the finish-line. The two great adversaries amicably shared the day's

bonuses before Coppi, for the sake of the team, conceded the stage win to his strongest rival: Bartali. This was obviously not quite what we'd imagined!

After spending all day beside Bartali, Coppi would hardly have demeaned himself by taking advantage of Gino's puncture to set off after the yellow jersey and the bonus awarded to the day's winner in Briançon. He'd now be leader in the general classification and nobody would have had the slightest objection to level at him. By acting the way he has, he has made a foolish bargain, because Bartali had started with a slight advantage and the spirit of sharing and entente they adopted allowed the wily Tuscan to hang on to his initial lead. So, no battle between the two big favourites.

BARTALI DIDN'T KNOW HE'D WON THE YELLOW JERSEY
BY ALBERT DE WETTER

BRIANÇON: Last night there was the inevitable queue into Bartali's room. At Briançon, Gino had too many friends to close the door. He was waiting for the visit of the President of Italy's cycling federation, the UVI, who had followed the stage. Bartali accepted the congratulations he received with that superior, slightly disenchanted air he likes to affect. Just once did his attitude light up into an immense joy, with, in his face, a glow of pride. It was when we showed him the general classification at the end of the day's stage from Cannes to Briançon. 'What,' he said, 'I'm on top? I'm in the yellow jersey. That means... I can't get over it!' 'You surely didn't doubt it?' we asked. 'Frankly, I had no idea,' he continued. 'I came back to the hotel almost as soon as I'd crossed the line. I was told that our lead was big, but I didn't think it would lose Magni the yellow jersey. He'd left Cannes with an advantage of more than twelve minutes over me.' Which suggests that Bartali's principal goal yesterday was not to take the race lead, but to show himself in a favourable light beside Coppi.

In any case, it was all agreed the previous night, we are assured. In the Italian camp, this first Alpine stage was intended to be about teamwork and defence. By breaking away in the morning, Kübler upset the Italian plan slightly. There was every reason to be alarmed by the buccaneering, dangerous initiative of this devil of a rider.

So at the top of the Col de Vars (the Allos having contributed almost nothing), we saw, less than four minutes behind Kübler, a group that was already very sparse, composed of Bartali and Coppi, plus a Franco-Belgian trio of Robic, Lazaridès and Ockers. It wasn't the attack that had been anticipated, but a counter-offensive which, in its material composition, looked just like it! The escapee's chances were narrowed by a couple of punctures, while the lightweights Ockers and Lazaridès descended the Vars badly and Robic had some slight mechanical problems coming out of Guillestre. This left the two Italian aces alone at the foot of the Izoard, without really having worked for it.

Brilliant on the Col de Vars, Kübler punctured on the climb up the Izoard. He finished 15 minutes behind Coppi and Bartali.

Having crossed the Izoard together, Bartali (leading) and Coppi finished in the same order in Briançon more than five minutes ahead of Robic. Without really testing their talent... or their rivalry!

Did they force the pace? We don't think so, and this (along with Bartali's puncture) probably explains why Lazaridès, Ockers and Marinelli finished in Briançon a bit closer than they were when they crossed the Izoard. Not very reassuring, in view of the next two stages! Yet who could overlook the fact that if Kübler, once joined by Bartali and Coppi, had managed to stay with them, he would probably be wearing the yellow jersey tonight? Two days from Switzerland, it had been a very dangerous episode for the men in white and red.

Briançon to Aosta: Bartali's in the lead, but he later suffered a puncture and a fall on the Petit-Saint-Bernard pass and had to let his rival Coppi go on to win and claim the yellow jersey.

Alfredo Binda (right) successfully blended the solidity of Bartali with the elegance of Coppi (centre).

Coppi walks in Bartali's footsteps

Sport has won. Coppi and Bartali made a triumphal entry to the Parc des Princes, which only displeased the one or two cranks who would like to blame them for the partisan incidents that took place on the descent of the Petit-Saint-Bernard pass and who, by so doing, place themselves on the same level as those brainless pests. Coppi has utterly dominated all his challengers, including his direct rival, towards whom he has behaved like a gentleman. Why this indulgence, One might be tempted to ask?

Without a doubt, the Bianchi rider was certainly reacting to a host of different feelings. Firstly, why rout an opponent who was already irremediably beaten, especially when this opponent is also a team-mate and compatriot? Secondly, why claim the yellow jersey too soon, and have to carry its onerous load over many long stages to follow? Finally, why not show some measure of

deference for the great champion under whose guidance he made his professional debut, for the star who has been his role model since his teenage years? It should be remembered that in 1940, when Coppi entered the big time, he was one of Bartali's auxiliaries.

Nor should it be forgotten that in that same year Coppi won the first Giro d'Italia he had entered, but only with the consent of Bartali, who had suffered a serious racing accident earlier. Their bitter rivalry began no earlier than 1946. Before this date they were friends and the younger of the two undeniably benefited greatly from the senior man's experience. Another question hangs over Coppi. Having reached the highest pinnacles; having achieved the unique feat of winning the Giro d'Italia and the Tour de France within weeks of each other; having won, in addition, Milan-San Remo and undoubtedly having formulated the plan to

end the season in the jersey of the World Champion – in the pursuit or on the road – will Coppi not now think it unnecessary to make such a relentless exertion again?

In short, does he envisage riding another Tour de France? In 1950, at least? The natural response to such a question is that the Tour is a drug and a rider once caught in its mechanism will never extricate himself. This calls to mind Apo Lazaridès who, standing contemplatively on the grass at the Parc, told us: 'In the future, I will only live for the Tour.' To which we replied that he certainly has what it takes to be a superb winner. Apo, as we know, had been keen to make his mark well before the finale in the Parc, but a fall put an end to his dreams.

So what can we say of the final stage, other than that it was very long, undoubtedly too long. 340 kilometres (211 miles) is such a distance that for over 150 km (93 miles), even the most daring riders were wary of trying their luck one last time. The organizer does not always do exactly as we like, however, and it must be recognized that it was quite an achievement to place the last peak only 24 hours from Paris! Van Steenbergen won, and deserves great credit, firstly because it was his second stage win and secondly because Bartali had very evidently attempted the impossible and tried to seize the stage. We should now list all the qualities, both great and small, of all the other surviving competitors, but as such a task would take for ever, let's concentrate for a moment on the man who has become the most popular cyclist in France after Coppi: Jacques Marinelli. He set the pace in the early stages, was the leader until the Pyrenees and then fell behind, but little Jacques had the immense courage not to abandon himself to fate – he wanted to finish as brilliantly as he had started. And so he did, ranked first among the French riders, finishing one place behind last year's champion and one place ahead of the 1947 champion. It was on the Colmar to Nancy stage that he especially astonished us. One small criticism, however, in his direction. Or rather, the expression of a fear, already articulated after the Les Sables to La Rochelle stage: the young champion seems to adore using huge gear ratios. It has to be said that this preference does not really suit his build or physical strength and if he continues in this manner, he may find that his career is cut short.

Major companies quickly realized the commercial value of participating in the Tour de France publicity caravan. Its popularity with the public could be seen at the roadside every day.

Already wearing the *maillot jaune*, Marinelli (leading) headed a 240-kilometre (149-mile) breakaway between Rouen and Saint-Malo with Dupont, Tacca, Gauthier and Kübler, who won at the sprint.

Kübler, after a crisis

After the domination of Coppi and Bartali in 1949, race director Jacques Goddet reduced the time bonuses at the top of the mountain passes, as well as the time limits, to force *domestiques* to make a continuous effort. Ten-man teams represented Belgium, France, Italy, and the French regions; Luxembourg, the Netherlands, Switzerland and French North Africa (Morocco and Algeria) sent six-man teams. The Belgian and Italian B teams also comprised six riders.

The Italians sent a formidable team, despite the absence of Coppi, who had been injured at the Giro d'Italia. Italians won stages two, three, five and seven, before Bartali rose majestically over the Pyrenees. Anticipating yet more Italian domination, the French crowds were growing impatient. On the Tourmalet, the day's second climb, insults were hurled from the roadside; the Belgian Stan Ockers and France's Jean Robic shielded Bartali from the threats. On the next climb, the Aspin, bottle tops and stones rained over the Italians. As the riders approached the finish-line, the road was blocked. Bartali was thrown to the floor. Robic collided with him and broke a wheel. Race director Jacques Goddet arrived in a vehicle, wielding a walking stick to keep the crowds at bay.

The group containing Magni reached the leaders, and with the road now cleared by the police, the stage was allowed to finish. On a slight incline, Bartali sprinted away for the win, his team-mate Fiorenzo Magni, who had won the stage into Niort five days earlier, on his wheel. Bartali jumped from nineteenth to sixth overall; Magni took over the yellow jersey. The prospect of a repeat of 1949, with two Italians dominating France's national fête, loomed.

That evening, Binda withdrew the Italian teams from the Tour. Jacques Goddet visited Binda and the Italians, and even offered to disguise them in neutral jerseys. But Binda was adamant; it was a lost opportunity both for Magni and for Gino Bartali. The organizers immediately re-routed the Tour, removing San Remo from the itinerary and replacing it with Menton.

The yellow jersey fell on the shoulders of Switzerland's Ferdi Kübler, who set off a great offensive with Stan Ockers between Perpignan and Nîmes. Louison Bobet, suffering in the heat, lost ten minutes on the stage, but a heroic solo win at Briançon brought him back into contention. Bobet made his bid for victory the following day on the road to Saint-Étienne, speeding through the feed zone at Pont de Claix, 180 km (112.5 miles) from the stage finish, with his team-mates Géminiani and Lazaridès. Kübler pursued frantically. Crossing the Rhône, Bobet rode into the wind, and began to flag. Kübler overtook him without a glance. In the time trial between Saint-Étienne and Lyon, Kübler, wearing his leather cap and with his mouth foaming, overtook him again.

GENERAL CLASSIFICATION

1. **Ferdi Kübler** (SUI) Switzerland, 4,775 km in 145h.36m.56s; Average speed: 32.778 kph
2. **Constant 'Stan' Ockers** (BEL) Belgium, at 9m.30s.
3. Louison Bobet (FRA) France, at 22m.19s.
4. Raphaël Géminiani (FRA) France, at 31m.14s.
5. Jean Kirchen (LUX) Luxembourg, at 34m.21s.
6. Kléber Piot (FRA) North-East-Île-de-France, at 41m.35s.
7. Pierre Cogan (FRA) South-West, at 52m.22s.
8. Raymond Impanis (BEL) Belgium, at 53m.34s.
9. Georges Meunier (FRA) South-West-Central, at 54m.29s.
10. Jean Goldschmit (LUX) Luxembourg, at 55m.21s.
11. Pierre Brambilla (FRA) South-East, at 57m.14s.
12. Jean Robic (FRA) West, at 59m.45s.
13. Roger Lambrecht (BEL) Belgium, at 1h.0m.29s.
14. André Brule (FRA) North-East-Île-de-France, at 1h.5m.29s.
15. Marcel Versuchueren (BEL) Belgium B, at 1h.5m.50s.
16. Marcel De Mulder (BEL) Belgium B, at 1h.11m.38s.
17. Bernard Gauthier (FRA) South-East, at 1h.13m.29s.
18. Jean 'Bim' Diederich (LUX) Luxembourg, at 1h.14m.56s.
19. Robert Castelin (FRA) South-East, at 1h.25m.12s.
20. Attilio Redolfi (FRA) North-East-Île-de-France, at 1h.28m.57s.

37TH TOUR DE FRANCE, 22 STAGES – 4,775 KM

Stage	Date	Distance		STAGE WINNER	YELLOW JERSEY
Stage 1	Thursday 13 July	307 km	Paris – Metz	J. Goldschmit (LUX)	J. Goldschmit
Stage 2	Friday 14 July	241 km	Metz – Liège (BEL)	A. Leoni (ITA)	J. Goldschmit
Stage 3	Saturday 15 July	232.5 km	Liège (BEL) – Lille	A. Pasotti (ITA)	B. Gauthier
Stage 4	Sunday 16 July	231 km	Lille – Rouen	C. Ockers (BEL)	B. Gauthier
Stage 5	Monday 17 July	316 km	Rouen – Dinard	G. Corrieri (ITA)	B. Gauthier
Stage 6	Wednesday 19 July	78 km	Dinard – Saint-Brieuc (TT)	F. Kübler (SUI)	J. Goldschmit
Stage 7	Thursday 20 July	248 km	Saint-Brieuc – Angers	N. Lauredi (FRA)	B. Gauthier
Stage 8	Friday 21 July	181 km	Angers – Niort	F. Magni (ITA)	B. Gauthier
Stage 9	Saturday 22 July	206 km	Niort – Bordeaux	A. Pasotti (ITA)	B. Gauthier
Stage 10	Sunday 23 July	202 km	Bordeaux – Pau	M. Dussault (FRA)	B. Gauthier
Stage 11	Tuesday 25 July	230 km	Pau – Saint-Gaudens	G. Bartali (ITA)	F. Magni
Stage 12	Wednesday 26 July	233 km	Saint-Gaudens – Perpignan	M. Blomme (BEL)	F. Kübler
Stage 13	Thursday 27 July	215 km	Perpignan – Nîmes	M. Molines (FRA)	F. Kübler
Stage 14	Friday 28 July	222 km	Nîmes – Toulon	C. Dos Reis (FRA)	F. Kübler
Stage 15	Saturday 29 July	205.5 km	Toulon – Menton	J. Diederich (LUX)	F. Kübler
Stage 16	Sunday 30 July	98 km	Menton – Nice	F. Kübler (SUI)	F. Kübler
Stage 17	Tuesday 1 August	239 km	Nice – Gap	R. Geminiani (FRA)	F. Kübler
Stage 18	Wednesday 2 August	165 km	Gap – Briançon	L. Bobet (FRA)	F. Kübler
Stage 19	Thursday 3 August	291 km	Briançon – Saint-Étienne	R. Geminiani (FRA)	F. Kübler
Stage 20	Saturday 5 August	98 km	Saint-Étienne – Lyon (TT)	F. Kübler (SUI)	F. Kübler
Stage 21	Sunday 6 August	233 km	Lyon – Dijon	G. Sciardis (ITA)	F. Kübler
Stage 22	Monday 7 August	314 km	Dijon – Paris	E. Baffert (FRA)	F. Kübler

Ferdi Kübler rode the time trial between Saint-Étienne and Lyon like a man possessed, winning by nearly six minutes and guaranteeing overall victory by a huge margin.

Toulon to Menton: The collective plunge by half the peloton into the waters of the Gulf of Saint-Tropez is a legendary moment in the Tour. 'Surely the cyclists should have been acquiring, or re-acquiring, the rudiments of their strenuous profession, instead of indulging in these carnival antics?' Or so Jacques Goddet thought.

The Italians fall into line with Bartali's decision

PERPIGNAN: This morning, just one hour before the start of the Saint-Gaudens to Perpignan stage, Fiorenzo Magni delivered the final 'No' which deprived the Tour de France of its entire Italian contingent of riders and followers. Right up to the last minute, first in the hotel, then in the hotel gardens in the small health resort of Loures, the debate had been heated. There were still hopes that, despite Gino Bartali's voluntary withdrawal, a few of the Italians would continue the fight. But on the stroke of 8 o'clock, the final decision was taken.

Gino told Alfredo Binda, who sympathized with his attitude: 'I don't want to set off again feeling I've been the victim of acts of violence that aren't compatible with sport. The sport I practise is dangerous. It will become even more so, judging by the hostility that was shown towards us by some of the spectators in the Pyrenees.'

Binda felt he should try to calm Gino down and make him understand that what had happened in the Pyrenees was, perhaps, the work of a minority, and that the real

sports enthusiasts who were aware of it would try to restrain the few fanatics in future. 'I talked with Gino all last evening,' Binda told us, 'and with his team-mates until 3 o'clock in the morning. They all stand by their leader. What more can I do?'

However, Binda, that old *campionissimo*, had told us during the night that there was a chance Magni might agree to continue. The organizers met with the Italian team to try to reconcile everyone's interests. Most of the Italian riders were up at the crack of dawn this morning. The B-team declared themselves ready to continue the fight if necessary. Magni seemed very hesitant.

It was then suggested to Alfredo Binda that he should form a team without any official status, re-clothed in jerseys of a different colour. In short, they asked Binda, who had the final say in the matter, to release both the B-team and the Internationals from their obligations so that they could be included as official guests of the organizers. It was evident, at this point, that Magni was dithering more and more, that Leoni was the most

eager to escape from Bartali's authority, and that others, including the B-team and one or two Internationals, would be willing to support Magni if he agreed to take over from Gino. 'You are on form, Fiorenzo,' urged Leoni, 'you can win the Tour. Go on! Ask Bindi for your freedom.' 'It's yours,' was the Italian's technical director's reply.

So now the unfortunate Magni found himself on the horns of a dilemma. 'I deeply regret that, as the race leader, I can't accept,' he said. 'I can't go back on the promises I gave Bartali before the start of the Tour. I was taken on to help Bartali and not to win the Tour de France. I can't stay on while Bartali has withdrawn, nowhere near defeated yet. What would I be taken for? A usurper!' So at 8 o'clock, in front of his friends and compatriots – journalists, mechanics and *soigneurs* – Magni honoured his promise, obliging his team-mates and the dismayed Italian followers to pack up as well. When we left Bartali, he told us sadly: 'I doubt I'll race in France again now.'

At the finish in Saint-Gaudens, Bartali (centre, in raincoat) hardly has the look of a stage winner. Feeling that French spectators had put him in danger, he abandoned the Tour de France, taking the rest of the Italians with him.

The time trial crowns Kübler

LYON: We'd long been thinking, since that spring day when we'd had the chance to reconnoitre the route, that the Saint-Étienne to Lyons time-trial would turn out to be the decisive stage of the 1950 Tour. On Saturday, we were proved right after just 20 km (12.4 miles). 'Ferdi' was certainly the best man in the race; Ockers merited second place (in spite of the reticence he had shown at various times); and Louison Bobet was their worthy companion. But, we had been wrong to think there would be fluctuations in the overall result from the stage in which the stopwatch is the only judge.

At Croix-Chaubouret, Kübler was leading Ockers by 1min 10secs, Bobet was trailing at 3mins 27secs, and we were still only a fifth of the way through the course! While 'Ferdi' was displaying extraordinary power, Louison seemed to be in much poorer condition than in the past few days. Pale, tense, he pushed on with his usual courage, but with none of the ease he had shown on the Izoard.

To cap it all he got a puncture when, at the start of the descent, Kübler was already on his heels, having closed to within four seconds. By the time he'd changed machine, Kübler was in front; during another change of machine a few miles further on, the Swiss rider disappeared from view!

At that moment, the Frenchman seemed to be facing a real disaster, namely the loss of his third place overall. But showing marvellous determination and class, Bobet managed to pull himself back together in the Rhône Valley. From then on, he succeeded in halting the downward spiral to which he had seemed to be condemned. In the end, he finished in Lyon 8mins 45secs behind Kübler, obviously a huge deficit, but only 3mins 11secs behind Ockers, which reduced the damage in the most obvious way. What's more, he still had the means to take sixth place, preceding men like Lambrecht and Géminiani. A miracle!

However, 'Ferdi' crossed the line bathed in glory! The Swiss champion had demonstrated his superiority in spectacular fashion. Not only had his yellow jersey not been in jeopardy for a moment, but he had repeated his Saint-Brieuc triumph with even more panache. He had authoritatively extended his lead. In short, he had become invincible.

Kübler belonged to the breed of great champions, yet until 1950 the man Jacques Goddet had described as a 'cycling demon' had never yet proved this with his results. Mission accomplished!

'MY YELLOW JERSEY'
BY 'FERDI' KÜBLER

'When I started the Tour de France, I must admit I felt a certain apprehension. I'd never been particularly successful in this great event. It had left me with some fairly painful memories and I was anxiously wondering how I was going to get through those 22 stages littered with formidable difficulties. In France, I was seen as dangerous but erratic, unstable and sometimes unreliable. The forecasts ranked me behind Bartali, Robic, Bobet, Ockers and Magni. People were wondering if I really was capable of finishing such a punishing circuit, and in the circumstances, I was asking myself the same question.

'So I was embarking on an adventure with a very uncertain outcome. But this role I was playing meant a lot to me. In my heart, I had a burning desire to do well. Switzerland had just won its own Tour and the Giro with Hugo Koblet. This gave me a unique opportunity to complete a marvellous trilogy. Our country had never achieved this before. For three weeks I lurched from hope to doubt and back. Bartali was always dangerous,

Magni menacing. There was Goldschmit, whose wonderful form I'd admired in the Tour of Switzerland, and Bobet, absolutely transformed since this event. These were very powerful adversaries against whom it was always difficult to fight.

'It was after the first time trial that I seriously envisaged winning for the first time. The famous Perpignan to Nîmes stage boosted my hopes, especially as I was improving as the kilometres went by. The second time trial was the high point for me. I was fired up, and exhilarated too by enthusiasm, a sports loving public which cheered me on just like its pet champions Bobet and Robic. It felt like a dream. That really warm reception from such sympathetic crowds lining the beautiful French roads ranks in my memories as the finest of victories.

'And the great frenzy at the finish! It's something I'll never forget. That's why it's such a joy for me to recount my story for French sports-people and for the readers of L'Équipe who are all my friends.'

Koblet, without a hair out of place

The 1951 Tour de France discarded the established geography of the race route, distancing itself from the six faces of France's hexagon, and penetrated the heart of the nation. Twelve riders represented Italy, Belgium, France and four French regions, while Luxembourg, the Netherlands, Spain, Switzerland and North Africa sent eight men each.

For the first time since 1926, the *Grand Départ* took place outside Paris and its environs. As the riders gathered in Metz, French hopes surrounded Louison Bobet, who had won the springtime classic between Milan and San Remo. In Fausto Coppi, Gino Bartali and Fiorenzo Magni, Italy had three contenders. Coppi, however, was in a state of bewilderment, a stranger to himself and to the world around him, mourning the death of his brother Serse, who had died in a fall at the Tour of Piedmont on 29 June 1951, five days before the Tour began.

Neither Coppi nor Bobet shaped the race; instead, on stage eleven from Brive-la-Gaillarde to Agen, Switzerland's Hugo Koblet escaped alone with 135 kilometres (84 miles) left on the stage, and, incredibly, held off a chasing group containing Coppi, Bobet, Bartali, Magni, Géminiani, Ockers and Robic – the very cream of world professional cycling at the time. Despite taking turns at the front and co-operating completely,

they saw the gap increase. Koblet, with such fluid, supple style that there was no impression of effort, rested his automobile goggles on his forehead or draped over his left forearm, and intermittently cooled his brow with a sponge from his shirt pocket. On the finish-line, he started his stopwatch, suavely ran a comb through his hair, and waited for his pursuers to appear. Jacques Grello, a French singer with a column in *L'Équipe*, dubbed Koblet 'le pédaleur de charme'; the charming champion was now third overall, 2mins 35secs ahead of his greatest rivals.

A time-keeping error deprived East South-East France rider Gilbert Bauvin of a day in the yellow jersey that night. Three days later, the first Dutchman ever to don the *maillot jaune*, Win Van Est, suffered even worse misfortune, sliding from the pass over the Aubisque into a deep ravine. With a towrope and all the Dutch team's spare tyres, he was pulled out.

The following day, Koblet took over the race lead at Luchon after winning a two-man sprint against Fausto Coppi. The Swiss rider was in complete control; the Italian suffered an emotional breakdown on stage sixteen and almost finished outside the time limit. Coppi was sufficiently composed on the stage to Briançon to win the great Alpine stage of the race, but it was too late to challenge Hugo Koblet.

GENERAL CLASSIFICATION:

1. **Hugo Koblet** (SUI) Switzerland, 4,697 km in 142h.20m.14s; Average speed: 32.979 kph
2. **Raphaël Géminiani** (FRA) France, at 22m.
3. **Lucien Lazaridès** (FRA) France, at 24m.16s.
4. Gino Bartali (ITA) Italy, at 29m.9s.
5. Constant 'Stan' Ockers (BEL) Belgium, at 32m.53s.
6. Pierre Barbotin (FRA) France, at 36m.40s.

7. Fiorenzo Magni (ITA) Italy, at 39m.14s.
8. Gilbert Bauvin (FRA) East South-East, at 45m.53s.
9. Bernardo Ruiz (SPA) Spain, at 45m.55s.
10. Fausto Coppi (ITA) Italy, at 46m.51s.
11. Nello Lauredi (FRA) France, at 57m.19s.
12. Jean 'Bim' Diederich (LUX) Luxembourg, at 59m.29s.
13. Marcel De Mulder (BEL) Belgium, at 1h.4m.18s.

14. Édouard Van Ende (BEL) Belgium, at 1h.7m.18s.
15. Serafino Biagioni (ITA) Italy, at 1h.8m.52s.
16. Georges Meunier (FRA) West South-West, at 1h.13m.36s.
17. Roger Decock (BEL) Belgium, at 1h.13m.57s.
18. Marcel Verschueren (BEL) Belgium, at 1h.14m.36s.
19. Pierre Cogan (FRA) West South-West, at 1h.15m.30s.
20. Louison Bobet (FRA) France, at 1h.24m.9s.

38TH TOUR DE FRANCE, 24 STAGES – 4,697 KM

			STAGE	STAGE WINNER	YELLOW JERSEY
Stage 1	Wednesday 4 July	185 km	Metz – Reims	G. Rossi (SUI)	G. Rossi
Stage 2	Thursday 5 July	228 km	Reims – Gand (BEL)	J. Diederich (LUX)	J. Diederich
Stage 3	Friday 6 July	219 km	Gand (BEL) – Le Tréport	G. Meunier (FRA)	J. Diederich
Stage 4	Saturday 7 July	188 km	Le Tréport – Paris	R. Lévêque (FRA)	J. Diederich
Stage 5	Sunday 8 July	215 km	Paris – Caen	S. Biagioni (ITA)	S. Biagioni
Stage 6	Monday 9 July	182 km	Caen – Rennes	E. Muller (FRA)	R. Lévêque
Stage 7	Tuesday 10 July	85 km	La Guerche – Angers (TT)	H. Koblet (SUI)	R. Lévêque
Stage 8	Wednesday 11 July	241 km	Angers – Limoges	A. Rosseel (BEL)	R. Lévêque
Stage 9	Friday 13 July	236 km	Limoges – Clermont-Ferrand	R. Géminiani (FRA)	R. Lévêque
Stage 10	Saturday 14 July	216 km	Clermont-Ferrand – Brive-la-Gaillarde	B. Ruiz (SPA)	R. Lévêque
Stage 11	Sunday 15 July	177 km	Brive-la-Gaillarde – Agen	H. Koblet (SUI)	R. Lévêque
Stage 12	Monday 16 July	185 km	Agen – Dax	W. Van Est (HOL)	W. Van Est
Stage 13	Tuesday 17 July	201 km	Dax – Tarbes	S. Biagioni (ITA)	G. Bauvin
Stage 14	Wednesday 18 July	142 km	Tarbes – Luchon	H. Koblet (SUI)	H. Koblet
Stage 15	Thursday 19 July	213 km	Luchon – Carcassonne	A. Rosseel (BEL)	H. Koblet
Stage 16	Friday 20 July	192 km	Carcassonne – Montpellier	H. Koblet (SUI)	H. Koblet
Stage 17	Sunday 22 July	224 km	Montpellier – Avignon	L. Bobet (FRA)	H. Koblet
Stage 18	Monday 23 July	173 km	Avignon – Marseille	F. Magni (ITA)	H. Koblet
Stage 19	Tuesday 24 July	208 km	Marseille – Gap	A. Baeyens (BEL)	H. Koblet
Stage 20	Wednesday 25 July	165 km	Gap – Briançon	F. Coppi (ITA)	H. Koblet
Stage 21	Thursday 26 July	201 km	Briançon – Aix-les-Bains	B. Ruiz (SPA)	H. Koblet
Stage 22	Friday 27 July	97 km	Aix-les-Bains – Genève (SUI) (TT)	H. Koblet (SUI)	H. Koblet
Stage 23	Saturday 28 July	197 km	Genève (SUI) – Dijon	G. Derycke (BEL)	H. Koblet
Stage 24	Sunday 29 July	322 km	Dijon – Paris	A. Deledda (FRA)	H. Koblet

Between Brive and Agen, Switzerland's Hugo Koblet attacked, 135 kilometres (84 miles) from the stage finish and held off the chasing group. Crossing the Lot at Villeneuve-sur-Lot, he had a three-minute lead.

Koblet's audacious attack

Dubbed 'the pedaller of charm' by songster Jacques Grello and 'Apollo on a bike' by *L'Équipe*, Koblet's performance between Brive and Agen justified all the epithets.

AGEN: There's no way of being absolutely sure that we haven't just witnessed, on the smiling roads between Brive and Agen, the greatest exploit of the 1951 Tour. In any case, the outstanding highlight of this second weekend has been the performance of Hugo Koblet, highly athletic as far as quality is concerned, and dazzling in terms of the spectacle it produced. Imagine a great champion managing to break away, alone, some 135 km (84 miles) from the finish and then holding out to the end against a furious pursuit involving all the other top riders, sceptical and disconcerted at first, then utterly mortified and fiercely vindictive. Koblet's lead had stretched to something over four minutes. At the finish he retained 2mins 35secs, which, with the bonus awarded to the stage winner, gave him third place in the general classification, 2mins 27secs behind Lévêque. Yet it's almost shameful to worry about these statistics. What matters isn't that the brilliant rider on Team Perle-Hutchinson has improved his position. *Au contraire*, the amazing thing is the evident lack of calculating forethought behind Koblet's enterprise. What spoke through him was an admirable fighting temperament. What he deserves credit for is the impression shown by the likes of Coppi, Magni, Bobet and Géminiani that his display of power and control was a distressing moral blow. Was Hugo right or wrong, considering what is to come? Anyone with his class and his powers of recuperation, anyone who is riding his first Tour, has everything to gain from trying to break with tradition, instead of seeking refuge in the conventionality nurtured by the top riders, for whom experience doesn't necessarily end up being the best counsellor.

Of course, Koblet risks paying dearly for his audacity. He has displeased his adversaries; he has wounded their pride, without winning an astronomical time advantage. He has even weakened his own team by causing the elimination of two *domestiques*. Yet he has achieved something which we had rarely, if ever, seen. Not wanting to wait until the high mountains, a great rider has attempted the kind of breakaway normally risked only by riders with a major disadvantage in the general classification and therefore likely to benefit from more or less unanimous tolerance. Coppi has succeeded in such exploits before, in the Tour and the Giro, but in the mountains where the chasers are necessarily individual and where the other contenders are in no position to work together. The difference is enormous.

It's no exaggeration to say that the Swiss champion has opened a new chapter in the history of the Tour de France and if he were to set a trend, we would soon find ourselves facing a revolution in the art of riding this great event. Koblet served up a delight. He rode harmoniously, with suppleness, his elbows with a slight outward flex, his arms absorbing the vibrations coming up from the road.

Brive-Agen: Behind Koblet, the chase is taking shape. The contenders took it upon themselves to close the gap, yet Bobet, Géminiani and Coppi work in vain.

Meanwhile, he's perfectly placed as the race reaches the mountains and, as everyone knows, he's entirely capable of coping with their gradients.

You'd have thought you were watching a time trial, a Grand Prix des Nations. The road belonged to him, the climbs didn't exist for him, and the descents gave him new impetus. There wasn't a moment to relax: at the finish, his average speed was nearly 39 kph (24.2 mph). How did fortune favour him? Without a doubt, at the start of his attack, when his lead had stabilized at around 1min 15secs, and he was making a great effort to hold it there, Bobet punctured. At that moment, Lucien Lazaridès and Lauredi were spear-heading the chase, in the company of Ruiz and Milano. Left to his own devices in the fray, Bobet was in grave danger. Jean Bidot therefore halted the two Frenchmen, who together with the others who were available, including the steadfast Barbotin, paced the French national champion back. During this time the chase lost its momentum, as the Italians were left at the head of the group and couldn't accept the monumental task imposed by the fugitive on his pursuers. Koblet was now able to consolidate his lead and get his second wind. This was the only contribution luck made to Koblet's ride, for the fall involving Coppi and Magni, which happened much later, didn't play a decisive role as the final result was already beyond doubt.

Only the gutsy and spirited Deprez had managed to go with him. But he was soon shaken off; Kübler's countryman and great rival was simply unstoppable.

DRAMA ON THE AUBISQUE

TARBES: Have you ever seen racing cyclists plummet from the crest of a pass into the valley? It's breathtaking. As the French has it, it's like diving into an open grave, an expression that is no exaggeration. Poor old Wim Van Est! On the ascent, he defended his yellow jersey with all his strength. The so-called kings of the mountain weren't so far ahead of him when he crossed the col. Without giving exhaustion or danger a second thought, he catapulted down after them at terrifying speed.

The descent of the Aubisque is thought of as the most dangerous of all. On one side of the narrow road there's a wall of rock; on the other, an abyss. The hairpin bends are often disguised by the rock-face. Hurtling down at 50 to 60 kph (31 to 37 mph), Van Est slipped once, and set off again. A few hundred metres further on, he was flung into a dramatic somersault and with his bike, plunged into the ravine, but clambered back up and continued his infernal pursuit. His third fall was like a scene from a nightmare. Massip, Langarica and Decock had caught him. Massip was on his wheel, then let out a sudden cry, shattering the silence of the mountains. Van Est had lurched into the void, between the rock-faces of the precipice. The others went flying past, yelling with alarm, at dizzying speed. Decock stopped to warn the chasing riders, careering down flat out, unaware of the drama. They dismounted and ran over, hearts in their mouths. At the bottom of the ravine, they made out the minuscule figure of the yellow jersey, lying on a rock. The ravine must have been 100 metres (328 ft) deep. Van Est and his bike had hit a steep strip of earth and then tumbled down the slope. There were no signs of life. Pellenaers, the Dutch *directeur sportif,* stopped too. He shouted 'Van Est, Van Est!'

but the only reply was an indifferent echo. However, some deity must have been watching over Wim Van Est. First one arm lifted, then the other! Bent double, he picked himself up and staggered towards his bicycle. Dragging it on all fours, he tried to climb back up. The followers on the edge of the precipice, sick with anxiety, could hardly believe what they were seeing. Our colleagues Coste, Persin, Commissaire Bourbon and Van Irland, the driver of the Dutch jeep, scrambled all the way down to Van Est's rock to rescue the miraculous survivor of the Aubisque. Albert de Wetter, Pellenaers and several others managed to make a rope out of tyres. With great effort, they hauled Van Est up onto the side of the road. Grazed and bleeding he collapsed, weeping and crying 'Thank you!'.

Next time, watch them plummet down the cols: it can be quite unforgettable!

Hugo Koblet's charm offensive

We thought this would be a high speed Tour. That was to underestimate the rudeness of the course, an intentional hardiness, calculated, judiciously distributed, slightly terrifying. Any journalist who has just come full circle on the Tour and looks back over the recent past, can't disassociate himself from certain feelings of admiration and respect for the men who have just collected, at the Parc des Princes, their reward for so much effort and, it has to be said, so much pain. Without exception, all have been eclipsed by Hugo Koblet, alone among the contenders in overcoming every obstacle with a smile – although they all deserved credit for fighting without losing heart. Some had their sights set on a high placing in the general classification; others, a stage win; still others, a particular honour – the prize as the best climber, or the defence of team positions gained in the Challenge Desgranges-Colombo. Others were riding for love of the sport and its battles.

Its battles… They're what bring us here. If this hasn't been a high speed Tour, it has been full of fight. Koblet set the tone (and he set it, remember, when he decided to allow himself the luxury of a solo breakaway which was indulged, even regarded with a certain degree of disdain, by the other favourites), but he constantly found imitators. Diederich and the Belgian lads riding for Sylvère Maes did so in stage two; Meunier, at the finish in Tréport; Lévêque, a slightly disparaged leader but nevertheless one full of passion and conviction; little Bauvin, who fixed his sights on the yellow jersey and finally claimed it in Tarbes; Bobet, who narrowly lost the first time-trial but made amends superbly between Mont Ventoux and Avignon; Géminiani, who snatched the first Auvergne stage brilliantly; Rosseel, who finished the lightning-fast breakaway to Limoges like an arrow; B. Ruiz, who beat everyone at Brive; Van Est, who donned the yellow jersey in Dax and wore it for his great leap on the descent of the Aubisque the following day; Lucien Lazaridès, who conquered Mont Ventoux;

EXPRESSIONS OF JOY IN SWITZERLAND

BY VICO RIGASSI

GENEVA: News of the overall victory of the young Swiss rider, Hugo Koblet, in the 38th Tour de France, has been greeted in Switzerland with great expressions of joy, which have in fact been going on non-stop since Friday, when Koblet finished in triumph at Geneva, after winning the time trial. However, the Swiss press and radio are taking great satisfaction over stressing, on the one hand, the perfect organization of this 38th Tour de France, and on the other, the exceptionally sporting attitude shown by the French crowds, and especially in Paris. This victory, coming one year after Kübler's, places Swiss cycling at the forefront of international cycling and allows the directors who will be receiving Koblet in Geneva on Monday and Zurich on Tuesday to face the World Road Racing championships (due to take place on 2 September in Varese, Italy) with justified optimism. A great cortege with Koblet in an open-topped car will parade through the streets of Geneva tomorrow and Zurich on Tuesday, to give the public the opportunity to express their admiration for the young rider from Zurich and the marvellous feat he has just performed.

little Baeyens who did a Géminiani at the finish in Gap; Coppi, who became an eagle once more on the Vars and the Izoard, etc.

A sensational pace, indeed, with this little lot. Doldrums? Yes, if you mean the days when the results had no direct impact on the top of the general classification. No, if you consider that there was always something going on, either early on in the stage, or at the stage finish. If the race of great sprinters is tending to die out (as we've had occasion to point out), this is mainly because the race of the privateers has developed strongly.

This last observation immediately leads us to mention afresh Koblet's great talents. Let us salute this truly great cycling champion. He has everything: elegance, intelligence, pure quality. He could be World Champion. He could beat the world hour record. M.K. Senn, the chairman of the SRB, has found himself an admirable standard-bearer for Swiss cycling.

Switzerland may have found its hero, but Koblet's mother (in the crowd) is still his biggest fan.

A capable climber, Koblet limited his losses on the Izoard behind Coppi.

A relentless *rouleur*, Koblet used the time trials to his advantage.

HUGO KOBLET
STAR OF THE CINEMA?
BY ALBERT DE WETTER

The certainty that he would win the Tour has meant that Koblet has received many propositions over the past few days. Propositions, that is, of every imaginable kind. He has been invited, among other things, to follow the next Tour... of Mexico, for amateurs (in October), and to give a series of lectures there. If he accepted, Koblet would travel to Mexico by boat, which would allow him to enjoy an enforced rest. But he is hesitating, because he's being offered the opportunity to shoot a film in Italy around the same time, a prospect he finds rather tempting. Among his other winter projects, Koblet envisages riding a Six-Days before the end of the year and, after a spell of winter sports in Davos, riding another in March (probably in Paris) to dive back into the pool of competitive cycling.

Koblet never neglected his physical appearance, in or out of competition.

Koblet's talent and conviviality captivated the crowds at the 1951 Tour.

At the finish-line, Koblet checked the time gaps himself.

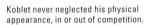

Fausto Coppi in a race of his own

If the 1951 Tour route had broken with tradition, the 1952 route began a new phase in Tour de France planning, drawing increasingly complex lines across the nation, and deliberately seeking new stage towns and novel obstacles, which this year included three first ascents of Alpe-d'Huez, Sestriere and the Puy de Dôme, and two time trials which, at around 60 kilometres (37 miles), were shorter than in the past.

The organizers dreamed of pitting Coppi, Kübler, Koblet and Bobet against each other. Only the first started; illness kept his rivals away. As early as stage five, Coppi broke away on the road to Namur and finished second, scattering his rivals out in his slipstream. The following day, Magni took over the yellow jersey with a stage win that gained him eight minutes on the main peloton. Coppi responded with victory in the first time trial, moving into third place overall. The day before Alpe-d'Huez, Sandrino Carrea, one of the riders known as 'Coppi's Angels' for their unswerving loyalty to the champion, donned the yellow jersey temporarily after joining a long breakaway to Lausanne. Then Coppi went into action; after a short acceleration by Robic at the foot of Alpe-d'Huez, he rose out of the saddle and forged ahead with elegance and power, head tucked down between his shoulders. From the roadside, a huge public witnessed the perfect, miraculous fusion of man and machine. Coppi's image even graced the first TV pictures from the Tour de France. Robic, second on the stage, lost 1min 20secs. Stan Ockers, third, lost 3mins 22secs. Coppi took the yellow jersey, just five seconds ahead of his team-mate Carrea. The next day, on the road to Sestrières, Coppi broke away on the Galibier, sped past the breakaway rider Jean Le Guilly without a second glance, and reached the bottom of the climb to Sestrières alone. By the time he reached the stage finish, his lead in the overall classification was three seconds short of twenty minutes. In response, the organizers doubled the prize money for second place, creating a race within the race with Fausto Coppi, the undisputed *campionissimo*, in a category of his own. From Sestrières to Monaco, he added four more minutes to his lead; in the Pyrenees, he extended it to twenty-seven with the stage win at Pau. He stretched it to over half an hour by winning on the Puy de Dôme, then allowed Stan Ockers to scratch a few seconds back on the final time trial. Even Gino Bartali, fourth for the second year running after giving his former rival a wheel, had to agree: Coppi had been simply magnificent.

GENERAL CLASSIFICATION

1. **Fausto Coppi** (ITA) Italy, 4,827 km in 151h.57m.20s; Average speed: 31.871 kph
2. **Constant 'Stan' Ockers** (BEL) Belgium, at 28m.17s.
3. **Bernardo Ruiz** (SPA) Spain, at 34m.38s.
4. Gino Bartali (ITA) Italy, at 35m.25s.
5. Jean Robic (FRA) France, at 35m.36s.
6. Fiorenzo Magni (ITA) Italy, at 38m.25s.
7. Alex Close (BEL), Belgium, at 38m.32s.
8. Jean-Baptiste 'Jean' Dotto (FRA) France, at 48m.1s.
9. Andrea Carrea (ITA) Italy, at 50m.20s.
10. Antonio Gelabert (SPA) Spain, at 58m.16s.
11. Raphaël Géminiani (FRA) France, at 1h.2m.47s.
12. Gottfried Weilenmann (SUI) Switzerland, at 1h.4m.19s.
13. Alois De Hertog (BEL) Belgium, at 1h.7m.15s.
14. Édouard Van Ende (BEL) Belgium, at 1h.17m.37s.
15. Jan Nolten (HOL) Holland, at 1h.30m.34s.
16. Jean Goldschmit (LUX) Luxembourg, at 1h.49m.47s.
17. Wilhem Van Est (HOL) Holland, at 1h.50m.54s.
18. Marcel Zelasco (FRA) North Africa, at 1h.51m.2s.
19. Nello Laurédi (FRA) France, at 1h.59m.43s.
20. Vincent Vitetta (FRA) South-East, at 2h.1m.17s.

39TH TOUR DE FRANCE, 23 STAGES – 4,827 KM

			STAGE	STAGE WINNER	YELLOW JERSEY
Stage 1	Wednesday 25 June	246 km	Brest – Rennes	R. Van Steenbergen (BEL)	R. Van Steenbergen
Stage 2	Thursday 26 June	181 km	Rennes – Le Mans	A. Rosseel (BEL)	R. Van Steenbergen
Stage 3	Friday 27 June	189 km	Le Mans – Rouen	N. Laurédi (FRA)	N. Laurédi
Stage 4	Saturday 28 June	232 km	Rouen – Roubaix	P. Molinéris (FRA)	N. Laurédi
Stage 5	Sunday 29 June	197 km	Roubaix – Namur (BEL)	J. Diederich (LUX)	N. Laurédi
Stage 6	Monday 30 June	228 km	Namur (BEL) – Metz	F. Magni (ITA)	F. Magni
Stage 7	Tuesday 1 July	60 km	Metz – Nancy (TT)	F. Coppi (ITA)	N. Laurédi
Stage 8	Wednesday 2 July	252 km	Nancy – Mulhouse	R. Géminiani (FRA)	F. Magni
Stage 9	Thursday 3 July	238 km	Mulhouse – Lausanne (SUI)	W. Diggelmann (SUI)	A. Carrea
Stage 10	Friday 4 July	266 km	Lausanne (SUI) – L'Alpe-d'Huez	F. Coppi (ITA)	F. Coppi
Stage 11	Sunday 6 July	182 km	Bourg-d'Oisans – Sestrières (ITA)	F. Coppi (ITA)	F. Coppi
Stage 12	Monday 7 July	251 km	Sestrières (ITA) – Monaco	J. Nolten (HOL)	F. Coppi
Stage 13	Tuesday 8 July	214 km	Monaco – Aix-en-Provence	R. Rémy (FRA)	F. Coppi
Stage 14	Wednesday 9 July	178 km	Aix-en-Provence – Avignon	J. Robic (FRA)	F. Coppi
Stage 15	Thursday 10 July	275 km	Avignon – Perpignan	G. Decaux (FRA)	F. Coppi
Stage 16	Friday 11 July	200 km	Perpignan – Toulouse	A. Rosseel (BEL)	F. Coppi
Stage 17	Sunday 13 July	204 km	Toulouse – Bagnères-de-Bigorre	R. Géminiani (FRA)	F. Coppi
Stage 18	Monday 14 July	149 km	Bagnères-de-Bigorre – Pau	F. Coppi (ITA)	F. Coppi
Stage 19	Tuesday 15 July	195 km	Pau – Bordeaux	H. Dekkers (HOL)	F. Coppi
Stage 20	Wednesday 16 July	228 km	Bordeaux – Limoges	J. Vivier (FRA)	F. Coppi
Stage 21	Thursday 17 July	245 km	Limoges – Puy de Dôme	F. Coppi (ITA)	F. Coppi
Stage 22	Friday 18 July	63 km	Clermont-Ferrand – Vichy (TT)	F. Magni (ITA)	F. Coppi
Stage 23	Saturday 19 July	354 km	Vichy – Paris	A. Rolland (FRA)	F. Coppi

Fausto Coppi prepared painstakingly for the Tour de France 1952. He won in magnificent style on the three great mountain stages and left the runner-up, Belgium's Stan Ockers, stranded at 28mins 17secs.

Robic provokes the master

For the first time, the Tour de France visits Alpe-d'Huez. The final 15-km (9.3-mile) stretch from Bourg-d'Oisans, 1,000 metres (3,281 ft) of climbing on a poor quality road, was a daunting prospect for the riders.

What happened between Bourg-d'Oisans and Alpe-d'Huez? The story is quickly told: a brusque acceleration by Robic a third of the way up the climb, an almost immediate response from Coppi, although he didn't catch Robic immediately; a brief moment wheel to wheel, and then, exactly six kilometres (3.7 miles) from the finish, Coppi attacked. During this attack, the great Italian ace didn't immediately destroy the little Frenchman; rather, he progressively extended his lead, without flying away. Over the first three kilometres (1.9 miles), he gained 50 seconds; over the final three, he added 30 more. Fausto appeared very much at ease, but we have to conclude that Robic was riding extremely strongly. It's a gratifying, and also a saddening observation. If France's best rider, in good condition, riding at his limit, lost 1min 20secs to Coppi on a 15-kilometre (9.3-mile) climb, how will he do in the gigantic challenge to be held the day after tomorrow? More importantly, how will everyone else do?

Which riders distinguished themselves behind Coppi and Robic? At first, Géminiani tried to hang on, but he was quickly forced to capitulate. Despite being well beaten (by nearly seven minutes at the finish), he didn't leave a bad impression. Eventually, a small group formed with Carrea, Ockers, Dotto and Gelabert. Le Guilly was also a member of this pack, but showed a terrible lack of judgement. Wanting to break away from his companions, he attacked with too much zest, accelerating violently in a tiny gear. He gained 30 metres in the blink of an eye, then, when he should have been pursuing his effort at a more normal pace, he ran out of breath. Dotto, keen to defend his reputation as a climber, and also anxious to protect his friend Robic, unleashed some of his great power to help ensure that the young upstart was neutralized.

Behind this group came Géminiani and Nolten. While 'Gém' was definitely on the decline, the young Dutchman achieved a veritable feat by shaking off the Frenchman well before the summit. He came in eighth, beaten on the line by a remarkable Molinéris (while Raphaël Géminiani came 13th). Even further back came Magni, Close and Bartali, the two Italian champions having been delayed by a minor fall. Who are the first revelations in the mountains? Apart from Nolten, we still hadn't seen anyone, except for Close, who is doing particularly well. Let us go further down: we see Laurédi, Weilenmann and Lazaridès, who were jumped before the finish by De Hertog, Massip and Deledda, the last of

whom must have been particularly satisfied with his climb. But it has to be said that this unique climb, which sliced through the general classification like a blade, could never be particularly favourable to new-comers who have not yet familiarized themselves with the terrain. With that proviso, the Spanish achieved a good all round result, with Gelabert coming in fourth, Ruiz 11th and Massip 16th. But the great lesson of today is that only on the climb, the last 15 km (9.3 miles) of the entire stage, was battle joined. This (even if we shouldn't prop up a categorical judgement with an isolated case) does nothing to promote high-altitude finishes.

Returning to the riders themselves, there were some disappointments: Gil, Mirando and Marinelli, for example. As for Dotto, whose role we have described, let's just assume that he hasn't revealed his full potential yet and that we won't be able to pass a definitive judgement until the circumstances of the race have allowed him a chance to prove himself! But taking the race situation as a whole, we have to admit that it has become much clearer and that we now know where we stand. The ascent of the Alpe-d'Huez (where we finally find the ideal cool conditions for a rest day) was the first real test, and it has proved most eloquent.

Coppi is plainly the best man in the race, in terms of sheer physical capacity. Robic is certainly the most reliable Frenchman, and Ockers is, for his part, the man on whom Belgian hopes can once more be pinned. Our own Laurédi and Géminiani have not been unworthy, but their placings are rather lowly (it's not impossible that the situation will change after a few stages, but we must go on present form). And we can see Close and De Hertog playing a very similar role among our Belgian friends. The Spanish and

Top: On the first hairpins of the climb to Alpe d'Huez, Robic attacked and broke away. Above: Coppi came back and then dropped him decisively 6 km (3.7 miles) from the summit. Of the favourites, only Robic and Ockers resisted. By this point, Bartali was already nearly 14 minutes behind his great rival.

the Dutch are decidedly better than might have been anticipated. Leaving aside Molinéris and Le Guilly, the French regionals are far from being brilliant. Also the Swiss aren't in as much distress as might have been feared, for one or other out of Weilenmann, Metzger and Diggelmann always finds a way not to pass unnoticed.

This is where we are now, and our round-up will be complete once we have broached the perennial problem of the Italian *squadra*. To tell the truth, the problem seems on the point of resolving

itself. Coppi has installed himself in the lead, which was easily predictable, and the only reason Carrea and Magni remain in overall contact is because at the start of the climb they stood above him in the general classification.

As for Bartali, he is now disappearing from the list of potential winners, and regarding the rather particular issue of Italian team spirit it doesn't appear that Coppi will have anything to fear from him in the future. At the start of the Tour, Gino could count on a degree of adulation that

might have been detrimental to Fausto. But opinion is fickle; after today's performance it appears that Coppi may have won many doubters over.

We are blithely reporting all this because it's a fascinating subject, but we don't deny that the first consequence of increased coherence in the Italian bloc will be to threaten French and Belgian positions. However, in truth, it is the mountains which will have the final say in the days to come; tactics will be relegated to the sidelines for a while.

Coppi triumphs *en solitaire*

SESTRIÈRES: Stretched out in the tub, Fausto Coppi lets his trainer wash him. Head hung back, he breathes gently, his narrow but deep rib cage inflating impressively. Then, he savagely expels the air through his nose as if he wanted to rid his nostrils and lungs of the dust of the road. After four or five breaths like this, Coppi seems refreshed, reinvigorated. 'It does me good,' he says with a smile.

'That stage was really tough,' he adds, anticipating our questions. Looking at his face, which shows scarcely a sign of effort, it seems an odd confession. There is no longer room for doubt: Coppi has indeed

recovered his tremendous form of 1949 and the last Giro d'Italia. Seeing him this calm and relaxed, the exploit he has just inscribed in the annals of the Tour seems almost natural.

'All the same,' he says, 'I didn't intend to attack on the Galibier.

'I wanted to wait for the final climb, and just to try to gain the bonuses at the summit of the Croix-de-Fer, the Galibier and the Montgenèvre. But the French, particularly Géminiani, roused me with their attacks on the Galibier. I counter-attacked and, since I was feeling very good, I kept going.' Coppi made this declaration so calmly that you might have believed it had been a matter of

Before the Tour, Fausto Coppi had some reservations about riding with Bartali. After Sestrières, Gino became a valued team-mate.

GINO GIVES HIS WHEEL TO FAUSTO!

MONACO: A moment that will enter Italian cycling legend. Fausto Coppi had three punctures in quick succession in less than 20 kilometres (12.5 miles). After one of these, Gino Bartali himself stopped to offer his wheel, saying that he was, like the rest of the team, at the leader's service. The incident seemed to confirm the power of the yellow jersey yet again. The three photographs (above) document the scene. Firstly, Bartali dismounts, about to remove his wheel with his team leader approaching in the background. Next, Coppi accepts Gino's wheel and fits it to his bicycle. Friendship between the two men may have been forged at this precise moment.

Above: On the ascent of the Col du Télégraphe, Coppi was still accompanied by Géminiani and Le Guilly (right). Below: On the Galibier he launched a decisive attack and began a stunning demonstration, culminating in a lead of almost 12 minutes on arrival at Sestrières.

'Coppi climbing is like a ski-lift gliding up its steel cable' marvelled Jacques Goddet, awed by Fausto's performance at Sestrières.

mere formality for him. Back in his room, Zambrini, the Bianchi team's commercial director, is preparing iced yoghurt, something Fausto always enjoys after racing. The conversation resumes, but this time the Tour leader has to answer ten questions at once; supporters and reporters from Italy and France have joined the first journalists on the scene.

Had he been worried about the last pass? 'No,' Fausto confesses. 'I was familiar with it. I'd already won at Sestrières in the 1949 Giro, with a 12-minute lead. But we finished on the descent the other side of the pass,' he emphasizes. Was he worried about the news of Robic's comeback in the Montgenèvre? Yes and no. He was surprised but expected that Robic might experience problems after his tough comeback.

Coppi is also surprised to learn that the Breton had to dismount six times on the Col de Sestrières to inflate his rear tyre. He shakes his head in admiration. We realize that he has changed his mind about 'Biquet'. Coppi is pressed to be more specific about the chief reasons for his attacking. Wasn't it because he wanted to put in a really good performance in front of Zambrini, who was following the stage in the Director-General's car? Didn't he want

With Coppi (overall winner and King of the Mountains) and the Challenge Desgrange-Colombo, the Italian team sweeps the board.

to win the stage because we were arriving in Italy? Coppi seeks to deny this, repeating that he felt well and that he had deemed it preferable to break away in order to gain, via bonus points, a precious lead which would cushion him from a hard knock or a crisis, the only thing that he now seems to fear.

As we leave, someone tells Coppi, 'We're going to visit your victims.'

'Well, ask them if they're as tired as I am,' says Fausto. 'You, tired?' says our colleague, 'with that relaxed, smiling face?' Coppi comments genially, 'But if I smile, it's because I've won, without that...' The phrase trails off. But you could guess what the Bianchi ace was thinking. He didn't want anyone to imagine that he was tempting fate. And yet...

Bobet, at last!

After winning a gruelling Giro d'Italia in June, reigning Tour de France champion Fausto Coppi, now aged 34, decided against defending his title. Louison Bobet had also ridden the Giro d'Italia, abandoning on the final stage with saddle sores. But by the start of the Tour, Bobet had recovered, and led the French national team, one of twelve ten-man teams contesting the 1953 Tour de France. The Tour celebrated its fiftieth year with the introduction of the *maillot vert*, the green jersey, awarded to the leader in the new points competition. Switzerland's Fritz Schaer headed the points competition and the general classification after winning the first two stages. By the evening of stage eleven, he had lost the yellow jersey definitively but twelve days later he earned a place in Tour history as the first winner of the points competition.

Meanwhile, the last-minute inclusion of Bobet in the French national team triggered off a bitter quarrel; Raphaël Géminiani (second in 1951), Nello Laurédi (eighth in 1953), Jean Dotto (eighth in 1952) and Édouard Teisseire refused to work for another leader. With the national team divided, Jean Robic, riding for West France, took the race lead at Luchon.

Robic's success was taken as an insult by Louison Bobet and by the French *directeur sportif* Marcel Bidot. Robic was a mere regional rider, banished from the ranks of the national team; now he posed the greatest threat. Bidot hatched a plan for stage thirteen; his riders followed it to the letter. At the stage start, Géminiani, Bobet, Rolland, Laurédi, Astrua and Malléjac attacked. On the way out of Albi, Robic had already missed the break; he finally arrived at Béziers thirty-eight minutes late. Bobet, meanwhile, had been squeezed into third place by his team-mates Laurédi and Géminiani, who gained time bonuses of a minute and thirty seconds respectively. He was livid. Marcel Bidot asked his riders, 'Who among you is sure he can win the yellow jersey in Paris?' Only Bobet raised his hand. The matter was settled. Transformed by his promise, Bobet used the great mountains stage from Gap to Briançon as his springboard. He dropped Gilbert Bauvin on the Col de Vars, sped across the Guil valley and followed his team-mate Adolphe Deledda's wheel to the foot of the Izoard. There, Bobet climbed with relentless power to reach Briançon with a five-minute lead. Famous for his one-day victories, Louison Bobet had finally won the Tour on his sixth attempt. For one of his most illustrious predecessors, Gino Bartali, this Tour marked the end of a beautiful era; he finished eleventh, thirty-two minutes behind the winner.

GENERAL CLASSIFICATION

1. **Louison Bobet** (FRA) France, 4,476 km in 129h.23m.25s; Average speed: 34.593 kph
2. **Jean Malléjac** (FRA) West, at 14m.18s.
3. **Giancarlo Astrua** (ITA) Italy, at 15m.2s.
4. Alex Close (BEL) Belgium, at 17m.35s.
5. Wout Wagtmans (HOL) Holland, at 18m.5s.
6. Fritz Schaer (SUI) Switzerland, at 18m.44s.
7. Antonin Rolland (FRA) France, at 23m.3s.
8. Nello Laurédi (FRA) France, at 26m.3s.
9. Raphaël Géminiani (FRA) France, at 27m.18s.
10. François Mahé (FRA) West, at 28m.26s.
11. Gino Bartali (ITA) Italy, at 32m.
12. Joseph Mirando (FRA) South-East, at 38m.21s.
13. Wim Van Est (HOL) Holland, at 39m.
14. José Serra (SPA) Spain, at 40m.32s.
15. Fiorenzo Magni (ITA) Italy, at 40m.47s.
16. Gilbert Bauvin (FRA) North-East Central, at 42m.3s.
17. Gerrit Voorting (HOL) Holland, at 44m.2s.
18. Marcel Ernzer (LUX) Luxembourg, at 46m.41s.
19. Jan Nolten (HOL) Holland, at 47m.29s.
20. Ugo Anzile (FRA) North-East Central, at 50m.38s.

40TH TOUR DE FRANCE, 22 STAGES – 4,476 KM

			STAGE	STAGE WINNER	YELLOW JERSEY
Stage 1	Friday 3 July	195 km	Strasbourg – Metz	F. Schaer (SUI)	F. Schaer
Stage 2	Saturday 4 July	227 km	Metz – Liège (BEL)	F. Schaer (SUI)	F. Schaer
Stage 3	Sunday 5 July	221 km	Liège (BEL) – Lille	S. Bober (FRA)	F. Schaer
Stage 4	Monday 6 July	188 km	Lille – Dieppe	G. Voorting (HOL)	F. Schaer
Stage 5	Tuesday 7 July	200 km	Dieppe – Caen	J. Malléjac (FRA)	R. Hassenforder
Stage 6	Wednesday 8 July	206 km	Caen – Le Mans	M. Van Geneugden (BEL)	R. Hassenforder
Stage 7	Thursday 9 July	181 km	Le Mans – Nantes	L. Isotti (ITA)	R. Hassenforder
Stage 8	Friday 10 July	345 km	Nantes – Bordeaux	J. Nolten (HOL)	R. Hassenforder
Stage 9	Sunday 12 July	197 km	Bordeaux – Pau	F. Magni (ITA)	F. Schaer
Stage 10	Monday 13 July	103 km	Pau – Cauterets	J. Lorono (SPA)	F. Schaer
Stage 11	Tuesday 14 July	115 km	Cauterets – Luchon	J. Robic (FRA)	J. Robic
Stage 12	Wednesday 15 July	228 km	Luchon – Albi	A. Darrigade (FRA)	F. Mahé
Stage 13	Thursday 16 July	189 km	Albi – Béziers	N. Laurédi (FRA)	J. Malléjac
Stage 14	Friday 17 July	214 km	Béziers – Nîmes	B. Quennehen (FRA)	J. Malléjac
Stage 15	Saturday 18 July	173 km	Nîmes – Marseille	M. Quentin (FRA)	J. Malléjac
Stage 16	Sunday 19 July	236 km	Marseille – Monaco	W. Van Est (HOL)	J. Malléjac
Stage 17	Tuesday 21 July	261 km	Monaco – Gap	W. Wagtmans (HOL)	J. Malléjac
Stage 18	Wednesday 22 July	165 km	Gap – Briançon	L. Bobet (FRA)	L. Bobet
Stage 19	Thursday 23 July	227 km	Briançon – Lyon	G. Meunier (FRA)	L. Bobet
Stage 20	Friday 24 July	70 km	Lyon – Saint-Étienne (TT)	L. Bobet (FRA)	L. Bobet
Stage 21	Saturday 25 July	210 km	Saint-Étienne – Montluçon	W. Wagtmans (HOL)	L. Bobet
Stage 22	Sunday 26 July	328 km	Montluçon – Paris	F. Magni (ITA)	L. Bobet

Louison Bobet celebrated his Tour victory by winning the final time trial on undulating
roads between Lyon and Saint-Étienne, watched by his wife Christiane (left).
The Tour was his, at the sixth attempt.

France falls for Louison

The 1954 Tour de France started in Amsterdam, the first of many foreign *Grands Départs*. Louison Bobet's campaign for his second Tour was simplified by the absence of Italian competition. After a riders' strike at the Giro d'Italia, the Italian Cycling Federation refused to authorize a team. A number of Italian riders sought independent commercial sponsorship, only to be refused entry by the French Cycling Federation, which opposed what were described as 'extra-sportive' interests in cycling. Coppi, in any case, was injured; he had been knocked down by a fugitive lorry wheel.

The Dutchman Wout Wagtmans celebrated the Amsterdam start by winning stage one. Bobet moved to within a second of him by winning stage two. On the morning of day four, Schaer, Koblet and Kübler, the three stars of the Swiss team, dominated the team time trial. Then, Gilbert Bauvin, the leader of the regionals from North-East and Central France, won stages ten and twelve, came second in stage eleven, and took the race lead. Of the main contenders, only Bobet counter-attacked to limit Bauvin's advantage on the punishing stage from Pau to Luchon.

Kübler lost five minutes; Koblet fell three times and lost nearly twenty-five. The following day, exhausted and injured, Koblet abandoned. Bauvin's appearance was a gift for the press. He made fun of the French national team, who responded with jibes about his northern accent and his bald head. The comedy ended when Bauvin punctured on the Montjaux between Toulouse and Millau, and lost contact with the winning break. Ferdi Kübler won the stage and Bobet took the yellow jersey.

In the Alps, Bobet rode with authority, using the Izoard to construct a brilliant win at Briançon, where he extended his advantage over Kübler to thirteen minutes – a lead he would keep all the way to Paris. Meanwhile, a Spanish maverick named Federico Bahamontes caught the public imagination with some extraordinary solo ascents. At Romeyère, he stole an ice-cream from an ice-cream seller and ate it at the roadside, waiting for the chasers to reach him. 'He's a very good climber,' conceded Jesús Loroño, his team-mate, 'but completely mad.' It was the obsession, close to madness, of a man determined to make his mark on history.

GENERAL CLASSIFICATION

1. **Louison Bobet** (FRA) France, 4,865.4 km in 140h.6m.5s; Average speed: 34.639 kph
2. **Ferdi Kübler** (SUI) Switzerland, at 15m.49s.
3. **Fritz Schaer** (SUI) Switzerland, at 21m.46s.
4. Jean-Baptiste 'Jean' Dotto (FRA) South-East, at 28m.21s.
5. Jean Malléjac (FRA) West, at 31m.38s.
6. Constant 'Stan' Ockers (BEL) Belgium, at 36m.2s.
7. Louis Bergaud (FRA) South-West, at 37m.55s.
8. Vincent Vitetta (FRA) South-East, at 41m.14s.
9. Jean Brankart (BEL) Belgium, at 42m.8s.
10. Gilbert Bauvin (FRA) North-East Central, at 42m.21s.
11. Nello Laurédi (FRA) France at 42m.42s.
12. Carlo Clerici (SUI) Switzerland, at 56m.36s.
13. Jean-Apôtre 'Apo' Lazaridès (FRA) South-East, at 1h.4m.3s.
14. Jan Nolten (HOL) Holland, at 1h.4m.15s.
15. François Mahé (FRA) West, at 1h.9m.3s.
16. Wilhem Van Est (HOL) Holland, at 1h.9m.13s.
17. Gerrit Voorting (HOL) Holland, at 1h.10m.20s.
18. Bernardo Ruiz (SPA) Spain, at 1h.11m.28s.
19. Antonin Rolland (FRA) France, at 1h.12m.20s.
20. Hein Van Breenen (HOL) Holland, at 1h.19m.10s.

41ST TOUR DE FRANCE, 23 STAGES – 4,865.4 KM

		STAGE		STAGE WINNER	YELLOW JERSEY
Stage 1	Thursday 8 July	216 km	Amsterdam (HOL) – Brasschaat (BEL)	W. Wagtmans (HOL)	W. Wagtmans
Stage 2	Friday 9 July	255 km	Beveren (BEL) – Lille	L. Bobet (FRA)	W. Wagtmans
Stage 3	Saturday 10 July	219 km	Lille – Rouen	M. Dussault (FRA)	W. Wagtmans
Stage 4 (1)	Sunday 11 July	104 km	Les Essarts – Les Essarts (TTT)	Switzerland	L. Bobet
Stage 4 (2)	Sunday 11 July	131 km	Rouen – Caen	W. Van Est (HOL)	L. Bobet
Stage 5	Monday 12 July	224 km	Caen – Saint-Brieuc	F. Kübler (SUI)	L. Bobet
Stage 6	Tuesday 13 July	179 km	Saint-Brieuc – Brest	D. Forlini (FRA)	L. Bobet
Stage 7	Wednesday 14 July	211 km	Brest – Vannes	J. Vivier (FRA)	L. Bobet
Stage 8	Thursday 15 July	190 km	Vannes – Angers	A. De Bruyne (BEL)	W. Wagtmans
Stage 9	Friday 16 July	343 km	Angers – Bordeaux	H. Faanhof (HOL)	W. Wagtmans
Stage 10	Sunday 18 July	202 km	Bordeaux – Bayonne	G. Bauvin (FRA)	W. Wagtmans
Stage 11	Monday 19 July	241 km	Bayonne – Pau	C. Ockers (BEL)	W. Wagtmans
Stage 12	Tuesday 20 July	161 km	Pau – Luchon	G. Bauvin (FRA)	G. Bauvin
Stage 13	Wednesday 21 July	203 km	Luchon – Toulouse	A. De Bruyne (BEL)	G. Bauvin
Stage 14	Thursday 22 July	225 km	Toulouse – Millau	F. Kübler (SUI)	L. Bobet
Stage 15	Friday 23 July	197 km	Millau – Le Puy	D. Forlini (FRA)	L. Bobet
Stage 16	Saturday 24 July	194 km	Le Puy – Lyon	J. Forestier (FRA)	L. Bobet
Stage 17	Monday 26 July	182 km	Lyon – Grenoble	L. Lazaridès (FRA)	L. Bobet
Stage 18	Tuesday 27 July	216 km	Grenoble – Briançon	L. Bobet (FRA)	L. Bobet
Stage 19	Wednesday 28 July	221 km	Briançon – Aix-les-Bains	J.-B. Dotto (FRA)	L. Bobet
Stage 20	Thursday 29 July	243 km	Aix-les-Bains – Besançon	L. Teisseire (FRA)	L. Bobet
Stage 21 (1)	Friday 30 July	134 km	Besançon – Épinal	F. Mahé (FRA)	L. Bobet
Stage 21 (2)	Friday 30 July	72 km	Épinal – Nancy (TT)	L. Bobet (FRA)	L. Bobet
Stage 22	Saturday 31 July	216 km	Nancy – Troyes	A. De Bruyne (BEL)	L. Bobet
Stage 23	Sunday 1 August	180 km	Troyes – Paris	R. Varnajo (FRA)	L. Bobet

After a long courtship, Bobet finally caught the heart of the French public. In Brest, the champion's popularity was sky high.

A new Tour, with a new competitive spirit

The superiority of one man, however fascinating in itself, and the absence of real competition inevitably diminish the attraction of the struggle for the yellow jersey. Don't let us reproach Louison Bobet, our illustrious winner, for having established his dominance from Briançon onwards! To do so, he had to confront and overcome all the difficulties that beleaguer those who compete in stage races. For despite his victory last year, he didn't start the race with any special rights, or with the power to conduct the race as he pleased. According to the laws that govern the Tour de France, demanding absolute equality of opportunity and treatment, Louison had to toil hard, boldly traversing the storms that blew at the start of the race, imposing his will by demonstrating his quality as a rider, performing his personal share of the hard work and achieving his results on merit. Now, the day after his superb victory, I am

sure he is happy that he was obliged to conquer all this. His victory is worth all the more since it was not willed by those who planned the route, nor influenced by public opinion, nor, in short, forced on his competitors. You know what I'm talking about: the embarrassing hegemony of a *campionissimo*, recognized before the start and sustained whatever the circumstances. The Tour de France honours its champions by not granting them any special favours.

On the contrary, this year, more than ever, we wanted to frustrate the predictions and put the riders to the test by opening up the race. It took a man of Koblet's qualities to profit from the restlessness and force the pace, and we had such a high-speed start that the early stages down the Atlantic seaboard had a profound effect on the overall battle and its conclusion. For this attacking start sapped the strength of many riders, including Wagtmans, Schaer, Bauvin,

even Kübler and perhaps also Koblet himself, and induced their crises, just as it caused Bobet's sudden collapse, shortly before the summit of the Peyresourde. Let's not forget this incident. The precipitating factor was Bahamontes' devastating attack; if it had come 5 kilometres (3 miles) earlier, our poor Louison would have certainly lost at least 15 minutes there and then. The result would have been a completely different race.

The old guard will say that all this proves that the best riders in the 1954 Tour have occasionally been guilty of allowing themselves to get carried away and that there should be a return to the time-established methods of yesteryear: no breakaways before the major stages, contained energy output... in short, economize, economize, economize. But that would be too simple.

Nor should we forget that the Giro showed an inclination, in its early stages at least, to surrender its customary respect for cycling's sacred cows, with the result that Messrs Coppi, Koblet, Magni and cycling's celebrity A-list suddenly found themselves chasing a deficit of more than half an hour, which they never managed to win back! So from now on, they have to commit themselves to playing their part. Perhaps the best tactic, the most reasonable, is to lead, to take the initiative. Riding defensively demands just as much effort, achieves only negative results and serves the majority of riders who are content to draft along in the slipstream of the team, which is obliged to react to every attack. It took all Bobet's astonishing mastery, his foresight and the magnificent physical form in which he found himself for him to succeed in closing all the gaps that his rampant Swiss adversaries had opened up on the way to Pont Aven. In other words, until our Louison's energy, brio and swiftness of response forced the red devils to calm down.

At its present pace, the Tour can only be won by the all-round rider. It requires presence of mind, exemplary vigilance, the courage to take up the racing, perfectly balanced health, fitness that grows throughout the race and the full range of abilities that distinguish the cycling athlete: climbing, riding powerfully on the flat and sprinting.

Grenoble to Briançon: After definitively dropping Ferdi Kübler, Louison Bobet takes flight on the Col de l'Izoard and wins the stage at Briançon with a lead of nearly two minutes over his adversary.

Yvette Horner, the famous accordionist, was in a lively mood at the distribution of jerseys. She seemed keen on getting to know Louison Bobet better...

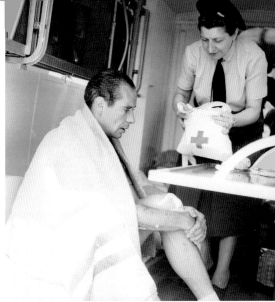

Koblet, already injured in a fall, suffered another on the Aubisque and abandoned the race at Toulouse.

Again cursed by bad luck, Jean Robic crashed at the stage finish at Caen. He quit the Tour.

We believe that the main threat to the attraction of a stage race as popular as the Tour de France is its conservatism. We no longer wanted it to be won at any particular point, fixed in advance; nor did we want successive stages that lacked any obvious difficulties. The peloton ended the 1954 Tour visibly tired. The time gaps were huge. Every face was drawn. Nevertheless, in future it will not be possible to slow the pace of the battle, and waiting and seeing amounts to surrendering to those prepared to take their fate in their own hands – it will be up to the riders to prepare better for their Tour and to apply themselves more rigorously to the demands of their profession.

Bobet did not triumph over exhaustion and his rivals simply by pedalling steadily between Amsterdam and Paris, via Bayonne and Briançon; he had the strength of character to distance himself from the normal way of life of a man of his age, which in his case has meant turning his back on the countless offers and temptations that fame brought him. We have all seen how exceptionally gifted riders like Hassenforder, Le Guilly or Nolten squander their great fortune through undisciplined behaviour, and we can take comfort in knowing that beyond the stage results, the classifications and the statistics, the rigours endured during the Tour de France serve to establish ethical rules of conduct that provide an example to all who practise sport – as well as everyone else.

ALL HOLLAND MAKES THE *GRAND DÉPART* A TRIUMPH

The entire population of the Netherlands seemed to have turned out along the roads of Wassenaar, Delft, Rotterdam and Breda: in all the towns and villages through which the Tour passed yesterday.

Many tens of thousands of spectators squeezed together in serried rows that remained unbroken for miles, brandishing little blue, white and red flags, clapping and cheering everyone and everything involved in the Tour: the riders, the motorcyclists and the vehicles front and aft. Was it a crowd of die-hard Tour fans? Probably not. These people weren't carrying programmes. They weren't trying to make out the numbers on the cyclists' backs and identify them. They were greeting the Tour which, for the first time ever, was paying them a visit and, from the first stage, they made it a triumph...

Bobet through the pain barrier

In 1955, the finish-lines were equipped for the first time with photo-finish cameras, and recorded television images reached homes in the major French cities within hours of the stage finishes. And with a short transfer from Poitiers to Châtellerault for the final time trial, the route ceased to be continuous, setting another trend for the future.

Bobet was the overwhelming favourite to win his third consecutive Tour de France. In August 1954, soon after winning his second Tour de France, he had won the World Championship; in March 1955, wearing the rainbow jersey of the World Champion, he had defeated the Flemish hard man Rik Van Steenbergen over the cobbles of the Tour of Flanders.

After Miguel Poblet won the opening stage, the yellow jersey graced the shoulders of a Spaniard for the first time. Dutchmen Wout Wagtmans and Wim Van Est briefly led the general classification, but when France's Antonin Rolland took over the race lead with Bobet twelve minutes behind, the race favourite had to observe team discipline. As far as Mont Ventoux, that is. Through the pine forest on the lower slopes, Bobet rode prudently. When he saw Luxembourg's climbing specialist Charly Gaul in difficulty, he forced the pace and emerged onto the rubble-strewn desert of its heights alone. He rode the final hour to Avignon like a time trial, preserving a fifty-second lead over his nearest rival, Belgium's Jean Brankart, after an intense effort. Rolland was still in yellow but psychologically Bobet was winning the Tour.

The Ventoux conferred a sacramental aura on Bobet's victory. Stan Ockers and Gilbert Bauvin lost all their illusions on its slopes. Jean Malléjac fell into the boulders and lapsed into doping-induced semi-consciousness. The race doctor had to unlock his jaw before he could administer first aid.

Ferdi Kübler, meanwhile, had become a victim of self-sabotage by attacking its gradient with his customary lack of restraint. Géminiani, an inveterate raconteur, dined off his version of events for years:

'Be careful, Ferdi; the Ventoux is not like other passes.'

'And Ferdi is not like other riders!'

Kübler was soon zigzagging across the road, his cap dishevelled, his expression demented, saliva dripping from his lips, until he took refuge in a café, then took to the road again, this time in the wrong direction. Somewhere between tragedy and comedy, the episode effectively ended his career.

The Pyrenees found in Bobet's favour, despite agonizing saddle sores that forced him to ride out of the saddle. Jean Brankart regained over two minutes in the final time trial, but by then, Bobet had done enough to win the Tour.

GENERAL CLASSIFICATION

1. **Louison Bobet** (FRA) France, 4,476 km in 130h.29m.26s; Average speed: 34.639 kph
2. **Jean Brankart** (BEL) Belgium, at 4m.53s.
3. **Charly Gaul** (LUX) Luxembourg-Mixed, at 11m.30s.
4. Pasquale Fornara (ITA) Italy, at 12m.44s.
5. Antonin Rolland (FRA) France, at 13m.18s.
6. Raphaël Géminiani (FRA) France, at 15m.1s.
7. Giancarlo Astrua (ITA) Italy, at 18m.13s.
8. Constant 'Stan' Ockers (BEL) Belgium, at 27m.13s.
9. Alex Close (BEL) Belgium, at 31m.10s.
10. François Mahé (FRA) France, at 36m.27s.
11. Maurice Quentin (FRA) West, at 36m.52s.
12. Agostino Coletto (ITA) Italy, at 39m.14s.
13. Raymond Impnis (BEL) Belgium, at 46m.3s.
14. Jean Bobet (FRA) France, at 1h.0m.5s.
15. Wilhem Van Est (HOL) Holland, at 1h.4m.50s.
16. Vincent Vitetta (FRA) South-East, at 1h.5m.18s.
17. Alfred De Bruyne (BEL) Belgium, 1h.5m.29s.
18. Gilbert Bauvin (FRA) North-East Central, at 1h.9m.58s.
19. Wout Wagtmans (HOL) Holland, at 1h.10m.16s.
20. Jesús Loroño (SPA) Spain, at 1h.19m.25s.

42ND TOUR DE FRANCE, 22 STAGES – 4,476 KM

			STAGE	STAGE WINNER	YELLOW JERSEY
Stage 1 (1)	Thursday 7 July	102 km	Le Havre – Dieppe	M. Poblet (SPA)	M. Poblet
Stage 1 (2)	Thursday 7 July	12.5 km	Dieppe – Dieppe (TTT)	Pays-Bas	M. Poblet
Stage 2	Friday 8 July	204 km	Dieppe – Roubaix	A. Rolland (FRA)	W. Wagtmans
Stage 3	Saturday 9 July	210 km	Roubaix – Namur (BEL)	L. Bobet (FRA)	W. Wagtmans
Stage 4	Sunday 10 July	225 km	Namur (BEL) – Metz	W. Kemp (LUX)	A. Rolland
Stage 5	Monday 11 July	229 km	Metz – Colmar	R. Hassenforder (FRA)	A. Rolland
Stage 6	Tuesday 12 July	195 km	Colmar – Zurich (SUI)	A. Darrigade (FRA)	A. Rolland
Stage 7	Wednesday 13 July	267 km	Zurich (SUI) – Thonon-les-Bains	J. Hinsen (HOL)	W. Van Est
Stage 8	Thursday 14 July	253 km	Thonon-les-Bains – Briançon	C. Gaul (LUX)	A. Rolland
Stage 9	Friday 15 July	275 km	Briançon – Monaco	R. Géminiani (FRA)	A. Rolland
Stage 10	Sunday 17 July	240 km	Monaco – Marseille	L. Lazaridès (FRA)	A. Rolland
Stage 11	Monday 18 July	198 km	Marseille – Avignon	L. Bobet (FRA)	A. Rolland
Stage 12	Tuesday 19 July	240 km	Avignon – Millau	A. Fantini (ITA)	A. Rolland
Stage 13	Wednesday 20 July	205 km	Millau – Albi	D. De Groot (HOL)	A. Rolland
Stage 14	Thursday 21 July	156 km	Albi – Narbonne	L. Caput (FRA)	A. Rolland
Stage 15	Friday 22 July	151 km	Narbonne – Ax-les-Thermes	L. Pezzi (ITA)	A. Rolland
Stage 16	Sunday 24 July	123 km	Ax-les-Thermes – Toulouse	R. Van Steenbergen (BEL)	A. Rolland
Stage 17	Monday 25 July	249 km	Toulouse – Saint-Gaudens	C. Gaul (LUX)	L. Bobet
Stage 18	Tuesday 26 July	206 km	Saint-Gaudens – Pau	J. Brankart (BEL)	L. Bobet
Stage 19	Wednesday 27 July	195 km	Pau – Bordeaux	W. Wagtmans (HOL)	L. Bobet
Stage 20	Thursday 28 July	243 km	Bordeaux – Poitiers	J. Forestier (FRA)	L. Bobet
Stage 21	Friday 29 July	68.6 km	Châtellerault – Tours (TT)	J. Brankart (BEL)	L. Bobet
Stage 22	Saturday 30 July	229 km	Tours – Paris	M. Poblet (SPA)	L. Bobet

After catching and dropping Géminiani and Kübler, Bobet, in the jersey of the World Champion, attacked on Mont Ventoux and won the stage at Avignon.

A historic moment for Spain and Poblet: by winning the stage at Dieppe, the Spanish sprinter became the first Spaniard to wear the yellow jersey.

Dieppe-Roubaix: Antonin Rolland beat Wagtmans in the sprint. The latter took the yellow jersey. Rolland climbed to fourth place in the general classification.

Malléjac out cold

AVIGNON: The most pitiable episode we witnessed during the murderous ascent of Mont Ventoux, under a fiery sun, was undoubtedly Malléjac's harrowing abandon. Still some 10 kilometres (6 miles) from the summit, he simply crumpled beside the road. With one foot still attached to a pedal, he continued to turn unconsciously the other leg like an automaton, groaning. Ducazeaux went to his aid, alarmed by the spectators who huddled round him. Malléjac was inanimate, his eyes rolled back, his skinny physique accentuated by a waxy pallor and drawn features. Jean Garnault was alerted and notified Dr Dumas. Malléjac's teeth had to be prised apart in an attempt to get him to drink and it was only some 15 minutes later, after he had been injected with Solu-Camphor and given oxygen, that he began to revive from his faint. He had still not fully recovered when he was taken away in an ambulance. Struggling, gesticulating and shouting, he wanted to leave the vehicle, demanded his bicycle, and had to be restrained. He is under observation in an Avignon clinic where, yesterday evening, his condition was described as improved.

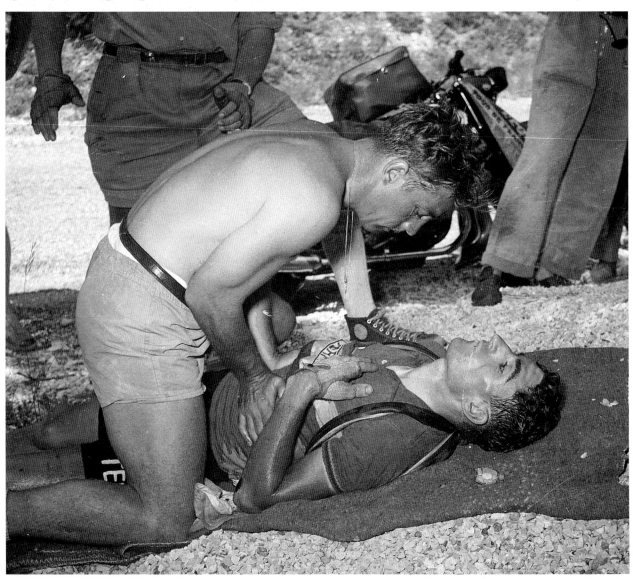

Eighth overall at the stage start, Malléjac was the victim of a spectacular but disturbing collapse while climbing Mont Ventoux. Dr Dumas gives him first aid.

Despite a brilliant climb up the Aubisque and crossing the summit first, Luxembourg's Charly Gaul (right) couldn't shake off Louison Bobet.

Louison Bobet joins Philippe Thys

Philippe Thys made an appearance at the Parc des Princes, joining the welcoming committee for the riders. Who would have thought this imposing gentleman, dressed in a tweed suit and with his hair slicked down, not very tall but solidly built, though without a pinch of fat, was 65 years old?

The winner of three Tours de France, in 1913, 1914 and again in 1920, was touring the Auvergne with friends when his wife passed on *L'Équipe*'s invitation to attend the finish of the Tour. 'So I left my companions at Limoges, took the train and disembarked in Paris,' he told us. Although composed, Thys was visibly affected by the atmosphere of the Parc; moved to emotion, even, as old memories returned. Evidently, his famous hat-trick in the Tour remains with him.

'Bobet will beat my record,' Thys said, when it was clear that Louison could no longer lose this Tour. 'I salute him because he is a great champion, but I think that if the war had never taken place, I too could have won three consecutive Tours.' The peloton suddenly darted into the Parc with Bobet...

The winner of the 1953, 1954 and 1955 Tours was surrounded, grabbed, photographed and embraced. He was presented with a brand-new Suze yellow jersey and a pennant, the Marseillaise was played, and

then Philippe Thys presented him with a bouquet to mark his three victories. The older man then took a lap of honour with Bobet: the two great men of the Tour's history sharing equal honours.

At Pau, at the end of a gruelling mountain stage, Jean Brankart defeats Bobet, Gaul and Géminiani in the sprint.

The triumph of modesty

Commercially-sponsored cycling teams, known to the French cycling establishment as the 'extra-sportifs', had begun in Italy at the end of 1953, when Fiorenzo Magni found himself facing unemployment when bicycle frame manufacturer Wilier-Triestina announced its withdrawal from team sponsorship. Magni approached the hand cream manufacturer Nivea, who agreed to fund his team. In France, Raphaël Géminiani approached the drinks manufacturer Saint-Raphaël-Quinquina (with whom he shared his forename), and secured a similar deal. The 'extra-sportifs' brought something new to cycling's established order; the Tour de France didn't immediately feel their influence, but a slow process had begun which would one day lead to the disappearance of national teams.

Other absences left the 1956 Tour de France wide open. Not yet recovered from an operation for his persistent saddle sores, Louison Bobet stayed away. So too did Jean Robic, convalescing after an accident, and the ageing heroes Coppi, Kübler and Koblet, in the twilight of their careers.

A new generation was waiting in the wings. Luxembourg's brilliant climber Charly Gaul was the favourite, but his rivalry with Stan Ockers and Federico Bahamontes for the title of King of the Mountains distracted him from the greater prize of the general classification. And when thirty-one riders broke away on stage seven and gained eighteen minutes on the peloton, the yellow jersey ended up with Roger Walkowiak, an honest worker on the regional French North-East Central team, who rode beside Bauvin and Géminiani in Saint-Raphaël colours.

Judiciously selecting the breakaways, André Darrigade fought his way back into contention, but a series of bitter rows between him and Gilbert Bauvin left the team with deep divisions. By hanging on in the Pyrenees, the Belgian Jan Adriaenssens took the yellow jersey from Darrigade, but on stage fifteen, Adriaenssens was among several Belgian riders who suffered food-poisoning and lost his lead. From Turin to Grenoble, Walkowiak rode with Bahamontes; by finishing fourth, he reclaimed the race lead. At his shoulder, however, was Gilbert Bauvin. At the Parc des Princes, the French *directeur sportif* Marcel Bidot was unable to hide his disappointment. 'If Darrigade had backed Bauvin up instead of going after the victory himself, Bauvin would have won the Tour.'

It had been a Tour without panache, and Walkowiak was panned as a second-rate winner of a second-rate race thanks to an error of judgement by the genuine contenders. Yet his critics forgot that Walkowiak was a resilient, reliable performer who had climbed well enough at the 1955 Tour to drop Louison Bobet on the slopes of the Côte du Laffrey.

GENERAL CLASSIFICATION

1. **Roger Walkowiak** (FRA) North-East Central, 4,527 km in 124h.1m.16s; Average speed: 36.268 kph
2. **Gilbert Bauvin** (FRA) France, at 1m.25s.
3. **Jan Adriaenssens** (BEL) Belgium, at 3m.44s.
4. Federico Bahamontes (SPA) Spain, at 10m.14s.
5. Nino Defilippis (ITA) Italy, at 10m.25s.
6. Wout Wagtmans (HOL) Holland, at 10m.59s.
7. Nello Laurédi (FRA) South-East, at 14m.1s.
8. Constant 'Stan' Ockers (BEL) Belgium, at 16m.52s.
9. René Privat (FRA) France, at 22m.59s.
10. A. Barbarosa Alves (POR) Luxembourg Mixed, at 26m.3s.
11. Gerrit Voorting (HOL) Holland, at 27m.16s.
12. Jean Forestier (FRA) France, at 30m.15s.
13. Charly Gaul (LUX) Luxembourg Mixed, at 32m.14s.
14. Brian Robinson (GBR) Luxembourg Mixed, at 33m.54s.
15. Daan De Groot (HOL) Holland, at 38m.40s.
16. André Darrigade (FRA) France, at 39m.51s.
17. Alex Close (BEL) Belgium, at 41m.47s.
18. Fernand Picot (FRA) West, at 42m.28s.
19. Jean-Baptiste 'Jean' Dotto (FRA) South-East, at 47m.19s.
20. Alfred De Bruyne (BEL) Belgium, at 49m.53s.

43RD TOUR DE FRANCE, 22 STAGES – 4,527 KM

			STAGE	STAGE WINNER	YELLOW JERSEY
Stage 1	Thursday 5 July	223 km	Reims – Liège (BEL)	A. Darrigade (FRA)	A. Darrigade
Stage 2	Friday 6 July	217 km	Liège (BEL) – Lille	A. De Bruyne (BEL)	A. Darrigade
Stage 3	Saturday 7 July	225 km	Lille – Rouen	A. Padovan (ITA)	G. Desmet
Stage 4 (1)	Sunday 8 July	151 km	Les Essarts – Les Essarts (TT)	C. Gaul (LUX)	G. Desmet
Stage 4 (2)	Sunday 8 July	125 km	Rouen – Caen	R. Hassenforder (FRA)	A. Darrigade
Stage 5	Monday 9 July	189 km	Caen – Saint-Malo	J. Morvan (FRA)	A. Darrigade
Stage 6	Tuesday 10 July	192 km	Saint-Malo – Lorient	A. De Bruyne (BEL)	A. Darrigade
Stage 7	Wednesday 11 July	244 km	Lorient – Angers	A. Fantini (ITA)	R. Walkowiak
Stage 8	Thursday 12 July	180 km	Angers – La Rochelle	M. Poblet (SPA)	R. Walkowiak
Stage 9	Friday 13 July	219 km	La Rochelle – Bordeaux	R. Hassenforder (FRA)	R. Walkowiak
Stage 10	Sunday 15 July	201 km	Bordeaux – Bayonne	A. De Bruyne (BEL)	G. Voorting
Stage 11	Monday 16 July	255 km	Bayonne – Pau	N. Defilippis (ITA)	A. Darrigade
Stage 12	Tuesday 17 July	130 km	Pau – Luchon	J.-P. Schmitz (LUX)	J. Adriaenssens
Stage 13	Wednesday 18 July	176 km	Luchon – Toulouse	N. Defilippis (ITA)	J. Adriaenssens
Stage 14	Thursday 19 July	231 km	Toulouse – Montpellier	R. Hassenforder (FRA)	J. Adriaenssens
Stage 15	Friday 20 July	204 km	Montpellier – Aix-en-Provence	J. Thomin (FRA)	W. Wagtmans
Stage 16	Sunday 22 July	203 km	Aix-en-Provence – Gap	J. Forestier (FRA)	W. Wagtmans
Stage 17	Monday 23 July	234 km	Gap – Turin (ITA)	N. Defilippis (ITA)	W. Wagtmans
Stage 18	Tuesday 24 July	250 km	Turin (ITA) – Grenoble	C. Gaul (LUX)	R. Walkowiak
Stage 19	Wednesday 25 July	173 km	Grenoble – Saint-Étienne	S. Ockers (BEL)	R. Walkowiak
Stage 20	Thursday 26 July	73 km	Saint-Étienne – Lyon (TT)	M. Bover (SPA)	R. Walkowiak
Stage 21	Friday 27 July	237 km	Lyon – Montluçon	R. Hassenforder (FRA)	R. Walkowiak
Stage 22	Saturday 28 July	331 km	Montluçon – Paris	G. Nencini (ITA)	R. Walkowiak

The unassuming Roger Walkowiak surprised everyone by wearing the yellow jersey into Paris without having won a stage. Disappointed with the Tour as a whole, the critics unjustly made Walkowiak a by-word for unworthy victory.

Walkowiak, the best strategist

The solitary exercise of power: 'Walko' in the yellow jersey during the Lyon time trial.

The yellow jersey is a heavy burden to bear, as Walkowiak discovered at the end of the Tour.

The '56 Tour was too frank with us for us not to be frank back. We shouldn't need to suppress a few home truths. Although it did not end plagued by ill health or uncertainty, the unfortunate impression at the Parc des Princes was that the last day had been a letdown. Riders who had been attacking all out on stages of 200 kilometres (124 miles), capable of seizing advantages of 15 minutes, didn't even open hostilities to challenge the 1min-25sec lead in 300 kilometres (186 miles) of racing.

This Tour had two stages too many, two grinding stages that rather weighed down a race that had been seductive for its highly competitive and revolutionary spirit. Don't misinterpret our meaning here: we are not calling for Walko's head. He deserves his victory, though he himself would probably have triumphed from one last, savage battle, by repulsing, for instance, the attacks of the Belgians or the French. All kinds of reasons for this pact of non-aggression will be sought; a few more or less disagreeable hypotheses will also be raised, no doubt.

To understand this Tour, we need to take the most simple, most direct route to the truth, and the only persuasive conclusion to be drawn from this unfinished finale is that the leaders of the classification were afraid of each other. We had credited Bauvin with

the boldness and belligerence of Jean Robic. But it's no use being more of a Bauvinist than Bauvin himself. We have to submit to the facts, and the facts say that the man from Nancy was suited to second place, and that's what he achieved. The riders who finished this infernal, devilish cycle had an excuse in their favour before which we're happy to bow: fatigue.

Physical lassitude may, in fact, have lowered the morale of the French and Belgian national teams; all the same, if we examine from today's standpoint the actions and deeds of the principal players, we discern that their teams lacked confidence in them. The only place any team spirit came into play was in the regional teams, especially the team representing North-East Central, and the West team. Walko was better served by a handful of faithful companions, such as the splendid Deledda, the courageous Huyghe and Bertolo (both carrying injuries) or the invaluable Scribante and Chupin, than Bauvin was by the French, or Adriaenssens by the Belgians. Walko, from Montluçon, had no ambitious deputies, so his place as leader could not provoke any jealousies. To a man, the NEC team was ready to make every sacrifice for him. Bauvin's attitude, on the other hand, created some personal qualms among his entourage. He was

frequently criticized for not being a good team member, and he needed to learn that one must give in order to receive. Furthermore, as he seemed content with a secondary role, his team wasn't motivated to go all out for him. The French team never really bonded. It had floated around Darrigade, a weak and sentimental leader who was never officially acknowledged, then it drifted around Bauvin, leader by mere force of circumstances, but one who, unlike Dacquois, was never the natural leader of the French team.

Bauvin and the French team sinned through lack of conviction. They were afraid of being the victims of the final offensive that they should have themselves unleashed. They stopped playing for victory and started playing for a placing. Walkowiak may have benefited from the rivalries inside the national teams, but it's just one more point in his credit that he knew how to exploit them. This 'little' Walko ended by earning the respect of the 'big' riders, and that's how he became one of them. He may have won a Tour without great names, but he did win a great Tour, and that, in our opinion, is even better.

Known for his skills as a climber, Walko was even able to contain the fiery Charly Gaul, who launched a magnificent offensive on the Croix-de-Fer.

The birth of a legend

On 23 May 1957, at Loreto in the Italian Marches, Louison Bobet, wearing the leader's jersey of Italy's national tour, the Giro d'Italia, announced that he would not take part in the Tour de France. With his iron discipline and unforgiving work ethic, the Breton had become a living symbol of France's post-war recovery. It was unthinkable that he shouldn't ride the Tour.

Two men replaced him: André Darrigade, an established star at 28, and a 23-year-old from Normandy named Jacques Anquetil, already famous for defeating Koblet in the Grand Prix des Nations, the greatest time trial in professional cycling.

Darrigade won stage one and the first yellow jersey. On stage two, Charly Gaul was overcome by the unbearable heat, and abandoned. Then Jacques Anquetil exploded into Tour de France history. He won stage four at his home town of Rouen, and took the yellow jersey temporarily at Charleroi. Then, on stage nine, he joined the winning breakaway and made up ten minutes on the race leader, his team-mate Jean Forestier. Through the Alps to Briançon, Anquetil made up Forestier's three-minute advantage, and added four more.

Saturday 13 July was, in theory at least, a rest day in the Catalan capital, Barcelona. Yet a 9.8-kilometre (6-mile) time trial had been arranged on Montjuich. No time bonuses were available, but Anquetil made it a point of principle to win the stage and defeat Forestier. Untouchable against the clock and on the flat stages, Anquetil was also an excellent climber. Nonetheless, the greatest threat to his dominance came in the Pyrenees. From Ax-les-Thermes to Saint-Gaudens, Jan Adriaenssens, Gastone Nencini and René Dotto launched probing attacks. Anquetil, with the help of his team-mates Louis Bergaud, Gilbert Bauvin and André Darrigade, struggled to respond. The following day, Anquetil launched an imprudent attack, climbing the Tourmalet at an infernal pace and dropping Nencini. Then, at the feed zone, he was handed the wrong musette; inside, instead of semolina and fruit, he found nothing but iced tea. On the Soulor, he ran out of energy. For 25 kilometres (15.5 miles), he rode at a snail's pace, as Janssens sped away in his bid for the yellow jersey. Da Silva, a Portuguese rider on the Luxembourg/Mixed team, led him through his crisis; 10 kilometres (6.2 miles) from Pau, Anquetil recovered, and powered towards the finish-line. He had lost 2mins 38secs, but the yellow jersey was safe. In the final time trial, Anquetil re-established his dominance and extended his margin of victory to nearly fifteen minutes. A star was born.

GENERAL CLASSIFICATION

1. **Jacques Anquetil** (FRA) France, 4,664 km in 135h.44m.42s; Average speed: 34.520 kph
2. **Marcel Janssens** (BEL) Belgium, at 14m.56s.
3. **Adolf Christian** (AUT) Switzerland, at 17m.20s.
4. Jean Forestier (FRA) France, at 18m.2s.
5. Jesús Loroño (SPA) Spain, at 20m.17s.
6. Gastone Nencini (ITA) Italy, at 26m.3s.
7. Nino Defilippis (ITA) Italy, at 27m.57s.
8. Wilhem Van Est (HOL) Holland, at 28m.10s.
9. Jan Adriaenssens (BEL) Belgium, at 34m.7s.
10. Jean-Baptiste 'Jean' Dotto (FRA) South-East, at 36m.31s.
11. François Mahé (FRA) France, at 39m.34s.
12. Marcel Rohrbach (FRA) North-East Central, at 42m.58s.
13. Fernand Picot (FRA) West, at 48m.26s.
14. Gilbert Bauvin (FRA) France, at 54m.48s.
15. Jean Bobet (FRA) Île-de-France, at 57m.48s.
16. Joseph Planckaert (BEL) Belgium, at 58m.52s.
17. Désiré Keteleer (BEL) Belgium, at 1h.0m.36s.
18. Joseph Thomin (FRA) West, at 1h.14m.38s.
19. Raymond Hoorelbeke (FRA) Île-de-France, at 1h.16m.18s.
20. Arrigo Padovin (ITA) Italy, at 1h.23m.17s.

44TH TOUR DE FRANCE, 23 STAGES – 4,664 KM

STAGE				STAGE WINNER	YELLOW JERSEY
Stage 1	Thursday 27 June	204 km	Nantes – Granville	A. Darrigade (FRA)	A. Darrigade
Stage 2	Friday 28 June	226 km	Granville – Caen	R. Privat (FRA)	R. Privat
Stage 3 (1)	Saturday 29 June	15 km	Caen – Caen (TTT)	France	R. Privat
Stage 3 (2)	Saturday 29 June	134 km	Caen – Rouen	J. Anquetil (FRA)	R. Privat
Stage 4	Sunday 30 June	232 km	Rouen – Roubaix	M. Janssens (BEL)	R. Privat
Stage 5	Monday 1 July	170 km	Roubaix – Charleroi (BEL)	G. Bauvin (FRA)	J. Anquetil
Stage 6	Tuesday 2 July	248 km	Charleroi (BEL) – Metz	A. Trochut (FRA)	J. Anquetil
Stage 7	Wednesday 3 July	223 km	Metz – Colmar	R. Hassenforder (FRA)	N. Barone
Stage 8	Thursday 4 July	192 km	Colmar – Besançon	P. Baffi (ITA)	J. Forestier
Stage 9	Friday 5 July	188 km	Besançon – Thonon-les-Bains	J. Anquetil (FRA)	J. Forestier
Stage 10	Sunday 7 July	247 km	Thonon-les-Bains – Briançon	G. Nencini (ITA)	J. Anquetil
Stage 11	Monday 8 July	267 km	Briançon – Cannes	R. Privat (FRA)	J. Anquetil
Stage 12	Tuesday 9 July	239 km	Cannes – Marseille	J. Stablinski (FRA)	J. Anquetil
Stage 13	Wednesday 10 July	160 km	Marseille – Alès	N.Defilippis (ITA)	J. Anquetil
Stage 14	Thursday 11 July	246 km	Alès – Perpignan	R. Hassenforder (FRA)	J. Anquetil
Stage 15	Friday 12 July	197 km	Perpignan – Barcelona (SPA)	R. Privat (FRA)	J. Anquetil
Stage 16	Saturday 13 July	9.8 km	Montjuich (SPA) – Montjuich (SPA) (TT)	J. Anquetil (FRA)	J. Anquetil
Stage 17	Sunday 14 July	220 km	Barcelona (SPA) – Ax-les-Thermes	J. Bourles (FRA)	J. Anquetil
Stage 18	Monday 15 July	236 km	Ax-les-Thermes – Saint-Gaudens	N.Defilippis (ITA)	J. Anquetil
Stage 19	Tuesday 16 July	207 km	Saint-Gaudens – Pau	G. Nencini (ITA)	J. Anquetil
Stage 20	Wednesday 17 July	194 km	Pau – Bordeaux	P. Baffi (ITA)	J. Anquetil
Stage 21	Thursday 18 July	66 km	Bordeaux – Libourne (TT)	J. Anquetil (FRA)	J. Anquetil
Stage 22	Friday 19 July	317 km	Libourne – Tours	A. Darrigade (FRA)	J. Anquetil
Stage 23	Saturday 20 July	227 km	Tours – Paris	A. Darrigade (FRA)	J. Anquetil

Considered a time trial specialist, Jacques Anquetil, congratulated here
by his manager Daniel Dousset (right), won the Tour at his first attempt.
His reign was only beginning...

Alex Virot dies

AX-LES-THERMES: 'Attention! Attention! We need an ambulance at the head of the race... A very serious accident has just occurred.' A dreadful silence followed these few words broadcast by Radio-Tour, which caused consternation among the officials. 'It's our colleague Alex Virot and his motorbike pilot who are the victims of the accident.' And yet everyone who heard this distressing message continued to hope; nobody dared think the worst. When we reached the fatal spot, we had to accept the evidence. There was nothing left to do. Two broken bodies lay on the rocks, far below the road. Alex Virot had breathed his last. René Wagner was still alive, despite the blood pouring from his mouth. But life was fading fast from his winded body and his face was the colour of wax. Dr Dumas had hurried quickly down, only to have to confirm the death of Alex Virot. The back of his skull had caved in; his body was covered by a blanket. René Wagner was taken away by Tour ambulance men, accompanied by Dr Dumas. His skull was fractured and he perished just before reaching the hospital.

The last person to see Alex Virot before he died was the rider Marcel Queheille: 'The motorbike began to accelerate, then, not far ahead of me, I saw it lose balance on the loose chippings. It started to zigzag, the driver tried to control it; it hit one stone marker, then another, then disappeared over the edge. I saw nothing more than two bodies in the air, and a pair of shoes that went flying. I'll never forget it for the rest of my life.' We cannot get used to the idea that we'll never hear Alex Virot's voice again, that we'll never again see him on the pillion seat of his motorbike with that huge stopwatch on a chain. René and Alex were a wonderful team and if you had to define that team in one word, it would be prudence. René Wagner, in his early 40s, was known for his composure and self-control, the safety of his driving, and for his generosity. He rode his motorbike every day but had never had an accident until today.

A fatal accident at the Tour de France: those first on the scene wait for help to arrive, without holding out great hope.

Jacques Anquetil's first Tour

Now that it's all over, many images flood back into our mind, but it would be wrong to select just one as a means of saying: 'Here it is, the moment Jacques Anquetil showed himself; the moment he won the Tour de France and became champion beside the very greatest champions.' All the images need to be gathered up. Legend can't bear instantaneity; it is constantly on the move, made up of a collection of deeds, in different colours, with different degrees of luminosity. All the strands need to be gathered together, like a sheaf of corn. Anquetil's harvest is singularly abundant. Memory records his every deed, his every action, and patiently assembles the beautiful, the admirable unity of his final victory. There were forward steps and also steps back, immense hopes, convictions which gave way to doubt and to the desire to say 'no more!'. The real courage wasn't so much in the exploit, but in the daily struggle, the hidden conflict with himself. It didn't take long to make an inventory of the things that sprang to eye and constituted the plot of our emotions. Memory replays the highlights of the race with high resolution.

Jacques Anquetil stamped the Tour with his authority. He set a new tone, with his youth (23 years old), his talent and his professionalism. Like a true Normandy

man, he's hard-headed in business; he even imposed his own conditions on his manager, the redoubtable Daniel Dousset. His sense of realism is manifest in the real estate he has purchased in Rouen. Yet, this pragmatism is masked by a totally disarming, choirboy gentleness and sociability. No wonder Anquetil ended up persuading his team-mates that, if they helped to bring him into the Parc as the winner, they would have more contracts with him than anyone. His style also lingers in the memory. Jacques Anquetil came to cycling as a natural vocation. He first took part in athletics while attending the technical college at Sotteville. An exceptional cardiovascular system gave him a preference for long distances. But Jacques discovered the bicycle on Sunday rides through the Normandy countryside with his friends. The rides soon turned into races and a local young rider, Dieullois, introduced him to racing. He made his debut in 1950 and the manager of A.C. Sotteville, André Boucher, immediately spotted his immense talent. Jacques Anquetil was 16 years old, the age at which everything begins. It took him only seven years to conquer his Everest...

Right: Anquetil accompanied by Georges Gay. With this young rider from Normandy, the Tour de France had found itself a new master.

A symbolic moment: Jacques Anquetil won his first stage in the Tour de France on home ground in Rouen, in suffocating heat, ahead of Georges Gay, Gastone Nencini and Federico Bahamontes.

His arm injured after a fall on the road to Thonon-les-Bains, Federico Bahamontes abandoned the Tour on the brink of nervous collapse.

The Tour was cut short for Charly Gaul. Shattered by the heat, he dismounts on the way into Coutances, after only a couple of days of racing.

With the first recorded television broadcasts, cycling found its voice in Robert Chapatte, the ex-rider turned reporter (with Darrigade, right).

After winning in Pau, the Italian Gastone Nencini confirmed his talents as both a climber and a descender and made a date with the future...

The Tour de Gaul

A year after his sensational debut in the Tour, Anquetil informed French *directeur sportif* Marcel Bidot he would ride alongside either Bobet or Géminiani, but not both. With a heavy heart, Bidot chose Bobet; Géminiani responded by posing for the press at the Universal Exhibition in Brussels beside a donkey baptized Marcel.

Riding for the Centre-Midi team, Géminiani launched a bruising attack on stage six to Saint-Brieuc, and seized the yellow jersey at Pau. The Tricolores didn't fight back. Jacques Anquetil was in poor health, and Louison Bobet, suffering from an intestinal complaint, had already lost seventeen minutes.

While the arguments continued among the French, Charly Gaul performed brilliantly against the clock, first in the downpour at Châteaulin, and then in the sun on the slopes of Mont Ventoux where he defeated Bahamontes by half a minute in a private contest minutes ahead of the rest. However, a day later a puncture on the road to Gap cost him fifteen minutes, reinforcing Géminiani's advantage in the general classification. It looked like the end of Gaul's hopes, and 'Gém', at 33, could finally believe the Tour was his. Then came the torturous stage across the Chartreuse massif from Briançon to Aix-Les-Bains.

The conditions were appalling when Gaul, who had told Bobet precisely where he was going to attack, darted ahead of the field on the Luitel. It was assumed he had set off to accumulate points for the mountains competition. But Gaul had his eye on bigger things. With a thin smile across his lips, he built up his lead over Géminiani: 5mins 30secs on the fog-bound Col de Porte, 7mins 50secs on the Cucheron, 12mins 20secs in the Granier, 14mins 35secs at Aix-les-Bains.

Far behind him, the French refused to come to Géminiani's aid. On the Luitel, Bobet either couldn't or wouldn't relay the ailing yellow jersey. Learning the scale of his defeat, Géminiani broke down in tears on the finish-line, and spat at his compatriots: 'Judases...' The yellow jersey passed to Italy's Vito Favero, who had a 39-second advantage over Géminiani and 1min 7secs over Gaul, who was by far the finest time-triallist of the three. Before it could begin, Anquetil, suffering congestion and coughing up blood, abandoned. Gaining 3mins 3secs on Géminiani and 3mins 17secs on Favero, Gaul won the stage, his fourth of the race, and the Tour de France.

GENERAL CLASSIFICATION

1. **Charly Gaul** (LUX) Holland-Luxembourg, 4,319 km in 116h.59m.5s; Average speed: 36.905 kph
2. **Vito Favero** (ITA) Italy, at 3m.10s.
3. **Raphaël Géminiani** (FRA) Centre-Midi, at 3m.41s.
4. Jan Adriaenssens (BEL) Belgium, at 7m.16s.
5. Gastone Nencini (ITA) Italy, at 13m.33s.
6. Joseph Planckaert (BEL) Belgium, at 28m.1s.
7. Louison Bobet (FRA) France, at 31m.39s.
8. Federico Bahamontes (SPA) Spain, at 40m.44s.
9. Louis Bergaud (FRA) France, at 48m.33s.
10. Jos Hoevenaers (BEL) Belgium, at 58m.26s.
11. Piet Damen (HOL) Holland-Luxembourg, at 1h.0m.40s.
12. Lothar Friedrich (SUI) Switzerland-Germany, at 1h.2m.13s.
13. Édouard Delberghe (FRA) Paris North-East, at 1h.2m.18s.
14. Jean Graczyk (FRA) Centre-Midi, at 1h04m.39s.
15. Gilbert Bauvin (FRA) France, at 1h.12m.51s.
16. Marcel Ernzer (LUX) Holland-Luxembourg, at 1h.16m.29s.
17. Henry Anglade (FRA) Centre-Midi, at 1h.24m.57s.
18. Joseph Thomin (FRA) West-South-West, at 1h.25m.44s.
19. Nino Catalano (ITA) Italy, at 1h.26m.5s.
20. Fernando Manzaneque (SPA) Spain, at 1h.29m.30s.

45TH TOUR DE FRANCE, 24 STAGES – 4,319 KM

			STAGE	STAGE WINNER	YELLOW JERSEY
Stage 1	Thursday 26 June	184 km	Bruxelles (BEL) – Gand (BEL)	A. Darrigade (FRA)	A. Darrigade
Stage 2	Friday 27 June	198 km	Gand (BEL)) – Dunkerque	G. Voorting (HOL)	J. Hoevenaers
Stage 3	Saturday 28 June	177 km	Dunkerque – Le Tréport	G. Bauvin (FRA)	W. Van Est
Stage 4	Sunday 29 June	205 km	Le Tréport – Versailles	J. Gainche (FRA)	W. Van Est
Stage 5	Monday 30 June	232 km	Versailles – Caen	T. Sabbadini (FRA)	G. Bauvin
Stage 6	Tuesday 1 July	223 km	Caen – Saint-Brieuc	M. Van Geneugden (BEL)	G. Voorting
Stage 7	Wednesday 2 July	170 km	Saint-Brieuc – Brest	B. Robinson (GBR)	G. Voorting
Stage 8	Thursday 3 July	46 km	Châteaulin – Châteaulin (TT)	C. Gaul (LUX)	G. Voorting
Stage 9	Friday 4 July	206 km	Quimper – Saint-Nazaire	A. Darrigade (FRA)	A. Darrigade
Stage 10	Saturday 5 July	255 km	Saint-Brévin – Royan	P. Baffi (ITA)	A. Darrigade
Stage 11	Sunday 6 July	137 km	Royan – Bordeaux	A. Padovan (ITA)	A. Darrigade
Stage 12	Monday 7 July	161 km	Bordeaux – Dax	M. Van Geneugden (BEL)	A. Darrigade
Stage 13	Tuesday 8 July	230 km	Dax – Pau	L. Bergaud (FRA)	R. Géminiani
Stage 14	Wednesday 9 July	129 km	Pau – Luchon	F. Bahamontes (SPA)	V. Favero
Stage 15	Thursday 10 July	176 km	Luchon – Toulouse	A. Darrigade (FRA)	V. Favero
Stage 16	Friday 11 July	187 km	Toulouse – Béziers	P. Baffi (ITA)	V. Favero
Stage 17	Saturday 12 July	189 km	Béziers – Nîmes	A. Darrigade (FRA)	V. Favero
Stage 18	Sunday 13 July	21.5 km	Bédouin – Mont-Ventoux (TT)	C. Gaul (LUX)	R. Géminiani
Stage 19	Monday 14 July	178 km	Carpentras – Gap	G. Nencini (ITA)	R. Géminiani
Stage 20	Tuesday 15 July	165 km	Gap – Briançon	F. Bahamontes (SPA)	R. Géminiani
Stage 21	Wednesday 16 July	219 km	Briançon – Aix-les-Bains	C. Gaul (LUX)	V. Favero
Stage 22	Thursday 17 July	237 km	Aix-les-Bains – Besançon	A. Darrigade (FRA)	V. Favero
Stage 23	Friday 18 July	74 km	Besançon – Dijon (TT)	C. Gaul (LUX)	C. Gaul
Stage 24	Saturday 19 July	320 km	Dijon – Paris	P. Baffi (ITA)	C. Gaul

A magnificent ride by Charly Gaul in the freezing rain between Briançon and Aix-les-Bains put him in contention for overall victory. He finished, numb but happy, with a lead of more than seven minutes over Belgium's Adriaenssens.

Who dares wins

Charly Gaul beat Jacques Anquetil by seven seconds in the time trial over the uneven terrain of the Châteaulin circuit. It was a real achievement, accomplished with an average speed of 41 kph (25.6 mph), and proved Gaul was a complete rider.

It was one of our last assignments: over the long slopes of Bièvres, en route to Paris, the local rider Tino Sabbadini began an attack. Two hundred metres (218 yds) behind, Charly Gaul and the men in the peloton took up the chase.

The man from Luxembourg, however, had very little left to fear from his opponents, visibly resigned to defeat. He knew it. The morning hours had only confirmed his opinion. The great Raphaël Géminiani had lost faith, the Italian Favero was thinking he would be happy to finish second and Adriaenssens was thinking of nothing but the three million francs for the Challenge Martini team competition. But Charly had learned to be suspicious after losing last year's Giro; the Carpentras-Gap stage, where Anquetil and Géminiani left him behind by a quarter of an hour, repeated the lesson. That's why we saw him set the pace on the slopes of Bièvres with the entire peloton in his slipstream.

The final time trial allowed him to again demonstrate the superiority he'd shown at Aix-les-Bains. As Géminiani began to show signs of weakness towards the summit of the Izoard, the new yellow jersey, and the freshest man in the peloton, surfaced in a truly dazzling fashion. He emerged the winner from that battle, after being knocked back at Gap, but then allowed himself respite on the road to Briançon, in order to deliver an even harder punch the following day.

If Gaul appears to be something of a slugger, however, he also has a calculating mind and is capable of sang-froid when things go wrong. In this Tour, Charly Gaul knew how to stay calm. His blows counted because they were delivered at the right time and in the best conditions: on the slopes of the Ventoux, during the second of the great Alpine stages, and against the clock. He returns to Luxembourg after four stage wins, including the three time trials, which sets him apart from Géminiani, Favero and Adriaenssens, three extremely reliable riders. These three men, gifted with great stamina and immense courage, laid the foundations of their campaigns in the same way that, in the boxing ring, Jean Despeaux used to build a points lead only to be suddenly felled by Marcel Cerdan's left hook.

It is quite clear what the first lesson to be drawn from this Tour is – always beware of the sluggers!

Opposite: A freak accident. Well-placed to carry off his sixth stage win in Paris, André Darrigade, had broken free of Baffi and Graczyk in the last 200 metres (218 yds) when he collided with the General Secretary of the Parc des Princes, Constant Wouters, who had unwisely stepped too close to the riders. Miraculously, André Darrigade emerged with only five stitches to his forehead and a dreadful headache. He was even able to offer his congratulations to Charly Gaul, the new Tour de France champion, several minutes after the accident. Wouters, however, was taken to the Boucicaut hospital where he died 11 days later.

Bahamontes, by default

With his slight physique, legs full of knots and dark looks intensified by suffering, Federico Bahamontes looked like one of El Greco's creations. Nicknamed 'El Picador' or 'The Eagle of Toledo' for his solo flights of fantasy over the mountain passes, he came from Castile in Spain, a region of meagre earth, bitter olives and little shelter from the sun. For years his ambitions went no further than the mountains competition; he would pause at each cusp in the road to eat ice-cream or watch the riders pass, like a simple spectator. Bahamontes came to the Tour for the mountains; he was too whimsical, too bohemian, too temperamental even to envisage wearing the yellow jersey into Paris. Until, in 1959, a unique opportunity presented itself to him.

The French team continued to tear itself apart; this year, Anquetil and the man who had beaten his world hour record, Roger Rivière, were at each other's throats. For the rest of the year, Anquetil led the team sponsored by Helyett-Potin, and Rivière rode on Géminiani's Saint-Raphaël team. At the Tour, they were asked to ride shoulder to shoulder. Anquetil told the organizers: 'I'll ride against him anyway!' Marcel Bidot tried hard to achieve some form of accommodation between his two leaders, but with little success. Rivière got the upper hand on his rival in the first time trial. Then, on stage seven, France Centre-Midi regional rider Henri Anglade escaped and gained five minutes on the peloton. When, on stage thirteen, the World Champion Ercole Baldini attacked, Anglade, Anquetil and Bahamontes went with him. At the stage finish, Anglade outsprinted Anquetil. Anquetil had overtaken Rivière in the general classification, but Anglade looked capable of winning the Tour.

Bahamontes won the mountain time trial on the Puy de Dôme, finished second behind Gaul at Grenoble, and took the yellow jersey with an advantage of 4mins 51secs over Anglade, 9mins 16secs over Anquetil and 11mins 36secs over Rivière. The 1959 Tour was decided on stage eighteen. At the head of the race, Anquetil and Rivière had joined a breakaway and dropped Bahamontes by four minutes. However, each refused to co-operate for fear of helping the other. Bahamontes was allowed to claw his way back into contention, and from that moment, in addition to his second King of the Mountains title, the little Spanish climber had effectively won the Tour. Far behind them, Louison Bobet climbed the Iseran alone and abandoned his final Tour de France where he had once risen like a spirit of the air. Jean Robic's Tour de France career ended two days later, in less dignified circumstances; he was disqualified at Chalon-sur-Saône for missing the time limit. Bahamontes became the first Spaniard to win the Tour de France.

GENERAL CLASSIFICATION

1. **Federico Bahamontes** (SPA) Spain, 4,358 km in 123h.46m.45s; Average speed: 35.474 kph
2. **Henry Anglade** (FRA) Centre-Midi, at 4m.1s.
3. **Jacques Anquetil** (FRA) France, at 5m.5s.
4. Roger Rivière (FRA) France, at 5m.17s.
5. François Mahé (FRA) West-South-West, at 8m.22s.
6. Ercole Baldini (ITA) Italy, at 10m.18s.
7. Jan Adriaenssens (BEL) Belgium, at 10m.18s.
8. Jos Hoevenaers (BEL) Belgium, at 11m.2s.
9. Gérard Saint (FRA) West-South-West, at 17m.40s.
10. Jean Brankart (BEL) Belgium, at 20m.38s.
11. Eddy Pauwels (BEL) Belgium, at 22m.20s.
12. Charly Gaul (LUX) Holland-Luxembourg, at 23m.59s.
13. Louis Bergaud (FRA) Centre-Midi, at 36m.54s.
14. Fernando Manzaneque (SPA) Spain, at 57m.29s.
15. Jean-Baptiste 'Jean' Dotto (FRA) Centre-Midi, at 1h.0m.4s.
16. André Darrigade (FRA) France, at 1h.3m.1s.
17. Joseph Planckaert (BEL) Belgium, at 1h.5m.
18. Lothar Friedrich (GER) Switzerland-Germany, at 1h.11m.51s.
19. Brian Robinson (GBR) International, at 1h.12m.11s.
20. Michel Vermeulin (FRA) Paris-North-East, at 1h.16m.10s.

46TH TOUR DE FRANCE, 22 STAGES - 4,358 KM

Stage	Date	Distance	STAGE	STAGE WINNER	YELLOW JERSEY
Stage 1	Thursday 25 June	238 km	Mulhouse – Metz	A. Darrigade (FRA)	A. Darrigade
Stage 2	Friday 26 June	240 km	Metz – Namur (BEL)	V. Favero (ITA)	A. Darrigade
Stage 3	Saturday 27 June	217 km	Namur (BEL) – Roubaix	R. Cazala (FRA)	R. Cazala
Stage 4	Sunday 28 June	230 km	Roubaix – Rouen	D. Bruni (ITA)	R. Cazala
Stage 5	Monday 29 June	286 km	Rouen – Rennes	J. Graczyk (FRA)	R. Cazala
Stage 6	Tuesday 30 June	45.3 km	Blain – Nantes (TT)	R. Rivière (FRA)	R. Cazala
Stage 7	Wednesday 1 July	190 km	Nantes – La Rochelle	R. Hassenforder (FRA)	R. Cazala
Stage 8	Thursday 2 July	201 km	La Rochelle – Bordeaux	M. Dejouhannet (FRA)	R. Cazala
Stage 9	Friday 3 July	207 km	Bordeaux – Bayonne	M. Queheille (FRA)	E. Pauwels
Stage 10	Sunday 5 July	235 km	Bayonne – Bagnères-de-Bigorre	M. Janssens (BEL)	M. Vermeulin
Stage 11	Monday 6 July	119 km	Bagnères-de-Bigorre – Saint-Gaudens	A. Darrigade (FRA)	M. Vermeulin
Stage 12	Tuesday 7 July	184 km	Saint-Gaudens – Albi	R. Graf (SUI)	M. Vermeulin
Stage 13	Wednesday 8 July	219 km	Albi – Aurillac	H. Anglade (FRA)	J. Hoevenaers
Stage 14	Thursday 9 July	231 km	Aurillac – Clermont-Ferrand	A. Le Dissez (FRA)	J. Hoevenaers
Stage 15	Friday 10 July	12.5 km	Clermont-Ferrand – Puy de Dôme (TT)	F. Bahamontes (SPA)	J. Hoevenaers
Stage 16	Saturday 11 July	210 km	Clermont-Ferrand – Saint-Étienne	D. Bruni (ITA)	E. Pauwels
Stage 17	Monday 13 July	197 km	Saint-Étienne – Grenoble	C. Gaul (LUX)	F. Bahamontes
Stage 18	Tuesday 14 July	243 km	Le Lautaret – Saint-Vincent d'Aoste (ITA)	E. Baldini (ITA)	F. Bahamontes
Stage 19	Wednesday 15 July	251 km	Saint-Vincent d'Aoste (ITA) – Annecy	R. Graf (SUI)	F. Bahamontes
Stage 20	Thursday 16 July	202 km	Annecy – Chalon-sur-Saône	B. Robinson (GBR)	F. Bahamontes
Stage 21	Friday 17 July	69.2 km	Seurre – Dijon (TT)	R. Rivière (FRA)	F. Bahamontes
Stage 22	Saturday 18 July	331 km	Dijon – Paris	J. Groussard (FRA)	F. Bahamontes

At Roubaix, Robert Cazala (right) beat Annaert in the sprint to take the yellow jersey.

At Aurillac, the astonishing Henry Anglade (right) defeated Jacques Anquetil.

After riding 160 km (100 miles) alone, Robic arrived at Chalon-sur-Saône outside the time limit.

Bobet abandons on the summit of the Iseran, unable to breathe.

Federico Bahamontes (far right) can laugh: Anquetil and Rivière cancelled each other out, while the determination of the French national riders to stop Anglade, a regional rider, from winning the Tour, served him victory on a plate.

Nencini, overshadowed by tragedy

On 9 June 1960, Jacques Anquetil defeated Gastone Nencini to win the Giro d'Italia by just eight seconds. Seventeen days later, the forty-seventh Tour de France started at Lille. Anquetil did not start; his place was filled by Roger Rivière. He and Nencini made an immediate impression; on stage two, a 27.8-kilometre (17.3-mile) time trial, Rivière took the stage win and Nencini the yellow jersey.

Within days, Henry Anglade, now riding for the national team after finishing second the previous year as a regional rider, had taken the race lead. Yet Rivière attacked audaciously on stage six, turning a huge gear and dragging Nencini and Jan Adriaenssens in his wake. Anglade appealed to his *directeur sportif* Marc Bidot to stop the attack, but Rivière was deaf to his pleas. By the time Anglade reached the finish-line, Adriaenssens had replaced him as race leader, followed by Nencini and Rivière. Anglade prophesied: 'We've just lost the Tour.' Rivière, three times the World Pursuit Champion on the track, had the power but not the roadcraft to win the Tour. 'He'll make mistakes,' Anglade explained. 'He'll try to follow Nencini on the descents, and one day it'll go wrong. You saw how close he came to losing control on the Aspin last year.'

The events of stage fourteen proved him right. Careering through the Cévennes, Nencini and Rivière were locked in a personal battle. The Italian, renowned as one of the most skilful downhill riders in the peloton, plummeted down from the Perjuret with the Frenchman on his heels. Some said he was intent on dealing the Italian a psychological blow by beating him on his favourite terrain. Others said it was mere bravado; Rivière was simply seduced by his own power. Edging beyond the limits of control, he lost adhesion, lurched off the road and catapulted through the air. His team-mate Louis Rostollan saw the fall and rode back up the road waving outstretched arms above his head and shouting, 'Roger's fallen! Roger's fallen!' His friend's body was lying in a bed of creepers, brambles and dried leaves. He couldn't make the slightest movement: his back was broken. That funereal Sunday, the Belgian Martin Van Geneugden's victory at Avignon went unnoticed, burnt out by the obvious question: why had Rivière insisted on trying to follow Nencini? Pills were found in the pocket of his jersey. Rivière, it was rumoured, occasionally used the opiate Palfium, an analgesic that could have affected his reaction time.

Rivière's Tour, and his career as a professional athlete, were over. Nencini, who had ridden in the shadow of the giants Bartali and Coppi, defended his race lead to Paris.

GENERAL CLASSIFICATION

1. **Gastone Nencini** (ITA), Italy, 4,173 km in 112 h.8m.42s; Average speed: 37.210 kph
2. **Graziano Battistini** (ITA) Italy, at 5m.2s.
3. **Jan Adriaenssens** (BEL) Belgium, at 10m.24s.
4. Hans Junkermann (GER) Germany, at 11m.21s.
5. Joseph Planckaert (BEL) Belgium, at 13m.2s.
6. Raymond Mastrotto (FRA) France, at 16m.12s.
7. Arnaldo Pambianco (ITA) Italy, at 17m.58s.
8. Henry Anglade (FRA) France, at 19m.17s.
9. Marcel Rohrbach (FRA) Centre-Midi, at 20m.2s.
10. Imerio Massignan (ITA) Italy, at 23m.28s.
11. Fernando Manzaneque (SPA) Spain, at 25m.59s.
12. Albertus Geldermans (HOL) Holland, at 26m.33s.
13. Jean Graczyk (FRA) France, at 26m.55s.
14. François Mahé (FRA) France, at 32m.36s.
15. Louis Rostollan (FRA) France, at 34m.18s.
16. André Darrigade (FRA) France, at 34m.23s.
17. Antonio Suárez (SPA) Spain, at 39m.15s.
18. Édouard Delberghe (FRA) France, at 44m.25s.
19. René Pavard (FRA) France, at 48m.13s.
20. Carmelo Morales (SPA) Spain, at 50m.44s.

47TH TOUR DE FRANCE
21 STAGES – 4,173 KM

STAGE			STAGE	STAGE WINNER	YELLOW JERSEY
Stage 1 (1)	Sunday 26 June	108 km	Lille – Bruxelles (BEL)	J. Schepens (BEL)	J. Schepens
Stage 1 (2)	Sunday 26 June	27.8 km	Bruxelles (BEL) – Bruxelles (TT)	R. Rivière (FRA)	G. Nencini
Stage 2	Monday 27 June	206 km	Bruxelles (BEL) – Malo-les-Bains	R. Privat (FRA)	G. Nencini
Stage 3	Tuesday 28 June	209 km	Malo-les-Bains – Dieppe	N. Defilippis (ITA)	J. Groussard
Stage 4	Wednesday 29 June	211 km	Dieppe – Caen	J. Graczyk (FRA)	H. Anglade
Stage 5	Thursday 30 June	189 km	Caen – Saint-Malo	A. Darrigade (FRA)	H. Anglade
Stage 6	Friday 1 July	191 km	Saint-Malo – Lorient	R. Rivière (FRA)	J. Adriaenssens
Stage 7	Saturday 2 July	244 km	Lorient – Angers	G. Battistini (ITA)	J. Adriaenssens
Stage 8	Sunday 3 July	240 km	Angers – Limoges	N. Defilippis (ITA)	J. Adriaenssens
Stage 9	Monday 4 July	225 km	Limoges – Bordeaux	M. Van Geneugden (BEL)	J. Adriaenssens
Stage 10	Tuesday 5 July	228 km	Mont-de-Marsan – Pau	R. Rivière (FRA)	G. Nencini
Stage 11	Wednesday 6 July	161 km	Pau – Luchon	K. Gimmi (SUI)	G. Nencini
Stage 12	Thursday 7 July	176 km	Luchon – Toulouse	J. Graczyk (FRA)	G. Nencini
Stage 13	Friday 8 July	224 km	Toulouse – Millau	L. Proost (BEL)	G. Nencini
Stage 14	Sunday 10 July	217 km	Millau – Avignon	M. Van Geneugden (BEL)	G. Nencini
Stage 15	Monday 11 July	187 km	Avignon – Gap	M. Van Aerde (BEL)	G. Nencini
Stage 16	Tuesday 12 July	172 km	Gap – Briançon	G. Battistini (ITA)	G. Nencini
Stage 17	Wednesday 13 July	229 km	Briançon – Aix-les-Bains	J. Graczyk (FRA)	G. Nencini
Stage 18	Thursday 14 July	215 km	Aix-les-Bains – Thonon-les-Bains	F. Manzaneque (SPA)	G. Nencini
Stage 19	Friday 15 July	83 km	Pontarlier – Besançon (TT)	R. Graf (SUI)	G. Nencini
Stage 20	Saturday 16 July	229 km	Besançon – Troyes	P. Beuffeuil (FRA)	G. Nencini
Stage 21	Sunday 17 July	200 km	Troyes – Paris	J. Graczyk (FRA)	G. Nencini

4

1

5

6

2   3

1. Stage 14, Millau-Avignon: On the descent from the Perjuret in the Cévennes, Roger Rivière plunged off the road. With a severe spinal injury and unable to move his legs, Rivière was lifted onto a stretcher, carried back up to the road and rushed to hospital in Montpellier.

2. After Rivière's fall, the Tour belonged to Nencini, the great descender, already the winner of the Giro d'Italia. Here he leads Massignan.

3. Over the final stages of the Tour, Nencini only had to monitor the Belgian Adriaenssens (right), third overall in Paris.

4. A unique moment in the Tour de France: the peloton stops to salute Général de Gaulle in his home village.

5. A bad year for Bahamontes, who retired at Malo-les-Bains.

6. Gastone Nencini receives his victory bouquet from Marcel Bidot, the French team manager. Nencini never forgot Roger Rivière's tragic accident.

Anquetil's masterclass

Since his victorious Tour debut in 1957, Jacques Anquetil had abandoned one Tour due to illness (1958), finished a poor third in another thanks to his fratricidal antipathy towards Roger Rivière (1959), and opted out of another completely (1960). In 1961, however, he was back. Fourteen days before the *Grand Départ* from his home town, Rouen, he had finished second in the Tour of Italy. Now he was hungry not only for victory, but for a greater goal: he planned to seize the yellow jersey on day one, and wear it all the way to Paris.

Stage one consisted of two parts; the second, a time trial through the streets of Versailles, would allow him to put his plan into practice. In the morning, he joined the fifteen riders who formed the winning breakaway, dropping his rivals Gaul, Adriaenssens, Massignan and Planckaert by more than five minutes. His team-mate André Darrigade won the Tour's opening stage for the fifth time. Then, by winning the afternoon time trial, Anquetil took over the yellow jersey.

His open bid for crushing victory mobilized the opposition, but the French national team suppressed all attacks, especially from the regional teams. The public and the race organizers accused Anquetil and the French *directeur sportif* Marcel Bidot of smothering the race. Between Belfort and Chalon, seventeen riders broke away, controlled by Anquetil's team-mates

Stablinski and Groussard. Their lead reached worrying proportions, but when Marcel Bidot suggested stopping Groussard and Stablinski, Anquetil objected. Instead, he launched a devastating counter-attack, dragging the chasing group along for more than 30 kilometres (19 miles) to reel in the breakaway, as if the task fell to him alone.

Charly Gaul launched his bid for victory in the Chartreuse, the scene of his triumphant incursion through the torrential rain in 1958. But he never rode well in brilliant sunshine; Anquetil loved it. Gaul won the stage, but gained just 1min 40secs on the yellow jersey. The Belgian Eddy Pauwels won an epic five-man breakaway over the Pyrenees from Luchon to Pau, but the win had no impact on Anquetil's lead. Anquetil's superiority intimidated the opposition. In a famous editorial, Jacques Goddet condemned those who didn't dare attack the yellow jersey as 'repulsive dwarves... impotent, submissive, satisfied in their mediocrity'. The editorial formed the basis of a quarrel between the Tour's boss, Goddet and its master, Anquetil.

Then, between Bergerac and Périgueux, Anquetil rode the final time trial like a master, distancing Gaul by 2mins 59secs and extending his winning margin to over twelve minutes. His commitment to the Tour had been questioned in the past, but now there was no doubt it belonged to Jacques Anquetil.

GENERAL CLASSIFICATION

1. **Jacques Anquetil** (FRA) France, 4,397 in 122h.1m.33s; Average speed: 36.033 kph
2. **Guido Carlesi** (ITA) Italy, at 12m.14s.
3. **Charly Gaul** (LUX) Switzerland-Luxembourg, at 12m.16s.
4. Imerio Massignan (ITA) Italy, at 15m.59s.
5. Hans Junkermann (GER) Germany, at 16m.9s.
6. Fernando Manzaneque (SPA) Spain, at 16m.27s.
7. José Pérez Francés (SPA) Spain, at 20m.41s.
8. Jean-Baptiste 'Jean' Dotto (FRA) Centre-Midi, at 21m.44s.
9. Eddy Pauwels (BEL) Belgium, at 26m.57s.
10. Jan Adriaenssens (BEL) Belgium, at 28m.5s.
11. Jos Hoevenaers (BEL) Belgium, at 28m.27s.
12. Alfred Ruegg (SUI) Switzerland-Luxembourg, at 32m.14s.
13. Michel Van Aerde (BEL) Belgium, at 40m.34s.
14. Jean Gainche (FRA) West-South-West, at 41m.26s.
15. Joseph Planckaert (BEL) Belgium, at 41m.53s.
16. Adriano Zamboni (ITA) Italy, at 43m.26s.
17. Frans Aerenhouts (BEL) Belgium, at 45m.52s.
18. Henry Anglade (FRA) France, at 47m.38s.
19. Raymond Mastrotto (FRA) France, at 53m.19s.
20. André Foucher (FRA) West-South-West, at 58m.8s.

48TH TOUR DE FRANCE, 21 STAGES – 4,397 KM

Stage	Date	Distance	STAGE	STAGE WINNER	YELLOW JERSEY
Stage 1 (1)	Sunday 25 June	136.5 km	Rouen – Versailles	A. Darrigade (FRA)	A. Darrigade
Stage 1 (2)	Sunday 25 June	28.5 km	Versailles – Versailles (TT)	J. Anquetil (FRA)	J. Anquetil
Stage 2	Monday 26 June	230,5 km	Pontoise – Roubaix	A. Darrigade (FRA)	J. Anquetil
Stage 3	Tuesday 27 June	197.5 km	Roubaix – Charleroi (BEL)	É. Daems (BEL)	J. Anquetil
Stage 4	Wednesday 28 June	237.5 km	Charleroi (BEL) – Metz	A. Novak (FRA)	J. Anquetil
Stage 5	Thursday 29 June	221 km	Metz – Strasbourg	L. Bergaud (FRA)	J. Anquetil
Stage 6	Friday 30 June	180.5 km	Strasbourg – Belfort	J. Planckaert (BEL)	J. Anquetil
Stage 7	Saturday 1 July	214.5 km	Belfort – Chalon-sur-Saône	J. Stablinski (FRA)	J. Anquetil
Stage 8	Sunday 2 July	240.5 km	Chalon-sur-Saône – Saint-Étienne	J. Forestier (FRA)	J. Anquetil
Stage 9	Monday 3 July	230 km	Saint-Étienne – Grenoble	C. Gaul (LUX)	J. Anquetil
Stage 10	Tuesday 4 July	250.5 km	Grenoble – Turin (ITA)	G. Ignolin (FRA)	J. Anquetil
Stage 11	Wednesday 5 July	225 km	Turin (ITA) – Antibes	G. Carlesi (ITA)	J. Anquetil
Stage 12	Thursday 6 July	199 km	Antibes – Aix-en-Provence	M. Van Aerde (BEL)	J. Anquetil
Stage 13	Friday 7 July	177.5 km	Aix-en-Provence – Montpellier	A. Darrigade (FRA)	J. Anquetil
Stage 14	Sunday 9 July	174 km	Montpellier – Perpignan	E. Pauwels (BEL)	J. Anquetil
Stage 15	Monday 10 July	206 km	Perpignan – Toulouse	G. Carlesi (ITA)	J. Anquetil
Stage 16	Tuesday 11 July	208 km	Toulouse – Superbagnères	I. Massignan (ITA)	J. Anquetil
Stage 17	Wednesday 12 July	197 km	Luchon – Pau	E. Pauwels (BEL)	J. Anquetil
Stage 18	Thursday 13 July	207 km	Pau – Bordeaux	M. Van Geneugden (BEL)	J. Anquetil
Stage 19	Friday 14 July	74.5 km	Bergerac – Périgueux (TT)	J. Anquetil (FRA)	J. Anquetil
Stage 20	Saturday 15 July	309.5 km	Périgueux – Tours	A. Darrigade (FRA)	J. Anquetil
Stage 21	Sunday 16 July	252.5 km	Tours – Paris	R. Cazala (FRA)	J. Anquetil

Anquetil powers off in search of the *maillot jaune* in the time trial on the afternoon of day one.

Imerio Massignan (on Anquetil's left), the winner at Superbagnères, won the King of the Mountains title without ever threatening the overall classification.

After a year's absence, Anquetil won his second Tour and wore the yellow jersey from day one like Bottechia, Frantz and Maes, who had accomplished the same feat before him.

Cazala leads Anquetil through the outskirts of Paris. Anquetil offered him victory on the final stage as a reward for his devotion.

Like a metronome

After six years of negotiations, the Tour de France finally allowed commercially-sponsored teams to benefit from its ample shop window. All sorts of anxieties surrounded the decision; it was even feared that the wealthiest teams would form pacts and stifle the racing. More to the point, Jacques Anquetil's role in the ranks of Saint-Raphaël was the subject of speculation. He had refused to co-habit with Bobet in the French national team; how would he respond to sharing the leadership of Saint-Raphaël at his own national Tour with a German, Rudy Altig? After all, it was no secret that Anquetil had abandoned the Tour of Spain in April to avoid witnessing Altig's triumph. As the Tour approached, Anquetil asked the team sponsors to replace *directeur sportif* Raphaël Géminiani with Mickey Wiegant for the duration of the Tour, but his employers emphatically rebutted the attempted coup. The Mercier camp was delighting in its rival's unrest until Mercier team leader Raymond Poulidor broke his left hand in training and had to start the Tour in a plaster cast.

The great Belgian sprinter Rik Van Looy started his first Tour de France by treating each stage like a spring classic; incredibly, at Herentals, his home town, he lost his chance of winning stage two after taking a wrong turn. Van Looy's aggressive style even had Anquetil on his back foot, but the duel was cut short by an accident. On stage eleven, as the race entered the Pyrenees, Van Looy was knocked down by a motorbike. With blood in his urine, he had to withdraw. The following day, Tom Simpson joined the winning break and became the first English-speaker to wear the yellow jersey. The mountain time trial from Luchon to Superbagnères was Bahamontes' speciality, but second place was good enough for Belgium's Josef Planckaert to take the yellow jersey. Anquetil stayed in contention by finishing third. After Nencini and several other riders abandoned on stage fourteen with food poisoning, the main obstructions blocking Anquetil's path to victory were cleared. As in 1961, the Alps had little influence on the overall race: Gaul was no longer the genius he had been in 1958; Bahamontes gained time on the climbs but lost it on the descents. Only Raymond Poulidor resisted, attacking over the Chartreuse and winning the stage by two and a half minutes. Everyone else was inhibited by Anquetil, whose performance in the Lyon time trial was superlative; he won the stage by three clear minutes and assumed the yellow jersey by five gaping minutes.

GENERAL CLASSIFICATION

1. **Jacques Anquetil** (FRA) St-Raphaël-Helyett, 4,274 km in 114h.31m.54s. Average speed: 37.317 kph
2. **Joseph Planckaert** (BEL) Faema-Flandria, at 4m.59s.
3. **Raymond Poulidor** (FRA) Mercier-BP, at 10m.24s.
4. Gilbert Desmet (BEL) Carpano, at 13m.1s.
5. Albertus Geldermans (HOL), St-Raphaël-Helyett, at 14m.4s.
6. Tom Simpson (GBR) Leroux-Gitane, at 17m.9s.
7. Imerio Massignan (ITA) Legnano Pirelli, at 17m.50s.
8. Ercole Baldini (ITA) Ignis, at 19m.
9. Charly Gaul (LUX) Gazzola, at 19m.11s.
10. Eddy Pauwels (BEL) Wiels-Groene-Leeuw, at 23m.4s.
11. Jean-Claude Lebaube (FRA) Leroux-Gitane, at 23m.33s.
12. Henry Anglade (FRA) Liberia-Grammont, at 26m.33s.
13. Émile Daems (BEL) Philco, at 27m.17s.
14. Federico Bahamontes (ESP) Margnat-Paloma, at 34m.16s.
15. Rolf Wolfshohl (GER) Leroux-Gitane, at 35m.23s.
16. Armand Desmet (BEL) Faema-Flandria, at 39m.10s.
17. Victor Van Schil (BEL) Mercier-BP, at 42m.1s.
18. Jos Hoevenaers (BEL) Philco, at 42m.28s.
19. Guido Carlesi (ITA) Philco, at 43m.29s.
20. François Mahé (FRA) Pelforth-Sauvage-Lejeune, at 45m.36s.

49TH TOUR DE FRANCE, 22 STAGES – 4,274 KM

Stage	Date	Distance	STAGE	STAGE WINNER	YELLOW JERSEY
Stage 1	Sunday 24 June	253 km	Nancy – Spa (BEL)	R. Altig (GER)	R. Altig
Stage 2 (1)	Monday 25 June	147 km	Spa (BEL) – Herentals (BEL)	A. Darrigade (FRA)	A. Darrigade
Stage 2 (2)	Monday 25 June	23 km	Herentals (BEL) – Herentals (TTT)	F. Flandria	A. Darrigade
Stage 3	Tuesday 26 June	210 km	Bruxelles (BEL) – Amiens	R. Altig (GER)	R. Altig
Stage 4	Wednesday 27 June	196.5 km	Amiens – Le Havre	W. Van den Berghen (BEL)	R. Altig
Stage 5	Thursday 28 June	215 km	Pont l'Evêque – Saint-Malo	E. Daems (BEL)	R. Altig
Stage 6	Friday 29 June	235.5 km	Dinard – Brest	R. Cazala (FRA)	A. Geldermans
Stage 7	Saturday 30 June	201 km	Quimper – Saint-Nazaire	H. Zilverberg (HOL)	A. Geldermans
Stage 8 (1)	Sunday 1 July	155 km	Saint-Nazaire – Luçon	M. Minieri (ITA)	A. Darrigade
Stage 8 (2)	Sunday 1 July	43 km	Luçon – La Rochelle (TT)	J. Anquetil (FRA)	A. Darrigade
Stage 9	Monday 2 July	214 km	La Rochelle – Bordeaux	A. Bailetti (ITA)	W. Schroeders
Stage 10	Tuesday 3 July	184.5 km	Bordeaux – Bayonne	W. Vannitsen (BE)	W. Schroeders
Stage 11	Wednesday 4 July	155.5 km	Bayonne – Pau	E. Pauwels (BEL)	W. Schroeders
Stage 12	Thursday 5 July	207.5 km	Pau – Saint-Gaudens	R. Cazala (FRA)	T. Simpson
Stage 13	Friday 6 July	18.5 km	Luchon – Superbagnères (TT)	F. Bahamontes (SPA)	J. Planckaert
Stage 14	Saturday 7 July	215 km	Luchon – Carcassonne	J. Stablinski (FRA)	J. Planckaert
Stage 15	Sunday 8 July	196.5 km	Carcassonne – Montpellier	W. Vannitsen (BEL)	J. Planckaert
Stage 16	Monday 9 July	185 km	Montpellier – Aix-en-Provence	E. Daems (BEL)	J. Planckaert
Stage 17	Tuesday 10 July	201 km	Aix-en-Provence – Antibes	R. Altig (GER)	J. Planckaert
Stage 18	Wednesday 11 July	241.5 km	Antibes – Briançon	E. Daems (BEL)	J. Planckaert
Stage 19	Thursday 12 July	204.5 km	Briançon – Aix-les-Bains	R. Poulidor (FRA)	J. Planckaert
Stage 20	Friday 13 July	68 km	Bourgoin – Lyon (TT)	J. Anquetil (FRA)	J. Anquetil
Stage 21	Saturday 14 July	232 km	Lyon – Nevers – Pougues-les-Eaux	D. Bruni (ITA)	J. Anquetil
Stage 22	Sunday 15 July	271 km	Pougues-les-Eaux – Paris	R. Benedetti (ITA)	J. Anquetil

Anquetil started three minutes after Poulidor in the time trial between Bourgoin and Lyon. Halfway through the 68 kilometres (42.2 miles), he forged past Poulidor without even glancing at his rival.

Anquetil, hero and anti-hero

Several hundred spectators jeered at Jacques Anquetil during his lap of honour on Sunday. It wasn't the first time: last year, we saw something similar. Having paid their entry fee to the Parc des Princes, these protesters felt they were free to express publicly their sentiments, which in the event meant their resentment. Free to do so, they emphatically were: we doubt neither their rights nor their good faith, while holding serious reservations about their good manners. We recognize their right to question the merits of the champion. We only ask, in return, that they grant us the right not to share their opinions. If Jacques Anquetil were enjoying his first success in the Tour, if his victory could be seen as a one-off,

the result of circumstances, then perhaps we'd find room for uncertainty. He has won this event three times. Taken on at the last minute by Marcel Bidot in 1957, he compensated for Louison Bobet's absence by winning two mass start stages and bringing the yellow jersey back to Saint-Adrien. Last year he made an impetuous wager and achieved the impossible by wearing the *maillot jaune* for 22 days. He was accused of stifling the Tour and exploiting his team-mates for his own benefit, and all manner of other things. This year, however, Jacques Anquetil took on the Tour under very different conditions. He had failed in the Vuelta and suffered in the Criterium du Dauphin Libéré. His team-mates had begun

to lose confidence in him. However, his excellent all-round performance over the first few days immediately guaranteed the assistance of Raphaël Géminiani. Reassured over Anquetil's health and aware of the natural limits of the other competitors in the team, Géminiani made sure 'Maître Jacques' enjoyed the most favourable conditions. In the Pyrenees and especially in the Alps, Anquetil hauled himself up to the level of his rival 'climbers' and sorted the sheep from the goats himself during the climb up the Izoard. Despite this, several hundred dissatisfied spectators jeered him during his lap of honour, perhaps the same people who booed Bobet in 1953. It was not deserved...

1. Over the 18.5 km (11.5 miles) separating Luchon from Superbagnères, Anquetil finished third behind Bahamontes and Planckaert, but ahead of Gaul and Poulidor, the mountain specialists.

2. A first: Tom Simpson, the good-humoured Englishman, took the yellow jersey at Saint-Gaudens.

3. Poulidor dropped Anquetil and Lebaube and headed alone towards victory at Aix-les-Bains.

4. Junkermann (being pushed) was one of the riders who dropped out at Carcassonne 'poisoned' by fish. Doping was suspected.

5. Victim of a motorbike, Van Looy had to abandon at Pau. The Tour lost one of its main protagonists.

2 3

1 4 5

Anquetil checkmates the climbers

By 1963, Anquetil's dominance had begun to concern the organizers. To make his task rather more difficult they reduced the length of the individual time trials to 79 kilometres (49 miles) compared with 111 km (69 miles) the year before, and set the finish-lines of the mountain stages near the last climb, to reinforce the challenge of the climbers. The intended beneficiaries were the 35-year-old Federico Bahamontes, the winner of five King of the Mountains titles, and Raymond Poulidor, whom Jacques Anquetil refused to consider a worthy adversary. Yet Poulidor created a sensation by finishing within forty-five seconds of Anquetil over the 24.5-kilometre (15.3-mile) time trial at Angers.

But it was in the Pyrenees that Anquetil raised eyebrows, outsprinting Pérez-Francés, Poulidor and Bahamontes at Bagnères, after climbing the Tourmalet. The stage win, and the time bonus that came with it, put Anquetil third overall. Poulidor, an ever-increasing threat, had promised to attack on the Grand-Saint-Bernard pass. Raphaël Géminiani, now Anquetil's trusted *directeur*, reassured his protégé: fierce head-winds on the descent made the Saint-Bernard no place for solo

attacks. Moreover, 'Gém' had heard that a rockslide had diverted the race up the old Forclaz, an unpaved goat-track with sections where the gradient reached 18%. The regulations allowed for no changes of equipment except after mechanical failure. But Géminiani was an expert in circumventing the rules. At the bottom of the Saint Bernard, as Poulidor fought the gale ahead of him, Anquetil raised his arm and feigned an accident.

'My derailleur!'

'*Merde!*' choked Géminiani. 'Anquetil's in trouble!'

The commissaire noted a snapped gear cable, not imagining that the mechanic had severed the line with wire-cutters. Anquetil attacked the Forclaz on a bike set up for climbing. On the climb, pandemonium reigned. Bahamontes attacked; Poulidor collapsed, finally crossing the col four minutes behind Anquetil, who descended on his first machine, to which the mechanic had fitted a new cable, won the stage and the yellow jersey at Chamonix, just ahead of Bahamontes. Two days later, Anquetil scored another superb time trial victory, and, on 14 July, claimed his fourth Tour before a Parisian public that was finally warming to him.

GENERAL CLASSIFICATION

1. **Jacques Anquetil** (FRA) St-Raphaël-Gitane, 4,138 km in 113m.30m.5s; Average speed: 36.456 kph
2. **Federico Bahamontes** (SPA) Margnat-Paloma, at 3m.35s.
3. **José Pérez-Francés** (SPA) Ferrys, at 10m.14s.
4. Jean-Claude Lebaube (FRA) St-Raphaël-Gitane, at 11m.55s.
5. Armand Desmet (BEL) Faema-Flandria, at 15m.
6. Angelino Soler (SPA) Faema-Flandria, at 15m.4s.
7. Renzo Fontona (ITA) Ibac, at 15m.27s.
8. Raymond Poulidor (FRA) Mercier-BP, at 16m.46s.
9. Hans Junkermann (GER) Wiels-Groene-Leeuw, at 18m.53s.
10. Rik Van Looy (BEL) GBC-Libertas, at 19m.24s.
11. Henry Anglade (FRA) Pelforth-Sauvage-Lejeune, at 21m.39s.
12. Fernando Manzaneque (SPA) Ferrys, at 22m.30s.
13. Eddy Pauwels (BEL) Wiels-Groene-Leeuw, at 25m.3s.
14. Francisco Gabica (SPA) KAS, at 26m.44s.
15. Dieter Puschel (GER) Wiels-Groene-Leeuw, at 28m.20s.
16. A. Ramsbottom (GBR) Pelforth-Sauvage-Lejeune, at 30m.36s.
17. Miguel Pacheco (SPA) KAS, at 31m.36s.
18. Graziano Battistini (ITA) Ibac, at 32m.6s.
19. François Mahe (FRA) Pelforth-Sauvage-Lejeune, at 33m.50s.
20. Jean Gainche (BEL) Mercier-BP, at 35m.38s.

50TH TOUR DE FRANCE, 21 STAGES – 4,138 KM

			STAGE	STAGE WINNER	YELLOW JERSEY
Stage 1	Sunday 23 June	152.5 km	Paris – Épernay	E. Pauwels (BEL)	E. Pauwels
Stage 2 (1)	Monday 24 June	185.5 km	Reims – Jambes (BEL)	R. Van Looy (BEL)	E. Pauwels
Stage 2 (2)	Monday 24 June	21.6 km	Jambes (BEL) – Jambes (TTT)	Pelforth-Sauvage-Lejeune	E. Pauwels
Stage 3	Tuesday 25 June	223.5 km	Jambes (BEL) – Roubaix	S. Elliott (IRL)	S. Elliott
Stage 4	Wednesday 26 June	235.5 km	Roubaix – Rouen	F. Melckenbeeck (BEL)	S. Elliott
Stage 5	Thursday 27 June	285 km	Rouen – Rennes	A. Bailetti (ITA)	S. Elliott
Stage 6 (1)	Friday 28 June	118.5 km	Rennes – Angers	R. De Breucker (BEL)	S. Elliott
Stage 6 (2)	Friday 28 June	24.5 km	Angers – Angers (TT)	J. Anquetil (FRA)	G. Desmet
Stage 7	Saturday 29 June	236 km	Angers – Limoges	J. Janssen (HOL)	G. Desmet
Stage 8	Sunday 30 June	231.5 km	Limoges – Bordeaux	R. Van Looy (BEL)	G. Desmet
Stage 9	Monday 1 July	202 km	Bordeaux – Pau	P. Cerami (BEL)	G. Desmet
Stage 10	Tuesday 2 July	148.5 km	Pau – Bagnères-de-Bigorre	J. Anquetil (FRA)	G. Desmet
Stage 11	Wednesday 3 July	131 km	Bagnères-de-Bigorre – Luchon	G. Ignolin (FRA)	G. Desmet
Stage 12	Thursday 4 July	172.5 km	Luchon – Toulouse	A. Darrigade (FRA)	G. Desmet
Stage 13	Friday 5 July	234 km	Toulouse – Aurillac	R. Van Looy (BEL)	G. Desmet
Stage 14	Sunday 7 July	236.5 km	Aurillac – Saint-Étienne	G. Ignolin (FRA)	G. Desmet
Stage 15	Monday 8 July	174 km	Saint-Étienne – Grenoble	F. Bahamontes (SPA)	G. Desmet
Stage 16	Tuesday 9 July	202 km	Grenoble – Val-d'Isère	F. Manzaneque (SPA)	F. Bahamontes
Stage 17	Wednesday 10 July	225.5 km	Val-d'Isère – Chamonix	J. Anquetil (FRA)	J. Anquetil
Stage 18	Thursday 11 July	225 km	Chamonix – Lons-le-Saunier	F. Brands (BEL)	J. Anquetil
Stage 19	Friday 12 July	54.5 km	Arbois – Besançon (TT)	J. Anquetil (FRA)	J. Anquetil
Stage 20	Saturday 13 July	233.5 km	Besançon – Troyes	R. De Breucker (BEL)	J. Anquetil
Stage 21	Sunday 14 July	185.5 km	Troyes – Paris	R. Van Looy (BEL)	J. Anquetil

At full throttle on the Aubisque, Anquetil then cruised over the Tourmalet to win a great mountain stage ahead of the specialists at Bagnères-de-Bigorre.

Anquetil returns transformed

The quality of the Tour de France doesn't always reflect the quality of the champion. Setting a record of four victories which, most probably, only he will be able to surpass, Jacques Anquetil, a man cut from the same cloth as the greatest champions, succeeded in honouring the 50th Tour de France not just with the brilliance of his performance, his spirit and kindness (much appreciated by our itinerant community), but also by the strength of the opposition he was able to eliminate, day by day. In my opinion the finest achievement of Saint-Raphaël-Gitane's incomparable champion, who has finally endeared himself to the public, was the astonishing psychological transformation he underwent when, having ruled out the Tour this year because of the apprehension it inspired in him, he suddenly had a courageous change of heart and decided to confront his fears rather than run away from them. From that moment on, something approaching a miraculous cure had been found for the perpetual uneasiness suffered by a star burdened with moral obligations and besieged by the spectre of public opinion. As Georges Bernanos used to say, the only way to triumph over life is to love it. Such was the Tour for our hero. He has learned to love the Tour, to love the unyielding executioner that is his bicycle, to love the struggle, the suffering, perhaps because, once loved, it allows him to truly enjoy the profound joys of a hard-won, honest victory. This victory, his fourth, was won by a totally changed man, a man with renewed morale and an entirely fresh outlook.

From now on, just watch this new rider, suddenly dazzled by the nature of his destiny, enjoying at last the finest of pleasures, that of pleasing others, as he takes his career in a different direction, the path that leads to the sun and the stars, the heavenly counterpart of the jersey he brought back to Paris yesterday.

You might think we are exaggerating the merit of such a narrow victory, that was finally won by only a very small margin over an old rival of 35 years of age. That would be to underestimate the tactical skill of a rider like Anquetil. He always plans his race in great detail to ensure victory, whilst taking all necessary precautions. It was not simply by chance that, at the old *L'Auto* headquarters at 10, Faubourg Montmartre, in the very place where Henri Desgrange devoted his life and talents to a great work of journalism and a great sporting event, the man from Normandy known as 'The Head and the Legs', was awarded a unique trophy, made specially to celebrate the 50th Tour de France. Desgrange, whose initials are inscribed on the famous yellow jersey – knew full well that cycling is also a display of intelligence, a proof of knowledge and a demonstration of strategic skill.

Over the last three weeks, Jacques has been the true master of the race, assessing the abilities of his main opponents, keeping tight control of their movements and limiting the risks of their attacks. In many ways his behaviour has been reminiscent of Juan Manuel Fangio, the greatest racing driver ever known, taking risks only when necessary, avoiding mechanical breakdowns, contenting himself, skilfully and intelligently, with giving each challenger the response needed to silence him.

Anquetil only really met one rider truly in his class; our old acquaintance, Federico Bahamontes. It might seem, therefore, that all in all, this champion so unreservedly admired by the experts did not really face any tough opposition. But that would be neither fair nor true, as he was forced to defend himself on every front right up until the two masterly stages between Grenoble and Chamonix that decided the final outcome for everyone.

The downside of this Tour, however, was that it hasn't brought us any of what must be sport's most valuable asset: revelations. It hasn't brought fresh compost to our journalistic pasture, revealing previously unknown names, adolescent faces and dreams, or undisciplined passion. There were too many seasoned competitors, used to playing the underdog and submitting, whose disenchantment led to apathy. Thankfully, at the same time and in the same circumstances, the amateurs on the Tour de l'Avenir, far from being indifferent, were full of expectation, valiently fighting their own battle.

Anquetil gains the upper hand in his duel with Bahamontes, winning with panache in the rain at Chamonix.

Above: On the Grand-Saint-Bernard pass, Poulidor dropped Bahamontes and Anquetil. But by the end of the stage he paid the price for this supreme effort.
Below: 10 kilometres (6.2 miles) from Chamonix, Bahamontes and Anquetil broke free of the pack. Anquetil led once more, carrying Bahamontes along with him.

Anquetil takes five

A fortnight before the 1964 Tour de France, Jacques Anquetil had won his second Giro d'Italia. He began the Tour at Rennes with a double in mind, something that only Coppi had achieved before him. Anquetil knew he would have to ride flawlessly to beat Raymond Poulidor, whose status as darling of France rankled with the champion.

The flaws began, however, on stage seven, when Poulidor gained 34 seconds on Anquetil. The following day, Anquetil was close to collapsing on the Galibier, then flatted, allowing Poulidor to pocket the 30-second time bonus for finishing second in the stage. On stage nine, Anquetil, only beginning to recover from the Giro, led 22 riders, including Poulidor and Bahamontes, away from the field, and over the final kilometres, forcing them to ride at an incredible tempo. When they reached the track in Monaco, Poulidor sprinted a lap too soon, allowing Anquetil to win the stage. Anquetil was closing in on his rivals.

On the rest day in Andorra, Anquetil created a sensation by appearing at a barbecue given by a local radio station, and getting into a drinking competition with his *directeur sportif*, Géminiani. Since an astrologer named Belline had announced in *France-Soir* that Anquetil would be killed in a fall on stage fourteen, Anquetil had been behaving like a condemned man.

The fateful stage began with the Col d'Envalira. Poulidor and Bahamontes attacked immediately. Anquetil was unable to follow; swaddled in dense mist, he dwelled on the prophesy. Then, reaching the summit, he hurtled blindly, almost suicidally, down into the whiteout, guessing the path of the road from the rear lights of the cars, until he reached yellow jersey Georges Groussard, and a group of team-mates helping him defend his lead. The group relayed him up to Poulidor; then, against all expectation, the balance of power shifted. After changing a wheel, Poulidor's mechanic gave him a push, and Poulidor went down. The accident cost him two minutes. The Pyrenees and stage-seventeen time trial left Anquetil 56 seconds ahead of Poulidor, with the Puy de Dôme still to climb. There, before 500,000 spectators, Poulidor and Anquetil staged a legendary duel, locked in combat, perfectly matched, neither able to gain an inch on the other, up the brunt of the climb. Then, almost in sight of the finish, Poulidor edged ahead, opened a small lead, then stretched up and away. When Anquetil crossed the line, his race lead was 14 seconds. 'If he had taken the jersey from me, I would have gone home,' Anquetil later confessed. But the final time trial gave him his fifth win, watched by the television cameras covering the whole event for the first time.

GENERAL CLASSIFICATION

1. **Jacques Anquetil** (FRA) St-Raphaël-Gitane, 4,505 km in 127h.9m.44s; Average speed: 35.419 kph
2. **Raymond Poulidor** (FRA) Mercier-BP, at 55s.
3. **Federico Bahamontes** (SPA) Margnat-Paloma, at 4m.44s.
4. Henry Anglade (FRA) Pelforth-Sauvage-Lejeune, at 6m.42s.
5. Georges Groussard (FRA) Pelforth-Sauvage-Lejeune, at 10m.34s.
6. André Foucher (FRA) Pelforth-Sauvage-Lejeune, at 10m.36s.
7. Julio Jiménez (SPA) Kas, at 12m.13s.
8. Gilbert Desmet (BEL) Wiels-Groene-Leeuw, at 12m.17s.
9. Hans Junkermann (GER) Wiels-Groene-Leeuw, at 14m.2s.
10. Vittorio Adorni (ITA) Salvarani, at 14m.19s.
11. Esteban Martín (SPA) Margnat-Paloma, at 25m.11s.
12. Fernando Manzaneque (SPA) Ferrys, at 32m.09s.
13. Francisco Gabica (SPA) Kas, at 41m.47s.
14. Tom Simpson (GBR) Peugeot-BP, at 41m.50s.
15. Rudi Altig (GER) St-Raphaël-Gitane, at 42m.8s.
16. Karl-Heinz Kunde (GER) Wiels-Groene-Leeuw, at 42m.16s.
17. Joaquín Galera (SPA) Kas, at 43m.47s.
18. Henri Duez (FRA) Peugeot-BP, at 46m.16s.
19. Joseph Novales (FRA) Margnat-Paloma, at 48m.49s.
20. Eddy Pauwels (BEL) Margnat-Paloma, at 50m.2s.

51ST TOUR DE FRANCE, 22 STAGES – 4,505 KM

Stage	Date	Distance	STAGE	STAGE WINNER	YELLOW JERSEY
Stage 1	Monday 22 June	215 km	Rennes – Lisieux	E. Sels (BEL)	E. Sels
Stage 2	Tuesday 23 June	208 km	Lisieux – Amiens	A. Darrigade (FRA)	E. Sels
Stage 3 (1)	Wednesday 24 June	196.5 km	Amiens – Forest (BEL)	B. Van de Kerckhove (BEL)	B. Van de Kerckhove
Stage 3 (2)	Wednesday 24 June	21.3 km	Forest (BEL) – Forest (TTT)	Kas	B. Van de Kerckhove
Stage 4	Thursday 25 June	291.5 km	Forest (BEL) – Metz	R. Altig (GER)	B. Van de Kerckhove
Stage 5	Friday 26 June	161.5 km	Lunéville – Fribourg-en-Brisgau (GER)	W. Derboven (BEL)	R. Altig
Stage 6	Saturday 27 June	200 km	Fribourg-en-Brisgau (GER) – Besançon	H. Nijdam (HOL)	R. Altig
Stage 7	Sunday 28 June	195 km	Champagnole – Thonon-les-Bains	J. Janssen (HOL)	R. Altig
Stage 8	Monday 29 June	248.5 km	Thonon-les-Bains – Briançon	F. Bahamontes (SPA)	G. Groussard
Stage 9	Tuesday 30 June	239 km	Briançon – Monaco	J. Anquetil (FRA)	G. Groussard
Stage 10 (1)	Wednesday 1 July	187.5 km	Monaco – Hyères	J. Janssen (HOL)	G. Groussard
Stage 10 (2)	Wednesday 1 July	20.8 km	Hyères – Toulon (TT)	J. Anquetil (FRA)	G. Groussard
Stage 11	Thursday 2 July	250 km	Toulon – Montpellier	E. Sels (BEL)	G. Groussard
Stage 12	Friday 3 July	174 km	Montpellier – Perpignan	J. De Roo (HOL)	G. Groussard
Stage 13	Saturday 4 July	170 km	Perpignan – Andorra (AND)	J. Jiménez (SPA)	G. Groussard
Stage 14	Monday 6 July	186 km	Andorra (AND) – Toulouse	E. Sels (BEL)	G. Groussard
Stage 15	Tuesday 7 July	203 km	Toulouse – Luchon	R. Poulidor (FRA)	G. Groussard
Stage 16	Wednesday 8 July	197 km	Luchon – Pau	F. Bahamontes (SPA)	G. Groussard
Stage 17	Thursday 9 July	42.6 km	Peyrehorade – Bayonne (TT)	J. Anquetil (FRA)	J. Anquetil
Stage 18	Friday 10 July	187 km	Bayonne – Bordeaux	A. Darrigade (FRA)	J. Anquetil
Stage 19	Saturday 11 July	215.5 km	Bordeaux – Brive	E. Sels (BEL)	J. Anquetil
Stage 20	Sunday 12 July	237.5 km	Brive – Puy de Dôme	J. Jiménez (SPA)	J. Anquetil
Stage 21	Monday 13 July	311 km	Clermont-Ferrand – Orléans	J. Stablinski (FRA)	J. Anquetil
Stage 22 (1)	Tuesday 14 July	118.5 km	Orléans – Versailles	B. Beheyt (BEL)	J. Anquetil
Stage 22 (2)	Tuesday 14 July	27.5 km	Versailles – Paris (TT)	J. Anquetil (FRA)	J. Anquetil

Briançon to Monaco: On the Col de Restefond, the three hard men of
the 1964 Tour, Bahamontes, Poulidor and Anquetil, broke away and
gave chase to Rostollan.

Puy de Dôme: 'We were side by side. I slowed down; he slowed down. I attacked, he responded. It was astounding.' Poulidor finally inched away from Anquetil after their legendary elbow-to-elbow duel.

One of the great rivalries

At the end of a legendary Tour, Raymond Poulidor and Jacques Anquetil ride a lap of honour around the Parc together, applauded by a public won over by their duel.

PARC DES PRINCES: Here we are, exhausted and gasping for breath, having experienced the intensity of one of the greatest moments ever seen in cycling or in any sport, despite its wealth of epic tales. The two champions, ferociously battling out the last few kilometres to win the 'Tour of Tours', after weeks of suffering, drew an enormous crowd who passionately cheered them on, but with a sense of restraint that left the very last word to sport. We will never forget the vast crowds gathered all along the route to the Parc, who, excitedly noting each rider go past, celebrated the extraordinary and spectacular athletic exploits of two champions who took outlandish risks and threw every ounce of strength into this heroic battle.

By the early hours of the afternoon, we began to sense the thrilling atmosphere that builds up when something out of the ordinary is about to occur. It felt as if we were waiting for the start of an Olympic final, our hearts beating, nerves tingling, sensations heightened by the gathering storm. The

moments leading up to the hour of reckoning were just as tense for the two riders! They had to seize the upper hand in this battle of nerves and maintain perfect self-control.

After reaching the finish of the first half-stage, Jacques Anquetil took a rest. 'I needed to focus myself,' he said. 'Yesterday, after the long stage from Clermont to Orléans, I didn't really feel that I was in the Tour. I needed to get a hold on myself and focus on the goal.' Jacques then had a light, but nutritious, lunch, after which, accompanied by Raphaël Géminiani and his *soigneur* Vergami, he went by car to reconnoitre the route, as he was not familiar with the terrain. He was still not sure which gear to use, as Géminiani confided to us: 'We set off with the idea of using a bottom gear of 49 x 17 (6.15 m or 20 ft 2 ins), but we changed our minds on the way and finally decided upon the 47 x 17 (5.90 m or 19 ft 4 ins). That's the reason why Jacques lost some ground during the hillier parts of the race.'

After surveying the course, Anquetil took another rest. He got up about three-quarters

of an hour before he was scheduled to start and rode a dozen or so kilometres (seven or eight miles) to warm up. Everything had also been put in place to enable communication during the race. Knowing he would have trouble reaching his rider, Géminiani had equipped himself with a slate. If Anquetil was in the lead, he had to chalk up a figure preceded by the + sign, in enormous letters, and a figure preceded by the - sign if he was behind. The minus sign wasn't needed. But after than 20 kilometres (12.5 miles) Géminiani's emotions switched from hope to fear as Anquetil's early advantage began to diminish.

At the bottom of the Sèvres descent, he sounded his horn. Jacques turned his head slightly and read '+3'. He bent his back, tensed his face, kept his eyes fixed a few feet in front of him and, giving his all, cranked up his biggest gear, the 54 x 13 (8.74 m or 28.6 ft 8 ins).

'I knew that I could gain time over Raymond Poulidor in this part of the race, which was more suited to me than to him,' acknowledged Anquetil frankly. 'I won the Tour definitively in the last five kilometres (three miles). I am glad nothing happened to disrupt such an important race in which I really had to give my all.'

He paused and then added: 'I gave 100 percent. I have rarely used such force. I had to go beyond my own limits in order to beat Raymond Poulidor, so I must pay tribute to him. I am proud to have beaten such a very great champion, in the hardest Tour I have ever known.' And the two fierce combatants and brotherly rivals spontaneously embraced and congratulated each other.

There was a nobility in this gesture that was completely devoid of affectation, which isn't part of either man's style. It touched us to core and underlined this superb duel. The public was right to admire both racers equally and give such a magnificent ovation to the two men, who rode side by side for the lap of honour.

As for the joyous Jacques Anquetil, he had realized a dream close to his heart: to emulate Fausto Coppi by winning the double – the Giro and the Tour de France in the same year.

After catching the Spanish rider Gabica on the Col du Portillon, Raymond Poulidor dropped him and reached Luchon, after a fantastic descent, with a 2min-43sec lead (including the time bonus) over his rivals. The Tour was wide open again!

From the very start of the Tour, Anquetil could see from the signs carried by the fans that his rivalry with Poulidor had split France in two.

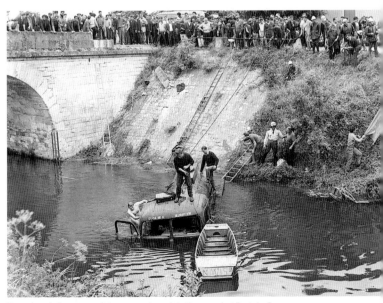

Tragedy: a helicopter assistance van drove into the crowd at Port-de-Couze, killing eight.

Gimondi, a *campionissimo* in the making?

In 1965, Jacques Anquetil won the pre-Tour Dauphiné Libéré in the Alps. Then, the evening after the final stage, he flew across France, started the Bordeaux-Paris shortly after midnight, and won it the following day. He didn't even start the Tour de France, reasoning: 'My contracts won't increase if I win a sixth Tour. And if I fail, I've everything to lose.' It looked as if a new opportunity was opening for Poulidor, although some wondered whether, far from being subjugated by Anquetil's tyranny, he had actually benefited from it. Poulidor had been beaten in the Vuelta a España by Rolf Wolfshohl, and critics were beginning to question his tactical abilities and speculate about the mistakes he would make. The first was to underestimate the abilities of a 22-year-old Italian, Felice Gimondi, riding his first Tour de France. Gimondi had finished third in the Giro d'Italia earlier that June, and in 1964 he'd won the Tour de l'Avenir, the amateur version of the Tour de France, ahead of Lucien Aimar. Included in the Salvarani team at the last moment, it was Gimondi who initiated the first attack on the road to Roubaix. He took the yellow jersey the next day at Rouen, with a lead of more than three minutes.

In the Pyrenees the burning heat of the Aubisque took many victims. Gimondi's team-leader Vittorio Adorni collapsed into the grass in tears with unbearable stomach pains. A few bends higher up, Lucien Aimar had tumbled on the asphalt, with irregular breathing and crossed arms, apparently suffering from sunstroke. During the same stage, Bahamontes, Wolfshol, Van de Kerckhove and Den Hartog also abandoned. The carnage led, together with the 'poisoned fish' episode of 1962, to suspicions that doping was increasing in the professional peloton.

On the ascent of Mount Ventoux, Poulidor showed signs of recovery. At Le Chalet-Reynard, he broke away with Julio Jiménez, Bahamontes, designated successor, but Gimondi managed to limit his advantage and retained the yellow jersey by 34 seconds. This was largely thanks to Henry Anglade, who was accused by French supporters of riding for Gimondi, where Anglade was only defending his own position in the general classification; he finished fourth in Paris. Poulidor didn't make a drama out of his relative failure. He believed he was still capable of taking control of the race on the mountain time trial up Mont Revard. Against all expectations, Gimondi roundly defeated him by 33 seconds, despite mechanical problems, and added a 20-second time bonus for the stage win. Gimondi had won the Tour de France at his first attempt.

GENERAL CLASSIFICATION

1. **Felice Gimondi** (ITA) Salvarini, 4,188 km in 116h.42m.6s; Average speed: 35.882 kph
2. **Raymond Poulidor** (FRA) Mercier-BP, at 2m.40s.
3. **Gianni Motta** (ITA) Molteni, at 9m.18s.
4. Henry Anglade (FRA) Pelforth-Sauvage-Lejeune, at 12m.43s.
5. Jean-Claude Lebaube (FRA) Ford-France, at 12m.56s.
6. José Pérez-Francés (SPA) Ferrys, at 13m.15s.
7. Guido De Rosso (ITA) Molteni, at 14m.48s.
8. Frans Brands (BEL) Flandria-Romeo, at 17m.36s.
9. Jan Janssen (HOL) Pelforth-Sauvage-Lejeune, at 17m.52s.
10. Francisco Gabica (SPA) Kas, at 19m.11s.
11. Karl-Heinz Kunde (GER) Wiels-Groene-Leeuw, at 19m.21s.
12. Roger Pingeon (FRA) Peugeot-BP, at 20m.32s.
13. Valentín Uriona (SPA) Kas, at 24m.34s.
14. Henri Duez (FRA) Peugeot-BP, at 25m.7s.
15. Renzo Fontona (ITA) Ignis, at 25m.31s.
16. Gilbert Desmet (BEL) Wiels-Groene-Leeuw, at 28m.4s.
17. André Zimmermann (FRA) Peugeot-BP, at 29m.35s.
18. André Foucher (FRA) Pelforth-Sauvage-Lejeune, at 29m.53s.
19. Arnalso Pambianco (ITA) Salvarini, at 32m.48s.
20. Louis Rostolan (FRA) Ford-France, at 34m.51s.

52ND TOUR DE FRANCE, 22 STAGES – 4,188 KM

			STAGE	STAGE WINNER	YELLOW JERSEY
Stage 1 (1)	Tuesday 22 June	149 km	Cologne (GER) – Liège (BEL)	R. Van Looy (BEL)	R. Van Looy
Stage 1 (2)	Tuesday 22 June	22.5 km	Liège (BEL) – Liège (BEL) (TT)	Ford-France	R. Van Looy
Stage 2	Wednesday 23 June	200.5 km	Liège (BEL) – Roubaix	B. Van de Kerckhove (BEL)	B. Van de Kerckhove
Stage 3	Thursday 24 June	240 km	Roubaix – Rouen	F. Gimondi (ITA)	F. Gimondi
Stage 4	Friday 25 June	227 km	Caen – Saint-Brieuc	E. Sorgeloos (BEL)	F. Gimondi
Stage 5 (1)	Saturday 26 June	147 km	Saint-Brieuc – Châteaulin	C. Van Espen (HOL)	F. Gimondi
Stage 5 (2)	Saturday 26 June	26.7 km	Châteaulin – Châteaulin (TT)	R. Poulidor (FRA)	F. Gimondi
Stage 6	Sunday 27 June	210.5 km	Quimper – La Baule	G. Reybrouck (BEL)	F. Gimondi
Stage 7	Monday 28 June	219 km	La Baule – La Rochelle	E. Sels (BEL)	B. Van De Kerckhove
Stage 8	Tuesday 29 June	197.5 km	La Rochelle – Bordeaux	J. De Roo (HOL)	B. Van De Kerckhove
Stage 9	Wednesday 30 June	226.5 km	Dax – Bagnères-de-Bigorre	J. Jiménez (SPA)	F. Gimondi
Stage 10	Thursday 1 July	222.5 km	Bagnères-de-Bigorre – Ax-les-Thermes	G. Reybrouck (BEL)	F. Gimondi
Stage 11	Friday 2 July	240.5 km	Ax-les-Thermes – Barcelone (SPA)	J. Pérez Francés (SPA)	F. Gimondi
Stage 12	Sunday 4 July	219 km	Barcelone (SPA) – Perpignan	J. Janssen (HOL)	F. Gimondi
Stage 13	Monday 5 July	164 km	Perpignan – Montpellier	A. Durante (ITA)	F. Gimondi
Stage 14	Tuesday 6 July	173 km	Montpellier – Mont Ventoux	R. Poulidor (FRA)	F. Gimondi
Stage 15	Wednesday 7 July	167.5 km	Carpentras – Gap	G. Fezzardi (ITA)	F. Gimondi
Stage 16	Thursday 8 July	177 km	Gap – Briançon	J. Galera (SPA)	F. Gimondi
Stage 17	Friday 9 July	193.5 km	Briançon – Aix-les-Bains	J. Jiménez (SPA)	F. Gimondi
Stage 18	Saturday 10 July	26.9 km	Aix-les-Bains – Mont Revard (TT)	F. Gimondi (ITA)	F. Gimondi
Stage 19	Sunday 11 July	165 km	Aix-les-Bains – Lyon	R. Van Looy (BEL)	F. Gimondi
Stage 20	Monday 12 July	298.5 km	Lyon – Auxerre	M. Wright (GBR)	F. Gimondi
Stage 21	Tuesday 13 July	225.5 km	Auxerre – Versailles	G. Karstens (HOL)	F. Gimondi
Stage 22	Wednesday 14 July	37.8 km	Versailles – Paris (TT)	F. Gimondi (ITA)	F. Gimondi

Transformed by the yellow jersey, Gimondi won the Revard time trial in spite of mechanical problems.

Poulidor is congratulated by Magne (right) on the summit of Mont Ventoux. Here, overall victory was still within Poulidor's reach.

It was a sweltering day on the road to Barcelona, where José Pérez-Francés won the stage after a solo breakaway of 223 kilometres (138.5 miles).

A good haul for Jan Janssen: ninth overall and the green jersey.

Aimar's strategic victory

After a year's absence, Jacques Anquetil returned to the Tour in 1966 – unlike most of the Italians, who stayed away in protest at the anti-doping controls. Anquetil had started the season by defeating Poulidor on the final stage of Paris-Nice, winning the race for the fifth time. In post-race interviews, Poulidor had accused Anquetil of unsporting conduct. Anquetil and Poulidor hadn't been on speaking terms since, and at the *Grand Départ* at Nancy, the enmity was still smouldering. It didn't take long to surface: on stage two, Poulidor was involved in a banal fall. Anquetil launched a blistering attack, stringing the peloton out and forcing Poulidor into a frantic chase. The hostilities had begun.

Over the opening stages, second-ranking riders took centre stage: Willy Planckaert, a Flemish rider, beat Van Looy by two lengths at Dieppe, and Jean-Claude Lebaube, who took the yellow jersey at Luchon before giving it up to the diminutive German Karl-Heinz Kunde, predictably dubbed the 'Yellow Dwarf'. At Bordeaux, Poulidor became the first rider to take anti-doping tests at the Tour. The riders, with Anquetil at their head, staged a protest. It was the start of a long battle.

Then one of Anquetil's team-mates on the Ford team, Lucien Aimar, slipped into a large breakaway group on the road to Pau. Poulidor and Anquetil lost seven minutes, and Antonin Magne, Poulidor's *directeur sportif*, criticized Anquetil's lack of response. Géminiani observed, 'It wasn't Jacques' job to chase down his team-mate. The mistake was Poulidor's, yet again.'

With seven stages left Dutch rider Jan Janssen, best placed of the Pau escapees, seemed poised to win the Tour. But events took an unexpected turn. Poulidor defeated Anquetil by seven seconds in the Vals-les-Bains time trial. The following day, on the stage from Privas to Bourg-d'Oisans, Anquetil, suffering from bronchitis, conceded a further 63 seconds to Poulidor. Recognizing that he had lost the Tour, Anquetil put himself in the service of Aimar, who caught Janssen and Poulidor off guard on the road to Turin, and broke away to take the yellow jersey. The next day, Poulidor escaped and gained 49 seconds. But Aimar, with Anquetil's support, retained control. A day later, Anquetil, weakened by a cold and weathering a rainstorm, took a comb from his pocket and tidied his hair before making a final farewell to the Tour de France in front of the cameras.

GENERAL CLASSIFICATION

1. **Lucien Aimar** (FRA) Ford-France, 4,329 km in 117h.34m.21s; Average speed: 36.819 kph
2. **Jan Janssen** (HOL) Pelforth-Savage-Lejeune, at 1m.7s.
3. **Raymond Poulidor** (FRA) Mercier-BP, at 2m.2s.
4. José-Antonio Momene (SPA) Kas, at 5m.19s.
5. Marcello Mugnaini (ITA) Filotex, at 5m.27s.
6. Herman Van Springel (BEL) Mann-Grundig, at 5m.44s.
7. Francisco Gabica (SPA) Kas, at 6m.25s.
8. Roger Pingeon (FRA) Peugeot-BP, at 8m.22s.
9. Karl-Heinz Kunde (GER) Peugeot-BP, at 9m.6s.
10. Martin Van Den Bossche (BEL) Smith's, at 9m.57s.
11. Antonio Gomez Del Moral (SPA) Kas, at 10m.18s.
12. Rudi Altig (GER) Molteni, at 11m.18s.
13. Julio Jiménez (SPA) Ford-France, at 11m.18s.
14. Valentín Uriona (SPA) Kas, at 11m.59s.
15. Joaquín Galera (SPA) Kas, at 13m.2s.
16. Jozef Huysmans (BEL) Mann-Grundig, at 14m.39s.
17. Franco Bitossi (ITA) Filitex, at 16m.35s.
18. Domingo Perurena (SPA) Fagor, at 17m.29s.
19. Willy Monty (BEL) Pelforth-Savage-Lejeune, at 18m.23s.
20. Mariano Diaz (SPA) Fagor, at 19m.58s.

53RD TOUR DE FRANCE, 22 STAGES - 4,329 KM

			STAGE	STAGE WINNER	YELLOW JERSEY
Stage 1	Tuesday 21 June	208.5 km	Nancy – Charleville	R. Altig (GER)	R. Altig
Stage 2	Wednesday 22 June	198 km	Charleville – Tournai (BEL)	G. Reybroeck (BEL)	R. Altig
Stage 3 (1)	Thursday 23 June	20.8 km	Tournai (BEL) – Tournai (BEL) (TTT)	Televizier	R. Altig
Stage 3 (2)	Thursday 23 June	131.5 km	Tournai (BEL) – Dunkerque	G. Karstens (HOL)	R. Altig
Stage 4	Friday 24 June	205 km	Dunkerque – Dieppe	W. Planckaert (BEL)	R. Altig
Stage 5	Saturday 25 June	178.5 km	Dieppe – Caen	F. Bitossi (ITA)	R. Altig
Stage 6	Sunday 26 June	216.5 km	Caen – Angers	E. Sels (BEL)	R. Altig
Stage 7	Monday 27 June	252.5 km	Angers – Royan	A. Van Vlierberghe (BEL)	R. Altig
Stage 8	Tuesday 28 June	137.5 km	Royan – Bordeaux	W. Planckaert (BEL)	R. Altig
Stage 9	Wednesday 29 June	201 km	Bordeaux – Bayonne	G. Karstens (HOL)	R. Altig
Stage 10	Thursday 30 June	234.5 km	Bayonne – Pau	T. De Pra (ITA)	T. De Pra
Stage 11	Friday 1 July	188 km	Pau – Luchon	M. Mugnaini (ITA)	J.-C. Lebaube
Stage 12	Sunday 3 July	218.2 km	Luchon – Revel	R. Altig (GER)	K.-H. Kunde
Stage 13	Monday 4 July	191.5 km	Revel – Sète	G. Vandenberghe (BEL)	K.-H. Kunde
Stage 14 (1)	Tuesday 5 July	144 km	Montpellier – Aubenas	J. De Roo (HOL)	K.-H. Kunde
Stage 14 (2)	Tuesday 5 July	20 km	Vals-les-Bains – Vals-les-Bains (TTT)	R. Poulidor (FRA)	K.-H. Kunde
Stage 15	Wednesday 6 July	203.5 km	Privas – Bourg-d'Oisans	L. Otano (SPA)	K.-H. Kunde
Stage 16	Thursday 7 July	148.5 km	Bourg-d'Oisans – Briançon	J. Jiménez (SPA)	J. Janssen
Stage 17	Friday 8 July	160 km	Briançon – Turin (ITA)	F. Bitossi (ITA)	L. Aimar
Stage 18	Sunday 10 July	188 km	Ivréa (ITA) – Chamonix	E. Schutz (LUX)	L. Aimar
Stage 19	Monday 11 July	264.5 km	Chamonix – Saint-Étienne	F. Bracke (BEL)	L. Aimar
Stage 20	Tuesday 12 July	223.5 km	Saint-Étienne – Montluçon	H. Nijdam (HOL)	L. Aimar
Stage 21	Wednesday 13 July	232.5 km	Montluçon – Orléans	P. Beuffeuil (FRA)	L. Aimar
Stage 22 (1)	Thursday 14 July	111 km	Orléans – Rambouillet	E. Sels (BEL)	L. Aimar
Stage 22 (2)	Thursday 14 July	51.3 km	Rambouillet – Paris (TTT)	R. Altig (GER)	L. Aimar

Above: A final consultation between the master, Anquetil, and his pupil, Aimar, under the paternalistic eye of Géminiani.
Below: Between Bordeaux and Bayonne, the riders dismounted to protest against the implementation of the anti-doping laws. The previous night, doctors and police had burst into their rooms to carry out the first controls in history.

Pingeon proves he's no ugly duckling

With his slender legs punctuated by knotted knees, Roger Pingeon resembled a wading bird. Inconsistent and subject to sudden mood changes, at the beginning of the season he had bowed out of the Tour of Corsica and announced his retirement. Then he'd had another rush of blood to the head during the Dauphiné Libéré, preferring to abandon rather than carry water for his team-mate Tom Simpson. Yet at the pre-Tour Midi Libre, although the organizer had organized an alliance of teams to prevent him from winning, he had ridden so strongly that Raymond Poulidor regarded him as the best French challenger for the Tour de France, where Pingeon would not have to help Simpson: the race had resorted to national teams for two more years, until the definitive return to commercially-sponsored teams in 1969.

As early as stage five, Pingeon showed his hand, making a spectacular breakaway on the way to Jambes. He swooped down on a group of twelve riders, and, carried along by a combination of skill, bravado and luck, left them behind almost without realizing it. At the end of a brilliant 60-kilometre (37.5-mile) solo breakaway, he had gained more than six minutes on all the favourites. Unruffled, Poulidor refocused his ambitions on the Belfort stage, which finished on the mythical Ballon d'Alsace. Breaking his usual custom, he announced his plan to the other members of the French team. As luck would have it, on the descent of the Platzerwasel, Poulidor fell. The support car of the French team had broken down, converting a simple accident into a pivotal moment in Poulidor's Tour. After a long delay, he finally got back in the saddle on someone else's bike.

Far ahead, Gimondi, Janssen, Aimar and Letort were taking turns at the front. To make matters worse, they were riding headlong into the wind from the valley and Poulidor was struggling hard to pedal on a bike whose toe-clips were too narrow for him. By the time he crossed the line, 11 minutes behind the winner of the stage, Aimar, Poulidor's Tour was in tatters. Yet he responded to his misfortune by putting himself at the service of Pingeon, now in yellow. On the tortuous ascent of the Galibier, he shepherded his team-mate up, turning to encourage him and spurring him on each time Pingeon seemed to be dropping the pace. By the time they reached Briançon, Pingeon, finally released from his demons, had won the Tour.

GENERAL CLASSIFICATION

1. **Roger Pingeon** (FRA) France, 4,779 km in 136h.53m.50s; Average speed: 34.775 kph
2. **Julio Jiménez** (SPA) Spain, at 3m.40s.
3. **Franco Balmamion** (ITA) Primavera, at 7m.23s.
4. Désiré Letort (FRA) Bleuets, at 18m.18s.
5. Jan Janssen (HOL) Holland, at 9m.47s.
6. Lucien Aimar (FRA) France, at 9m.47s.

7. Felice Gimondi (ITA) Italy, at 10m.14s.
8. Jozef Huysmans (BEL) Belgium, at 16m.45s.
9. Raymond Poulidor (FRA) France, at 18m.18s.
10. Fernando Manzaneque (SPA) Esperanza, at 19m.22s.
11. Hans Junkermann (GER) Germany, at 23m.2s.
12. Willy Monty (BEL) Belgium, at 23m.6s.
13. Frans Brands (BEL) Belgium, at 25m.8s.

14. Cees Haast (HOL) Holland, at 26m.23s.
15. Franco Bodrero (ITA) Primavera, at 26m.30s.
16. Noël Van Clooster (BEL) Diables Rouges, at 26m.40s.
17. José Samyn (FRA) Bleuets, at 28m.42s.
18. Ginés García (SPA) Spain, at 28m.56s.
19. André Bayssiere (FRA) Coqs, at 29m.23s.
20. Johnny Schleck (LUX) Switzerland-Luxembourg, at 32m.9s.

54TH TOUR DE FRANCE, 22 STAGES – 4,779 KM

			STAGE	STAGE WINNER	YELLOW JERSEY
Prologue	Thursday 29 June	5.8 km	Angers – Angers	J. M. Errandonea (SPA)	J. M. Errandonea
Stage 1	Friday 30 June	185.5 km	Angers – Saint-Malo	W. Godefroot (BEL)	J. M. Errandonea
Stage 2	Saturday 1 July	180 km	Saint-Malo – Caen	W. Van Neste (BEL)	W. Van Neste
Stage 3	Sunday 2 July	248 km	Caen – Amiens	M. Basso (ITA)	G. Polidori
Stage 4	Monday 3 July	191 km	Amiens – Roubaix	G. Reybroeck (BEL)	J. Spruyt
Stage 5 (1)	Tuesday 4 July	172 km	Roubaix – Jambes (BEL)	R. Pingeon (FRA)	R. Pingeon
Stage 5 (2)	Tuesday 4 July	17 km	Jambes (BEL) – Jambes (TTT)	Belgium	R. Pingeon
Stage 6	Wednesday 5 July	238 km	Jambes (BEL) – Metz	H. Van Springel (BEL)	R. Pingeon
Stage 7	Thursday 6 July	205.5 km	Metz – Strasbourg	M. Wright (GBR)	R. Riotte
Stage 8	Friday 7 July	215 km	Strasbourg – Belfort	L. Aimar (FRA)	R. Pingeon
Stage 9	Sunday 9 July	238.5 km	Belfort – Divonne-les-Bains	G. Reybroeck (BEL)	R. Pingeon
Stage 10	Monday 10 July	243 km	Divonne-les-Bains – Briançon	F. Gimondi (ITA)	R. Pingeon
Stage 11	Tuesday 11 July	197 km	Briançon – Digne	J. Samyn (FRA)	R. Pingeon
Stage 12	Wednesday 12 July	207.5 km	Digne – Marseille	R. Riotte (FRA)	R. Pingeon
Stage 13	Thursday 13 July	211.5 km	Marseille – Carpentras	J. Janssen (HOL)	R. Pingeon
Stage 14	Friday 14 July	201.5 km	Carpentras – Sète	B. Hoban (GBR)	R. Pingeon
Stage 15	Sunday 16 July	230.5 km	Sète – Toulouse	R. Wolfshohl (GER)	R. Pingeon
Stage 16	Monday 17 July	188 km	Toulouse – Luchon	F. Manzaneque (SPA)	R. Pingeon
Stage 17	Tuesday 18 July	250 km	Luchon – Pau	R. Mastrotto (FRA)	R. Pingeon
Stage 18	Wednesday 19 July	206.5 km	Pau – Bordeaux	M. Basso (ITA)	R. Pingeon
Stage 19	Thursday 20 July	217 km	Bordeaux – Limoges	J. Stablinski (FRA)	R. Pingeon
Stage 20	Friday 21 July	222 km	Limoges – Clermont-Ferrand	F. Gimondi (ITA)	R. Pingeon
Stage 21	Saturday 22 July	359 km	Clermont-Ferrand – Fontainebleau	P. Leméteyer (FRA)	R. Pingeon
Stage 22 (1)	Sunday 23 July	104 km	Fontainebleau – Versailles	R. Binggeli (SUI)	R. Pingeon
Stage 22 (2)	Sunday 23 July	46 km	Versailles – Paris	R. Poulidor (FRA)	R. Pingeon

On the road to Jambes, Roger Pingeon took advantage of the climb up the cobbled Thuin to strike out alone in pursuit of the yellow jersey.

He collapsed into the boulders...

CARPENTRAS: We'd left Tom Simpson laughing and joking in front of the town hall in Marseille. A few hours later, there he was, rigid and already cold, lying in compartment no. 3 in the mortuary at Sainte-Marthe Hospital, Avignon.

Yet everything that could have been done to save this man's life had been done. As soon as Simpson fell, some 3 kilometres (1.8 miles) from the summit of Ventoux, Dr Dumas performed cardiac massage while a spectator carried out standard mouth-to-mouth resuscitation. Shortly afterwards, Simpson was transferred to a helicopter and Dr Macorigh took over until they landed near Pont Saint-Bénézet. The attempts at resuscitation continued in the waiting ambulance. Seconds later, Simpson was receiving treatment in Dr Soubeyrand's intensive care unit, even though he was already thought to be dead.

Despite the most up-to-date resuscitation technology used at the hospital, the unfortunate rider was pronounced dead at 5.40pm. The medical authorities at the hospital and the Tour doctors, Dumas and Macorigh, refused to issue a burial certificate without indication of the cause of death.

A little later, the Tour de France Directors, Jacques Goddet and Félix Lévitan, as well as Gaston Plaud, Simpson's technical director and friend, came to pay their respects at the hospital.

For nearly 40 minutes Dr Dumas tried to revive Tom Simpson, both on the road and in the helicopter on the way to the hospital in Avignon, but to no avail. Simpson died at 5.40pm.

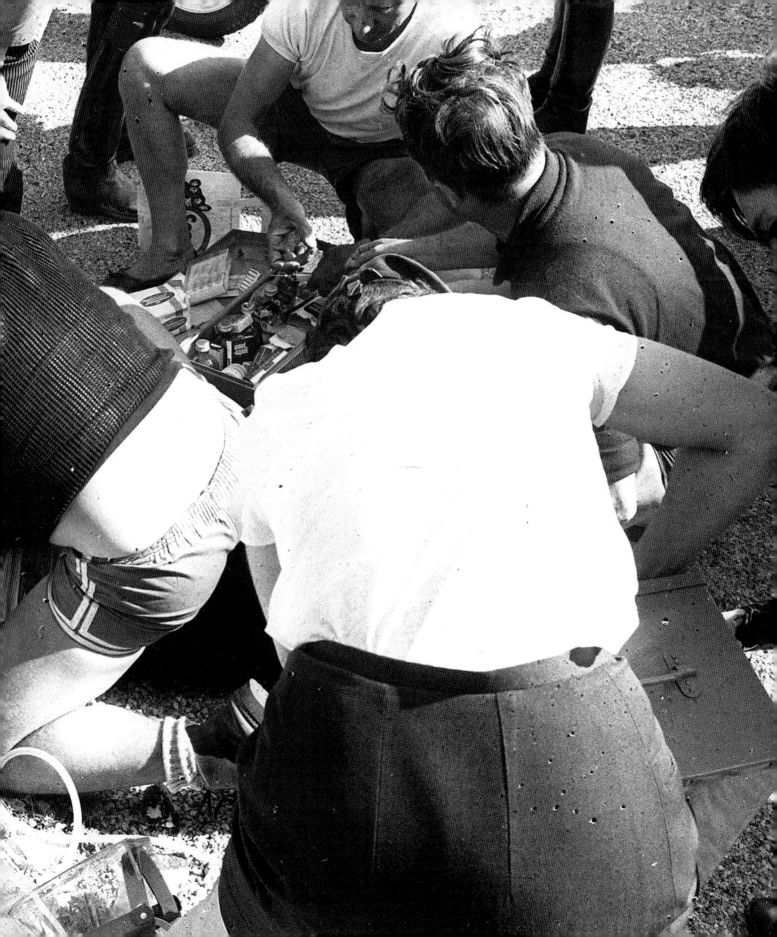

A cyclist is dead...
...and our grief is as profound as our horror

A cyclist is dead... and our grief is as profound as our horror. Tommy was one of the most cheerful fellows on the road. He had adapted the British sense of humour to the banter of the peloton. He was also a champion. But he wanted victory too badly, with everything that it could add to his happiness as a husband and father. We had already been wondering whether this athlete, who often seemed to be in pain when riding hard, was looking after himself properly. Was it doping? The doctors will tell us whether he was using drugs and in what conditions and to what degree, but the fact that they refused to issue a burial certificate leads us to presume the worst. We dread, therefore, the public revelation of a tragedy caused by this scourge, not just on cycling, but on sport and on modern life itself. Hardly a day goes by without the press denouncing the damaging effects of drugs, which attack not just a person's health but his very personality. Simpson's case comes at a time when all the legal, moral, spiritual and scientific communities need to join forces to restore the moral order. But today, let us weep for Tom Simpson, a decent chap who probably simply feared defeat.

Tom Simpson dragged himself up the slopes of the Ventoux with great difficulty. He fell once, was put back in the saddle by the spectators, then fell a second time. This time, he did not get up.

The day after the tragedy, the peloton allowed the British rider Barry Hoban to claim victory.

A moment of contemplation on the starting line. The British riders Hoban, Denson and Lewis have sewn black armbands onto their jerseys.

Under the plane trees of Carpentras, Gimondi wept over the loss of Simpson, who had been due to join him on the Salvarani team the following year.

Roger Pingeon, at long last free of the troubles that had plagued him, joined his wife Dany in the VIP stand, with Tour director Félix Lévitan (far left).

Roger Pingeon:
'I dedicate this victory to my wife Dany'

PARC DES PRINCES: The most important Sunday of Roger Pingeon's life ended in glory. He's confirmed the promise he'd first shown during his long breakaway on the road to Jambes. He's added panache to his athleticism and character. He fought to the end, even when victory was already his; witness his presence at the side of Julio Jiménez, whom he had caught on a road lined with an enormous, passionate and impetuous crowd, through which both men had difficulty cutting a path. It is easy to imagine what this supreme victory must represent for this courageous athlete, a latecomer to top cycling competition. It was achieved with the kind of flawless determination the public never ceases to admire. Now he's triumphed in such a dazzling fashion, we can appreciate the significance of his earlier sacrifices – he is conscientious, honest and meticulous, and these qualities have finally borne fruit. On his own, it might never have happened; Pingeon was on the verge of quitting the sport. Fortunately, he had his wife at his side with the words

he needed to encourage him and to rekindle his ambition. She was watching from the VIP stand, radiant with joy in her summer dress, having arrived that morning from Hauteville in the Ain region. She never lost confidence in him. With her at his side, Pingeon's joy was complete. Asked about his impressions of the Tour, what it meant to him and how he had won it, all he could say was 'This success that is more than I ever dreamed of, I owe it all to my wife Dany: I dedicate it to her.'

This clear-headed, outwardly calm athlete, who'd planned his race with great diligence right up to the final time trial – he'd studied every detail of the complicated route and even knew which way the wind would blow at any point – is ultimately a man who follows his heart. He does not open up easily, like most people from his part of the country, but he's utterly dependable.

One unforgettable image remains of that last day – more private than the image in the Parc, more discreet than the ovation of the crowd or the congenial

post-Tour receptions and the friendly team dinners. We were in the gymnasium at the Versailles stadium, transformed into a waiting room for the final time trial. The only remaining competitors were the overall leaders: Letort on a camp bed, leaning anxiously on his elbows; Janssen chatting with some friends; Gimondi with his team director; Jiménez resigned in a corner; Aimar enjoying a lengthy massage; Balmamion impatient, it seemed, to get going. There weren't enough massage tables and Duchesne, the trainer, had given up on the pommel horse, too uncomfortable for the tall Pingeon, and settled him on a bench covered by a mattress. Pingeon was impressively calm, very sure of himself. Then Poulidor came back from riding.

'I like it,' he said, 'this course suits me.'

'It's yours,' said Pingeon.

A look full of mutual esteem and human warmth passed between them – in fact, there was a very moving sense of comradeship between these enemies bound by so many things in common.

Janssen's hijack

Since Tom Simpson's death in 1967, the cycling world had been debating the intractable problem of drug taking. Fearing a repeat of the previous year's tragedy, the Tour organizers had taken Mont Ventoux off the route and had dubbed the race 'le Tour de la santé' – 'the Tour for good health'. The *Grand Départ* was symbolically staged at the mineral water town of Vittel. None of the three most recent Giro d'Italia winners, Gianni Motta, Felice Gimondi and Eddy Merckx – the comfortable winner of the June 1968 Giro, and the reigning world champion – started. Raymond Poulidor was counting on the help of Roger Pingeon, who had promised to support him in return for services rendered the previous year. Their team-mate Charly Grosskost won the Prologue ahead of Janssen and Poulidor, as well as stage one. Then, the Tour descended into monotony. With riders completing stages en masse, the journalists became bored and criticized the planning of the route. Speaking on a private radio station outside France, the organizer Félix Lévitan accused them of having 'stale eyes'. The journalists responded by staging a strike that remains unique in the history of the Tour, boycotting the first 70 kilometres (43.5 miles) of the stage between Bordeaux and Bayonne.

The Belgian sprinter Georges Vandenberghe had the race lead when Roger Pingeon launched a remarkable solo attack of 193 kilometres (119.9 miles) on the road to Albi. Behind him, Poulidor dropped Jan Janssen, Ferdi Bracke and Lucien Aimar, only for misfortune to intervene yet again in his Tour career, when he was mown down by a press motorbike. With blood pouring from his nose, elbow and knee, Poulidor could scarcely breathe. He managed to limit his delay to a minute, but he had lost the Tour. The next day, Lucien Aimar attacked. The rebel leader of the France B-team dragged 15 riders in his wake, including Janssen, Bracke and his team-mate Van Springel, Germany's Rolf Wolfshohl and the Spaniard Gregorio San Miguel. For the French national team it was a catastrophe. Pingeon was relegated by nine minutes; Poulidor, covered in bandages, abandoned at Saint-Étienne. A valiant solo stage win by Pingeon at Grenoble did nothing to change the overall result; the yellow jersey went from Wolfshohl to San Miguel, and then to Belgium's Van Springel. Paralysed by the stakes, he lost his 16-second lead in the final time trial from Melun to Paris, to Jan Janssen, who became the first Dutchman to win the Tour de France, despite never once having worn the yellow jersey.

GENERAL CLASSIFICATION

1. **Jan Janssen** (HOL) Holland,
   4,492 km in 133h.49m.42s; Average speed: 34.894 kph
2. **Herman Van Springel** (BEL) Belgium, at 38s.
3. **Ferdinand Bracke** (BEL) Belgium B, at 3m.3s.
4. Gregorio San Miguel (SPA) Spain, at 3m.17s.
5. Roger Pingeon (FRA) France, at 3m.29s.
6. Rolf Wolfshohl (GER) Germany, at 3m.46s.
7. Lucien Aimar (FRA) France B, at 4m.44s.
8. Franco Bitossi (ITA) Italy, at 4m.59s.
9. Andrés Gandarias (SPA) Spain, at 5m.5s.
10. Ugo Colombo (ITA) Italy, at 7m.55s.
11. Antonio Gómez Del Moral (SPA) Spain, at 8m.11s.
12. Georges Pintens (BEL) Belgium, at 10m.26s.
13. Aurelio Gonzáles (SPA) Spain, at 10m.42s.
14. André Poppe (BEL) Belgium, at 12m.31s.
15. Silvano Schiavon (ITA) Italy, at 14m.9s.
16. Tony Houbrechts (BEL) Belgium B, at 17m.23s.
17. Charles 'Charly' Grosskost (FRA) France B, at 17m.26s.
18. Georges Vandenberghe (BEL) Belgium B, at 18m.2s.
19. Flaviano Vicentini (ITA) Italy, at 18m.19s.
20. Walter Godefroot (BEL) Belgium B, at 18m.28s.

55TH TOUR DE FRANCE, 22 STAGES – 4,492 KM

	STAGE		STAGE WINNER	YELLOW JERSEY
Prologue Thursday 27 June 6,1 km	Vittel – Vittel		C. Grosskost (FRA)	C. Grosskost
Stage 1 Friday 28 June 89 km	Vittel – Esch-sur-Alzette (LUX)		C. Grosskost (FRA)	C. Grosskost
Stage 2 Saturday 29 June 210.5 km	Arlon (BEL) – Forest (BEL)		E. De Vlaeminck (BEL)	C. Grosskost
Stage 3 (1) Sunday 30 June 22 km	Forest (BEL) – Forest (BEL) (TTT)		Belgium A	H. Van Springel
Stage 3 (2) Sunday 30 June 112 km	Forest (BEL) – Roubaix		W. Godefroot (BEL)	H. Van Springel
Stage 4 Monday 1 July 238 km	Roubaix – Rouen		G. Chappe (FRA)	J.-P. Genet
Stage 5 (1) Tuesday 2 July 165 km	Rouen – Bagnoles-de-l'Orne		A. Desvages (FRA)	G. Vandenberghe
Stage 5 (2) Tuesday 2 July 154.5 km	Bagnoles-de-l'Orne – Dinard		J. Dumont (FRA)	G. Vandenberghe
Stage 6 Wednesday 3 July 188 km	Dinard – Lorient		A. Gonzáles (SPA)	G. Vandenberghe
Stage 7 Thursday 4 July 190 km	Lorient – Nantes		F. Bitossi (ITA)	G. Vandenberghe
Stage 8 Friday 5 July 223 km	Nantes – Royan		D. Van Ryckeghem (BEL)	G. Vandenberghe
Stage 9 Sunday 7 July 137.5 km	Royan – Bordeaux		W. Godefroot (BEL)	G. Vandenberghe
Stage 10 Monday 8 July 202.5 km	Bordeaux – Bayonne		G. Bellone (FRA)	G. Vandenberghe
Stage 11 Tuesday 9 July 183.5 km	Bayonne – Pau		D. Van Ryckeghem (BEL)	G. Vandenberghe
Stage 12 Wednesday 10 July 226.5 km	Pau – Saint-Gaudens		G. Pintens (BEL)	G. Vandenberghe
Stage 13 Thursday 11 July 208.5 km	Saint-Gaudens – Seo De Urgell (SPA)		H. Van Springel (BEL)	G. Vandenberghe
Stage 14 Friday 12 July 231.5 km	Seo De Urgell (SPA) – Canet-Plage		J. Janssen (HOL)	G. Vandenberghe
Stage 15 Sunday 14 July 250.5 km	Font-Romeu – Albi		R. Pingeon (FRA)	G. Vandenberghe
Stage 16 Monday 15 July 199 km	Albi – Aurillac		F. Bitossi (ITA)	R. Wolfshohl
Stage 17 Tuesday 16 July 236.5 km	Aurillac – Saint-Étienne		J.-P. Genet (FRA)	R. Wolfshohl
Stage 18 Wednesday 17 July 235 km	Saint-Étienne – Grenoble		R. Pingeon (FRA)	G. San Miguel
Stage 19 Thursday 18 July 200 km	Grenoble – Sallanches		B. Hoban (GBR)	H. Van Springel
Stage 20 Friday 19 July 242.5 km	Sallanches – Besançon		J. Huysmans (BEL)	H. Van Springel
Stage 21 Saturday 20 July 242 km	Besançon – Auxerre		E. Leman (BEL)	H. Van Springel
Stage 22 (1) Sunday 21 July 136 km	Auxerre – Melun		M. Izier (FRA)	H. Van Springel
Stage 22 (2) Sunday 21 July 55.2 km	Melun – Paris (TT)		J. Janssen (HOL)	J. Janssen

At the start of the final time trial, Melun-Paris, the suspense was palpable. Nine riders finished within two minutes of each other, but it was a non-specialist, the Dutchman Jan Janssen, who won the stage and the Tour.

Van Springel, inconsolable after losing the *maillot jaune* on the final day, implied that Janssen had perhaps evaded the anti-doping control.

Poulidor, run down by a motorbike on the way to Albi, suffered a fractured nose. Another Tour lost, yet again.

Merckx!

In 1964, Eddy Merckx had become the world amateur champion. By the time he rode his first Tour de France in 1969, he had won the Giro d'Italia, three Milan-San Remos, two Gent-Wevelgems, a Tour of Flanders, a Flèche Wallonne, a Paris-Roubaix, and the professional World Championship title. Aged barely twenty-five, Merckx was the finest rider in the sport; now he was ready for the sport's greatest race.

However, on 2 June he had been ejected from the 1969 Giro d'Italia after a positive dope test in circumstances that stank of conspiracy. Merckx started the Tour at Roubaix an angry, bitter man, bent on restoring his name. For three weeks, he channelled this rage into a war on all fronts, and proved himself a man of many faces. The Merckx who took his first yellow jersey in front of the Belgian crowd after the team time trial at Woluwe-Saint-Pierre was a sentimentalist; the Merckx who humiliated his opponents on the Ballon d'Alsace was a tyrant; the Merckx who confirmed his dominance in the Divonne time trial was the powerful *rouleur*; the Merckx who allowed Pingeon to win the stage at Chamonix was a giver of mercy; and the Merckx who, with the Tour already in his pocket, sped away on the Tourmalet, riding 130 kilometres (81 miles) alone in the yellow jersey was Merckx the omnipotent.

Years later, an explanation for this incredible feat in the Pyrenees did eventually surface. Merckx had learned that his Faema team-mate Martin Van den Bossche had accepted an offer from another team, creating a conflict of interest. Instead of allowing Van den Bossche to take the mountains points, Merckx decided to humiliate him on his favourite terrain. He later regretted his decision, but the result was one of the greatest feats in Tour history. After the summit, as Roger Pingeon later remembered, 'He shot down the descent like a stone. A small gap opened, and gradually grew. I looked at Poulidor; he shrugged his shoulders as if to say that Merckx had no reason to continue his break. There were still another 130 kilometres to go.' This stage win outshone every other rider on the Tour de France, and even the Tour de France itself. At Mourenx, there was an eight-minute wait before Michele Dancelli flew into view with Pingeon, Poulidor, Theillière, Zimmermann, Bayssière and Van den Bossche. Gimondi and Janssen lost nearly a quarter of an hour. Merckx's competitors would never quite get over it.

GENERAL CLASSIFICATION

1. **Eddy Merckx** (BEL) Faema, 4,117 km in 116h.16m.2s; Average speed: 35.296 kph
2. **Roger Pingeon** (FRA) Peugeot-BP, at 17m.54s.
3. **Raymond Poulidor** (FRA) Mercier-BP, at 22m.13s.
4. Felice Gimondi (ITA) Salvarani, at 29m.24s.
5. Andrés Gandarias (SPA) Kas, at 33m.4s.
6. Marinus Wagtmans (HOL) Willem II-Gazelle, at 33m.57s.
7. Pierfranco Vianelli (ITA) Molteni, at 42m.40s.
8. Joaquim Agosthino (POR) Frimatic De Gribaldy, at 51m.24s.
9. Désiré Letort (FRA) Peugeot-BP, at 51m.41s.
10. Jan Janssen (HOL) Bic, at 52m.56s.
11. Joaquín Galera (SPA) Fagor, at 54m.47s.
12. Lucien Van Impe (BEL) Sonolor-Lejeune, at 56m.17s.
13. Jean-Claude Theillière (FRA) Sonolor-Lejeune, at 1h.4m.58s.
14. Wladimiro Panizza (ITA) Salvarani, at 1h.5m.16s.
15. Eddy Schutz (LUX) Molteni, at 1h.6m.58s.
16. Jean Dumont (FRA) Peugeot-BP, at 1h.7m.25s.
17. Paul Gutty (FRA) Frimatic De Gribaldy, at 1h.8m.5s.
18. Herman Van Springel (BEL) Mann-Grundig, at 1h.10m.11s.
19. Eduardo Castello (SPA) Kas, at 1h.14m.4s.
20. Michele Dancelli (ITA) Molteni, at 1h.17m.36s.

56TH TOUR DE FRANCE, 22 STAGES – 4,117 KM

			STAGE	STAGE WINNER	YELLOW JERSEY
Prologue	Saturday 28 June	10.4 km	Roubaix – Roubaix	R. Altig (GER)	R. Altig
Stage 1 (1)	Sunday 29 June	147 km	Roubaix – Woluwe-Saint-Pierre (BEL)	M. Basso (ITA)	R. Altig
Stage 1 (2)	Sunday 29 June	15.6 km	Woluwe – Woluwe (BEL) (TTT)	Faema	E. Merckx
Stage 2	Monday 30 June	181.5 km	Woluwe (BEL) – Maastricht (HOL)	J. Stevens (BEL)	J. Stevens
Stage 3	Tuesday 1 July	213.5 km	Maastricht (HOL) – Charleville	É. Leman (BEL)	J. Stevens
Stage 4	Wednesday 2 July	214 km	Charleville – Nancy	R. Van Looy (BEL)	J. Stevens
Stage 5	Thursday 3 July	193.5 km	Nancy – Mulhouse	J. Agostinho (POR)	D. Letort
Stage 6	Friday 4 July	133.5 km	Mulhouse – Belfort	E. Merckx (BEL)	E. Merckx
Stage 7	Saturday 5 July	241 km	Belfort – Divonne-les-Bains	M. Diaz (SPA)	E. Merckx
Stage 8 (1)	Sunday 6 July	8.8 km	Divonne-les-Bains – Divonne (TT)	E. Merckx (BEL)	E. Merckx
Stage 8 (2)	Sunday 6 July	136.5 km	Divonne-les-Bains – Thonon-les-Bains	M. Dancelli (ITA)	E. Merckx
Stage 9	Monday 7 July	111 km	Thonon-les-Bains – Chamonix	R. Pingeon (FRA)	E. Merckx
Stage 10	Tuesday 8 July	220.5 km	Chamonix – Briançon	H. Van Springel (BEL)	E. Merckx
Stage 11	Wednesday 9 July	198 km	Briançon – Digne	E. Merckx (BEL)	E. Merckx
Stage 12	Thursday 10 July	161.5 km	Digne – Aubagne	F. Gimondi (ITA)	E. Merckx
Stage 13	Friday 11 July	195.5 km	Aubagne – La Grande-Motte	G. Reybroeck (BEL)	E. Merckx
Stage 14	Saturday 12 July	234.5 km	La Grande-Motte – Revel	J. Agostinho (POR)	E. Merckx
Stage 15	Sunday 13 July	18.5 km	Revel – Revel (TT)	E. Merckx (BEL)	E. Merckx
Stage 16	Monday 14 July	199 km	Castelnaudary – Luchon	R. Delisle (FRA)	E. Merckx
Stage 17	Tuesday 15 July	214.5 km	Luchon – Mourenx	E. Merckx (BEL)	E. Merckx
Stage 18	Wednesday 16 July	201 km	Mourenx – Bordeaux	B. Hoban (GBR)	E. Merckx
Stage 19	Thursday 17 July	192.5 km	Libourne – Brive	B. Hoban (GBR)	E. Merckx
Stage 20	Friday 18 July	198 km	Brive – Puy de Dôme	P. Matignon (FRA)	E. Merckx
Stage 21	Saturday 19 July	329.5 km	Clermont-Ferrand – Montargis	H. Van Springel (BEL)	E. Merckx
Stage 22 (1)	Sunday 20 July	111.5 km	Montargis – Créteil	J. Spruyt (BEL)	E. Merckx
Stage 22 (2)	Sunday 20 July	36.8 km	Créteil – Paris (TT)	E. Merckx (BEL)	E. Merckx

After a legendary 130-kilometre (81-mile) solo breakaway, Eddy Merckx arrived in Mourenx nearly eight minutes ahead of his rivals and sealed his first Tour win.

Merckxissimo!

MOURENX-VILLE-NOUVELLE: Nothing can ever compare to this; there will only ever be one Eddy Merckx in the history of cycling. He is a mystery of human creation – 'It is extraordinary that so much brilliance can contain so much mystery,' as the poet Mallarmé said of Gauguin. What this magnificent cyclist achieved yesterday was different from anything that has ever been seen in the history of road cycling. It was a gratuitous act, one without premeditation or preparation; an act which annihilated everything and everyone in its path, from the responses of the other riders to the very idea of the race itself.

Was it his intention to humiliate the other riders, crushing them under his wheels like insects? Is this the vanity of a megalomaniac wanting to dominate, conquer and possess

'Eddy Merckx, young superman of the road, pursues the destiny prescribed by the natural play of his uncommon gifts.' The writer Antoine Blondin is bowled over by the Merckx phenomenon.

everything he sees? Merckx is certainly motivated by pride, as without pride there can be no true spark or competition. But what is really behind his need to attack is the desire to pay tribute to his sport, a physical sport, to do his job, and also the fundamental need to have an outlet for his physical strength. To this straightforward and direct young man, holding back or saving his strength would be seen as a sign of laziness, even cowardice and certainly hypocrisy.

So when he realized, between Luchon and Mourenx, that the race was dragging and that the giants of the Pyrenees, who not long ago had haunted the dreams of his childhood, were just spinning easily up the gradient (even if, in such conditions, they were wreaking havoc, forcing a pale and unwell Gimondi to drop off the pace), he felt the need to act. The Peyresourde and the Aspin had been cleared by the peloton bunched together and the terrible slopes of the Tourmalet had then sorted the wheat from the chaff. Eddy paid his respects to this famous pass with a dazzling sprint. So dazzling in fact that, ahead once more by several seconds, the man of the Tour dashed headlong to the bottom in his lithe, skilful manner, at the kind of insane speed that this exceptional cyclist can produce.

At the narrow gorge of the Pau valley that runs towards the foot of the Aubisque, there really did not appear to be anything premeditated about his actions; his demeanour was that of a rider making the most of his lead and taking it easy while waiting for his fellow cyclists to catch up. These were only Pingeon and Poulidor flanked by Bayssière, a Peugeot-BP team-mate, Theillière and Zimmermann, two French riders from the Sonolor-Lejeune group, at last in a role of some value, and Merckx's mountain lieutenant, the tall, thin Van den Bossche.

RESOLVE

But the solitary descent by the man in the yellow jersey had unwittingly created a huge gap. As he looked back, he realized how ridiculous and lacking in dignity it would be to wait. He pushed on so that, at the very least, the Tour de France he was going to win

would not be tarnished or damaged by this incident. The others would surely catch up with him and at least in the meantime it would seem like a race.

When Eddy is in the saddle, especially when he is alone – as then there is nothing to restrict his speed – it is something quite out of the ordinary, even if several others are in league against him. The gap quickly stretches to one minute, approaching one and a half minutes at Argèles, the foot of the tough ramp that climbs up to the long plateau before the start of the Soulor. There, the advantage of numbers was no longer apparent as he reached 3mins 30secs at the base of the Soulor, 4mins 55secs at its summit, the antechamber of the Aubisque, and seven minutes at the Aubisque itself! He finished at Mourenx-Ville-Nouvelle, not having weakened once over the last 75 kilometres (46.5 miles), with a lead of eight minutes over the next riders to cross the line and nearly a quarter of an hour over a group containing men of the class of Gimondi and Janssen.

It was the performance of a world-beating athlete, who always maintains his devastating form. His long, slender legs, lacking in sharp muscular contours and glistening with perspiration, seemed to be mechanically propelled. On the mountains, he was living proof of a new type of climber. The classic climbers and their graceful dashes, heroes of an outdated age, were consigned to oblivion and replaced by Merckx's rhythmic pedalling at a constant speed, only the movement of his shoulders disturbing his streamlined flow, precisely articulating each pedal thrust, right, left, right, left, but in such harmony that the general elegance of his pace was not affected.

It was also a truly marvellous display of character – to perform so well in the Tour de France required great determination. Merckx's position was already unassailable, but this morning we will head back to Paris with the general classification showing incredible time gaps, reminiscent of the legendary early adventures of the Tour. He also took an enormous risk. He could well have done himself some real harm in the blazing sun of that scorching day. He could have exhausted all his energy reserves as the route got even tougher, especially in that

Merckx, looking relaxed, mechanically distances his competitors. A position they were to frequently find themselves in over the next few years.

Merckx '...like those matadors thirsty for blood who provoke the bull simply to feel the thrill of excitement,' as so eloquently expressed by the journalist Pierre Chany that same day.

heat, which is capable of causing a great deal of damage. He could also have made himself a figure of hate for all those miserable wretches he had upset and diminished and who, thanks to Merckx, must have been losing their taste for this tough profession...

BEATEN AND EXHAUSTED

The dreamlike ride of this trailblazing cyclist certainly seemed to have deadened the pace of his rivals, an incorrect term perhaps for the men who knew there was no longer any reason to try to compete with him. It was surprising, however, to note that Pingeon and Poulidor, having descended the Tourmalet without great enthusiasm, did not immediately try to catch up with their torturer during the 18 kilometres (11 miles) of the Pau valley, even though they had the chance to pursue a common goal together, free of Gimondi and with the friendly support of Bayssière, Theillière and Zimmermann, their three unexpected companions, all former French hopes...

Instead, over the whole 130 kilometres (81 miles), including the stretch over the Aubisque, we witnessed a sad, gloomy march of resigned men, totally demoralized by the cruel nature of the situation. They did not quite throw in the towel, but they did economize in order to avoid the even worse defeat of a failed pursuit by five or even six against one when Dancelli, the only true fighter of the day, came up from behind. It was not an attitude to be proud of, but perhaps we can sympathize with the disillusionment of these men, aware of their relative inadequacy in the face of such fundamental genius.

This feeling was certainly shared by all those still trying to navigate their way across the troubled waters of this insulting rout. At the rear, it was a complete débâcle – the gaps got wider and wider and the Spaniards, passing along their own border, disappeared. Significantly, one has the distinct impression that the amazing feat achieved by this unique athlete did not, in the end, exhaust him as much as the badly coordinated, pitiful march trailing in his wake broke the spirits of these wretched stragglers.

Never again will we be able to say that the Tour is not won until Paris. Eddy Merckx has destroyed that legend too.

A victory after thirty long years

The La Cipale velodrome in Paris was Belgian yesterday. Merckx's supporters did not wait for him to return to his country; they were ahead of him forming a guard of honour all the way from Créteil to Vincennes. The event has such importance for Belgium that its national holiday will also be a holiday in celebration of Eddy Merckx.

The President of the Ligue Vélocipédique Belge, Maurice Moyson, placed the situation in its national context, telling us: 'I received a telephone call from King Baudoin's private office. He is anxious to be the first Belgian to officially receive Eddy Merckx before the national holiday procession. This victory, which we have spent 30 years waiting for, has an importance that we don't yet fully understand. We would never have dared hope for

such honour for Belgian cycling. Thirty years is a long time, but at the end of the day, our patience has been rewarded. We obviously had to wait for a super-champion before we could win again.' Mr Vandenbak, the secretary of the LVB, added some more information to this statement, saying 'The fact that His Majesty King Baudoin, the chief patron of the LVB and the World Championships, wishes to receive Eddy Merckx and his team shows how prestigious this victory is. Merckx will also be received at the town hall, a rare honour, and by the Minister for Culture.' Yesterday, the ordinary people from Brussels, Liège and Antwerp became Parisians. We spoke to one of them on a packed Metro train – an 80-year-old former singer named Mr Veeckmans, who said, 'Merckx has given me

the chance to see Paris again for the first time in 20 years. I didn't want to miss this great day for Belgium, especially with such a great champion!' Romain Maes, the last Belgian winner of the Tour still alive (now 57 and living on a private income), still fairly trim and youthful looking, arrived from Ostend where he was on holiday, to relive the adventure. He won the Tour in 1935, having victoriously defended his yellow jersey from the first stage through to the last.

'When I returned home after my victory it was also a national holiday and the King invited me to the Brussels World Fair, which was taking place at the time. But I think that it will be an even bigger occasion for Eddy Merckx...Yes, it's an event for Belgium, a truly unique event!' And so long awaited...

Eddy Merckx had to use all his skills to carry off his first big attack on the stretch between Mulhouse and Belfort. All his opponents caved in. Only Altig (left), Galera and De Vlaeminck (in order, behind) managed to limit the damage until the foot of the Ballon d'Alsace.

Looking more tense than usual, Eddy Merckx nevertheless managed to finish the Tour de France with another comfortable victory in the time trial between Créteil and Paris. His domination was total.

Merckx takes control

One year on from his crushing dominance of the 1969 Tour, and 19 days after winning his second Giro d'Italia, Merckx arrived at Limoges as the overwhelming favourite. Yet the previous September, Merckx had crashed on the track at Blois while being motor-paced. He suffered a head wound, but more seriously, the accident had jarred his pelvis; for the rest of his career, he nursed persistent back pain. 'Before Blois,' Merckx said, 'climbing had been a pleasure. Now it is a torment.' The opposition had also been decimated by illness and injury. Roger Pingeon had a knee problem, Raymond Poulidor had shingles and Gimondi, runner-up to Merckx at the Giro d'Italia, was too downhearted even to start the Tour.

Put briefly, Merckx won the short Prologue; his Faema team-mate Italo Zilioli won stage three and took over the yellow jersey; then Merckx took it back for the final eighteen days.

The only upset was the victory of a little-known Spaniard, José González Linares, in the short time trial at Forest. Three days later, on the road to Divonne-les-Bains, Merckx staged a show of strength. Among the few riders able to follow him was the little-known Dutchman Joop Zoetemelk.

On Mont Ventoux, Merckx scattered the peloton behind him. He dropped Poulidor and two promising younger riders, France's Bernard Thévenet and the Belgian Lucien Van Impe, as he approached the landmark Chalet Reynard. The heat was suffocating. When his former team-mate Martin Van den Bossche and Portugal's Joaquim Agostinho finally dropped off his wheel, Merckx had no competition left. He had the presence of mind to remove his cap as he passed the Tom Simpson Memorial, but then his pedalling became disturbingly irregular. He levered himself awkwardly out of the saddle at the foot of the observatory marking the summit and won the stage. But as he headed towards the podium, his legs began to collapse beneath him, and he started to faint. He was taken to an ambulance and given oxygen. Several minutes later, he emerged, white as a sheet, and admitted that he had been very afraid. But of what? Losing the Tour? Or losing his life, like Simpson himself? Thankfully, Merckx had soon recovered, and in Paris he celebrated his second crushing victory in the Tour de France. Behind him, Joop Zoetemelk finished second, not for the last time in his career.

GENERAL CLASSIFICATION

1. **Eddy Merckx** (BEL) Faema, 4,369 km in 119h.31m.45s; Average speed: 35.589 kph
2. **Joop Zoetemelk** (HOL) Mars-Flandria, at 12m.41s.
3. **Gösta Pettersson** (SWE) Ferretti, at 15m.54s.
4. Martin Van den Bossche (BEL) Molteni, at 18m.53s.
5. Marinus Wagtmans (HOL) Willem II-Gazelle, at 19m.54s.
6. Lucien Van Impe (BEL) Sonolor-Lejeune, at 20m.34s.

7. Raymond Poulidor (FRA) Fagor-Mercier, at 20m.35s.
8. Tony Houbrechts (BEL) Salvarini, at 21m.34s.
9. Francisco Galdós (SPA) Kas, at 21m.45s.
10. Georges Pintens (BEL) Mann-Grundig, at 23m.23s.
11. Raymond Delisle (FRA) Peugeot-BP, at 23m.59s.
12. Franco Balmamion (ITA) Salvarini, at 25m.10s.
13. Italo Zilioli (ITA) Faema, at 26m.17s.

14. J. Agostinho (POR) Frimatic De Gribaldy, at 26m.52s.
15. Luis Zubero (SPA) Kas, at 28m.11s.
16. Willy Van Neste (BEL) Mann Grundig, at 29m.17s.
17. Lucien Aimar (FRA) Sonolor-Lejeune, at 29m.22s.
18. Wladimiro Panizza (ITA) Salvarini, at 31m.2s.
19. Johnny Schleck (LUX) Bic, at 32m.19s.
20. Andrés Gandarias (SPA) Kas, at 35m.22s.

57TH TOUR DE FRANCE, 23 STAGES – 4,369 KM

	STAGE		STAGE WINNER	YELLOW JERSEY
Prologue	Friday 26 June	7.4 km	Limoges – Limoges	E. Merckx (BEL)	E. Merckx
Stage 1	Saturday 27 June	224.5 km	Limoges – La Rochelle	C. Guimard (FRA)	E. Merckx
Stage 2	Sunday 28 June	200 km	La Rochelle – Angers	I. Zilioli (ITA)	I. Zilioli
Stage 3 (1)	Monday 29 June	10.7 km	Angers – Angers (TTT)	Faemino	I. Zilioli
Stage 3 (2)	Monday 29 June	140 km	Angers – Rennes	M. Basso (ITA)	I. Zilioli
Stage 4	Tuesday 30 June	229 km	Rennes –Lisieux	W. Godefroot (BEL)	I. Zilioli
Stage 5 (1)	Wednesday 1 July	94.5 km	Lisieux – Rouen	W. Godefroot (BEL)	I. Zilioli
Stage 5 (2)	Wednesday 1 July	113 km	Rouen – Amiens	J. Spruyt (BEL)	I. Zilioli
Stage 6	Thursday 2 July	135.5 km	Amiens – Valenciennes	R. De Vlaeminck (BEL)	E. Merckx
Stage 7 (1)	Friday 3 July	119 km	Valenciennes – Forest (BEL)	E. Merckx (BEL)	E. Merckx
Stage 7 (2)	Friday 3 July	7.2 km	Forest – Forest (BEL) (TT)	J. González Linares (SPA)	E. Merckx
Stage 8	Saturday 4 July	232.5 km	Ciney (BEL) – Felsberg (GER)	A. Vasseur (FRA)	E. Merckx
Stage 9	Sunday 5 July	269.5 km	Sarrlouis (GER) – Mulhouse	M. Frey (DAN)	E. Merckx
Stage 10	Monday 6 July	241 km	Belfort – Divonne-les-Bains	E. Merckx (BEL)	E. Merckx
Stage 11 (1)	Tuesday 7 July	8.8 km	Divonne – Divonne (TT)	E. Merckx (BEL)	E. Merckx
Stage 11 (2)	Tuesday 7 July	139.5 km	Divonne-les-Bains – Thonon-les-Bains	M. Basso (ITA)	E. Merckx
Stage 12	Wednesday 8 July	194 km	Thonon-les-Bains – Grenoble	E. Merckx (BEL)	E. Merckx
Stage 13	Thursday 9 July	195.5 km	Grenoble – Gap	P. Mori (ITA)	E. Merckx
Stage 14	Friday 10 July	170 km	Gap – Mont Ventoux	E. Merckx (BEL)	E. Merckx
Stage 15	Saturday 11 July	144.5 km	Carpentras – Montpellier	M. Wagtmans (HOL)	E. Merckx
Stage 16	Sunday 12 July	259.5 km	Montpellier – Toulouse	A. Van Vlierberghe (BEL)	E. Merckx
Stage 17	Monday 13 July	190 km	Toulouse – Saint-Gaudens	L. Ocaña (SPA)	E. Merckx
Stage 18	Tuesday 14 July	135.5 km	Saint-Gaudens – La Mongie	B. Thévenet (FRA)	E. Merckx
Stage 19	Wednesday 15 July	185.5 km	Bagnères-de-Bigorre – Mourenx	C. Raymond (FRA)	E. Merckx
Stage 20 (1)	Thursday 16 July	231 km	Mourenx – Bordeaux	R. Wolfshohl (GER)	E. Merckx
Stage 20 (2)	Thursday 16 July	8.2 km	Bordeaux – Bordeaux (TT)	E. Merckx (BEL)	E. Merckx
Stage 21	Friday 17 July	191.5 km	Ruffec – Tours	M. Basso (ITA)	E. Merckx
Stage 22	Saturday 18 July	238.5 km	Tours – Versailles	J.-P. Danguillaume (FRA)	E. Merckx
Stage 23	Sunday 19 July	54 km	Versailles – Paris (TT)	E. Merckx (BEL)	E. Merckx

On Mont Ventoux, in suffocating heat, Merckx passed the monument commemorating Tom Simpson at the very moment Jacques Goddet left a bouquet. Merckx was inscribing his own name in Ventoux's awful history.

Eddy Merckx suffered terribly on the upper slopes of Mont Ventoux, and was close to collapse as he dismounted.

By winning at La Mongie, shrouded in dense mist, Bernard Thévenet emerged as a promising stage racer for the future.

Luis Ocaña, despite illness, won 'his' stage on the road to Saint-Gaudens. He was determined not to leave it at that...

Ocaña's unfinished masterpiece

In 1969, only the disunity of his team had kept Luis Ocaña from victory in the Vuelta a España. He had won the pre-Tour Midi Libre, but a heavy fall in the first mountain stage of the Tour had prevented him from challenging Merckx. In 1970, Ocaña had finally won the Vuelta a España, but sickness had again prevented him from riding at full strength in the Tour. In 1971, weeks before the Tour, Ocaña had had Merckx on the ropes in the mountains of the pre-Tour Dauphiné Libéré. 'I shook him off climbing the Granier, but I coundn't finish off the job on the next climb, the Forclaz, because it started to rain.' At the Tour de France, there was an aura of expectation surrounding Eddy Merckx. Not: 'Could he win the Tour?' But: 'Could he lose?' Ocaña thought so. He won stage eight on the Puy de Dôme, then seized the moment on the stage from Grenoble to Orcières-Merlette. Ascending with remarkable agility, Ocaña, the leader of the Bic team, gained nearly nine minutes on Merckx and seized the yellow jersey. On the next stage, Merckx responded by attacking at the stage start immediately. Two hundred and fifty kilometres later, Merckx entered the old port of Marseille; he had regained just two minutes.

Three days later, on the Pyrenean stage from Revel to Luchon, where Ocaña was expected to attack, it was Merckx who went on the offensive. However, each time he accelerated, Ocaña pulled him back with ease. Soon, a storm broke out, and their battle continued in dreadful conditions. Streams of mud ran onto the road; hailstones pounded the riders' backs. Their brakes became useless, and they had to brake with their feet. Merckx was the first to fall; unhurt, he climbed back into the saddle again and set off. Then Ocaña went down. As he was picking himself up, Zoetemelk slid into him at high speed. The collision was sickening; Ocaña bent double and collapsed into the dirt, muttering unintelligibly. Perhaps remembering Roger Rivière's accident in 1960, Maurice De Muer, Ocaña's *directeur sportif*, later commented: 'I feared the worst: spinal damage, paralysis...' Merckx learned of Ocaña's plight at the foot of Le Portillon, under a hail of spittle and stones from Ocaña's fans, who held him responsible. At Luchon Merckx refused to don the yellow jersey out of sympathy for Ocaña. He considered abandoning, and in an evocative post-stage interview, expressed his bitterness. 'Whatever happens, I have lost the Tour. The doubt will always remain.' The drama on the Col de Mente had given him an unassailable lead, but had deprived him of the opportunity of winning the Tour by virtue of athletic superiority alone.

GENERAL CLASSIFICATION

1. **Eddy Merckx** (BEL) Molteni,
   3,608 km in 96h.45m.14s; Average speed: 37.290 kph
2. **Joop Zoetemelk** (HOL) Mars-Flandria, at 9m.51s.
3. **Lucien Van Impe** (BEL) Sonolor-Lejeune, at 11m.6s.
4. Bernard Thévenet (FRA) Peugeot-BP, at 14m.50s.
5. Joaquim Agostinho (POR) Hoover De Gribaldy, at 21ms.
6. Leif Mortensen (DEN) Bic, at 21m.38s.
7. Cyrille Guimard (FRA) Fagor-Mercier, at 22m.58s.
8. Bernard Labourdette (FRA) Bic, at 30m.7s.
9. Lucien Aimar (FRA) Sonolor-Lejeune, at 32m.45s.
10. Vicente López Carril (SPA) Kas, at 36m.
11. Francisco Galdós (SPA) Kas, at 41m.59s.
12. Primo Mori (ITA) Salvarani, at 47m.44s.
13. Antonio Martos (SPA) Werner, at 48m.13s.
14. Herman Van Springel (BEL) Molteni, at 48m.20s.
15. Agustin Tamames (SPA) Werner, at 49m.19s.
16. Marinus Wagtmans (HOL) Molteni, at 52m.50s.
17. Désiré Letort (FRA) Bic, at 57m.53s.
18. Jean-Pierre Danguillaume (FRA) Peugeot-BP, at 59m.10s.
19. Mauro Simonetti (ITA) Ferretti, at 1h.3m.6s.
20. Jean Dumon (FRA) Peugeot-BP, at 1h.3m.49s.

58TH TOUR DE FRANCE, 20 STAGES - 3,585 KM

			STAGE	STAGE WINNER	YELLOW JERSEY
Prologue	Saturday 26 June	11 km	Mulhouse – Mulhouse (TTT)	Molteni	E. Merckx
Stage 1 (1)	Sunday 27 June	59.5 km	Mulhouse – Bâle (SUI)	E. Leman (BEL)	M. Wagtmans
Stage 1 (2)	Sunday 27 June	90 km	Bâle (SUI) – Fribourg-en-Brisgau (GER)	G. Karstens (HOL)	E. Merckx
Stage 1 (3)	Sunday 27 June	74.5 km	Fribourg-en-Brisgau (GER) – Mulhouse	A. Van Vlierberghe (BEL)	E. Merckx
Stage 2	Monday 28 June	144 km	Mulhouse – Strasbourg	E. Merckx (BEL)	E. Merckx
Stage 3	Tuesday 29 June	165.5 km	Strasbourg – Nancy	M. Wagtmans (HOL)	E. Merckx
Stage 4	Wednesday 30 June	242 km	Champigneulles – Marche-en-Famenne (BEL)	J.-P. Genet (FRA)	E. Merckx
Stage 5	Thursday 1 July	208.5 km	Dinant (BEL) – Roubaix	P. O. Guerra (ITA)	E. Merckx
Stage 6 (1)	Friday 2 July	127.5 km	Roubaix – Amiens	E. Leman (BEL)	E. Merckx
Stage 6 (2)	Friday 2 July	133.5 km	Amiens – Le Touquet	M. Simonetti (ITA)	E. Merckx
Stage 7	Sunday 4 July	257.5 km	Rungis – Nevers	E. Leman (BEL)	E. Merckx
Stage 8	Monday 5 July	221 km	Nevers – Puy de Dôme	L. Ocaña (SPA)	E. Merckx
Stage 9	Tuesday 6 July	153 km	Clermont-Ferrand – Saint-Étienne	W. Godefroot (BEL)	E. Merckx
Stage 10	Wednesday 7 July	188.5 km	Saint-Étienne – Grenoble	B. Thévenet (FRA)	J. Zoetemelk
Stage 11	Thursday 8 July	134 km	Grenoble – Orcières-Merlette	L. Ocaña (SPA)	L. Ocaña
Stage 12	Saturday 10 July	251 km	Orcières-Merlette – Marseille	L. Armani (ITA)	L. Ocaña
Stage 13	Sunday 11 July	16.3 km	Albi – Albi (TT)	E. Merckx (BEL)	L. Ocaña
Stage 14	Monday 12 July	214.5 km	Revel – Luchon	J. Manuel Fuente (SPA)	E. Merckx
Stage 15	Tuesday 13 July	19.6 km	Luchon – Superbagnères	J. Manuel Fuente (SPA)	E. Merckx
Stage 16 (1)	Wednesday 14 July	145 km	Luchon – Gourette	B. Labourdette (FRA)	E. Merckx
Stage 16 (2)	Wednesday 14 July	57.5 km	Gourette – Pau	H. Van Springel (BEL)	E. Merckx
Stage 17	Thursday 15 July	188 km	Mont-de-Marsan – Bordeaux	E. Merckx (BEL)	E. Merckx
Stage 18	Friday 16 July	244 km	Bordeaux – Poitiers	J.-P. Danguillaume (FRA)	E. Merckx
Stage 19	Saturday 17 July	185 km	Blois – Versailles	J. Krekels (HOL)	E. Merckx
Stage 20	Sunday 18 July	53.8 km	Versailles – Paris (TT)	E. Merckx (BEL)	E. Merckx

Drama in the Tour de France. Luis Ocaña, the race leader, fell on the descent from the Col de Mente. As he was getting up, Zoetemelk ploughed into him. Ocaña abandoned with severe bruising.

Merckx pays homage: 'Ocaña was extraordinary'

ORCIÈRES-MERLETTE: It could always be construed as patronizing to say that a champion has emerged from defeat with increased stature. Firstly, because in his career Eddy Merckx has reached heights that it is difficult to surpass; and secondly, because it must be of scant comfort to the person in question. But what an example he showed us, what a masterly way to overcome adversity: alone, surrounded by a small pack, most of whom were of no threat to him at all whilst others, led by Maurice De Muer, were doing their best to make his position even more difficult. Our sense of astonishment as we watched this man, this athlete who drew on his champion's pride for his last reserves of strength to fight with the energy of despair, was gradually transformed into unparalleled admiration the further we followed him into the valleys with their harsh, overbearing mountain slopes. Following his comprehensive defeat,

the Belgian champion conducted himself with absolute dignity and exemplary sportsmanship, just as he had on the road under the blazing sun.

He did not look for excuses: 'Of course, I wasn't good from the start,' he confided. 'I had stomach pains and didn't feel too strong; I didn't feel able to react. If you were to ask me if at any moment I was tempted to give up and get off my bike, I would have to say that it crossed my mind. If my strength really had deserted me, as I thought it might do at the start of the stage, I wouldn't have been able to continue... but I didn't give up.'

Merckx was speaking with the injured pride of a champion, but he was undoubtedly also concerned not to diminish his opponent's victory in any way. Of all the praise that can be heaped on Luis Ocaña, Eddy Merckx surely awarded him the highest accolade of all: 'What he did was extraordinary, believe me; he really was head

and shoulders above the rest of us. You can only bow down before a champion of his calibre. That's sport for you. Even if I had been fit, I don't think I would have been able to keep up with him. It was a fantastic achievement – he took risks but gained ground. I had already noticed him during the Dauphiné Libéré and he has now reached maturity as an athlete. Things like this happen in sport, there's nothing else you can say. That's the way it goes and you have to be able to recognize it. He prepared himself admirably for this Tour and he's at the peak of his physical powers.'

In spite of the huge disappointment he had suffered and then overcome thanks to his strength of character, Merckx was not thinking of giving up.

'Given the lead that Luis Ocaña has I don't see how, at the moment, the Tour de France could possibly slip through his fingers. It's virtually impossible for me to make up my deficit, unless I find new strength from somewhere or unless he performs very badly. But I don't want to think about that, I don't believe it will happen.'

It almost seemed that Eddy did not want to believe it. He knew that all kinds of things can happen in the Tour de France, but his last hope depended not on the collapse of Ocaña but on his own revival.

'We'll see over the next few days,' he said. 'Having a rest day helps you to reflect on things. I've been doing far too much for some years now. All the classics, the stage races, the winter track events, two major Tours a year, it's too much. You end up paying for it.' Along the way, Eddy, like the true gentleman he is, excused his team-mates; in fact, he even defended them. Merckx, who for so many years has been the one to beat, the one to bring down from his pedestal, finds himself alone, facing his own questions. It is still too early to know what he will do. It will probably not be until the autumn, when he is peacefully settled at home with his wife and daughter, that Eddy will make his decisions.

There can surely be nothing more touching than witnessing the moment that comes, sooner or later, to all great champions: the turning point of their career.

Stage 11: Just before the Col du Noyer in the Alps, Ocaña gave Zoetemelk, Agostinho and Van Impe the slip, then he simply flew away. By the end of the day he was in yellow.

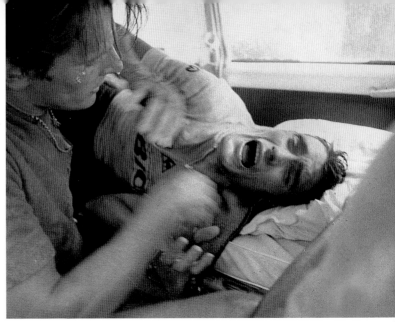

On the Portet d'Aspet, Merckx (in white) tried in vain to drop Ocaña. But the weather took a turn for the worse and the path became dangerous.

Five minutes after the accident, Dr Judet (left) was the first to treat Luis Ocaña and took the decision to transfer him to hospital.

A Tour to restore the legend of the Giants of the Road

Starting at Mulhouse this year, the great July journey was dubbed 'Merckx's Tour'. Some authoritative figures even suggested to the organizers that there should also be a prize for first place after Merckx in the Tour, with a considerable financial reward.

However, the most glorious of champions was destined to face a series of severe tests. Firstly, there was his prodigious reputation, which didn't allow him any chance of respite; then there was the accumulation of grudges held against him as a result of so many humiliations inflicted on so many opponents. Added to this was the very quality of the competitors, their number and, in particular, their prowess in the mountains, in a Tour that favoured the climbers. Finally there was his own character, that determination to establish his superiority in every classification, that desire to stand out from the crowd and that admirable spirit that makes him ready to suffer at all moments and in all circumstances. In his first Tour in 1969, he accomplished magnificent feats in the mountains; but that was because there were no brilliant climbers in the race, and due to the way the high-altitude stages were organized, with more opportunities to recover: more descents, more intermediate flat sections and finishing lines some way from the last peak. What's more, Eddy was unquestionably much younger then, from an athletic point of view (but that will get me back on my high horse about the use of excessive gears, which slowly and

inevitably wear the body down). On analysis, the conclusions to be drawn from this Tour are fairly clear. The Molteni ace maintained his solid, unsparing dominance on the plains. From the second day, crossing the slopes of the Alsace vineyards, he laid the ground for a large-scale breakaway, leading and animating it himself. He then had the audacity not just to compete in a sprint more suited to acrobats than riders, but to win it! He made sure no major expeditions were launched, controlled the race in person, and chased after every time bonus going. And although his opponents were disparaged for not launching any real attacks before the mountains, my feeling was that the error belonged to Eddy himself, who should have played his cards in the early stages, knowing the difficulties he would face in the mountains.

And then Ocaña – a superb Ocaña, a thoroughbred athlete, with a clear under-standing of the situation that faced him – surged forward. He battered his illustrious rival on the Puy de Dôme, shook him up on the Chartreuse, where Merckx suffered an untimely puncture, and then finished him off on the third day, when he realized that the 'Cannibal' was having difficulty digesting his breakfast on the slopes of the Côte de Laffrey. Sizing up both his opponent and himself, Ocaña was sure of himself and of his own ascendancy – both perhaps enhanced by the state of cruel disarray in which he'd left his rival – and was destined to carry off the final

victory. Everything that happened after his distressing withdrawal confirms this view. Merckx was at full-stretch in the testing race up the slopes of Superbagnères and didn't attack during the whole of the next stage over any of the cols. I am positive that Ocaña, the Bic leader, would have reinforced his position on these two occasions. I am also inclined to believe that he would have learned his lesson from the breakaway, that spurt of power on the springboard of Merietia with which Eddy Merckx counter-attacked the man who had dealt him such a mortal blow two days earlier, embarking on a magnificent 250-kilometre (155-mile) attack, showcasing a temperament and determination worthy of the praise and admiration of everyone on the Tour.

What a great Tour this has been, to have two riders of such class and calibre locked in competition and digging deep into their innermost reserves of strength. When sport creates such magnificent clashes, it is reminiscent of the legendary days of the great cycling champions. And when an apocalyptic storm in the middle of the race tests our heroes even further, the Tour takes on the aspect of a heroic epic once more, one with long echoes in the popular imagination, one that brings another dimension to human existence. This Tour showed how a sport that has become so professional in every aspect can still provide excitement and instruction for mankind.

Merckx wins the rematch

Twelve months after Ocaña's accident on the Col de Mente had handed Merckx victory, the cycling world awaited the rematch. The two men had been trading abuse through the press, Ocaña because he was convinced he should have won the previous year, Merckx because his rival's abandon had prevented him from proving his physical superiority. In the spring, Merckx had won four one-day classics and his third Giro d'Italia. Ocaña had won the pre-Tour Dauphiné Libéré and the Spanish national championship. Both men started the Tour in peak condition.

But before their contest could begin, Cyrille Guimard won the first stage and took the yellow jersey. Guimard, riding for the Gan team, was wearing the yellow jersey again at the foot of the Pyrenees when he began to complain of knee pain. The Tour doctor diagnosed synovitis, or water on the knee. Daily injections of Novocaine allowed him to ignore the pain as far as the Alps, but soon Guimard was being carried on a chair to the stage starts. Eventually he was forced to abandon.

By then, the contest between Merckx and Ocaña had already come to an abrupt end at precisely the point where it should have begun: on stage seven, in the Pyrenees. As in 1971, the conditions were dreadful, with icy rain lashing the riders'

backs. After stopping on the Soulor to change a wheel, Ocaña caught Thévenet and Van Impe. The three men were on the point of catching the group containing Merckx when they came out of a bend to find a line of cars blocking the way. Ocaña went down; Thévenet, Van Impe and Alain Santy followed him. Santy stayed down with a serious back injury; Thévenet was concussed, but set off again, only recovering his senses several kilometres further on. Ocaña sped away to the finish-line in Pau with his jersey covered with blood. He had only lost a minute to Merckx, but a lung infection forced him to abandon. For the second time, bad luck, poor bike handling, or the relentless pressure Merckx subjected him to, had cost Ocaña the Tour.

At Luchon, Roger Pingeon's withdrawal from the race passed almost without mention. Pingeon's *directeur sportif*, Gaston Plaud, had wanted the former champion to ride on in support of Bernard Thévenet, the leader of a younger generation now catching up with its elders. Thévenet's time would come; for now, Merckx had no serious challengers left in the race and cruised to his fourth Tour victory, taking the points and the combined classifications with it. In Paris, he symbolically offered the green points jersey to Guimard. With such dominance, he could afford to be generous.

GENERAL CLASSIFICATION

1. **Eddy Merckx** (BEL) Molteni, 3,846 km in 108h17m.18s; Average speed: 35.514 kph
2. **Felice Gimondi** (ITA) Salvarini, at 10m.41s
3. **Raymond Poulidor** (FRA) Gan-Mercier, at 11m.34s
4. Lucien Van Impe (BEL) Sonolor, at 16m.45s
5. Joop Zoetemelk (HOL) Beaulieu-Flandria, at 19m.09s
6. Mariano Martínez (FRA) Magniflex-De Gribaldy, at 21m.31s.

7. Yves Hezard (FRA) Sonolor, at 21m.52s.
8. J. Agostinho (POR) Magniflex-De Gribaldy, at 34m.16s.
9. Bernard Thévenet (FRA) Peugeot-BP, at 37m.11s.
10. Édouard Janssens (BEL) Magniflex-De Gribaldy, at 42m.33s.
11. Raymond Delisle (FRA) Peugeot-BP, at 46m.27s.
12. Leif Mortensen (DEN) Bic, at 46m.39s.
13. Tony Houbrechts (BEL) Salvarini, at 47m.37s.

14. Roger Swertz (BEL), Molteni, at 49m.24s.
15. Martin Van Den Bossche (BEL), Molteni, at 59m.29s.
16. Frans Verbeeck (BEL) Watney-Avia, at 1h.0m.9s.
17. Lucien Aimar (FRA) Rokado, at 1h.3m.41s.
18. Tino Tabak (HOL) Goudsmit-Hoff, at 1h.5m.9s.
19. Michel Périn (FRA) Gan-Mercier, at 1h.6m.19s.
20. Karl-Heinz Kunde (GER) Rokado, at 1h.10m.9s.

59TH TOUR DE FRANCE, 20 STAGES – 3,846 KM

			STAGE	STAGE WINNER	YELLOW JERSEY
Prologue	Saturday 1 July	7.2 km	Angers – Angers	E. Merckx (BEL)	E. Merckx
Stage 1	Sunday 2 July	235.5 km	Angers – Saint-Brieuc	C. Guimard (FRA)	C. Guimard
Stage 2	Monday 3 July	206.5 km	Saint-Brieuc – La Baule	R. Van Linden (BEL)	C. Guimard
Stage 3 (1)	Tuesday 4 July	161 km	Pornichet – Saint-Jean-de-Monts	E. Gualazzini (ITA)	C. Guimard
Stage 3 (2)	Tuesday 4 July	16.2 km	Merlin-Plage – Merlin-Plage (TTT)	Molteni	E. Merckx
Stage 4	Wednesday 5 July	236 km	Merlin-Plage – Royan	C. Guimard (FRA)	C. Guimard
Stage 5 (1)	Thursday 6 July	133.5 km	Royan – Bordeaux	W. Godefroot (BEL)	C. Guimard
Stage 5 (2)	Thursday 6 July	12.7 km	Bordeaux-le-Lac – Bordeaux-le-Lac (TT)	E. Merckx (BEL)	C. Guimard
Stage 6	Friday 7 July	205 km	Pessac – Bayonne	L. Duyndam (HOL)	C. Guimard
Stage 7	Sunday 9 July	220.5 km	Bayonne – Pau	Y. Hézard (FRA)	C. Guimard
Stage 8	Monday 10 July	163.5 km	Pau – Luchon	E. Merckx (BEL)	E. Merckx
Stage 9	Tuesday 11 July	179 km	Luchon – Colomiers	J. Huysmans (BEL)	E. Merckx
Stage 10	Wednesday 12 July	210 km	Castres – La Grande-Motte	W. Teirlinck (BEL)	E. Merckx
Stage 11	Thursday 13 July	207 km	Carnon-Plage – Mont Ventoux	B. Thévenet (FRA)	E. Merckx
Stage 12	Friday 14 July	192 km	Carpentras – Orcières-Merlette	L. Van Impe (BEL)	E. Merckx
Stage 13	Sunday 16 July	201 km	Orcières-Merlette – Briançon	E. Merckx (BEL)	E. Merckx
Stage 14 (1)	Monday 17 July	51 km	Briançon – Valloire	E. Merckx (BEL)	E. Merckx
Stage 14 (2)	Monday 17 July	151 km	Valloire – Aix-les-Bains	C. Guimard (FRA)	E. Merckx
Stage 15	Tuesday 18 July	28 km	Aix-les-Bains – Mont Revard	C. Guimard (FRA)	E. Merckx
Stage 16	Wednesday 19 July	198.5 km	Aix-les-Bains – Pontarlier	W. Teirlinck (BEL)	E. Merckx
Stage 17	Thursday 20 July	213 km	Pontarlier – Ballon d'Alsace	B. Thévenet (FRA)	E. Merckx
Stage 18	Friday 21 July	257.5 km	Vesoul – Auxerre	M. Wagtmans (HOL)	E. Merckx
Stage 19	Saturday 22 July	230 km	Auxerre – Versailles	J. Bruyère (BEL)	E. Merckx
Stage 20 (1)	Sunday 23 July	42 km	Versailles – Versailles (TT)	E. Merckx (BEL)	E. Merckx
Stage 20 (2)	Sunday 23 July	89 km	Versailles – Paris	W. Teirlinck (BEL)	E. Merckx

Merckx leads De Schoenmacker, Huysmans, Sweerts and Bruyère in the Merlin-
Plage team time trial.

At 36, Raymond Poulidor (left) was still leading out
the best riders on the 1972 Tour de France.
In the centre, Eddy Merckx.

Eddy Merckx wanted to win at Briançon in the
tradition of the Greats of the Tour. He achieved
his goal in style.

'This green jersey is yours: you deserve it. The credit is yours. Take it.' On arrival at La Cipale, Merckx paid homage to his rival
Cyril Guimard, who cannot hide his emotion.

Ocaña, driven by Spanish pride

Luis Ocaña could have been forgiven for thinking he was cursed by the gods. A fall on the Ballon d'Alsace had ruined his 1969 Tour; the storm on the Col de Mente had cost him victory in 1971; the downpour on the Soulor had forced him out in 1972. He, like everyone else, rode in the massive shadow cast by Eddy Merckx, although, proud and persistent, he was less overshadowed than most. In 1973, Merckx completed a historic double by winning the Tours of Spain and Italy in the spring, and decided not to defend his title at the Tour. For Ocaña, the stage was set.

On stage two, he was brought down by a dog, and was lucky to escape with superficial bruising. Then, on the cobblestones of Querenaing, near the Belgian border between Roubaix and Reims, he joined Cyrille Guimard and four of Guimard's Bic team-mates on the attack. Guimard won the stage, his team-mate José Catieau took over the yellow jersey, but the real victor was Ocaña. He had gained two minutes on Poulidor, Thévenet, Zoetemelk and Van Impe, and seven on the fine Spanish stage racer José Manuel Fuente. With this lead, Ocaña entered the Alps with a huge appetite for victory. He won the short stage from Divonne to Gaillard, then took up José Manuel Fuente's challenge on the road to the ski station at Les Orres. It was an epic duel. At the top of the climb to Les Orres, Ocaña emerged the victor, but was so exhausted that he went straight to his room, too tired to eat or change his clothes. Thévenet and his compatriot Mariano Martínez had managed to limit their losses, but among the rest of the peloton, the race schedule of three severe mountain stages in two days had wrought havoc. The Tour had been decimated, and the peloton was bristling with defiance. Ocaña was among them. 'If you take the coach and train transfers into account, we get less than six hours' sleep a night. And after that, they ask us to climb mountains!' The Spaniard consolidated his lead over the Pyrenees to Luchon, on a stage that almost proved fatal to Poulidor. On the descent from the Portet d'Aspet, the 37-year-old Frenchman plunged into a ravine, taking a vicious blow to the head and crawling out only with a helping hand from the race director Jacques Goddet.

The Tour, meanwhile, belonged to Ocaña, a flamboyant winner and a complex man, whose drive was fed, in part, by the desire to avenge his father's exile from Franco's Spain.

GENERAL CLASSIFICATION

1. **Luis Ocaña** (SPA) Bic, 4,150 km in 122h.25m.34s; Average speed: 33.407 kph
2. **Bernard Thévenet** (FRA) Peugeot-BP, at 15m.51s.
3. **José Manuel Fuente** (SPA) Kas, at 17m.15s.
4. Joop Zoetemelk (HOL) Gitane-Frigécrème, at 26m.22s.
5. Lucien Van Impe (BEL) Sonolor, at 30m.20s.
6. Herman Van Springel (BEL) Rokado, at 32m.1s.
7. Michel Périn (FRA) Gan-Mercier, at 33m.2s.
8. Joaquim Agostinho (POR) Bic, at 35m.51s.
9. Vicente López Carril (SPA) Kas, at 36m.18s.
10. Régis Ovion (FRA) Peugeot-BP, at 36m.59s.
11. Raymond Delisle (FRA) Peugeot-BP, at 37m.43s.
12. Mariano Martínez (FRA) Gan-Mercier, at 40m.49s.
13. Pedro Torres (SPA) La Casera-Bahamontes, at 47m.30s.
14. José Catieau (FRA) Bic, at 49m.12s.
15. Antonio Martos (SPA) Kas, at 49m.20s.
16. Tony Houbrechts (BEL) Rokado, at 49m.38s.
17. Lucien Aimar (FRA) De Kova-Lejeune, at 49m.54s.
18. F. Mendes (POR) Carpenter-Shimano-Flandria, at 51m.22s.
19. Leif Mortensen (DEN) Bic, at 52m.18s.
20. Francisco Galdós (SPA) Kas, at 53m.5s.

60TH TOUR DE FRANCE, 20 STAGES – 4,150 KM

			STAGE	STAGE WINNER	YELLOW JERSEY
Prologue	Saturday 30 June	7.1 km	Scheveningen (HOL) – Scheveningen (HOL)	J. Zoetemelk (HOL)	J. Zoetemelk
Stage 1 (1)	Sunday 1 July	84 km	Scheveningen (HOL) – Rotterdam (HOL)	W. Teirlinck (BEL)	W. Teirlinck
Stage 1 (2)	Sunday 1 July	137.5 km	Rotterdam (HOL) – St Nicolas (BEL)	J. Catieau (FRA)	H. Van Springel
Stage 2 (1)	Monday 2 July	12.5 km	St Nicolas (BEL) – St Nicolas (BEL) (TTT)	Watney-Maes	H. Van Springel
Stage 2 (2)	Monday 2 July	138 km	St Nicolas (BEL) – Roubaix	E. Verstraeten (BEL)	H. Van Springel
Stage 3	Tuesday 3 July	226 km	Roubaix – Reims	C. Guimard (FRA)	J. Catieau
Stage 4	Wednesday 4 July	214 km	Reims – Nancy	J. Zoetemelk (HOL)	J. Catieau
Stage 5	Thursday 5 July	188 km	Nancy – Mulhouse	W. Godefroot (BEL)	J. Catieau
Stage 6	Friday 6 July	244.5 km	Belfort – Divonne-les-Bains	J.-P. Danguillaume (FRA)	J. Catieau
Stage 7 (1)	Sunday 8 July	86.5 km	Divonne-les-Bains – Aspro-Gaillard	L. Ocaña (SPA)	L. Ocaña
Stage 7 (2)	Sunday 8 July	150.5 km	Aspro-Gaillard – Méribel-les-Allues	B. Thévenet (FRA)	L. Ocaña
Stage 8	Monday 9 July	237.5 km	Méribel-les-Allues – Les Orres	L. Ocaña (SPA)	L. Ocaña
Stage 9	Tuesday 10 July	234.5 km	Embrun – Nice	V. López Carril (SPA)	L. Ocaña
Stage 10	Wednesday 11 July	222.5 km	Nice – Aubagne	M. Wright (GBR)	L. Ocaña
Stage 11	Thursday 12 July	238 km	Montpellier – Argelès-sur-Mer	B. Hoban (GBR)	L. Ocaña
Stage 12 (1)	Friday 13 July	28.3 km	Perpignan – Thuir (TT)	L. Ocaña (SPA)	L. Ocaña
Stage 12 (2)	Friday 13 July	76 km	Thuir – Pyrénées 2000	L. Van Impe (BEL)	L. Ocaña
Stage 13	Sunday 15 July	235 km	Bourg-Madame – Luchon	L. Ocaña (SPA)	L. Ocaña
Stage 14	Monday 16 July	227.5 km	Luchon – Pau	P. Torres (SPA)	L. Ocaña
Stage 15	Tuesday 17 July	137 km	Pau – Fleurance	W. David (BEL)	L. Ocaña
Stage 16 (1)	Wednesday 18 July	210 km	Fleurance – Bordeaux	W. Godefroot (BEL)	L. Ocaña
Stage 16 (2)	Wednesday 18 July	12.4 km	Bordeaux-le-Lac – Bordeaux-le-Lac (TT)	J. Agostinho (POR)	L. Ocaña
Stage 17	Thursday 19 July	248 km	Sainte-Foix-la-Grande – Brive	C. Tollet (FRA)	L. Ocaña
Stage 18	Friday 20 July	216.5 km	Brive – Puy de Dôme	L. Ocaña (SPA)	L. Ocaña
Stage 19	Saturday 21 July	233.5 km	Bourges – Versailles	B. Hoban (GBR)	L. Ocaña
Stage 20 (1)	Sunday 22 July	16 km	Versailles – Versailles (TT)	L. Ocaña (SPA)	L. Ocaña
Stage 20 (2)	Sunday 22 July	89 km	Versailles – Paris	B. Thévenet (FRA)	L. Ocaña

On the slopes of the Télégraphe, after containing
Fuente's repeated accelerations, Ocaña profited from
his rival's puncture and attacked him.

1. Victory for Luis Ocaña, who shared the podium with the other prize winners: Zoetemelk (white jersey for the combined competition), Thévenet (runner-up) and Van Springel (green jersey).

2. Uncompromising and irrepressible, Ocaña withstood Fuente's attacks on the final sections of the climb to Les Orres and won the stage with less than a minute's lead over his rival that day.

3. The start of the Brive to Clermont-Ferrand stage was disturbed by a cattle farmers' demonstration. Zoetemelk took the time to read their pamphlet.

4. 48 hours from the finish, Ocaña was keen to achieve a victory *à la Merckx* on the Puy de Dôme. Neither Lucien Van Impe nor Bernard Thévenet, the runner-up, could stop him.

5. Between Perpignan and Thuir, on a 28.3-kilometre (17.5-mile) time-trial course that suited him well, Ocaña beat Poulidor by 30 seconds and Fuente by 1min 39secs.

Merckx overtakes Leducq

In June 1974, Merckx had won his fifth Giro d'Italia. Then, the day after winning the Tour of Switzerland, he had undergone a delicate operation on his perineum. At Brest for the *Grand Départ* of the 1974 Tour de France, the wound had still not healed. 'After the Prologue, the lining of my racing shorts was soaked in blood. It was to stay that way for the duration of the Tour,' he recalled.

Luis Ocaña, in talks with his employer, had not started; nor had Joop Zoetemelk, who was recovering from serious injuries after a crash during the pre-Tour Midi Libre. In their absence, Merckx left the yellow jersey to his team-mate Joseph Bruyère and busied himself by amassing points at every sprint. The pure sprinters grew frustrated at what they saw as Merckx's greed; others optimistically divined in his strategy a man uncertain of his abilities in the approaching mountains. They were stripped of their illusions when Merckx won the first two mountain stages at Aspro-Gaillard and Aix-les-Bains. On the ascent of the Mont du Chat, Raymond Poulidor, now 38 years old, caused a storm by dropping Merckx, only to falter on the Galibier. Nonetheless, Poulidor spared the Tour from monotony by winning at Saint-Lary-Soulan in the Pyrenees, although he could offer no sustained challenge to Merckx's overall dominance. The Belgian had won at Seo de Urgell, and six days later, won again with an extraordinary show of strength on the stage from Vouvray to Orléans, when, with 14 kilometres to go, he simply rode away from the rest of the peloton. Jacques Anquetil, providing commentary for French radio, expressed his amazement. 'I have known a few champions, men like Coppi, Van Looy and Altig, but none of them could have dropped the entire peloton like Merckx did today. On the other hand, it is not acceptable for the peloton to surrender like that. There must be riders out there lacking in self-esteem!' Hardly surprising, given Merckx's supremacy. Some hours later, an ungainly young Belgian named Michel Pollentier defeated Merckx in the Orléans time trial. Poulidor finished the Tour second overall, five seconds ahead of the veteran Spaniard Vicente López Carril. By wining eight stages, Merckx set a new record of 32 stage wins, passing André Leducq's mark of 25.

GENERAL CLASSIFICATION

1. **Eddy Merckx** (BEL) Molteni, 4,098 km in 116h.16m.58s; Average speed: 35.661 kph
2. **Raymond Poulidor** (FRA) Gan-Mercier, at 8m.4s.
3. *Vicente López Carril* (SPA) Kas, at 8m.9s.
4. Wladimiro Panizza (ITA) Brooklyn, at 10m.59s.
5. Gonzalo Aja (SPA) Kas, at 11m.24s.
6. Joaquim Agostinho (POR) Bic, at 14m.24s.
7. Michel Pollentier (BEL) Carpenter-Confortluxe, at 16m.34s.
8. Mariano Martínez (FRA) Sonolor-Gitane, at 18m.33s.
9. Alain Santy (FRA) Gan-Mercier, at 19m.55s.
10. H. Van Springel (BEL) M.I.C.-Ludo-De Gribaldy, at 24m.11s.
11. Roger Pingeon (FRA) Jobo-Lejeune, at 27m.7s.
12. Raymond Delisle (FRA) Peugeot-BP, at 28m.59s.
13. Jean-Pierre Danguillaume (FRA) Peugeot-BP, at 29m.43s.
14. Juan Zurano (SPA) La Casera-Bahamontes, at 30m.20s.
15. André Romero (FRA) Jobo-Lejeune, at 31m.35s.
16. Michel Périn (FRA) Gan-Mercier, at 31m.57s.
17. Miguel María Lasa (SPA) Kas, at 32m.55s.
18. Lucien Van Impe (BEL) Sonolor-Gitane, at 37m.35s.
19. Andrés Olivia (SPA) La Casera-Bahamontes, at 37m.48s.
20. Bernard Labourdette (FRA) Bic, at 38m.2s.

61ST TOUR DE FRANCE, 22 STAGES – 4,098 KM

			STAGE	STAGE WINNER	YELLOW JERSEY
Prologue	Thursday 27 June	7.1 km	Brest – Brest	E. Merckx (BEL)	E. Merckx
Stage 1	Friday 28 June	144 km	Brest – Saint-Pol-de-Léon	E. Gualazzini (ITA)	J. Bruyère
Stage 2	Saturday 29 June	163.7 km	Plymouth (GBR) – Plymouth (GBR)	H. Poppe (HOL)	J. Bruyère
Stage 3	Sunday 30 June	190 km	Morlaix – Saint-Malo	P. Sercu (BEL)	J. Bruyère
Stage 4	Monday 1 July	184.5 km	Saint-Malo – Caen	P. Sercu (BEL)	E. Merckx
Stage 5	Tuesday 2 July	165 km	Caen – Dieppe	R. De Witte (BEL)	G. Karstens
Stage 6 (1)	Wednesday 3 July	239 km	Dieppe – Harelbeke (BEL)	J.-L. Molinéris (FRA)	P. Sercu
Stage 6 (2)	Wednesday 3 July	9 km	Harelbeke (BEL) – Harelbeke (TTT)	Molteni	G. Karstens
Stage 7	Thursday 4 July	221.5 km	Mons (BEL) – Châlons-sur-Marne	E. Merckx (BEL)	E. Merckx
Stage 8 (1)	Friday 5 July	136 km	Châlons-sur-Marne – Chaumont	C. Guimard (FRA)	E. Merckx
Stage 8 (2)	Friday 5 July	152 km	Chaumont – Besançon	P. Sercu (BEL)	E. Merckx
Stage 9	Saturday 6 July	241 km	Besançon – Aspro-Gaillard	E. Merckx (BEL)	E. Merckx
Stage 10	Sunday 7 July	131.5 km	Aspro-Gaillard – Aix-les-Bains	E. Merckx (BEL)	E. Merckx
Stage 11	Tuesday 9 July	199 km	Aix-les-Bains – Serre-Chevalier	V. López Carril (SPA)	E. Merckx
Stage 12	Wednesday 10 July	231 km	Savine-le-Lac – Orange	J. Spruyt (BEL)	E. Merckx
Stage 13	Thursday 11 July	126 km	Avignon – Montpellier	B. Hoban (GBR)	E. Merckx
Stage 14	Friday 12 July	248.5 km	Lodève – Colomiers	J.-P. Genet (FRA)	E. Merckx
Stage 15	Sunday 14 July	225 km	Colomiers – Seo de Urgell (SPA)	E. Merckx (BEL)	E. Merckx
Stage 16	Monday 15 July	209 km	Seo de Urgell (SPA) – Saint-Lary-Soulan	R. Poulidor (FRA)	E. Merckx
Stage 17	Tuesday 16 July	119 km	Saint-Lary-Soulan – Le Tourmalet	J.-P. Danguillaume (FRA)	E. Merckx
Stage 18	Wednesday 17 July	141.5 km	Bagnères-de-Bigorre – Pau	J.-P. Danguillaume (FRA)	E. Merckx
Stage 19 (1)	Thursday 18 July	195.5 km	Pau – Bordeaux	F. Campaner (FRA)	E. Merckx
Stage 19 (2)	Thursday 18 July	12.4 km	Bordeaux-le-Lac – Bordeaux-le-Lac (TT)	E. Merckx (BEL)	E. Merckx
Stage 20	Friday 19 July	117 km	Saint-Gilles-Croix-de-Vie – Nantes	Gérard Vianen (HOL)	E. Merckx
Stage 21 (1)	Saturday 20 July	1125 km	Vouvray – Orléans	E. Merckx (BEL)	E. Merckx
Stage 21 (2)	Saturday 20 July	37.5 km	Orléans – Orléans (TT)	M. Pollentier (BEL)	E. Merckx
Stage 22	Sunday 21 July	146 km	Orléans – Paris	E. Merckx (BEL)	E. Merckx

Having won at Aspro-Gaillard, Eddy Merckx won again the following day at Aix-les-Bains, beating Martínez, Poulidor and Aja, in the sprint. Of the three, it was Poulidor who proved to represent the greatest threat.

Eight kilometres (5 miles) from Saint-Lary-Soulan, Poulidor escaped from López Carril and Merckx, to win the stage.

Au revoir, peleton! In the first part of the penultimate stage, Vouvray to Orléans, Eddy Merckx broke away 10 kilometres (6.2 miles) from the finish.

Poulidor, Merckx and López Carril take a lap of honour. The Spaniard, who lost second place by a few seconds on the penultimate stage, looks rather sombre.

Thévenet ends an era

Merckx came to the 1975 Tour de France intent on beating Jacques Anquetil's record of five Tour wins. He imposed his usual tyranny from the start. On the Côte d'Alsemberg, one of the feared, cobbled climbs from the Paris-Brussels classic, he tore the peloton apart; on the cobble-stones of Roubaix, he made mincemeat of his rivals. Victory in the first time trial stage at Merlin Plage won Merckx the yellow jersey, and a narrow, nine-second win over Thévenet in the second, at Auch, seemed to confirm his dominance.

However, on the Puy de Dôme, he finally began to flag. Dropped by Van Impe and Thévenet, and with Zoetemelk hot on his heels, Merckx was attempting to close the gap when, within sight of the summit, a spectator leapt from the crowd and punched him in the kidneys. Doubled up by the violence of the blow, Merckx finished the stage barely able to breathe. He conceded less than a minute to Van Impe and Thévenet, but the blow was more than physical; the incident was indicative of the widespread feeling against Merckx in France. His fellow competitors were weary of his domination, and accused him of leaving not even the smallest crumbs.

However, Merckx remained Merckx, and between Nice and the Pra-Loup, he rode head-to-head against Thévenet, who launched at least six darting attacks on the ascent of the Col des Champs. Every time, Merckx responded, before launching his own attack on the Col d'Allos. Thévenet had no answer. Merckx had opened a slender, eight-second lead and the Tour seemed to have been decided when the unthinkable happened; on the final climb of the day, Merckx simly ran out of energy. An incredulous Felice Gimondi was the first to catch him up, soon followed by Thévenet, who then set off to win the yellow jersey. Merckx was beaten. Later it became apparent that he was still suffering from the punch on the Puy de Dôme and from the blood-thinning effect of the medication he was subsequently prescribed. More bad luck followed when Merckx collided with Denmark's Ole Ritter at the stage start in Valloire, and fractured his jaw. Yet he refused to abandon; to do so would have devalued Thévenet's victory. Like Bobet years before, Thévenet won the Tour on his sixth attempt. He was greeted like a hero by the French crowds at the first ever Tour finish on the Champs-Elysées in central Paris.

GENERAL CLASSIFICATION

1. **Bernard Thévenet** (FRA) Peugeot-BP, 4,000 km in 114h.35m.31s; Average speed: 34.906 kph
2. **Eddy Merckx** (BEL) Molteni, at 2m.47s.
3. **Lucien Van Impe** (BEL) Gitane-Campagnolo, at 5m.1s.
4. Joop Zoetemelk (HOL) Gan-Mercier, at 6m.42s.
5. Vicente López Carril (SPA) Kas, at 19m.29s.
6. Felice Gimondi (ITA) Bianchi, at 23m.5s.
7. Francesco Moser (ITA) Filotex, at 24m.13s.
8. Joseph Fuchs (SUI) Filotex, at 25m.51s.
9. Édouard Janssens (BEL) Molteni, at 32m.1s.
10. Pedro Torres (SPA) Super Ser, at 35m.36s.
11. Hennie Kuiper (HOL) Frisol, at 40m.45s.
12. André Romero (FRA) Jobo-Sabliere, at 44m.24s.
13. Georges Talbourdet (FRA) Gan-Mercier, at 44m.49s.
14. Mariano Martínez (FRA) Gitane-Campagnolo, at 45m.41s.
15. J. Agostinho (POR) Sporting-Sotto-Mayor, at 50m.46s.
16. Raymond Delisle (FRA) Peugeot-BP, at 55m.21s.
17. Joseph Deschoenmaeker (BEL) Molteni, at 55m.24s.
18. Fedor Den Hertog (HOL) Frisol, at 56m.45s.
19. Raymond Poulidor (FRA) Gan-Mercier, at 58m.57s.
20. Ferdinand Julien (FRA) Sporting-Sotto-Mayor, at 1h.5m.27s.

62ND TOUR DE FRANCE, 22 STAGES – 4,000 KM

			STAGE	STAGE WINNER	YELLOW JERSEY
Prologue	Thursday 26 June	6.3 km	Charleroi (BEL) – Charleroi (BEL)	F. Moser (ITA)	F. Moser
Stage 1 (1)	Friday 27 June	94 km	Charleroi (BEL) – Molenbeek (BEL)	C. Priem (HOL)	F. Moser
Stage 1 (2)	Friday 27 June	108.5 km	Molenbeek (BEL) – Roubaix	R. Van Linden (BEL)	F. Moser
Stage 2	Saturday 28 June	121.5 km	Roubaix – Amiens	R. De Witte (BEL)	F. Moser
Stage 3	Sunday 29 June	169.5 km	Amiens – Versailles	K. Rottiers (BEL)	F. Moser
Stage 4	Monday 30 June	224 km	Versailles – Le Mans	J. Esclassan (FRA)	F. Moser
Stage 5	Tuesday 1 July	222.5 km	Sablé-sur-Sarthe – Merlin-Plage	T. Smit (HOL)	F. Moser
Stage 6	Wednesday 2 July	16 km	Merlin-Plage – Merlin-Plage (TT)	E. Merckx (BEL)	E. Merckx
Stage 7	Thursday 3 July	235.5 km	Saint-Gilles-Croix-de-Vie – Angoulême	F. Moser (ITA)	E. Merckx
Stage 8	Friday 4 July	134 km	Angoulême – Bordeaux	B. Hoban (GBR)	E. Merckx
Stage 9 (1)	Saturday 5 July	131 km	Langon – Fleurance	T. Smit (HOL)	E. Merckx
Stage 9 (2)	Saturday 5 July	37.4 km	Fleurance – Auch (TT)	E. Merckx (BEL)	E. Merckx
Stage 10	Monday 7 July	206 km	Auch – Pau	F. Gimondi (ITA)	E. Merckx
Stage 11	Tuesday 8 July	160 km	Pau – Saint-Lary-Soulan	J. Zoetemelk (HOL)	E. Merckx
Stage 12	Wednesday 9 July	242 km	Tarbes – Albi	G. Knetemann (HOL)	E. Merckx
Stage 13	Thursday 10 July	260 km	Albi – Super-Lioran	M. Pollentier (BEL)	E. Merckx
Stage 14	Friday 11 July	173.5 km	Aurillac – Puy de Dôme	L. Van Impe (BEL)	E. Merckx
Stage 15	Sunday 13 July	217.5 km	Nice – Pra-Loup	B. Thévenet (FRA)	B. Thévenet
Stage 16	Monday 14 July	107 km	Barcelonnette – Serre-Chevalier	B. Thévenet (FRA)	B. Thévenet
Stage 17	Tuesday 15 July	225 km	Valloire – Morzine-Avoriaz	V. López Carril (SPA)	B. Thévenet
Stage 18	Wednesday 16 July	40 km	Morzine – Châtel (TT)	L. Van Impe (BEL)	B. Thévenet
Stage 19	Thursday 17 July	229 km	Thonon-les-Bains – Chalon-sur-Saône	R. Van Linden (BEL)	B. Thévenet
Stage 20	Friday 18 July	256 km	Pouilly-en-Auxois – Melun	G. Santambrogio (ITA)	B. Thévenet
Stage 21	Saturday 19 July	220.5 km	Melun – Senlis	R. Van Linden (BEL)	B. Thévenet
Stage 22	Sunday 20 July	163.4 km	Paris – Paris	W. Godefroot (BEL)	B. Thévenet

A historic moment. Thévenet passes Merckx on the Pra-Loup climb. The once invincible champion is unable to respond. In 2.5 km (1.5 miles), Merckx lost nearly two minutes.

A magnificent and controversial mass sprint at
Le Mans, won by Jacques Esclassan (centre),
who collided with Van Linden (to his left) after
crossing the finishing line.

Thévenet's long march

The Belgian Lucien Van Impe (left, wearing the polka-dot jersey), the best climber on the Tour de France, was an implacable opponent for Bernard Thévenet.

The successes of 1973 confirmed his talents: winning a long mountain stage in the Spanish Vuelta in front of Merckx and Ocaña, becoming champion of France at Plumelec and then, in the Tour itself, winning at Méribel-les-Allues and on the last day in Paris, taking advantage of the climb leading up to the La Cipale velodrome. At the end of 1973 – 'my best year until 1975' – Thévenet could look to the future with enthusiasm. He had taken an important step forward: 'I now believe,' he said, 'that in the next few years I'll be capable of realizing my dream – to win the Tour de France.'

He has now raised himself up to the level of the true greats of our times. He is more consistent in his efforts and also more vigilant, and has established himself as team leader in the major stage races. He is confident of his fitness and the solidity of the principles governing his life. Although he contracted shingles during the Spanish Vuelta, which affected him both physically and mentally for many months, he had clearly recovered by the time of the Dauphiné Libéré. As he told us that evening in Briançon: 'This second mountain stage has taught me something crucial to my career: I now find it easier to recover. I am ready for the Tour, fate has brought me here and I am going to race to win...'

We met up with him again at Briançon during the Tour, the evening after climbing the Izoard. He confided: 'During the last 5 kilometres (3 miles) of the Izoard, I said to myself maybe this is where I am going to win the Tour and so I gave it everything I had.'

The following day Bernard made a personal pilgrimage. Descending the Col du Télégraphe, he passed the exact same spot where, the year before, he had had to pull out of the race. He recognized it by the substation on the side of the road. Time stood still. This time, however, he was full of hope. Such is the race and such is life, when men make the decision not to give in to adversity.

Close to the finish at Clermont-Ferrand, Eddy Merckx was winded by a punch to the kidneys from a violent spectator. Merckx recognized his assailant at the finish-line and had him arrested.

As a child, he read the biographies of the great *routiers* of the past. Without really having a role model, he compared himself with them, and said that the cyclist whose career most closely resembled his own was Louison Bobet. Bernard Thévenet made his debut in 1963, winning six youth events that year, and, with victory in the Trophée du Progrès de Lyon, very quickly established himself as a force to be reckoned with in regional competition. However, 1966 was the year when he really began to confirm his reputation as a name for the future, causing a revelation at the Grand Prix de France by coming in fourth and earning selection to the

Grand Prix des Nations, where he finished third, bringing his total number of wins to 23. It was already apparent that he was a good rider, gifted in the hills, where he often streaked ahead of his opponents to victory well ahead of the pack. In January 1970, he turned professional, joining Peugeot-BP. It was not long before the young cyclist on 1,000 francs a month was making his name known. On 7 March 1970 he won the Mont Faron hill climb, an achievement all the more impressive given that he was competing against, among others, Gimondi, Pingeon and Merckx, who came in second (although he had, admittedly, suffered a fall).

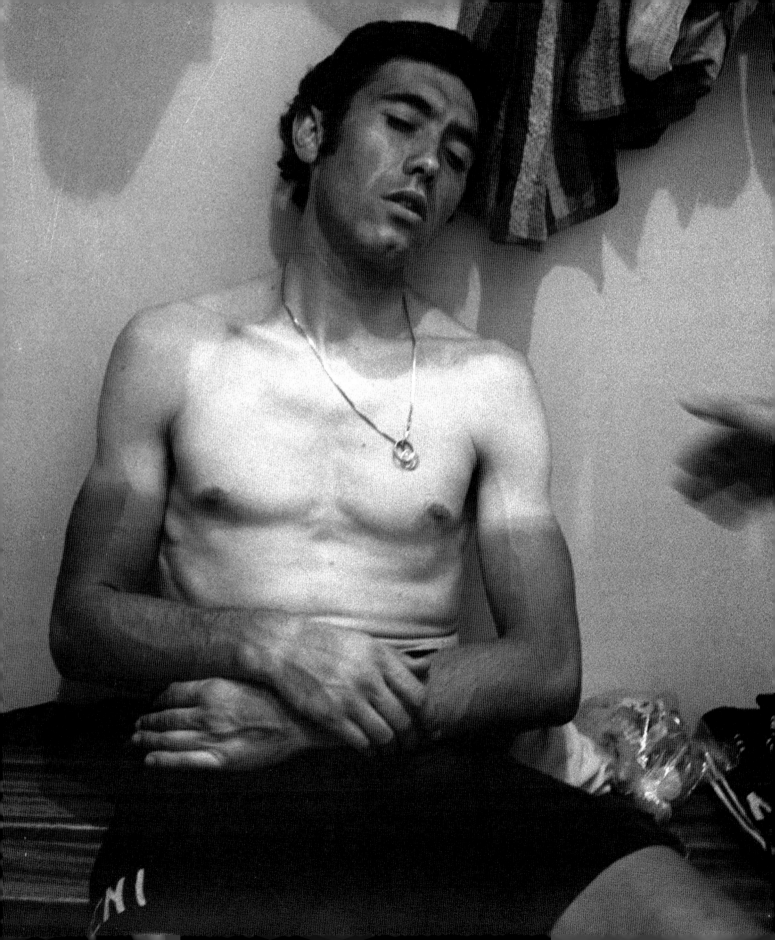

Van Impe climbs to victory

Eddy Merckx started 1976 by winning his seventh Milan-San Remo classic. The victory merely blinded him, and the cycling world, to the truth. At the Giro d'Italia in May and June, he could finish no higher than eighth; his superhuman strength seemed to have abandoned him. When injury ruled him out of the Tour de France, it was clear that an era had ended. His absence cleared the way for the favourites: Thévenet, who had just won the pre-Tour Dauphiné Libéré, and Ocaña, who had lost the Vuelta a España by barely a minute in May.

The outside favourites included the Belgian Lucien Van Impe. Van Impe had won the mountains competition three times, and had finished on the final podium twice; this year he had improved his riding against the clock, and Merckx's absence left him full of ambition. For the first time since his professional debut in 1970, he could count on the unconditional support of his team, now directed by Cyrille Guimard.

The 1976 Tour also welcomed the brilliant Freddy Maertens, a ruthless sprinter capable of rivalling Merckx in the classics. Maertens had not come to assume Merckx's mantle but to take as many stage wins as possible on his way to the green jersey in Paris. In the scorching heat, he duly won the Prologue, the sprint finish in Angers, the time trial at Le Touquet, and another bunch sprint at Mulhouse. Then came the punishing, 258-kilometre (160-mile) marathon that finished on the slopes of Alpe-d'Huez. Zoetemelk and Van Impe attacked and counter attacked in a fascinating piece of choreography that allowed Zoetemelk to gain just three seconds on his rival. Twenty-four hours later, Zoetemelk won again at Montgenèvre ahead of Thévenet, Van Impe, and five more riders including Thévenet's team-mate Raymond Delisle. Thévenet, however, fell ill, and on the stage finishing at the ski station at Pyrenees 2000, Delisle attacked on the final climb and took over the yellow jersey.

On stage fourteen, a stinging attack by Luis Ocaña shattered the peloton. Ocaña catapulted up the Col du Portillon in pursuit of the leading group; behind him, Van Impe dropped Zoetemelk, caught the breakaway group, then darted off in search of Ocaña. The two men approached the final climb in intense heat, and Ocaña relayed Van Impe away from Zoetemelk, who had never assisted him in his struggles with Merckx. With Ocaña's help, Lucien Van Impe, who had started his career as a paper boy, finally won the Tour at his eighth attempt.

GENERAL CLASSIFICATION

1. **Lucien Van Impe** (BEL) Gitane-Campagnolo, 4,017km in 116h.22m.23s; Average speed: 34.518 kph
2. **Joop Zoetemelk** (HOL) Gan-Mercier, at 4m.14s.
3. **Raymond Poulidor** (FRA) Gan-Mercier, at 12m.8s.
4. Raymond Delisle (FRA) Peugeot-Esso, at 12m.17s.
5. Walter Riccomi (ITA) Scic-Fiat, at 12m.39s.
6. Francisco Galdós (SPA) Kas, at 14m.50s.

7. Michel Pollentier (BEL) Velda-Flandria, at 14m.59s.
8. Freddy Maertens (BEL) Velda-Flandria, at 16m.6s.
9. Fausto Bertoglio (ITA) Jollyceramica, at 16m.36s.
10. Vicente López Carril (SPA) Kas, at 19m.28s.
11. José Pesarrodona (SPA) Kas, at 21m.14s.
12. José Martins (POR) Kas, at 21m.45s.
13. Wladimiro Panizza (ITA) Scic-Fiat, at 22m.8s.

14. Luis Ocaña (SPA) Super Ser, at 25m.8s.
15. Raymond Martin (FRA), Gitane-Campagnolo, at 25m.35s.
16. Giancarlo Bellini (ITA) Brooklyn, at 26m.43s.
17. Pedro Torres (SPA) Super Ser, at 32m.44s.
18. Ronald De Witte (BEL) Brooklyn, at 34m.21s.
19. Ferdinand Julien (FRA) Lejeune-BP, at 36m.29s.
20. Robert Bouloux (FRA) Jobo La France, at 39m.54s.

63RD TOUR DE FRANCE, 22 STAGES – 4,017 KM

			STAGE	STAGE WINNER	YELLOW JERSEY
Prologue	Thursday 24 June	8 km	St-Jean-de-Monts – St-Jean-de-Monts	F. Maertens (BEL)	F. Maertens
Stage 1	Friday 25 June	173 km	St-Jean-de-Monts – Angers	F. Maertens (BEL)	F. Maertens
Stage 2	Saturday 26 June	236.5 km	Angers – Caen	G. Battaglin (ITA)	F. Maertens
Stage 3	Sunday 27 June	37 km	Le Touquet – Le Touquet (TT)	F. Maertens (BEL)	F. Maertens
Stage 4	Monday 28 June	258 km	Le Touquet – Bornem (BEL)	H. Kuiper (HOL)	F. Maertens
Stage 5 (1)	Tuesday 29 June	4.3 km	Louvain (BEL) – Louvain (BEL) (TTT)	Ti-Raleigh	F. Maertens
Stage 5 (2)	Tuesday 29 June	144 km	Louvain (BEL) – Verviers (BEL)	M.-M. Lasa (SPA)	F. Maertens
Stage 6	Wednesday 30 June	209 km	Bastogne (BEL) – Nancy	A. Parecchini (ITA)	F. Maertens
Stage 7	Thursday 1 July	207.5 km	Nancy – Mulhouse	F. Maertens (BEL)	F. Maertens
Stage 8	Friday 2 July	220.5 km	Valentigney – Divonne-les-Bains	J. Esclassan (FRA)	F. Maertens
Stage 9	Sunday 4 July	258 km	Divonne-les-Bains – L'Alpe-d'Huez	J. Zoetemelk (HOL)	L. Van Impe
Stage 10	Monday 5 July	158 km	Bourg-d'Oisans – Montgenèvre	J. Zoetemelk (HOL)	L. Van Impe
Stage 11	Tuesday 6 July	224 km	Montgenèvre – Manosque	J. Luis Viejo (SPA)	L. Van Impe
Stage 12	Thursday 8 July	205.5 km	Port-Barcarès – Pyrénées 2000	R. Delisle (FRA)	R. Delisle
Stage 13	Friday 9 July	188 km	Font-Romeu – Saint-Gaudens	W.Teirlinck (BEL)	R. Delisle
Stage 14	Saturday 10 July	139 km	Saint-Gaudens – Saint-Lary-Soulan	L. Van Impe (BEL)	L. Van Impe
Stage 15	Sunday 11 July	195 km	Saint-Lary-Soulan – Pau	W. Panizza (ITA)	L. Van Impe
Stage 16	Monday 12 July	152 km	Pau – Fleurance	M. Pollentier (BEL)	L. Van Impe
Stage 17	Tuesday 13 July	38.8 km	Fleurance – Auch (TT)	F. Bracke (BEL)	L. Van Impe
Stage 18 (1)	Wednesday 14 July	86 km	Auch – Langon	F. Maertens (BEL)	L. Van Impe
Stage 18 (2)	Wednesday 14 July	123 km	Langon – Lacanau-Océan	F. Maertens (BEL)	L. Van Impe
Stage 18 (3)	Wednesday 14 July	70.5 km	Lacanau-Océan – Bordeaux	G. Karstens (HOL)	L. Van Impe
Stage 19	Thursday 15 July	219.5 km	Sainte-Foix-la-Grande – Tulle	H. Mathis (FRA)	L. Van Impe
Stage 20	Friday 16 July	220 km	Tulle – Puy de Dôme	J. Zoetemelk (HOL)	L. Van Impe
Stage 21	Saturday 17 July	145.5 km	Montargis – Versailles	F. Maertens (BEL)	L. Van Impe
Stage 22 (1)	Sunday 18 July	6 km	Paris – Paris (TT)	F. Maertens (BEL)	L. Van Impe
Stage 22 (2)	Sunday 18 July	90.7 km	Paris – Paris	G. Karstens (HOL)	L. Van Impe

Cyrille Guimard (left) knew how to manage Lucien Van Impe, notably ordering him not to hang on Delisle's wheel on the climb up to Pyrenees 2000. A risky move, but a winning one.

Approaching the summit of the Puy de Dôme, Zoetemelk attacked, dropped Van Impe and won the stage by 12 seconds.

Climbing the Col de Peyresourde, Van Impe and Ocaña, his ally of convenience, found themselves alone and ahead of the field. Van Impe attacked, and not only won the stage, but also pulled on the yellow jersey.

At Angers, Freddy Maertens takes the first of eight stage wins at the 1976 Tour. Gualazzini (left) was third; Karstens (right) finished fourth.

Thévenet, with a little help

The 1977 Tour de France took the riders over the Pyrenees on day two. The favourites, Zoetemelk, Van Impe and Thévenet hesitated, allowing the young German Dietrich Thurau to reap the benefits. Victory in the Prologue and stage two put him in yellow for seventeen days, until the mountain time trial on the slopes of Avoriaz revealed his limitations and the race began in earnest. Van Impe won the stage, but Bernard Thévenet took the race lead.

Van Impe, bolstered by victory the previous year, was more audacious than ever, and chose the stage from Chamonix to Alpe-d'Huez to try to reverse the situation. On the Col du Glandon, he attacked, but was held back by the fierce headwind blowing out of the valley. On the final ascent of the Alpe, he lost a large part of his lead when a television reporter's car struck him from behind and threw him into the ditch. Van Impe rose immediately and set off without hesitation, but his wheel was buckled. As his mechanic changed it, Van Impe could only look on in distress as Hennie Kuiper passed, pursued by Thévenet.

Thévenet lost 41 seconds; nine more and he would have lost the race lead. For Van Impe, third across the line 2mins 25secs behind the yellow jersey, the Tour was lost. Still further back, Eddy Merckx lost nearly a quarter of an hour. He had been suffering the symptoms of dysentery since Fribourg, four days earlier. Riding his last Tour, Merckx knew how to lose as well as how to win; he insisted on finishing. Sixth place overall, more than most professional cyclists could hope for, represented the end of his Tour de France career. At Saint-Étienne, Merckx was even awarded the stage win after the first and second placed riders were disqualified after failing anti-doping tests. Indeed, the Tour ended in an atmosphere of suspicion. A list of riders suspected of doping circulated clandestinely. The Tour organizers published a statement clearing Thévenet, who had tested positive in March during the Paris-Nice, of all suspicion. But months later Thévenet admitted that he had taken cortisone, which was still undetectable. Criticized by his employer and his peers, Thévenet never again played a major role in the Tour.

GENERAL CLASSIFICATION

1. **Bernard Thévenet** (FRA) Peugeot-Esso, 4,096 km in 115h.38m.30s; Average speed: 35.393 kph
2. **Hennie Kuiper** (HOL) Ti-Raleigh, at 48s.
3. **Lucien Van Impe** (BEL) Lejeune-BP, at 3m.32s.
4. Francisco Galdós (SPA) Kas, at 7m.45s.
5. Dietrich Thurau (GER) Ti-Raleigh, at 12m.24s.
6. Eddy Merckx (BEL) Fiat, at 12m.38s.
7. Michel Laurent (FRA) Peugeot-Esso, at 17m.42s.
8. Joop Zoetemelk (HOL) Miko-Mercier, at 19m.22s.
9. Raymond Delisle (FRA) Miko-Mercier, at 21m.32s.
10. Alain Meslet (FRA) Gitane-Campagnolo, at 27m.31s.
11. Raymond Maertin (FRA) Miko-Mercier, at 28m.35s.
12. Hubert 'Bert' Pronk (HOL) Ti-Raleigh, at 30m.6s.
13. Joaquim Agostinho (POR) Teka, at 33m.13s.
14. Gonzalo Aja (SPA) Teka, at 36m.11s.
15. P.-R. Villemiane (FRA) Gitane-Campagnolo, at 36m.42s.
16. José Martins (POR) Kas, at 38m.53s.
17. Edouard Janssens (BEL) Fiat, at 46m.13s.
18. Enrique Martínez-Heredia (SPA) Kas, at 47m.30s.
19. Pedro Torres (SPA) Teka, at 47m.39s.
20. Bernard Vallet (FRA) Miko-Mercier, at 48m.41s.

64TH TOUR DE FRANCE,

			STAGE	STAGE WINNER	YELLOW JERSEY
Prologue	Thursday 30 June	5 km	Fleurance – Fleurance	D. Thurau (GER)	D. Thurau
Stage 1	Friday 1 July	237 km	Fleurance – Auch	P.-R. Villemiane (FRA)	D. Thurau
Stage 2	Saturday 2 July	253 km	Auch – Pau	D. Thurau (GER)	D. Thurau
Stage 3	Sunday 3 July	248.2 km	Oloron-Sainte-Marie – Vitoria (SPA)	J. Nazabal (SPA)	D. Thurau
Stage 4	Monday 4 July	256 km	Vitoria (SPA) – Seignosse-le-Penon	R. Delépine (FRA)	D. Thurau
Stage 5 (1)	Tuesday 5 July	138.5 km	Morcenx – Bordeaux	J. Esclassan (FRA)	D. Thurau
Stage 5 (2)	Tuesday 5 July	30.2 km	Bordeaux – Bordeaux (TT)	D. Thurau (GER)	D. Thurau
Stage 6	Thursday 7 July	225.5 km	Bordeaux – Limoges	J. Raas (HOL)	D. Thurau
Stage 7 (1)	Friday 8 July	139.5 km	Jauney-Clan – Angers	P. Sercu (BEL)	D. Thurau
Stage 7 (2)	Friday 8 July	4.5 km	Angers – Angers (TTT)	Fiat	D. Thurau
Stage 8	Saturday 9 July	246.5 km	Angers – Lorient	G. Santambrogio (ITA)	D. Thurau
Stage 9	Sunday 10 July	187 km	Lorient – Rennes	K.-Peter Thaler (GER)	D. Thurau
Stage 10	Monday 11 July	174 km	Bagnoles-de-l'Orne – Rouen	F. Den Hertog (HOL)	D. Thurau
Stage 11	Tuesday 12 July	242.5 km	Rouen – Roubaix	J.-P. Danguillaume (FRA)	D. Thurau
Stage 12	Wednesday 13 July	192.5 km	Roubaix – Charleroi (BEL)	P. Sercu (BEL)	D. Thurau
Stage 13 (1)	Friday 15 July	46 km	Fribourg-en-Brisgau – Fribourg-en-B. (GER)	P. Sercu (BEL)	D. Thurau
Stage 13 (2)	Friday 15 July	159.5 km	Altkirch – Besançon	J.-P. Danguillaume (FRA)	D. Thurau
Stage 14	Saturday 16 July	230 km	Besançon – Thonon-les-Bains	B. Quilfen (FRA)	D. Thurau
Stage 15 (1)	Sunday 17 July	105 km	Thonon-les-Bains – Morzine	P. Wellens (BEL)	D. Thurau
Stage 15 (2)	Sunday 17 July	14 km	Morzine – Avoriaz (TT)	L. Van Impe (BEL)	B. Thévenet
Stage 16	Monday 18 July	121 km	Morzine – Chamonix	D. Thurau (GER)	B. Thévenet
Stage 17	Tuesday 19 July	184.5 km	Chamonix – L'Alpe-d'Huez	H. Kuiper (HOL)	B. Thévenet
Stage 18	Wednesday 20 July	199.5 km	Voiron – Saint-Étienne	E. Merckx (BEL)	B. Thévenet
Stage 19	Thursday 21 July	171.5 km	Saint-Trivier – Dijon	G. Knetemann (HOL)	B. Thévenet
Stage 20	Friday 22 July	50 km	Dijon – Dijon (TT)	B. Thévenet (FRA)	B. Thévenet
Stage 21	Saturday 23 July	141.5 km	Montereau – Versailles	G. Knetemann (HOL)	B. Thévenet
Stage 22 (1)	Sunday 24 July	6 km	Paris – Paris (TT)	D. Thurau (GER)	B. Thévenet
Stage 22 (2)	Sunday 24 July	90.7 km	Paris – Paris	A. Meslet (FRA)	B. Thévenet

At Alpe-d'Huez Thévenet pushed himself to the limit to defend his race lead from Hennie Kuiper.

The rumours grow...

The Peugeot-Esso-Michelin team, managed discreetly and efficiently by Maurice de Muer, brought two prestigious jerseys – yellow for Thévenet and green for Esclassan – back to the Champs-Élysées.

Bernard Thévenet towed Hennie Kuiper and Joop Zoetemelk up the Alpe-d'Huez. At the finishing line, a furious Thévenet called them *petits coureurs* – insignificant riders.

Time does not change men: in old age, we are essentially the same people as we were in short trousers. Primary school sneaks quickly turn into informers, and the young boy with high principles is bound to be taken for an imbecile one day. But let's let it pass. The past, that enclave of often hypocritical nostalgia, is presented to us by fools as a great healer, although its real effect, in the vast majority of cases, is to act like a grindstone that slowly erases the rough patches. But once more, let's let it pass.

For one day in July 1939, lost in the crowd and bicycle in hand, we watched the Belgian Sylvère Maes cross the slopes of the Corbeil, the *maillot jaune* on his back, pursued by the vanquished René Vietto. And since then 30 Tours de France experienced through day-to-day interaction with the riders have convinced us that true glory does not come from the laboratory. We'd taken at face value the results of the last few weeks. And yet a rumour is growing. It seems that our trust has been abused. In Versailles on Saturday we learned – even though we had already heard the information unofficially two days previously – that Zoetemelk had been penalized following a drugs test on the Alpe-d'Huez. He now joins Bernard Thévenet, who was penalized for an identical result the day after the Paris-Nice earlier this year. The rumours continued to grow.

Raphaël Géminiani proclaimed that 'If the rules are going to be enforced they should be enforced all round.' Then a caustic Henry Anglade suggested that perhaps the Tour was not lost for Van Impe after all! A simple mind would be perturbed by less than this. Lists of names were passed round furtively – unreliable lists from unverifiable sources, bearing the names of seven or eight competitors suspected of taking drugs.

A more official list was delivered to us under a Saharan tent, in the green and white stripes of the medical profession – colours of purity and hope. An ironic touch, unless the decorator made a mistake. This list contained four names: Joaquim Agostinho, Luis Ocaña, Antonio Menéndez and Fernando Mendes. The 'foreigners' do not have much luck it seems, bearing in mind a comment made by one of the Tour doctors the day before: 'You want to know the names of the riders who have taken drugs? Let me enlighten you – there are 54!' We didn't have time to ask him any more questions as he shrugged his shoulders and walked away. It was a joke of course (yet another one), for we live in a world that does not like getting to the bottom of things. However, those who had heard it could not stop wondering if there was some truth in it. We had heard Géminiani's complaints, seen the look in Cyrille Guimard's eye that hinted at possible new developments, and could not fail to notice the distress of Louis Caput, Joop Zoetemelk's director.

On the Champs-Élysées, however, free rein was given to exuberant triumphalism, as if nothing had happened and nothing would happen. Remember that Al Capone was arrested by the Feds on a simple charge of tax evasion and that a thousand eminent citizens were ready to swear to the fact that 'good old Al' had never killed a soul. It's the same thing here – the incomplete manner in which the drugs tests are administered is an outrageous fraud. Poachers do not stop poaching, they simply try to get around the gamekeeper. This is how we have ended up

today in this farcical situation (which not long ago would have been unthinkable), with 200 disillusioned journalists waiting to be handed a press release telling them whether, after three weeks of following the cyclists' progress, Bernard Thévenet has won the Tour and whether Hennie Kuiper deserves second place. The press release confirmed that Thévenet had indeed won. After seeing him put his heart and soul into the climb up the Alpe-d'Huez and stamp his authority once more on the Dijon time trial, we are glad he won an honest victory. This is the Thévenet we want to see, not the Thévenet we saw at Paris-Nice in March. We hope with all our hearts that he will come back and win a third Tour, not a Tour overshadowed by the shame of Zoetemelk, Ocaña or Agostinho, but a Tour that will still be talked about with joy and without regrets 20 years from now.

Dietrich Thurau, the revelation of the Tour, wore the *maillot jaune* for 15 days.

It was the last Tour de France for Eddy Merckx. Nevertheless, he finished in sixth place.

Hinault strikes the first blow

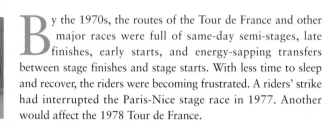

By the 1970s, the routes of the Tour de France and other major races were full of same-day semi-stages, late finishes, early starts, and energy-sapping transfers between stage finishes and stage starts. With less time to sleep and recover, the riders were becoming frustrated. A riders' strike had interrupted the Paris-Nice stage race in 1977. Another would affect the 1978 Tour de France.

On 29 June 1978, the Tour celebrated its 75th anniversary in the Dutch town of Leiden. A Dutchman, Jan Raas, won the Prologue, and two more Dutchmen, Hennie Kuiper and Joop Zoetemelk, were among the favourites, together with a Belgian, Michel Pollentier, and a talented Frenchman who was starting his first Tour de France. But Bernard Hinault was no ordinary 23-year-old. He had emerged the previous year, establishing himself as a brilliant one-day classics rider by winning the Liège-Bastogne-Liège and the Gent-Wevelgem. By conquering the prestigious Grand Prix des Nations, he had also proved himself as an exceptional time triallist. And by triumphing in the Dauphiné Libéré, a mountainous pre-Tour de France stage race, he had demonstrated the climbing prowess and powers of recovery that would make him an excellent stage racer. Two months before the 1978 Tour de France, he had won the

three-week Vuelta a España. He also set off from Leiden as the newly crowned Champion of France.

The first decisive stage was the time trial between Saint-Émilion and Sainte-Foy-la-Grande. Hinault won the stage, although Belgium's Joseph Bruyère, one of Merckx's former lieutenants, retained his race lead by finishing in second place. Despite his triumph in Spain, doubt still surrounded Hinault's abilities to climb at altitude. During the great Pyrenean stage at Saint-Lary-Soulan, Hinault proved the doubters wrong; the mountain specialist Mariano Martínez won the stage by five seconds, but Hinault controlled his rivals, the expert climbers Pollentier and Zoetemelk, with pitiless sang-froid.

At Valence-d'Agen, the riders dismounted with the finish-line in view, with Hinault at the head of the striking peloton. As the most visible figurehead, he was derided by the critics. But the scandal of the strike paled into insignificance after an energetic Pollentier won the yellow jersey at Alpe-d'Huez, then was caught trying to pass off someone else's urine as his own during the drugs test. With Pollentier out, Zoetemelk inherited the yellow jersey with a 14-second lead over Hinault. Overwhelming supremacy in the final time trial gave Hinault triumph in his first Tour de France, like Anquetil and Merckx.

GENERAL CLASSIFICATION

1. **Bernard Hinault** (FRA) Renault-Gitane, 3,908 km in 108h.18s; Average speed: 36.084 kph
2. **Joop Zoetemelk** (HOL) Miko-Mercier, at 3m.56s.
3. **Joaquim Agostinho** (POR) Velda-Flandria, at 6m.54s.
4. Joseph Bruyère (BEL) C&A, at 9m.4s.
5. Christian Seznec (FRA) Miko-Mercier, at 12m.50s.
6. Paul Wellens (BEL) Ti-Raleigh, at 14m.38s.
7. Francisco Galdós (SPA) Kas, at 17m.8s.
8. Henk Lubberding (HOL) Ti-Raleigh, at 17m.26s.
9. Lucien Van Impe (BEL) C&A, at 21m.1s.
10. Mariano Martínez (FRA) Jobo-Superia, at 22m.58s.
11. Sven-Ake Nilsson (SUE) Miko-Mercier, at 23m.
12. Raymond Martin (FRA) Miko-Mercier, at 32m.58s.
13. Freddy Maertens (BEL) Velda-Flandria, at 34m.26s.
14. Michel Laurent (FRA) Peugeot-Esso, at 40m.
15. André Romero (FRA) Jobo-Superia, at 49m.34s.
16. Édouard Janssens (BEL) C&A, at 51m.19s.
17. Yves Hézard (FRA) Peugeot-Esso, at 53m.20s.
18. Antonio Menéndez (SPA) Teka, at 53m.28s.
19. René Bittinger (FRA) Velda-Flandria, at 53m.47s.
20. Joseph Deschoemaecker (BEL) C&A, at 54m.14s.

65TH TOUR DE FRANCE, 22 STAGES – 3,908 KM

			STAGE	STAGE WINNER	YELLOW JERSEY
Prologue	Thursday 29 June	5.2 km	Leiden (HOL) – Leiden (HOL) (TT)	J. Raas (HOL)	J. Raas
Stage 1 (1)	Friday 30 June	135 km	Leiden (HOL) – Sint-Willebrord (HOL)	J. Raas (HOL)	J. Raas
Stage 1 (2)	Friday 30 June	100 km	Sint Willebrord (HOL) – Bruxelles (BEL)	W. Planckaert (BEL)	J. Raas
Stage 2	Saturday 1 July	199 km	Bruxelles (BEL) – Saint-Amand-les-Eaux	J. Esclassan (FRA)	J. Raas
Stage 3	Sunday 2 July	243.5 km	St-Amand-les-Eaux – St-Germain-en-Laye	K.-P. Thaler (GER)	J. Bossis
Stage 4	Monday 3 July	153 km	Évreux – Caen (TTT)	Ti-Raleigh	K.-P. Thaler
Stage 5	Tuesday 4 July	244 km	Caen – Mazé-Montgeoffroy	F. Maertens (BEL)	K.-P. Thaler
Stage 6	Wednesday 5 July	162 km	Mazé-Montgeoffroy – Poitiers	S. Kelly (IRL)	G. Knetemann
Stage 7	Thursday 6 July	242 km	Poitiers – Bordeaux	F. Maertens (BEL)	G. Knetemann
Stage 8	Friday 7 July	59.3 km	St-Émilion – Sainte-Foy-la-Grande (TT)	B. Hinault (FRA)	J. Bruyère
Stage 9	Saturday 8 July	233 km	Bordeaux – Biarritz	M.-M. Lasa (SPA)	J. Bruyère
Stage 10	Monday 10 July	191.5 km	Biarritz – Pau	H. Lubberding (HOL)	J. Bruyère
Stage 11	Tuesday 11 July	161 km	Pau – Saint-Lary-Soulan	M. Martínez (FRA)	J. Bruyère
Stage 12 (1)	Wednesday 12 July	158 km	Tarbes – Valence-d'Agen	J. Bruyère (BEL)	J. Bruyère
Stage 12 (2)	Wednesday 12 July	96 km	Valence-d'Agen – Toulouse	J. Esclassan (FRA)	J. Bruyère
Stage 13	Thursday 13 July	221.5 km	Figeac – Superbesse	P. Wellens (BEL)	J. Bruyère
Stage 14	Friday 14 July	52.5 km	Besse-en-Chandesse – Puy de Dôme	J. Zoetemelk (HOL)	J. Bruyère
Stage 15	Saturday 15 July	196 km	Saint-Dier-d'Auvergne – Saint-Étienne	B. Hinault (FRA)	J. Bruyère
Stage 16	Sunday 16 July	240.5 km	Saint-Étienne – L'Alpe-d'Huez	H. Kuiper (HOL)	J. Zoetemelk
Stage 17	Tuesday 18 July	225 km	Grenoble – Morzine	C. Seznec (FRA)	J. Zoetemelk
Stage 18	Wednesday 19 July	137.5 km	Morzine – Lausanne (SUI)	G. Knetemann (HOL)	J. Zoetemelk
Stage 19	Thursday 20 July	181.5 km	Lausanne (SUI) – Belfort	M. De Meyer (BEL)	J. Zoetemelk
Stage 20	Friday 21 July	72 km	Metz – Nancy (TT)	B. Hinault (FRA)	B. Hinault
Stage 21	Saturday 22 July	207.5 km	Épernay – Senlis	G. Knetemann (HOL)	B. Hinault
Stage 22	Sunday 23 July	161.5 km	St-Germain-en-Laye – Paris	G. Knetemann (HOL)	B. Hinault

Nothing could prevent the irresistible rise of Bernard Hinault, even
if Joop Zoetemelk was still wearing the yellow jersey in the Alps.

1978

Exhausted by the early morning starts, the numerous transfers, the increased number of half-stages and the lack of consultation, the peloton dismounted in protest. Hinault is in the front line.

Hinault: the vitality of youth

The evening after his fabulous victory in the time trial at Nancy, a win which guaranteed his victory in the Tour, a relaxed Bernard Hinault, bursting with vitality ('I feel so good I could race another three months like that, I'm feeling better and better every day'), with a brand new *maillot jaune* on his lap, was carefully examining some photos he'd been presented with of his latest achievement. 'Look at this,' he muttered, 'my shorts really are too long. Several times during the race I had to pull them up. I must get some made that fit better than this.' The reason for relating this trivial tale is precisely because it reveals an aspect of the champion that is often ignored – that of the perfectionist, concerned with every minute detail, always on the lookout for improvement, neglecting nothing.

Many opinions have been bandied around about Bernard Hinault, often malicious. Some that initially seem presumptuous turn out later on to hit the mark. He's earned a reputation for wading in where he's not wanted, which did him a lot of harm during the strike at Valence-d'Agen. But, surely, isn't there something laudable in an eagerness to engage in discussion, in an uncontrollable urge to speak one's mind, in an age of indifference in which people are unenthusiastic and reluctant to take up a position?

'I knew this Tour would be long and full of risk,' he said, 'and that it would be won by the person with the stamina to keep going right to the end and that, if you had to pick a point along the way, the time trial between Metz and Nancy would be decisive.

'The first major test was the first long time trial between Saint-Émilion and Sainte-Foy-la-Grande. I knew I had to get the upper hand here so that I could then afford to stand back a little, watch out for the attacks and control them. To prepare for this stage, we stayed at Villemiane's house. Knowing I'd reconnoitred the route, I felt relaxed; it gave me an advantage, and that fed my confidence. Later, when I was climbing up to Saint-Lary, I knew I couldn't be beaten on the mountains; I'd held on to my psychological advantage.

'But then I had to deal with my most serious crisis of the Tour. I supported the riders who decided on the spur of the moment to strike at Valence-d'Agen, but to say I was the ringleader is just not true. All the comments made about me and the harsh criticisms that followed really affected me deeply. I was in an extreme state of nervous tension, I couldn't sleep properly for several days – I felt as if I was on a tightrope.

'It was in this state of anxiety that I approached the time trial at the Puy de Dôme, where I did badly. That gave me a real slap in the face, which actually did me good for the rest of the Tour.'

One of Hinault's great qualities is his sensitivity to injustice, so when his plain speaking backfired on him, he felt the unfairness of it keenly. At Valence-d'Agen, when he was trying to reason with everyone, the town's chief councillor turned to him and said, 'You do not deserve to wear the jersey of the champion of France.' It hit him hard. But the sign of a true champion is one who in the face of adversity and defeat can still find the will to win. The way in which Bernard reacted to his slap in the face on the Puy de Dôme by going on to win the next day in Saint-Étienne goes to show that he is truly one of the greatest.

We should be grateful to him. At a time when the world of sport is undermined by so many doubts, Bernard Hinault's irresistible youth has made them all disappear.

1. Joop Zoetemelk, who'd been in yellow since Alpe-d'Huez, put up a decent fight, but it wasn't enough to stop the impudent young Hinault, who clinched the decision in the Nancy time trial.

2. Bernard Hinault could also sprint like a true specialist. At the finish of the Saint-Dier-d'Auvergne to Saint-Étienne stage, Sean Kelly (right) was an expert witness.

3. The *maillot jaune* after Alpe-d'Huez, Michel Pollentier, was disqualified the same evening, after he was caught cheating during the drugs test.

4 Joop Zoetemelk inherited the yellow jersey after Pollentier's disqualification. But Bernard Hinault had confidence in his strength.

5. The champion of France took the first of 28 career stage wins in the time trial between St-Émilion and Ste-Foy-la-Grande.

6. Holland's Jan Raas won a popular home victory in the Prologue at Leiden.

7. Freddy Maertens, points champion, dominated the sprints, as here at Mazé-Montgeoffroy.

1

2

3

4

5

6

7

Hinault finds glory in the Champs-Élysées

In 1979, many expected Bernard Hinault to win the Prologue, take the yellow jersey, and defend it all the way to Paris. The Tour de France is rarely so simple. The World Champion, Holland's Gerrie Knetemann, had won the final stage of the 1978 Tour, and started the 1979 edition with victory in the Prologue. The following day, Hinault's team-mate Jean-René Bernaudeau took over the race lead. Then Hinault sprang into action. Following the blueprint of the 1977 Tour, the 1979 race started with the challenge of the Pyrenees. More than that, the second stage consisted of an unforgiving mountain time trial up the pass to the Superbagnères ski station. It was made for Hinault, whose victory over the 37-year-old Portuguese rider Joaquim Agostinho gave him his first yellow jersey. When Pau saw Hinault's second stage win the following day, his second Tour de France success seemed certain. The good performance of his team, Renault-Gitane, in the two team time trials – the speciality of the powerful Dutchmen of Ti-Raleigh – reinforced the conviction.

That was before Hinault punctured on the cobblestones between Amiens and Roubaix, and Joop Zoetemelk seized the yellow jersey and a 2min-8sec cushion as Hinault pursued in vain. However, even before the Alps, Hinault had whittled Zoetemelk's lead down to 49 seconds. There, a mammoth mountain time trial from Evian to the ski resort at Avoriaz awaited one of the more remarkable exploits of Hinault's career. Far longer than a conventional mountain time trial, the 54.2-kilometre (33.7-mile) stage had been designed to deliver huge differences between the protagonists. Measuring his power output with the precision of a high-performance engine, Hinault devoured Zoetemelk's lead, gaining 1min 17secs over the first 40 kilometres (25 miles) before the Dutchman suffered mechanical problems and had to change bikes twice. Zoetemelk lost 2mins 37secs on the stage. Only seven riders could finish within five minutes of Hinault's remarkable time.

Alpe-d'Huez welcomed two stage finishes on consecutive days. The stage winners, Agostinho on stage 17 and Zoetemelk the following day, ensured that the podium roster would repeat the previous year's result: Hinault, Zoetemelk, Agostinho. Hinault, who had started so strongly, finished the Tour with a flourish by winning the penultimate stage. Then, on the last day, Zoetemelk launched his final attack. Hinault reacted strongly, crossing single-handed to the Dutchman, and together, they battled on the Champs-Élysées. Hinault won the sprint, and the Tour reached the perfect conclusion.

GENERAL CLASSIFICATION

1. **Bernard Hinault** (FRA) Renault-Gitane, 3,765 km in103h.6m.50s; Average speed: 36.512 kph
2. **Joop Zoetemelk** (HOL) Miko-Mercier, at 3m.7s.
3. **Joaquim Agostinho** (POR) Flandria-Ca Va Seul, at 26m.53s.
4. Hennie Kuiper (HOL) Peugeot-Esso, at 28m.2s.
5. Jean-René Bernaudeau (FRA) Renault-Gitane, at 32m.43s.
6. Giovanni Battaglin (ITA) Inoxpran, at 38m.12s.
7. Jo Maas (HOL) DAF Trucks, at 38m.39s.
8. Paul Wellens (BEL) Ti-Raleigh, at 39m.6s.
9. Claude Criquielion (BEL) Kas, at 40m.38s.
10. Dietrich Thurau (GER) Ijsboerke-Warncke, at 44m.35s.
11. Lucien Van Impe (BEL) Kas, at 47m.26s.
12. Sven-Ake Nilsson (SWE) Miko-Mercier, at 48m.16s.
13. P.-R. Villemiane (FRA) Renault-Gitane, at 59m.9s.
14. Johan Van Der Velde (HOL) Ti-Raleigh, at 59m.13s.
15. Eddy Schepers (BEL) DAF Trucks, at 59m.51s.
16. Mariano Martínez (FRA) La Redoute, at 1h.1m.36s.
17. Yves Hézard (FRA) Peugeot-Esso, at 1h.3m.5s.
18. Henk Lubberding (HOL) Ti-Raleigh, at 1h.3m.9s.
19. Robert Alban (FRA) Fiat-La France, at 1h.6m.47s.
20. Bernard Vallet (FRA) La Redoute, at 1h.8m.25s.

66TH TOUR DE FRANCE, 24 STAGES – 3,765 KM

			STAGE	STAGE WINNER	YELLOW JERSEY
Prologue	Wednesday 27 June	5 km	Fleurance – Fleurance (TT)	G. Knetemann (HOL)	G. Knetemann
Stage 1	Thursday 28 June	225 km	Fleurance – Luchon	R. Bittinger (FRA)	J.-R. Bernaudeau
Stage 2	Friday 29 June	23.9 km	Luchon – Superbagnères (TT)	B. Hinault (FRA)	B. Hinault
Stage 3	Saturday 30 June	180.5 km	Luchon – Pau	B. Hinault (FRA)	B. Hinault
Stage 4	Sunday 1 July	87.5 km	Captieux – Bordeaux (TTT)	Ti-Raleigh	B. Hinault
Stage 5	Monday 2 July	145.5 km	Neuville-de-Poitou – Angers	J. Raas (HOL)	B. Hinault
Stage 6	Tuesday 3 July	238.5 km	Angers – Saint-Brieuc	J. Jacobs (BEL)	B. Hinault
Stage 7	Wednesday 4 July	158.2 km	St-Hilaire-du-Harcouët – Deauville	L. Van Vliet (HOL)	G. Knetemann
Stage 8	Thursday 5 July	90.2 km	Deauville – Le Havre (TTT)	Ti-Raleigh	B. Hinault
Stage 9	Friday 6 July	201.2 km	Amiens – Roubaix	L. Delcroix (BEL)	J. Zoetemelk
Stage 10	Saturday 7 July	122.2 km	Roubaix – Bruxelles (BEL)	J. Maas (HOL)	J. Zoetemelk
Stage 11	Sunday 8 July	33.4 km	Bruxelles (BEL) – Bruxelles (BEL) (TTT)	B. Hinault (FRA)	J. Zoetemelk
Stage 12	Monday 9 July	193 km	Rochefort (BEL) – Metz	C. Seznec (FRA)	J. Zoetemelk
Stage 13	Tuesday 10 July	202 km	Metz – Ballon d'Alsace	P.-R. Villemiane (FRA)	J. Zoetemelk
Stage 14	Thursday 12 July	248.2 km	Belfort – Evian	M. Demeyer (BEL)	J. Zoetemelk
Stage 15	Friday 13 July	54.2 km	Evian – Morzine-Avoriaz (TT)	B. Hinault (FRA)	B. Hinault
Stage 16	Saturday 14 July	201.3 km	Morzine – Les Menuires	L. Van Impe (BEL)	B. Hinault
Stage 17	Sunday 15 July	166.5 km	Moûtiers – L'Alpe-d'Huez	J. Agostinho (POR)	B. Hinault
Stage 18	Monday 16 July	118.5 km	L'Alpe-d'Huez – L'Alpe-d'Huez	J. Zoetemelk (HOL)	B. Hinault
Stage 19	Tuesday 17 July	162 km	Bourg-d'Oisans – Saint-Priest	D. Thurau (GER)	B. Hinault
Stage 20	Wednesday 18 July	239.6 km	Saint-Priest – Dijon	S. Parsani (ITA)	B. Hinault
Stage 21	Thursday 19 July	48.8 km	Dijon – Dijon (TT)	B. Hinault (FRA)	B. Hinault
Stage 22	Friday 20 July	189 km	Dijon – Auxerre	G. Knetemann (HOL)	B. Hinault
Stage 23	Saturday 21 July	205 km	Auxerre – Nogent-sur-Marne	B. Hinault (FRA)	B. Hinault
Stage 24	Sunday 22 July	180.3 km	Le Perreux – Paris	B. Hinault (FRA)	B. Hinault

On the final stage, Zoetemelk launched one last attack but Hinault, too strong for the Dutchman, responded. The result was this sumptuous tête-à-tête on the Champs-Élysées.

Bernard Hinault – a monster let loose

Zoetemelk gets a good deal, riding in Thurau's slipstream over the cobblestones of the Amiens-Roubaix stage. Delayed by a puncture, Hinault loses the jersey, but saves the Tour.

At 37, Joaquim Agostinho was still bursting with energy. He won at Alpe-d'Huez, which was crossed twice within 24 hours, and finished in third place in Paris.

A world champion used to doing well on the Tour: on the cinder track at Dijon, the Dutchman Gerrie Knetemann beats the Italian climber Giovanni Battaglin.

In an editorial column in the *Gazzetta dello Sport* yesterday morning, Bruno Raschi wrote this of Bernard Hinault: 'He is a rider who tries to copy Merckx faithfully, but doesn't have the ability to do so.' This from someone who'd love to be like the great Italian sports writer Malaparte, but does not have the talent. This radical pronounce-ment will come as a surprise to the Tour champion, who is in fact very careful not to imitate anyone, especially not the inimitable Merckx – even more so as it comes from the pen of a part-timer who disappeared from the press convoy before the race had even got past the halfway mark. This said, however, it's perfectly true that Bernard Hinault, winner of his second consecutive Tour before he has even celebrated his 25th birthday, can be identified with the great Belgian champion in some respects. Like Merckx, he is famous for his performance in the one-day classics and at the Grand Prix des Nations, as tough a test as any. Whether the abilities of the man from Brittany can be compared to Merckx or not is of little importance – we will have to wait until the end of his career and examine his list of achievements in order to do that. Until such time as the Tour champion reaches his peak and begins to display the unmistakeable signs of decline, all comparisons with past greats will remain highly questionable. The rash claims of a passing oracle who bends the truth to suit his own ends really have no basis in reality.

Let's limit ourselves to the actual facts and briefly remind ourselves of the main events in the Hinault-Zoetemelk battle. Hinault, 'the Badger', ultimately wore his opponent down,

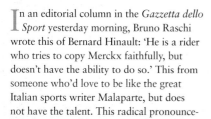

Joop Zoetemelk played his part as the challenger wherever possible, but especially on the mountains. However, Bernard Hinault (in the middle ground with Van Impe) was unassailable.

AN EXTRA GEAR

BELFORT: For the second day in a row, Joop Zoetemelk and Sven-Ake Nilsson have been using a hub armed with seven gears, instead of the more normal six. Why?

'It gives us an extra cog on the mountain stages,' explained the yellow jersey. 'It's also reassuring. It also means we can bring the gear ratios closer together so that, for example, we can use a 13, 14 and 15 in the valleys and a 19, 20, 21 or 22 on the mountains. It's much less tiring for the muscles.'

Zoetemelk, the Miko-Mercier team leader, is delighted with the results so far, and intends to carry on using this system until the end of the Tour.

12 July: Hinault used the mountain time trial to Avoriaz to swap his green jersey for a yellow one.

but not before proving himself his superior in all the key moments of the race. It was a complete victory over an opponent who made some very wise strategic decisions and who never gave up, as shown by his repeated attacks on the final day.

It was already clear from the outset that the riders who had ridden hard at the start of the season, and those who had emerged exhausted from the Giro d'Italia, would have little chance – very little – against the leader of the Renault-Gitane team. Hinault was the best athlete, and his meticulous preparation had all been geared towards his one over-riding goal – the *maillot jaune*. No one had any doubts, least of all Joop Zoetemelk, that the route of the 1979 Tour would leave no scope at all for heroics or admit any unmerited outcomes. This explains the Dutchman's

watchful, cautious attitude; he lay in wait, watching for his opportunity without forcing his hand, putting his hopes on the increasing fatigue of an opponent highly sensitive to displays of skill, inclined to grandiose gestures even, and therefore vulnerable to attack. A stroke of luck fell Zoetemelk's way as the riders entered the 'Hell of the North' on the ninth stage between Amiens and Roubaix, when Hinault punctured more than 100 kilometres (62 miles) from the finish. Everyone knows what happened next. Zoetemelk pushed on towards Roubaix accompanied by Thurau, Delcroix, Dierickx, Pollentier and Vanoverschelde – a high-quality bunch – while Hinault had to make a long, depressing and exhausting effort, chasing them down alone, like a lamb defying his slaughterer. The Frenchman ended up 3mins 26secs

behind and the *maillot jaune* landed on the shoulders of the Dutchman.

'That was the day when Hinault won the Tour. Or rather, the day he didn't lose it, as he would have done if he hadn't shown such extraordinary strength in adversity,' explained Jacques Anquetil at the finish-line on the Champs-Élysées. If he made sure he didn't lose the Tour at Roubaix, he made certain of winning it in the time trials. All things considered, Hinault proved himself to be more complete than last year, reaping the fruit of months of hard training. He's improved in the mountains above 1,500m (5,000ft), producing intense, sustained efforts at the high-altitude finishing lines and out-sprinting the sprinters in the group finishes. In this respect, Hinault is an imitator of Merckx – but it would be ridiculous to reproach him for it.

Zoetemelk, at last!

When Bernard Hinault won the first Tour de France Prologue of his career at Frankfurt in 1980, a sense of inevitability descended on the race. Merckx's years of domination had followed close on those of Anquetil. Now a new era of dominance had begun to suffocate the spirit of sporting tension. In the first individual time trial, he sped to victory, his Renault colours at home on the smooth asphalt of the Spa-Francorchamps racing circuit. His victory the next day, on the longest stage of the race in the rain and cold over the jarring cobblestones of North-East France vividly illustrated his prowess. It was 'inhuman' in Hinault's word's, over 'ce cochonnerie de pavé' – 'those swinish cobbles'. The predictable Ti-Raleigh victory in the team time trial temporarily deprived him of the yellow jersey, which passed to Belgium's Rudy Pevenage after a swashbuckling breakaway through driving rain on the stage from Frankfurt to Metz. Appalling conditions characterized the entire first half of the Tour, and tendonitis soon reached epidemic proportions. Bernard Hinault felt the first symptoms during the stage from Lille to Compiègne. The following day, he went through the pain barrier to stay with his Renault-Gitane team-mates during the team time trial.

The Ti-Raleigh team, strengthened by the arrival of Joop Zoetemelk, took the semi-stage and gained 1min 35secs on Renault-Gitane. But in the long time trial between the Gascon villages of Damazan and Laplume, he finally retrieved the yellow jersey, despite riding far below his usual level and achieving fifth place behind the winner, Zoetemelk. Twenty-four hours later, Hinault quit the race while still in yellow. The man who inherited the race lead, Joop Zoetemelk, initially refused to wear the yellow jersey out of respect for the champion.

Zoetemelk was a man with a remarkable Tour de France record. In his first Tour de France in 1970, he'd finished second behind Merckx. The following year, he did the same. Second again in '76, '78 and '79, fourth in '73 and '75 and fifth in 1972, his record was testimony to remarkable athletic gifts, and to a career that coincided first with Merckx and then with Hinault. In 1979, he had won the Vuelta a España; now, aged 33 and on his tenth Tour, Zoetemelk was in the driving seat. With the strongest team in the race to protect his lead, Zoetemelk added authority to his win by taking the final time trial around St-Étienne. He was the first Dutchman to win the jersey since Jan Janssen in 1968, his undespairing patience rewarded.

GENERAL CLASSIFICATION

1. **Joop Zoetemelk** (HOL) Ti-Raleigh, 3,842 km in 109h.19m.14s; Average speed: 35.068 kph
2. **Hennie Kuiper** (HOL) Peugeot-Esso, at 6m.55s.
3. **Raymond Martin** (FRA) Miko-Mercier, at 7m.56s.
4. Johan De Muynck (BEL) Splendor, at 12m.24s.
5. Joaquim Agostinho (POR) Puch, at 15m.37s.
6. Christian Seznec (FRA) Miko-Mercier, at 16m.16s.
7. Sven-Ake Nilsson (SWE) Miko-Mercier, at 16m.33s.
8. Ludo Peeters (BEL) Ijsboerke, at 20m.45s.
9. Pierre Bazzo (FRA) La Redoute, at 21m.3s.
10. Henk Lubberding (HOL) Ti-Raleigh, at 21m.10s.
11. Robert Alban (FRA) La Redoute, at 22m.41s.
12. Johan Van der Velde (HOL) Ti-Raleigh, at 25m.28s.
13. Claude Criquielion (BEL) Splendor, at 27m.43s.
14. Jostein Willmann (NOR) Puch, at 28m.4s.
15. Régis Ovion (FRA) Puch, at 29m.48s.
16. Lucien Van Impe (BEL) Marc-I.W.C., at 32m.55s.
17. Bernard Thévenet (FRA) Teka, at 32m.59s.
18. Ludo Loos (BEL) Marc-I.W.C., at 36m.36s.
19. Jo Maas (HOL) DAF Trucks, at 36m.44s.
20. Vicente Belda (SPA) Kelme, at 42m.42s.

67TH TOUR DE FRANCE, 22 STAGES – 3,842 KM

	STAGE			STAGE WINNER	YELLOW JERSEY
Prologue	Thursday 26 June	7.6 km	Frankfurt (GER) – Frankfurt (GER)	B. Hinault (FRA)	B. Hinault
Stage 1 (1)	Friday 27 June	133 km	Frankfurt (GER) – Wiesbaden (GER)	J. Raas (HOL)	B. Hinault
Stage 1 (2)	Friday 27 June	45.8 km	Wiesbaden (GER) – Frankfurt (GER) (TTT)	Ti-Raleigh	Ti-Raleigh
Stage 2	Saturday 28 June	276 km	Frankfurt (GER) – Metz	R. Pevenage (BEL)	Y. Bertin
Stage 3	Sunday 29 June	282.5 km	Metz – Liège (BEL)	H. Lubberding (HOL)	R. Pevenage
Stage 4	Monday 30 June	34.6 km	Spa-Francorchamps (BEL) – Spa-Francorchamps (BEL) (TT)	B. Hinault (FRA)	R. Pevenage
Stage 5	Tuesday 1 July	249.3 km	Liège (BEL) – Lille	B. Hinault (FRA)	R. Pevenage
Stage 6	Wednesday 2 July	215.8 km	Lille – Compiègne	J.-L. Gauthier (FRA)	R. Pevenage
Stage 7 (1)	Thursday 3 July	65 km	Compiègne – Beauvais (TTT)	Ti-Raleigh	R. Pevenage
Stage 7 (2)	Thursday 3 July	92 km	Beauvais – Rouen	J. Raas (HOL)	R. Pevenage
Stage 8	Friday 4 July	164.2 km	Flers – Saint-Malo	B. Oosterbosch (HOL)	R. Pevenage
Stage 9	Sunday 6 July	205.3 km	Saint-Malo – Nantes	J. Raas (HOL)	R. Pevenage
Stage 10	Monday 7 July	163 km	Rochefort-sur-Mer – Bordeaux	C. Priem (HOL)	R. Pevenage
Stage 11	Tuesday 8 July	51.8 km	Damazan – Laplume (TT)	J. Zoetemelk (HOL)	B. Hinault
Stage 12	Wednesday 9 July	194.1 km	Agen – Pau	G. Knetemann (HOL)	B. Hinault
Stage 13	Thursday 10 July	200.4 km	Pau – Luchon	R. Martin (FRA)	J. Zoetemelk
Stage 14	Friday 11 July	189.5 km	Lézignan-Corbières – Montpellier	L. Peeters (BEL)	J. Zoetemelk
Stage 15	Saturday 12 July	160 km	Montpellier – Martigues	B. Vallet (FRA)	J. Zoetemelk
Stage 16	Sunday 13 July	208.6 km	Trets – Pra-Loup	J. Deschoenmaecker (BEL)	J. Zoetemelk
Stage 17	Monday 14 July	242 km	Le Lautare – Morzine	M. Martínez (FRA)	J. Zoetemelk
Stage 18	Wednesday 16 July	198.8 km	Morzine – Prapoutel-les-Sept-Laux	L. Loos (BEL)	J. Zoetemelk
Stage 19	Thursday 17 July	139.7 km	Voreppe – Saint-Étienne	S. Kelly (IRL)	J. Zoetemelk
Stage 20	Friday 18 July	34.5 km	Saint-Étienne – Saint-Étienne (TT)	J. Zoetemelk (HOL)	J. Zoetemelk
Stage 21	Saturday 19 July	208 km	Auxerre – Fontenay-sous-Bois	S. Kelly (IRL)	J. Zoetemelk
Stage 22	Sunday 20 July	186.1 km	Fontenay-sous-Bois – Paris	P. Verschuere (HOL)	J. Zoetemelk

After carrying a knee injury for several days, Bernard Hinault abandoned the Tour at Pau in order not to ruin the rest of his season. The way was now clear for Joop Zoetemelk.

The day after Bernard Hinault abandoned Joop Zoetemelk refused to wear the yellow jersey, but from now on he would have little to trouble him on his way to Paris.

Joop Zoetemelk was a worthy successor to Bernard Hinault. He dominated the two time trials, at Gascogne and then at Saint-Étienne.

On the final podium, Kuiper stands next to Zoetemelk and the Frenchman Martin (left), best climber.

Hinault, the showman

A year after his forced abandon at Pau, Bernard Hinault returned to the Tour de France. He had made up for the Tour by winning the World Championship, and despite his setback the previous year, he arrived at the *Grand Départ* at Nice as the outstanding favourite. His rivals were all older than him: Zoetemelk, as ever, Agostinho, and the 1976 champion Van Impe. Jean-René Bernaudeau, two years Hinault's junior and now with Peugeot, led the new generation.

Hinault took the yellow jersey on day one, winning the Prologue by 7 seconds, a wide margin given the length of the stage. On stage 2, Ti-Raleigh won its sixth consecutive Tour de France team time trial, taking the yellow jersey for Gerrie Knetemann, and three days later made it seven consecutive team time trial wins. Hinault's rivalry with Bernaudeau didn't quite materialize, but an unexpected adversary emerged in Phil Anderson, an aggressive, 23-year-old Australian riding his first Tour. By matching Hinault in the Pyrenean stage, Anderson became the first Australian to wear the yellow jersey. By distancing Anderson by just 30 seconds in the Pau time trial the following day, Hinault won it back. It was sweet revenge for having had to abandon there the previous year, and it was the first of three time trial victories for Hinault at the 1981 Tour.

The second, at Mulhouse, nine days later, gave him a decisive lead even before the Tour reached the Alps. There, Hinault contented himself with a steady, controlling ride, since his margin was so great. On Alpe-d'Huez, the semi-professional Dutchman Peter Winnen gained eight seconds on Hinault. Lucien van Impe, second overall, was already more than nine minutes down; Robert Alban, the winner at Morzine and third overall, more than ten. Hinault's dominance earned him comparison with Anquetil. On the final climb of the final Alpine stage, Hinault led the Belgian Fons De Wolf and Bernaudeau for two-thirds of the climb. Then, with 4.5 kilometres (2.8 miles) to the stage finish, he swung round a hairpin bend, fixed them with the look of a man about to commit murder, and darted up the road. De Wolf offered no resistance; Bernaudeau gave chase, and had nearly reached the leader when Hinault accelerated again. It was pure Gallic panache. The time trial at Saint-Priest allowed Hinault to seal his third Tour de France victory. His 14min-34sec advantage over Van Impe represented the greatest margin of victory recorded between 1973 and 2003.

The formidable Belgian sprinter Freddy Maertens won his third green jersey with five stage victories, including the final stage on the Champs-Élysées.

GENERAL CLASSIFICATION

1. **Bernard Hinault** (FRA) Renault-Elf, 3,758 km in 96h.19m.38s; Average speed: 37.844 kph
2. **Lucien Van Impe** (BEL) Boston-Mavic, at 14m.34s.
3. **Robert Alban** (FRA) La Redoute, at 17m.4s.
4. Joop Zoetemelk (HOL) Ti-Raleigh, at 18m.21s.
5. Peter Winnen (HOL) Capri Sonne, at 20m.26s.
6. Jean-René Bernaudeau (FRA) Peugeot-Esso, at 23m.2s.
7. Johan De Muynck (BEL) Splendor, at 24m.25s.
8. Sven-Ake Nilsson (SWE) Splendor, at 24m.37s.
9. Claude Criquielion (BEL) Splendor, at 26m.18s.
10. Phil Anderson (AUS) Peugeot-Esso, at 27m.0s.
11. Alfons 'Fons' De Wolf (BEL) Vermeer-Thijs, at 28m.53s.
12. Johan Van der Velde (HOL) Ti-Raleigh, at 29m.46s.
13. Marcel Tinazzi (FRA) Sem, at 30m.3s.
14. Paul Wellens (BEL) Sunair, at 32m.9s.
15. Mariano Martinez (FRA) La Redoute, at 32m.16s.
16. Eddy Schepers (BEL) DAF Trucks at 33m.27s.
17. Raymond Martin (FRA) Miko-Mercier, at 33m.41s.
18. Michel Laurent (FRA) Peugeot-Esso, at 34m.41s.
19. Jean-François Rodriguez (FRA) Renault-Elf, at 38m.32s.
20. Graham Jones (GBR) Peugeot-Esso, at 41m.6s.

68TH TOUR DE FRANCE, 24 STAGES – 3,758 KM

			STAGE	STAGE WINNER	YELLOW JERSEY
Prologue	Thursday 25 June	5.9 km	Nice – Nice (TT)	B. Hinault (FRA)	B. Hinault
Stage 1	Friday 26 June	97 km	Nice – Nice	F. Maertens (BEL)	B. Hinault
Stage 2	Friday 26 June	40 km	Antibes – Nice (TTT)	Ti-Raleigh	G. Knetemann
Stage 3	Saturday 27 June	254 km	Nice – Martigues	J. Van de Velde (HOL)	G. Knetemann
Stage 4	Sunday 28 June	232 km	Martigues – Narbonne	F. Maertens (BEL)	G. Knetemann
Stage 5	Monday 29 June	77.2 km	Narbonne – Carcassonne (TTT)	Ti-Raleigh	G. Knetemann
Stage 6	Tuesday 30 June	117.5 km	Saint-Gaudens – Saint-Lary-Soulan	L. Van Impe (BEL)	P. Anderson
Stage 7	Wednesday 1 July	26.7 km	Nay – Pau (TT)	B. Hinault (FRA)	B. Hinault
Stage 8	Thursday 2 July	227 km	Pau – Bordeaux	U. Freuler (SUI)	B. Hinault
Stage 9	Friday 3 July	182 km	Rochefort-sur-Mer – Nantes	A. Wijnands (HOL)	B. Hinault
Stage 10	Sunday 5 July	196.5 km	Nantes – Le Mans	R. Martens (BEL)	B. Hinault
Stage 11	Monday 6 July	264 km	Le Mans – Aulnay-sous-Bois	A. Wijnands (HOL)	B. Hinault
Stage 12	Tuesday 7 July	246 km	Compiègne – Roubaix	D. Willems (BEL)	B. Hinault
Stage 13	Wednesday 8 July	107.3 km	Roubaix – Bruxelles (BEL)	F. Maertens (BEL)	B. Hinault
Stage 14	Wednesday 8 July	137.8 km	Bruxelles (BEL) – Zolder (BEL)	E. Planckaert (BEL)	B. Hinault
Stage 15	Thursday 9 July	157 km	Beringen (BEL) – Hasselt (BEL)	F. Maertens (BEL)	B. Hinault
Stage 16	Friday 10 July	38.5 km	Mulhouse – Mulhouse (TT)	B. Hinault (FRA)	B. Hinault
Stage 17	Saturday 11 July	231 km	Besançon – Thonon-les-Bains	S. Kelly (IRL)	B. Hinault
Stage 18	Sunday 12 July	199.5 km	Thonon-les-Bains – Morzine	R. Alban (FRA)	B. Hinault
Stage 19	Tuesday 14 July	230.5 km	Morzine – L'Alpe-d'Huez	P. Winnen (HOL)	B. Hinault
Stage 20	Wednesday 15 July	134 km	L'Alpe-d'Huez – Le Pleynet	B. Hinault (FRA)	B. Hinault
Stage 21	Thursday 16 July	117.5 km	Veurey – Saint-Priest	D. Willems (BEL)	B. Hinault
Stage 22	Friday 17 July	46.5 km	Saint-Priest – Saint-Priest (TT)	B. Hinault (FRA)	B. Hinault
Stage 23	Saturday 18 July	207 km	Auxerre – Fontenay-sous-Bois	J. Van de Velde (HOL)	B. Hinault
Stage 24	Sunday 19 July	186.8 km	Fontenay-sous-Bois – Paris	F. Maertens (BEL)	B. Hinault

A killing look. The public expected Hinault to show his class with
a great victory in the mountains. At Pleynet-Les-Sept-Laux,
he gave them what they wanted.

Coasting

At the *Grand Départ* from Basel, Switzerland, the 1982 Tour de France set a new record of 169 starters. Jacques Goddet, impressed by the excitement aroused by Italy's win in the FIFA World Cup, created a stir in the pages of *L'Équipe* by arguing for a return to national teams, every four years, for a globalized Tour. The idea was to bring together the traditional nations and the 'new' cycling countries – including Colombia and teams from Eastern Europe – in a race with stages in the USA, Great Britain, across Europe, and just nine in France (including, of course, the grand finale on the Champs-Élysées), all with the aim of bringing cycling to a wider, global audience.

At least one rider from beyond the heartlands of European cycling, Australia's Phil Anderson, made a huge impact on the 1982 Tour, winning the stage from Basel to Nancy and taking the yellow jersey for ten days. The Ti-Raleigh team was robbed of another team time trial victory when stage five, through the industrial north from Orchies to Fontaine-au-Pire, was cancelled due to striking steel-workers. Five days later, the team time trial from Lorient to Plumelec gave the Dutch formation its chance to add another to its formidable series of wins. Then, Ti-Raleigh's Gerrie Knetemann won the individual time trial at Valence-d'Agen, where Bernard Hinault made it a point of honour to retrieve the yellow jersey in the town where, four years earlier, he had led the riders' strike.

Hinault had won his second Giro d'Italia in June; tendonitis had robbed him of the Italian-French double at the 1980 Tour, and now he intended to rectify the matter; victory would also take him past Louison Bobet's milestone of three Tour wins. He pursued his goal with such singularity of purpose that the opposition barely made any impact. Hinault won two more time trials at Martigues and Saint-Priest, where he covered the last kilometre in precisely one minute: 60 kilometres an hour (37.2 mph)! Even more memorably, he triumphed for the second time in his career on the Champs-Élysées itself, three years after his memorable breakaway with Zoetemelk. This time he beat the whole peloton in a bunch sprint, proving his unquestionable superiority. Zoetemelk finished second for the sixth time, and two more Dutchmen, Johan Van der Velde and Peter Winnen, took the next two places, while, by winning his first green jersey, the great Irish classics rider Sean Kelly began to build another legend. Yet this had been the easiest of all Hinault's victories, and it was hard to see where the challenge to his supremacy could come from in the foreseeable future.

GENERAL CLASSIFICATION

1. **Bernard Hinault** (FRA) Renault-Elf, 3,507 km in 93h.43m.44s; Average speed: 37.458 kph
2. **Joop Zoetemelk** (HOL) Coop-Mercier, at 6m.21s.
3. **Johan Van der Velde** (HOL) Ti-Raleigh, at 8m.59s.
4. Peter Winnen (HOL) Capri-Sonne, at 9m.24s.
5. Phil Anderson (AUS) Peugeot-Shell, at 12m.16s.
6. Beat Breu (SUI) Cilo-Aufina, at 13m.21s.
7. Daniel Willems (BEL) Sunair, at 15m.33s.
8. Raymond Martin (FRA) Coop-Mercier, at 15m.35s.
9. Hennie Kuiper (HOL) Daf, at 17m.1s.
10. Alberto Fernández (SPA) Teka, at 17m.19s.
11. Robert Alban (FRA) La Redoute, at 17m.21s.
12. Bernard Vallet (FRA) La Redoute, at 19m.52s.
13. Jean-René Bernaudeau (FRA) Peugeot-Shell, at 20m.2s.
14. Sven-Ake Nilsson (SWE), Wolber, at 25m.11s.
15. Sean Kelly (IRL) Sem, at 27m.17s.
16. Charly Berard (FRA) Renault-Elf, at 31m.35s.
17. Kim Andersen (DEN) Coop-Mercier, at 31m.57s.
18. Jacques Michaud (FRA) Coop-Mercier, at 32m.21s.
19. Théo De Rooy (HOL) Capri-Sonne, at 32m.37s.
20. Pascal Simon (FRA) Peugeot-Shell, at 34m.22m.

69TH TOUR DE FRANCE, 21 STAGES – 3,507 KM

			STAGE	STAGE WINNER	YELLOW JERSEY
Prologue	Friday 2 July	7.4 km	Basel (SUI) – Basel (TT)	B. Hinault (FRA)	B. Hinault
Stage 1	Saturday 3 July	207 km	Shupfart-Möhlin (SUI) – Shupfart-Möhlin	L. Peeters (BEL)	L. Peeters
Stage 2	Sunday 4 July	250 km	Basel (SUI) – Nancy	P. Anderson (AUS)	P. Anderson
Stage 3	Monday 5 July	134 km	Nancy – Longwy	D. Willems (BEL)	P. Anderson
Stage 4	Tuesday 6 July	219 km	Beauraing (BEL) – Mouscron (BEL)	G. Knetemann (HOL)	P. Anderson
Stage 5	Wednesday 7 July	73 km	Orchies – Fontaine-au-Pire (TTT)	Stage cancelled	P. Anderson
Stage 6	Thursday 8 July	233 km	Lille – Lille	J. Raas (HOL)	P. Anderson
Stage 7	Saturday 10 July	234.5 km	Cancale – Concarneau	P. Verschuere (BEL)	P. Anderson
Stage 8	Sunday 11 July	200.8 km	Concarneau – Châteaulin	F. Hoste (BEL)	P. Anderson
Stage 9 (1)	Monday 12 July	69 km	Lorient – Plumelec (TTT)	Ti-Raleigh	P. Anderson
Stage 9 (2)	Monday 12 July	138.5 km	Plumelec – Nantes	S. Mutter (SUI)	P. Anderson
Stage 10	Tuesday 13 July	147.2 km	Saintes – Bordeaux	P.-R. Villemiane (FRA)	P. Anderson
Stage 11	Wednesday 14 July	57.3 km	Valence-d'Agen – Valence-d'Agen (TT)	G. Knetemann (HOL)	B. Hinault
Stage 12	Thursday 15 July	249 km	Fleurance – Pau	S. Kelly (IRL)	B. Hinault
Stage 13	Friday 16 July	122 km	Pau – Saint-Lary-Soulan	B. Breu (SUI)	B. Hinault
Stage 14	Sunday 18 July	32.5 km	Martigues – Martigues (TT)	B. Hinault (FRA)	B. Hinault
Stage 15	Monday 19 July	208 km	Manosque – Orcières-Merlette	P. Simon (FRA)	B. Hinault
Stage 16	Tuesday 20 July	123 km	Orcières-Merlette – L'Alpe d'Huez	B. Breu (SUI)	B. Hinault
Stage 17	Wednesday 21 July	251 km	Bourg-d'Oisans – Morzine-Avoriaz	P. Winnen (HOL)	B. Hinault
Stage 18	Thursday 22 July	233 km	Morzine – Saint-Priest	H. V. Houwelingen (HOL)	B. Hinault
Stage 19	Friday 23 July	48 km	Saint-Priest – Saint-Priest (TT)	B. Hinault (FRA)	B. Hinault
Stage 20	Saturday 24 July	161 km	Sens – Aulnay-sous-Bois	D. Willems (BEL)	B. Hinault
Stage 21	Sunday 25 July	186.8 km	Fontenay-sous-Bois – Paris	B. Hinault (FRA)	B. Hinault

Bernard Hinault coasted to victory in the fourth and easiest of his Tour de France victories, spending ten days in the yellow jersey.

The Tour is part of the times. Above, the peloton waits for angry farmers to lift the blockades holding up the stage start at Orcières-Merlette.

Industrial action meant the team time trial between Orchies and Fontaine-au-Pire had to be cancelled with several teams already on the road.

The Ti-Raleigh team left a permanent mark in the annals of cycling. Peeters, Lubberding, Raas and Hoste were also highly successful as individual riders.

Fignon leads the next wave

Jacques Goddet's grandiose plans for a globalized Tour de France with teams from cycling's furthest-flung nations and stages around the planet amounted, not to nothing, but to an invitation to Colombia's national team. Some even considered the Colombian leader, Alfonso Flórez, the winner of the 1980 Tour de l'Avenir, the amateur cousin of the Tour de France, a dark horse, and the 1983 Tour favourites were all dark horses; Hinault had announced that the tendonitis he had suffered winning the Tour of Spain in May would prevent him from starting.

Éric Vanderaerden, a semi-professional from Belgium, won the Prologue at Fontenay-sous-Bois. After stage three and the first real breakaway of the race, Kim Andersen became the first Dane in Tour history to wear the yellow jersey. Scotland's Robert Millar, riding his first Tour, won the first mountain stage in the Pyrenees, but he had fallen on stage three, losing over 15 minutes, and posed no threat in the general classification – it was a shame, for he was the strongest rider in the Pyrenees. It was Millar's Peugeot team-mate Pascal Simon who assumed the race lead after finishing third at Pau. The next day, the complexion of the race was transformed when Simon fell and dislocated his shoulder, finishing the stage in great pain. He soldiered on for six days, as the Tour crossed the Massif Central; his pains were heroic, but in vain, and his fate was decided on the mountain time trial up the Puy de Dôme. Spanish and Colombian climbers squabbled over the stage win, with the real race taking place behind them; Pascal Simon struggled pitifully up the steepest sections and lost 3mins 10secs of his 4min-14sec lead over Laurent Fignon. He kept first place overall, but it was now only a matter of time before he was overhauled; unable to put on the yellow jersey without intense pain, he was permitted to dispense with the post-stage jersey presentation.

Simon's ordeal ended on stage seventeen on the road to Alpe-d'Huez. The Dutchman Peter Winnen, who had won on the Alpe in 1981, took the stage win just ahead of Bernaudeau. Two minutes behind them, riding alongside Van Impe and the little-known Spaniard Pedro Delgado, a cerebral 23-year-old from Paris named Laurent Fignon climbed into the yellow jersey. Fignon had finished 15th in the Giro d'Italia in June, and nobody had named him among the favourites for the Tour. Yet by winning the final time trial, Fignon proved himself a worthy winner of the Tour de France at his first attempt.

GENERAL CLASSIFICATION

1. **Laurent Fignon** (FRA) Renault-Git, 3,860 km in 107h.31m.58s; Average speed: 36.230 kph
2. **Angel Arroyo** (SPA) Reynolds, at 4m.4s.
3. **Peter Winnen** (HOL) Ti-Raleigh, at 4m.9s.
4. Lucien Van Impe (BEL) Metauromobili, at 4m.16s.
5. Robert Alban (FRA) La Redoute, at 7m.53s.
6. Jean-René Bernaudeau (FRA) Wolber, at 8m.59s.
7. Sean Kelly (IRL) Sem, at 12m.9s.
8. Marc Madiot (FRA) Renault-Git, at 14m.55s.
9. Phil Anderson (AUS) Peugeot-Shell, at 16m.56s.
10. Henk Lubberding (HOL) Ti-Raleigh, at 18m.55s.
11. Joaquim Agostinho (POR) Sem, at 19m. ;
12. Jonathan Boyer (USA) Sem, at 19m.57s.
13. Stephen Roche (IRL) Peugeot-Shell, at 21m.30s.
14. Robert Millar (GBR) Peugeot-Shell, at 23m.29s.
15. Pedro Delgado (SPA) Reynolds, at 25m.44s.
16. Edgar Corredor Alvarez (COL) Colombia Varta, at 26m.8s.
17. Patrocinio Jiménez (COL) Colombia Varta, at 28m.5s.
18. Claude Criquielion (BEL) Splendor, at 33m.29s.
19. Jacques Michaud (FRA) Coop Mercier, at 35m.44s.
20. Christian Seznec (FRA) Wolber, at 39m.49s.

70TH TOUR DE FRANCE, 22 STAGES – 3,860 KM

			STAGE	STAGE WINNER	YELLOW JERSEY
Prologue	Friday 1 July	5.5 km	Fontenay-sous-Bois – Fontenay-s.-B.(TT)	É. Vanderaerden (BEL)	É. Vanderaerden
Stage 1	Saturday 2 July	163 km	Nogent-sur-Marne – Créteil	F. Pirard (HOL)	É. Vanderaerden
Stage 2	Sunday 3 July	100 km	Soissons – Fontaine-au-Pire (TTT)	Coop-Mercier	J.-L. Gauthier
Stage 3	Monday 4 July	152 km	Valenciennes – Roubaix	R. Matthijs (BEL)	K. Andersen
Stage 4	Tuesday 5 July	300 km	Roubaix – Le Havre	S. Demierre (SUI)	K. Andersen
Stage 5	Wednesday 6 July	257 km	Le Havre – Le Mans	D. Gaigne (FRA)	K. Andersen
Stage 6	Thursday 7 July	58.5 km	Châteaubriant – Nantes (TT)	B. Oosterbosch (HOL)	K. Andersen
Stage 7	Friday 8 July	216 km	Nantes – Île d'Oléron	R. Magrini (ITA)	K. Andersen
Stage 8	Saturday 9 July	222 km	La Rochelle – Bordeaux	B. Oosterbosch (HOL)	K. Andersen
Stage 9	Sunday 10 July	207 km	Bordeaux – Pau	P. Chevallier (FRA)	S. Kelly
Stage 10	Monday 11 July	201 km	Pau – Bagnères-de-Luchon	R. Millar (GBR)	P. Simon
Stage 11	Tuesday 12 July	177 km	Bagnères-de-Luchon – Fleurance	R. Clere (FRA)	P. Simon
Stage 12	Wednesday 13 July	261 km	Fleurance – Roquefort-sur-Soulzon	K. Andersen (DEN)	P. Simon
Stage 13	Thursday 14 July	210 km	Roquefort-sur-Soulzon – Aurillac	H. Lubberding (HOL)	P. Simon
Stage 14	Friday 15 July	149 km	Aurillac – Issoire	P. Le Bigaut (FRA)	P. Simon
Stage 15	Saturday 16 July	15.6 km	Clermont-Ferrand – Puy de Dôme (TT)	A. Arroyo (SPA)	P. Simon
Stage 16	Sunday 17 July	144.5 km	Issoire – Saint-Étienne	M. Laurent (FRA)	P. Simon
Stage 17	Monday 18 July	223 km	La Tour-du-Pin – L'Alpe-d'Huez	P. Winnen (HOL)	L. Fignon
Stage 18	Wednesday 20 July	247 km	Bourg-d'Oisans – Morzine	J. Michaud (FRA)	L. Fignon
Stage 19	Thursday 21 July	15 km	Morzine – Avoriaz (TT)	L. Van Impe (BEL)	L. Fignon
Stage 20	Friday 22 July	291 km	Morzine – Dijon	P. Leleu (FRA)	L. Fignon
Stage 21	Saturday 23 July	50 km	Dijon – Dijon (TT)	L. Fignon (FRA)	L. Fignon
Stage 22	Sunday 24 July	195 km	Alfortville – Paris	G. Glaus (SUI)	L. Fignon

A new star appeared in the firmament of international cycling.
A strong personality, too, older than his 23 years.

SIMON'S VIA DOLOROSA

Pascal Simon, wearer of the *maillot jaune* since Bagnères-de-Luchon, abandoned the Tour de France yesterday. Eight other Tour leaders have been victims of the same misfortune. The first was in 1929 when Victor Fontan, having been awarded the jersey at Luchon, dropped out after a fall the very next day. In 1937, Sylvère Maes withdrew from the race in Bordeaux as an expression of dissent at a decision by the officials to sanction him by a mere ten seconds. Magni withdrew in the same fashion in 1950 when Bartali caused his whole team to drop out after he had been pushed and threatened on the Col d'Aspin. The following year, Van Est fell into a ravine on the Soulor. In 1965, it was Van de Kerckhove's turn, withdrawing in the ninth stage due to illness. In more recent times, we will certainly never forget Luis Ocaña's dramatic fall on the Col de Mente. The Spanish rider was leading at the time and had dropped Merckx by eight minutes! In 1978, Pollentier dropped out of the Tour at the Alpe-d'Huez following his notorious fraud in the drugs test. Finally, three years ago, Bernard Hinault, suffering from tendonitis of the knee, left the Tour one evening in July.

This village near Arpajon-sur-Cère (above) was one of the 'stations of the cross' for Pascal Simon, following his fall 50 km (31 miles) from Fleurance. For five days he tried to hide his suffering – each day finished was victory in itself. France was won over by the courage of its hero (left). But it was all too much. On the slopes of the Chapelle Blanche, heading towards the Alpe-d'Huez, Simon dismounted once and for all (below and left).

Laurent Fignon exercises his power in the mountains.

Although he failed to win a mountain stage, there was no doubting Fignon's climbing credentials.

Fignon silenced his critics by winning the last time trial from Dijon to Prenois in style.

A *maillot jaune* in every way

By one of those coincidences to which life is so partial, we found ourselves yesterday morning following that wide avenue in Créteil where the valiant Fritz Pirard won the first stage of the 1983 Tour de France on Saturday 2 July. A Sunday morning calm stilled the air, a nightingale was singing in the shrubbery and two whitewashed slogans were still legible on the tarmac: 'Allez Fignon!' The authors of these encouraging words knew that their favourite had worn the jersey of the Union Sportive de Créteil for several years, but they could surely never have imagined what was to come. They were undoubtedly in attendance on the Champs-Élysées yesterday, their voices blending in with the multitude of cheers that greeted the bespectacled champion. For Laurent Fignon, who started the Tour cautiously, then became more conspicuous as the action unfolded, has been acclaimed by the public as a fully-fledged champion, worthy to rank alongside his illustrious predecessors. From the crossing of the Alps, where he held the climbers in check and rebuffed the concerted attack launched by Winnen and Arroyo, he won the public's sympathy, although sympathy is obviously only a small part of the esteem in which a sporting champion is held. Panache must also play a major part in ensuring fame (there must be a good reason why Fausto Coppi is more admired than Nicolas Frantz, although both won the Tour twice, and why Rik Van Looy is more popular than several others with a nonetheless admirable *palmarès*).

On Saturday morning, the day of the last time trial from Dijon to Prenois, there was still some doubt over the verdict to be passed on this otherwise extremely credible young man, full of potential for the future. He was certainly going to win the Tour on his first attempt, like Coppi in 1949, Koblet in 1951, Anquetil in 1957, Merckx in 1969 and Hinault in 1978. Noble company indeed, but what about the less glorious names of those who had won the Tour without a single stage victory to their credit? In the past, it used to be said that a great champion had to win in the Alps; later, it was acknowledged that if he could not win one of the major mountain stages, a true champion had to assert his individual superiority in the time trials.

This, therefore, is why Laurent Fignon's performance on the uneven, scorching circuit at Dijon was so important. He crowned his fair and honest overall victory with a demonstration of strength that silenced all attempts to play down his win. An average performance by the yellow jersey wearer would have brought back the recent memories of Bernard Hinault, prevented from starting by tendonitis, and Pascal Simon, who dropped out after his fall, and Laurent Fignon's reputation would have suffered as a result. Instead of this, however, he was able to take control of the situation with the authority that comes from a perfect balance of body and spirit. He has established himself not as a champion of circumstance, but as the very best among all those who competed against him, none of whom can claim that they were able to raise themselves up to Fignon's level.

A new champion mounted the podium on the Champs-Élysées, where Laurent Fignon, receiving his trophy from Mme. Edwige Avice, the Minister for Sport (left), discovered glory.

Fignon, by a generation

The 1984 Tour de France was presented as a generational clash between Bernard Hinault, now 29, and Laurent Fignon, still only 23. At the end of 1983, Bernard Hinault had left his inspirational *directeur sportif* Cyrille Guimard and joined a new team, La Vie Claire, owned by the flamboyant Bernard Tapie, who introduced big business values and wages in line with other global sports to the world of cycling. Back at Guimard's Renault-Elf team, Laurent Fignon had finished second in the Giro d'Italia, losing the race lead on the final stage, and came into the Tour having just won the French national championship. But it was Hinault who struck first, winning the Prologue three seconds ahead of Fignon. Guimard's riders made a deep impression on the race, first through Marc Madiot's win on stage two, second with victory in the team time trial the following day, and then when Vincent Barteau took the *maillot jaune* by finishing second on stage four, 17 minutes ahead of the peloton; his advantage raised the possibility of a win after the fashion of Roger Walkowiak in 1956.

Guimard skilfully exploited the situation, keeping Fignon in the wings and sending Pascal Jules, Pascal Poisson and Pierre-Henri Menthéour out to win stages. Barteau showed enough strength to hold on to the yellow jersey until the Alps. The contest for overall victory, meanwhile, had begun in earnest with the long time trial on stage seven. The route should have favoured Hinault, but it was Fignon who took the stage, 49 seconds ahead of him. In the Alps, Fignon won three stages out of five: the mountain time trial at La Ruchère, 25 seconds ahead of the Colombian Lucho Herrera; La Plagne, convincingly and alone; and Crans-Montana. As in 1983, he assumed the race lead on the slopes of Alpe-d'Huez. Hinault had launched a series of long-range solo attacks to unsettle his young rival, but the stronger Fignon confidently bided his time and overwhelmed his opponent, despite an irresistible climb by Lucho Herrera, who, on the Tour's most mythical ascent, achieved the first stage win by an amateur in Tour de France history.

The transfer of power felt definitive; Fignon, six years Hinault's junior, took his second Tour win. Hinault finally won favour with the French public, not, as he saw it, by losing the Tour, but by showing bravery even in defeat. In third place, Greg Lemond became the first American to climb the podium in Paris, where he also met his compatriot, Marianne Martin, the winner of the first women's Tour.

GENERAL CLASSIFICATION

1. **Laurent Fignon** (FRA) Renault-Elf, 4,021 km in 112h.3m.40s; Average speed: 34.906 kph
2. **Bernard Hinault** (FRA) La Vie Claire, at 10m.32s.
3. **Greg Lemond** (USA) Panasonic, at 11m.46s.
4. Robert Millar (GBR) Peugeot-Shell, at 14m.42s.
5. Sean Kelly (IRL) Skil, at 16m.35s.
6. Angel Arroyo (SPA) Reynolds, at 19m.22s.
7. Pascal Simon (FRA) Peugeot-Shell, at 21m.17s.
8. Pedro Muñoz (SPA) Teka, at 26m.17s.
9. Claude Criquielion (BEL) Splendor, at 29m.12s.
10. Phil Anderson (AUS) Panasonic, at 29m.16s.
11. Niki Ruttimann (SUI) La Vie Claire, at 30m.58s.
12. Rafael Acevedo (COL) Colombia-Varta, at 33m.32s.
13. Jean-Marie Grezet (SUI) Skil, at 33m.41s.
14. Éric Caritoux (FRA) Skil, at 36m.28s.
15. Patrocinio Jiménez (COL) Teka, at 37m.49s.
16. Gerard Veldscholten (HOL) Panasonic, at 41m.54s.
17. Michel Laurent (FRA) Coop-Hoonved, at 44m.33s.
18. Alfonso Flores (COL) Colombia-Varta, at 45m.33s.
19. Antonio Agudelo (COL) Colombia-Varta, at 49m.25s.
20. Bernard Gavillet (SUI) Cilo-Aufina, at 51m.2s.

71ST TOUR DE FRANCE, 23 STAGES - 4,021 KM

			STAGE	STAGE WINNER	YELLOW JERSEY
Prologue	Friday 29 June	5.4 km	Montreuil – Noisy-le-Sec (TT)	B. Hinault (FRA)	B. Hinault
Stage 1	Saturday 30 June	148.5 km	Bondy – Saint-Denis	F. Hoste (BEL)	L. Peeters
Stage 2	Sunday 1 July	249 km	Bobigny – Louvroil	M. Madiot (FRA)	J. Hanegraaf
Stage 3	Monday 2 July	51 km	Louvroil – Valenciennes (TTT)	Renault-Elf	J. Hanegraaf
Stage 4	Monday 2 July	83 km	Valenciennes – Béthune	F. Van Den Haute (BEL)	A. Van Der Poel
Stage 5	Tuesday 3 July	207 km	Béthune – Cergy-Pontoise	P. Ferreira (POR)	V. Barteau
Stage 6	Wednesday 4 July	202 km	Cergy-Pontoise – Alençon	F. Hoste (BEL)	V. Barteau
Stage 7	Thursday 5 July	67 km	Alençon – Le Mans (TT)	L. Fignon (FRA)	V. Barteau
Stage 8	Friday 6 July	192 km	Le Mans – Nantes	P. Jules (FRA)	V. Barteau
Stage 9	Saturday 7 July	338 km	Nantes – Bordeaux	J. Raas (HOL)	V. Barteau
Stage 10	Sunday 8 July	198 km	Langon – Pau	E. Vanderaerden (BEL)	V. Barteau
Stage 11	Monday 9 July	226.5 km	Pau – Guzet-Neige	R. Millar (GBR)	V. Barteau
Stage 12	Tuesday 10 July	111 km	Saint-Girons – Blagnac	P. Poisson (FRA)	V. Barteau
Stage 13	Wednesday 11 July	220.5 km	Blagnac – Rodez	P. -H. Menthéour (FRA)	V. Barteau
Stage 14	Thursday 12 July	227.5 km	Rodez – Domaine du Rouret	A. De Wolf (BEL)	V. Barteau
Stage 15	Friday 13 July	241.5 km	Domaine du Rouret – Grenoble	F. Vichot (FRA)	V. Barteau
Stage 16	Sunday 15 July	22 km	Les Échelles – La Ruchère-en-Chartreuse (TT)	L. Fignon (FRA)	V. Barteau
Stage 17	Monday 16 July	151 km	Grenoble – L'Alpe-d'Huez	L. Herrera (COL)	L. Fignon
Stage 18	Tuesday 17 July	185.5 km	Bourg-d'Oisans – La Plagne	L. Fignon (FRA)	L. Fignon
Stage 19	Wednesday 18 July	186 km	La Plagne – Morzine	A. Arroyo (SPA)	L. Fignon
Stage 20	Thursday 19 July	140.5 km	Morzine – Crans-Montana (SUI)	L. Fignon (FRA)	L. Fignon
Stage 21	Friday 20 July	320.5 km	Crans-Montana (SUI) – Villefranche-en-Beaujolais	F. Hoste (BEL)	L. Fignon
Stage 22	Saturday 21 July	51 km	Villié-Morgon – Villefranche-en-Beaujolais (TT)	L. Fignon (FRA)	L. Fignon
Stage 23	Sunday 22 July	196.5 km	Pantin – Paris	E. Vanderaerden (BEL)	L. Fignon

Above: A clash of generations between Bernard Hinault and Laurent Fignon, who took possession of the yellow jersey at Alpe-d'Huez, witnessed by the climbers Lucho Herrera (left), Beat Breu (centre) and Robert Millar (behind). Below: Hinault gave it everything he had, but Fignon left him for dead at Alpe-d'Huez.

When a true champion dominates the Tour

Do we love the Tour for itself, for the competition it gives rise to? Is a good Tour de France one that is full of closely fought confrontations that leave the final result hanging in the air until the very end? Or is a good Tour one that has become the plunder of an extraordinary individual, a cycling maestro, one of those champions who can forge legends? In short, does the victory of a great champion stamp a Tour with greatness?

The 1984 Tour will be considered an excellent vintage, in my opinion, and we can truly declare that the six letters F, I, G, N, O and N will be inscribed into the history, not just of the Tour, but of cycling itself. And despite achieving, in the end, utter domina-tion, this headstrong young man avoided removing all interest from the race. He left the field open to the point that, eight days before the finish, on the rest day at Grenoble, he'd still not been universally acknowledged as the race favourite. As, all around him, riders hit significant peaks and troughs, Fignon showed not the slightest hint of weakness. The most remarkable thing about this young man is the robust health he showed at the end of a particularly tough route. His physical freshness is in perfect harmony with his state of mind, his clarity of judgement and his responsible attitude – everything about him displays balance and reason. He also managed to keep his resources intact. His performance in Saturday's time trial among the vineyards of Beaujolais, in the face of so many highly motivated and fiercely combative opponents, was both outstanding and convincing.

Fignon's reputation has been vigorously reinforced by his battle with his former team leader, the man who until now carried the entire reputation of modern cycling on his shoulders – Bernard Hinault. Fignon's vic-tory in 1983 was won in Hinault's absence and after Pascal Simon's accident, which made it difficult to ascertain his true level with any precision. A reputation needs to be confirmed. However, the domination shown by this year's *maillot jaune*, and his faultless mastery of the decisive week (just think: first at La Ruchère, second at the Alpe-d'Huez, first at La Plagne, in the lead group at Morzine, first at Crans-Montana and then first at Villefranche!) helped him to achieve a series of stage wins that has almost certainly never been accomplished before in the his-tory of the Tour – anoraks, to the archives! All with such *savoir-faire* and style. And with such ease: not forced, but gliding – especially in the face of such strong resist-ance that it almost felt like a war was being waged. Without Hinault, without the combative attitude of a man frantically trying to rediscover the formula for his past superiority, Fignon would have been nothing more than a sporting tyrant, reigning over insignificant opponents and quickly reducing them to submission. We'd have tired of his dominance and the Tour would have lost its substance. But Hinault, admirable in the humanity of his reactions, grittily determined not to accept defeat, or rather refusing to no longer be Number One, fought hard. He tried to introduce disorder, to make it a trial of strength. It was deeply moving, indeed heart-rending, when we understood that these impromptu, tactically irrational attacks had something derisory about them, all very quickly dissolving into nothing. Hinault was rewarded by the respect that he earned from such a brave performance. I am sure that his sensitive nature, which his sardonic veneer only heightens, will have been deeply touched by an article pubished in *L'Équipe* entitled, 'And now, let us love him'.

Although rivals, Hinault and Fignon, former team-mates, had great respect for each other. In the 1984 Tour, the fight was fair and honest.

Barteau, the Portuguese rider Ferreira and Le Guilloux gained a massive lead in the stage from Béthune to Cergy-Pontoise: 17 minutes!

The Renault team, led by Barteau and Madiot, reach maximum speed in the team time trial at Valenciennes.

Laurent Fignon riding ahead of the pack. His dominance did not stop him from giving it everything he had.

Pascal Jules finished first at Nantes. In Cyrille Guimard's Renault-Elf team, everyone had their chance!

On the lowest ramps of Alpe-d'Huez, Lucho Herrera attacked. On the other side of the planet the Colombian climber instantly became a hero.

Into the Pantheon of the Greats

Hinault's absence in 1983 had cleared the way for Fignon's first Tour win. In May 1985, Fignon underwent an operation on an inflamed Achilles tendon, forfeiting the chance to defend his title and leaving Hinault, written off the previous year as a geriatric, as the outstanding favourite. Hinault had won the Giro d'Italia in June, and was aiming for his second Italian-French double. The 1985 Tour de France started in Hinault's beloved Brittany, at the tiny village of Plumelec, and Hinault duly won his fifth Tour Prologue before home crowds. Three days later his team, La Vie Claire, proved its strength by winning the team time trial at Fougères. Hinault won back the yellow jersey at the long individual time trial between Sarrebourg and Strasbourg, which he won by the considerable margin of 2mins 20secs over Ireland's Stephen Roche. On the first alpine stage, Hinault attacked so strongly that only Herrera could go with him. The two men shared the lead for most of the day, and when Herrera kicked for the stage win Hinault didn't fight him. The following day, Herrera spent another eight hours at the front, accompanying his countryman Fabio Parra to another Colombian stage win. The day after the second time trial, in which Hinault finished second, Herrera again sped off the front irresistibly. On the final descent into Saint-Étienne, he fell, opening a deep cut over his left eye. He remounted, and won the stage with rivulets of blood covering his face. Over two minutes later, Hinault's group was accelerating to sprinting speed when there was a touch of wheels and they all fell. Hinault spent minutes on the ground, while the medical team and also Jacques Goddet, the Tour's Director, attended him. Eventually, he crawled over the line and was taken to hospital, where he encountered Herrera. Hinault had a fracture at the base of the nose, and it obstructed his breathing for the rest of the Tour, preventing him from building on his lead. In the Pyrenees, as Hinault struggled up the Aubisque, La Vie Claire's *directeur sportif*, Paul Koechli, had to give orders to Hinault's American team-mate Greg Lemond not to co-operate with the stage leader Stephen Roche. The atmosphere was tense and Lemond declared on American radio: 'Koechli made me lose the Tour on the day I could have won it!'

Hinault emerged from the Pyrenees with his race lead intact, and although Greg Lemond won the time trial around the Lac de Vassivière, the first American stage win in the Tour, he gained only five seconds on Hinault. Aged 30, Bernard Hinault achieved his second Giro-Tour double and claimed his fifth Tour de France, equalling Anquetil and Merckx.

GENERAL CLASSIFICATION

1. **Bernard Hinault** (FRA) La Vie Claire, 4,109 km in 113h.24m.23s; Average speed: 36.232 kph
2. **Greg Lemond** (USA) La Vie Claire, at 1m.42s.
3. **Stephen Roche** (IRL) La Redoute, at 4m.29s.
4. Sean Kelly (IRL) Skil, at 6m.26s.
5. Phil Anderson (AUS) Panasonic, at 7m.44s.
6. Pedro Delgado (SPA) Seat-Orbea at 11m.53s.
7. Lucho Herrera (COL) Café de Colombia, at 12m.53s.
8. Fabio Parra (COL) Café de Colombia, at 13m.35s.
9. Eduardo Chozas (SPA) Reynolds, at 13m.56s.
10. Steve Bauer (CAN) La Vie Claire, at 14m.57s.
11. Robert Millar (GBR) Peugeot-Shell, at 15m.10s.
12. Joop Zoetemelk (HOL) Kwantum at 15m.24s.
13. Niki Ruttimann (SUI) La Vie Claire, at 16m.2s.
14. Eddy Schepers (BEL) Lotto, at 16m.13s.
15. Peter Winnen (HOL) Panasonic, at 17m.35s.
16. Robert Forest (FRA) Peugeot-Shell, at 17m.51s.
17. Celestino Prieto (SPA) Reynolds, at 19m.48s.
18. Claude Criquielion (BEL) Hitachi, at 21m.12s.
19. Alvaro Pino (SPA) Zor, at 21m.35s.
20. Pascal Simon (FRA) Peugeot-Shell, at 23m.30s.

72ND TOUR DE FRANCE, 22 STAGES – 4,109 KM

			STAGE	STAGE WINNER	YELLOW JERSEY
Prologue	Friday 28 June	6.8 km	Plumelec – Plumelec (TT)	B. Hinault (FRA)	B. Hinault
Stage 1	Saturday 29 June	256 km	Vannes – Lanester	R. Matthijs (BEL)	E. Vanderaerden
Stage 2	Sunday 30 June	242 km	Lorient – Vitré	R. Matthijs (BEL)	E. Vanderaerden
Stage 3	Monday 1 July	73 km	Vitré – Fougères (TTT)	La Vie Claire	E. Vanderaerden
Stage 4	Tuesday 2 July	239 km	Fougères – Pont-Audemer	G. Solleveld (HOL)	K. Andersen
Stage 5	Wednesday 3 July	224 km	Neufchâtel-en-Bray – Roubaix	H. Manders (HOL)	K. Andersen
Stage 6	Thursday 4 July	221.5 km	Roubaix – Reims	F. Castaing (FRA)	K. Andersen
Stage 7	Friday 5 July	217.5 km	Reims – Nancy	L. Wijnants (BEL)	K. Andersen
Stage 8	Saturday 6 July	75 km	Sarrebourg – Strasbourg (TT)	B. Hinault (FRA)	B. Hinault
Stage 9	Sunday 7 July	173.5 km	Strasbourg – Épinal	M. Ducrot (HOL)	B. Hinault
Stage 10	Monday 8 July	204.5 km	Épinal – Pontarlier	J. -V. Pedersen (DEN)	B. Hinault
Stage 11	Tuesday 9 July	195 km	Pontarlier – Morzine-Avoriaz	L. Herrera (COL)	B. Hinault
Stage 12	Wednesday 10 July	269 km	Morzine – Lans-en-Vercors	F. Parra (COL)	B. Hinault
Stage 13	Thursday 11 July	31.8 km	Villard-de-Lans – Villard-de-Lans (TT)	E. Vanderaerden (BEL)	B. Hinault
Stage 14	Saturday 13 July	179 km	Autrans – Saint-Étienne	L. Herrera (COL)	B. Hinault
Stage 15	Sunday 14 July	237.5 km	Saint-Étienne – Aurillac	E. Chozas (ESP)	B. Hinault
Stage 16	Monday 15 July	247 km	Aurillac – Toulouse	F. Vichot (FRA)	B. Hinault
Stage 17	Tuesday 16 July	209.5 km	Toulouse – Luz-Ardiden	P. Delgado (SPA)	B. Hinault
Stage 18 (1)	Wednesday 17 July	52.5 km	Luz-Saint-Sauveur – Col d'Aubisque	S. Roche (IRL)	B. Hinault
Stage 18 (2)	Wednesday 17 July	83.5 km	Laruns – Pau	R. Simon (FRA)	B. Hinault
Stage 19	Thursday 18 July	203 km	Pau-Bordeaux	E. Vanderaerden (BEL)	B. Hinault
Stage 20	Friday 19 July	225 km	Montpon-Ménestérol – Limoges	J. Lammerts (HOL)	B. Hinault
Stage 21	Saturday 20 July	47.5 km	Lac de Vassivière – Lac de Vassivière (TT)	G. Lemond (USA)	B. Hinault
Stage 22	Sunday 21 July	196 km	Orléans – Paris	R. Matthijs (BEL)	B. Hinault

Above: Bernard Hinault states his intent at the Prologue in Plumelec, to the great joy of the Brittany public. He's already heading for his fifth Tour victory.

Bernard Hinault, concussed after his fall at Cours Fauriel. With injuries to the face and scalp, he nevertheless continued the Tour.

A visit from Hinault's mother to the podium on the Champs-Élysées; La Vie Claire's one-two left Lemond with a distinctly equivocal look.

A young Miguel Induráin, aged just 21, made his debut in the Tour. He finished 100th in the Prologue and abandoned on stage four.

Hand in hand

The 1986 Tour de France offered Bernard Hinault the opportunity to win a record sixth Tour. But as he started the Prologue in Boulogne, a promise hung over him, one he'd made to his young co-leader Greg Lemond a year before, after Lemond had put his ambitions on hold for Hinault's benefit. His judgement overcome by the euphoria of his fifth victory, Hinault had made a show of generosity that might have seemed sincere at the time: 'In '86,' he had told the American, 'the Tour will be for you. I'll be there to help you.'

Still, the moment the race reached the Pyrenees, Hinault launched a stinging attack. The Spanish climber Pedro Delgado, not yet a contender for the overall classification, took the stage win, but Hinault's prize was bigger: a 4min-36sec advantage over his team-mate Lemond.

The following day, Hinault increased the pressure by attacking on the descent from the Tourmalet and had 2mins 20secs over Lemond as he crossed the Aspin, but he was caught and dropped before the final climb to Superbagnères, where Greg Lemond won the stage and beat Hinault by precisely 4mins 36secs – the time he had lost the previous day. Hinault emerged from the Pyrenees in yellow, but the atmosphere in La Vie Claire was tense, despite the efforts of the media-conscious Bernard Tapie to play down the discord.

In the Alps, Lemond took the yellow jersey from his team-mate on stage seventeen, the Col du Granon, but these were uneasy times for the American. He knew all about Hinault's opportunism and recognized in him a sense of anticipation. Sure enough, on the descent from the Galibier, Hinault broke away alone, throwing down the final, decisive gauntlet. Lemond joined the Canadian Steve Bauer and bridged the gap, and when Bauer was dropped, Hinault and Lemond were alone, and over the Croix-de-Fer and on the climb up to Alpe-d'Huez history was made. Hinault rode on the front, dragging the American along in his slipstream and leaving the opposition far behind them. As they approached the finish line at Alpe-d'Huez, Hinault paused to join hands with his team-mate, before Lemond, knowing the Tour was his, pushed the Frenchman ahead to take the stage. Hinault won the final time trial, gaining 25 seconds on Lemond, and in Paris, both men achieved something special. Greg Lemond became the first American to win the Tour de France, while Bernard Hinault ended his Tour de France career on a high note.

GENERAL CLASSIFICATION

1. **Greg Lemond** (USA) La Vie Claire, 4,084 km in 110h.35m.19s; Average speed: 37.020 kph
2. **Bernard Hinault** (FRA) La Vie Claire, at 3m.10s.
3. Urs Zimmermann (SUI) Carrera, at 10m.54s.
4. Andrew Hampsten (USA) La Vie Claire, at 18m.44s.
5. Claude Criquielion (BEL) Hitachi, at 24m.36s.
6. Ronan Pensec (FRA) Peugeot-Shell, at 25m.59s.
7. Niki Ruttimann (SUI) La Vie Claire, at 30m.52s.
8. Alvaro Pino (SPA) Zor B.H., at 33m.
9. Steven Rooks (HOL) P.D.M., at 33m.22s.
10. Yvon Madiot (FRA) Système U, at 33m.27s.
11. Samuel Cabrera (COL) Reynolds, at 35m.28s.
12. Jean-François Bernard (FRA) La Vie Claire, at 35m.45s.
13. Pascal Simon (FRA) Peugeot-Shell, at 37m.44s.
14. Eduardo Chozas (SPA) Teka, at 38m.48s.
15. Reynel Montoya (COL) Postobon, at 45m.36s.
16. Charly Mottet (FRA) Système U, at 45m.58s.
17. Thierry Claveyrolat (FRA) R.M.O., at 46m .
18. Marino Lejarreta (SPA) Seat-Orbea, at 49m.9s.
19. Jean-Claude Bagot (FRA) Fagor, at 51m.38s.
20. Eric Caritoux (FRA) Fagor, at 52m.39s.

73RD TOUR DE FRANCE, 23 STAGES - 4,084 KM

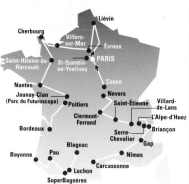

			STAGE	STAGE WINNER	YELLOW JERSEY
Prologue	Friday 4 July	4.6 km	Boulogne-Billancourt – Boulogne-Billancourt	T. Marie (FRA)	T. Marie
Stage 1	Saturday 5 July	85 km	Nanterre – Sceaux	P. Verschuere (BEL)	A. Stieda
Stage 2	Saturday 5 July	56 km	Meudon – St-Quentin-en-Yvelines (TTT)	Système U	T. Marie
Stage 3	Sunday 6 July	214 km	Levallois-Perret – Liévin	D. Phinney (USA)	T. Marie
Stage 4	Monday 7 July	243 km	Liévin – Évreux	P. Ruiz-Cabestany (SPA)	D. Gaigne
Stage 5	Tuesday 8 July	124.5 km	Évreux – Villers-sur-Mer	J. Van Der Velde (HOL)	J. Van Der Velde
Stage 6	Wednesday 9 July	200 km	Villers-sur-Mer – Cherbourg	G. Bontempi (ITA)	J. Van Der Velde
Stage 7	Thursday 10 July	201 km	Cherbourg – St-Hilaire-du-Harcouët	L. Peeters (BEL)	J. Pedersen
Stage 8	Friday 11 July	204 km	St-Hilaire-du-Harcouët – Nantes	E. Planckaert (BEL)	J. Pedersen
Stage 9	Saturday 12 July	61.5 km	Nantes – Nantes (TT)	B. Hinault (FRA)	J. Pedersen
Stage 10	Sunday 13 July	183 km	Nantes – Futuroscope	A. José Sarrapio (SPA)	J. Pedersen
Stage 11	Monday 14 July	258.5 km	Poitiers – Bordeaux	R. Dhaenens (BEL)	J. Pedersen
Stage 12	Tuesday 15 July	217.5 km	Bayonne – Pau	P. Delgado (SPA)	B. Hinault
Stage 13	Wednesday 16 July	186 km	Pau – Superbagnères	G. Lemond (USA)	B. Hinault
Stage 14	Thursday 17 July	154 km	Luchon – Blagnac	N. Ruttimann (SUI)	B. Hinault
Stage 15	Friday 18 July	225.5 km	Carcassonne – Nîmes	F. Hoste (BEL)	B. Hinault
Stage 16	Saturday 19 July	246.5 km	Nîmes – Gap	J.-F. Bernard (FRA)	B. Hinault
Stage 17	Sunday 20 July	179.5 km	Gap – Le Granon	E. Chozas (SPA)	G. Lemond
Stage 18	Monday 21 July	162.5 km	Briançon – L'Alpe-d'Huez	B. Hinault (FRA)	G. Lemond
Stage 19	Wednesday 23 July	179.5 km	Villard-de-Lans – St-Étienne	J. Gorospe (SPA)	G. Lemond
Stage 20	Thursday 24 July	58 km	St-Étienne – St-Étienne (TT)	B. Hinault (FRA)	G. Lemond
Stage 21	Friday 25 July	190 km	St-Étienne – Puy de Dôme	E. Maechler (SUI)	G. Lemond
Stage 22	Saturday 26 July	194 km	Clermont-Ferrand – Nevers	G. Bontempi (ITA)	G. Lemond
Stage 23	Sunday 27 July	255 km	Cosne-sur-Loire – Paris	G. Bontempi (ITA)	G. Lemond

Greg Lemond and Bernard Hinault recorded for posterity. At Alpe-d'Huez,
the American clinched the Tour, and the Frenchman achieved a glorious end
to his career. The two leaders of La Vie Claire finished hand in hand.

Roche paints the Emerald Isle yellow

By 1 July 1987, as the riders prepared to start the Prologue of the Tour de France in a still-divided Berlin, Bernard Hinault had retired, Greg Lemond was recovering from gunshot wounds sustained in a serious hunting accident and Laurent Fignon was suffering from a catastrophic loss of form. Cycling had entered a period of transition, and the Tour de France was more open than ever.

No Tour had ever had so many stages (25), and none had seen so many different riders wear the yellow jersey; eight, an all-time record, with nine changes of leader. The powerful Dutch *rouleur* Jelle Nijdam won the Prologue, before Poland's Lech Piasecki became the first East European to lead the Tour. Switzerland's Erich Maechler took over from him, but the real race hierarchy was established during the incredibly long Saumur-Futuroscope time trial (87.5 km/54 miles). Ireland's Stephen Roche won it, but France's Charly Mottet took the yellow jersey, and wore it through the Pyrenees, after swapping it briefly with by his Système U team-mate Martial Gayant.

The mountain time trial on Mont Ventoux was eagerly awaited, and the French time trial specialist Jean-François Bernard relegated the brilliant Colombian climber Herrera to second place by nearly two minutes. Bernard took the yellow jersey, and looked likely to wear it all the way to Paris until he punctured the next day on the road to Villard-de-Lans, and was dropped by the leading group. Delgado won the stage but the race lead passed to Stephen Roche. The following day, Delgado used the climb up to Alpe-d'Huez to wrestle the yellow jersey from the Irishman. A day later, on the climb to La Plagne, the suspense reached fever pitch. Laurent Fignon launched a formidable attack, suddenly striding up the general classification. In his wake, Roche and Delgado rode themselves to the verge of collapse, and at the finish the Irishman had to be given oxygen. But he recovered fast enough to leave the Spaniard behind the next day on the descent from Joux-Plane and clawed back 18 seconds. At the start of the the final time trial, the yellow jersey was just 21 seconds away. Jean-François Bernard won the stage convincingly, but the real race was behind him. Roche, second, ended the day with the race lead by the tiny margin of 40 seconds. He had won Ireland's first Tour victory in a year in which he was simply irrepressible, winning the Tours of Italy and France, and then, on 6 September, the World Championship. Only Eddy Merckx, in 1974, had achieved a similar feat.

GENERAL CLASSIFICATION

1. **Stephen Roche** (IRL) Carrera, 4,331 km in 115h.27m.42s; Average speed: 36.644 kph
2. **Pedro Delgado** (SPA) P.D.M., at 40s.
3. **Jean-François Bernard** (FRA) Toshiba, at 2m.13s.
4. Charly Mottet (FRA) Système U, at 6m.40s.
5. Lucho Herrera (COL) Café de Colombia, at 9m.32s.
6. Fabio Parra (COL) Café de Colombia, at 16m.53s.
7. Laurent Fignon (FRA) Système U, at 18m.24s.
8. Anselmo Fuerte Abelenda (SPA) B.H., at 18m.33s.
9. Raúl Alcalá (MEX) 7 Eleven, at 21m.49s.
10. Marino Lejarreta (SPA) Caja Rural, at 26m.13s.
11. Claude Criquielion (BEL) Hitachi, at 30m.32s.
12. Federico Echave (SPA) B.H., at 31m.6s.
13. Martin Alonso Ramirez (COL) Café de Colombia, at 36m.55s.
14. Gerhard Zadrobilek (AUT) Brianzoli, at 40m.35s.
15. Luciano Loro (ITA) Del Tongo, at 43m.52s.
16. Andrew Hampsten (USA) 7 Eleven, at 44m.7s.
17. Jean-René Bernaudeau (FRA) Fagor, at 47m.16s.
18. Rafael Acevedo (COL) Café de Colombia, at 50m.33s.
19. Robert Millar (GBR) Panasonic, at 50m.47s.
20. Denis Roux (FRA) Z Peugeot, at 52m.13s.

74TH TOUR DE FRANCE, 25 STAGES – 4,331 KM

			STAGE	STAGE WINNER	YELLOW JERSEY
Prologue	Wednesday 1 July	6.1 km	Berlin (GER) – Berlin (GER) (TT)	J. Nijdam (HOL)	J. Nijdam
Stage 1	Thursday 2 July	105.5 km	Berlin (GER) – Berlin (GER)	N. Verhoeven (HOL)	L. Piasecki
Stage 2	Thursday 2 July	40 km	Berlin (GER) – Berlin (GER) (TTT)	Carrera	L. Piasecki
Stage 3	Saturday 4 July	219 km	Karlsruhe (GER) – Stuttgart (GER)	A. Da Silva Mura (POR)	E. Maechler
Stage 4	Sunday 5 July	79 km	Stuttgart (GER) – Pforzheim (GER)	H. Frison (BEL)	E. Maechler
Stage 5	Sunday 5 July	112.5 km	Pforzheim (GER) – Strasbourg	M. Sergeant (BEL)	E. Maechler
Stage 6	Monday 6 July	169 km	Strasbourg – Épinal	C. Lavainne (FRA)	E. Maechler
Stage 7	Tuesday 7 July	211 km	Épinal – Troyes	M.-J. Dominguez (SPA)	E. Maechler
Stage 8	Wednesday 8 July	205.5 km	Troyes – Épinay-sous-Sénart	J.-P. Van Poppel (HOL)	E. Maechler
Stage 9	Thursday 9 July	260 km	Orléans – Renazé	A. Van Der Poel (HOL)	E. Maechler
Stage 10	Friday 10 July	87.5 km	Saumur – Futuroscope (TT)	S. Roche (IRL)	C. Mottet
Stage 11	Saturday 11 July	255 km	Futuroscope – Chaumeil	M. Gayant (FRA)	M. Gayant
Stage 12	Sunday 12 July	228 km	Brive – Bordeaux	D. Phinney (USA)	M. Gayant
Stage 13	Monday 13 July	219 km	Bayonne – Pau	E. Breukink (HOL)	C. Mottet
Stage 14	Tuesday 14 July	166 km	Pau – Luz-Ardiden	D.-O. Lauritzen (NOR)	C. Mottet
Stage 15	Wednesday 15 July	164 km	Tarbes – Blagnac	R. Golz (GER)	C. Mottet
Stage 16	Thursday 16 July	216.5 km	Blagnac – Millau	R. Clere (FRA)	C. Mottet
Stage 17	Friday 17 July	239 km	Millau – Avignon	J.-P. Van Poppel (HOL)	C. Mottet
Stage 18	Sunday 19 July	36.5 km	Carpentras – Mont Ventoux (TT)	J.-F. Bernard (FRA)	J.-F. Bernard
Stage 19	Monday 20 July	185 km	Valréas – Villard-de-Lans	P. Delgado (SPA)	S. Roche
Stage 20	Tuesday 21 July	201 km	Villard-de-Lans – L'Alpe-d'Huez	F. Echave (SPA)	P. Delgado
Stage 21	Wednesday 22 July	185.5 km	Bourg-d'Oisans – La Plagne	L. Fignon (FRA)	P. Delgado
Stage 22	Thursday 23 July	186 km	La Plagne – Morzine	E. Chozas (SPA)	P. Delgado
Stage 23	Friday 24 July	224.5 km	Saint-Julien-en-Genevois – Dijon	R. Clere (FRA)	P. Delgado
Stage 24	Saturday 25 July	38 km	Dijon – Dijon (TT)	J.-F. Bernard (FRA)	S. Roche
Stage 25	Sunday 26 July	192 km	Créteil – Paris	J. Pierce (USA)	S. Roche

Roche captured the yellow jersey the day after Bernard's brilliant performance on the Ventoux, but soon lost it to Delgado on the road to Alpe-d'Huez.

Berlin: At the foot of the wall still separating Eastern from Western Europe, Colombian Lucho Herrera poses for the photographers.

Jean-François Bernard's victory in the Mont Ventoux time trial promised much, but proved to be the summit of his career.

The Delgado affair

The only past winner to start the 1988 Tour de France was Laurent Fignon, although his form was wildly inconsistent. Much was expected of Lucho Herrera, a past winner of the Vuelta a España, and the American Andy Hampsten, the winner of the Giro d'Italia in June, but the hot favourite was Pedro Delgado. Second to Stephen Roche in 1987, Delgado had already won a three-week tour in 1985, when he took the Vuelta a España, and he had finished seventh in the recent Giro d'Italia without even trying to win it. He was ready to challenge for the Tour de France.

Stage one left Steven Bauer in the yellow jersey, the second Canadian to wear it after Alex Stieda in 1986. Another English-speaker, Sean Yates, won the first individual time trial on stage six. But as so often, it was the stage finishing on Alpe-d'Huez that transformed the general classification. A Spaniard (Delgado), a Colombian (Fabio Parra) and two Dutchmen (team-mates Steven Rooks and Gert-Jan Theunisse) led up the final climb. Parra attacked repeatedly but was baulked by the race officials and camera crews on motorbikes, and lost impetus. Then Rooks attacked, finding a way through and riding off to victory. Delgado came in 17 seconds later to take the yellow jersey. He strengthened his position the following day by winning the second individual time trial. Through the Pyrenees, his favourite terrain, he consolidated his lead, until, on the eve of the Bordeaux stage, it was revealed on French TV that Delgado, by now the certain winner, had tested positive in an anti-doping test. Two days later, at Clermont-Ferrand, the counter-analysis confirmed the test result. But it transpired that although the offending substance, probenecid, was included on the International Olympic Committee's list of prohibited substances, cycling's world governing body, the Union Cycliste Internationale (UCI), had not updated its own list. According to the letter of the law, Delgado had broken no regulation, even though probenecid could be used as a masking agent for anabolic steroids. On the other hand, Delgado had been tested at least ten times during the Tour, and traces of probenicid had shown up just once. He escaped unpunished, despite the fact that another rider who failed an anti-doping test, the Dutchman Theunisse, was awarded a 10-minute time penalty. Pedro Delgado continued on his way to Paris, mostly receiving warm public support as he went, and a jubilant Spain celebrated the latest successor to Federico Bahamontes and Luis Ocaña.

GENERAL CLASSIFICATION

1. **Pedro Delgado** (SPA), Reynolds, 3,286 km in 84h.27m.53s; Average speed: 38.909 kph
2. **Steven Rooks** (HOL) P.D.M., at 7m.13s.
3. **Fabio Parra** (COL) Kelme, at 9m.58s.
4. Steve Bauer (CAN) Weinmann-La Suisse, at 12m.15s.
5. Eric Boyer (FRA) Système U, at 14m.4s.
6. Lucho Herrera (COL) Café de Columbia, at 14m.36s.
7. Ronan Pensec (FRA) Z-Peugeot, at 16m.52s.
8. Alvaro Pino (SPA) B.H., at 18m.36s.
9. Peter Winnen (HOL) Panasonic, at 19m.12s.
10. Denis Roux (FRA) Z-Peugeot, at 20m.8s.
11. Gert-Jan Theunisse (HOL) P.D.M., at 22m.46s.
12. Erik Breukink (HOL) Panansonic, at 23m.6s.
13. Laudelino Cubino Gonzalez (SPA) B.H., at 23m.46s.
14. Claude Criquielion (BEL) Hitachi, at 24m.32s.
15. Andrew Hampsten (USA) 7-Eleven, at 26m.
16. Marino Lejarreta (SPA) Caja Rural, at 26m.36s.
17. Pascal Simon (FRA) Système U, at 28m.39s.
18. Éric Caritoux (FRA) Kas, at 29m.4s.
19. Jérôme Simon (FRA) Z-Peugeot, at 28m.39s.
20. Raúl Alcalá (MEX) 7 Eleven, at 31m.14s.

75TH TOUR DE FRANCE, 22 STAGES – 3,286 KM

		STAGE		STAGE WINNER	YELLOW JERSEY
Prologue	Sunday 3 July	6 km	Pornichet – La Baule (TT)	G. Bontempi (ITA)	G. Bontempi
Stage 1	Monday 4 July	91.5 km	Pontchâteau – Machecoul	S. Bauer (CAN)	S. Bauer
Stage 2	Monday 4 July	48 km	La-Haye-Fouassière – Ancenis (TTT)	Panasonic	T. Van Vliet
Stage 3	Tuesday 5 July	213.5 km	Nantes – Le Mans	J.-P. Van Poppel (HOL)	T. Van Vliet
Stage 4	Wednesday 6 July	158 km	Le Mans – Évreux	A. Da Silva Mura (POR)	T. Van Vliet
Stage 5	Thursday 7 July	147.5 km	Neufchatel-en-Bray – Liévin	J. Nijdam (HOL)	H. Lubberding
Stage 6	Friday 8 July	52 km	Liévin – Wasquehal (TT)	S. Yates (GBR)	J. Nijdam
Stage 7	Saturday 9 July	225.5 km	Wasquehal – Reims	V. Tebaldi (ITA)	J. Nijdam
Stage 8	Sunday 10 July	219 km	Reims – Nancy	R. Golz (GER)	S. Bauer
Stage 9	Monday 11 July	160.5 km	Nancy – Strasbourg	J. Simon (FRA)	S. Bauer
Stage 10	Tuesday 12 July	149.5 km	Belfort – Besançon	J.-P. Van Poppel (HOL)	S. Bauer
Stage 11	Wednesday 13 July	232 km	Besançon – Morzine	F. Parra (COL)	S. Bauer
Stage 12	Thursday 14 July	227 km	Morzine – L'Alpe-d'Huez	S. Rooks (HOL)	P. Delgado
Stage 13	Friday 15 July	38 km	Grenoble – Villard-de-Lans (TT)	P. Delgado (SPA)	P. Delgado
Stage 14	Sunday 17 July	163 km	Blagnac – Guzet-Neige	M. Ghirotto (ITA)	P. Delgado
Stage 15	Monday 18 July	187.5 km	Saint-Girons – Luz-Ardiden	L. Cubino Gonzalez (SPA)	P. Delgado
Stage 16	Tuesday 19 July	38 km	Luz-Ardiden – Pau	A. Van der Poel (HOL)	P. Delgado
Stage 17	Tuesday 19 July	210 km	Pau – Bordeaux	J.-P. Van Poppel (HOL)	P. Delgado
Stage 18	Wednesday 20 July	93.5 km	Ruelle-sur-Touvre – Limoges	G. Bugno (ITA)	P. Delgado
Stage 19	Thursday 21 July	188 km	Limoges – Puy de Dôme	J. Weltz (DEN)	P. Delgado
Stage 20	Friday 22 July	223.5 km	Clermont-Ferrand – Chalon-sur-Saône	T. Marie (FRA)	P. Delgado
Stage 21	Saturday 23 July	46 km	Santenay – Santenay (TT)	J. Martinez Oliver (SPA)	P. Delgado
Stage 22	Sunday 24 July	172.5 km	Nemours – Paris	J.-P. Van Poppel (HOL)	P. Delgado

Despite distractions, Pedro Delgado remained focused on winning the Tour de France to the end. But 'L'affaire Delgado' tarnished his victory and foreshadowed the doping scandals to come.

In spite of everything, the Spanish flag flies over Paris: Pedro Delgado and his Reynolds team-mates take a lap of honour on the Champs-Élysées. He succeeded Federico Bahamontes and Luis Ocaña.

Theunisse and Delgado elbow-to-elbow. There was anti-doping incoherence as the Dutchman was penalized and the Spaniard was cleared.

Eight seconds

In Spain, the 1988 champion Pedro Delgado was a hero. In the offices of the Société du Tour de France, the race organizer, he was a villain. Jean-Marie Leblanc, a former Tour rider and now one of the key Tour officials, wrote an article for *L'Équipe* entitled 'The Rules of the Game', arguing: 'Sport comes first… may the Tour de France no longer have to tolerate those who don't give it the respect it deserves.'

Delgado himself played the part of the slighted champion determined to clear his name. But his Tour went very wrong before it had even begun. He signed in 20 minutes before his Prologue start time, gave a TV interview and disappeared into the crowd to sign autographs. But his start time had come and gone when, mortified, he finally appeared and set off, 2mins 40 secs late. Incredibly, his time for the loop around the city of Luxembourg was only 14 seconds slower than the winner, but his title defence started with a self-imposed handicap of nearly three minutes. The next day, Delgado suffered a catastrophic loss of form. His team nursed him to the finish-line; after just two days, the reigning champion was 9mins 57secs behind the race leader, Acacio Da Silva, a Portuguese rider brought up in Luxembourg and riding on his home streets.

From then on, Delgado cut his losses with style, finishing second in the first long time trial, gaining 27 seconds on Lemond and Fignon on the road to Cauterets (his young teammate Miguel Induráin won the stage), and three and a half minutes on Fignon, now the race leader, on stage ten to Superbagnères. On stage 15, a time trial to Orcières, he gained eight seconds on Lemond, who had now replaced Fignon in yellow, and nearly a minute on Fignon. By the end of the stage, Fignon lay 40 seconds behind Lemond, and Delgado lay just 2 mins 28 secs behind Lemond, his place on the podium assured.

No more than seven seconds had separated Lemond and Fignon between Rennes (stage five) and Gap (stage 14). By the final time trial between Versailles and Paris, Fignon was back in yellow, just 50 seconds ahead of Lemond. The American, stretched aerodynamically over innovative handlebar extensions, set a new speed record for a Tour de France time trial, yet by the time Fignon, riding last, reached the Place de la Concorde, the Tour was still his by two seconds. The ride up the Champs-Élysées brought the most unforgettable of turnarounds. Greg Lemond won the Tour de France by the narrowest margin ever: eight seconds.

GENERAL CLASSIFICATION

1. **Greg Lemond** (USA) ADR-Agrigel, 4,021 km in 87h.38m.35s; Average speed: 37.487 kph
2. **Laurent Fignon** (FRA) Super U, at 8s.
3. **Pedro Delgado** (SPA) Reynolds, at 3m.34s.
4. Gert-Jan Theunisse (HOL) P.D.M., at 7m.30s.
5. Marino Lejarreta (SPA) Caja Rural, at 9m.39s.
6. Charly Mottet (FRA) RMO, at 10m.6s.
7. Steven Rooks (HOL) P.D.M., at 11m.10s.
8. Raúl Alcalá (MEX) P.D.M., at 14m.21s.
9. Sean Kelly (IRL) P.D.M., at 18m.25s.
10. Robert Millar (GBR) Z-Peugeot, at 18m.46s.
11. Gianni Bugno (ITA) Château-Dax, at 24m.12s.
12. Éric Caritoux (FRA) RMO, at 28m.14s.
13. Pascal Simon (FRA) Super U, at 28m.28s.
14. Bruno Cornillet (FRA) Z-Peugeot, at 28m.31s.
15. Steve Bauer (CAN) Helvetia, at 31m.16s.
16. Alvaro Pino (SPA) B.H., at 31m.17s.
17. Miguel Induráin (SPA) Reynolds, at 31m.21s.
18. Jérôme Simon (FRA) Z-Peugeot, at 34m.10s.
19. Lucho Herrera (COL) Café de Colombia, at 36m.15s.
20. Alberto Camargo (COL) Café de Colombia, at 37m.13s.

76TH TOUR DE FRANCE, 21 STAGES – 4,021 KM

			STAGE	STAGE WINNER	YELLOW JERSEY
Prologue	Saturday 1 July	7.8 km	Luxembourg – Luxembourg (TT)	E. Breukink (HOL)	E. Breukink
Stage 1	Sunday 2 July	135.5 km	Luxembourg – Luxembourg	A. Da Silva (POR)	A. Da Silva
Stage 2	Sunday 2 July	46 km	Luxembourg – Luxembourg (TTT)	Super U	A. Da Silva
Stage 3	Monday 3 July	241 km	Luxembourg – Spa-Francorchamps (BEL)	R. Alcalá (MEX)	A. Da Silva
Stage 4	Tuesday 4 July	255 km	Liège (BEL) – Wasquehal	J. Nijdam (HOL)	A. Da Silva
Stage 5	Thursday 6 July	73 km	Dinard – Rennes (TT)	G. Lemond (USA)	G. Lemond
Stage 6	Friday 7 July	259 km	Rennes – Futuroscope	J. Pelier (FRA)	G. Lemond
Stage 7	Saturday 8 July	258.5 km	Poitiers – Bordeaux	E. De Wilde (BEL)	G. Lemond
Stage 8	Sunday 9 July	157 km	La Bastide d'Armagnac – Pau	M. Earley (IRL)	G. Lemond
Stage 9	Monday 10 July	147 km	Pau – Cauterets	M. Induráin (SPA)	G. Lemond
Stage 10	Tuesday 11 July	136 km	Cauterets – Luchon-Superbagnères	R. Millar (GBR)	L. Fignon
Stage 11	Wednesday 12 July	158.5 km	Luchon – Blagnac	M. Hermans (HOL)	L. Fignon
Stage 12	Thursday 13 July	242 km	Toulouse – Montpellier	V. Tebaldi (ITA)	L. Fignon
Stage 13	Friday 14 July	179 km	Montpellier – Marseille	V. Barteau (FRA)	L. Fignon
Stage 14	Saturday 15 July	240 km	Marseille – Gap	J. Nijdam (HOL)	L. Fignon
Stage 15	Sunday 16 July	39 km	Gap – Orcières-Merlette (TT)	S. Rooks (HOL)	G. Lemond
Stage 16	Tuesday 18 July	175 km	Gap – Briançon	P. Richard (SUI)	G. Lemond
Stage 17	Wednesday 19 July	165 km	Briançon – L'Alpe-d'Huez	G. -J. Theunisse (HOL)	L. Fignon
Stage 18	Thursday 20 July	91.5 km	Bourg-d'Oisans – Villard-de-Lans	L. Fignon (FRA)	L. Fignon
Stage 19	Friday 21 July	125 km	Villard-de-Lans – Aix-les-Bains	G. Lemond (USA)	L. Fignon
Stage 20	Saturday 22 July	130 km	Aix-les-Bains – L'Isle-d'Abeau	G. Fidanza (ITA)	L. Fignon
Stage 21	Sunday 23 July	24.5 km	Versailles – Paris (TT)	G. Lemond (USA)	G. Lemond

On the banks of the Seine, Lemond, stretched aerodynamically over his tri-bars, rapidly reduced the 50-second deficit separating him from Fignon.

Tour tennis

The 1989 Tour will be remembered for the exciting hand-to-hand struggle between Greg Lemond and Laurent Fignon. Each wore the yellow jersey at least eight times, but it was the American who had the last word, emerging victorious in the Tour by eight slender seconds – the narrowest winning margin ever recorded. Before the sensational dénouement on the final day of the Tour, Fignon and Lemond had been locked in combat, the margin between them never exceeding 53 seconds. There were eight key points during this duel:

DEUCE in the Luxembourg prologue when Fignon (2nd) and Lemond (4th) finished with the same time.

ADVANTAGE FIGNON after the second Luxembourg stage, a team time trial won by Fignon's Super U, which gave him a 51-second lead over Lemond.

ADVANTAGE LEMOND after the fifth stage (Dinard-Rennes), an individual time trial won by Lemond who took the race leader's yellow jersey with a five-second margin.

ADVANTAGE FIGNON at the end of the tenth stage, which finished at the top of Superbagnères and put Fignon back in yellow with a seven-second lead.

ADVANTAGE LEMOND, who retook the lead after the 15th stage, the Orcières-Merlette time trial, with a margin of 40 seconds.

ADVANTAGE LEMOND at the finish in Briançon (stage 16), he increased his lead to 53 seconds.

ADVANTAGE FIGNON he regained the yellow jersey on the Alpe-d'Huez (stage 17) with a margin of 26 seconds.

ADVANTAGE FIGNON after stage ten at Villard-de-Lans, increasing his lead by 24 seconds to a total of 50 seconds.

LAST WORD TO LEMOND when he reversed the situation in the final Versailles-Paris time trial and won the Tour by just eight seconds!

Above: On the ascent to the Pyrenean resort of Cauterets, a certain Miguel Induráin took his first stage win in the Tour de France.

Right: Fignon accelerates, dropping Lemond and taking back the yellow jersey at Superbagnères. A closely fought battle to the last.

Lemond: the other side of suspense

Sunny Paris. Sleepy Paris. It's 2.55pm on the deserted Quai Saint-Exupéry, and the Tour de France's little princes ride in solitude along the deserted river banks. Gendarmes and crowds doze. Two more hours to go. Two more hours to bid '*Au revoir!*' to De Wilde and Blindi. Two more hours to bid 'Goodbye!' to the Tour, 'Farewell!' to the *Grande Boucle*.

3.02pm: the temperature rises little by little. The sky seems to descend, heavy with heat. A brass band celebrates Ronan Pensec's passage with a fanfare. 3.33pm: the Arc de Triomphe surveys the endless succession of riders that pass its feet with an impassive gaze, before giving its blessing. Time slips by in its burning hour-glass. It's 4pm.

The last few grains of time slip through the hour-glass. Fifty more seconds until 4.12pm, when Greg Lemond will catapult out of the sweltering start-house cockpit and reach for

the stars, 20 years after fellow American Neil Armstrong landed on the moon. Lemond has half an hour to change the course of history and defy the laws of this stifling, Parisian gravity that weighs heavily on the motionless crowd. 4.22pm: all eyes are already on the Lemonnier underpass. But they're as likely to see Lemond emerge from the tunnel as they are an astronaut: he's still far down the road at Issy.

Some 10 kilometres (6 miles) away, near the Arc de Triomphe, his wife Kathy is biting her nails. Something tells her that his mission impossible may not be impossible. At the second checkpoint, 13 kilometres (8 miles) from the end of this trial of strength, opposite the offices of *L'Équipe*, a page of Tour history begins to turn. Lemond has a 21-second lead over Fignon, who started two minutes behind him. Two seconds better than at the previous checkpoint. 4.25pm: time's running out.

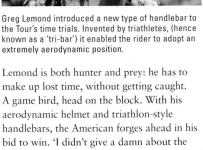

Greg Lemond introduced a new type of handlebar to the Tour's time trials. Invented by triathletes, (hence known as a 'tri-bar') it enabled the rider to adopt an extremely aerodynamic position.

Lemond is both hunter and prey: he has to make up lost time, without getting caught. A game bird, head on the block. With his aerodynamic helmet and triathlon-style handlebars, the American forges ahead in his bid to win. 'I didn't give a damn about the checkpoints. I was simply giving it all I'd got.'

It's breathtaking. As Lemond heads for the expressway, flying along with a gear ratio of 54 x 12, Fignon is perceptibly losing ground. The margin has increased to 24 seconds after 14 km (8.7 miles). 4.28pm: Fignon's hopes are not the only things going up in smoke. Cigarette after cigarette is lit in the press room and, as the tension mounts, typewriters misspell words, stopwatches overheat. In the Concorde underpass, Laurent Fignon begins to struggle. six kilometres (3.7 miles) from the finish, 35 seconds separate the two men. 4.32pm: distance itself elongates before the Parisian; Lemond is flying. 4.35pm: the pavements of the Place de la Concorde are crowded with people. When the first cheer breaks out, Lemond is 45 seconds ahead of Fignon, turning onto the Champs-Élysées, three kilometres (1.85 miles) from the finish. A difficult climb still stands between Lemond and the finish-line where the crowd can see his outline taking shape with every passing second. Then he finishes. Time stops. The clock reads 4.38.57pm.

Lemond is trying not to smile. Millions of pairs of eyes hang on the luminous digits: forty eight, forty nine... A collective gasp roars over the bitumen. On the greatest avenue in the world the blue-eyed American has signed one of the most beautiful exploits in Tour history. Now we know why Fignon hated the idea of the Tour finishing with a time trial.

Lemond could hardly believe his eyes as Laurent Fignon's time was posted. By eight seconds, he'd won the Tour de France on the Champs-Élysées!

Greg Lemond, armed with his new handlebars, aerodynamic helmet and an iron will, heads for the launch ramp for the last time trial.

It's all too much for Fignon – losing the Tour by seconds on the last day. His pain was all the greater as preparations had already been made for his victory celebrations.

Fignon corners beneath the Arc de Triomphe. The climb up the Champs-Élysées would give the Tour a new winner.

Rarely has victory been so sweet and defeat so bitter.

Lemond makes it three

By inviting the Soviet Union team sponsored by Alpha-Lum, the 1990 Tour de France took the most important stepin the internationalisation of modern cycling since 1983, when the Colombian team rode the Tour as amateurs. The Soviet riders made an immediate impact: in the Prologue, Viatcheslav Ekimov won the white jersey of the best young rider and retained it for the next ten stages. Dmitri Konychev led the mountains competition for four stages, then won stage 18 from Lourdes to Pau. An East German, Olaf Ludwig, won a stage and the points competition at his first Tour.

The Tour had started dramatically, when the peloton allowed four riders, and not just any four, to break away on stage one and end the day 10 mins 35 secs ahead of the race favourites. The stage winner, Dutchman Frans Maassen, wasn't considered dangerous, but the riders who finished with him had serious stage-racing credentials: France's Ronan Pensec had finished sixth and seventh at the Tour de France in 1986 and 1988; Canada's Steve Bauer had finished fourth overall in 1988; and Italy's Claudio Chiappucci had won the King of the Mountains competition in the 1990 Giro d'Italia, three weeks earlier. Bauer, with the best Prologue time of the four, took the overall race lead, and wore the yellow jersey all the way to the Alps.

One favourite abandoned as early as stage five; Laurent Fignon, unable to find his true form, dropped back quietly to his team car and dismounted. Two days later, Mexican Raúl Alcalá won the time trial at Épinal by 1 min 24 secs from a fast improving Miguel Induráin.

At St-Gervais in the shadow of Mont Blanc, Ronan Pensec celebrated his 27th birthday by stripping Steve Bauer of the yellow jersey. The following day, on Alpe-d'Huez, Pensec finished tenth, only 48 seconds behind the stage winner Gianni Bugno, and many began to believe he could win the Tour, despite the ambitions of his team-mate and leader, Greg Lemond. But the clash of interests subsided after the mountain time trial at Villard-de-Lans, where the third member of the stage one breakaway, Claudio Chiappucci, seized the lead. The Italian lost time on the way to Saint-Étienne, but showed terrific panache in the Pyrenees, attacking on the Col d'Aspin, retaining a slight lead at the Tourmalet, but slipping back at Luz-Ardiden, where Miguel Induráin won his second Pyrenean stage (following Cauterets in 1989) and Greg Lemond crept to within five seconds of the yellow jersey. By finishing fourth in the final time trial beside Lac de Vassivière, Lemond took the overall lead and his third Tour de France title, without ever winning a stage.

GENERAL CLASSIFICATION

1. **Greg Lemond** (USA) Z, 3,504 km in 90h.43m.20s; Average speed: 38.621 kph
2. **Claudio Chiappucci** (ITA) Carrera Jeans, at 2m.16s.
3. **Erik Breukink** (HOL) P.D.M., at 2m.29s.
4. Pedro Delgado (SPA) Banesto, at 5m.1s.
5. Marino Lejarreta (SPA) ONCE, at 5m.5s.
6. Eduardo Chozas (SPA) ONCE, at 9m.14s.

7. Gianni Bugno (ITA) Château D'Ax, at 9m.39s.
8. Raúl Alcalá (MEX) P.D.M., at 11m.14s.
9. Claude Criquielion (BEL) Lotto, at 12m.14s.
10. Miguel Induráin (SPA) Banesto, at 12m.47s.
11. Andrew Hampsten (USA) 7-Eleven, at 12m.54s.
12. Pello Ruiz-Cabestany (SPA) ONCE, at 13m.39s.
13. Fabio Parra (COL) Kelme, at 14m.35s.

14. Fabrice Philipot (FRA) Castorama-Raleigh, at 15m.49s.
15. Gilles Delion (FRA) Helvetia-La Suisse, at 16m.57s.
16. William Palacio (COL) Ryalcao-Postobon, at 19m.43s.
17. Johan Bruyneel (BEL) Lotto, at 20m.24s.
18. Roberto Conti (ITA) Ariostea, at 20m.43s.
19. Éric Boyer (FRA) Z, at 22m.9s.
20. Ronan Pensec (FRA) Z, at 22m.54s.

77TH TOUR DE FRANCE, 21 STAGES – 3,504 KM

			STAGE	STAGE WINNER	YELLOW JERSEY
Prologue	Saturday 30 June	6.3 km	Futuroscope – Futuroscope (TT)	T. Marie (FRA)	T. Marie
Stage 1	Monday 2 July	138.5 km	Futuroscope – Futuroscope	F. Maassen (HOL)	S. Bauer
Stage 2	Monday 2 July	44.5 km	Futuroscope – Futuroscope (TTT)	Panasonic	S. Bauer
Stage 3	Tuesday 3 July	233 km	Poitiers – Nantes	M. Argentin (ITA)	S. Bauer
Stage 4	Wednesday 4 July	203 km	Nantes – Mont-Saint-Michel	J. Museeuw (BEL)	S. Bauer
Stage 5	Thursday 5 July	301 km	Avranches – Rouen	G. Solleveld (HOL)	S. Bauer
Stage 6	Friday 6 July	202.5 km	Sarrebourg – Vittel	J. Nijdam (HOL)	S. Bauer
Stage 7	Saturday 7 July	61.5 km	Vittel – Épinal (TT)	R. Alcalá (MEX)	S. Bauer
Stage 8	Sunday 8 July	181.5 km	Épinal – Besançon	O. Ludwig (GER)	S. Bauer
Stage 9	Monday 9 July	196 km	Besançon – Genève (SUI)	M. Ghirotto (ITA)	S. Bauer
Stage 10	Tuesday 10 July	118.5 km	Genève (SUI) – St-Gervais-Mont-Blanc	T. Claveyrolat (FRA)	R. Pensec
Stage 11	Wednesday 11 July	182.5 km	Saint-Gervais – L'Alpe-d'Huez	G. Bugno (ITA)	R. Pensec
Stage 12	Thursday 12 July	33.5 km	Fontaine – Villard-de-Lans (TT)	E. Breukink (HOL)	C. Chiappucci
Stage 13	Saturday 14 July	149 km	Villard-de-Lans – Saint-Étienne	E. Chozas (SPA)	C. Chiappucci
Stage 14	Sunday 15 July	205 km	Le Puy-en-Velay – Millau-Causses noirs	M. Lejarreta (SPA)	C. Chiappucci
Stage 15	Monday 16 July	170 km	Millau – Revel	C. Mottet (FRA)	C. Chiappucci
Stage 16	Tuesday 17 July	215 km	Blagnac – Luz-Ardiden	M. Induráin (SPA)	C. Chiappucci
Stage 17	Wednesday 18 July	150 km	Lourdes – Pau	D. Konyshev (RUS)	C. Chiappucci
Stage 18	Thursday 19 July	202 km	Pau – Bordeaux	G. Bugno (ITA)	C. Chiappucci
Stage 19	Friday 20 July	182.5 km	Castillon-la-Bataille – Limoges	G. Bontempi (ITA)	C. Chiappucci
Stage 20	Saturday 21 July	45.5 km	Lac de Vassivière – Lac de Vassivière (TT)	E. Breukink (HOL)	G. Lemond
Stage 21	Sunday 22 July	182 km	Brétigny-sur-Orge – Paris	J. Museeuw (BEL)	G. Lemond

Above: The present and the future meet on the climb to Luz-Ardiden, where Induráin (left) and Lemond attacked together.
Below: Chiappucci leads stage one's escapade in the company of Bauer (left), Ronan Pensec (right) and Frans Maassen (hidden).

The start of a new reign

The 1991 Tour de France started with a Prologue win for Thierry Marie, the third of his career. Five days later, Marie recaptured the yellow jersey after an epic 234-kilometre (145-mile) breakaway between Arras and Le Havre. The previous race leader, Denmark's Rolf Sörensen, had abandoned wearing the yellow jersey after colliding with a traffic island at Valenciennes. The reigning champion Greg Lemond finished second in the first individual time trial at Alençon, just 8 seconds behind Spain's Miguel Induráin, and took over the yellow jersey. At Rennes the following day, Mauro Ribeiro became the first Brazilian to win a Tour stage. At Quimper, the entire PDM team abandoned, reportedly due to food poisoning, amid suspicion that the abuse of doping products had backfired on them.

It was in the Pyrenees that the Tour reached its crux. On the Tourmalet climb, Lemond and the temporary race leader Luc Leblanc were visibly tired. Shortly before the summit, Lemond dropped off the pace of the leading group, crossing the peak 17 seconds behind. He closed the gap on the descent, but Induráin had broken away alone, with Italy's Claudio Chiappucci giving energetic pursuit. At the base of the Aspin, Induráin waited for the Italian, and the pair shared the workload equally on the

climb to Val Louron. Chiappucci took his first Tour de France stage win and Induráin took his first yellow jersey. He would wear it again no fewer than 59 times.

It was Induráin's seventh Tour de France, and the victory rewarded a long, patient apprenticeship under José Miguel Echavarri, his *directeur sportif* at Reynolds and now Banesto. Aged 27, Miguel Induráin became only the fourth Spaniard to win the Tour de France after Federico Bahamontes (1959), Luis Ocaña (1973) and Pedro Delgado (1988), whom he had served as a faithful *domestique*.

Induráin defended his yellow jersey like Jacques Anquetil. He shadowed the fine Italian rider Gianni Bugno up to Alpe-d'Huez, where Bugno had won in 1990, and took the final time trial, 27 seconds ahead of Bugno and 48 seconds ahead of Chiappucci; these three filled the podium places, with Lemond trailing in seventh. Riding the Tour for the second time, the former Soviet riders performed excellently: Ekimov and Konychev were both stage winners, while the powerful Uzbek sprinter Djamolidine Abdoujaparov won two stages and the points competitions, despite falling at top speed in the final kilometre of the Champs-Élysées, and crossing the line 15 minutes after the peloton, aided by medical staff.

GENERAL CLASSIFICATION

1. **Miguel Induráin** (SPA) Banesto, 3,914 km in 101h.1m.20s; Average speed: 38.747 kph
2. **Gianni Bugno** (ITA) Gatorade-Château-Dax, at 3m.36s.
3. **Claudio Chiappucci** (ITA) Carrera Jeans, at 5m.56s.
4. Charly Mottet (FRA) RMO, at 7m.37s.
5. Luc Leblanc (FRA) Castorama, at 10m.10s.
6. Laurent Fignon (FRA) Castorama, at 11m.27s.

7. Greg Lemond (USA) Z, at 13m.13s.
8. Andrew Hampsten (USA) Motorola, at 13m.40s.
9. Pedro Delgado (SPA) Banesto, at 20m.10s.
10. Gérard Rué (FRA) Helvetia, at 20m.13s.
11. Eduardo Chozas (SPA) ONCE, at 21m.
12. Abelardo Rondon (COL) Banesto, at 26m.47s.
13. Gert-Jan Theunisse (HOL) TVM, at 27m.10s.

14. Jean-François Bernard (FRA) Banesto, at 28m.57s.
15. Maurizio Fondriest (ITA) Panasonic, at 30m.9s.
16. Denis Roux (FRA) Toshiba, at 30m.40s.
17. Éric Caritoux (FRA) RMO, at 32m.39s.
18. Alberto Camargo (COL) Ryalcao, at 32m.54s.
19. Alvaro Mejia Castrillona (COL) Ryalcao, at 33m.52s.
20. Frédéric Vichot (FRA) Castorama, at 36m.43s.

78TH TOUR DE FRANCE, 22 STAGES – 3,914 KM

			STAGE	STAGE WINNER	YELLOW JERSEY
Prologue	Saturday 6 July	5.3 km	Lyon – Lyon	T. Marie (FRA)	T. Marie
Stage 1	Sunday 7 July	114.5 km	Lyon – Lyon	D. Abdoujaparov (UZB)	G. Lemond
Stage 2	Sunday 7 July	36.5 km	Bron – Chassieu-Eurexpo (TTT)	Ariostea	R. Sörensen
Stage 3	Monday 8 July	210.5 km	Villeurbanne – Dijon	E. De Wilde (BEL)	R. Sörensen
Stage 4	Tuesday 9 July	286 km	Dijon – Reims	D. Abdoujaparov (UZB)	R. Sörensen
Stage 5	Wednesday 10 July	149.5 km	Reims – Valenciennes	J. Nijdam (HOL)	R. Sörensen
Stage 6	Thursday 11 July	259 km	Arras – Le Havre	T. Marie (FRA)	T. Marie
Stage 7	Friday 12 July	167 km	Le Havre – Argentan	J. -P. Van Poppel (HOL)	T. Marie
Stage 8	Saturday 13 July	73 km	Argentan – Alençon (TT)	M. Induráin (SPA)	G. Lemond
Stage 9	Sunday 14 July	161 km	Alençon – Rennes	M. Ribeiro (BRA)	G. Lemond
Stage 10	Monday 15 July	207.5 km	Rennes – Quimper	P. Anderson (AUS)	G. Lemond
Stage 11	Tuesday 16 July	246 km	Quimper – Saint-Herblain	C. Mottet (FRA)	G. Lemond
Stage 12	Thursday 18 July	192 km	Pau – Jaca (SPA)	C. Mottet (FRA)	L. Leblanc
Stage 13	Friday 19 July	232 km	Jaca (SPA) – Val-Louron	C. Chiappucci (ITA)	M. Induráin
Stage 14	Saturday 20 July	172.5 km	Saint-Gaudens – Castres	B. Cenghialta (ITA)	M. Induráin
Stage 15	Sunday 21 July	235 km	Albi – Alès	M. Argentin (ITA)	M. Induráin
Stage 16	Monday 22 July	215 km	Alès – Gap	M. Lietti (ITA)	M. Induráin
Stage 17	Tuesday 23 July	125 km	Gap – L'Alpe-d'Huez	G. Bugno (ITA)	M. Induráin
Stage 18	Wednesday 24 July	255 km	Bourg-d'Oisans – Morzine	T. Claveyrolat (FRA)	M. Induráin
Stage 19	Thursday 25 July	177 km	Morzine – Aix-les-Bains	D. Konyshev (RUS)	M. Induráin
Stage 20	Friday 26 July	160 km	Aix-les-Bains – Mâcon	V. Ekimov (RUS)	M. Induráin
Stage 21	Saturday 27 July	57 km	Lugny – Mâcon (TT)	M. Induráin (SPA)	M. Induráin
Stage 22	Sunday 28 July	178 km	Melun – Paris	D. Konyshev (RUS)	M. Induráin

Despite his physical size, Miguel Induráin
dictated the pace in the mountains.

The end of an era

VAL-LOURON: The race was blown apart to the deafening sound of car horns, shouting and helicopter blades – that unique cacophony that accompanies the most exciting moments of the Tour. It was all enacted over the last 500 metres to the top of the Col du Tourmalet between a gauntlet of shaking fists, waving arms and faces distorted with excitement. A moment earlier, the Banesto team car had pulled alongside Miguel Induráin who asked a simple question: 'Who's struggling?' 'Leblanc!' yelled José Miguel Echavarri through the window. 'And Lemond, I think...'

At that moment there was a noticeable increase in tempo among the eight surviving riders in the leading group. People were about to witness one of the most furious battles in recent Tour history. With just 500 metres to go, Greg Lemond suddenly sat down on the saddle. Then he stood up on his pedals, sat down again, got up again. He wasn't pushing down on the pedals any more; he was leaning on them. It's painful to see him in such dire straits.

He managed to cross the top of the mountain a mere 17 seconds behind Chiappucci, Induráin, Hampsten, Mottet, Bugno, Leblanc, who was holding his own, and Rué, who had completely recovered, and immediately flung himself down the other side. After three or four vertiginous hairpin bends, he caught up with the leading group, just before La Mongie, only to find that Induráin had gone. He shot away from the group, selecting a huge gear that showed what great reserves he still had in store. Five kilometres (3 miles) further on, at the foot of the Col d'Aspin, Induráin was in sight.

But his efforts were in vain. By the base of the climb to Val Louron cycling's new generation had asserted itself. Induráin and Chiappucci had broken away and nothing now could stop them. The Italian was heading for a historic stage win and the Spanish titan knew he would take the yellow jersey.

Top: On the Col du Tourmalet, Greg Lemond slips away from the back of the leading group in which Luc Leblanc is still wearing yellow.
Below: In Val Louron, Miguel Induráin (right) and Claudio Chiappucci shared the work that would take the Spaniard to his first yellow jersey.

In Reims, a duel reminiscent of the East European Peace Race: the Uzbek Djamolidine Abdoujaparov, in green, beats Olaf Ludwig (East Germany).

Samba! The popular Brazilian Mauro Ribeiro comes out of the leading group to take the stage win in Rennes, ahead of the young Laurent Jalabert (right).

Martin Earley, from Ireland, and the rest of the Dutch P.D.M. team packed their bags and mysteriously left the Tour.

Sprinting at full-speed for a Champs-Élysées stage win, Abdoujaparov hit an advertising hoarding. He kept the green jersey since the rules allow for accidents that occur in the final kilometre.

Simply sublime!

On 14 June 1992, Miguel Induráin rode victoriously into Milan, having won the Giro d'Italia by virtue of extraordinary aggression in the time trials, impenetrable defence in the mountains and an almost infallible ability to read the race. On 4 July, he brought the same skills to the 1992 Tour de France, and won the Prologue at San Sebastián, in front of massive and adoring Basque crowds. Two seconds behind him, a young Swiss rider, Alex Zülle, riding for the Spanish team ONCE, took second place, and the following day took over the yellow jersey. Zülle was among several younger riders who emerged during the 1992 Tour and went on to define the 1990s. Richard Virenque, riding his first Tour, had been selected to ride at the last moment by his team owner, Marc Braillon, and justified the decision by wearing the yellow jersey at the end of stage two. Virenque's team-mate Pascal Lino took over the yellow jersey in Bordeaux, after joining the winning breakaway. Yet another swashbuckling young Frenchman, Zülle's French team-mate Laurent Jalabert, took his first Tour de France stage win at Brussels on stage six.

The first ten days allowed other riders to taste glory at the Tour: Gilles Delion rode to victory in Valkenburg (Netherlands) in front of a huge crowd; the Belgian Jan Nevens won at Coblence (Germany). Holland's Jean-Paul Van Poppel won a bunch sprint at Strasbourg, the crossroads of Europe. But it was all peripheral: Induráin imposed stark clarity on the race, allowing others crumbs from his table, but dominating the key moments with absolute assurance. On the 65-kilometre (41-mile) time trial around Luxembourg, he was in a dimension of his own. He overtook Laurent Fignon, who had set off six minutes earlier, and distanced the second-placed rider, his own team-mate Armand de Las Cuevas, by three minutes. Among his potential rivals, only Gianni Bugno could finish within four minutes of him. Induráin's most serious rival was the tiny climber Claudio Chiappucci. Chiappucci had finished second in two Giros (1991 and 1992), and second and third in the Tour de France (1990 and 1991), and after crossing the Iseran and Mont-Cenis on the road to Sestrières, he launched his bid for victory and broke away alone for the last 125 kilometres (78 miles), spurred on by the Italian crowd. The media paid due homage to this brilliant stage win, but Induráin had contained Chiappucci's advantage, allowing him to take back 1 min 45 secs, and with the long final time trial ahead of him, was imperious in yellow. In the final time trial, with 18 gruelling stages behind him, he could still ride 64 kilometres (39.7 miles) at the incredible speed of 52.349 kph (32.51 mph).

GENERAL CLASSIFICATION

1. **Miguel Induráin** (SPA) Banesto, 3,983 km in 100h.49m.30s; Average speed: 36.504 kph
2. **Claudio Chiappucci** (ITA) Carrera-Jeans Tassoni, at 4m.35s.
3. **Gianni Bugno** (ITA) Gatorade-Chateau D'Ax, at 10m.49s.
4. Andrew Hampsten (USA) Motorola, at 13m.40s.
5. Pascal Lino (FRA) RMO, at 14m.37s.
6. Pedro Delgado (SPA) Banesto, at 15m.16s.
7. Erik Breukink (HOL) PDM, at 18m.51s.
8. Giancarlo Perini (ITA) Carrera-Jeans Tassoni, at 19m.16s.
9. Stephen Roche (IRL) Carrera-Jeans Tassoni, at 20m.23s.
10. Jens Heppner (GER) Telekom, at 25m.30s.
11. Franco Vona (ITA) GBM, at 25m.43s.
12. Éric Boyer (FRA) Z, at 26m.16s.
13. Gert-Jan Theunisse (HOL) TVM, at 27m.07s.
14. Eddy Boumwans (HOL) Panasonic, at 28m.35s.
15. Gérard Rué (FRA) Castorama, at 28m.48s.
16. Franco Chioccioli (ITA) GEM, at 30m.31s.
17. Steven Rooks (HOL) Buckler, at 31m.09s.
18. Robert Millar (GBR) TVM, at 31m.19s.
19. Francisco Mauleon (SPA) CLAS, at 31m.27s.
20. Arsenio Gonzales (SPA) CLAS, at 31m.51s.

79TH TOUR DE FRANCE, 21 STAGES - 3,983 KM

			STAGE	STAGE WINNER	YELLOW JERSEY
Prologue	Saturday 4 July	8 km	San Sebastián – San Sebastián (SPA)	M. Induráin (SPA)	M. Induráin
Stage 1	Sunday 5 July	194.5 km	San Sebastián – San Sebastián (SPA)	D. Arnould (FRA)	A. Zülle
Stage 2	Monday 6 July	255 km	San Sebastián (SPA) – Pau	J. Murguialday (SPA)	R. Virenque
Stage 3	Tuesday 7 July	210 km	Pau – Bordeaux	R. Harmeling (HOL)	P. Lino
Stage 4	Wednesday 8 July	63.5 km	Libourne – Libourne (TTT)	Panasonic	P. Lino
Stage 5	Thursday 9 July	196 km	Nogent-sur-Oise – Wasquehal	G. Bontempi (ITA)	P. Lino
Stage 6	Friday 10 July	167 km	Roubaix – Bruxelles (BEL)	L. Jalabert (FRA)	P. Lino
Stage 7	Saturday 11 July	196.5 km	Bruxelles (BEL) – Valkenburg (HOL)	G. Delion (FRA)	P. Lino
Stage 8	Sunday 12 July	206.5 km	Valkenburg (HOL) – Coblence (GER)	J. Nevens (BEL)	P. Lino
Stage 9	Monday 13 July	65 km	Luxembourg – Luxembourg (LUX) (TT)	M. Induráin (SPA)	P. Lino
Stage 10	Tuesday 14 July	217 km	Luxembourg (LUX) – Strasbourg	J.-P. Van Poppel (HOL)	P. Lino
Stage 11	Wednesday 15 July	249.5 km	Strasbourg – Mulhouse	L. Fignon (FRA)	P. Lino
Stage 12	Friday 17 July	267.5 km	Dole – St-Gervais-Mt-Blanc	R. Jaermann (SUI)	P. Lino
Stage 13	Saturday 18 July	254.5 km	St-Gervais – Sestrières (ITA)	C. Chiappucci (ITA)	M. Induráin
Stage 14	Sunday 19 July	186.5 km	Sestrières – L'Alpe-d'Huez	A. Hampsten (USA)	M. Induráin
Stage 15	Monday 20 July	198 km	Bourg-d'Oisans – St-Étienne	F. Chioccioli (ITA)	M. Induráin
Stage 16	Tuesday 21 July	212 km	St-Étienne – La Bourboule	S. Roche (IRL)	M. Induráin
Stage 17	Wednesday 22 July	189 km	La Bourboule – Montluçon	J.-C. Colotti (FRA)	M. Induráin
Stage 18	Thursday 23 July	212 km	Montluçon – Tours	T. Marie (FRA)	M. Induráin
Stage 19	Friday 24 July	64 km	Tours – Blois (TT)	M. Induráin (SPA)	M. Induráin
Stage 20	Saturday 25 July	222 km	Blois – Nanterre	P. De Clercq (BEL)	M. Induráin
Stage 21	Sunday 26 July	141 km	La Défense – Paris	O. Ludwig (GER)	M. Induráin

Laurent Jalabert had to fight to the bitter end to head off Johan Museeuw and take his first green jersey in Paris.

Richard Virenque attacks in the mountains of the Basque Country, beginning a long and passionate relationship with the Tour de France.

Claudio Chiappucci celebrates his masterpiece at Sestrières, after a 200-kilometre (128 mile) breakaway, most of which he rode alone.

The Luxembourg time trial, in which Miguel Induráin became the symbol of the strength of the solitary rider.

A gentle sort of panache

In 1992 Miguel Induráin had completed the double, winning the Tours of Italy and France in the same year. By winning the 1993 Tour of Italy in June, Induráin had completed the first part of another double. Only Coppi, Anquetil, Merckx, and Hinault had achieved the feat twice, and none had done so in consecutive years. The Spaniard's remarkable consistency set him apart even from their auspicious company. Twenty days later after riding victoriously into Milan, Induráin won the Prologue of the 1993 Tour de France, finishing 8 seconds ahead of Alex Zülle and 11 seconds ahead of Gianni Bugno. For the first eight days, the sprinters squabbled over the yellow jersey: Mario Cipollini snatched it from Wilfried Nelissen, Nelissen took it back, Cipollini seized it again, then Museeuw grabbed it for a couple of days. At Amiens, Johan Bruyneel won the fastest stage in Tour history; the following day, Denmark's Bjarne Riis was the stage winner; and a day later at Verdun, Lance Armstrong became the youngest Tour de France stage winner since the war. All three men would leave their mark on Tour history – but that was in the future.

Comedians in the press tent dubbed the first long time trial, around the Lac de Madine just south of Metz, 'the Induráin sandwich': Miguel Induráin won by 2mins 11secs from Gianni Bugno, despite a puncture. His brother Prudencio Induráin trailed in last; only Miguel's puncture allowed Prudencio to finish inside the time limit. By that stage, the French were in need of a sense of humour; Pascal Lino's sole French stage win of the 1993 Tour didn't come until 18 July. Despite expectations, the greatest threat to Induráin came from neither Bugno nor Zülle, but from another Swiss rider, Tony Rominger, who won successive mountain stages in the Alps. On both occasions, Induráin was in close attendance, but with his eyes fixed firmly on the overall prize, he graciously refused to challenge his rival for the stage win. His was a soft flamboyance, a gentle panache that often passed unrecognized: only a true champion can afford to show magnanimity.

In the Pyrenees, Poland's Zenon Jaskula won the stage finishing at St-Lary-Soulan: by finishing third in the final time trial, he edged Lance Armstrong's Colombian team-mate Álvaro Mejía off the podium and became the first East European to stand on the final podium of the Tour de France. Tony Rominger had already won the mountains competition when he defeated Induráin by 42 seconds in the final time trial to the south of Paris.

GENERAL CLASSIFICATION

1. **Miguel Induráin** (SPA) Banesto, 3,714 km in 95h,57m.9s; Average speed: 38.709 kph
2. **Tony Rominger** (SUI) CLAS, at 4m.59s.
3. **Zenon Jaskula** (POL) G.B.M., at 5m.48s.
4. Álvaro Mejía Castrillona (COL) Motorola, at 7m.29s.
5. Bjarne Riis (DEN) Ariostea, at 16m.26s.
6. Claudio Chiappucci (ITA) Carrera, at 17m.18s.
7. Johan Bruyneel (BEL) ONCE, at 18m.4s.
8. Andrew Hampsten (USA) Motorola, at 20m.14s.
9. Pedro Delgado (SPA) Banesto, at 23m.57s.
10. Vladimir Poulikov (UKR) Carrera, at 25m.29s
11. Gianni Faresin (ITA) Mobili, at 29m.5s.
12. Antonio Martin Velasco (SPA) Amaya, at 29m.51s.
13. Stephen Roche (IRL) Carrera, at 29m.53s.
14. Roberto Conti (ITA) Ariostea, at 30m.5s.
15. Jean-Philippe Dojwa (FRA) Festina, at 30m.24s.
16. Oliviero Rincon Quintana (COL) Amaya, at 33m.19s.
17. Alberto Elli (ITA) Ariostea, at 33m.29s.
18. Jon Unzanga (SPA), CLAS, at 38m.9s.
19. Richard Virenque (FRA) Festina, at 38m.12s.
20. Gianni Bugno (ITA) Gatorade, at 40m.8s.

80TH TOUR DE FRANCE, 20 STAGES – 3,714 KM

STAGE				STAGE WINNER	YELLOW JERSEY
Prologue	Saturday 3 July	6.8 km	Le Puy-du-Fou – Le Puy-du-Fou (TT)	M. Induráin (SPA)	M. Induráin
Stage 1	Sunday 4 July	215 km	Luçon – Les Sables-d'Olonne	M. Cipollini (ITA)	M. Induráin
Stage 2	Monday 5 July	227.5 km	Les Sables-d'Olonne – Vannes	W. Nelissen (BEL)	W. Nelissen
Stage 3	Tuesday 6 July	189.5 km	Vannes – Dinard	D. Abdoujaparov (UZB)	W. Nelissen
Stage 4	Wednesday 7 July	81 km	Dinard – Avranches (TTT)	G.B.-M.G.-Maglífico	M. Cipollini
Stage 5	Thursday 8 July	225.5 km	Avranches – Évreux	J. Skibby (DEN)	W. Nelissen
Stage 6	Friday 9 July	158 km	Évreux – Amiens	J. Bruyneel (BEL)	M. Cipollini
Stage 7	Saturday 10 July	199 km	Péronne – Châlons-sur-Marne	B. Riis (DEN)	J. Museeuw
Stage 8	Sunday 11 July	184.5 km	Châlons-sur-Marne – Verdun	L. Armstrong (USA)	J. Museeuw
Stage 9	Monday 12 July	59 km	Lac de Madine – Lac de Madine (TT)	M. Induráin (SPA)	M. Induráin
Stage 10	Wednesday 14 July	203 km	Villard-de-Lans – Serre-Chevalier	T. Rominger (SUI)	M. Induráin
Stage 11	Thursday 15 July	180 km	Serre-Chevalier – Isola 2000	T. Rominger (SUI)	M. Induráin
Stage 12	Friday 16 July	287.5 km	Isola 2000 – Marseille	F. Roscioli (ITA)	M. Induráin
Stage 13	Saturday 17 July	182.5 km	Marseille – Montpellier	O. Ludwig (GER)	M. Induráin
Stage 14	Sunday 18 July	224 km	Montpellier – Perpignan	P. Lino (FRA)	M. Induráin
Stage 15	Monday 19 July	231.5 km	Perpignan – Andorre (AND)	O. Rincon (COL)	M. Induráin
Stage 16	Wednesday 21 July	230.5 km	Andorre (AND) – Saint-Lary-Soulan	Z. Jaskula (POL)	M. Induráin
Stage 17	Thursday 22 July	189.5 km	Tarbes – Pau	C. Chiappucci (ITA)	M. Induráin
Stage 18	Friday 23 July	200.5 km	Orthez – Bordeaux	D. Abdoujaparov (UZB)	M. Induráin
Stage 19	Saturday 24 July	48 km	Brétigny-sur-Orge – Montlhéry (TT)	T. Rominger (SUI)	M. Induráin
Stage 20	Sunday 25 July	196.5 km	Viry-Châtillon – Paris	D. Abdoujaparov (UZB)	M. Induráin

Above: Miguel Induráin was criticized as lacking panache but his climbing power was immense, as demonstrated on the Galibier where he dominated (right to left) Mejía, Hampsten, Jaskula and Rominger. Below: In the Alps, whether climbing or descending, Induráin and Rominger couldn't be separated.

Lance Armstrong: over the moon!

A first stage win at Verdun for the young Lance Armstrong, wearing the jersey of the US champion.

VERDUN: Lance Armstrong wasn't even born when the American astronaut, Neil Armstrong, took the first step on the moon, on 20 July 1969. It was, in the expression of the time, a giant step for mankind.

Yesterday, on 11 July 1993, Lance Armstrong won the eighth stage of the Tour de France in Verdun. He, too, bearing in mind the difference in scale, is taking giant steps forward in his cycling apprenticeship. 'He dreams of a great career and he's well on his way,' we reported on Saturday morning in our profile of the American rider. He needed no longer than 48 hours to demonstrate his outstanding talent. No doubt about it, this young man is an exceptional find for American cycling at a time when the career of his compatriot Greg Lemond, three-times winner of the Tour, is waning.

Armstrong won the stage in great style, winning the sprint when he was practically wedged between the barriers and Ronan Pensec, who seemed to have the upper hand.

He had climbed the Côte de Douaumont among the leaders and then, 6 kilometres (3.7 miles) from the finish, closed with Alcalá and Pensec on the leading trio, Perini, Roche and Arnould. In the final sprint, he came up from fourth place to win and, as he crossed the finish, he raised his hands to heaven as if reaching for his own personal moon. 'Just before the finish, it was Arnould who worried me most. Then, as the sprint got started, I moved to the right so he couldn't get on my wheel, because he was just behind me.' He relived the last few metres with a wry smile, sitting in the interview bus.

Born on 16 September 1971, Lance Armstrong is the youngest rider on this Tour. But he has guts. He wasn't the slightest bit intimidated and answered the journalists' questions confidently, even raising a smile.

Q: Will you be a second Lemond?
A: No, I'll be the first Lance Armstrong.
Q: Are you married, do you have children?
A: No, I'm not married, and I don't think I have any children.
Q: What do you expect of this Tour?
A: I came to learn and to win a stage. I've already learnt a lot and I've won a stage. Now I'll carry on learning so I can win again.

A quick look at Armstrong's career gives a clear picture of this young man from Austin, Texas, who loves to joke but is well aware of his own ability. He was first seen in Europe at the World Junior Championships at the famous Krylatscoye Olympic route at Moscow in 1989. With one lap to go, Armstrong was in the leading group but lost the race when Heinrich Trumheller and his Soviet team launched an all-out attack. Lance returned to Europe in 1992 as one of the favourites for the Barcelona Olympics. He was never in the running, but consoled himself with the fact that he had already signed a contract with Motorola. A week later, he rode his first professional race, the San Sebastián Classic, and came last. Two weeks later he came second in the Championship of Zurich and then went on to Italy where he won a race held before beating some of the best Italians in the sprint.

'You know,' he was saying the other day, 'I gotta go back to San Sebastián to get my revenge. I gotta win there. For a proud Texan like me, coming last, being whistled at and pointed at, is unbearable. So I'll go back there and show them I'm a winner.'

On Saturday 7 August, he'll go back and this time, he certainly won't finish last.

Among his other ambitions, he wants to win the Championship of Zurich and the Tour of Lombardy, and beat the favourites in the World Championships in Oslo. Lance Armstrong is going to be a force to be reckoned with. With a name like Armstrong, it's only a matter of time...

Lance Armstrong in difficulty in the mountains, a few days after his stage win at Verdun. At only 22, the young American still had a lot to learn.

1. Tony Rominger won the Brétigny-Montlhéry time trial with an average speed of 50.495 kph (31.376 mph) – 42 seconds up on Induráin. Nevertheless he sportingly admitted the Spaniard's superiority in this Tour.

2. Johan Bruyneel on his way to the fastest recorded mass-start Tour stage – run at an average speed of 49.417kph (30.7mph).

3. With an impressive time trial performance at Médine, Miguel Induráin puts himself ahead of Rominger by almost three minutes!

4. Rominger took the win at Isola 2000, when Induráin was criticized for his magnanimity.

5. Two years after his fall, Abdoujaparov won on the Champs-Élysées, ahead of Moncassin.

6. Bjarne Riis, stage winner at Châlons-sur-Marne, was one of the new faces on the 1993 Tour destined to make history.

7. In the Alps, Miguel Induráin kept an eye on the main prize – the yellow jersey – and left the stage wins for Tony Rominger (left).

Induráin, stronger than ever

The 1994 Tour de France started with a question: was the Induráin era coming to an end? At the Tour of Italy in June, a young Russian rider, Evgeni Berzin, had defeated him in every time trial on the way to overall victory, while a brilliant young climbing specialist, Marco Pantani, had edged the giant Spaniard into third place. It was the end of three invincible years, for Induráin had not lost a three-week tour since finishing second in the the 1991 Vuelta a España, shortly before his first Tour de France win.

On 2 July, at the Prologue in Lille, the omens were not good. Berzin was not riding the Tour, but in his absence, another newcomer, England's Chris Boardman, distanced Induráin by 15 seconds and took the yellow jersey on the first day of his Tour de France career. Drama of another kind marred the Armentières finish on stage one, when a gendarme armed with a camera lurched into the path of sprinters Wilfried Nelissen and Laurent Jalabert and caused a horrific accident.

By the time the Tour reached Dover via the Channel Tunnel, the yellow jersey had passed from an Englishman to a Belgian (Museeuw). The day after the Tour left England, another Englishman, Sean Yates, took over the yellow jersey for a day.

Once again, the greatest challenge to Miguel Induráin seemed to come from Tony Rominger, who had been in fine form since the early season stage races, winning the Paris-Nice

and the Tour of the Basque Country. However, another extraordinary performance by Induráin in the time trial between Périgueux and Bergerac saw him win the stage with a 2-minute advantage over Rominger and more than 5 minutes over time-trial specialist Boardman, who finished fifth!

Indeed, as Induráin stamped his authority on the high mountain stages, Rominger fell ill and abandoned. Forty-six years after Gino Bartali, another devout Catholic, Luc Leblanc, won the stage to Lourdes, with Induráin monitoring his progress two seconds behind. Leblanc's Festina team-mate, Richard Virenque won the mountains competition after a buccaneering Pyrenean stage victory at Luz-Ardiden, but Induráin's superiority was not questioned again. It remained unchallenged both at Ventoux, and Alpe-d'Huez. The Russian-speaking Latvian Piotr Ugrumov was the best of the rest: he finished second on stage 17, won stage 18, then dominated the mountain time trial on the slopes of Avoriaz, beating Pantani by 1min 38secs and Induráin by 3mins 16secs. Ugrumov had ridden the 1990 Tour for the Soviet team sponsored by Alfa-Lum. Now he had finished second. In third place, the 24-year-old Marco Pantani seemed to hold the future in his hands. However, Induráin's fourth Tour de France victory was one of his most accomplished, and as the Tour ended, the idea that Induráin was in decline seemed more absurd than ever.

GENERAL CLASSIFICATION

1. **Miguel Induráin** (SPA) Banesto, 3,978 km in 103h.38m.38s; Average speed: 38.381 kph
2. **Piotr Ugrumov** (LAT) Gewiss-Ballan, at 5m.39s.
3. **Marco Pantani** (ITA) Carrera, at 7m.19s.
4. Luc Leblanc (FRA) Festina, at 10m.3s.
5. Richard Virenque (FRA) Festina, at 10m.10s.
6. Roberto Conti (ITA) Lampre, at 12m.29s.

7. Alberto Elli (ITA) G.B.-M.G., at 20m.17s.
8. Alex Zülle (SUI) ONCE, at 20m.35s.
9. Udo Bolts (GER) Telekom, at 25m.19s.
10. Vladimir Poulnikov (UKR) Carrera, at 25m.28s.
11. Pascal Lino (FRA) Festina, at 30m.1s.
12. Fernando Escartín (SPA) Mapei-Clas, at 30m.38s.
13. Gianluca Bortolami (ITA) Mapei-Clas, 32m.35s.

14. Bjarne Riis (DEN) Gewiss-Ballan, at 33m.32s.
15. Oscar Pellicioli (ITA) Polti, at 34m.55s.
16. Nelson Rodriguez Serna (COL) ZG-Mobili, at 35m.18s.
17. Jean-François Bernard (FRA) Banesto, at 36m.44s.
18. Hernan Buenahora (COL) Kelme, at 38m.
19. Rolf Sörensen (DEN) G.B.-M.G., at 42m.39s.
20. Bo Hamburger (DEN) TVM, at 43m.44s.

81ST TOUR DE FRANCE, 21 STAGES – 3,978 KM

			STAGE	STAGE WINNER	YELLOW JERSEY
Prologue	Saturday 2 July	7.2 km	Lille – Lille	C. Boardman (GBR)	C. Boardman
Stage 1	Sunday 3 July	234 km	Lille – Armentières	D. Abdoujaparov (UZB)	C. Boardman
Stage 2	Monday 4 July	203.5 km	Roubaix – Boulogne-sur-Mer	J.-P. Van Poppel (HOL)	C. Boardman
Stage 3	Tuesday 5 July	66.5 km	Calais – Eurotunnel (TTT)	G.B.-M.G. Technogym	J. Museeuw
Stage 4	Wednesday 6 July	204.5 km	Dover (GBR) – Brighton (GBR)	F. Cabello (SPA)	F. Vanzella
Stage 5	Thursday 7 July	187 km	Portsmouth (GBR) – Portsmouth (GBR)	N. Minali (ITA)	F. Vanzella
Stage 6	Friday 8 July	270.5 km	Cherbourg – Rennes	G. Bortolami (ITA)	S. Yates
Stage 7	Saturday 9 July	259.5 km	Rennes – Futuroscope	J. Svorada (SLO)	J. Museeuw
Stage 8	Sunday 10 July	218.5 km	Poitiers – Trélissac	B. Hamburger (DEN)	J. Museeuw
Stage 9	Monday 11 July	64 km	Périgueux – Bergerac (TT)	M. Induráin (SPA)	M. Induráin
Stage 10	Tuesday 12 July	160.5 km	Bergerac – Cahors	J. Durand (FRA)	M. Induráin
Stage 11	Wednesday 13 July	263.5 km	Cahors – Lourdes-Hautacam	L. Leblanc (FRA)	M. Induráin
Stage 12	Friday 15 July	204.5 km	Lourdes – Luz-Ardiden	R. Virenque (FRA)	M. Induráin
Stage 13	Saturday 16 July	223 km	Bagnères-de-Bigorre – Albi	B. Riis (DEN)	M. Induráin
Stage 14	Sunday 17 July	202 km	Castres – Montpellier	R. Sörensen (DEN)	M. Induráin
Stage 15	Monday 18 July	231 km	Montpellier – Carpentras	E. Poli (ITA)	M. Induráin
Stage 16	Tuesday 19 July	224.5 km	Valréas – L'Alpe-d'Huez	R. Conti (ITA)	M. Induráin
Stage 17	Wednesday 20 July	149 km	Bourg-d'Oisans – Val-Thorens	N. Rodriguez Serna (COL)	M. Induráin
Stage 18	Thursday 21 July	174.5 km	Moûtiers – Cluses	P. Ugrumov (LAT)	M. Induráin
Stage 19	Friday 22 July	47.5 km	Cluses – Avoriaz (TT)	P. Ugrumov (LAT)	M. Induráin
Stage 20	Saturday 23 July	208.5 km	Morzine – Lac de Saint-Point	D. Abdoujaparov (UZB)	M. Induráin
Stage 21	Sunday 24 July	175 km	Disneyland – Paris	E. Seigneur (FRA)	M. Induráin

The perfect Prologue by Chris Boardman, a Tour de France newcomer, won him the yellow jersey at Lille. Boardman was the very archetype of a Prologue specialist.

Despite the challenge of Festina's French contingent, led by Richard Virenque (left) and Luc Leblanc, Induráin rode with greater authority than ever in the mountains.

Marco Pantani finished third, aged 24, and still with a few hairs left.

At Armentières, the Tour brushed with disaster (above, left). Among the victims (above, right) were Laurent Jalabert (left) and Fabiano Fontanelli. Jalabert, with serious head injuries and blood loss, was forced to abandon. The Tour de France lost its best French rider on stage one.

Big Mig joins the greats

The 1995 Tour de France began in Brittany, with a Prologue around the picturesque town of St-Brieuc. In the damp twilight, the prologue specialist Chris Boardman gave no quarter to the conditions, crashed heavily, and broke his ankle. Victory fell to an early starter riding before the rain, France's Jacky Durand. Miguel Induráin took no chances: this was his chance to enter the elite club of five-time winners beside Jacques Anquetil, Eddy Merckx and Bernard Hinault. Induráin explained, with characteristic modesty, that 'No one can ever match up to their idols.' His approach to this historic opportunity was no different from the four previous Tours, he claimed, although he had steered clear of the Giro d'Italia, won by his old rival Tony Rominger.

A time bonus earned in an early intermediate sprint gave Laurent Jalabert the first yellow jersey of his career, before the real racing had begun. It did so not, as expected, with the individual time trial on stage eight, but the previous evening, when Miguel Induráin exploded out of the peloton in the Ardennes, dragging Johan Bruyneel along in his wake and gaining a 50-second advantage over his shell-shocked rivals. Bruyneel took the stage win and the yellow jersey at Liège, depriving Induráin of victory in a mass-start stage, something that had been missing from his *palmarès* since his reign began back in 1991. That marauding attack may have taken the edge off his time

trial performance the following day; he won by just 12 seconds over Bjarne Riis, with Rominger third at 58 seconds. Nonetheless, Induráin was in yellow, right on schedule.

In the first Alpine stage, Alex Zülle attacked early and took the stage win. Behind him, Induráin dropped his rivals with consummate ease and gave chase alone, finishing two minutes behind Zülle, but 2mins 9secs ahead of the third-placed rider, Russia's Pavel Tonkov. Only once did the yellow jersey come under credible attack, and it wasn't in the high mountains. On the transitional stage between Saint-Étienne and Mende, on 14 July, Bastille Day, the great Spanish rival of Induráin's Banesto team, ONCE, launched an all-out attack, finished off brilliantly by Laurent Jalabert after a 198-kilometre (123-mile) breakaway. In the Pyrenees, the young Italian Fabio Casartelli, gold-medallist at the Barcelona Olympics, lost control on a hairpin bend on the descent from the Portet d'Aspet. A sickening collision with a concrete marker left him curled in a fetal position at the roadside. He was rushed to hospital, but shortly after arrival, he died. The day after the tragedy, the peloton held a day of mourning and rode in moving silence to Pau. On stage 18, Casartelli's friend and team leader, Lance Armstrong, honoured his memory with an inspirational stage win at Limoges. Induráin won the final time trial to seal his achievement as the first rider to win the Tour de France on five consecutive occasions.

GENERAL CLASSIFICATION

1. **Miguel Induráin** (SPA) Banesto, 3,635 km in 92h.44m.59s. Average speed: 39.191 kph
2. **Alex Zülle** (SUI) ONCE, at 4m.35s.
3. **Bjarne Riis** (DEN) Gewiss-Ballan, at 6m.47s.
4. Laurent Jalabert (FRA) ONCE, at 8m.24s.
5. Ivan Gotti (ITA) Mapei-GB, at 11m.34s.
6. Melchor Mauri (SPA) Mapei-GB, at 15m.20s.

7. Fernando Escartín (SPA) Festina, at 15m.49s.
8. Tony Rominger (SUI) Kelme-Avianca, at 16m.46s.
9. Richard Virenque (FRA) Carrera-Jeans-Tassoni, at 17m.31s.
10. Hernan Buenahora (COL) Castorama, at 18m.50s.
11. Claudio Chiappucci (ITA), Carrera-Jeans-Tassoni, at 18m.55s.
12. Laurent Madouas (FRA) Brescialat, at 20m.37s.
13. Marco Pantani (ITA) Gewiss-Ballan, at 26m.20s.

14. Paolo Lanfranchi (ITA) Motorola, at 29m.41s.
15. Bruno Cenghialta (ITA) Gewiss-Ballan, at 29m.55s.
16. Álvaro Mejía (COL) TVM, at 33m.40s.
17. Bo Hamburger (DEN) Novell, at 34m.49s.
18. Vjatceslav Ekimov (RUS) Festina, at 39m.51s.
19. Laurent Dufaux (SUI) ONCE, at 45m.55s.
20. Erik Breukink (HOL) ONCE, at 47m.27s.

82ᵀᴴ TOUR DE FRANCE, 20 STAGES – 3,635 KM

			STAGE	STAGE WINNER	YELLOW JERSEY
Prologue	Saturday 1 July	7.3 km	Saint-Brieuc – Saint-Brieuc (TT)	J. Durand (FRA)	J. Durand
Stage 1	Sunday 2 July	233.5 km	Dinan – Lannion	F. Baldato (ITA)	J. Durand
Stage 2	Monday 3 July	235.5 km	Perros-Guirec – Vitré	M. Cipollini (ITA)	L. Jalabert
Stage 3	Tuesday 4 July	67 km	Mayenne – Alençon (TTT)	Gewiss-Ballan	L. Jalabert
Stage 4	Wednesday 5 July	162 km	Alençon – Le Havre	M. Cipollini (ITA)	I. Gotti
Stage 5	Thursday 6 July	261 km	Fécamp – Dunkerque	J. Blijlevens (HOL)	I. Gotti
Stage 6	Friday 7 July	202 km	Dunkerque – Charleroi (BEL)	E. Zabel (GER)	B. Riis
Stage 7	Saturday 8 July	203 km	Charleroi (BEL) – Liège (BEL)	J. Bruyneel (BEL)	J. Bruyneel
Stage 8	Sunday 9 July	54 km	Huy (BEL) – Seraing (BEL) (TT)	M. Induráin (SPA)	M. Induráin
Stage 9	Tuesday 11 July	160 km	Aime-La Plagne – La Plagne	A. Zülle (SUI)	M. Induráin
Stage 10	Wednesday 12 July	162.5 km	Aime-La Plagne – L'Alpe-d'Huez	M. Pantani (ITA)	M. Induráin
Stage 11	Thursday 13 July	199 km	Bourg-d'Oisans – Saint-Étienne	M. Sciandri (GBR)	M. Induráin
Stage 12	Friday 14 July	222.5 km	Saint-Étienne – Mende	L. Jalabert (FRA)	M. Induráin
Stage 13	Saturday 15 July	245 km	Mende – Revel	S. Outschakov (UKR)	M. Induráin
Stage 14	Sunday 16 July	164 km	St-Orens – Guzet-Neige	M. Pantani (ITA)	M. Induráin
Stage 15	Tuesday 18 July	206 km	St-Girons – Cauterets-Crêtes-du-Lys	R. Virenque (FRA)	M. Induráin
Stage 16	Wednesday 19 July	237 km	Tarbes – Pau	Stage annulled	M. Induráin
Stage 17	Thursday 20 July	246 km	Pau – Bordeaux	E. Zabel (GER)	M. Induráin
Stage 18	Friday 21 July	166.5 km	Montpon-Ménestérol – Limoges	L. Armstrong (USA)	M. Induráin
Stage 19	Saturday 22 July	46.5 km	Lac de Vassivière – Lac de Vassivière (TT)	M. Induráin (SPA)	M. Induráin
Stage 20	Sunday 23 July	155 km	Ste-Geneviève-des-Bois – Paris	D. Abdoujaparov (UZB)	M. Induráin

In the Ardennes, Miguel Induráin, wearing a helmet as Belgian law prescribes, went on the attack. It was a demonstration of the strength he was sometimes criticized for using with excessive moderation.

Day of mourning

CAUTERETS: We'll never forget the minute of silence observed at Tarbes. Time seemed to stand still. The moment was unbearable for some riders who, like Marco Pantani, went off to grieve alone in a corner. No one will ever forget the crossing of the Pyrenees during the 1995 Tour. No one should ever forget it. A rider died and, the following day, his 119 colleagues, most of whom didn't know him, came together to honour his memory. For a day, they abandoned the race, the prizes, their profession and their ambitions, great or small. It was a day of mourning, and was poignant and admirable.

Was it the right thing to do? Was it the only course of action to take? Everyone has a right to their own opinion. For example, Bjarne Riis considered that the harm had been done and there was no point adding to it, a point of view that is as valid as any other. However, the Dane mourned with everyone else. In these days of excessive selfishness, the peloton gave a great lesson in solidarity.

Some members of the general public, who had got up early to see the racing, didn't understand, nor did some of the street

The peloton paid homage in Pau, allowing Fabio's team, Motorola, to cross the line first.

vendors who make money out of the Tour. But the riders didn't sell anyone short. The Tour is the only free sporting event and it was not time wasted to follow a peloton so unanimously determined to pay their respects. Being a professional means respecting your profession, respecting other people and those who pay your wages and, in this respect, professional cyclists, who suffer more than most top-level athletes, have nothing to learn from anyone. For 15 days, they've given us a sometimes exceptional competition and, on the sixteenth, they decided that reason dictated equally exceptional restraint.

Being a professional also means setting an example, presenting the best possible image of yourself and your sport. And what more tragically fine example could there be than Andrea Peron, the other Italian in the American Motorola team and friend of Fabio Casartelli, symbolically crossing the finish ahead of the peloton in Béarn?

But the show must go on, and the Tour will recommence where it left off. There will be more falls, like Abdou on the Champs-Élysées, like Jalabert and Nelissen at Armentières, and there will be more great athletic feats. Wherever he is now, Fabio Casartelli can say that he was a member of one of the finest professions in the world.

Above: The day after the tragedy, the peloton is in shock. At the start in Tarbes, the yellow jersey and Casartelli's team (Armstrong second from the right), during the minute's silence.

Left: The appalling sight of Fabio Casartelli, fatally injured, on the Portet d'Aspet.

311

Welcome to the Pantheon of the Greats

He's done it! And even now, he doesn't consider himself better than anyone. Put simply, Miguel Induráin likes a job well done, and he's performed this one to perfection – for the fifth time! With great wisdom (Induráin is also a wise champion) and with an innate sense of measure, he simply tries to do the job fate has meted out as best he can. If he'd been a ploughman, he'd have taken care to plough the perfect furrow. And he'd have adapted perfectly to such a life because it would have been healthy, and he would have been just as happy at the end of each long working day.

He's well aware of the debt he owes nature, which endowed him with the quiet strength that has brought him to this sporting pinnacle. But he often says that a victory or a brilliant performance isn't inherently better than an object produced by the hand of a skilled craftsman. For Induráin it is the skill and care that a man puts into his work that shows his worth. But Miguel Induráin is no craftsman, he's

an artist, and his work has already entered the gallery of cycling, and also of sport as a whole. Today, as the winner of this Tour de France, the Spanish champion rightly occupies the place reserved for him alongside Jacques Anquetil, Eddy Merckx and Bernard Hinault, as a five-time winner of the Tour. He could almost be regarded a step above them, in that he's unique in having won five consecutive Tours, although he'd be the first to insist there's no comparison; each of these giants was great in his own way.

Miguel Induráin's racing style has become familiar to us over the past five years. It hasn't changed much, merely improved with time. But his route to fame, from strapping adolescent to accomplished champion, is highly atypical compared with his famous predecessors. Jacques Anquetil (1957), Eddy Merckx (1969) and Bernard Hinault (1978) all won the Tour at their first attempt.

Miguel Induráin, for his part, learned patience in the good company of Pedro

Delgado, which gave José Miguel Echavarri time to chisel out, tiny blow by tiny blow, an immense champion from the raw material he'd acquired. Aged 31, Induráin has just ridden his eleventh Tour, reminding us that his apprenticeship extended over six Tours. Armed with the profound knowledge these long years provided, he was able to make full use of his astonishing athletic potential.

Was this Tour the easiest, even though his team-mates were for once momentarily overwhelmed by the ambition of the great ONCE team and the brilliance of Jalabert on the road to Mende? It's hard to say. What is clear is that Induráin's margin over his closest challenger has always been in the relatively small range of between three and five minutes – 4mins 35secs in this case. But there's no particular conclusion to draw from this, other than that this incomparable *rouleur* achieved a slightly lower margin in his speciality, the time trial, than in the past: Denmark's Bjarne Riis, third on the Champs-Élysées podium, lost only, and exactly, one minute over the two long time trials.

Less devastating against the clock, it nevertheless seems to us that Miguel Induráin has brought added value this year, compared to his earlier wins. It's hard to say whether the general public thinks he has ridden with real flair since he still hasn't won a mass-start stage; the only two to his name are Cauterets in 1989 and Luz-Ardiden in 1990, both in the years before he won the Tour. However, he was certainly inspiring on at least two occasions:

1) during the stage to Liège, on the Côte des Forges, where his beautifully improvised attack was one of the finest moments of his Tour de France career.

2) on the spectacular climb to La Plagne, where he showed his superiority over all his rivals. When he dropped his hands onto the lower curve of the handlebars he was immune to all but the irresistible accelerations of a climber of genius like Marco Pantani, as happened the day after La Plagne, at Alpe-d'Huez and in the Pyrenees near Guzet-Niege.

Miguel Induráin, in yellow as usual. On either side, Richard Virenque is wearing the polka-dot jersey and Laurent Jalabert has won his second green jersey.

For the fifth time in a row, Miguel Induráin rode along
the Champs-Élysées in the yellow jersey – a record.

A new chapter begins

Stage seven of the 1996 Tour de France, a gruelling ride through the Eastern Alps from Chambéry, the old capital of the Dukes of Savoy, to the modern ski station of Les Arcs, was truly a journey from one era into another. There was drama from the start: the yellow jersey, Stéphane Heulot of the Gan team, abandoned; reigning Vuelta a España champion Laurent Jalabert was dropped at the foot of the Col de la Madeleine, the very first pass of the day; his team-mate Alex Zülle, another potential challenger, was involved in two serious falls, blinded by the rain; and Johan Bruyneel slid into a gully after swerving to avoid a rock. All of which paled into insignificance when, just minutes from the stage finish, Miguel Induráin, whose face had betrayed no trace of strain or fatigue for six years, was suddenly transfigured with pain. It soon became clear that he was in trouble, and he eventually struggled across the line in sixteenth place, 4mins 19secs behind the stage winner Luc Leblanc. He had been suffering the pangs of hunger, and low blood sugar was the immediate cause of his poor stage finish. However, the Val-d'Isère time trials the following day seemed to confirm that this could be an irreversible decline. He could only finish fifth, 1min 1sec behind the race leader Evgeni Berzin, the blond-haired Russian who, as a 23-year-old, had defeated Induráin in the 1994 Tour of Italy. Berzin was a credible race leader, and a plausible successor to the great Spaniard; there was, as yet, no way of knowing how brief the Berzin era was to be.

The day after the time trial, the 190-kilometre (118-mile) epic from Val-d'Isère to Sestrières was shortened due to heavy snow on the Iseran and Galibier, leaving a 46-kilometre (28-mile) sprint. This time, Bjarne Riis dropped Induráin and Rominger by 28 seconds, and took over the yellow jersey when Berzin crossed the line 1min 23secs off the pace. In the Pyrenees, Riis became the first yellow jersey to win a mass-start stage since Laurent Fignon in 1989, and Induráin lost the chance of ever outshining the likes of Jacques Anquetil, Eddy Merckx and Bernard Hinault. On stage 17 he rode past the family farm at Villava in a group of stragglers, but was greeted by rapturous crowds in Pamplona at the stage finish. The time trial at Saint-Émilion revealed the ability of Riis's young German team-mate, Jan Ullrich, who at only 22 years of age finished runner-up in Paris, with Richard Virenque on the bottom step of the podium. As well as being the first Dane ever to win the Tour, Bjarne Riis had the honour of bringing Induráin's long reign to an end.

GENERAL CLASSIFICATION

1. **Bjarne Riis** (DEN) Telekom, 3,765 km in 95h.57m.16s; Average speed: 39.235 kph
2. **Jan Ullrich** (GER) Telekom, at 1m.41s.
3. **Richard Virenque** (FRA) Festina, at 4m.37s.
4. Laurent Dufaux (SUI) Festina, at 5m.53s.
5. Peter Luttenberger (AUT) Carrera, at 7m.7s.
6. Luc Leblanc (FRA) Polti, at 10m.3s.
7. Piotr Ugrumov (LAT) Roslotto, at 10m.4s.
8. Fernando Escartín (SPA) Kelme, at 10m.26s.
9. Abraham Olano (SPA) Mapei, at 11m.
10. Tony Rominger (SUI) Mapei, at 11m.53s.
11. Miguel Induráin (SPA) Banesto, at 14m.14s.
12. Patrick Jonker (HOL) ONCE, at 18m.58s.
13. Bo Hamburger (DEN) TVM, at 22m.19s.
14. Udo Bolts (GER) Telekom, at 25m.56s.
15. Alberto Elli (ITA) MG-Technologym, at 26m.18s.
16. Manuel Fernandez Gines (SPA) Mapei, at 26m.28s.
17. Leonardo Piepoli (ITA) Refin, at 27m.36s.
18. Laurent Brochard (FRA) Festina, at 32m.11s.
19. Michele Bartoli (ITA) MG-Technologym, at 37m.18s.
20. Evgueni Berzin (RUS) Gewiss, at 38m.

83RD TOUR DE FRANCE, 21 STAGES – 3,765 KM

's-Hertogenbosch
Wasquehal
Nogent-sur-Oise
Soissons
PARIS
Palaiseau
Lac de Madine
Besançon
Arc-et-Senans
Les Arcs
Bourg-Saint-Maurice
Brive-la-Gaillarde
Besse
Aix-les-Bains
Tulle
Val-d'Isère
Saint-Émilion
Chambéry
Bordeaux
Turin
Sestrières
Superbesse-Sancy
Valence
Agen
Villeneuve-sur-Lot
Le-Puy-en-Velay
Gap
Hendaye
Lourdes-Hautacam
Pampelune
Argelès-Gazost

STAGE		STAGE WINNER	YELLOW JERSEY
9.4 km		A. Zülle (SUI)	A. Zülle
209 km		F. Moncassin (FRA)	A. Zülle
247.5 km		M. Cipollini (ITA)	A. Zülle
195 km		E. Zabel (GER)	F. Moncassin
232 km		C. Saugrain (FRA)	S. Heulot
242 km		J. Blijlevens (HOL)	S. Heulot
207 km		M. Boogerd (HOL)	S. Heulot
200 km		L. Leblanc (FRA)	E. Berzin
30.5 km		E. Berzin (RUS)	E. Berzin
46 km		B. Riis (DEN)	B. Riis
208.5 km		E. Zabel (GER)	B. Riis
202 km		J.J. González (COL)	B. Riis
143.5 km		P. Richard (SUI)	B. Riis
177 km		R. Sörensen (DEN)	B. Riis
186.5 km		D. Abdoujaparov (UZB)	B. Riis
176 km		M. Podenzana (ITA)	B. Riis
199 km		B. Riis (DEN)	B. Riis
262 km		L. Dufaux (SUI)	B. Riis
154.5 km		B. Voskamp (HOL)	B. Riis
226.5 km		F. Moncassin (FRA)	B. Riis
63.5 km		J. Ullrich (GER)	B. Riis
147.5 km		F. Baldato (ITA)	B. Riis

This time, Miguel Induráin had to give way. The champion had fallen, but his dignity remained intact as Bjarne Riis put an end to an era.

Somewhere in the Franche-Comté, in pouring rain, Lance Armstrong removes his number and abandons the race. A few months later, he learned he was riddled with cancer.

Above: The moving homage paid by the people of Navarre to their champion. Miguel Induráin arrived in Pamplona behind the leaders, but still received an enormous ovation.

Left: For Bjarne Riis, 32, the first Danish Tour winner, the danger came from his young team-mate, Jan Ullrich.

Jan Ullrich: the start of a new era?

The 1997 Tour de France departed from Rouen, where the surviving five-time Tour winners, Eddy Merckx, Bernard Hinault and Miguel Induráin, visited Jacques Anquetil's grave. From the start the reigning champion Bjarne Riis, a Dane riding for Deutsche Telekom, could feel the previous year's runner-up, his German team-mate Jan Ullrich, breathing down his neck. The Prologue specialist Chris Boardman achieved his task with just two seconds to spare; Ullrich was right behind him. The charismatic Italian sprinter Mario Cipollini seized the yellow jersey with the first of two stage wins, before France's Cédric Vasseur broke away alone to win stage five by two and a half minutes. Twenty-seven years earlier, Vasseur's father Alain had won a stage in the Tour. Vasseur the Younger gallantly defended his race lead for four days until Ullrich demonstrated his superiority with Teutonic detachment by taking the race to pieces on the punishing climb of Arcalis into Andorra. Ullrich's takeover signalled the arrival of a new star. He drove the point home in Saint Étienne by winning the time trial, overtaking Richard Virenque, who had set off three minutes before him. Virenque, fighting for his fourth King of the Mountains title as well as the overall race win, rode with such determination that he took second place.

With the Alps still to be crossed, Virenque refused to surrender, despite Ullrich's lead of over five minutes. But it was the tiny Italian climber Marco Pantani who stole the show on Alpe-d'Huez and again on the stage finishing at Morzine; both days, he finished alone, far ahead of Ullrich and Virenque. His performance earned him third place overall. Virenque, meanwhile, fought so hard that it sometimes seemed he could threaten Ullrich's lead. He summoned his Festina team-mates to launch a carefully choreographed offensive on the Glandon, forcing the stewards to extend the time limit in order to avoid eliminating a pack of 93 riders. Virenque needled Ullrich all day, until just the two of them remained, locked in combat on the climb up to Courchevel. Magnanimously, Ullrich allowed him the stage victory. Nonetheless, Ullrich went through difficult moments, notably in the Vosges, where Virenque and his team-mates missed a golden opportunity to seize the *maillot jaune*, despite Didier Rous taking Festina's fourth stage victory. The French public was overcome with 'Virenquemania', although it was Ullrich who became the first German winner of the Tour with a comfortable lead of 9 mins 9 secs. At twenty three and a half years old, everything suggested this would be a very long reign.

GENERAL CLASSIFICATION

1. **Jan Ullrich** (GER) Telekom, 3,950 km in 100h.30m.35s; Average speed: 39.237 kph
2. **Richard Virenque** (FRA) Festina, at 9m.9s.
3. **Marco Pantani** (ITA) Mercatone-Uno, at 14m.03s.
4. Abraham Olano (SPA) Banesto, at 15m.55s.
5. Fernando Escartín (SPA) Kelme, at 20m.32s.
6. Francesco Casagrande (ITA) Saeco, at 22m.47s.
7. Bjarne Riis (DEN) Telekom, at 26m.34s.
8. José María Jiménez (SPA) Banesto, at 31m.17s.
9. Laurent Dufaux (SUI) Festina, at 31m.55s.
10. Roberto Conti (ITA) Mercatone-Uno, at 32m.26s.
11. Beat Zberg (SUI) Mercatone-Uno, at 35m.41s.
12. Oscar Camenzind (SUI) Mapei-GB, at 35m.52s.
13. Peter Luttenberger (AUT) Rabobank, at 45m.39s.
14. Manuel Beltran (SPA) Banesto, at 49m.34s.
15. Jean-Cyril Robin (FRA) US Postal, at 58m.35s.
16. Michael Boogerd (HOL) Rabobank, at 1h.0m.33s.
17. Bobby Julich (USA) Cofidis, at 1h.1m.10s.
18. Daniele Nardello (ITA) Mapei, at 1h.1m.30s.
19. Christophe Moreau (FRA) Festina, at 1h.2m.48s.
20. Stéphane Heulot (FRA) Française Des Jeux, at 1h.6m.13s.

84TH TOUR DE FRANCE, 21 STAGES – 3,950 KM

			STAGE	STAGE WINNER	YELLOW JERSEY
Prologue	Saturday 5 July	7.3 km	Rouen – Rouen (TT)	C. Boardman (GBR)	C. Boardman
Stage 1	Sunday 6 July	192 km	Rouen – Forges-les-Eaux	M. Cipollini (ITA)	M. Cipollini
Stage 2	Monday 7 July	262 km	Saint-Valéry-en-Caux – Vire	M. Cipollini (ITA)	M. Cipollini
Stage 3	Tuesday 8 July	224 km	Vire – Plumelec	E. Zabel (GER)	M. Cipollini
Stage 4	Wednesday 9 July	223 km	Plumelec – Le Puy-du-Fou	N. Minali (ITA)	M. Cipollini
Stage 5	Thursday 10 July	261.5 km	Chantonnay – La Châtre	C. Vasseur (FRA)	C. Vasseur
Stage 6	Friday 11 July	215 km	Le Blanc – Marennes	J. Blijlevens (HOL)	C. Vasseur
Stage 7	Saturday 12 July	194 km	Marennes – Bordeaux	E. Zabel (GER)	C. Vasseur
Stage 8	Sunday 13 July	161.5 km	Sauternes – Pau	E. Zabel (GER)	C. Vasseur
Stage 9	Monday 14 July	182 km	Pau – Loudenvielle	L. Brochard (FRA)	C. Vasseur
Stage 10	Tuesday 15 July	252.5 km	Luchon – Andorre-Arcalis (AND)	J. Ullrich (GER)	J. Ullrich
Stage 11	Wednesday 16 July	192 km	Andorre (AND) – Perpignan	L. Desbiens (FRA)	J. Ullrich
Stage 12	Friday 18 July	55 km	Saint-Étienne – Saint-Étienne (TT)	J. Ullrich (GER)	J. Ullrich
Stage 13	Saturday 19 July	203.5 km	Saint-Étienne – L'Alpe-d'Huez	M. Pantani (ITA)	J. Ullrich
Stage 14	Sunday 20 July	148 km	Bourg-d'Oisans – Courchevel	R. Virenque (FRA)	J. Ullrich
Stage 15	Monday 21 July	208.5 km	Courchevel – Morzine	M. Pantani (ITA)	J. Ullrich
Stage 16	Tuesday 22 July	181 km	Morzine – Fribourg (SUI)	C. Mengin (FRA)	J. Ullrich
Stage 17	Wednesday 23 July	218.5 km	Fribourg (SUI) – Colmar	N. Stephens (AUS)	J. Ullrich
Stage 18	Thursday 24 July	175.5 km	Colmar – Montbéliard	D. Rous (FRA)	J. Ullrich
Stage 19	Friday 25 July	172 km	Montbéliard – Dijon	M. Traversoni (ITA)	J. Ullrich
Stage 20	Saturday 26 July	63 km	Disneyland – Disneyland (TT)	A. Olano (SPA)	J. Ullrich
Stage 21	Sunday 27 July	149.5 km	Disneyland – Paris	N. Minali (ITA)	J. Ullrich

Jan Ullrich showed tremendous power in the mountains. With his incredible athletic potential, the young German seemed to dominate the future of the Tour.

Ullrich, a German Colossus

Ullrich's show of strength during the climb to the Andorran resort of Arcalis exchanged his German champion's jersey for the yellow jersey.

ANDORRA: The sweat trickles down his boyish cheeks, the freckles hidden beneath a hint of flame-coloured beard. Even if his eyes were bright with happiness, there was no real winner's smile. It's just after 5.15pm and Jan Ullrich has just joined the ranks of the cycling greats, the hermetically-sealed circle of the yellow jerseys, but he doesn't welcome this new covenant with a tear. His first thought is to clean his face and put on a pair of tracksuit bottoms. It isn't simply to make himself presentable for the cameramen and photographers, this young man with the look of an adolescent behaves like an adult – above all, he doesn't want to catch cold. On the Tour, every little detail counts. A little later, at the press conference, after a heartfelt embrace from Riis, the deposed hero, he even tucked himself up in his Telekom team jacket with a huge matching pink towel round his neck. The yellow

jersey is no longer visible. Not to worry, there'll be plenty of time to see it during the race.

He's like that, the new leader of the Tour; mature, even if he was only born in 1973. He is already sitting on the wheel of Anquetil, Merckx and Hinault. In their image, a great future is predicted. But what prophet could have foretold such a future for his mother, a few weeks before Christmas 1973, when the nurse brought her this cute little baby with ginger curls?

In Rostock, a town swept by the winds that roar across the Baltic, his mother struggled to bring up her family as best she could. Her husband, a stonemason, was not wealthy, and her secretary's wages did not stretch to luxuries. Even so, their three sons wanted for nothing. Stefan, the eldest, was passionate about athletics. He achieved good results and benefited from the coaching system employed in East Germany. Jan was originally interested in football and didn't take up cycling until the age of nine when he won a cycling race organized at school. He left the other competitors standing on a 'bit of a hill', much as he has just done in the Tour. Only this time the 'bit of a hill' had become a mountain pass, the fifth of the day, leaden with heat.

'Before the start of the stage, it was decided, with Riis, that we'd set a fairly fast pace, like yesterday, and establish a small leading group,' Ullrich explains. 'It worked and I kept up the pace. But towards the end, when I turned round, there was no one behind me. So I just kept going.' Simply, quietly, almost completely relaxed. He added: 'They say I climbed well, but I could have gone faster. Even so, I put in a fair amount of effort.' His face, however, seems smooth, unmarked by the dreadful contortions of intense effort. The face of the rider digging deep into his physical reserves is not yet part of his repertoire. And this young man has plenty of reserves, built up through hard work over the past ten years, ever since the East German system caught up with him and the course of his life was mapped out. At the age of 12, he packed his bags to go and join SC Dynamo Berlin. His mother wasn't worried, she'd entrusted him to the

system and Peter Beckker, the coach, had taken a shine to the lad. His real father didn't care one way or the other: he'd left too long before to give a damn.

From that point on, Ullrich's life was entirely devoted to cycling, punctuated by bursts of training and body-building sessions in a small, austere room where good old East German methods and weights worked wonders. 'But I was happy,' confirms the new yellow jersey, 'and I couldn't really see much difference with the West. As a sportsman I was privileged and the collapse of the Berlin

The yellow jersey asserts himself ahead of Richard Virenque; the French climber skilfully managed to create the illusion of a duel.

A transfer of power within the German Telekom team. For Bjarne Riis, the 1996 Tour winner, the power was short lived.

Richard Virenque and Jan Ullrich locked in battle on the climb to Courchevel. The yellow jersey was magnanimous towards the courageous French climber.

Wall didn't change my life very much.' But it did change one or two things. Instead of straining his eyes trying to make out images of cycle races recorded secretly from Western television, he could now watch these races at the click of a button. He could also admit to having new idols since, while he was still just as enthusiastic about the Peace Race and professional riders such as Ludwig and Ampler, he could now openly admire Lemond, Fignon and Co. The two heroes of the 1989 Tour had inspired his ambition to win the yellow jersey. 'They were competing for yellow and, as I watched them on TV, I wanted to be like them,' he admitted. He's achieved that ambition sooner than he thought... In 1992, Peter Beckker took his young protégés from Berlin to Hamburg and, the following year, saw Ullrich win the World Amateur Championships in Oslo. But he never had the pleasure of seeing him race in the rainbow jersey. Without sponsors, and therefore without funding, Beckker had to shut up shop. Ullrich was forced to turn professional in a very short space of time. After winning a bronze medal in the World

Time Trial Championships (behind Chris Boardman and Andrea Chiurato) in the summer of 1994, Ullrich found himself in the German Telekom team which, without realizing it, had probably made one of the best deals of the late 1990s, although Ullrich's professional debut was not exactly brilliant. Life had too many temptations for the young East German, fast cars in particular. But a serious encounter with the police, the love of a young Bavarian girl named Gaby and a new home in Merdingen, near the French border, have put Ullrich back on track. Walter Godefroot and his assistants didn't waste time teaching him about life on a bike, its demands and its code of practice. Having missed the Tour in 1995, he shone in 1996 when his natural abilities came to the fore – his strength, speed, altruism and above all his calm which, according to his close friends, was the secret of his success. Ullrich has no doubt; he doesn't know the meaning of anxiety, and he always did what he was told. When they told him to help Riis, he helped Riis. And when they gave him his chance... he took it.

Three cheers for Germany's Erik Zabel – at Plumelec, Bordeaux and Pau. Green seems to suit him!

Scandal!

It all began with the arrest of a *soigneur* named Willy Voet at the Franco-Belgian border. Voet was driving a Festina team car bound for Dublin and the start of the 1998 Tour de France. Inside, French customs officers found a huge stockpile of drugs and associated products, most notably EPO, a hormone that helps oxygenate the blood. The greatest scandal in the history of cycling, perhaps of all sport, had just broken, and the world was about to learn just how widespread and sophisticated the techniques, products and practices of modern doping had become. Bruno Roussel, Festina's *directeur sportif*, and Dr Eric Rijckaert, Festina's team doctor, were questioned and incarcerated. Roussel's confession led to the Festina team being suspended from the Tour in Brive. The following day, the highest profile Festina rider, and the most defiant, Richard Virenque, burst into tears before the television cameras.

With *l'affaire Festina* providing the media with more material than it could publish, the race itself took a low priority. Chris Boardman had taken his customary Prologue win before his customary crash out on stage two. Mario Cipollini had taken his usual couple of stage wins, and Jan Ullrich had emulated Miguel Induráin by kick-starting the race-proper with victory in the first long time trial. Amid daily revelations about the peloton and its lifestyle, courtroom hearings and police searches, the event became a bizarre sporting soap opera. The TVM team were taken in for questioning. Italy's Rodolfo Massi, leader of the mountains competition, was charged with selling doping products after a large stash was found in his hotel room. Morale in the peloton was ebbing. On two occasions the Tour was nearly abandoned. At Tarascon-sur-Ariège, some of the riders went on strike, and between Albertville and Aix-les-Bains, the peloton stopped several times to express solidarity with the TVM team who were being investigated. The stage was annulled, but the Tour continued all the way to Paris, albeit without the Spanish teams who quit the race.

Ullrich's expected cakewalk to Paris was interrupted not just by the Festina affair, but by the brilliant climber Marco Pantani, who inflicted a devastating defeat over Jan Ullrich on the climb to Les Deux Alpes. Pantani had won the Giro d'Italia in June, and was the first to attempt the double since Induráin in 1995, the year in which the first of a series of appalling injuries had threatened to end Pantani's career. In an age in which powerful time triallists dominated the Tour, Pantani's inspired climbing broke a psychological barrier and caught the public imagination. Presented as the saviour of the Tour de France, his win had to be set against the reality of a severely disrupted Tour. Just 96 cyclists finally reached Paris.

GENERAL CLASSIFICATION

1. **Marco Pantani** (ITA) Mercatone Uno, 3,875 km in 92h.49m.46s; Average speed: 39.983 kph
2. **Jan Ullrich** (GER) Telekom, at 3m.21s.
3. **Bobby Julich** (USA) Cofidis, at 4m.8s.
4. Christophe Rinero (FRA) Cofidis, at 9m.16s.
5. Michael Boogerd (HOL) Rabobank, at 11m.26s.
6. Jean-Cyril Robin (FRA) US Postal, at 14m.57s.
7. Roland Meier (SUI) Mapei-Bricobi, at 15m.13s.
8. Daniele Nardello (ITA) Mapei-Bricobi, at 16m.7s.
9. Giuseppe Di Grande (ITA) Polti, at 17m.35s.
10. Axel Merckx (BEL) Polti, at 17m.39s.
11. Bjarne Riis (DEN) Telekom, at 19m.10s.
12. Dariusz Baranowski (POL) US Postal, at 19m.58s.
13. Stéphane Heulot (FRA) La Française Des Jeux, at 20m.57s.
14. Leonardo Piepoli (ITA) Saeco, at 22m.45s.
15. Bo Hamburger (DEN) Casino, at 26m.39s.
16. Kurt Van De Wouwer (BEL) Lotto-MobiStar, at 27m.20s.
17. Kevin Livingston (USA) Cofidis, at 34m.3s.
18. Jörg Jaksche (GER) Polti, at 35m.41s.
19. Peter Farazjin (BEL) Lotto-MobiStar, at 36m.10s.
20. Andreï Teteriouk (KAZ) Lotto-MobiStar, at 37m.3s.

85TH TOUR DE FRANCE, 21 STAGES – 3,875 KM

			STAGE	STAGE WINNER	YELLOW JERSEY
Prologue	Saturday 11 July	5.6 km	Dublin (IRL) – Dublin (IRL) (TT)	C. Boardman (GBR)	C. Boardman
Stage 1	Sunday 12 July	180.5 km	Dublin (IRL) – Dublin (IRL)	T. Steels (BEL)	C. Boardman
Stage 2	Monday 13 July	205.5 km	Enniscorthy (IRL) – Cork (IRL)	J. Svorada (CZE)	E. Zabel
Stage 3	Tuesday 14 July	169 km	Roscoff – Lorient	J. Heppner (GER)	B. Hamburger
Stage 4	Wednesday 15 July	252 km	Plouay – Cholet	J. Blijlevens (HOL)	S. O'Grady
Stage 5	Thursday 16 July	228.5 km	Cholet – Châteauroux	M. Cipollini (ITA)	S. O'Grady
Stage 6	Friday 17 July	204.5 km	La Châtre – Brive	M. Cipollini (ITA)	S. O'Grady
Stage 7	Saturday 18 July	58 km	Meyrignac-l'Église – Corrèze (TT)	J. Ullrich (GER)	J. Ullrich
Stage 8	Sunday 19 July	190.5 km	Brive – Montauban	J. Durand (FRA)	L. Desbiens
Stage 9	Monday 20 July	210 km	Montauban – Pau	L. Van Bon (HOL)	L. Desbiens
Stage 10	Tuesday 21 July	196.5 km	Pau – Luchon	R. Massi (ITA)	J. Ullrich
Stage 11	Wednesday 22 July	170 km	Luchon – Plateau de Beille	M. Pantani (ITA)	J. Ullrich
Stage 12	Friday 24 July	222 km	Tarascon-sur-Ariège – Cap d'Agde	T. Steels (BEL)	J. Ullrich
Stage 13	Saturday 25 July	196 km	Frontignan-la-Peyrade – Carpentras	D. Nardello (ITA)	J. Ullrich
Stage 14	Sunday 26 July	186.5 km	Valréas – Grenoble	S. O'Grady (AUS)	J. Ullrich
Stage 15	Monday 27 July	189 km	Grenoble – Les Deux-Alpes	M. Pantani (ITA)	M. Pantani
Stage 16	Tuesday 28 July	204 km	Vizille – Albertville	J. Ullrich (GER)	M. Pantani
Stage 17	Wednesday 29 July	149 km	Albertville – Aix-les-Bains	Stage annulled	M. Pantani
Stage 18	Thursday 30 July	218.5 km	Aix-les-Bains – Neufchâtel (SUI)	T. Steels (BEL)	M. Pantani
Stage 19	Friday 31 July	242 km	La Chaux-de-Fonds (SUI) – Autun	M. Backstedt (SWE)	M. Pantani
Stage 20	Saturday 1 August	52 km	Montceau-les-Mines – Le Creusot (TT)	J. Ullrich (GER)	M. Pantani
Stage 21	Sunday 2 August	147.5 km	Melun – Paris	T. Steels (BEL)	M. Pantani

Storm clouds hung over the Tour in Tarascon-sur-Ariège as Pantani and the other
riders refused to start the twelfth stage. For the first time in Tour de France history,
the race was nearly prevented from reaching Paris.

A sorry affair

DUBLIN: This is without doubt only the beginning of an affair that will see many new developments over the days, or even weeks, to come. The Tour de France has been rocked by the announcement that a significant quantity of doping products have been seized from a car sporting Festina's team colours, travelling to Dublin.

We have learned that one part of the haul consisted of more than 400 bottles, capsules and doping products bought in Germany and Switzerland. The team's trainer, Willy Voet, had gone to collect one of the official cars allotted to the Festina team from Paris, close to the Tour de France head offices. He was detained by French-Belgian customs, at Neuville-en-Ferrain, with the equivalent of 250 doses of EPO (a hormone which facilitates the transport of oxygen in the blood), as well as around a hundred or so doses of anabolic steroids (Saizen and Pantestone), bottles of substances that have yet to be identified and material for their administration – syringes and solutions for injections.

Willy Voet, the Festina *soigneur*, was the first to be imprisoned, and the first to talk.

Miguel Rodríguez, Festina's managing director, learned the bad news while he was surfing the net in Paris. He immediately called Bruno Roussel, his *directeur sportif*, to assure him of his support, and is alleged to have said: 'We are there to win the race. Don't worry about the rest. I trust you. Reassure the team.' Nevertheless, Rodríguez, duped once before when his team was predominantly Dutch, has always maintained that he would not be fooled again. How he will react if the company's image is damaged by this affair, no one can say. Furthermore, he has signed contracts until 2001, which would not withstand the 'gross misconduct' of certain individuals. There are precedents, including the affair involving the Italian MG-Technogym team last year, which withdrew in similar circumstances.

It is too soon to have already forgotten the sad end of MG-Technogym, a team under the direction of Giancarlo Ferretti, one of the peloton's very best *directeurs sportifs*. The 1997 Giro was at Cavalese when the Italian narcotics squad (NAS) raided the hotel where the MG team was staying in the early hours of the morning. They found twenty boxes of anabolic steroids, three boxes of growth hormones and a number of syringes in a trainer's room. The decision to withdraw from the race was taken immediately by MG-Technogym executives. It took many hours of questioning before Ferretti was exonerated.

Today, it is important to underline that the French Cycling Federation has opted to side with the Public Prosecutor in a court action, joining the plaintiffs, presumably in a plea for immediate punishment. The forthcoming confrontation between Bruno Roussel and his trainer, requested by the Public Prosecutor's office, may prove critical. The regional crime squad, who have been on Willy Voet's trail for some time, are convinced that he was not working for Roussel. So who was he working for? One theory put forward was that he was part of a network unrelated to cycling. A member of the Festina team said that Voet should have set off for Calais as soon as he had left the Tour de France garage 'in convoy with other Festina cars' and that nobody knew where he had gone. Bruno Roussel denied everything: 'Let the courts decide,' he said. 'I want to wait for more information before coming to any decision.' It's difficult to imagine that the management of the Tour de France would ban Festina from the race as has been rumoured. The Tour's director, Jean-Marie Leblanc, taking the opportunity to re-affirm his anti-doping stance, qualified what had been said: 'This matter has nothing to do with a cyclist from the Tour de France, it did not take place at the Tour de France, and the inquiry is ongoing.'

Be that as it may, the Tour is in shock, as is Richard Virenque and his team. It will be down to the inquiry to confirm that they're above suspicion – a move that would swiftly relieve the burden that weighs heavily upon the event.

VOET TALKS...

He has confessed. And his revelations could be devastating. After being stopped at the France-Belgium border with almost 400 doping substances in his car, Willy Voet, Festina's trainer, was charged with 'illegally importing and trafficking prohibited goods' and later imprisoned in Loos prison on the outskirts of Lille. Despite his initial statement that the substances he was transporting, including EPO, anabolic steroids (Saizen and Pantestone) and other unidentified substances, were for his own personal use, Voet later explained to police from the Lille regional crime squad that he had in fact acted on the orders of Festina and that he had been entrusted with this kind of assignment many times before. However, it is not only accusations from their *soigneur* that have put Festina in an awkward position. The search, led by customs officers in Lille only a matter of hours after questioning Voet at Festina's race headquarters in Meyzieu in the Rhône, is said to have resulted in the seizure of 18 different substances, some of which were similar to those found in the trainer's car. The distress caused by this affair has never seemed so overwhelming for one of the event's top-ranking teams as it has done during this last week.

1   2

1. Cyclists are taken into police custody at Lyon.

2. The whole caravan of the Tour's officials under surveillance. Highly disturbing.

3. 31 July. The TVM team leave the Tour.

4. A tearful Richard Virenque announced, in a bar close to the time trial finish-line, that the Festina team was withdrawing from the race.

5. 29 July. Jalabert and ONCE pack their bags.

6. Saturday, 18 July. Tour director Jean-Marie Leblanc, announced that the Festina team are banned from the race. He admitted to 'embarrassed relief'.

7. Will they stay or will they go? The riders consult.

3   4

5   6   7

Pantani climbs to the heavens

LES DEUX ALPES: Crossing the line, he closed his eyes and stretched out his arms, like Christ on the cross. This is a man forged by suffering. He's known fractures to the thumb, collarbone, metatarsal, tibia and fibula, two cranial traumas, a dislocated shoulder, prolapsed lumbar vertebrae and cartilage damage. He lost the Giro in 1997 when a black cat crossed his path. In October 1995, in the exercise of his profession, he destroyed his leg and battered his body. He came close to death, but yesterday, he breathed new life into cycling. This was no miracle; it was an extraordinary lesson in perseverance, courage and greatness, from a champion who brought both madness and humanity back to the event. His charisma and genius were reminiscent of legendary climbers like Fausto Coppi or Charly Gaul, the outstanding cyclist from Luxembourg who was his original inspiration.

Marco Pantani broke away 5.5 kilometres (approximately 3.5 miles) from the peak of the Col du Galibier and 48 kilometres (30 miles) from Les Deux Alpes. What followed will go down in the history of the Tour: riding the lightest bicycle in the peloton, with a frame weighing only one kilo, he overtook the six front-runners, who had sprinted ahead early in the race, one by one. A month earlier, the same machine, manufactured by Bianchi, had carried him to victory

Ullrich fought back after his crisis at Les Deux Alpes. With Pantani in close attendance, they rode in perfect harmony on the Madeleine. Ullrich took the stage win at Albertville, helping Pantani consolidate his lead.

in the Giro during its first test-run in the Dolomites. He surged into first position on the Galibier, at which point Jan Ullrich had already conceded 2mins 50secs. On the descent, he stopped to put on a waterproof, allowing Escartín, Serrano, Rinero, Jiminez and Massi to overtake him. Massi proving to

be a true friend, clearly collaborated with Pantani to increase their lead on the yellow jersey (who had, admittedly, suffered a puncture) to 4mins 6secs at the foot of the final climb up to Les Deux Alpes. The yellow jersey, his first, appeared to be in the bag and during the final 9 kilometres (5.5 mile) climb Ullrich conceded almost five extra minutes.

Asked his impressions of the German cyclist, Pantani said: 'His strength lay in his ability to repress his emotions. My determination pushed him over the edge.' With this win, he did not have the cheek to suggest that he was feeling less than 100 percent as he had still been insisting five days earlier, on the final ascent towards the Plateau de Beille. He simply stated: 'This is the greatest day of my career,' and he dedicated his win to Luciano Pezzi, who led the last Italian tour winner, Felice Gimondi, to victory in 1965. Pezzi had always believed in Marco Pantani. He had inspired him with confidence following that appalling accident in October 1995. Sadly, Pezzi died a month ago.

Mission accomplished: Gimondi (left) had been waiting for a successor since 1965.

Star find. Christophe Rinero: first French rider overall (fourth place) and best climber.

Opposite: The dominant force on Les Deux Alpes, Marco Pantani realized a dream and took the yellow jersey, forcing Ullrich to admit defeat.

The second life of Lance Armstrong

On the morning of 5 June 1999, the day before what would have been a brilliant win in the Giro d'Italia, Marco Pantani was suspended when routine blood tests showed suspect readings. It was the gravest in a succession of incidents that threatened cycling's future. The Festina scandal was still vivid in the collective memory, and the idea of suspending the Tour for a year had its supporters. Some were anxious to announce an over-hasty return to 'normality'; others were evidently unable to break out of the old habits. The Tour organizers had declared several cyclists 'unwelcome', including Richard Virenque, regarded as a symbol of doping. Cycling's world governing body, the UCI, overruled them, and as the 1999 Tour de France convened at Puy-du-Fou in the normally sleepy Loire Valley, the atmosphere was tense.

The Prologue was won by a rider who had missed the 1998 Tour. In October 1996, Lance Armstrong had been diagnosed with testicular cancer. His chances of survival were low, and of competing as a professional athlete were negligible. Armstrong had persevered with incredible self-belief, yet despite finishing fourth in the Vuelta a España in September 1998, few considered him a likely Tour de France contender. The first week consisted of seven massive sprints in as many days, with four in

a row won by Mario Cipollini, who set a record average speed of 50.355 kph (31.29 mph) in the stage from Laval to Blois. The Estonian sprinter Jan Kirsipuu wore yellow for a week, before Armstrong won the individual time trial at Metz, gaining nearly a minute on Alex Zülle. Zülle, who would prove Amrstrong's greatest rival, had already lost more than six minutes in a fall on the treacherous Passage de Gois, a cobbled pathway on the Vendée coast that is submerged at high tide. Armstrong had proven himself the best time-triallist in the Tour; the following day he proved himself the best climber, catching and then dropping Zülle, Escartín and Virenque on the climb to Sestrières.

Armstrong's transformation was impressive. Once a stocky one-day champion, he had become an unbeatable time-triallist while re-introducing the fluid, high-cadence pedalling of the classic climbers. Perhaps inevitably given cycling's recent past, Armstrong's sheer supremacy attracted suspicion and hostility from a French public starved of success (for the first time since 1926 French riders failed to win even a stage). Armstrong was the second American to win the Tour, nine years after Greg Lemond's third and final victory. Lemond's recovery had been dramatic; Armstrong's was the comeback of the century.

GENERAL CLASSIFICATION

1. **Lance Armstrong** (USA) US Postal, 3,686.8 km in 91h.32m.16s; Average Speed: 40.276 kph
2. **Alex Zülle** (SUI), Banesto, at 7m.37s.
3. **Fernando Escartín** (SPA) Kelme, at 10m.26s.
4. Laurent Dufaux (SUI) Saeco, at 14m.43s.
5. Angel Luis Casero (SPA) Vitalicio Seguros, at 15m.11s.
6. Abraham Olano (SPA) ONCE, at 16m.47s.

7. Daniele Nardello (ITA) Mapei, at 17m.2s.
8. Richard Virenque (FRA) Polti, at 17m.28s.
9. Wladimir Belli (ITA) Festina, at 17m.37s.
10. Andrea Peron (ITA) ONCE, at 23m.10s.
11. Kurt Van De Wouwer (BEL) Lotto, at 23m.32s.
12. David Etxebarria (SPA) ONCE, at 26m.41s.
13. Tyler Hamilton (USA) US Postal, at 26m.53s.

14. Stéphane Heulot (FRA) La Française Des Jeux, at 27m.58s.
15. Roland Meier (SUI) Cofidis, at 28m.44s.
16. Benoît Salmon (FRA) Casino, at 28m.59s.
17. Alberto Elli (ITA) Telecom, at 33m.39s.
18. Paolo Lanfranchi (ITA) Mapei, at 34m.14s.
19. Carlos Contreras (COL) Kelme, at 34m.53s.
20. Georg Totschnig (AUT) Telecom, at 37m.10s.

86TH TOUR DE FRANCE, 20 STAGES – 3,686.8 KM

			STAGE	STAGE WINNER	YELLOW JERSEY
Prologue	Saturday 3 July	6.8 km	Le Puy-du-Fou – Le Puy-du-Fou (TT)	L. Armstrong (USA)	L. Armstrong
Stage 1	Sunday 4 July	208 km	Montaigu – Challans	J. Kirsipuu (SPA)	L. Armstrong
Stage 2	Monday 5 July	176 km	Challans – Saint-Nazaire	T. Steels (BEL)	J. Kirsipuu
Stage 3	Tuesday 6 July	194.5 km	Nantes – Laval	T. Steels (BEL)	J. Kirsipuu
Stage 4	Wednesday 7 July	191 km	Laval – Blois	M. Cipollini (ITA)	J. Kirsipuu
Stage 5	Thursday 8 July	233.5 km	Bonneval – Amiens	M. Cipollini (ITA)	J. Kirsipuu
Stage 6	Friday 9 July	171.5 km	Amiens – Maubeuge	M. Cipollini (ITA)	J. Kirsipuu
Stage 7	Saturday 10 July	227 km	Avesnes-sur-Helpe – Thionville	M. Cipollini (ITA)	J. Kirsipuu
Stage 8	Sunday 11 July	56.5 km	Metz – Metz (TT)	L. Armstrong (USA)	L. Armstrong
Stage 9	Tuesday 13 July	213.5 km	Le Grand-Bornand – Sestrières (ITA)	L. Armstrong (USA)	L. Armstrong
Stage 10	Wednesday 14 July	220.5 km	Sestrières (ITA) – L'Alpe-d'Huez	G. Guerini (ITA)	L. Armstrong
Stage 11	Thursday 15 July	198.5 km	Bourg-d'Oisans – Saint-Étienne	L. Dierckxsens (BEL)	L. Armstrong
Stage 12	Friday 16 July	201.5 km	Saint-Galmier – Saint-Flour	D. Etxebarria (SPA)	L. Armstrong
Stage 13	Saturday 17 July	236.5 km	Saint-Flour – Albi	S. Commesso (ITA)	L. Armstrong
Stage 14	Sunday 18 July	199 km	Castres – Saint-Gaudens	D. Konyshev (RUS)	L. Armstrong
Stage 15	Tuesday 20 July	173 km	Saint-Gaudens – Piau-Engaly	F. Escartín (SPA)	L. Armstrong
Stage 16	Wednesday 21 July	192 km	Lannemezan – Pau	D. Etxebarria (SPA)	L. Armstrong
Stage 17	Thursday 22 July	200 km	Mourenx – Bordeaux	T. Steels (BEL)	L. Armstrong
Stage 18	Friday 23 July	187 km	Jonzac – Futuroscope	G.P. Mondini (ITA)	L. Armstrong
Stage 19	Saturday 24 July	57 km	Futuroscope – Futuroscope (TT)	L. Armstrong (USA)	L. Armstrong
Stage 20	Sunday 25 July	143.5 km	Arpajon – Paris	R. McEwen (AUS)	L. Armstrong

By winning alone at Sestrières at the end of the first alpine stage, Lance Armstrong opened a major gap in the general classification, leading Olano by more than six minutes.

The comeback of the century

At one time, everyone has wanted to slip a foot into one of Neil Armstrong's asbestos boots, or snap their fingers to the music of Louis Armstrong's trumpet, but as yet no one has ever been able to get to the heart of Lance Armstrong. The Armstrongs of this world seem to travel the odyssey of our species together, leaving indelible traces in our collective memory, be it with a footstep on the moon, a timeless rhythm or, now, in man's conquest of man.

The triumph of the latest Armstrong can only be described as a miracle, and not just a medical one. This man awoke the intrepid child in each of us when, at the age of 21, he stole the rainbow from the grey skies above him at the 1993 Oslo World Championships. In July 1995 he over-whelmed us with emotion when, with his stage victory in Limoges, he tearfully searched the skies for any sign of Fabio Casartelli, killed on the sharp bends of Portet-d'Aspet three days earlier. He brought a lump to our throats when he lifted his lashless eyes from the catheter piercing his thorax following a chemotherapy session in November 1996. But at last, he has dominated the stars, their signs, their eclipses and their dark side, exposing the brilliant sun of the fibres of this jersey, and leaving us all reflecting deeply. Armstrong, a light year ahead.

Life, all of life, nothing but life. Lance Armstrong is a gesture of defiance in the face of gravity, a response to the cynical, a refusal to bow to the inevitable.

All those witnesses privileged to watch him surmount his obstacles recognize the strength of his character, starting with his mother Linda, who became pregnant at 17 by a father soon forgotten. Linda, now 45, remembers his conquering spirit: 'Even as a child, he knew what he wanted.' She intro-duced him to running near the Texan town of Plano, and looked on as he precociously showed his talent. 'His friends then got him interested in swimming, which is why he's got such broad shoulders,' she smiled. There was only one missing link, one side of the triangle before he could achieve his first goal: the triathlon. 'His first bike; he bought it when he was 16 with his pocket money. He wasn't made for university, but for sport, that much

was clear from the start.' So Armstrong Jr. became a professional triathlete, as if he already knew how to suffer more than normal. He switched to cycling in 1991, aged 19, when he joined the brand new Montgomery amateur team. 'I spotted him a year later in the Tour Dupont,' said Jim Ochowicz, then team manager of 7-Eleven, the first professional American team to cross the Atlantic – a true milestone. 'Lance hadn't achieved anything special that year, but I liked his spirit.'

Ochowicz was one of the pioneers of a perilous quest to conquer Europe. During their apprenticeship, before they could earn acceptance, he and his team had to show energy, optimism, hope and learn to face ridicule. They had to believe an El Dorado existed at the end of the adventure. Perhaps he saw a bit of himself in this ambitious kid with long hair, who already spoke with pride and confidence. Sam Abt, our American colleague at the *Herald Tribune*, was one of the first to take an interest in this restless youth. Lance Armstrong had told him quite plainly: 'No, I won't be the next Greg Lemond, I'll be the first Lance Armstrong.'

Lance was ready to take the plunge and knew where he would land. 'He wanted to turn pro, you could see it in his eyes.' A 10,000 francs a month contract signed on the corner of a table during the 1991 World Championships in Stuttgart, and the big break was only a matter of time. Just one year later, on 8 August 1992, he started his professional career at the San Sebastian Classic, the Spanish leg of the World Cup. He jumped in feet first and finished 111th in the Basque race – in other words, last. Others as cocky as him might have been demoralized. Not Lance. 'He was wound up like a cuckoo clock,' said Ochowicz. 'He kept on saying that next time he would kick their butts.' For four days Ochowicz looked on amused, but was amazed by what followed, as the boy stormed down the streets of Cangas to take a stage win in the Tour of Galicia. Eleven days later, Armstrong finished second behind Ekimov in another World Cup race, the Championship

The final time trial at Futuroscope gave Armstrong his fourth stage win of the race and proved him a worthy winner of the 1999 Tour.

Absent from the peloton since 1996, Lance Armstrong had to battle cancer before he could return to the Tour. He came back with his eyes firmly fixed on the yellow jersey.

of Zurich. Ochowicz was stunned.

The brash Armstrong had only 12 wins under his belt, seven borne of sheer perseverance brought from faraway America, when he took part in his first professional World Championship. Oslo, with its cold rain, stunning blondes, good King Harald V, rainbow jerseys and a new champion standing proud on the podium between Miguel Induráin and Olaf Ludwig – two regents forced to relinquish their thrones. Armstrong smoothed the vivid colours adorning his chest and held his head high to the first notes of the Star Spangled Banner, his fist clenched tightly to his heart.

Armstrong reached the height of his powers in 1996. Not only did he mark his stage-racing territory by winning five stages and the overall classification in the Tour Dupont, but his success in the Flèche Wallonne, followed four days later by second place in the Liège-Bastogne-Liège, ranked him among the most accomplished champions of his time. In August, he had just walked off with two top five places in the World Cup races (fourth in both the Wincanton Classic and the Swiss Grand Prix) when he finished second in the Tour of the Netherlands on the 31 August. The next day at the Grand Prix Eddy Merckx, he finished hot on the wheels of Chris Boardman, just five days before the Briton beat the world hour record. Armstrong was flying.

Doctor Reeves, urologist at Saint David's hospital, Austin, did not beat about the bush when he saw the young cyclist on the afternoon of 2 October 1996. An hour before going to his clinic, Armstrong, ranked sixth in the world, was only concerned about the traces of blood he was coughing up. Three weeks earlier, he had signed a lucrative deal with the Cofidis team and was living life to the full. Returning with the results of the tests, carried out in a neighbouring laboratory, the doctor broke the news that he had testicular cancer. 'At that moment, I thought I was going to die.' His world had just crumbled beneath his feet; every ounce of energy had been sapped from him. The initial prognosis was 50/50; life or death. The next day he underwent a two-hour operation to remove the diseased testicle, but the cancer had spread: the abdomen, kidneys, lungs, his whole body was riddled with malignant cells. Then came the marks that appeared on his forearms, followed by two shadows on an x-ray – cancerous lesions surrounding his brain. As he's often said, 'Only people who have been through this understand how it feels.' The chemotherapy sessions in Indianapolis, four weeks of torture spread over three months: the clammy nights when he resisted sleep for fear of never waking up again; the body, once so proud, now

Cipollini clinches his fourth successive stage win, a feat unaccomplished since 1930.

Three stage wins for Steels. In the final 200 metres, Cipollini was his only rival.

In Challans, Estonian Jaan Kirsipuu took his first stage victory in the Tour de France.

On the Passage du Gois, linking the Île de Noirmoutier with the mainland, the Tour was cut in two when a group of riders toppled over the edge, leaving many favourites, including Zülle, Boogerd, Gotti and Rinero, lagging behind.

shrivelling up; the endless days of distress, crying out for help in a soundless nightmare; his skin, growing paler; his body hair falling out; the life-saving chemicals that made him vomit up his very insides; the shadow of death which threatened to engulf him. But he never gave up. It was only a matter of a few weeks before he stopped shaking with fear in his sweat-drenched sheets and altered the course of destiny. He progressed from 'Why me?' to 'Why not me?' Rather than resigning himself to the statistics, he decided to thrust himself into the hands of fate. Louis Armstrong never played a requiem, Neil Armstrong came back from the darkness of space, Lance Armstrong was determined to fight his way out of the valley of death.

He may just have been another convalescent, struggling to move, hiding his scars beneath a baseball cap, but at least his shattered heart had regained its strength. At the beginning of 1997, his contract with Cofidis was renegotiated and he felt that everyone had abandoned him. It was perhaps for this reason that he decided to take a step back from the cycling world. He took up golf, messed about with his Harley Davidson, and took out his speedboat, which was moored on the Colorado River, adjacent to his plush Austin villa. He dabbled in stocks and shares on his computer and invested time and money in the organization he founded for children with cancer, setting up a charity bike ride, the Ride for the Roses, which raised $1.1 million in May last year. But, most importantly, he began to live, little by little pushing away the constant shadow of death.

Armstrong was away from cycling for over a year and a half, 518 days to be precise, a time that he used to reflect upon the world around him, a world that he would rejoin in time for the Ruta del Sol in February 1998. He finished fifteenth, but his miraculous recovery appeared short-lived when ten days later, for no apparent reason, he pulled out of Paris-Nice during the first stage. 'I don't know, I wasn't in the right frame of mind that day.' The man had regained his strength but the champion remained fragile. Once again he headed home to Texas to 'build himself up'. His inner circle, including Ochowicz, Chris Carmichael (his first coach), his mother, and Kristin (whom he married in May 1998 and who will give birth to their first child in three months' time), helped him bridge the gap between doubt and determination.

Armstrong then took off where he had left off; his gaze fixed firmly on the horizon. Victories at the Tour of Luxembourg, the Tour de Rhénanie in June, then fourth in the Vuelta a España and the World Championships (fourth in the road race and the time trial) reinforced his conviction. He would be the next cyclist to win the Tour de France. To stage the most fabulous comeback in the history of sport, Armstrong relied purely on his obsession. In May he became the first man in history to devote two solid weeks to familiarizing himself with twelve stages of the Tour. He was the first to believe that one could battle with cancer and emerge stronger than ever.

This determination rendered a recent advertising campaign on the part of an American sports manufacturer all the more moving when it first hit the screens across America last Friday. Over an image of Armstrong cycling furiously came the words: 'According to recent statistics, Lance Armstrong should be dead. He'll never win the Tour de France,' then: 'Just do it.' Yes, Armstrong 'just did it'. Not simply by securing four stage wins and riding his way into the cycling hall of fame nor by sending our doubts crashing to the ground with his powerful message, but by overcoming the scourge of the human condition. His seemingly impossible journey, as he quite candidly pointed out, was 'a true story'. Like Neil, Lance Armstrong is also out of this world. Having made up so much ground, he won the tour nine years after the third and final victory of his fellow American Greg Lemond and, most remarkable of all, only two and a half years after he was diagnosed with cancer. It was the comeback of the century.

His solitary win at Sestrières was a demonstration of Lance Armstrong's extraordinary power. It was his first mountain victory in the Tour.

A triumph foretold

How to celebrate the new millennium? Schemes were drawn up for the grandest *Grand Départ* ever, from New York or somewhere similar, but it was not to be. Plans for long-haul transfers to stages all over the planet never got off the ground. The 2000 Tour made just two concessions to the future; one was to freeze the anti-doping urine samples for re-testing in the future when an effective EPO test had been introduced. The second was to start the race at the Futuroscope, admittedly by now a hackneyed feature of the Tour de France scenery. Other time-honoured landmarks on the route included three of the great monuments: Mont Ventoux, the Izoard and the Galibier.

The 2000 Tour pitted the winners of the three previous Tours de France against each other. Injury had prevented Jan Ullrich from starting the 1999 Tour. Shame had kept Marco Pantani away. Many believed that had they competed, Armstrong would never have won. The Texan lost the Prologue by two seconds to Scotland's David Millar. Victory in the team time trial by the Spanish team ONCE gave Laurent Jalabert the yellow jersey, the Dutch classics specialist Erik Dekker won three stages, and at Limoges, Christophe Agnolutto gave France its first stage victory in the Tour for two years.

Then Armstrong established his overwhelming superiority on a stage he didn't even win. On the first major climb, Pantani attacked. Armstrong's response was instant and categorical. He caught and dropped Pantani, sped past the leading group of climbers and finished alone at Hautacam, 42 seconds behind the Spaniard Javier Otxoa, who won the stage after a long solo breakaway. Armstrong was in yellow; right on time.

The long mountain stage to Briançon saw the emergence of Colombia's Santiago Botero, a worthy successor to Lucho Herrera and Fabio Parra. The following day, Armstrong and Pantani duelled again on Mont Ventoux. Armstrong claimed he allowed the Italian to win the stage, Pantani retorted that to say so betrayed a lack of respect. At Courchevel, Pantani won his second stage; at Morzine, Richard Virenque was the victor, as Armstrong suffered a moment of relative weakness on the Joux-Plane, losing nearly two minutes to his closest rival, Jan Ullrich. His tribulations on the stage suggested Armstrong was vulnerable; the final time trial suggested the opposite: in front of Ullrich's fans between Fribourg, in Germany, and Mulhouse, Armstrong averaged 53.986 kph (33.525 mph), a new Tour record, on his way to the stage win. Armstrong won the Tour by over six minutes without ever being put under pressure.

GENERAL CLASSIFICATION

1. **Lance Armstrong** (USA) US Postal, 3,662 km in 92h.33m.8s; Average speed: 39.545 kph
2. **Jan Ullrich** (GER) Telekom, at 6m.2s.
3. **Joseba Beloki** (SPA) Festina, at 10m.4s.
4. Christophe Moreau (FRA) Festina, at 10m.34s.
5. Roberto Heras (SPA) Kelme, at 11m.50s.
6. Richard Virenque (FRA) Polti, at 13m.26s.
7. Santiago Botero (COL) Kelme, at 14m.18s.
8. Fernando Escartín (SPA) Kelme, at 17m.21s.
9. Francisco Mancebo (SPA) Banesto, at 18m.9s.
10. Daniele Nardello (ITA) Mapei, at 18m.25s.
11. Manuel Beltran (SPA) Mapei, at 21m.11s.
12. Pascal Herve (FRA) Polti, at 23m.13s.
13. Javier Otxoa Palacios (SPA) Kelme, at 25m .
14. Felix Manuel García Casas (SPA) Festina, at 32m.4s.
15. Alexandre Vinokourov (KAZ) Telekom, at 32m.26s.
16. Roberto Conti (ITA) Vini Caldirola, at 34m.18s.
17. Kurt Van De Wouwer (BEL) Lotto, at 34m.29s.
18. Guido Trentin (ITA) Vini Caldirola, at 35m.57s.
19. Jean-Cyril Robin (FRA) Bonjour, at 43m.12s.
20. Geert Verheyen (BEL) Lotto, at 46m.24s.

87TH TOUR DE FRANCE, 21 STAGES – 3,662 KM

			STAGE	STAGE WINNER	YELLOW JERSEY
Stage 1	Saturday 1 July	16.5 km	Futuroscope – Futuroscope (TT)	D. Millar (GBR)	D. Millar
Stage 2	Sunday 2 July	194 km	Futuroscope – Loudun	T. Steels (BEL)	D. Millar
Stage 3	Monday 3 July	161.5 km	Loudun – Nantes	T. Steels (BEL)	D. Millar
Stage 4	Tuesday 4 July	70 km	Nantes – Saint-Nazaire (TTT)	ONCE Deutsche Bank	L. Jalabert
Stage 5	Wednesday 5 July	202 km	Vannes – Vitré	M. Wust (GER)	L. Jalabert
Stage 6	Thursday 6 July	198.5 km	Vitré – Tours	L. Van Bon (HOL)	A. Elli
Stage 7	Friday 7 July	205.5 km	Tours – Limoges	C. Agnolutto (FRA)	A. Elli
Stage 8	Saturday 8 July	203.5 km	Limoges – Villeneuve-sur-Lot	E. Dekker (HOL)	A. Elli
Stage 9	Sunday 9 July	181 km	Agen – Dax	P. Bettini (ITA)	A. Elli
Stage 10	Monday 10 July	205 km	Dax – Lourdes-Hautacam	J. Otxoa Palacios (SPA)	L. Armstrong
Stage 11	Tuesday 11 July	218.5 km	Bagnères-de-Bigorre – Revel	E. Dekker (HOL)	L. Armstrong
Stage 12	Thursday 13 July	149 km	Carpentras – Mont Ventoux	M. Pantani (ITA)	L. Armstrong
Stage 13	Friday 14 July	185.5 km	Avignon – Draguignan	V. Garcia-Acosta (SPA)	L. Armstrong
Stage 14	Saturday 15 July	249.5 km	Draguignan – Briançon	S. Botero (COL)	L. Armstrong
Stage 15	Sunday 16 July	173.5 km	Briançon – Courchevel	M. Pantani (ITA)	L. Armstrong
Stage 16	Tuesday 18 July	196.5 km	Courchevel – Morzine	R. Virenque (FRA)	L. Armstrong
Stage 17	Wednesday 19 July	155 km	Évian – Lausanne (SUI)	E. Dekker (HOL)	L. Armstrong
Stage 18	Thursday 20 July	246 km	Lausanne – Fribourg-en-Brisgau (GER)	S. Commesso (ITA)	L. Armstrong
Stage 19	Friday 21 July	58.5 km	Fribourg-en-Brisgau (GER) – Mulhouse (TT)	L. Armstrong (USA)	L. Armstrong
Stage 20	Saturday 22 July	254.5 km	Belfort – Troyes	E. Zabel (GER)	L. Armstrong
Stage 21	Sunday 23 July	138 km	Paris – Paris	S. Zanini (ITA)	L. Armstrong

At an average speed of 53.986 kmh (33.525 mph), Lance Armstrong finally took his first stage win in this Tour in the Mulhouse time trial, despite a brilliant Jan Ullrich.

Jan Ullrich's tribute:
'Armstrong was better prepared than me'

MULHOUSE: Ullrich's homage came after the stage in which he finished second, twenty-five seconds behind Lance Armstrong. Above all, he felt he'd done everything in his power to challenge the American. 'I've nothing to reproach myself for in the time trial,' he announced. 'It was a fast stage and I couldn't have done any better. I didn't want to know any of Armstrong's splits; I didn't want to clutter my mind with them. Each time I passed the displays at each of the timing points, I could see that I was leading but the yellow jersey had set off after me. At any rate, I knew what I had to do.'

Ever the realist, Ullrich certainly didn't want to have any regrets; he just let slip a hint of sadness that he hadn't been able to shine on his home ground. 'It was a goal for the final phase of the Tour de France. It's a pity I couldn't offer this victory to my compatriots.'

Walter Godefroot, Ullrich's *directeur sportif*, did not want to speak in terms of failure. 'If we are disappointed, then how must the others feel?' he laughed. 'Seriously, we have no regrets. Today was always going to boil down to a battle between Jan and Armstrong. With every passing kilometre, there was only a matter of a few tenths of a second between them. It was easy to see that Armstrong was marginally faster than Jan. They are two of a kind; there wasn't much in it today.' The Belgian later admitted that he had long believed that his cyclist should win this part of the race: 'It was a prestigious stage, and Jan was really motivated.'

Some wondered if Ullrich's impressive form over the last few days might have been better suited to a slightly longer race. An extremely calm Ullrich scotched any speculation. 'The Tour lasts three weeks,' he announced 'and you have to be prepared; Lance Armstrong showed that today, and watching his performance, there is really nothing to regret.'

Rudy Pevenage, Telekom's other *directeur sportif*, acknowledged Armstrong's supremacy: 'Twenty-five seconds isn't much, but we really can't complain. Sure, the yellow jersey had a slight advantage because he could see Jan's times, but this is no excuse.'

1

2

1. With his success in the Prologue, young David Millar was one of the Tour's brightest discoveries.

2. The ONCE team rode well in the team time trial, putting Jalabert in the yellow jersey.

3. Three years after his triumph at Courcheval, Richard Virenque greeted his supporters on the finishing line at Morzine: revenge in the form of sweet victory.

4. Once again, the ascent of Mont Ventoux confirmed the supremacy of two riders: Armstrong and Pantani.

5 & 6. On the final climb towards Hautacam, Armstrong caught the leading group of (left to right) Virenque, Escartín and Jiménez, and dropped them without challenge.

7. The incredible Lance Armstrong! His second Tour de France win was as dominant as his first, outclassing his opponents through out the race.

3

4

7

5   6

The Armstrong monopoly

The 2001 Tour de France started with a French win at Dunkirk, where Christophe Moreau won the Prologue. Although Moreau was destined to withdraw at the foot of the Pyrenees, his compatriot Laurent Jalabert continued to attract the crowds. Jalabert won at Verdun on stage four, again at Colmar on Bastille Day, and then stormed through the Pyrenees to take a commanding lead in the King of the Mountains competition, previously the spoils of Richard Virenque, now serving a ban for his part in the Festina affair.

Then, 48 hours before the race reached the Alps, on a rainy Sunday on the way to Pontarlier, a large breakaway group was allowed to escape and open a 30-minute lead. Australia's Stuart O'Grady took over the yellow jersey, to be replaced by the French all-rounder François Simon. But the real threat was a rider from the emerging cycling superpower of Kazakhstan, Andreï Kivilev. Kivilev was an excellent climber, and had all the credentials to become a latter-day Roger Walkowiak.

Armstrong, as ever, remained cool, even giving Jan Ullrich an unforgettable lesson in gamesmanship. On the Col de Glandon, he grimaced with pain, hanging on the back of the leading group as Ullrich's Telekom team put down the hammer. The moment the leading riders reached the foot of Alpe-d'Huez, Armstrong turned to the German, flashed a murderous look deep into Ullrich's eyes, and severed his ties with gravity. Ullrich struggled up behind, losing two minutes on the final climb; the Spaniard Joseba Beloki lost ten seconds more. It was sport as empirical science, and the experiment yielded the same results day after day: on Alpe-d'Huez, in the mountain time trial to Chamrousse the next day, and again later at St-Lary-Soulan, where he finally took the yellow jersey, Armstrong proved he was a class above Ullrich, who proved he was a class above Beloki, who proved he was a class above everyone else. Crossing the line on the summit of Luz-Ardiden, Ullrich and Armstrong shook hands. The German had never been in better form since winning the Tour de France in 1997, yet he had no answer to the Texan's dominance.

On the final stage, Germany's Erik Zabel won a compelling points competition, pipping Stuart O'Grady at the post and taking his sixth green jersey. Sprinter turned King of the Mountains, Laurent Jalabert eventually finished just nineteenth overall, but he had delighted the crowd in the process. Armstrong, meanwhile, had won three of the five mountain stages, the final time trial, and had carried off his third consecutive Tour de France with absolute authority.

GENERAL CLASSIFICATION

1. **Lance Armstrong** (USA) US Postal, 3,453 km in 86h.17m.28s; Average speed: 40.070 kph
2. **Jan Ullrich** (GER) Team Deutsche Telekom, at 6m.44s.
3. **Joseba Beloki** (SPA) ONCE-Eroski, at 9m.5s.
4. Andreï Kivilev (KAZ) Cofidis, at 9m.53s.
5. Igor González de Galdeano (SPA) ONCE-Eroski, at 13m.28s.
6. François Simon (FRA) Bonjour, at 17m.22s.
7. Oscar Sevilla (SPA) Kelme-Costa, at 18m.30s.
8. Santiago Botero (COL) Kelme-Costa, at 20m.55s.
9. Marcos Serrano (SPA) ONCE-Eroski, at 21m.45s.
10. Michael Boogerd (HOL) Rabobank, at 22m.38s.
11. Didier Rous (FRA) Bonjour, at 24m.22s.
12. Inigo Chaurreau (SPA) Euskatel, at 28m.9s.
13. Francisco Mancebo (SPA) Ibanesto, at 28m.33s.
14. Stefano Garzelli (ITA) Mapei, at 29m.
15. Roberto Heras (SPA) US Postal, at 30m.44s.
16. Alexandre Vinokourov (KAZ) Team Deutsche Telekom, at 33m.55s.
17. Alexandre Botcharov (RUS) AG2R Prévoyance, at 41m.15s.
18. Bobby Julich (USA) Crédit Agricole, at 48m.4s.
19. Laurent Jalabert (FRA) CSC-Tiscali, at 50m.6s.
20. Carlos Sastre (SPA) ONCE-Eroski, at 50m.20s.

88TH TOUR DE FRANCE, 20 STAGES – 3,453 KM

			STAGE	STAGE WINNER	YELLOW JERSEY
Prologue	Saturday 7 July	8.2 km	Dunkerque – Dunkerque (TT)	C. Moreau (FRA)	C. Moreau
Stage 1	Sunday 8 July	194.5 km	Saint-Omer – Boulogne-sur-Mer	E. Zabel (GER)	C. Moreau
Stage 2	Monday 9 July	218.5 km	Calais – Anvers (BEL)	M. Wauters (BEL)	M. Wauters
Stage 3	Tuesday 10 July	198.5 km	Anvers (BEL) – Seraing (BEL)	E. Zabel (GER)	S. O'Grady
Stage 4	Wednesday 11 July	215 km	Huy (BEL) – Verdun	L. Jalabert (FRA)	S. O'Grady
Stage 5	Thursday 12 July	67 km	Verdun – Bar-le-Duc (TTT)	Crédit Agricole	S. O'Grady
Stage 6	Friday 13 July	211.5 km	Commercy – Strasbourg	J. Kirsipuu (EST)	S. O'Grady
Stage 7	Saturday 14 July	162.5 km	Strasbourg – Colmar	L. Jalabert (FRA)	J. Voigt
Stage 8	Sunday 15 July	222.5 km	Colmar – Pontarlier	E. Dekker (HOL)	S. O'Grady
Stage 9	Monday 16 July	185 km	Pontarlier – Aix-les-Bains	S. Ivanov (RUS)	S. O'Grady
Stage 10	Tuesday 17 July	209 km	Aix-les-Bains – L'Alpe-d'Huez	L. Armstrong (USA)	F. Simon
Stage 11	Wednesday 18 July	32 km	Grenoble – Chamrousse (TT)	L. Armstrong (USA)	F. Simon
Stage 12	Friday 20 July	166.5 km	Perpignan – Ax-les-Thermes	F. Cardenas (COL)	F. Simon
Stage 13	Saturday 21 July	194 km	Foix – Saint-Lary-Soulan	L. Armstrong (USA)	L. Armstrong
Stage 14	Sunday 22 July	141.5 km	Tarbes – Luz-Ardiden	R. Laiseka (SPA)	L. Armstrong
Stage 15	Tuesday 24 July	232.5 km	Pau – Lavaur	R. Verbrugghe (BEL)	L. Armstrong
Stage 16	Wednesday 25 July	229.5 km	Castelsarrasin – Sarran	J. Voigt (GER)	L. Armstrong
Stage 17	Thursday 26 July	194 km	Brive-la-Gaillarde – Montluçon	S. Baguet (BEL)	L. Armstrong
Stage 18	Friday 27 July	61 km	Montluçon – Saint-Amand-Montrond (TT)	L. Armstrong (USA)	L. Armstrong
Stage 19	Saturday 28 July	149.5 km	Orléans – Évry	E. Zabel (GER)	L. Armstrong
Stage 20	Sunday 29 July	160.5 km	Corbeil-Essonnes – Paris	J. Svorada (CZE)	L. Armstrong

Dunkerque
Calais
Anvers
Boulogne-sur-Mer
Huy
Seraing
Saint-Omer
PARIS
Verdun
Évry
Strasbourg
Corbeil-Essonnes
Orléans
Bar-le-Duc
Colmar
Commercy
Pontarlier
Saint-Amand-Montrond
Aix-les-Bains
Montluçon
L'Alpe-d'Huez
Grenoble
Brive-la-Gaillarde
Sarran
Chamrousse
Castelsarrasin
Pau
Lavaur
Tarbes
Foix
Luz-Ardien
Perpignan
Saint-Lary-Soulan
Ax-les-Thermes
Pla d'Adet
plateau de Bonascre

Luz-Ardiden: behind the Basque Roberto Laiseka who won the stage, Lance Armstrong matched Jan Ullrich pedal-stroke for pedal-stroke. From this moment on, Ullrich knew he'd lost the Tour de France. Sportingly, he admitted as much.

Lance Armstrong: 'I'm at my best'

This is your third victory in the Tour de France. Is the feeling this time the same as your first two successes?

The feelings are very alike, but they each have a different significance for me. The first had the element of novelty and surprise. I still couldn't believe it the following morning when I woke up in my hotel room in Paris. The second was a confirmation, similar to the first, but with a different message. We've never worked as hard as we did this year to achieve our goal; I've never waited so long to take the yellow jersey and I've never been so happy. In any case, every new Tour is surprising; five years ago I wasn't sure I'd even survive. They all have a place in my heart and it would be impossible for me to say any one has been better than the others.

Would you agree that this year without doubt, for the first time, your performance bordered on perfection?

That's not for me to say. I just tried to eliminate any mistakes, like Soulor in 1999 or Joux-Plane last year, and of course to avoid any falls, injuries or illness. The past two years I felt vulnerable during the last days in the mountains. Physically I was tired, and psychologically I was on a downhill slope. This year, I wanted to avoid all that. So we trained hard, very hard; we practically learned the stages by heart and the team became much stronger. If you only knew how reassuring it feels to have two team-mates at your side at the bottom of a final climb...

But during the last three weeks at no time did you encounter any difficulty. Was this Tour easy to win?

I'd never say it is easy to win the Tour de France. Never. There is so much work beforehand, so many hours sacrificed. It is true though, that, during my first two Tours, I was sometimes pushed to my limit. Last year, for example, on the Madeleine, I wasn't great; around Courcheval I was nothing special, it was the same on the Izoard. Not enough to make me fail, but enough to make me feel unsafe.

Nevertheless, the impression was that this year the standard was not as high and that no one, with the exception of Jan Ullrich, seemed capable of getting the upper hand...

Don't you think that's enough? This was the second time I have been confronted by Ullrich and there is no doubt: this year he was stronger than ever, much stronger than I had thought, and let me tell you he is a constant source of worry. He is the only competitor who really frightens me, the only one I couldn't keep up with when he's having a great day. Otherwise, my team, which has gone through highs and lows, played its role of controlling the peloton perfectly. In fact, my only regret is the absence of Marco Pantani. I missed his strong personality on the course; it acts like a stimulant and makes me perform even better.

There are two Lance Armstrongs: the one before the cancer, and the one who wins the Tour de France. How much of the first is still here today?

I always say that you can never change someone's soul. There are virtues that I have kept: tenacity, aggression, love of hard work. But since my illness, my priorities have changed because I have been given a second chance. That is why I work so hard, why I am so determined. My illness taught me to make the most of the moment and to do everything within my power to make it as sweet as possible.

You said last year that it was out of the question to attempt to beat the record five victories of Jacques Anquetil, Eddy Merckx, Bernard Hinault and Miguel Induráin. But you are not even 30. Why give up when you are doing so well?

For the moment I enjoy what I do and I'm not thinking about retiring yet. But I'm not someone who makes long-term plans. The only thing I can say is that when I decide to stop competing in the Tour de France, I will have decided to end my career. As long as I am racing, the Tour will be my only goal. I will definitely be here again next year, but that may be the last time. As for the record, I never think about it. I am not on the same level as a Coppi, an Anquetil or a Merckx.

1. On 14 July, Frenchman Laurent Jalabert repeated his 1995 Bastille Day victory with a stage win at Colmar. He entered the Tour to enjoy himself; and it worked!

2. After three days as a hero, François Simon handed the yellow jersey to Lance Armstrong at Saint-Lary-Soulan.

3. On the road to Luz-Ardiden, Basque supporters celebrated for Roberto Laiseka and bowed before Lance Armstrong.

4. Armstrong has just taken off at the foot of l'Alpe-d'Huez, dropping Jan Ullrich and Andrei Kivilev. He soon caught Laurent Roux and struck out alone in the lead. He took almost two minutes out of Ullrich.

5. A record-breaking sixth con-secutive green jersey for Erik Zabel. His battle with O'Grady was nail-biting to the last moment.

6. In yellow on the Champs-Élysées for the third time in a row, Lance Armstrong concentrates on the closing moments of the 2001 Tour de France, and prepares to savour his success.

4

5

6

Armstrong in a class of his own

As the 2002 Tour de France convened at Luxembourg, long-term injury had ruled out Jan Ullrich and no new contender had emerged to challenge Lance Armstrong. When the American won the Prologue at a canter, the race seemed almost over. Armstrong refused the temptation to defend the jersey and a young Swiss rider, Rubens Bertogliati, took over the race lead on stage one. When team time trial specialists ONCE won stage four, the Spaniard Igor González de Galdeano took the yellow jersey for eight days. Then, in Lorient, the Colombian Santiago Botero rode a muscular time trial defeating Armstrong by 11 seconds. It was a slender margin, but a defeat nonetheless, the first in a long time trial since Armstrong's Tour reign began. Had a chink opened in the Texan's armour? The answer came two days later in the Pyrenees, where Armstrong's team imposed a suffocating pace for the final 90 minutes, before his mountain lieutenants José Luis Rubiera and Roberto Heras led him up the final climb to La Mongie at a sprint, leaving his challengers panting at the wayside in their wake. The last to go was the Basque, Joseba Beloki, who resisted valiantly, but was plainly inferior to the champion. Armstrong was quite simply in a class of his own.

The following day, the performance was repeated on the Plateau de Beille. On the climb up to the Plateau, the leading group passed Laurent Jalabert. The 34-year-old Frenchman had already announced his decision to retire at the end of the season, and the Tour was his lap of honour. Over three consecutive days, riding through his home region in South-West France, he led the Tour for 429 km (268 miles), to the delight of crowds who made it clear that they did not want him to go.

After his spat with Pantani two years before, Armstrong was desperate to win the stage to Mont Ventoux, but Richard Virenque had joined a breakaway group 200 kilometres (125 miles) from the stage finish, and had a large advantage at the foot of the climb. Armstrong ascended at phenomenal speed, to abuse from Virenque's fans. He failed to catch the Frenchman, but tightened his grip on the race lead still further. The next day, Botero powered up to Les Deux-Alpes to win the stage; unfortunately for the Colombian, a terrible loss of form on Mont Ventoux had cost him 15 minutes, and he no longer represented a threat. As the race left the Alps, it was all over. Armstrong's US Postal Service team, the strongest team ever to support him, had guaranteed him victory. In the final time trial, Armstrong extended his advantage over Beloki to 7mins 17secs. With his fourth victory Armstrong had overtaken Thys, Bobet and Lemond, winners of three Tours and at the age of 30 was just one step behind the greats, Anquetil, Merckx, Hinault and Induráin, whose glorious ranks he will attempt to join in the centenary year, 2003.

GENERAL CLASSIFICATION

1. **Lance Armstrong** (USA) US Postal, 3,276 km in 82h.5m.12s; Average speed: 39.909 kph
2. **Joseba Beloki** (SPA) ONCE, at 7m.17s.
3. **Raimondas Rumsas** (LIT) Lampre, at 8m.17s.
4. Santiago Botero (COL) Kelme, at 13m.10s.
5. Igor González de Galdeano (SPA) ONCE, at 13m.54s.
6. José Azevedo (POR) ONCE, at 15m.44s.
7. Francisco Mancebo (SPA) Ibanesto. com, at 16m.5s.
8. Levi Leipheimer (USA) Rabobank, at 17m.11s.
9. Roberto Heras (SPA) US Postal, at 17m.12s.
10. Carlos Sastre (SPA) CSC Tiscali, at 19m.5s.
11. Ivan Basso (ITA) Fassa Bortolio, at 19m.18s.
12. Michael Boogerd (HOL) Rabobank, at 20m.33s.
13. David Moncoutié (FRA) Cofidis, at 21m.8s.
14. Massimiliano Lelli (ITA) Cofidis, at 27m.51s.
15. Tyler Hamilton (USA) CSC Tiscali, at 28m.38s.
16. Richard Virenque (FRA) Domo-Farm Frites, at 28m.42s.
17. Stéphane Goubert (FRA) Jean Delatour, at 29m.51s.
18. Unaï Osa (SPA) Ibanesto.com, at 30m.17s.
19. Nicolas Vogondy (FRA) FDJeux.com, at 32m.44s.
20. Nicki Sörensen (DEN) CSC Tiscali, at 32m.56s.

89TH TOUR DE FRANCE, 20 STAGES – 3,276 KM

			STAGE	STAGE WINNER	YELLOW JERSEY
Prologue	Saturday 6 July	7 km	Grand-duché de Luxembourg (LUX) (TT)	L. Armstrong (USA)	L. Armstrong
Stage 1	Sunday 7 July	192.5 km	Luxembourg – Luxembourg	R. Bertogliati (SUI)	R. Bertogliati
Stage 2	Monday 8 July	181 km	Luxembourg – Sarrebruck	O. Freire (SPA)	R. Bertogliati
Stage 3	Tuesday 9 July	174.5 km	Metz – Reims	R. McEwen (AUS)	E. Zabel
Stage 4	Wednesday 10 July	67.5 km	Épernay – Château-Thierry (TTT)	ONCE (SPA)	I. González de Galdeano
Stage 5	Thursday 11 July	195 km	Soissons – Rouen	J. Kirsipuu (EST)	I. González de Galdeano
Stage 6	Friday 12 July	198 km	Forges-les-Eaux – Alençon	E. Zabel (GER)	I. González de Galdeano
Stage 7	Saturday 13 July	176 km	Bagnoles-de-l'Orne – Avranches	B. McGee (AUS)	I. González de Galdeano
Stage 8	Sunday 14 July	217.5 km	Saint-Martin-de-Landelles – Plouay	K. Kroon (HOL)	I. González de Galdeano
Stage 9	Monday 15 July	52 km	Lanester – Lorient (TT)	S. Botero (COL)	I. González de Galdeano
Stage 10	Wednesday 17 July	147 km	Bazas – Pau	P. Halgand (FRA)	I. González de Galdeano
Stage 11	Thursday 18 July	158 km	Pau – La Mongie	L. Armstrong (USA)	L. Armstrong
Stage 12	Friday 19 July	199.5 km	Lannemezan – Plateau de Beille	L. Armstrong (USA)	L. Armstrong
Stage 13	Saturday 20 July	171 km	Lavelanet – Béziers	D. Millar (GBR)	L. Armstrong
Stage 14	Sunday 21 July	221 km	Lodève – Mont Ventoux	R. Virenque (FRA)	L. Armstrong
Stage 15	Tuesday 23 July	226.5 km	Vaison-la-Romaine – Les Deux-Alpes	S. Botero (COL)	L. Armstrong
Stage 16	Wednesday 24 July	179.5 km	Les Deux-Alpes – La Plagne	M. Boogerd (HOL)	L. Armstrong
Stage 17	Thursday 25 July	142 km	Aime – Cluses	D. Frigo (ITA)	L. Armstrong
Stage 18	Friday 26 July	176.5 km	Cluses – Bourg-en-Bresse	T. Hushovd (NOR)	L. Armstrong
Stage 19	Saturday 27 July	50 km	Régnié-Durette – Mâcon (TT)	L. Armstrong (USA)	L. Armstrong
Stage 20	Sunday 28 July	144 km	Melun – Paris	R. McEwen (AUS)	L. Armstrong

Lance Armstrong won the yellow jersey on the stage to La Mongie. The following day, after an equally spectactular win on the Plateau de Beille, he consolidated his lead. Beloki, second, now trailed by 1min 4secs.

On the way up

What's new, after three weeks? Not much that's likely to alter the landscape of international cycling, or upset the established hierarchy. When Lance Armstrong presented himself at the start in Luxembourg, he was a stonger favourite than ever. Three weeks later he won his fourth consecutive Tour de France, probably his easiest, certainly his calmest.

He started the race with no clearly identified challenger, and he failed to find one *en route*. His opponents promised to attack, and they did. Joseba Beloki, the runner-up, and his team, ONCE, who didn't want to reach the race end with any regrets, performed their duty; or rather, they did what little they could. Put end to end, the attacks by the Portuguese rider Azevedo and the Spaniard Beloki, first on the Ventoux, and then under the *flamme rouge* on Les Deux-Alpes, added up a lead of no more than about 100 metres. It would have taken more than that to bring down Lance Armstrong.

Of the fairly dense group of dark horses brought together at the start, only two were missing from the 153 survivors who appeared yesterday on the Champs-Élysées (the greatest number of finishers since 1991): Christophe Moreau and Oscar Sevilla. The Frenchman had pulled out, overwhelmed and discouraged by the many difficulties along the way. He'd been France's best chance of securing a place on the podium, which seemed a reasonable ambition given his performance at the Critérium du Dauphiné Libéré. There were other disappointments, too, including the Kazakh Andreï Kivilev, fourth last year, 21st this. Nor did any spectacular new riders emerge, the one new development being the improvement of Lithuania's Raimondas Rumsas, who battled to his last breath on the Champs-Élysées to improve his position. He finally appeared in third place on the podium, a good result for a novice, even if he is already 30.

Armstrong knew the world was watching out for the slightest sign of decline, but no conclusion can be drawn from his first defeat in a long time trial, two weeks ago, in Lorient. He set the record straight in Beaujolais; his opponents next year will have to keep their eye on the big picture as well as stage wins.

Armstrong is often criticized for targeting the Tour alone, but like Merckx in 1971 and Induráin in 1995, he won the Midi Libre and the Dauphiné Libéré in the run up to the Tour, and performed excellently in several one-day classics.

Was Armstrong stronger this year, or has he just maintained his previous peak? Make no mistake, he is unbeatable in the mountains, despite the fact that he never opens enormous gaps on his direct rivals because he will only attack on the final climb (he gained 1min 4secs and 1min 45secs on Beloki on the Plateau de Beille and on the Ventoux respectively). On those two stages, his performance was up to the level of Sestrières in 1999, Hautacam in 2000 and Alpe-d'Huez in 2001. Armstrong pushed the runner-up, Joseba Beloki, back to regulation distance (7mins 17secs); keeping him in the same position as his predecessors (Zülle finished 7 mins 37 secs behind in 1999, Ullrich finished 6mins 2secs and 6mins 44secs behind in the past two years). Such is the margin of his superiority.

His story has not evolved much, either. He seized the yellow jersey at the Luxembourg Prologue, temporarily ceding it with good grace to the young Swiss rider Bertogliati, then Eric Zabel and then to the Spaniard Igor González de Galdeano, for a full week. But he retrieved it as soon as the race reached its first summit, and spent ten days in yellow (compared to 15 in 1999, 12 in 2000 and eight in 2001, a total of 45).

He demanded his customary tariffs: his usual four victories (the exception being 2000, when he made do with the final time trial, having gifted Ventoux to Pantani). The Luxembourg Prologue, his grand slam in the Pyrenees (La Mongie, Plateau de Beille) and the Mâcon time trial brought his personal score to 15 stage victories including Prologues, a record among active riders.

All the time, the American champion continues to climb the stairway that brings him ever closer to the elite group of five-time champions. He has just past the storey where Thys, Bobet and Lemond reside. Nobody has stopped at four, and he's no more than a step away from the pantheon of the great. And since history has always rejected those who tried to go higher, including Anquetil (who pulled out in 1966), Merckx (beaten by Thévenet in 1975), Hinault (his knee in 1980, beaten by Fignon in 1984 and by Lemond in 1986) and Induráin (faltering in 1996, the year of Riis); could Lance

Lance Armstrong wanted to win on Mont Ventoux, perhaps to erase memories of his defeat there by Pantani in 2000, but Richard Virenque beat him to the summit with a perfectly calculated long-range break.

The ONCE team charges, as one, towards victory in the team time trial between Épernay and Château-Thierry.

Already a stage winner at Lorient, the Colombian Santiago Botero had no trouble winning on Les Deux-Alpes as well.

Stage 6, Alençon: Eric Zabel leaves (left to right) McEwen, Ivanov, Cooke and Freire trailing in his wake. He would eventually lose the green jersey to McEwen.

Armstrong be the first to take six victories? The question may seem premature, but it's natural to ask it, when you consider that when we look for a potential rival, the cupboard seems decidedly bare. If we can identify no one to rival him now, can we find someone to succeed him when he is no longer here? Was his successor on the podium (Beloki, Rumsas)? Is he still lost in the peloton, for example Basso, winner of the young riders' white jersey, eleventh and all the same some way behind Mancebo and Sevilla, his two predecessors? Is he still hidden further down the GC (Millar)? Is he still practically a debutant like the French Casar or Chavanel, who competed in a Tour for their age group? Was he absent or suspended (Ullrich, Garzelli, Simoni)? Or has he not yet even ridden the Tour (Cadel Evans)? Today, we have few indications, but a lot can happen in two years.

At the top of the table, the reorganization was minimal despite four new arrivals in the

Lance Armstrong was never really attacked, but can you blame his outmatched opponents? At Ventoux, Joseba Beloki (behind) attempted to challenge the yellow jersey. Lance Armstrong responded immediately and categorically, putting him back in his place. Right: Armstrong on his way to a solo stage win at Plateau de Beille.

Laurent Jalabert was a fast enough descender to attack on the way down – a daily occurrence on the final Pyrenean stages of his illustrious career.

top ten (Rumsas, Azevedo, Leipheimer and Sastre), and Mancebo and Heras regained their positions after a year of being sidelined. The only place where we saw a really significant change was with the green jersey, where Erik Zabel's series of six consecutive wins, a definitive record, was ended, but not without the German champion looking good on the Champs (7th) and winning his stage (Alençon). But Robbie McEwen was going far too fast for him. The Australian, already a stage winner at Reims, reaffirmed his status on the Champs-Élysées where he dominated as he had done in 1999.

Laurent Jalabert had a magnificent final Tour. He is the only King of the Mountains, apart from Merckx and Hinault, to have also won the green jersey, in 1992 and 1995.

Deprived of the yellow jersey during the first week, Jalabert devised for himself the best possible farewell Tour by travelling across France in the lead (429 kilometres [267 miles] in breakaways over three days starting from the Pyrenees). He was still competitive, and wanted his stage win. He had to concentrate his efforts on the polka-dot jersey, greatly justified on the Aubisque

and elsewhere, as he wiped out all the bad memories that the Tour, unfairly, held for him. We already know that the Tour will miss him a great deal. Perhaps this gave us, and the public, an even more acute sense of the gap that he will leave behind.

Richard Virenque was still there, for a certain amount of time. Paradoxically, he had to work hard in the passes where he previously he seemed at ease, and would have had one of his worst Tours to date (16th overall), if he hadn't pulled off one of the masterstrokes of his career at Ventoux.

As a result of his consistency, David Moncoutié (13th) had the honour of being the first Frenchman (he had come between 12th and 14th place in the mountains on four occasions), but that is not to say that this is the high point of his career; he has the potential to aim a little higher.

French cycling (two stages with Halgand and Virenque) did not do too badly, especially the teams (five out of six did not come back empty-handed). All the same, it has been 17 years since a Frenchman has won the Tour. Already, a whole generation of young people have no recollection of Bernard Hinault; it would be a pity if this gap meant that fewer and fewer young people showed an interest in the Tour.

Hardship and triumph

For the centennial Tour de France, Jean-Marie Leblanc's masterstroke lay in postponing the first long time trial until after the Alps. This, and Lance Armstrong's inability to kill the race on its first mountain finish, made it a classic.

In March, the Kazakh Andrei Kivilev – fourth in 2001 – had died after a banal fall. Cycling's governing body acted by making helmets compulsory. It gave the 2003 peloton a new look. New too was the star of the week one sprints: Alessandro Petacchi, who resisted any comparison to Mario Cipollini until he'd taken four stage wins, and pointedly remarked, 'Not even Cipollini has won 6 Giro stages and 4 stages in the same year.' Then, Cipollini-style, he abandoned on the first major climb.

The team time trial gave Armstrong a time advantage over his expected rivals. He took the yellow jersey on Alpe-d'Huez, but only after a rally of attacks launched by the persistent Joseba Beloki, the heroic Tyler Hamilton – riding with a double fracture to his right collarbone after a fall on stage one – and the electrifying Iban Mayo, who was followed home by the revelation of the race, Alexandre Vinokourov. Victory at Gap the next day put the Kazakh within 21 seconds of Armstrong. The valiant Beloki ended the day with a broken femur, elbow and wrist after slipping on a road surface liquefied in the heat.

Then, on 18 July, in the cauldron of Cap' Découverte, Jan Ullrich came back from the dead. As Armstrong became severely dehydrated, Kaiser Jan made up 1min 36secs on him. Vinokourov lost only 30 seconds and took back 43 seconds two days later *en route* for Loudenvielle. After 14 stages, the three leaders were within 18 seconds of each other: unprecedented in 100 years of Tour history. And the best was yet to come.

The stage to Luz-Ardiden was one of the highpoints of Tour de France history. On the mythical Tourmalet, Vinokourov attacked. Armstrong reeled him in, before an irresistible acceleration by Ullrich saw the American lose 50 metres (160 feet) before slowly clawing his way back up to Ullrich's wheel. Then, at the foot of the final climb, he launched his own offensive, with Mayo on his wheel. Suddenly, Armstrong and Mayo were on the ground: Armstrong's handlebar had caught the shoulder strap of a child's bag in the crowd. His Tour reign seemed to be over. Ullrich avoided the fallers, and in an act of cycling chivalry, slowed up to allow them to recover. Armstrong righted himself, regained the waiting group and attacked again. No-one could follow him and he powered away to win the stage by 40 seconds. It was classic Armstrong.

Ullrich started the final time trial at incredible speed, gaining 6 seconds in the first 2 kilometres. But in the pouring rain, he fell heavily on the run in to the finish at Nantes. Armstrong had already made up the lost time, and was able to coast safely to the finish, secure of his yellow jersey and his place in history.

GENERAL CLASSIFICATION

1. **Lance Armstrong** (USA) US Postal-Berry Floor, 3,361 km in 83h.41m.12s; Average Speed 40.94 kph
2. **Jan Ullrich** (GER) Team Bianchi, at 1m.01s
3. **Alexandre Vinokourov** (KAZ) Team Telekom, at 4m.14s
4. Tyler Hamilton (USA) Team CSC, at 6m.17s.
5. Haimar Zubeldia (SPA) Euskaltel-Euskadi, at 6m.51s.
6. Iban Mayo (SPA) Euskaltel-Euskadi, at 7m.06s.
7. Ivan Basso (ITA) Fassa Bortolo, at 10m.12s.
8. Christophe Moreau (FRA) Credit Agricole, at 12m.28s.
9. Carlos Sastre (SPA) Team CSC, at 18m.49s.
10. Francisco Mancebo (SPA) iBanesto.com, at 19m.15s.
11. Denis Menchov (RUS) iBanesto.com, at 19m.44s.
12. Georg Tötschnig (AUT) Gerolsteiner, at 21m.32s.
13. Peter Luttenberger (AUT) Team CSC, at 22m.16s.
14. Manuel Beltran (SPA) US Postal-Berry Floor, at 23m.03s.
15. Massimiliano Lelli (ITA) Cofidis, at 24m.00s.
16. Richard Virenque (FRA) Quick-Step Davitamon, at 25m.31s.
17. Jörg Jaksche (GER) ONCE-Eroski, at 27m.22s.
18. Roberto Laiseka (SPA) Euskaltel-Euskadi, at 29m.15s.
19. José Luis Rubiera (SPA) US Postal-Berry Floor, at 29m.37s.
20. Didier Rous (FRA) Brioches La Boulangere, at 30m.14s.

90TH TOUR DE FRANCE, 20 STAGES – 3,361 KM

			STAGE	STAGE WINNER	YELLOW JERSEY
Prologue	Saturday 5 July	6.5 km	Paris (TT)	B. McGee (AUS)	B. McGee
Stage 1	Sunday 6 July	160 km	Saint-Denis/Montgeron – Meaux	A. Petacchi (ITA)	B. McGee
Stage 2	Monday 7 July	195 km	La Ferté-sous-Jouarre – Sedan	B. Cooke (AUS)	B. McGee
Stage 3	Tuesday 8 July	160 km	Charleville-Mézières – Saint-Dizier	A. Petacchi (ITA)	J.-P. Nazon
Stage 4	Wednesday 9 July	68 km	Joinville – Saint-Dizier (TTT)	US Postal (USA)	V. H. Pena
Stage 5	Thursday 10 July	196 km	Troyes – Nevers	A. Petacchi (ITA)	V. H. Pena
Stage 6	Friday 11 July	230 km	Nevers – Lyon	A. Petacchi (ITA)	V. H. Pena
Stage 7	Saturday 12 July	226.5 km	Lyons – Morzine	R. Virenque (FRA)	R. Virenque
Stage 8	Sunday 13 July	211 km	Sallanches – L'Alpe-d'Huez	I. Mayo (SPA)	L. Armstrong
Stage 9	Monday 14 July	184.5 km	Bourg d'Oisans – Gap	A. Vinokourov (KAZ)	L. Armstrong
Stage 10	Tuesday 15 July	195 km	Gap – Marseille	J. Piil (DEN)	L. Armstrong
Stage 11	Thursday 17 July	160 km	Narbonne – Toulouse	J. A. Flecha (SPA)	L. Armstrong
Stage 12	Friday 18 July	48.5 km	Galliac – Cap' Découverte (TT)	J. Ullrich (GER)	L. Armstrong
Stage 13	Saturday 19 July	197.5 km	Toulouse – Plateau de Bonascre	C. Sastre (SPA)	L. Armstrong
Stage 14	Sunday 20 July	191.5 km	Saint-Girons – Loudenvielle	G. Simoni (ITA)	L. Armstrong
Stage 15	Monday 21 July	159.5 km	Bagnères-de-Bigorre – Luz-Ardiden	L. Armstrong (USA)	L. Armstrong
Stage 16	Wednesday 23 July	197.5 km	Pau – Bayonne	T. Hamilton (USA)	L. Armstrong
Stage 17	Thursday 24 July	165 km	Dax – Bordeaux	S. Knaven (HOL)	L. Armstrong
Stage 18	Friday 25 July	200 km	Bordeaux – Saint-Maixent-l'École	P. Lastras (SPA)	L. Armstrong
Stage 19	Saturday 26 July	49 km	Pornic – Nantes (TT)	D. Millar (GBR)	L. Armstrong
Stage 20	Sunday 27 July	160 km	Ville-d'Avray – Paris	J.-P. Nazon (FRA)	L. Armstrong

Right: Despite wearing the yellow jersey from stage 8, Lance Armstrong was haunted by a series of mishaps and could only be sure of his fifth victory in the final metres of the Nantes time trial.

Above: In pursuit of Vinokourov on the descent into Gap, Armstrong had to leave the road to avoid Beloki's crash. Taking to the fields, he showed great presence of mind and excellent bike handling.

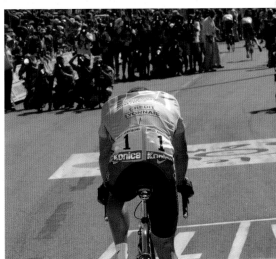

Stage 13: For the first time in five years, Armstrong's rivals had him in difficulties in the mountains.

Stage 15: Armstrong's first attack on Luz-Ardiden ended abruptly after a spectator's bag caught his handlebars.

347

Lance Armstrong: 'I don't ever want to go through another Tour like this.'

You have just won your fifth Tour de France, without doubt the hardest. Is this victory sweeter than the others?

Nothing could ever be like the first: it was a new experience, like suddenly winning the lottery. A strange feeling, like being on a cloud. I've never felt that way since. In 2001, I had a great feeling, it was a great year. Last year, the team was impeccable and everything went according to plan. This year, it's much nicer… Last night, alone in my room, I asked myself: 'Am I happy?' And then I thought: 'What would you be feeling if you'd lost, if you'd fallen?' And I realised just how happy I was. If I'd failed, the walk from my room to the dining room where my friends were waiting would have been long and tortuous. I went through it the evening after the time trial, when the only thing I could say to them was, 'I'm sorry.'

You're a perfectionist, and despite winning, this Tour has the flavour of something not quite won. That must bother you…

No one likes stress; I don't ever want to go through another Tour like this. If it ever happens, at least I'll have the experience of this one. But I hope it doesn't. I had a fright this year because nothing went according to plan.

It all began when you fell at the Dauphiné Libéré in June. What did you do between that fall and the start of the Tour?

Physically, the Dauphiné was hard, perhaps too hard, what with the mountains, the heat and of course the fall. It was too hard and I won't do it again. It's a great race, but when it takes so much out of you to win, it isn't good for you. Physically, obviously, because you have to control the race, but mentally too its stressful, because once I had the jersey, I didn't want to give it up. Perhaps it would have been better to let Mayo win… and also, for sure, not to fall. I paid for it. It took longer to recover from the fall than I hoped. Perhaps I'm getting older and my body no longer responds as readily. I hadn't taken antibiotics for six or seven years.

My body didn't respond well, I had stomach pains. At the end of the Dauphiné, I wasn't well. And that lasted until the Tour.

The week before the Tour started, you had gastroenteritis.

I had diarrhoea and I almost didn't recover in time, although mentally, I was pretty cool. I knew I could get over that type of problem in three or four days. If Alpe-d'Huez had been the first day, my Tour would have been over. I had the Prologue to get into the race: it's important, but it doesn't decide anything. What's more, I had hip pain because of some new shoes. The Thursday before the race start, I wore them to train on the time trial bike, but there was a tiny movement where the cleat meets the pedal. I've been changing shoes for twenty years without a problem, but this time, my hip tied up and I could hardly walk. At the team presentation on TV, I tried to look normal; I don't think anyone noticed. Can you imagine if they had? Armstrong is injured! He's going to lose the Tour! It took a week to heal, all the same.

It didn't look as if you started the prologue with the usual concentration.

The fact is, I dreamt about it. Before the Dauphiné, I said to Johan [*directeur sportif*]: 'I'm going to finish seventh in the Prologue.' It was a dream, but also an idea. Everyone was going to say, 'You see, he's not as strong, he's only seventh, he doesn't look good.' I rode it flat out and I finished… seventh! So I said to Johan: 'You see what I told you, it's happened!' And then I said: 'But in my dream, I won the Tour all the same.' I don't think he believed me, but I took it as a good sign.

All the same, at Meaux, you were in the fall. At the time, were you afraid you'd lost the Tour on the second day?

No, I wasn't afraid. But I was bruised because I took a heavy blow to the hip, which is a sensitive place for a cyclist. I suffered on the following stages, especially to Sedan, where I couldn't keep on the pace towards the end. But some strange stuff happened this year. At the presentation in Paris, a bird flew into the bus and shat on Johan's suit. Padrnos

US Postal shepherd the yellow jersey safely down the Col d'Izoard on stage 9.

immediately said it was a bad omen. Maybe he was right. And there were some strange technical things. My accident during the Dauphiné wasn't normal. The brakes were glued to the fork. Why? No mechanic ever does that. Then, on the descent from the Galibier, I realised my brake had been rubbing the rim for the whole climb. At Marseille, Padrnos' front wheel suddenly came loose. The same day, at the start, Ekimov noticed the same thing when he was checking his bike.

Given the security measures around your team, how was that possible?

Every morning, between the bus and the podium where we sign in, we always stop to sign autographs and take photos and give interviews. You're immediately surrounded by 50 people, and it couldn't be easier to touch the brakes. It's obviously my fault, because you should always check your bike. After that, I did it every day.

Were you worried about these bad vibes?

Whatever happens, you have to try to relax and be in control. A problem with the bike? Check the bike. A problem with food? Same thing. A physical problem? Get some treatment. I brought an osteopath over from Italy. If he'd been in Tunisia, or on the Moon, he'd have come, because it's the Tour de France. There's no limit. You try to control the negative things, and in the end, I had a few problems but also plenty of fortune.

Was there a day you thought your chances of winning were less than 50%? Did you ever doubt yourself?

Yes, after Bonascre. I was calm, but I was losing my footing. But my lowest moment in the Tour, the real moment I hit rock bottom, was the second split during the Cap' Découverte time trial. When I heard Ullrich's time, I said to myself, 'The Tour's over.' At that moment, I was in crisis, a deep crisis, almost giving up. At Joux-Plane in 2000, I had a difficult moment, but I had a seven minute advantage; that's the big difference.

Was the dehydration your own fault?

The mistake began ten days earlier. It wasn't an instantaneous dehydration, but an accumulation. Maybe I didn't keep enough of an eye on everything. Then again, when you think it's a done deal, you make mistakes. It's one of the big lessons of this Tour and I won't forget it.

Vinokourov and Ullrich pile the pressure on Armstrong on the climb to Bonascre in the Pyrenees.

When did you feel the tide was turning?

I'll tell you exactly when the Tour de France was won. The day of the time trial, I had a real off-day, a moment of intense suffering, the like of which I've experienced very rarely in my career. I was at the bottom of a deep hole. You don't get over a crisis like that so easily. The next day, I was a bit better, but not yet there, a little better at Loudenvielle – although not yet great, especially given that Ullrich seemed really strong on Peyresourde. Inside, I knew I was going to be better the following day. Every morning, I go for a coffee in the bus, because it's better than at the hotel. There, the morning of Luz-Ardiden, one of the boys who work for us at the Tour told me a story. He told me that a year ago, Rudy Pévenage [Ullrich's *directeur sportif*] asked him for one of my yellow jerseys, and that he'd asked again at Paris. And then, he said that the morning before Bonascre, Pévenage went to see him and said: 'Oh, you can forget that yellow jersey. We'll have our own pretty soon.' When I heard that, I told him, 'The Tour's finished! He'll never have it.' It really, really, REALLY motivated me! I went crazy – completely crazy. It was really a profound moment for me, because I felt personally hurt. So it became a challenge. Already, some of my friends in the peloton had told me they were going to attack at the foot of Luz-Ardiden because they were sure I was finished.

Yet Jan Ullrich attacked on the Tourmalet, a long way from the finish. With hindsight, how do you explain it?

I said to myself: 'Big mistake – huge mistake. But that was the responsibility of his *directeur sportif* in the car. If Johan had seen me go like that, he'd have shouted, 'What do you think you're doing? Where are you going? Are you nuts?' It's not a village criterium, it's the Tour de France. Their arrogance made them lose, because they were sure I wouldn't be able to follow. They were saying it everywhere: 'we'll attack and he'll get dropped.' But I'm not just anyone – I'm not some shitty rider. OK, at Bonascre, he dropped me, but to achieve what? He was riding flat out; not me. I followed at a distance, then came back.

On Friday, you had a setback in the time trial and on the two following days, you lost time on some of your rivals. At Luz-Ardiden, you seem to have been reborn. How do you explain it?

That morning, everything was up to scratch. There was only one thing to do if I wanted to win the Tour: attack. That's how we planned it, and I have to say the team was once again spectacular.

When Ullrich attacked on the Tourmalet – a long way from the finish – you didn't react immediately. Why not?

Firstly, because it was a very powerful attack. The fact is, I immediately said to myself that it wasn't the time to move. The Tourmalet is a long climb and there was still the descent and the climb to Luz-Ardiden. Tactically, I didn't want to lose my composure. It was better to shadow him from 10 seconds behind, hold guys like Mayo there,

349

Tyler Hamilton rode for 21 days with a broken collarbone, finishing fourth overall and taking a brilliant solo stage win at Bayonne.

TYLER HAMILTON

The stage winner yesterday and sixth in the GC, Tyler Hamilton is a strange kid. A small boy from another world who concentrates the quintessence of his strength in one small corner of his mind. Tyler is a Jedi knight, a warrior straight out of Star Wars. He bears a disarming tranquillity within him. He never swears, whether against those who don't believe in him or against the heavens which inflict such trials on him. He always says 'Thank you.' He thinks ceaselessly of others, and feels indebted to them each morning.

A funny man, out of time, out of fashion. When he moves, his gestures are slow, very slow. His eyelids are always half closed and his barely delineated lips scarcely move. He speaks like a ventriloquist, although his smile, rare, always opens with real purpose. He is just and good, because the Tour de France admits no lies – it reveals you as you are. Since his fall on the first Sunday of the month, analysed from every angle in the world's media, and destiny dictated that he ride the centenary Tour with a fractured collarbone, Tyler Hamilton has been divulging his truth despite himself, although he is as secretive as a tomb.

and come back gently at my own rhythm. But he was super strong, and I said to myself: 'If he continues at this rhythm, he'll win the Tour.'

Then you had a big scare when you fell, just as you were starting your attack. What happened?

When Iban Mayo attacked, I accelerated with him, and counter-attacked. I took a corner too tight, got too close to the public, and I think my handlebar caught a spectator's *musette*. It was my fault and I couldn't do a thing about it. I said to myself: 'Shit! This can't be happening! Not now!' At the time, I didn't think about the time loss; I thought about the state of my bike, if I needed to change it or if I could carry on with it. I tried to get up as quickly as I could, saw I wasn't hurt, apart from a cut on my elbow, checked the bike over, put the chain back on and set off. At times like that, instinct takes over.

Did you know at the time that Ullrich had waited for you?

Yes, I was told immediately and it didn't surprise me. I did the same thing two years ago, when Jan had a spectacular fall on the descent from the Col de Peyresourde. I was with some other guys and I said to them: 'It's impossible to go on until we know if it's serious or if he can rejoin the race.' I thank him for remembering that. What he did was the gesture of a gentleman and I appreciate it.

It looked as if the fall, and the subsequent pedal mishap made you angry, and that anger unleashed your strength…

My attack was made in desperation. Since the start of the Tour, nothing was going according to plan. I'd had lots of problems, but I believe in cycles and I knew this one would end. It was really a Tour of every type of problem, every type of drawback and disruption. Now my only wish is that it's behind me. So after the fall, I felt a huge rush of adrenaline. I said to myself: 'Lance, if you want to win the Tour, you better attack.'

This year, it looked as if you've changed you riding style. You don't jump onto everything that moves, you no longer give it everything when you attack.

It's inevitable as you get older. You no longer have the same punch, the same accel-

eration. So you use your experience, your head. I knew that this moment would arrive, perhaps not this year, but I was ready. At the Dauphiné, I said it in an interview with the *New York Times*: the day will come when a very strong, very aggressive young kid will attack again and again until he's got you cornered. Then you have to completely change your style.

If Beloki hadn't had to abandon, that would have changed something in the physiognomy of the race.

Sure. He was in great shape and he showed it in the Prologue. He'd never started the Tour in such good shape, and on Alpe-d'Huez he really impressed me. But no one can say how he would have progressed in the second part of the race because it was harder than the first. The speed on the climb up to Luz-Ardiden was high, much higher than on Alpe-d'Huez. It was very hot, and some of the tactics were strange. He'd have made the race simpler for us, without a doubt.

Did you make any tactical errors during the Tour?

One big one: Ullrich could and should have been eliminated on Alpe-d'Huez. He was ill that day and we should have made the most of it up front. At times, he was virtually at a stand still, but at the finish line, he lost only 1min 32sec, when I think that by raising our game, that could have been doubled. But you always learn from these mistakes.

You're coming back in 2004 to try to win your sixth Tour, which would make you unique in history. Does that matter to you?

What's important is to win the Tour de France. Number 1, number 2, number 6… who cares? That's why I get up in the morning, it's all that matters. If I win, the season is a success. If I lose, it's a disaster. To come second is no consolation, it's failure, for me, for the team, for the sponsor.

If you win next year, you'll be able to retire without ever being beaten. Is that something you think about?

It's a dream to retire undefeated. Lots of athletes try to achieve it and some don't know how to stop in time. I hope to recognise the moment. I want to win again, and to stop at the top. But one thing's for sure: I won't do a goodbye Tour.

Jan Ullrich attacked powerfully on the Tourmalet, but by the summit Lance Armstrong, Iban Mayo and Haimar Zubeldia were back on his wheel.

Jan Ullrich, Ivan Basso and Tyler Hamilton wait for the yellow jersey to rejoin their group after his crash on the slopes of Luz-Ardiden.

Lance Armstrong pushed himself to the very limit at Luz-Ardiden, taking an unforgettable stage win and putting 40 seconds into Jan Ullrich.

Six!

So compelling was the Centenary Tour that many predicted an even closer finish in 2004. Armstrong, at 32, was another year older and when Iban Mayo, the previous year's winner at Alpe d'Huez, thrashed Armstrong in a time trial on Mont Ventoux in June, speculation was rife that the Texan was no longer the athlete he had once been.

Armstrong lost the Prologue in Liège by two seconds to the Swiss rider Fabian Cancellara, but gained no less than 15 seconds on Ullrich and 16 on Tyler Hamilton – and these were the best of his expected rivals. Nonetheless, the heavily back-loaded race route, with a very demanding third week, fostered optimism that Armstrong's form would dip, his rivals' would improve, and the hoped-for close contest would emerge.

Any hope Armstrong's rivals had of riding into form during the first week were shattered by appalling conditions that saw regular falls and desperate chases in rain, hale, and gale-force winds. The first victim was Mayo, his Tour dreams destroyed by a fall as riders jockeyed for position before the first cobbled section of stage 3. Then, as if talent, experience and tactical acuity were not already on Armstrong's side, his team even benefited from a lull in the weather to dominate the team time trial and put him in the yellow jersey. However, for the first time in their Tour career, US Postal-Berry Floor didn't defend the yellow jersey. The next day, an evergreen Stuart O'Grady

took the stage from a breakaway group, but the real winner was 25-year-old Thomas Voeckler who took the yellow jersey and defended it in dashing fashion for ten days.

In the Pyrenees, before any lightning acceleration from the American could shatter the field, all the expected challengers – Ullrich, Hamilton, Heras, Sevilla – began to drop off the pace. Only the Italian Ivan Basso could follow Armstrong, taking the stage win at La Mongie. The following day at Plateau de Beille, the result went the other way. Meanwhile, Andreas Klöden, not Jan Ullrich, was emerging as T-Mobile's strongest challenger. At Villard-de-Lans, Armstrong again beat Basso to the line.

The long-awaited Alpe d'Huez time trial saw Armstrong take his third win, catching Basso, who had started two minutes before him, after 15.5 kilometres. Ullrich, second on the day, lost 61 seconds – his deficit after three weeks in 2003.

At Le Grand Bornand, Klöden seemed to have timed his sprint perfectly, only for the astonishing Armstrong to accelerate past him like a track sprinter and take his fourth stage win. The final time trial, won imperiously by Armstrong, decided the final placings: the valiant Basso conceded second place to Klöden, and confirmed Ullrich in fourth.

The following day, Armstrong left the five club, and started his own, one-man order as the only winner of six Tours de France in history. And there was no sign of him retiring!

GENERAL CLASSIFICATION

1. **Lance Armstrong** (USA) US Postal-Berry Floor
   3,391 km in 83h.36m.02s; Average Speed 40.56 kph
2. **Andreas Klöden** (GER) T-Mobile Team, at 6m.19s
3. **Ivan Basso** (ITA) Team CSC, at 6m.40s
4. Jan Ullrich (GER) T-Mobile Team, at 8m.50s
5. Jose Azevedo (POR) US Postal-Berry Floor, at 14m.30s
6. Francisco Mancebo (SPA) Illes Balears-Banesto, at 18m.01s
7. Georg Totschnig (AUT) Gerolsteiner, at 18m.27s
8. Carlos Sastre (SPA) Team CSC, at 19m.51s
9. Levi Leipheimer (USA) Rabobank, at 20m.12s
10. Oscar Pereiro (SPA) Phonak Hearing Systems, at 22m.54s
11. Pietro Caucchioli (ITA) Alessio-Bianchi, at 24m.21s
12. Christophe Moreau (FRA) Crédit Agricole, at 24m.36s
13. Vladimir Karpets (RUS) Illes Balears-Banesto, at 25m.11s
14. Michael Rasmussen (DEN) Rabobank, at 27m.16s
15. Richard Virenque (FRA) Quick Step-Davitamon, at 28m.11s
16. Sandy Casar (FRA) Fdjeux.com, at 28m.53s
17. Gilberto Simoni (ITA) Saeco, at 29m.00s
18. Thomas Voeckler (FRA) Brioches La Boulangère, at 31m.12s
19. Jose Luis Rubiera (SPA) US Postal-Berry Floor, at 32m.50s
20. Stéphane Goubert (FRA) AG2R Prévoyance, at 37m.11s

91ST TOUR DE FRANCE, 20 STAGES - 3,391 KM

			STAGE	STAGE WINNER	YELLOW JERSEY
Prologue	Saturday 3 July	6.1 km	Liège (TT) (BEL)	F.Cancellara (SWI)	F.Cancellara
Stage 1	Sunday 4 July	202.5 km	Liège – Charleroi (BEL)	J. Kirsipuu (EST)	F.Cancellara
Stage 2	Monday 5 July	197 km	Charleroi – Namur (BEL)	R. McEwen (AUS)	T. Hushovd
Stage 3	Tuesday 6 July	210 km	Waterloo (BEL) – Wasquehal	J.-P. Nazon (FRA)	R. McEwen
Stage 4	Wednesday 7 July	64.5 km	Cambrai – Arras (TTT)	US Postal-Berry Floor	L. Armstrong
Stage 5	Thursday 8 July	200.5 km	Amiens – Chartres	S. O'Grady (AUS)	T.Voeckler
Stage 6	Friday 9 July	196 km	Bonneval – Angers	T. Boonen (BEL)	T. Voeckler
Stage 7	Saturday 10 July	204.5 km	Chateaubriant – Saint Brieuc	F. Pozzato (ITA)	T. Voeckler
Stage 8	Sunday 11 July	168 km	Lamballe – Quimper	T. Hushovd (NOR)	T. Voeckler
Stage 9	Tuesday 13 July	160.5 km	St Leonard de Noblat – Guéret	R. McEwen (AUS)	T. Voeckler
Stage 10	Wednesday 14 July	237 km	Limoges – St Flour	R.Virenque (FRA)	T. Voeckler
Stage 11	Thursday 15 July	164 km	St Flour – Figeac	D. Moncoutié (FRA)	T. Voeckler
Stage 12	Friday 16 July	197.5 km	Castelsarrasin – La Mongie	I. Basso (ITA)	T. Voeckler
Stage 13	Saturday 17 July	205.5 km	Lannemezan – Plateau de Beille	L. Armstrong (USA)	T. Voeckler
Stage 14	Sunday 18 July	192.5 km	Carcassonne – Nimes	A.Gonzalez (SPA)	T. Voeckler
Stage 15	Tuesday 20 July	180.5 km	Valreas – Villard-de-Lans	L. Armstrong (USA)	L. Armstrong
Stage 16	Wednesday 21 July	15.5 km	Bourg d'Oisans – Alpe d'Huez (TT)	L. Armstrong (USA)	L. Armstrong
Stage 17	Thursday 22 July	204.5 km	Bourg d'Oisans – Le Grand Bornand	L. Armstrong (USA)	L. Armstrong
Stage 18	Friday 23 July	166.5 km	Annemasse – Lons le Saunier	J. M. Mercado (SPA)	L. Armstrong
Stage 19	Saturday 24 July	55 km	Besançon–Besançon (TT)	L. Armstrong (USA)	L. Armstrong
Stage 20	Sunday 25 July	163 km	Montereau–Paris-Champs-Elysees	T. Boonen (BEL)	L. Armstrong

Right: Lance Armstrong dominated 2004's Tour in the manner of Merckx and Hinault, taking five individual stage wins at (clockwise from left) L'Alpe d'Huez, Plateau de Beille, Villard-de-Lans, Le Grand Bornand and Besançon.

Lance Armstrong: '100 percent commitment'

For three weeks, Armstrong has put on a show like no champion before him. As an athlete, let there be no doubt, he's unique. However, what of the man behind the champion? He's a 'survivor,' as he has defined himself since beating cancer. He is also a power-broker, on intimate terms with the other power-brokers of cycling – he says 'Jean-Marie,' not 'Leblanc'. He's a great actor, too, meticulous about his appearance and rapier-like in his repartee. He's turned the Tour into a piece of American-style entertainment, a show straight out of Broadway, in which his close friend, the actor Robin Williams, plays a mere supporting role behind the rock star Sheryl Crow, the champion's new companion, who has been tracked everywhere by television cameras which have seen her racked with nerves during a time trial, agonizing over a climb, and exultant after a triumphant sprint.

What is the secret of Armstrong's astounding success? '100 percent commitment,' he says. He underlines the importance of his entourage, and, above all, Johan Bruyneel, rightly considered a brilliant strategist. Nor does he forget the devoted team-mates bound spiritually and contractually to the Texan. 'Our relationship lasts 365 days a year'.

Above all, Armstrong has shown an astonishing ability to rekindle his enthusiasm year after year. Unlike Bernard Hinault, who had retired from cycling by the same age, Armstrong is neither sated nor jaded by success. But will the spell wear off one day? Armstrong refuses to speculate. All he will say is: 'I've been here ten years, and I'm enjoying myself now more than ever.'

What he doesn't say is that he has revolutionised not only how to approach the Tour de France, with his meticulous, painstaking reconnaissance of strategic sections of the route, but also the spirit of the Tour. His great predecessors, from Jacques Anquetil to Eddy Merckx and Bernard Hinault, limited themselves to taking on their adversaries as the mood took them. Armstrong goes further. He doesn't merely take on Jan Ullrich or Iban Mayo; he takes on matter itself – he takes on his own limits in an unprecedented self-interrogation. 'He concedes nothing to instinct,' said former champion Felice Gimondi the other day. Gimondi considers Armstrong the

first 'pre-programmed' champion in history. Others regard him as something similar to a serial killer who visits, measures and scrutinises to the finest detail the site of his deeds – ten, twenty times, if necessary – in order to snuff out his rivals come the summer. 'In a way, I'm a slave to the Tour,' he smiles. There are riders like Ivan Basso who try to imitate him, reproducing his pedal technique, without ever quite succeeding. No one has married strength and speed better than Armstrong, and this explains his dominance both in the mountains and the time trials. He reigns absolutely, almost despotically, and is ready to excommunicate those who do not share his way of thinking. He's a tyrant who claims divine right with a Manichean fervour, and decrees right and wrong according to his vision of the world. If the public hisses when he passes, he doesn't care. Popularity isn't his forte – it isn't even part of the game. 'I understand that certain people don't like me, but plenty of champions before me haven't been the people's favourites,' he says, with some justification. The same public that shouts him down found Anquetil cold and distant, Hinault unrefined, and subscribed in the seventies to virulent Anti-Merckxism: 'what's the point of following the Tour if it's only to see who comes second?,' the papers of the time read, and these sentiments eventually translated into the senseless punch delivered from the roadside by a fan on the Puy de Dôme in 1975.

Whatever his personality, the reigning champion sooner or later becomes an irritant. It's a classic, long recognised symptom. This time around, Lance Armstrong had reason to fear for his safety. He felt threatened by German supporters ('a minority,' he stresses) who spat at him in the Alps, but it is worth asking to what extent he sowed the seeds of the antipathy he felt grow towards him. The difference of opinion that divided him from Filippo Simeoni are symptomatic of his double personality. Early in stage 18, Simeoni, a modest équipier, surged out of the peloton in pursuit of six breakaway riders – only to be chased down by Armstrong himself in the yellow jersey, and forced to curtail his attack. The final stage saw a repeat performance, with Armstrong deploying his superlative

Armstong's sixth Tour win confirms him as the world's most glamorous sports star: Sheryl Crow and...

...Robin Williams lead the cast of his superstar entourage, while the Times Square billboards...

... proclaim his triumphs to a spellbound crowd. What would Maurice Garin or Eugene Christophe make of this?

team to neutralise three attacks by the unfortunate Italian.

The differences between the two men lie in a court case unfolding with excruciating sluggishness in Italy. Under oath, Simeoni has effectively accused Dr Michele Ferrari of prescribing him doping products. But Ferrari is Armstrong's trainer, and the Texan has staunchly defended him: 'He's a misunderstood figure, an upright, intelligent man who knows more than anyone how to judge a performance.' Now, Ferrari could very well be both the doper described by Simeoni and the clean, scrupulous trainer depicted by Armstrong. He could very well have administered EPO to one and not the other. Did Armstrong have to venge himself on Simeoni on the road to Lons le Saunier? Did he have to flout every democratic tradition of the Tour and humiliate him? 'I have to confess I found it disappointing,' said former world champion Luc Leblanc. This episode – 'comical' in the view of Jean-Marie Leblanc, 'shocking' in that of the President of the Jury of Commissaires Mirco Monti, simply 'mean' to many other onlookers – did his image more harm than good.

The incident was not without precedent: in 1999, Amrstrong set the entire peloton against another humble rider, Christophe Bassons; in 2003, he did the same to Patrice Halgand, who had attacked when Armstrong was involved in a fall. This year, Armstrong's display of gracelessness came at the very moment when we should have been celebrating his sixth victory. From a man who has beaten cancer and acquired a wider vision of the world – from a man who in many respects embodies the future of sport – we would have liked to see magnanimity. We would have liked to see him rise above these petty feuds and show himself greater than the common run of his profession, dropping these vain, worthless quarrels and bringing warmth and humanity into a sport that has been deeply damaged by the unfolding of the Cofidis affair, the confessions of the Spanish rider Jesus Manzano, and the echoes of the Conconi trial. It was within Armstrong's ample grasp to do so, but he chose to pass on the opportunity. Perhaps he's saving such gestures for later in his career. Nonetheless, small, but unnecessary blemishes are left on the image of a truly great champion.

George Hincapie: the most faithful of the faithful. The only domestique to have helped his leader win six Tours.

The greatest individual in Tour history was surrounded by probably the greatest team: US Postal-Berry Floor.

10 days in yellow

The rain was beating down on the road to Chartres, and Thomas Voeckler had no idea that he had started a breakaway that would change his life. As the best placed in a group of five riders that also included Sandy Casar and Stuart O'Grady, the young Brioches la Boulangère rider was about the shed the jersey of the champion of France, acquired ten days earlier at Pont-du-Fossé, and don the most beautiful jersey in cycling: the prestigious yellow jersey, and with a lead of 9 minutes 43 seconds over Lance Armstrong. 'Why me?' he said, over and again, that evening. 'It could have been anyone of us. I'm not the exceptional rider on the team.' His first thoughts were of his team-mates – of offering them what he could of his moment of glory: 'I'm the one wearing the jersey, but it also belongs to them.' They served him well. For a week, the red and white train of Brioches La Boulangère

replaced the blue of US Postal at the front of the peloton, setting the pace, countering the attacks, and laughing a great deal. 'The media made a lot of it because we're at the Tour,' Voeckler recalls, 'but for us, it's like this all year round. Earpieces are for conveying tactical information and communicating when there's a problem, but we use them to have a laugh as well. Sometimes, when the racing is calm, it can be as boring as being in your room.'

Giving their all to defend the jersey, Thomas Voeckler and his team seduced thousands of spectators on the roads of France. 'With them, I'm experiencing the most thrilling moments of my life in cycling. Every day, I'm struck by the way they work for me, and, at the finish line, when I see their pride, I tell myself that this is the biggest prize of all – greater even than the yellow jersey.'

Yet, alone with Jacques Duchêne, his confident, Voeckler sometimes betrayed signs of the enormous pressure. 'I can't go on,' he confessed, after yet another interview and yet another late dinner. 'He worries about his team-mates,' Duchêne admits. 'He feels he is depriving them of a breakaway or a stage win.' It's the price you have to pay for defending the yellow jersey, but Thomas Voeckler finds it hard to accept that he must ride on his team-mates' wheels. He wants to act, and give his all. It's part of his character.

After six days of watching and waiting, the Pyrenean stages revealed Voeckler's formidable temperament. In particular, the stage up to Plateau de Beille made him a national hero. Dropped on the early slopes, he fought tenaciously, gritting his teeth and regained Armstrong's wheel. He attacked the final 16-kilometre climb, alongside the Texan with only 5 minutes to lose. At the summit, after something like a team time trial in which Jérôme Pineau and Sylvain Chavanel took monstruous pulls at the front to help their friend, the diminutive Thomas, aged 25, retained his jersey by 22 seconds. 'That final climb,' he confessed later, 'was vicious hand-to-hand combat and, when I reached the line, I really felt I'd accomplished my mission. I was up to the task: I proved that I was worthy of the jersey. Up to that point, apart from being the best placed rider in an attack that had got away, I had mainly benefited from race conditions and the hard work of my team. That day, I gave everything that was in me, and because of that, I feel at peace with myself.'

That's Thomas Voeckler, caught in the permanent struggle to be worthy of his ten days in yellow, which fell upon him like a gift from heaven. 'I must have a lucky star,' he smiles. Perhaps. But it isn't by chance that it lingered over this engaging rider, who arrived alone in France from Martinique aged 17. To be sure, exhausted by riding to his very limits, our young man finally surrendered his arms in the first Alpine stage. 'Ten days: that was my limit. I don't want anyone to think I could have won the Tour de France.' But if he refuses to dream, the public of the Tour de France will surely do so on his behalf.

Voeckler's celebration at Plateau de Beille recalled Armstrong's at Nantes a year earlier. Armstrong was celebrating winning the Tour, for Voeckler retaining his yellow jersey was no less an achievement.

By the time the race reached the Alps, Jan Ullrich was riding into form. But his valient attack on the road to Villard-de-Lans was too little, too late.

King of the Mountains for a record seventh time, Richard Virenque has now crested more cols at the head of the race than any other rider in Tour history.

TELECOM TROUBLE

Again, Jan Ullrich stood on the final podium. Again, it was not as the winner. This time, however, it was not even as runner-up: receiving the team prize was meager consolation for finishing fourth. T-Mobile's team manager Walter Godefroot tried to identify his leader's shortcomings.

'I would be lying if I said I was pleased with Ullrich's performance. He came to the Tour as the number one rival for Armstrong, and he's failed. He hasn't even won us a stage. We knew by La Mongie that Jan wasn't going to win the Tour. Jan just hasn't got the killer instinct. He's not a beast who's mentally capable of living like a monk. If he didn't allow himself certain things in the winter, he wouldn't be able to live with the stress of competition. It's a pity. With Erik Zabel's professionalism, Jan would be an Eddy Merckx.' The problem, however, extends beyond Ullrich's self-discipline and into the bizarre labyrinth of the T-Mobile team. Godefroot admits: 'I don't have much contact with him. I'm just in charge of the team. The person in charge of his training is Rudy Pevenage. Pevenage and Ullrich pass their decisions to Mario Kummer, who passes them on to me.' Asked why Andreas Klöden wasn't made team leader, Godefroot was frank: 'We had a choice to make, a commercial one. Jan's the star.'

Andreas Klöden: Ullrich's friend, compatriot, team-mate and now his successor as Tour runner-up.

Statistics

Year	Class	Points	Rider	Country
1903	1		Maurice Garin	FRA
	2		Lucien Pothier	FRA
	3		Fernand Augereau	FRA
1904	1		Henri Cornet	FRA
	2		Jean-Baptiste Dortignacq	FRA
	3		Aloïs Catteau	BEL
1905	1		Louis Trousselier	FRA
	2		Hippolyte Aucouturier	FRA
	3		Jean-Baptiste Dortignacq	FRA
1906	1		René Pottier	FRA
	2		Georges Passerieu	FRA
	3		Louis Trousselier	FRA
1907	1		Lucien Petit-Breton	FRA
	2		Gustave Garrigou	FRA
	3		Émile Georget	FRA
1908	1		Lucien Petit-Breton	FRA
	2		François Faber	LUX
	3		Georges Passerieu	FRA
1909	1		François Faber	LUX
	2		Gustave Garrigou	FRA
	3		Jean Alavoine	FRA
1910	1		Octave Lapize	FRA
	2		François Faber	LUX
	3		Gustave Garrigou	FRA
1911	1		Gustave Garrigou	FRA
	2		Paul Duboc	FRA
	3		Émile Georget	FRA
1912	1		Odile Defraye	BEL
	2		Eugène Christophe	FRA
	3		Gustave Garrigou	FRA
1913	1		Philippe Thys	BEL
	2		Gustave Garrigou	FRA
	3		Marcel Buysse	BEL
1914	1		Philippe Thys	BEL
	2		Henri Pélissier	FRA
	3		Jean Alavoine	FRA
1919	1		Firmin Lambot	BEL
	2		Jean Alavoine	FRA
	3		Eugène Christophe	FRA
1920	1		Philippe Thys	BEL
	2		Hector Heusghem	BEL
	3		Firmin Lambot	BEL
1921	1		Léon Scieur	BEL
	2		Hector Heusghem	BEL
	3		Honoré Barthélemy	FRA
1922	1		Firmin Lambot	BEL
	2		Jean Alavoine	FRA
	3		Félix Sellier	BEL
1923	1		Henri Pélissier	FRA
	2		Ottavio Bottecchia	ITA
	3		Romain Bellenger	FRA
1924	1		Ottavio Bottecchia	ITA
	2		Nicolas Frantz	LUX
	3		Lucien Buysse	BEL
1925	1		Ottavio Bottecchia	ITA
	2		Lucien Buysse	BEL
	3		Bartolomeo Aimo	ITA
1926	1		Lucien Buysse	BEL
	2		Nicolas Frantz	LUX
	3		Bartolomeo Aimo	ITA
1927	1		Nicolas Frantz	LUX
	2		Maurice De Waele	BEL
	3		Julien Vervaecke	BEL
1928	1		Nicolas Frantz	LUX
	2		André Leducq	FRA
	3		Maurice De Waele	BEL
1929	1		Maurice De Waele	BEL
	2		Giuseppe Pancera	ITA
	3		Joseph Demuysère	BEL
1930	1		André Leducq	FRA
	2		Learco Guerra	ITA
	3		Antonin Magne	FRA
	Team		France	
1931	1		Antonin Magne	FRA
	2		Joseph Demuysère	BEL
	3		Antonio Pesenti	ITA
	Team		Belgium	
1932	1		André Leducq	FRA
	2		Kurt Stoepel	GER
	3		Francesco Camusso	ITA
	Team		Italy	
1933	1		Georges Speicher	FRA
	2		Learco Guerra	ITA
	3		Giuseppe Martano	ITA
	Polka-dot	126 pts	Vicente Trueba	SPA
	Team		France	
1934	1		Antonin Magne	FRA
	2		Giuseppe Martano	ITA
	3		Roger Lapébie	FRA
	Polka-dot	111 pts	René Vietto	FRA
	Team		France	
1935	1		Romain Maes	BEL
	2		Ambrogio Morelli	ITA
	3		Félicien Vervaecke	BEL
	Polka-dot	118 pts	Félicien Vervaecke	BEL
	Team		Belgium	
1936	1		Sylvère Maes	BEL
	2		Antonin Magne	FRA
	3		Félicien Vervaecke	BEL
	Polka-dot	132 pts	Julian Berrendero	SPA
	Team		Belgium	
1937	1		Roger Lapébie	FRA
	2		Mario Vicini	ITA
	3		Léo Amberg	SUI
	Polka-dot	114 pts	Felicien Vervaecke	BEL
	Team		France	
1938	1		Gino Bartali	ITA
	2		Félicien Vervaecke	BEL
	3		Victor Cosson	FRA
	Polka-dot	108 pts	Gino Bartali	ITA
	Team		Belgium	
1939	1		Sylvère Maes	BEL
	2		René Vietto	FRA
	3		Lucien Vlaemynck	BEL
	Polka-dot	85 pts	Sylvère Maes	BEL
	Team		Belgium	
1947	1		Jean Robic	FRA
	2		Edouard Fachleitner	FRA
	3		Pierre Brambilla	ITA
	Polka-dot	98 pts	Pierre Brambilla	ITA
	Team		Italy	
1948	1		Gino Bartali	ITA
	2		Albéric 'Brik' Schotte	BEL
	3		Guy Lapébie	FRA
	Polka-dot	62 pts	Gino Bartali	ITA
	Team		Belgium	
1949	1		Fausto Coppi	ITA
	2		Gino Bartali	ITA
	3		Jacques Marinelli	FRA
	Polka-dot	81 pts	Fausto Coppi	ITA
	Team		Italy	
1950	1		Ferdi Kübler	SUI
	2		Constant 'Stan' Ockers	BEL
	3		Louison Bobet	FRA
	Polka-dot	58 pts	Louison Bobet	FRA
	Team		Belgium	
1951	1		Hugo Koblet	SUI
	2		Raphaël Géminiani	FRA
	3		Lucien Lazaridès	FRA
	Polka-dot	66 pts	Raphaël Géminiani	FRA
	Team		France	
1952	1		Fausto Coppi	ITA
	2		Constant 'Stan' Ockers	BEL
	3		Bernardo Ruiz	SPA
	Polka-dot	92 pts	Fausto Coppi	ITA
	Team		Italy	
1953	1		Louison Bobet	FRA
	2		Jean Malléjac	FRA
	3		Giancarlo Astrua	ITA
	Green	271 pts	Fritz Schaer	SUI
	Polka-dot	54 pts	Jésus Loroño	SPA
	Team		Holland	
1954	1		Louison Bobet	FRA
	2		Ferdi Kübler	SUI
	3		Fritz Schaer	SUI
	Green	215 pts	Ferdi Kübler	SUI
	Polka-dot	95 pts	Federico Bahamontes	SPA
	Team		Switzerland	
1955	1		Louison Bobet	FRA
	2		Jean Brankart	BEL
	3		Charly Gaul	LUX
	Green	322 pts	Constant 'Stan' Ockers	BEL
	Polka-dot	84 pts	Charly Gaul	LUX
	Team		France	
1956	1		Roger Walkowiak	FRA
	2		Gilbert Bauvin	FRA
	3		Jan Adriaenssens	BEL
	Green	280 pts	Constant 'Stan' Ockers	BEL
	Polka-dot	71 pts	Charly Gaul	LUX
	Team		Belgium	
1957	1		Jacques Anquetil	FRA
	2		Marcel Janssens	BEL
	3		Adolf Christian	AUT
	Green	301 pts	Jean Forestier	FRA
	Polka-dot	44 pts	Gastone Nencini	ITA
	Team		France	
1958	1		Charly Gaul	LUX
	2		Vito Favero	ITA
	3		Raphaël Géminiani	FRA
	Green	347 pts	Jean Graczyk	FRA
	Polka-dot	79 pts	Federico Bahamontes	SPA
	Team		Belgium	
1959	1		Federico Bahamontes	SPA
	2		Henry Anglade	FRA
	3		Jacques Anquetil	FRA
	Green	613 pts	André Darrigade	FRA
	Polka-dot	73 pts	Federico Bahamontes	SPA
	Team		Belgium	
1960	1		Gastone Nencini	ITA
	2		Graziano Battistini	ITA
	3		Jan Adriaenssens	BEL
	Green	74 pts	Jean Graczyk	FRA
	Polka-dot	56 pts	Imerio Massignan	ITA
	Team		France	
1961	1		Jacques Anquetil	FRA
	2		Guido Carlesi	ITA
	3		Charly Gaul	LUX
	Green	174 pts	André Darrigade	FRA
	Polka-dot	95 pts	Imerio Massignan	ITA
	Team		France	
1962	1		Jacques Anquetil	FRA
	2		Joseph Planckaert	BEL
	3		Raymond Poulidor	FRA
	Green	173 pts	Rudi Altig	GER
	Polka-dot	137 pts	Federico Bahamontes	SPA
	Team		St-Raphaël-Helyett	
1963	1		Jacques Anquetil	FRA
	2		Federico Bahamontes	SPA
	3		José Perez Francés	SPA
	Green	275 pts	Rik Van Looy	BEL
	Polka-dot	147 pts	Federico Bahamontes	SPA
	Team		St-Raphaël-Gitane	
1964	1		Jacques Anquetil	FRA
	2		Raymond Poulidor	FRA
	3		Federico Bahamontes	SPA
	Green	208 pts	Jan Janssen	HOL
	Polka-dot	173 pts	Federico Bahamontes	SPA
	Team		Pelforth Sauvage-Lejeune	
1965	1		Felice Gimondi	ITA
	2		Raymond Poulidor	FRA
	3		Gianni Motta	ITA
	Green	144 pts	Jan Janssen	HOL
	Polka-dot	133 pts	Julio Jimenez	SPA
	Team		KAS	
1966	1		Lucien Aimar	FRA
	2		Jan Janssen	HOL
	3		Raymond Poulidor	FRA
	Green	211 pts	Willy Planckaert	BEL
	Polka-dot	123 pts	Julio Jimenez	SPA
	Team		KAS	
1967	1		Roger Pingeon	FRA
	2		Julio Jimenez	SPA
	3		Franco Balmamion	ITA
	Green	154 pts	Jan Janssen	HOL
	Polka-dot	122 pts	Julio Jimenez	SPA
	Team		France	
1968	1		Jan Janssen	HOL
	2		Herman Van Springel	BEL
	3		Ferdinand Bracke	BEL
	Green	241 pts	Franco Bitossi	ITA
	Polka-dot	96 pts	Aurelio Gonzales	SPA
	Team		Spain	
1969	1		Eddy Merckx	BEL
	2		Roger Pingeon	FRA
	3		Raymond Poulidor	FRA
	Green	244 pts	Eddy Merckx	BEL
	Polka-dot	155 pts	Eddy Merckx	BEL
	Team		Faema	
1970	1		Eddy Merckx	BEL
	2		Joop Zoetemelk	HOL
	3		Gösta Pettersson	SWE
	Green	212 pts	Walter Godefroot	BEL
	Polka-dot	128 pts	Eddy Merckx	BEL
	Team		Salvarani	
1971	1		Eddy Merckx	BEL
	2		Joop Zoetemelk	HOL
	3		Lucien Van Impe	BEL
	Green	202 pts	Eddy Merckx	BEL
	Polka-dot	228 pts	Lucien Van Impe	BEL
	Team		BIC	
1972	1		Eddy Merckx	BEL
	2		Felice Gimondi	ITA
	3		Raymond Poulidor	FRA
	Green	196 pts	Eddy Merckx	BEL
	Polka-dot	229 pts	Lucien Van Impe	BEL
	Team		Gan-Mercier	
1973	1		Luis Ocaña	SPA
	2		Bernard Thévenet	FRA
	3		José Manuel Fuente	SPA
	Green	187 pts	Herman Van Springel	BEL